The Quark XPress Book

▼▼▼

Second Edition for Windows

The Quark XPress Book

Second Edition for Windows

by
David Blatner
&
Bob Weibel

edited by
Stephen F. Roth

AN OPEN HOUSE BOOK

PEACHPIT PRESS

The QuarkXPress Book, Second Edition for Windows
David Blatner and Bob Weibel
Edited by Stephen F. Roth

Peachpit Press, Inc.
2414 Sixth Street
Berkeley, CA 94710
510/548-4393
510/548-5991 (fax)

Copyright ©1994 by David Blatner and Bob Weibel

Editor: Stephen F. Roth
Copy Editor: Gaen Murphree
Cover design: Ted Mader & Associates
Interior design: Olav Martin Kvern
Production: Glenn Fleishman

Distribution

Peachpit Press books are distributed to the US book trade by Publishers Group West, 4065 Hollis, PO Box 8843, Emeryville, CA 94609, phone 800/788-3123 or 510/658-3453, fax 510/658-1834. Peachpit books are also available from wholesalers throughout the US including Baker & Taylor Books, Golden-Lee Book Distributors, and Ingram Book Company. Resellers outside the book trade can contact Peachpit directly at 800/980-8999.

Notice of Rights

All rights reserved. No part of this book may be reproduced or transmitted in any form by any means, electronic, mechanical, photocopying, recording, or otherwise, without the prior written permission of the publisher. For information on getting permission for reprints and excerpts, contact Trish Booth at Peachpit Press.

Notice of Liability

The information in this book is distributed on an "As Is" basis, without warranty. While every precaution has been taken in the preparation of the book, neither the author nor Peachpit Press, Inc., shall have any liability to any person or entity with respect to any loss or damage caused or alleged to be caused directly or indirectly by the instructions contained in this book or by the computer software and hardware products described in it.

ISBN 1-56609-135-7

9 8 7 6 5 4 3 2 1

Printed and bound in the United States of America

PRINTED ON RECYCLED PAPER

FOREWORD

QuarkXPress Secrets

▼▼▼▼▼▼▼▼▼▼▼▼▼▼▼▼▼▼▼▼▼▼▼▼▼▼▼▼▼▼▼▼▼▼▼

When we introduced QuarkXPress back in 1987, we had no idea of the broad impact it would have on the world of publishing. Now, if you look at any random collection of magazines and newspapers, the chances are that many of them were produced using QuarkXPress. From high-end publishing to newsletters and brochures, the methods used to produce high-quality documents have changed completely in the space of only a few years. And QuarkXPress has been a major force catalyzing that change. The power of QuarkXPress rivals, and in some cases surpasses, the power of older, expensive, high-end publishing systems.

At last we have moved QuarkXPress to the Windows platform. But when we develop documentation for the product, we take a very broad view of our audience. The QuarkXPress documentation takes you only so far. The uses of the product are as varied as the backgrounds of the users. To get all the information that everyone wants takes much more. That's where *The QuarkXPress Book* comes in.

When I was asked to write a foreword for *The QuarkXPress Book*, I thought, "Yeah, sure. I'll write something generic that says how nice the book is and that it will be a good addition to your library." Then, I actually got to read it. It's more than a good book on QuarkXPress. It's a great book. It explains everything about publishing with QuarkXPress in detail. Technical issues that you can read about nowhere else are discussed in depth.

The QuarkXPress Book for Windows has the same high quality as its Macintosh companion. But, this is more than just a book on QuarkXPress. It is a book on PC publishing. The information that's covered has broader uses. And with tips ranging from simple step-by-step procedures for creating fancy drop caps to advanced ways to customize your system, the information provided is invaluable. As far as I know, it has never been collected in one place before.

Users like David and Bob are one of the reasons that QuarkXPress has been successful. Making a great product takes more than just a bunch of clever people in research and development. It takes actual users telling us what we did right and what we did wrong. David and Bob both use QuarkXPress. This book was produced with QuarkXPress. Its quality is not a testament to what QuarkXPress can do; it is a testament to what QuarkXPress can do in the hands of skilled and knowledgeable operators. No matter what your level of expertise, this book will help you know more and work better. It will be one of the most useful books you own for QuarkXPress and your PC.

Tim Gill
Founder and Senior Vice President of
Research and Development
Quark, Inc.

PREFACE

The Amazon Explorers

▼▼▼▼▼▼▼▼▼▼▼▼▼▼▼▼▼▼▼▼▼▼▼▼▼▼▼▼▼▼▼

"You're doing what?"

"We've got one QuarkXPress document here to print the borders for each page, and then in this other document we have all the text in galleys. We tried to put them together, but because we don't know the program well enough, it's faster just to use our production people for pasteup."

"If you're just going to paste it up, why are you using QuarkXPress at all?"

"A consultant suggested we buy Windows and QuarkXPress. But we haven't had a chance to really learn it. Besides, QuarkXPress gives us a lot of control over the text."

It was a story both of us had heard before. Designers, ad agencies, small and large businesses bought Windows and QuarkXPress with the idea that everything was going to be easier, faster, and cooler. All that can be true, but let's face it: QuarkXPress is not a magical solution. Desktop publishing on personal computers requires knowledge, experience, and expertise.

It seems there is a need for a consultant who not only knows the computer and graphic design, but also one who can sit there, patiently, and—at 11 PM—walk you through building a better registration mark, making a drop cap, or explaining how master pages work—all for a $29.95 flat fee. That consultant is this book.

The Early Days

But how did this book come to be? What possessed us to write 200,000 words, more or less, on a piece of computer software? Let's start at the beginning of our QuarkXPress story.

The early days of desktop publishing were much simpler than they are now. When a new program came out, we asked some basic, hard-hitting questions.

- Can you put text on a page?
- Can you put graphics on a page?
- Does the page print?

Once we had satisfactory answers to those three questions, we could get down to brass tacks, ripping it to pieces to make it do all the things it wasn't designed to do. It was a wild time, much like trudging through the Amazon forests with only a machete and a match.

To be blunt, David's not ordinarily the quiet type. So it is telling that, when he saw the first copy of QuarkXPress 1.0 on the Macintosh, all he could say was, "Wow." Here was, at last, a program to use instead of PageMaker. No more eyeballing the measurements, no more relying on built-in algorithms. Those were the days of PageMaker 1.2, and QuarkXPress was a glimmer of hope in the dark ages.

But it was the beginning of the Macintosh Way, and we were so gung-ho that we would do almost anything not to look in the manuals. Even if we had wanted to peek every once in a while, peer pressure was stiff. No, we had to play by the rules and learn QuarkXPress the hard way.

But perhaps all those years of system crashes and blank pages coming out of the printer paid off. While frequenting cocktail parties, we can blithely hint at the magnificent techniques we've come upon for using QuarkXPress on both PCs and Macs in a networked environment. Our friends and family are amazed as we stand tall, knowing which menu to pull down to create style sheets. But is it really enough?

Making Pages

Even more important than fancy party talk has been the ability to use all our QuarkXPress tips and tricks to make good-looking pages quickly and efficiently. And a couple of years ago, we knew it was finally time to put finger to keyboard and get this information out to you, the newest real-world users of QuarkXPress. To find even more tips, tricks, and techniques for QuarkXPress users, especially Windows enthusiasts, we searched the on-line systems, looked through back issues of computer magazines, and even resorted to books on other Windows software.

But books full of tips and tricks tell just half the story. And we think the simple menu-by-menu approach that most computer books use deserves the phrase "tastes filling, less great!" We knew there should be more.

So we sat down and listed all the ways in which we use QuarkXPress in our work: books, magazines, newsletters, flyers, and brochures. The most striking thing we found was that we rarely use QuarkXPress by itself. Aldus FreeHand, CorelDraw, Adobe Illustrator, PostScript programming, Windows Notepad, Microsoft Word, Aldus PhotoStyler, and numerous other accessories and utilities play a large part in our publishing process. We figured that if we weren't publishing in a vacuum, you probably weren't either. So we've gathered up information about using those programs in conjunction with QuarkXPress.

Our idea has been to roll together tips and tricks, a full overview of the program, and in-depth discussions of core concepts behind using QuarkXPress in a real-world setting. So we've included discussions on fonts, PostScript and TrueType printing, color models, practical tips on using Windows, and much more, along with examples of how we've been using QuarkXPress for the past seven years. We also describe the way QuarkXPress operates and how to take advantage of its sometimes strange methods.

Of course, this is a lot of information for a single book. But what did you shell out $29.95 for? Chopped liver? No, this book is meant not only to be read, but to be used. We wanted to include a Post-It pad so you could mark the pages you'll use the most, but it didn't work out. But don't let that stop you.

About This Book

We have purposely taken a wide spectrum of potential readers into account, from Windows beginners to seasoned professionals. We did this because we've found that those seasoned professionals are delighted to learn new tricks, techniques, and concepts, and people who have used the PC very little sometimes surprise us with their intuitive grasp of the Big Picture.

Remember, this book was written for you. It's designed to work for you—as your personal consultant—whoever you are. It's also designed to help you get a sure footing on a sometimes uneven path, and to help you make pages like the pros.

Organization

We have organized this book to reflect what we think QuarkXPress is all about: producing final camera-ready output from your computer. So we start with an overview of the program, move on to building a structure for the document, then discuss the basics—such as putting text and pictures on a page. Next we move into some fine-tuning aspects of QuarkXPress, and finally, to printing. That's the speed-reading rundown; now here's a play-by-play of the chapters.

Introduction. In the Introduction we lay out QuarkXPress on the table, telling you what it is and what it does. We also include a rundown of the hardware and software requirements you should be aware of. It's a brief overview, but it should be helpful as an introduction to both the book and the product.

Chapter 1: QuarkXPress Basics. The first step in understanding QuarkXPress is learning about its structure from the ground up. This involves an investigation of QuarkXPress's menus, palettes, and dialog boxes. We also look at file management, navigating through your document, and the basics of the new libraries, grouping, and alignment controls.

Chapter 2: Document Construction. Without a sturdy foundation, your document won't be reliable or flexible. This chapter discusses the basics of making earthquake-proof infrastructures for your pages: opening a new document, creating master pages, and setting up column guides and linking for text flow.

Chapter 3: Word Processing. If you wanted a drawing program, you would have bought one. Words are what QuarkXPress is all about, and this chapter is where words start. We talk here about simple text input, the Find/Change feature, and QuarkXPress's spelling checker.

Chapter 4: Type and Typography. Once you've got those words in the computer, what do you do with them? Chapter 4 discusses the details of formatting text into type—fonts, sizes, styles, indents, widows, orphans, drop caps—the list goes on. This is, not surprisingly, the longest chapter in the book.

Chapter 5: Copy Flow. You bought the computer, so why not let it do the work for you? This chapter explains how to use style sheets to automate aspects of copy processing, and how to use importing and exporting effectively.

Chapter 6: Pictures. Who reads text anymore? We like to look at the pictures. And pictures are what Chapter 6 is all about. We discuss graphic file formats and how to work with them in your documents—including OLE (Object Linking and Embedding). We also cover rotating, skewing, and other manipulations of images.

Chapter 7: Where Text Meets Graphics. This is the frontierland, the border between the two well-discussed worlds of type and pictures. Life gets different on the edge, and in this chapter we discuss how to handle it with grace—using anchored boxes, paragraph rules, and text runaround.

Chapter 8: Modifying Images. Here's where a good eye can help you improve a bitmapped image, and a creative eye can help you make those graphics do flips. In this chapter we look at brightness, contrast, gamma correction, and halftoning for bit-mapped images such as scans.

Chapter 9: Color. QuarkXPress is well-known for its powerful color capabilities. This chapter covers color models, building custom colors, applying colors, and the first steps in understanding color separation.

Chapter 10: Printing. This is where everything we've talked about is leading: getting your document out of the machine and onto film or paper. In this chapter we cover every step of printing—from printer setup to color separations. We also discuss the finer points of working with service bureaus and how to troubleshoot your print job.

Appendix A: Windows and QuarkXPress. As we said, QuarkXPress doesn't exist in a vacuum. The main program that we use in conjunction with QuarkXPress is, of course, Microsoft Windows. This appendix covers all sorts of tips and tricks to make your life within Windows easier.

Appendix B: If You Use a Macintosh. QuarkXPress was originally a Macintosh product. In this Appendix we cover just about everything you need to know in order to move files between the two platforms. Also, we throw in some extra tips about using Windows from the perspective of a Macintosh user.

Appendix C: ANSI Codes. This third appendix is a listing of the ANSI codes in several typefaces. You'll need these codes in order to type special characters from within QuarkXPress.

Appendix D: XPress Tags. XPress Tags comprises a powerful method for editing, massaging, and controlling large amounts of text. In this appendix we cover all the XPress Tags and what they mean.

Appendix E: Resources. This appendix is an extensive directory of Quark XTensions, software, hardware, magazines, and publications that we've found useful while working with QuarkXPress.

**Appendix F: What's New in 3.3.** In early 1994, Quark shipped the long-awaited update to QuarkXPress for Windows: version 3.3. This version is now completely cross-platform compatible with the Macintosh version 3.3 (which shipped at about the same time). For the convenience of users of both 3.1 and 3.3, we've referenced the new features in this appendix throughout the book with the symbol in the margin at left.

Appendix G: EfiColor. With the release of version 3.3, Quark brought the EfiColor color-management system to Windows. Many of you will find the EfiColor system useful in keeping color consistent among scans, proofs, the screen, and final output.

Finding What You Need

There are many ways to read this book. First, there's the cover-to-cover approach. This is the best way to get every morsel we have included. On the other hand, that method doesn't seem to work for some people. As we said, this book is meant to be used, right off the shelf, no batteries needed.

We've done everything in our power to make it easy to find topics throughout this book. However, there's so much information that sometimes you might not know where to look. The table of contents breaks down each chapter into first- and second-level headings, so you can jump to a particular topic fast.

If it's a tip that you're looking for, you can look through the tips list at the beginning of the book. We've also started the tips in the text with the word "Tip" to make them stand out. Finally, if you can't find what you're looking for or you are trying to find an explanation for a single concept, try the index.

Acknowledgments

No book is an island. So many people have contributed directly and indirectly to this book's production that we would have to publish a second volume to thank them all. We do want to thank a few people directly, however.

First of all, great thanks to the people at Quark, who not only put out a great product, but also worked with us to get this book out to you with as much information in it as possible. In particular, Tim Gill, Fred Ebrahimi, Kathleen "hold on, I'll check" Thurston, Peter Warren, Dave Ambler, and PC support technicians Tad Hana, Cliff Zwart, Duane Schat, and Roy Brothwell for always coming through with the answers. We couldn't have gotten far without them.

And many thanks go to the many people who wrote, called, and e-mailed us their comments and suggestions. We've tried to incorporate their ideas into this Windows edition.

The People Who Made This Book

Guy Kawasaki wrote about Steve Roth in *The Macintosh Way*: "If you find an editor who understands what you are trying to do, brings the best out of you, and doesn't botch up your work, 'marry' him as fast as you can." We can't think of a better description of Steve, so that'll have to do. Steve's already married to Susie Hammond, who—along with Cindy Bell, Stephanie Izarek Smith, Gaen Murphree, and Steve's soon-to-be-famous managing editor Glenn Fleishman—was excellent in making sure our t's were dotted and our i's crossed, and most of all, making sure that we didn't sound like fools.

Eric Taub. Special thanks go to our New York correspondent, Eric Taub, who single-handedly tackled most of the word-processing and copy flow chapters, and contributed to both the *EfiColor* and *What's New in 3.3* appendixes. His steady hand and sturdy mouse helped enormously in getting this book out to you under the extreme time pressures we've all experienced. He's an Amazon XPress Demon without a doubt.

Mike Arst. What do you say about a guy who can move through QuarkXPress like Leonard Bernstein through Beethoven's Ninth? A guy who can create explanatory figures that are not just explanatory, but (occasionally) funny? A guy who can do more with a string of text than Houdini could do with a ball of string? What do you say? Thanks.

And a cast of thousands. We also want to thank everyone at Peachpit Press, including (but not limited to) Ted Nace, Gregor "Samsa" Clark, Keasley Jones, Cary "proud Honda-owner" Norsworthy, Paula Baker, John "world famous" Grimes, Trish Booth, Hanna Onstad, Paul Ellis, Bernhard "with a t" Schmidt, Roslyn Bullas, Carl and Jim Bruce, and Zigi Lowenberg. We gave it the wings, but they made it fly. Also, much appreciation and astonishment goes to our excellent book designer Olav Martin Kvern, our wordsmith Don "*Zap!*" Sellers, Steve "Magic Touch" Broback and Marci "Warlocks" Eversole of Thunder Lizard Productions, and other folks who helped poke and prod the book until it was done. The people at The Ashland Bakery and The Dexter Deli, for mind- and body-sustaining espresso. Doug "Aldus" Peltonen, for help with technical edits.

And, finally, some personal acknowledgments.

David: "My thanks to all those people even further behind the scenes who helped us along the road. Vincent Dorn at the former LaserWrite in Palo Alto, who said, 'Hey, let's go to Burger King.' Steve Herold at LaserGraphics in Seattle, who said, 'Meet Steve Roth.' Barbara and Richard, Adam and Allee, Alisa and Paul, Debbie, Mark and Toni, Don and Sarah, and other friends who were such a support over the past few decades. It wouldn't have happened without you."

Bob: "Years have passed, but I'm still indebted to Susan Gubernat, Jim Felici, Christine Whyte, and Erik Holsinger, all formerly of *Publish* magazine, for letting some of their skill and creativity rub off on me. Thanks also to my colleague and PC publishing guru, Dan Will-Harris. Without my wife Terry and 7-year-old son Simon life wouldn't be fun, and neither would my writing, so this book's for them. And another free copy to my parents—perpetually intrigued and highly supportive of my book-writing endeavors."

Thanks.

David Blatner
Bob Weibel

Contents

Foreword v
Preface: The Amazon Explorers vii

▼▼▼▼▼▼▼▼▼▼▼▼▼▼▼▼▼▼▼▼▼▼▼▼▼▼▼▼▼▼

Introduction 1
  What QuarkXPress Is 2
    Who QuarkXPress is For 2
  What QuarkXPress Does 2
  XTensions 4
  Requirements 4
    Hardware and System Software 5
    Hard Disks. 5
    Random Access Memory. 6
  Your Environment 6
  QuarkXPress and You 7

▼▼▼▼▼▼▼▼▼▼▼▼▼▼▼▼▼▼▼▼▼▼▼▼▼▼▼▼▼▼

Chapter 1   QuarkXPress Basics 9
  The Files 9
    Registration 10
    Customization 10
    Other Files 11
    Faith. 13
    File Management 13
    Opening Documents 13
    Closing Documents 14
    Saving Your Document 15
    Templates 16
    Locking Documents 17
    Revert To Saved. 18
    Multiple Documents 18
  QuarkXPress's Interface 20
    Menus 20
    Palettes 23
    Dialog Boxes. 27
  Using the Tools 29
    Items and Contents 29

- Text Boxes 30
- Picture Boxes 33
- Picture Box Attributes 35
- Transforming Picture Boxes 35
- Lines and Arrows 36
- Line Attributes 37
- Manipulating Items 38
- Moving Items 39
- Rotating Items 40
- Resizing and Reshaping Items 41
- Locking Items 45
- Duplicating Items 45
- Deleting Items 47
- Relationships Between Items 48
- Layering Items 48
- Grouping Objects 49
- Modifying Grouped Objects 50
- Constraining 52
- Aligning and Distributing Objects 54
- Getting Around Your Document 57
  - Scrolling 57
  - Zooming 60
  - Moving from Page to Page 61
- Manipulating Your Document 62
  - Menu Manipulations 62
  - Thumbnails 63
  - Document Layout Palette 64
  - Moving Items Between Documents 65
  - Moving Pages Between Documents 66
  - Linking 66
  - Linking Text Boxes 67
  - Unlinking Text Boxes 67
  - Guides and Rulers 69
  - Guides 70
  - Snap to Guides 71
  - Frames 72
  - Frame Weight 72
- Libraries 73
  - Manipulating Libraries 74
  - Adding and Moving Library Entries 74
  - Removing Library Items 75
  - Labeling Library Items 76
  - Saving Libraries 78
- XTensions 78
- Changing Defaults 79
  - Application Preferences 80
  - General Preferences 82

Tool Preferences	84
XPress Preferences	87
Moving On	89

Chapter 2 Document Construction 91

Building a New Document	92
Page Size	92
Margin Guides	93
Facing Pages	94
Column Guides	95
Automatic Text Box	97
Master Pages: Elementary	98
How PageMaker Does It	99
How QuarkXPress Does It	99
Your First Master Page	100
Parts of a Master Page	101
Master Guides	102
Automatic Text Link Icon	102
Automatic Text Link Box	103
Modifying Automatic Text Link Boxes	104
Creating Multiple Automatic Text Link Boxes	104
Unlinking Automatic Text Link Boxes	105
What to Put on a Master Page	106
Automatic Page Numbering	107
Graphics and Master Pages	108
Changing Master Page Items	108
Changes to Document Pages	109
Changes on Master Pages	109
Master Pages Preferences	110
Master Pages: Advanced	111
Document Layout Palette	111
Basing a New Master Page on Another	114
Applying Master Pages to Document Pages	115
Making Pages	115
Insert Pages	116
Document Layout Insertions	117
Modifying Your Pages	118
Changing Page Size	118
Changing Facing Pages	119
Changing Margins	119
Changing Column Guides	120
Automatic Page Insertion	121
Text Linking	122
Multiple Page Spreads	122
Sections and Page Numbering	122
Changing Your Page Numbering	123
Changing the Page-Numbering Style	124

CONTENTS

Prefixes 124
Automatic "Continued..." Pagination 125
    To Create a "Continued on..." Message 125
    To Create a "Continued from..." Message 126
Crop Marks and Print-Area Considerations. 127
    To Crop or.... 127
    Who Crops What 127
Foundations 128

Chapter 3   Word Processing 129

Entering Text 130
    Selecting and Navigating 130
    Using the Mouse 131
    Using the Keyboard 131
    Deleting Text. 133
Finding and Changing 133
    Where QuarkXPress Looks 133
    Specifying Text 134
    Specifying Attributes. 136
    What to Find, What to Change 136
    Finding and Changing Character Styles. 138
    Going to It 139
Spell-Checking. 140
    Checking a Word 140
    Checking a Story 141
    Checking a Document/Master Page 143
    Auxiliary Dictionaries 143
When Not to Use QuarkXPress. 147
    Slow Going. 147
    Modifying Preferences and Settings 149
    Using Dummy Text Boxes 150
Watching Your Words 152

Chapter 4   Type and Typography 153

Fonts. 154
    Adobe Type Manager and TrueType 154
    Screen Fonts. 155
    Printer Fonts. 155
    Type 1 vs. TrueType 156
Fonts and Windows. 158
    Managing TrueType 158
    Managing PostScript Fonts. 159
    WIN.INI Revealed 161
Formatting Text in QuarkXPress. 164
Character Formatting 164
    Selecting a Typeface 165

Font Size	166
Type Styles	167
Styling by Attributes Versus Font Choice	170
Color and Shade	171
Horizontal Scale	172
Kerning and Tracking	173
Kerning	174
Tracking	178
Baseline Shift	180
Paragraph Formatting	181
Alignment	182
Horizontal Alignment	182
Vertical Alignment	184
Indents	187
Leading	192
Specifying Leading	192
Leading Modes	195
Space Before and Space After	199
First Baseline	200
Tabs	200
Right Indent Tab	205
Hyphenation and Justification	207
The Basics of H&J	207
Auto Hyphenation	209
Justification	211
Setting Your Own H&J	212
Creating an H&J Setting	213
Applying an H&J Setting	213
Widow and Orphan Control	214
Keep With Next	215
Keep Lines Together	215
Baseline Grid	218
Maintain Leading	219
Fine-Tuning Type	220
Typographic Preferences	221
Kerning and Tracking Tables	223
Kerning Tables	224
Tracking Tables	226
Hyphenation	229
Suggested Hyphenation	229
Hyphenation Exceptions	229
Special Characters	231
Formatting Characters	231
Punctuation and Symbols	236
Foreign Punctuation and Accents	240
Math Symbols and the Symbol Font	241
Dingbats	242

Mismatched Character Sets 243
Typographic Special Effects. 245
    Fractions 245
    Initial Caps. 248
    Shadowed Type Alternatives 255
Text Handling 256
    Text Greeking 256
    Vector Above 256
Putting It Together 257

Chapter 5 Copy Flow 259

Managing Copy 259
    Working Smart 260
Style Sheets—What They Are, and Why You Need Them 261
    Warning: A Style Is a Style Sheet Is a Style. 261
    And Now, Back to the Show 262
    Tagging 262
    Local Formatting Versus Style Formatting 263
    Defining Styles 264
    Creating a New Style 265
    Normal Style and No Style 267
    Appending Styles 267
    Basing One Style on Another. 269
Style Palette. 270
    Combining Paragraphs For Run-in Heads 272
Importing Text 273
    What Filters Are, and How To Use Them 274
    When It Is Okay To Use QuarkXPress
    As Your Word Processor 274
    What Word Processor to Use? 275
    How QuarkXPress Works with Word 275
    How QuarkXPress Works with WordPerfect 277
Exporting Text 278
    How to Export Text 279
    Pitfalls 279
    Exporting to WinWord. 279
A Solution: XPress Tags 280
    Why Use XPress Tags? 281
Getting Your Stories Straight 283

Chapter 6 Pictures 285

Graphic File Formats. 286
    Bitmaps. 286
    Object-Oriented Graphics 289
    File Types 291
Importing Pictures into QuarkXPress 299

        The Clipboard 299
        Get Picture 300
        Object Linking and Embedding. 301
        Linking and Embedding 302
    What Happened to My Picture? 306
    Working with Your Picture 308
        Moving Your Picture Around. 308
        Rotating, Skewing, and Distorting 314
    Picture Management. 318
        To Represent. 318
        Picture Usage 319
        Greeking and Suppression 322
    Page as Picture. 323
        Using OPI. 323
        Page Size 325

Chapter 7   Where Text Meets Graphics 327

    Transparency. 328
    Text Runaround 328
        None. 329
        Item 330
        Auto Image. 330
        Manual Image. 331
        Inverting the Text Wrap 334
    Anchored Boxes 338
        Turning a Box into a Character 338
        Modifying Anchored Boxes. 340
        Working with Anchored Boxes. 345
    Anchored Rules 346
        Rule Above/Rule Below 346
    Poking and Prodding. 353

Chapter 8   Image Modification 355

    The Picture File 356
        Bitmapped Images. 356
    Modifying Images. 357
        Importing High-Resolution TIFF Graphics 358
    The Style Menu 359
    Contrast 361
        Picture Contrast Specifications Dialog Box. 365
        Halftones 370
        Making Halftones Work for You 372
        Preset Screen Combinations. 374
        Other Screen Option. 376
    Many Colorful Shades of Gray 378

Chapter 9 Color 379
- What You See and What You Get. 380
- Describing Color 382
  - Spot Versus Process Colors 382
  - Color Models 384
- Specifying Color 389
  - The Color List 390
  - New 390
  - Edit. 395
  - Duplicate 397
  - Delete 397
  - Append 397
  - Edit Trap 398
  - Save 398
  - Cancel 399
- Special Colors 399
  - Registration 400
  - Indeterminate 400
- Colors Palette 401
  - Color Blends 402
- Trapping 403
  - Edit Trap 405
  - Trap Information Palette 411
- Auto Trap Preferences 412
- Color from Outside Sources 416
  - Color TIFFs 417
  - Preseparating 417
  - Postseparating 420
  - Color EPS Files 420
  - Specifications in EPS Files 422
  - Deciding to Work in Color 423

Chapter 10 Printing 425
- PostScript 426
- Fonts 426
- Printer Fonts 427
  - Printing Ugly 428
  - More Font Downloading 429
- Choosing a Printer 430
- Printer Setup 430
  - Printer 431
  - Orientation 432
  - Paper 434
  - Image 435
  - Roll-Fed Printer Specifications 437
  - Options 441

        Advanced 445
        Memory. 448
        Graphics 449
        Conform to Adobe Document Structuring Convention 450
        Print PostScript Error Information 450
    Printing 450
        Printing Basics 451
        Output 452
        Tiling 463
        Print Status. 465
    Color Separations. 466
        The Basics of Color Separation 466
        Print Colors as Grays. 467
        Another Look at Colors 467
        Printing Color Separations 468
        The Rosette 469
        Dot Gain and Printer Calibration 470
        Working with a Service Bureau 472
        Sending Your Document 474
        Sending QuarkXPress Files 474
    Sending a PostScript Dump 480
        System Setup 481
        Starting the Print Job. 483
        Checklist for Sending PostScript Dumps 485
    Troubleshooting. 486
        Graphics Look Awful. 486
        Memory Problems 487
        PostScript Problems 489
        Big Ugly White Gaps Appear Between Colors 490
        Wrong Screen Frequency 490
        Not Enough Space Between Pages 490
        Fonts Come Out Wrong 490
        Registration Problems 491
    "Job Finished" 491

▼ ▼

Appendix A   **Windows and XPress** 493
    Memory Lane 493
        Use Extended Memory 494
        Virtual Memory 494
        Permanent Swap File 495
        Ram's the Thing 497
        Windows Resources 499
        Clip the Clipboard 500
    Speed-Ups 501
    Shortcuts 502

Appendix B If You Use a Macintosh 505
You May Get There From Here 505
File Names, Types, and Creators 507
    Moving from Pc to Mac 508
    Mac to Pc: Filenames and Extensions 509
What Does and Doesn't Transfer 511
    Transferring Graphics 516
Modern Myths 520

Appendix C Ansi Codes 521

Appendix D XPress Tags 527

Appendix E Resources 531
XTensions 531
Quark Lab-Paks 534
    Do You Qualify? 534
Quark Multi-Paks 535
Software 536
User Groups 539
Color-Matching Systems 539
Magazines and Publications 540

Appendix F What's New in Version 3.3 543
What Happened to 3.2? 545
QuarkXPress Basics 546
    Installing and Upgrading 546
    The New File and Library Commands 549
    Quick Item Deactivation 550
    Palettes 551
    By the Numbers 551
    Viewing Changes as You Make Them 553
    More Better Shortcuts 554
    Box Skew 555
    Flipping Out 556
    Polygonal Text Boxes 557
    InteractiveText Resizing 558
    Doing Windows 560
    Copying Linked Text Boxes 562
    Multiple-Item Undo 563
    Visually Accurate Rulers 563
    Application Preferences 564
    The Q and Didot Measurements 571
Document Construction 571

CONTENTS xxvii

  Document Layout Palette 572
Word Processing. 576
  Drag-and-Drop Editing 576
  Drag-and-Drop Text Import 576
  Get Text 576
Type and Typography 577
  Fonts. 579
  Indent Here 579
  Two-Character Tab Leaders 579
  New Typographic Preferences 581
  Horizontal and Vertical Scaling 581
  Kern to Space 582
  Keep with Next ¶ 583
  The H&Js of Paragraph Formatting. 583
Copy Flow. 584
  Styles and Local Formatting 584
  Next Style. 584
  Appending Styles 585
Where Text Meets Graphics. 589
Pictures 590
  Previews 590
  Suppressing Printout in Picture Usage 591
  Drag-and-Drop Picture Importing 592
  New Graphic File Formats 594
Color 597
  Drag-and-Drop Color Application 598
  Automatically Adding EPS Spot Colors 599
  Cool Blends 599
  Trapping Preferences 602
  Color Models 602
Printing 605
  New PostScript Options. 605
  Non-PostScript Printing 606
  Saving a Page as EPS 609
  Printer Setup Changes. 611
  Print Dialog Box Changes. 613
  Collect for Output 615
The Big 3.3 Picture 616

Appendix G EfiColor 619

Managing Color 620
  What EfiColor Attempts. 620
  Why Color Management "Can't" Work. 621
  "I Only Paint What I See" 622
  Color-Management Concepts 623
  From Device to Device 624
  Metric Color Tags (MCTS) 625

Using EfiColor 626
    Installing EfiColor 626
    What You Get 626
The EfiColor XTension 628
    Telling EfiColor About Your Monitor 628
    Telling EfiColor About Your Printers 627
Telling EfiColor About Pictures 631
    Selecting a Profile. 631
    Rendering Style 632
    Changing the Profiles for a Picture 634
    Pictures That EfiColor Understands 637
Editing Colors in QuarkXPress 638
    Target 638
    Gamut Alarm 639
    Rendering Style for Colors 640
EfiColor Preferences 642
Missing Profiles 644
    What To Do 644
    Printing with Missing Profiles 645
Before You Use EfiColor 646
    Performance 646
    Dollars and Sense 647
    Incompatible File Formats 648
    The Problem with OPI 649
    Quality of Character 649
Pros and Cons 650

▼ ▼

Index 651

Tips

Chapter 1 QuarkXPress Basics 9
    Clean up Your Subdirectory 11
    Where To Put All of Those Files 12
    Launching QuarkXPress. 14
    Resaving Templates 17
    Template Types 17
    Too Many Files Open 19
    Keyboard Palettes. 25
    Pushing Your Buttons 28
    Continuous Apply 28
    Specifying Measurements 28
    Quick Accurate Boxes 31
    That Ol' Specifications Dialog Box 32
    Careful With Those Ovals 36
    See It Happen While You Do It. 39
    Techniques for Item Placement 40
    Constraining Lines 44
    Making Line Joins Join. 44
    Moving Locked Items 45
    Clone Item 47
    Grab Down Deep 49
    Multilevel Grouping 50
    Modifying Frames for Groups 51
    Watch Out for What You Group 52
    "Live" Scrolling 59
    Use the Grabber Hand. 59
    Adjusting Your Pasteboard 59
    Fitting More in Your Window 61
    Deleting to End 63
    Moving and Deleting Multiple Pages. 64
    Unlinking a Text Box from the Middle of a Chain 69
    Adjusting Your Rulers 69
    Longer Guides. 71
    Grouping Library Items 77

TIPS

          Get to Those Tool Preferences Quickly 86
          Document Defaults Versus Program Defaults 86
          Resetting and Switching Preferences. 88
          Single Document Preferences 88

Chapter 2   Document Construction 91
          Page Size is Not Paper Size 93
          Check That New Dialog Box 98
          Assigning a Startup Font. 104
          Make Sure that You're Working with the Correct Pointer 105
          Use Step and Repeat to Copy Page Geometry 105
          Retrieving Document Layout Deletions 113
          Master Pages Naming Conventions. 114
          Ignoring the Guides 120
          Snap to Guides for Box Fitting 120
          Get to That Section Quickly. 123

Chapter 3   Word Processing 129
          Where Did the Rest of My Page Go?. 130
          Extend by Word 131
          The Lazy Man's Way to Follow a Text Chain. 132
          Seeing Text as It Is Found 140
          Getting a Word Count 143
          Editing Dictionaries the Fast Way. 145
          Editing Dictionaries in a Word Processor 145
          Adding Your Microsoft Word Dictionary. 146
          Use a Text-Editing Windows Accessory 148
          Use a Dummy Document 151

Chapter 4   Type and Typography 153
          Install ATM last 160
          Update Your Port 163
          Use FontMinder 163
          Use the Content Tool 164
          Precision Font Sizing 167
          Reversed Type 171
          Know Your Ems and Ens. 174
          What To Do with These Numbers 176
          Kerning the Kerned 178
          Tracking and the Single Word 179
          When To Track 180
          Centering Text 185
          Watch the Text Inset 188
          Hanging Indents 190
          When Black and White Is Colorful 196
          Leading Tips 196

Adding Extra Space 199
Hanging Tabs. 203
Don't Use Space Where You Really Want Tabs 205
Check for Rivers 208
Tighter and Looser H&Js 214
Other Orphan and Widow Controls. 217
Quick Kerning for Families 226
Watch Those Hyphens 230
Adding Hyphenation. 234
Finding and Replacing Ligatures 238
Character Mapping. 239
Get it Right for Overseas. 240
One-Stroke, One-Character Font Change 241
Ballot Boxes and Custom Dingbats 242
Checking Your Layout 256

Chapter 5 Copy Flow 259
Keys You Can Use for Style Shortcuts. 266
Macro Styles 268
Creating Styles by Example 268
Copy Styles from One Paragraph to Another 270
Creating New Styles 271
Totally Overriding Local Formatting 271
Use Search and Replace to Fake Character Styles 271
Start a Style at the Top 272
Don't Worry About Word Styles 277
Exporting Styles 280
Printing Your Style Sheet 280
Automate Your Copy Processing with XPress Tags 282
Importing Text from Ventura Publisher 282

Chapter 6 Pictures 285
Grab That Pencil. 301
If You Must Paste 305
Minimoves 310
Precision Placement 311
Rotating Your Picture Boxes 315
Faking Perspective 316
Making Multiple Changes to Your Picture. 316
Relinking with a New Picture. 322
Suppressing Pictures in Eps Pages 326

Chapter 7 Where Text Meets Graphics 327
Speed up Polygon Editing. 333
Picture Wrap with No Picture 334
Polygons from Empty Boxes 334

Disappearing Runaround Text 336
Full Wrapp'n' 336
Blend in Anchored Boxes 341
Anchored Figures on Their Own Line 343
Aligning Text in Anchored Boxes 343
Anchored Boxes as Initial Caps 344
Getting an Anchored Box Out Again 346
Reversed Type in Rules. 350
Vertical Rules. 350
Return of Vertical Rules 352
Vertical Rules Strike Back 352

Chapter 8 Image Modification 355
When the Style Menu Is Gray. 359
Making Your Grayscale Picture "Transparent" 360
Applying Your Changes 364
Continuous Apply. 364
Adjusting the Break Point on a High-Contrast Image. 369
Correcting Errors in the Curve 369
Gray Levels in Your Halftones 372

Chapter 9 Color 379
Taking a Color Reality Check 381
Color on Monochrome Monitors 382
Making Your Colors Stick Around 390
Make Your Pantones Look Right 393
Multiple Models 394
Color Tricks the Eye. 395
Returning to Your Origins 396
One More Way to Append a Color 398
Libraries of Colors 398
Adding Document Colors to the Default Palette. 398
Recovering from Color Boo-Boos 399
Editing the Registration Color 400
Unique Registration Colors 400
Trapping Small Type 408
Overprinting Black 409
Four-Color Black 409
Knockout Lettering from Rich Black 410
Trapping Tiny Objects 416
Making DCS Files on the Mac 418

Chapter 10 Printing 425
Save the Rc Trees 432
Negatives of Low Screen Frequency Halftones. 436
A Colorful Shade of Gray 438

Manually Download PostScript Header	444
Automatically Download PostScript Header	444
Get Your Memory Straight	448
From Beginning or End	452
Faster, Larger Thumbnails	454
Two Thumbnails per Page	454
Printing Double-Sided Documents	455
Printing Spreads in a Document	457
Printing for Saddle-Stitched Binding	458
Better Registration Marks	460
Additional Job Information	462
Printer as Magnifying Glass	465
Laserchecking with LaserCheck	471
Does Your Service Bureau Have a Densitometer	473
Some More Questions for Your Service Bureau	473
Catching All the Fonts and Pictures	478
Check Your Compatibility	479
When Your File Is Too Big	484

Appendix A Windows and XPress ... 493
Increase Your Picture Memory ... 498

Appendix B If You Use a Macintosh ... 505
Translations vs. Universal File Formats ... 507
Careful with Your Naming ... 510
Transferring Libraries ... 519

Appendix E Resources ... 531
Managing the Lab-Pak ... 535
Answer Your Mail ... 535

Appendix F What's New in 3.3 ... 543
Full Install with an Upgrader ... 547
Turning XTensions Off ... 548
If You Sell Out ... 549
Send Your Libraries, Not Your Pictures ... 550
Keeping Your Tools Around ... 551
Mix and Match Measurements ... 552
Moving an Item's Origin ... 552
Proportional Resizing by the Numbers ... 553
Spacing with Percentages ... 553
The Polygon Blues ... 556
Fitting More in Your Windows ... 561
Centering an Item when Zooming ... 561
Jump to View Percent ... 561
Getting Rid of Ruler Guides ... 563

Scale-Specific Guides 564
Scroll Speed 565
Revert to Last Minisave 568
Fill 'Er Up with Backups 569
Toggling Quotes 569
Erasing Preferences You've Made 570
Resetting and Switching Preferences 570
Avoiding Alerts 574
Big Page Numbers 574
Copying Master Pages 574
Basing a New Master Page on Another 575
Unintentional Multipage Spreads 575
Speed Spell-Checking 577
Formatting Tabs Quickly 577
Selecting Paragraphs 578
Formatting Past the Boundaries 578
Adjusting Leaders 580
Adjusting Space After Caps 582
Find/Change H&Js Settings 583
Deleting Styles 586
Overwriting Styles 587
Replacing Style Sheets 588
Style Sheet Page Breaks 588
Based on Differences 589
Use Polygonal Text Boxes 590
Adjusting Runarounds for Anchored Boxes 590
Finding Pictures Paths 593
Finding a Bunch of Missing Files 593
Duotones from Photoshop 598
Find/Change Colors 598
To Import or Not To Import 599
A New Dimension 600
Just (Don't) Do It 602
Turning Off Auto Trapping 602
Finding Your Device Name 609
Jump to Absolute Page Numbers 615

Appendix G   EfiColor 617

Non-PostScript Printers 630
Turn Calibrated Output Off 631
Matching Colors in Pictures 641
Pre-EfiColor Documents 646
Don't Convert Pantone Colors 649

INTRODUCTION

Trying to figure out exactly what type of program QuarkXPress is sometimes reminds us of a scene from an old "Saturday Night Live" episode, when a couple bickered over their new purchase. "It's a floor wax," said one. "No, it's a dessert topping," replied the other. The answer was clear: "It's a floor wax *and* a dessert topping." QuarkXPress is a program with the same predicament. Some people insist it's a typesetting application. Others bet their bottom dollar that it's a word processor. Still others make QuarkXPress a way of life.

The truth is that QuarkXPress is all these things, and more. However, no matter how you use it, it is never more than a tool. And a tool is never more than the person behind it.

We like to think of machetes. You can use a machete as an exotic knife to cut a block of cheese, or you can use it as your only means of survival hacking through the Amazon jungles. It's all up to you.

Here in the Introduction, we talk about the big picture: QuarkXPress and how it fits into the world of desktop publishing. Most importantly, we set the stage for the real thrust of this book: how to use QuarkXPress to its fullest.

What QuarkXPress Is

QuarkXPress for Windows combines word processing, typesetting, page layout, drawing, image control, and document construction in a single program. From text editing to typography, page ornamentation to picture manipulation, it offers precision controls that you'll be hard pressed to find in other programs.

Who QuarkXPress is For

Just because it has all these powers, though, doesn't mean that only trained publishing professionals or graphic designers can or should use it. Anyone who can run a personal computer can use it. In fact, many of the people who swear by QuarkXPress aren't even in the "publishing" business. They use it for internal corporate communications, product brochures, stationery, display advertisements, name tags, labels, forms, posters, announcements, and a hundred other things.

Of course, it does "real" publishing, too, and has become a top choice in that realm. It's used by book publishers such as Simon and Schuster and Peachpit Press; magazines such as *Newsweek, People, Spy, Smart, Rolling Stone,* and *Premiere;* newspapers such as *The New York Times,* USA *Today, The Washington Times,* and *The Denver Post;* design firms, art studios, advertising agencies, and documentation departments throughout the world.

What QuarkXPress Does

When it comes right down to it, QuarkXPress is built to make pages. You can place text and graphics on an electronic page and then print that out in a number of different formats. But how can you do that? What tools are at your disposal? Before we spend the rest of the book talking about how to use QuarkXPress and its tools, we had better introduce you to them. And perhaps the best way to introduce QuarkXPress in real-world terms is to provide a digest of some of its most basic options.

Page sizes. You can specify the page sizes for each of your documents, along with their margins. Page dimensions can range from one by one inch to 48 by 48 inches, and margins can be any size. QuarkXPress's main window presents you with a screen representation of your full page, and guidelines indicate margin areas. You can view pages at actual size or any scale from 10 percent to 400 percent. If your document consists of multiple pages, you can view them all by scrolling. If pages are larger than the maximum paper size handled by the target printer, QuarkXPress tiles the document, printing it in overlapping sections for you to assemble manually.

Page layout. QuarkXPress provides tools so you can design your pages by creating and positioning columns, text boxes, picture boxes, and decorative elements. There's a facility to set up "chains" for the automatic flow of text both around a page and between pages. QuarkXPress automates the insertion of new pages and new columns, the creation of elements that are common to all pages, and the page numbering/renumbering process itself.

Word processing. QuarkXPress's word processing tools let you type directly into pages and edit what you type, with your text appearing in either the full-page background (as on paper in a typewriter) or wrapping into overlaying text boxes that can be moved and resized. Text always automatically rewraps to fit into the new box boundaries.

Formatting type. You have full control over character-level formatting (font, size, style, etc.) and paragraph-level formatting (indents, leading, space before and after, etc.). You can also build style sheets for different types of paragraphs that include both character and paragraph formatting.

Importing text. Various import filters let you bring in formatted text from other programs (again, either onto full pages or smaller text boxes), while simultaneously reformatting, using style sheets.

Graphic elements. Drawing tools let you create lines, boxes, ovals, and polygons in different styles, sizes, and shapes, with different borders, fills, and colors.

Importing graphics. You can import computer graphics into picture boxes. These graphics can include scanned images, object-oriented and bitmapped graphics, in color, gray scale, or black and white. Once you've imported them into picture boxes, they can be cropped, fitted, rotated, skewed, and—with bitmaps—manipulated for brightness, contrast, and special effects.

XTensions

QuarkXPress allows for add-on modules called XTensions that add functionality to the program. Over 200 developers around the world are creating custom XTensions for either commercial sale or private use. But perhaps the most prolific of XTension developers is Quark itself. Quark has released several free XTensions already and will continue to do so as time goes on. Because they're free, you can typically get them from a user group or from an on-line service such as CompuServe (they're usually in the DTPFORUM libraries). We've also included several on the Quark Goodies Disk (see the tear-out card at the end of the book).

Requirements

To take advantage of all these great features in QuarkXPress, you need, at a minimum, a 66-MHz 80486 PC with 32Mb of RAM, a one gigabyte hard disk drive, twin removable hard drives, a 600Mb read/write optical drive and 2-gigabyte DAT storage system for secondary backup, a 32-bit color drum scanner, a high-resolution imagesetter with a PostScript Level II RIP, a 1000-dpi Laser Master Unity XL (for rough comps), a Tektronix PXi color printer, a 21-inch color monitor with 24-bit video and graphics accelerator cards, and of course, an NTSC video capture board and genlock control panel.

Just kidding! All you really need is a 386sx clone system. But, as few things are more frustrating than being all psyched up to start something only to discover that you can't for lack of an essential component, here is a résumé of the components you need to know about.

Hardware and System Software

QuarkXPress will, theoretically at least, run on any PC that can run Windows—with an 80286 processor or better, 5Mb of RAM, a hard disk, and Windows 3.1. No matter what PC model you have, 8Mb of RAM is *highly* recommended. Otherwise, you won't be able to effectively QuarkXPress and another application at the same time, speed will suffer greatly, and you will be limited in your use of utility programs (type and font managers, screen capture, font downloaders, and so on), some of which can seem practically indispensable once you've employed them. Note well that you must install Adobe Type Manager (ATM) if you intend to use PostScript fonts with QuarkXPress for Windows.

But let's be honest: We really can't recommend using QuarkXPress to its fullest on any PC model under a 25-MHz 80486. Anything less is just plain slow. Dave uses a 25-MHz 80386 clone and it's . . . OK. No major complaints. Bob hogs around on a 33-mHz 486 clone with 20Mb of RAM. With that, QuarkXPress moves along quite well, partly because the extra RAM gives QuarkXPress, and the other programs he runs along with it, enough memory to perform more of their functions in RAM. That way, they rely less on temporary—and slower—hard disk storage.

Hard Disks

The Iron Law of Hard Disk Storage is that your needs expand to equal and then exceed the storage capacity available. Get the biggest hard disk you can. If you think you'll never need more than 80Mb of storage, then get double that. You may be sorry later if you don't. Also, get a fast one, preferably one with at least a 20-millisecond average access time rating. Windows and QuarkXPress do a fair amount of disk access, and a slow disk becomes a real speed bottleneck.

Random Access Memory

As we hinted above, RAM is good. Put as much into your computer as you possibly can afford. Four megabytes is minimal, and you'll still only get minimal performance out of Windows and QuarkXPress. Most 386- and 486-based PCs can handle 16Mb, or even 32Mb of memory. If you're working with a lot of full-color scanned images, you'll want to max it out. If you're doing serious publishing, chances are you'll want to run QuarkXPress along with several other applications. You'll want the extra RAM so you can move around smoothly when you have those programs open along with much-needed extras like ATM and Ares Software's FontMinder.

Your Environment

If you ever call Quark technical support, you're almost sure to be asked about the hardware and software environment you're working with. The best way to find this out is to look at your QuarkXPress Environment dialog box (see Figure I-1; also see page 549 in Appendix F, *What's New in 3.3*). You can get to this dialog box by holding down the Control key while selecting About QuarkXPress from the Help menu.

The QuarkXPress Environment dialog box can tell you (and the technical support person) all sorts of things about the machine that you're working with, including what version of a printer driver is installed, how much RAM is loaded, and what your QuarkXPress for Windows serial number is.

Figure I-1
QuarkXPress 3.1 Environment dialog box

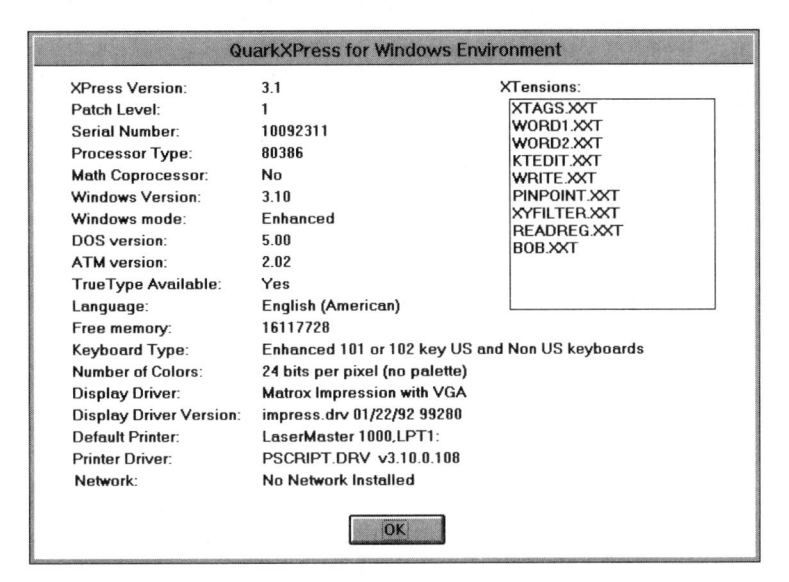

QuarkXPress for Windows Environment		
XPress Version:	3.1	XTensions:
Patch Level:	1	XTAGS.XXT
Serial Number:	10092311	WORD1.XXT
Processor Type:	80386	WORD2.XXT
Math Coprocessor:	No	KTEDIT.XXT
Windows Version:	3.10	WRITE.XXT
Windows mode:	Enhanced	PINPOINT.XXT
DOS version:	5.00	XYFILTER.XXT
ATM version:	2.02	READREG.XXT
TrueType Available:	Yes	BOB.XXT
Language:	English (American)	
Free memory:	16117728	
Keyboard Type:	Enhanced 101 or 102 key US and Non US keyboards	
Number of Colors:	24 bits per pixel (no palette)	
Display Driver:	Matrox Impression with VGA	
Display Driver Version:	impress.drv 01/22/92 99280	
Default Printer:	LaserMaster 1000,LPT1:	
Printer Driver:	PSCRIPT.DRV v3.10.0.108	
Network:	No Network Installed	

▼▼▼▼▼▼▼▼▼▼▼▼▼▼▼▼▼▼▼▼▼▼▼▼▼▼▼▼▼▼▼▼▼

QuarkXPress and You

Version 3 of QuarkXPress is clearly a pretty impressive package. But don't let it intimidate you. Remember, QuarkXPress is not only a machete, it's a Swiss Army machete. If you want to use it for writing letters home, you can do it. If you want to create glossy four-color magazines, you can do that, too. The tool is powerful enough to get the job done, but sometimes—if you're trying to get through that Amazon jungle—you need to wield your machete accurately and efficiently.

Let's look at how it's done.

CHAPTER 1

QUARKXPRESS BASICS

This book, like QuarkXPress, is for everyone who wants to create great documents. But in order to create great documents, you've got to know how to use the tools you've been given. That's what this chapter is really about. We start from the very beginning and move through every major tool and feature in QuarkXPress. It will take a little while for you to get through it, but we really think it'll be worthwhile in the long run. Even if you know QuarkXPress pretty well, you may find some really good tidbits of new information hidden throughout this chapter. Then, in the following chapters, we focus more on how to use the knowledge you've gained to build those documents on good, solid ground.

Let's start right at the beginning: opening the package.

The Files

When you take QuarkXPress out of the package, you're faced with five disks. If you're like us, you bypass the manual entirely and just start shoving disks into the computer to see what there is to see. We suggest starting with Disk 1. Just put it in, select "Run" from the Windows Program Manager's File menu, type

A:INSTALL (or B:INSTALL depending on your floppy disk drive setup), and press Enter.

Registration

New in 3.3 — See page 548

When you first install QuarkXPress, you are required to fill out a survey. The information you provide is saved onto a registration disk that you send back to Quark. There were myths circulating that Quark was secretly saving all sorts of other information on this disk, including what software you use and so on. This is not true. The registration disk does take one piece of information with it that it doesn't ask you for: your system configuration (what type of PC you use, what DOS and Windows version you use, and so on). Theoretically, this information could help the people in technical support, should you ever talk to them about a problem.

Customization

The QuarkXPress installation automatically installs a full-course version of QuarkXPress, including special XTensions, sample files, and a tutorial. However, you can also do an *a la carte* installation by clicking the Customize button in the QuarkXPress Installer opening screen. The aptly named Select Items to Install dialog box opens, and from there you can select which items—XTensions, sample files, tutorial, or QuarkXPress program—you'd like to install or not to install. Highlight the item in the Item list and then click in the Install Highlighted Item check box to activate or deactivate installation for that item. If, for a particular item, you'd like to have the Installer stash the related files into a subdirectory other than the default subdirectory shown in the Path: text box, simply enter a new subdirectory name over the old one.

You might want to custom install QuarkXPress without the tutorial (since you're the proud owner of this book). If you want to use the tutorial later to help train a co-worker, you can run the Installer and deselect all the choices except "Tutorial." That way, only the tutorial will get installed.

If you want to get even more specific about what you install during a custom installation, click the View Details button for one of the four main items. You'll see an expanded list of subitems that you can choose to install or not to install.

Other Files

When the installation is finished, you will find a slew of files on your hard disk. These include several files for getting text from word processors, a dictionary, and several other files that help QuarkXPress do its business. Figure 1-1 shows a disk subdirectory with all of Quark's programs and add-ons in it.

Figure 1-1
Our QuarkXPress subdirectory

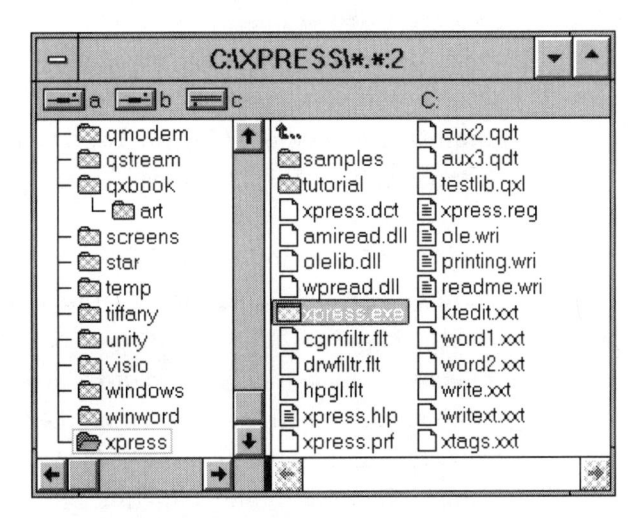

If you are new to QuarkXPress, you probably want to work through Quark's tutorials and look at their sample files. QuarkXPress installs them for you, unless you elect not to by using the Customize command mentioned earlier.

▼ ▼

Tip: Clean up Your Subdirectory. Unless you have and use more software than we do (which is hard to imagine), you don't need all of those files. We never seem to have enough room on our hard disks, so we have gotten into the habit of throwing away any files that we don't need.

If you only use Microsoft Word as your text editor, go ahead and throw away the WordPerfect, WordStar, and other text filters. The same applies for graphics filters; if you'll never use Hewlett-Packard Graphics Language (HPGL) plotter drawings in your documents, you might as well remove the HPGL filter. If you ever need to get them back, run the QuarkXPress Installer again, using the Customize command to perform a custom installation. In the Select Items to Install dialog box, highlight each item one at time, deselecting the Install Highlighted Item check box. Then select the QuarkXPress folder icon and click the View Details button. Deselect all of the options in the Item list until only the filters you want to reinstall are check marked. Then click OK, and QuarkXPress will install the filters. Unfortunately, you can't just copy the filters from Disk 1, since they're stored in a compressed format.

However, if you really don't want to throw out those files, at least put the ones you don't use in a different subdirectory. The more supplementary files you have floating around in QuarkXPress's subdirectory, the longer QuarkXPress takes to launch.

▼▼▼▼▼▼▼▼▼▼▼▼▼▼▼▼▼▼▼▼▼▼▼▼▼▼▼

Tip: Where To Put All of Those Files. Just a quick digression from the topic of hard disk management. Apparently, one of the most difficult techniques for PC users to understand and control is the effective management of hard disks files. Now, we know that *you* wouldn't do something like this, but there are those who just toss their files and applications all over their hard disks, sometimes into subdirectories and sometimes not. They are making their lives hard for themselves.

The Windows File Manager is designed to make life easy for you when it comes to using the PC's subdirectory file system provided by MS-DOS. We like to keep one subdirectory called XPRESS, which contains the actual QuarkXPress application and all of the filters and supplemental files we need. We have a subdirectory in the XPRESS directory for keeping extra add-on modules and filters that we sometimes need. Then, in a subdirectory different from XPRESS, we keep our QuarkXPress documents (usually a specific subdirectory for each project we're working on).

If you aren't familiar with subdirectories and how they work, we heartily suggest you look into the matter (see "File Management," below). You may not self-actualize from using subdirectories well, but your life is sure to be the better for it.

▼▼▼▼▼▼▼▼▼▼▼▼▼▼▼▼▼▼▼▼▼▼▼▼▼▼▼

Faith

Just to be honest with you, there's almost no way to explain one feature in QuarkXPress without explaining all the rest at the same time. But that would make for a pretty confusing book. We're asking you to take minor leaps of faith along the path of reading this chapter. If we mention a term or a function you don't understand, trust that we'll explain it further in later chapters. If you are able to do that, you will find that what we are discussing makes sense. For example, we're not going to talk about the details of creating a new document until the next chapter, *Document Construction*. But since we need to talk about working with documents now, we ask you to trust us while we go over the details of opening, closing, and saving your files.

File Management

Getting a good grasp on file management is essential to working most efficiently and happily with QuarkXPress. When we talk about file management with QuarkXPress, we are talking primarily about opening, closing, and saving your documents. These are pretty basic concepts, so if you've used other Windows programs you should feel right at home with it. If you haven't used a PC before, you'll soon learn a great way of organizing computer files.

Opening Documents

Remember that QuarkXPress is not the same as your document itself. There is the program—QuarkXPress—and then there are files that you create with QuarkXPress. We won't talk in depth about creating new files until Chapter 2, *Document Construction*. However, there are several QuarkXPress documents that are available to be opened in the Tutorial and Sample subdirectories, if you did a full installation.

There are two ways to open an existing QuarkXPress document. If you're not in QuarkXPress, you can double-click on the document's icon in the Windows File Manager, which launches QuarkXPress and opens the file. If you are in QuarkXPress, you can select Open from the File menu (or type Control-O). A pop-up menu at the bottom of the dialog box lets you choose whether you want to view either documents or templates—or both ("All Types"). We discuss templates and their function in "Saving Your Document," below.

Note that QuarkXPress only displays certain types of files in this dialog box, based on the file's three-letter extension and the List Files of Type control. If you saved a QuarkXPress document with some strange file extension, it won't appear in the dialog box unless you set List Files of Type to "All Types *.*". This can be frustrating at times, but it's generally helpful, as it cleans out the riff-raff of any subdirectory you're looking at.

▼ ▼

Tip: Launching QuarkXPress. When you launch QuarkXPress (double-click on the QuarkXPress icon), the program performs all sorts of operations while it's loading. For example, it figures out which fonts are in the system and which XTensions are available for its use. While it's doing all of this, you don't see too much activity on the screen. You know that the computer is ready to go when you see QuarkXPress's menu bar appear across the top of the screen and when the cursor turns into an arrow.

▼ ▼

Closing Documents

After you have finished working on a document, you must close it. You have three choices for closing a document: double-clicking the window control box in the upper-left corner of the document window, choosing Close from the File menu, or selecting Exit from the same menu. This last choice not only closes the file, but it also quits QuarkXPress. If changes have been made to the document since the last time you saved it, you'll see an alert box asking you if you want to save those changes.

Saving Your Document

Until you save your document to a disk, it exists only in the computer's temporary memory (called RAM), ready to disappear forever in the event of a power disruption or system crash. You should save any new document as soon as it opens, and make frequent saves during your work session. All it takes is Control-S. We suggest developing it into a nervous tic. We cannot tell you how many times our clients (and we) have lost hours of work because they didn't save frequently enough. David even made a little sign to post above his computer that read, "Save Every 10 Minutes."

Saving your document is so important, Quark gave you two different items on the File menu to do it: Save and Save As.

Save As. Selecting Save As from the file menu (or typing Control-Alt-S), lets you save the document you're working on under a different name. For example, David often saves different versions of a document with each version number attached. The first one might be called BROCHUR1, the next BROCHUR2, and so on. Whenever he decides to create a new version, he chooses Save As from the File menu, which brings up the Save As dialog box (see Figure 1-2). He types in a file name (or edits the one that's there), then clicks on the Save button to save it to disk. If you decide to do this, remember to delete earlier versions as soon as you decide you don't need them anymore, or else your hard disk will be so full, it'll burst at the seams.

Note that when you save a document, QuarkXPress automatically adds an appropriate three-letter extension to the name. However, you can add whatever extension you want by simply typing it after a period in the name. There's no reason you can't have a perfectly legitimate QuarkXPress document called DAVIDS.FIL. However, note that this file won't appear in the QuarkXPress Open dialog box unless you have "All Types *.*" selected.

As we said above, file management is an issue that too many people don't seem to get. The Save As dialog box is a key ingredient in file management. The important issue here is that your document is saved to whatever subdirectory is open in the Save

Figure 1-2
The Save As dialog box

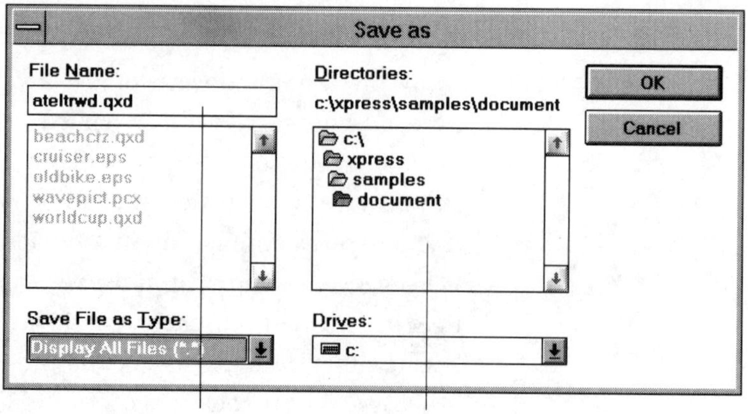

Type the name of the file here. *Your document is saved in whatever subdirectory is open here.*

As dialog box. If you want your document saved in a subdirectory called CRNTJOB, you must either navigate your way to that subdirectory or type the path name into the Save As dialog box. You have a few tools at your disposal for this. Table 1-1 shows several mouse and keyboard shortcuts.

Table 1-1
Navigating through the high seas

Do this...	To get here...
Up arrow	Move one item up on the displayed files list
Down arrow	Move one item down
Tab	Move to next field or button
Double-click	Open this subdirectory
Enter or Return	When a subdirectory is highlighted, open this subdirectory; if no subdirectory is highlighted, Save here

Save. If you want to save your document with the same name that it already has, you can select Save from the File menu (or press Control-S). If you haven't yet saved your document, and it is unnamed, selecting Save automatically reverts to the Save As function.

Templates

The concept of templates seems—to some people—shrouded in more mystery than the Druids of old. Here's an area that seems complicated because people make it complicated. But it's not.

Really. You have the choice of saving your document as a template when you're in the Save As dialog box.

When a file is saved as a template, nothing changes except that you cannot accidentally save over it. For example, let's say you create a document and save it as a normal document called NEWSLETR. Then, a couple of days later you go back into the document and create the newsletter. You make changes, flow text, and place pictures. You then select Save from the File menu. The file NEWSLETR is modified with the changes you made, and there is no way to go back to the original untouched file.

Okay, let's say you create that same NEWSLETR, then save it as a template by selecting "Template" in the Save As dialog box. Then, when you make changes to that document and select Save from the File menu, QuarkXPress doesn't automatically erase the old file and replace it with the new one. Instead, it gives you the Save As dialog box and lets you choose a different name.

▼ ▼

Tip: Resaving Templates. If QuarkXPress gives you the Save As dialog box when you try to save a document specified as a template, how can you change the template itself? Simple. You can replace the old template with a new one by giving it exactly the same name in the Save As dialog box (don't forget to select the Template button if you still want it to be a template).

▼ ▼

Tip: Template Types. As it turns out, there's really nothing special about a QuarkXPress template except for its three-letter filename extension. Rather than a typical ".QXD" extension, a template is named with a ".QXT" extension. You can use DOS or the File Manager to change a document's file extension by renaming the file, effectively changing the way that QuarkXPress deals with that file. For example, you can quickly change a document called FOOBIE.QXD into a template by renaming it FOOBIE.QXT.

▼ ▼

Locking Documents

There's one final method of insuring against undesirable changes to documents: locking the file. This is a function of the MS-DOS and Windows systems rather than QuarkXPress. You can lock an entire document so that changes will never be saved. Select the document while in the Windows File Manager (after closing the document); choose "Properties" from the File menu; and click the Read Only check box. The "Read Only" property means what it says: You can load the file (read it), but you can't save it (write it), which essentially "locks" the file. The only way to save a locked file is to perform a Save As under a different name.

Revert To Saved

NEW IN 3.3 — See page 568

As we said above, no changes are permanent until you save them. If you want to discard all changes made to a document since the last save, you can do it by closing the document (choose Close from the File menu) and telling QuarkXPress that you don't want to save the changes. Or, if you wish to continue working on it without interruption, choose "Revert to Saved" from the File menu. For example, if—in the name of improvement—you have managed to mess up your document beyond redemption, you can revert to the version that you last saved.

Multiple Documents

QuarkXPress lets you open up to seven documents at a time, each in a separate window. However, the actual number and size of documents you can have open depends on both the amount of memory available and the number of files open. (QuarkXPress internally opens more files than just the documents you work with; see "Tip: Too Many Files Open," below.)

NEW IN 3.3 — See page 560

Window Management. Managing all of those document windows can get confusing, but QuarkXpress gives you some help. If you have several windows open on your screen but can't select them because they're stacked up on top of one another, try using the commands under the Windows menu. The Tile command will automatically arrange the open document windows, resizing them so they all fit on the screen without overlapping (like floor tiles, get it?). The Cascade command neatly stacks the document windows on screen, offsetting each window so that you can see each file name on the top bar (like fanning a hand of cards; see Figure 1-3). You can then easily select whichever one you want.

Perhaps the fastest way to see what windows (documents) are open and switch between them is to select the document's name from the Window menu. To really sail between documents, try this keyboard shortcut. Press Alt-W to open the Windows menu, then enter the number (1, 2, 3, etc.) corresponding to the document window. QuarkXPress jumps to that document. You can also press Control-F6 to switch to the next document in the list (just keep typing it until you get the document you want).

Figure 1-3
Cascading windows

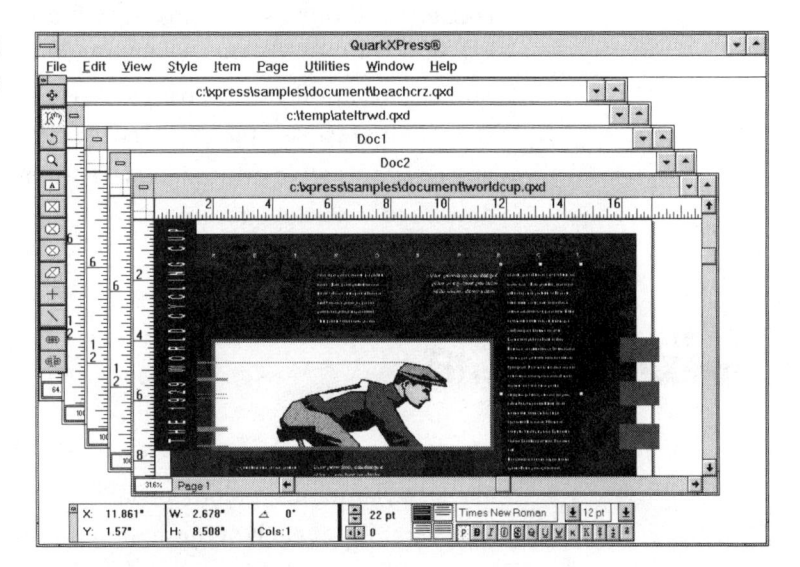

Tip: Too Many Files Open. Windows lets you have a lot of files open at one time, but not an unlimited number. First, you're limited by the amount of RAM and virtual memory you have available on your PC; each file uses memory. You're also limited by the amount of System Resources that Windows has available for keeping track of open files and windows (about 128K for Windows 3.1). You can still run out of memory, even if you have a zillion megabytes of RAM, should System Resources run low. You can see what percentage of System Resources you're currently using with the About Program Manager command under the Program Manager's Help menu. Obviously, the more applications you have running simultaneously, the more files you have open. This is especially true because many applications open "invisible" files that you don't ordinarily know about. For example, QuarkXPress opens one file for each XTension you have available in your QuarkXPress subdirectory, plus a file for the XPress Dictionary, XPress Hyphenation, and so on.

If you're running other Windows and DOS applications at the same time you're running QuarkXpress, well, you're obviously using a lot of system resources. You may have to close an application should you get a "low memory" message. You can also conserve resources by closing windows you're not actually using, while leaving the application running. Also, reduce the number of application groups you use in Program Manager. Often, when you hit the resource ceiling, you may have to take a more conservative approach: save all of your files, close Windows, and restart everything.

QuarkXPress's Interface

While working in QuarkXPress, you have access to its tools and features via menus, palettes, dialog boxes, and keystrokes. Let's look carefully at each of these methods and how you use them.

Menus

There are several conventions used with menus. One is the hierarchical menu, which we often call a submenu. These allow multiple items to be, literally, offshoots of the primary menu item. Another convention is the check mark . A check mark next to an item shows that the feature is enabled or activated. Selecting that item turns the feature off, (or disables it), and the check mark disappears. Figure 1-4 shows these two menu conventions. Other conventions are discussed as needed throughout the book.

We don't need to talk a great deal about menus and their contents here, because we discuss them throughout the book.

However, you should note that certain types of features fall under particular menus. Let's go through a quick rundown.

File. Items on the File menu relate to disk files (entire documents). Commands to open, save, and print disk files are located here.

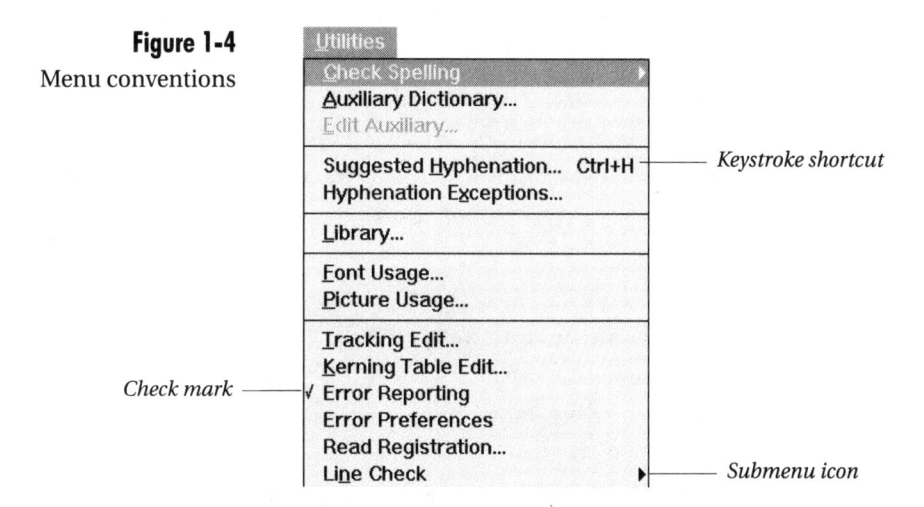

Figure 1-4
Menu conventions

```
Utilities
Check Spelling              ▶
Auxiliary Dictionary...
Edit Auxiliary...

Suggested Hyphenation...  Ctrl+H     ——— Keystroke shortcut
Hyphenation Exceptions...

Library...

Font Usage...
Picture Usage...

Tracking Edit...
Kerning Table Edit...
Check mark ——— √ Error Reporting
Error Preferences
Read Registration...
Line Check                  ▶      ——— Submenu icon
```

Edit. The Edit menu contains features for changing items within QuarkXPress. The last section of the Edit menu contains features to edit internal defaults on a document or on an application-wide level, such as the Color palette, the text style sheets, and the specifications for each tool on the Tool palette (see "Tool palette," below).

View. Almost every feature based on what you see and how you see it is located in the View menu. This menu also includes several other items, such as "Show Guides," that involve QuarkXPress's interface. (We'll be discussing these later in this chapter.)

Style. The Style menu changes depending on what item you have selected on your document page. Selecting a picture box results in one Style menu, selecting a text box results in a different one, and rules (lines) result in a third menu. The items on the Style menu let you change specific style attributes of the selected item.

Item. Whereas the Style menu contains commands for changing the contents of a picture or text box, the Item menu's commands change the box or rule itself. For example, changing the style of a picture box's contents might involve changing the shade of a picture. Changing an attribute of the box itself may involve changing the frame thickness of the picture box.

Page. The Page menu is devoted to entire pages in your document. Controls for master pages (see Chapter 2, *Document Construction*), as well as several features for adding, deleting, and navigating among pages are located here.

Utilities. This menu is, in many ways, a catch-all that contains assorted goodies for helping you make pages. The spell-checker, libraries, and so forth are kept here. Also, most XTensions add items to the Utilities menu, so the more XTensions you have, the longer the menu.

Window. As we mentioned above in the Window Management section, this menu has several commands for reducing the on-screen clutter when you're working with several documents simultaneously.

Help. Yes, help is just a click away. Don't reach for your manual until you've tried the QuarkXPress online help. Using the basic Windows Help engine, the XPress help screens are well-indexed and cross-referenced using a hypertext format.

Palettes

There is a part of QuarkXPress's interface that is incredibly powerful: palettes. The analogy to a painter's palette is helpful insofar as a palette contains a selection of usable and changeable items that you can place wherever it suits you best. A left-handed painter might hold a paint palette in her right hand, while a short, ambidextrous painter might place the palette on the floor. QuarkXPress has several palettes, each with a different function, that can be placed anywhere you like on the screen. These palettes are additional windows on the screen that—although they can overlap one another—never go "behind" a document window. Because of this, we call them floating palettes or *windoids*.

You can manipulate palettes in the same manner as you would move a window. For example, to move a palette, drag the window from the top, shaded area. To close a palette, double-click in the Close box in the upper-left corner.

QuarkXPress comes with four basic palettes: the Tool palette, the Measurements palette, the Document Layout palette, and the Library palette (see Figure 1-5). When you first launch QuarkXPress, you can see the Tool palette and the Measurements palette. QuarkXPress remembers which palettes are open or closed and where the palette is placed, so the location and the status of palettes remain from when you quit to when you next start up.

Let's take a look at each one of these palettes.

Tool palette. The Tool palette is the most elementary and most functional of the palettes. There's not much you can do without it. Here, you have the tools for making boxes in which you place your pictures and text, tools for rotating, tools for drawing lines, and tools for linking the text boxes together to allow the flow of text. Selecting a tool is easy: just click it (see "Tip: Keyboard Palettes," below). We won't go into each tool here, since we discuss them in "Using the Tools," later in this chapter.

Figure 1-5
QuarkXPress's four basic palettes

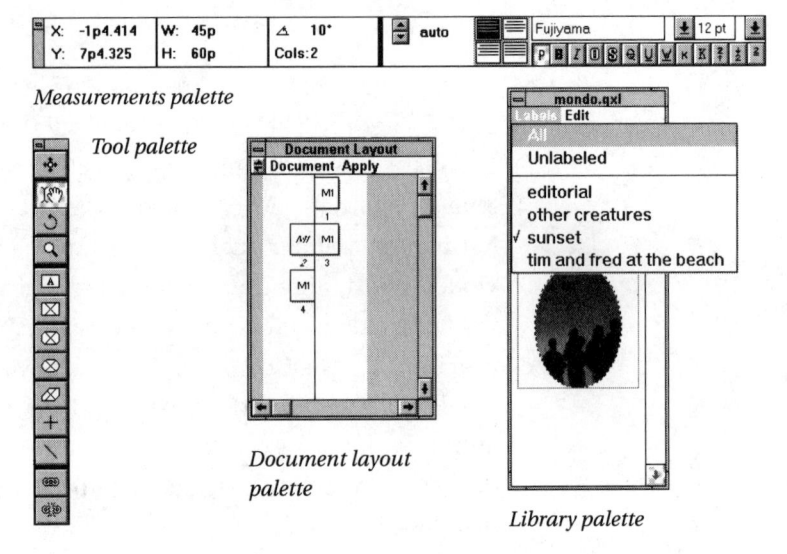

Measurements palette

Tool palette

Document layout palette

Library palette

NEW IN 3.3

See page 551

Measurements palette. Like the Style menu, the Measurements palette is dynamic: it changes depending on the type of item selected on your document page. Text boxes have one type of Measurements palette, picture boxes have a second type, and rules and lines have a third type (see Figure 1-6). The tool you have selected from the Tool palette also has an effect on how the Measurements palette looks. The Measurements palette's purpose in life is to show you an item's vital statistics and to save you a trip to the Style or Item menu for making changes to those page elements.

For example, if you select a text box, the Measurements palette shows the dimensions of the text box, the coordinates of its upper-left corner, the number of columns in the box, the rotation of the box, and the style, font, and size of the text you've selected in the box.

Not only does the Measurements palette display this information, but you can click on an item in the palette and change it. For example, if you want to rotate a picture box 10 degrees, you simply replace "0" with "10" and then type either Return or Enter (pressing Return or Enter tells QuarkXPress that you've finished; it's like clicking the OK button).

Note that the left half of a Measurements palette displays information about a page element (an "item"), and the right half

QUARKXPRESS BASICS   **25**

Figure 1-6
The Measurements palette

The palette changes depending on what type of page element you have selected.

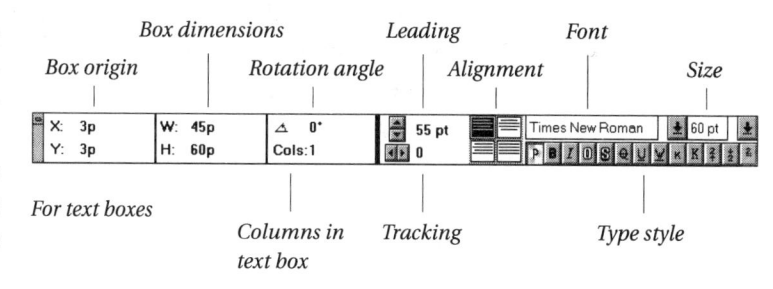

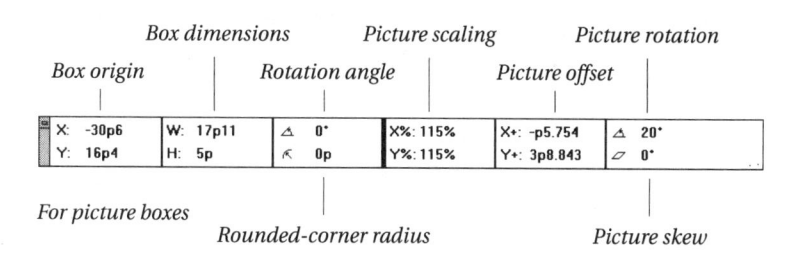

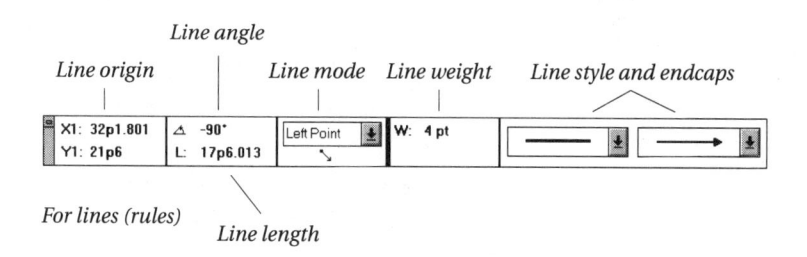

For text boxes: Box origin, Box dimensions, Rotation angle, Columns in text box, Leading, Alignment, Tracking, Font, Size, Type style

For picture boxes: Box origin, Box dimensions, Rotation angle, Rounded-corner radius, Picture scaling, Picture offset, Picture rotation, Picture skew

For lines (rules): Line origin, Line angle, Line length, Line mode, Line weight, Line style and endcaps

displays information about the contents or the style of the item (see "Items and Contents," later in this chapter).

▼ ▼

Tip: Keyboard Palettes. You can access and select items on either the Tool palette or the Measurements palette by using keyboard commands. You can jump to the first item on this palette by entering Control-Alt-M (this also opens the palette if it was closed). If you want to get to the font field of the palette quickly, you can press Control-Alt-Shift-M. To select the next tool on the Tool palette (to move down one), press Control-Tab. To select the next higher tool, press Control-Shift-Tab. If you have closed the Tool palette, you can open it by pressing either of these key commands. You also can use the Tab key to move through the Measurements palette.

David finds it much faster to toggle between items on the Tool palette using keystrokes, especially when moving between the Content tool and the Item tool. He hardly ever uses the mouse to click in the Measurements palette, preferring to press Control-Alt-M and through the items until he gets where he wants to be.

▼ ▼

NEW IN 3.3

See page 572

Document Layout palette. You can view the Document Layout palette by selecting "Show Document Layout" from the View menu. This palette displays a graphic, page-by-page representation of your document. When you first start using it, it's slightly weird, but the more you work with it, the more you realize how amazingly cool it is. We discuss the Document Layout palette in "Manipulating Your Document," later in this chapter, but—in a nutshell— you can use this palette for creating, deleting, and shuffling pages, assigning master pages, and creating multipage spreads. Generally, many of the functions of the Page menu can be performed by dragging icons in the Document Layout palette.

Library palette. Here's another QuarkXPress feature, which we discuss in much greater detail later in this chapter (we're not trying to tease; we're just taking things one step at a time). The Library palette lets you save page items, such as picture and text boxes, so that you can quickly access them later. It's a simple enough palette, but it has some very powerful uses. You can have more than one Library palette open at one time (each palette represents one Library file), and you are able to store up to 2,000 items in each library.

Other palettes. There are three additional palettes, for special uses: Trapping Information, Style Sheets, and Colors. They're not large, but you may find that you rarely use them all at once because the screen gets cluttered. We'll discuss in detail the Colors and Trapping Information palettes in Chapter 9, *Color*, and the Style Sheets palette in "Copy Flow," later in this chapter. For now, suffice it to say that each of these palettes can be shown or hidden by selecting items in the View menu. QuarkXPress remembers where each palette was when you quit or closed it, and puts each one back in the right place when you open them.

Dialog Boxes

You can perform almost every function in QuarkXPress with only the palettes and the menus. However, it is rarely efficient to work this way. Dialog boxes are areas in which you can usually change many specifications for an item at one time. For example, Figure 1-7 shows the Text Box Specifications dialog box. In this dialog box, you can modify any or every item quickly, then click OK to make those changes take effect.

Here's a quick lesson in terminology, if you're unfamiliar with dialog boxes. The area in which you enter a value is called a *field*. Often there are *check boxes* that can be set as on, off, or undefined. Many dialog boxes also contain *pop-up menus*, which act much like the menus at the top of the screen: Just position the cursor on them and press the mouse button. Then click the mouse button again on the item you want.

Typically, dialog boxes have two buttons: OK and Cancel. Clicking OK closes the dialog box and puts your changes into effect. Cancel closes the dialog box and ignores the changes you've made. Some dialog boxes have a Save option, which acts as OK. Other dialog boxes have an Apply button. Clicking on this

Figure 1-7
A typical dialog box

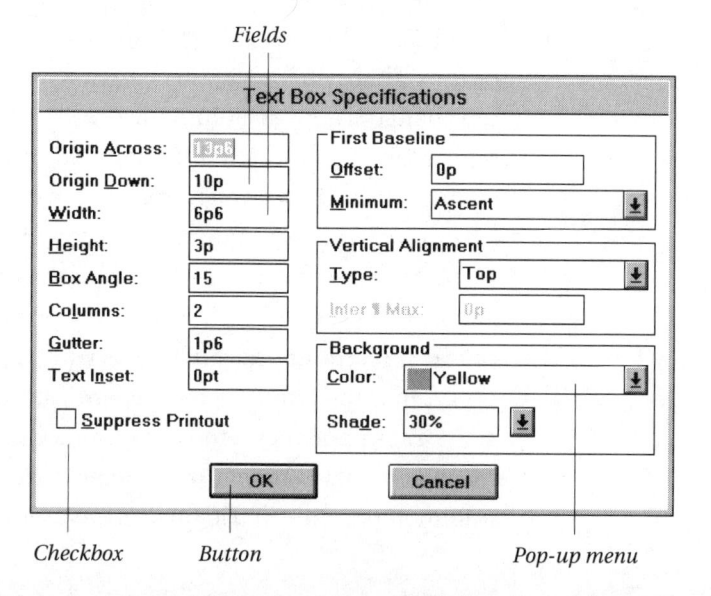

Checkbox *Button* *Pop-up menu*

button temporarily applies the settings you've made to the document so that you can see them. If you like what you see, you can then click OK. If you don't like it, you can usually type Control-Z to revert the dialog box to the last setting. In any case, you can click on Cancel to rid yourself of the dialog box and the changes you've made, even after using the Apply button.

▼▼▼▼▼▼▼▼▼▼▼▼▼▼▼▼▼▼▼▼▼▼▼▼▼▼▼

Tip: Pushing Your Buttons. Many choices in QuarkXPress's dialog boxes can be replaced with a keystroke. The keystroke is usually the first letter in the button's name. Look in the dialog box and you'll notice that the appropriate letter is underlined. For example, the Style dialog box has a Font list box with the "F" underlined; you can select the box by typing "F". When you're checking the spelling of a story, you can select the Skip button by typing "S". Note that any button that is highlighted (with a darker border than a normal button) can be selected by pressing Enter or Return (this is usually OK) , and you can almost always select Cancel with the Esc key.

▼▼▼▼▼▼▼▼▼▼▼▼▼▼▼▼▼▼▼▼▼▼▼▼▼▼▼

Tip: Continuous Apply. As we said earlier, the Apply button temporarily applies the change you made in a dialog box. You can then decide whether you want to actually make that change, revert back, or cancel the operation entirely. Holding down the Control key and clicking the Apply button speeds up the process some. When you do this, the Apply button changes to an Auto button. Then, whenever you change something in the dialog box, the change is applied automatically. Note that you might have to type a tab or move to a different field in the dialog box so that QuarkXPress knows you're ready to have the change entered. Also note that these changes, just like the Apply button changes, aren't permanent. You can always hit the Cancel button.

▼▼▼▼▼▼▼▼▼▼▼▼▼▼▼▼▼▼▼▼▼▼▼▼▼▼▼

Tip: Specifying Measurements. Unless you raise horses and measure everything in "hands," chances are that QuarkXPress and you share a common measurement system. QuarkXPress understands measurements in points, picas, inches, ciceros, centimeters, and millimeters. You can use these measurement units at any time, no matter what the default setting is (see "Changing Defaults," later in this chapter). Table 1-2 shows you how to specify a value for each system.

Table 1-2
Measurement systems

You can spec...	By typing...	For example...
points	pt or p	6pt or p6
picas	p	10p or 2p6 (2 picas, 6 points)
inches	"	6"
ciceros	c	2c or 6c3 (6 ciceros, 3 points)
centimeters	cm	3cm
millimeters	mm	210mm

You also can specify measurements with a plus or minus sign to build simple equations using one or more measurement units. For example, if a measurement is set to 10p, and you want to add 4cm, type "10p+4cm". Similarly, if you want to take away 1p2 (ever since calculators, our math skills have degenerated horribly), type "10p-1p2".

Using the Tools

Up until now, we have talked primarily about the general interface: this does this, that does that. Now our emphasis shifts toward the practical. The first step is learning about the tools on the Tool palette. Let's look at each tool on the Tool palette in turn.

Items and Contents

If you learn only one thing from this chapter, it should be the difference between items and contents. This is a concept that some people find difficult to understand, but it's really pretty simple. Moreover, the concept of items and contents is central to working efficiently in QuarkXPress.

Let's take it from the beginning. In order to place text on a page, you must place it in a text box. To put a graphic image on a page, you must place it in a picture box. A text box acts as a sort of corral that holds all of the words. There's almost no way a word can get outside the bounds of a Text box. Picture boxes act as a sort of window through which you can see a picture. In both cases, the content of the box is different from the box itself.

Boxes are *items*. What goes inside them is *content*. You can modify either one, but you need to use the correct tool at the correct time.

Item tool. The Item tool is the first tool on the Tool palette. It's used for selecting and moving items (picture and text boxes, rules, and so on). You can use the Item tool either by choosing it from the Tool palette or by holding down the Control key while any other tool is selected (though you can't select or work with multiple items unless you actually have the Item tool selected). We discuss all of the things you can do with items in "Manipulating Items," later in this chapter.

Content tool. The second tool on the Tool palette is the Content tool. This tool is used for adding, deleting, or modifying the contents of a Text or Picture box. Note that its palette icon consists of a text insert and a hand. When you have selected this tool from the Tool palette, QuarkXPress turns the cursor into one of these icons, depending on what sort of box you have highlighted (as we'll see in Chapter 6, *Pictures*, the hand is for moving images within a picture box).

Text Boxes

NEW IN 3.3
See page 557

In this chapter, we're talking mostly about items, which we sometimes call *page elements*. The first tool we encounter on the Tool palette that lets us make a page element is the Text Box tool. The method of creating text boxes is simple: Choose the Text Box tool from the Tool palette, then click and drag a text box. You can see exactly how large your text box is by watching the width and height values on the Measurements palette. Note that you can keep the text box a perfect square shape by holding down the Shift key while dragging.

Text boxes—as items—have six basic attributes: position, size, background color, columns, angle, and text inset. They also have border or frame attributes, which we discuss later in this chapter.

Position and size. All boxes are positioned by their upper-left corner. This point is called their *origin*. The first two fields in the Text Box Specifications dialog box (select the box and type Control-M) and the text box Measurements palette are the "Origin Across" and the "Origin Down." The size of the box is then specified by its width and height (the distances to the right and down from the origin).

▼ ▼

Tip: Quick Accurate Boxes. Some people tend to use a visual approach for creating and sizing boxes in QuarkXPress, while others work with a more mathematical or coordinate-based method. Fortunately, both methods work equally well. You can click and drag page elements to the size you want them, if you prefer to make a decision based on seeing what it looks like.

If you're working on a grid or have some other reason for needing a box of some specific size, you can draw a box to any size, and then go into the Measurements palette or Item Specifications dialog box to specify the origin coordinates, the width, and the height.

▼ ▼

Background color. Every box can have a background color set to any color on the color palette (see Chapter 9, *Color*) or set to None. Any background color other than None can be set to a specific tint. Note that 0 (zero) percent of a color is not transparent; it's opaque white.

The background color reaches to the inside edge of the frame around the box. There is a subtle distinction between going to the edge of the box and the edge of the frame: If you have specified a frame on a box, the background color only fills to the frame, rather than to the edge of the box (see "Frames," later in this chapter). If you have not specified a frame around a box, however, then the background color fills the box up to the border.

Columns. While the last two items were applicable to both text and picture boxes, the columns attribute is text-box-specific. Text boxes can be divided into a maximum of 30 columns. The size of each column is determined by the size of the gutter (blank space) between each column. You can set the gutter width only in the Text Box Specifications dialog box, although you can set the number of columns in either that dialog box or the Measurements palette.

Note that you cannot have columns with negative widths. In other words, the number of columns you can have is determined by the gutter width. For example, if your gutter width is 1 pica and your text box is 20 picas, you cannot have more than 11 columns. That leaves only 9 picas for all the columns—hardly enough for any text to fit on a line.

Text Inset. The last attribute particular to text boxes is "Text Inset." The Text Inset value determines how far your text is placed inside the four sides of the text box. For example, a Text Inset value of 0 (zero) places the text right up against the side of the text box. A Text Inset value of 3cm places the text no closer than 3 centimeters from the side of the box. The default setting is 1 point; we can't tell you why and find it rather obnoxious. We discuss how to change these default settings in "Changing Defaults". We usually just change the setting to zero text inset. You can only specify the Text Inset value in the Text Box Specifications dialog box.

▼ ▼

Tip: That Ol' Specifications Dialog Box. We use the Specifications dialog boxes for picture boxes, text boxes, and rules so often that we're glad to have some variance in how we get to it. You can open a Specifications dialog box for a page element in three ways.

- Double-click on the page element using the Item tool (remember, you can hold down the Control key to temporarily work with the Item tool).

- Select the item with either the Content or the Item tool and press Control-M.

- Select the item with either the Content or the Item tool and choose "Modify" from the Item menu.

Once you're in the dialog box, you can tab through the fields to get to the value you want to change. After a while, you start to memorize how many tabs it takes to get to a field, and you can type Control-M, tab, tab, tab, tab, tab, enter the value, press Return, and be out of there before QuarkXPress has time to catch up with you. That's when you know you're becoming an XPress Demon.

▼ ▼

Picture Boxes

As we said above, picture boxes are made to hold pictures. That's part of the truth, but let's hold off on that subject for a bit. Chapter 6, *Pictures*, tells us all about importing pictures. QuarkXPress gives us four different tools for creating picture boxes. Each tool makes a differently shaped box: rectangles, rounded-corner rectangles, ovals, and polygons. Let's take a brief look at each of these and why you should use them.

Rectangular Picture Box tool. This is the basic, no-frills picture box maker. As with the Text Box tool above, just click and drag a box to the size you want it. We use this box for 95 percent of the picture boxes we make.

Rounded-corner Picture Box tool. The Rounded-corner Picture Box tool makes rectangular picture boxes that have rounded corners. Is this of interest to you? Not to be biased, but some of the all-time worst designs that have come off a computer use rounded-corner picture boxes. We really dislike them. But then again, it's your design, and you can do what you like with it.

To be frank for a moment, this tool is redundant. Why? Any rectangular picture box can have rounded corners simply by making an adjustment to the Corner Radius value in the Picture Box Specifications dialog box or in the Measurements palette. Unless you use a lot of rounded-corner picture boxes (and if you do, we don't want to know about it), you could probably just use the Rectangular Picture Box tool and adjust the Corner Radius.

Oval Picture Box tool. When you need circles and ovals, the Oval Picture Box tool is the way to get them. Ovals are constrained to circles when you hold the Shift key down while dragging. Note that oval picture boxes are still defined by the rectangle that encloses them. That is, you modify an oval's shape by its height and width.

Polygon Picture Box tool. This function is…Wow! The Polygon Picture Box tool lets you make a picture box in almost any shape. The key is that the shape must be made of only straight lines.

The basic method for creating this type of frame is to click on the Polygon Picture Box tool, click where you want your first point to be (it doesn't matter which corner of the frame you begin with), then keep clicking at successive corners to create the shape you want. You'll notice that when the mouse hovers over the first point on the line, the cursor turns into a hollow circle. This indicates that QuarkXPress will close the path when you click and finish the polygon.

Polygonal picture boxes must have at least three points, but there's no limit that we can tell (and we've done some complex picture boxes; see "Tip: Making Your Gray-Scale Picture Transparent" in Chapter 8, *Modifying Images*).

Once you have created a polygon, QuarkXPress places an invisible rectangular border around it. The corner handles of this border, like the bounding border of ovals, define the polygon's height and width. Whenever you select the polygonal picture box, you see these corner handles. You can use them to stretch the polygonal picture box, but not to reshape it. To do that, use the Reshape Polygon command on the Item menu. We cover reshaping and resizing polygons and other picture boxes in "Manipulating Items," later in this chapter.

Picture Box Attributes

Picture boxes are similar to text boxes in several ways. First, they are positioned according to their origin (upper-left corner of the box). Second, they are generally sized by their width and height. Third, they have a background color (see "Text Boxes," above, for a discussion of these three items). However, some picture boxes have two attributes that text boxes don't: Corner Radius and Suppress Picture Printout. We'll hold off on covering the latter until Chapter 6, *Pictures*.

The Corner Radius attribute is applicable to rectangular and rounded-corner rectangle picture boxes. We've already told you how we feel about rounded corners on picture boxes, but—just in case you still want to make them—you can use this value to set the roundness of those corners should be. Literally, the "Corner Radius" defines the size of the radius of a circle tangent to the sides of the box (see Figure 1-8). You can change the corner radius of a rectangular picture box either in the Picture Box Specifications dialog box or in the Measurements palette.

Transforming Picture Boxes

Once you have a picture box created, you can change it into another type of picture box using the Picture Box Shape submenu under the Item menu (see Figure 1-9). For example, if you made a rectangular picture box on your page, you could turn it into an oval by first selecting the picture box, and then selecting the Oval Picture Box icon in the Picture Box Shape submenu.

This submenu has two other preset picture boxes that you might find useful. One is a bevelled corner picture box, and the other is a photo-frame picture box. The "depth" of the bevel or the concave curve depends on the Corner Radius setting.

The last item on the Picture Box Shape submenu is an icon representing a polygonal picture box. When you select a picture box and then choose this last icon, the picture box does not change in any obvious way. However, this is an extremely useful

Figure 1-8
Corner radius setting

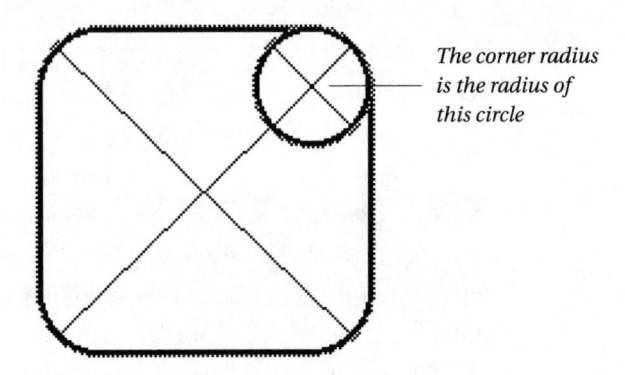

The corner radius is the radius of this circle

technique for making slight modifications to a picture box, as we'll see later in this chapter when we discuss the Reshape Polygon feature in "Resizing and Reshaping Picture Boxes."

▼ ▼

Tip: Careful With Those Ovals. Use the oval or polygon shaped boxes only when you must have that shape. Using a rectangle or square box for the majority of your pictures can cut your printing time in half, or even to a third of what it takes when you use ovals.

▼ ▼

Lines and Arrows

The Tool palette contains two tools to draw lines and arrows on your page: the Orthogonal Line tool and the Line tool. To be precise, you really only lines draw, but those lines can be in several styles and have arrowheads and tailfeathers. You can create these lines with any thickness between 0 (zero) and 504 points (that's a pretty thick line), and at any angle. A zero width line is the same as a "hairline," which QuarkXPress defines as .12 points.

Orthogonal Line tool. For those of you who aren't in arm's reach of a dictionary, orthogonal means that the lines you draw with this tool can be only horizontal or vertical. Drawing a line is easy: Choose this tool from the Tool palette, then click and drag to where you want the line to go. This tool is somewhat redundant, as you can constrain the movement of the Line tool orthogonally by holding down the Shift key. But since most of the rules we make are horizontal or vertical, it's nice to have this option.

Figure 1-9
Picture Box Shape submenu

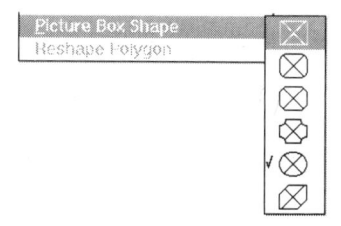

Line tool. The Line tool can make a line at any angle. If you hold down the Shift key while dragging out the line, you can constrain the line to 45 or 90 degrees.

Line Attributes

Once you have created a line, you can apply certain attributes to it, including line weight, style, endcaps, and color. Each of these can be specified in the Line Specifications dialog box. Several attributes can also be specified in the Measurements palette.

Line weight. We always use the word "weight" rather than "width," which is what QuarkXPress calls the thickness of a line. The line weight is centered on the line; that is, if you specify a 6-point line, 3 points fall on one side of the line you drew, and 3 points fall on the other side. This value appears in both the Line Specifications dialog box and the Measurements palette. However, we never use mundane methods like that; instead, we type Control-Shift-\ (backslash) to bring up the Line Width dialog box (which, as we discuss later, you can also use for specifying type size). Table 1-3 shows several other ways to change a line's weight with keystrokes. Note that these are the same keystrokes as for changing the size of type.

Table 1-3
Changing line weight

To change a line...	Type...
Increase weight by preset amount	Control-Shift-Period (>)
Increase weight by 1 point	Control-Shift-Alt-Period (>)
Decrease weight by preset amount	Control-Shift-Comma (<)
Decrease weight by 1 point	Control-Shift-Alt-Comma (<)

Color and shade. You can choose any color on your document's color palette (see Chapter 9, *Color*), then tint it to any value from 0 (zero) to 100 percent, in 1-percent increments (0 percent is white). This specification is only available in the Line Specifications dialog box.

Line Style and endcaps. Lines don't have to be boring; you can spice them up with a new style or add endcaps to turn them into arrows. You can choose one of 11 different line styles and one of six endcap combinations by selecting them from two pop-up menus in either the Style menu or the Measurements palette (see Figure 1-10).

Six of the line styles are defined as multiple lines. The weight of each line of the group is determined by a ratio. For example, each line in the double-line style is given a third of the total weight. So, if you specify the double line with a 12-point thickness, each black line is 4 points thick, and the white space between them is 4 points across.

Even though you have six to choose from, the endcap styles are limited—with arrowheads and tailfeathers or without them. Because QuarkXPress defines all of its lines as going from left to right or from top to bottom, you can control which side the arrowhead should be on by choosing the proper endcap from the pop-up menu. For example, if your line was drawn from left to right and you want the head of the arrow to be on the left end of the line, you should select an endcap that has the arrow pointing to the left.

Manipulating Items

Once you've created a page element (item) such as a picture box or a line, what can you do with it? A lot. In this section we talk about how to move, rotate, resize, reshape, lock, duplicate, and delete items. Remember that we're talking only about the items themselves here, so you need to select the items with the Item tool to perform most of these changes.

Figure 1-10
Line styles and endcaps

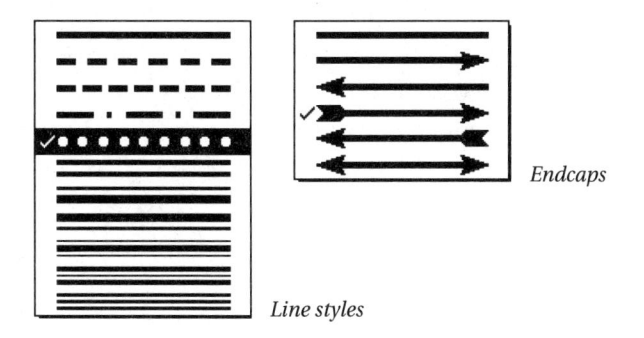

Endcaps

Line styles

Tip: See It Happen While You Do It. Note that if you hold down the mouse button for half a second, you can see the picture as it is cropped, moved, rotated, or scaled. No, you don't have to count out half a second; just wait until you see the object flash quickly before you start dragging.

Moving Items

You can move an entire page element in several ways. First, by selecting the Item tool, then clicking on the object and dragging it. This sometimes gets tricky if you have many different overlapping objects on a page. For example, normally you can click anywhere within an empty picture box to select it. However, if you're trying to select a picture box that has a picture in it, you must click on the picture itself.

The second method for moving an item is by changing its origin coordinates. We find this method especially useful if we need to move the item a specific amount. For example, let's say we have a text box with its origin at 3 picas across and 3 picas down. If we want to move a text box horizontally 1.5 inches, we change the Origin Across coordinate in the Measurements palette to 3p+1.5", then press Enter. The box is moved over an inch and a half.

A third method for moving items is to select them and use the arrow keys on the keyboard. Each time you press an arrow key, the item moves 1 point in that direction. Pressing Alt-arrow moves the item a tenth of a point.

▼▼▼▼▼▼▼▼▼▼▼▼▼▼▼▼▼▼▼▼▼▼▼▼▼▼▼▼

Tip: Techniques for Item Placement. If you have a style of placing and sizing your page elements—such as lines and picture boxes—that works for you, stick to it. To paraphrase, "a manner of picture box placement is a real possession in a changing world." Nonetheless, here are some basic guides that we've found helpful:

- Use pica/point measurements for everything except basic page size. This is the standard among designers and printers, and allows precision without having to deal with numbers like .08334 inches (which is 6 points, or half a pica). It also makes dealing with type on your page easier to think of in terms of picas and points, since that's how type is generally specified.

- Try to use round numbers for most of your measurements. Creating a box while at the Fit in Window size usually gives you measurements that have coordinates out to the thousandth of a point, such as 6p3.462. It might seem like a picky detail, but in the long run, it can come in handy to either create your boxes at Actual Size and then resize them if needed. Or, if you must work at a reduced or enlarged view, go into the Measurements palette or the Item Specifications dialog box (double-click on the box or type Control-M) and change the coordinates and the sizes to round numbers.

▼▼▼▼▼▼▼▼▼▼▼▼▼▼▼▼▼▼▼▼▼▼▼▼▼▼▼▼

Rotating Items

The rotation of an item is an attribute that can be specified in either the Item Specifications dialog box or in the Measurements palette. Note that positive rotation values rotate the object counter-clockwise; negative values rotate it clockwise. Most objects are rotated from their centers. This center may not be where you think it is, however. The center is defined as the middle of the object's bounding box. Figure 1-11 shows a sample of an object that's center is not where you might expect. The

Figure 1-11
Rotating items

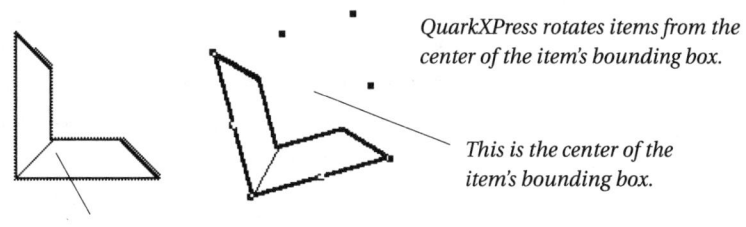

QuarkXPress rotates items from the center of the item's bounding box.

This is the center of the item's bounding box.

This is where we'd expect it to rotate.

Rotation tool, however, lets you select your own center of rotation by simply clicking on the point of rotation you want, even if it's outside the item's boundary.

Lines are the main exception when it comes to the center of rotation. Lines are rotated differently depending on their Mode (see "Lines," below). For example, if a line is in Right Point mode when you specify a rotation, the line rotates around the right endpoint.

If you are more visually minded, you can rotate items using the Rotation tool mentioned above as follows.

1. Select a page item.

2. Choose the Rotation tool from the Tool palette.

3. Click where you want the center of rotation.

4. Drag the Rotation tool. As you drag, the object is rotated in the direction you drag.

We don't like to use this tool, but that's just us and our bias. It may suit you well. However, it's significantly harder to control the rotation using the tool than by typing a specific rotation.

Resizing and Reshaping Items

Resizing an object is just about as simple as moving it. Reshaping it may be that simple, or it may be slightly more complex. Resizing and reshaping lines is a little different from resizing or reshaping picture or text boxes, so let's take them one at a time.

Picture and text boxes. Before we get into reshaping polygons, let's discuss the basics: resizing and reshaping rectangular and oval boxes. Once again, you have a choice between using QuarkXPress's interactive click-and-drag style, or working in measurements. To resize by clicking and dragging, you must place the screen cursor over one of the box's handles; a pointing finger cursor then appears. Boxes have eight handles (one on each side, one on each corner) that you can drag to resize. Dragging a side handle resizes the box in one direction—horizontally or vertically. Dragging a corner handle resizes the box in two directions—horizontally *and* vertically. As long as "Reshape Polygon" is not selected from the Item menu (if it's selected, it has a check mark next to it), you can resize polygons using this same click-and-drag method.

In order to maintain an item's width and height ratio, you can hold down the Alt and Shift keys while dragging. If you want to constrain the box into a square or circle, hold down only the Shift key while dragging (if the object is rectangular or oval, it snaps into a square or a circle).

The second method of resizing and reshaping picture and text boxes is to change their height and width values. These values are available in both the Item Specifications dialog box and the Measurements palette. Unless you're a math wizard, it's difficult to keep an object's aspect ratio (width-to-height) this way. Instead, this is a great way to make a box exactly the size you want it. For example, if you want an 8-by-10-inch picture box, you can draw one to any size you'd like, then change its width and height coordinates to 8 inches and 10 inches.

Polygonal picture boxes. Once you make that last segment of a polygon by clicking on its beginning/ending point, it seems as if the game is over. If the Reshape Polygon item is not selected from the Item menu, then QuarkXPress places a rectangular bounding box around the polygonal picture box, and there's no way to move a corner or a line segment. The key there, of course, is the Reshape Polygon feature from the Item menu. If you select a polygonal picture box and then enable Reshape Polygon, the bounding box disappears and each corner point gets its own handle.

To move a corner point, simply click on it and drag it someplace else. You also can move an entire line segment, including the two points on either end of it, by just clicking and dragging it. To add a new corner point, you can hold down the Control key and click where you want it. Or, if you want to delete a corner point that was already there, you can hold down the Control key and click on top of it.

Lines. Most people define lines by the two endpoints. However, QuarkXPress can define any line in four different ways. Each line description is called a mode (see Figure 1-12). The four modes are as follows.

- **Endpoints.** These describe the line by two sets of coordinates: X1,Y1 and X2,Y2. In the Line Specifications dialog box, these may be called the "Left Endpoint" and the "Right Endpoint," or the "Top Endpoint" and the "Bottom Endpoint," depending on how steep the line is.

- **Left Point mode.** In Left Point mode, QuarkXPress describes a line by three values: its left or bottom endpoint, its length, and its angle.

- **Right Point mode.** QuarkXPress uses the same three values for the Right Point mode, except it uses the right or top coordinate.

- **Midpoint.** The fourth mode, "Midpoint", defines lines with its length and angle based on the coordinate of the most central point; that is, if a line is 2 inches long, QuarkXPress draws the line 1 inch out on either side from the midpoint.

Figure 1-12
Line modes

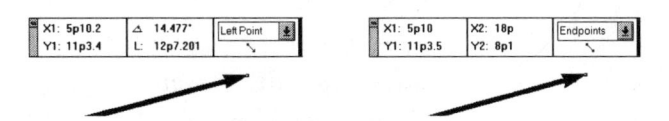

Any line can change mode, if you're in the mood. You can define a line while in one mode, modify it with another, and move it with another. For example, let's say you draw a line someplace on your page. You then find that you want to rotate it slightly. You have the choice to rotate the line from its left point, right point, or midpoint by selecting the proper mode from the Measurements palette or the Line Specifications dialog box, then to change the line's rotation value. If you want to move just the left point of the line over 3 points, you can switch to Endpoints mode and alter the X1,X2 coordinate.

▼▼▼▼▼▼▼▼▼▼▼▼▼▼▼▼▼▼▼▼▼▼▼▼▼▼▼▼

Tip: Constraining Lines. We all know that you can hold down the Shift key while you resize or reshape a line to hold the line horizontally and vertically. However, you also can constrain a line along its angle of rotation by holding down the Alt and Shift keys together while dragging an endpoint. This is similar to constraining boxes to their width/height proportions.

▼▼▼▼▼▼▼▼▼▼▼▼▼▼▼▼▼▼▼▼▼▼▼▼▼▼▼▼

Tip: Making Line Joins Join. We're putting a bid in here for a Line tool that can draw more than one segment at a time (like a polygon that doesn't have to be closed up). Until then, however, we are forced to use single-segment lines, carefully joining them at their corners. Note that if you place two lines' endpoints together, they won't necessarily join properly; that is, if two lines come together at a 90-degree angle, and their endpoints are specified exactly the same, the corner joint looks chiseled out (see Figure 1-13).

You can fill in this missing piece by moving the endpoint of one of the lines half the line thickness. For example, if you are using 12-point lines, one of the lines should be extended 6 points farther. Remember, you can adjust the line mode and specify an endpoint coordinate as an equation (for example, 45p3.6+6pt).

Also, note that you can simply use the Space/Align feature (which we'll discuss later in this chapter). However, this doesn't extend the line; instead, it actually moves it.

▼▼▼▼▼▼▼▼▼▼▼▼▼▼▼▼▼▼▼▼▼▼▼▼▼▼▼▼

Figure 1-13
Lines don't always join properly

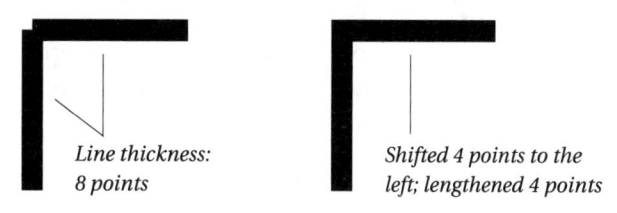

*Line thickness:
8 points*

Shifted 4 points to the left; lengthened 4 points

Extend the line to fill in the missing piece

Locking Items

There are times when you want an item to stay exactly as it is. For example, if you've painstakingly placed multiple text boxes on your page, you probably don't want to move or resize them accidentally. You can lock any page item down to its spot, making it invulnerable to being moved or resized with the Item tool. Just select the item with either the Item or the Content tool and choose "Lock" from the Item menu (or type Control-L).

If an item is locked, the Item tool cursor turns into a padlock when passed over it. You cannot move it by clicking and dragging either the item or its control handles. We find this feature especially helpful when we're working on a complex page and don't want an accidental click here or a drag there to ruin our work.

To unlock an item, select it and type Control-L again (or choose "Unlock" from the menu).

▼ ▼

Tip: Moving Locked Items. As usual, no matter how much we say you can't do something, there is a way to get around it. One way you can move a locked item is to change its Origin Across and Origin Down settings in the Item Specifications dialog box or in the Measurements palette (see "Resizing and Reshaping Items," above). You can also move a locked item through the Space/Align feature (discussed later in this chapter). Typically, QuarkXPress figures that if you go out of your way to move a locked item, it'll do it.

▼ ▼

Duplicating Items

The last set of features we discuss in this section on manipulating items revolves around duplicating items on your page. There are three ways of duplicating a page element such as a picture or text box: copy and paste it, duplicate it, or use "Step and Repeat."

Copy and paste. Selecting an item, copying it, and pasting it (Control-C and Control-V) is the QuarkXPress Way, though it's not always the most efficient or precise way. Many people get confused when they copy and paste picture and text boxes, because they don't use the correct tools. Remember, the Item tool is for working with items (boxes and lines), and the Content tool is for working with the contents of boxes. If you have the Content tool selected and you try to copy a text box, you only copy the text you may have inadvertently highlighted within the box, rather than the box itself. The Item tool actually copies the text box with the text in it.

When you paste the page item, the program places it in the middle of your screen, which is not always where you want it. Then you can use the methods we described earlier to move it around your page.

Duplicate. If you select an item with the Item tool or the Content tool, and choose "Duplicate" from the Item menu (or type Control-D), QuarkXPress duplicates that item, displacing it from the original with the horizontal and vertical offsets last used in "Step and Repeat" (see below). You can then move the new item to where you want it. The default setting for "Duplicate" is ¼ inch to the right and down from the original object.

Step and Repeat. The Step and Repeat feature can best be described as a powerhouse, and we wish every program had it. "Step and Repeat" under the Item menu (Control-Alt-D) lets you select one or more objects and duplicate them with specific horizontal and vertical offsets as many times as you like. For example, if you want 35 lines, each 9 points away from each other across the page, you select the line, choose "Step and Repeat" from the Item menu, and enter "35" in the Repeat Count field, "9 pt" in the Horizontal Offset field, and "0" (zero) in the Vertical Offset field. After you use "Step and Repeat," you can type Control-Z to undo all of the duplications.

Both "Duplicate" and "Step and Repeat" have certain limitations. You cannot duplicate an item so that any part of the duplicate is off the pasteboard. If you are working with constrained items, you cannot duplicate them so that any of the copies would fall outside of the constraining box (see "Constraining," later in this chapter.) Items that you do duplicate from within a constrained group become part of that constrained group. However, duplicating an item from a set of grouped objects does not necessarily include the copy in the group. If you duplicate a locked item, the duplicate is also locked.

▼ ▼

Tip: Clone Item. If you're an Aldus FreeHand user, you're probably familiar with the Control-C keystroke used to duplicate an item without any offset. This is called *cloning*. We can perform a similar operation in QuarkXPress by selecting "Step and Repeat" from the Item menu (we type Control-Alt-D because it's usually faster), then quickly typing "1-Tab-0-Tab-0-Enter" (the "Enter" is to press the OK button). This makes a duplicate of an item that sits precisely on top of the original.

▼ ▼

Deleting Items

As we suggested above, there is a difference between deleting the contents of a picture or text box and deleting the box itself. When the contents of a box—such as a picture or text—are deleted, the box still remains. When the box itself is deleted, everything goes. We think the easiest way to delete a page item is to select it (with either the Item or the Content tool) and type Control-K. This is the same as selecting "Delete" from the Item menu. The second easiest way to delete an item is to select it with the Item tool and press the Backspace key on your keyboard.

A third way to delete an item is to select it with the Item tool and then select Cut or Clear from the Edit menu. Of course, cutting it actually saves the item on the Clipboard so that you can place it somewhere else later.

The only one of these methods that works for deleting an item from a group is Control-K. That's because to remove this kind of page item, you must first select it with the Content tool, or else you end up deleting the entire group.

Relationships Between Items

When it comes to layout, QuarkXPress is both laid-back and uptight. Fortunately, we get to choose the mood. Sure, there are times when we want to position items freely and independently on the page. That's well and good, but when design calls for some consistent relationship between items, it's nice to know our layout program will automatically preserve some order for us.

Ahh…constraint: freedom from chaos. The beauty of QuarkXPress is that it lets us set or relax certain constraints between items. Strict or lax, QuarkXPress let's us proceed with each layout in the manner that suits it. A typical example is the "parent/child" relationship of text and picture boxes in QuarkXPress. Create a box within a box: If you want constraint, QuarkXPress keeps the newly created box (child) within the underlying box (parent), no matter where you move it. But you can turn this constraint off when it gets in your way. In this section, we talk about controlling the relationships between items: layering, grouping, constraining, and finally, positions on the page relative to other page elements.

Layering Items

QuarkXPress, like most electronic publishing programs, handles multiple objects on a page by layering them. Each page item (picture boxes, text boxes, and lines) is always on a higher or lower layer than the other page items. This is generally an intuitive approach to working with page elements; it's just what you would do if each of the objects were on little pieces of paper in front of you. The one difference is that, while you can have multiple objects on the same layer with each other on paper, each and every item is on its own layer on a QuarkXPress page. When you're placing objects on your page, you work from the bottom layer up. That is, the first object you place on your page is the back-most object, the second object is on top of it, and so on.

If none of your page elements touches or overlaps another, then layering has almost no relevance to you. However, when they do touch or overlap in some way, you want to be able to control which objects overlap each other. The primary methods for controlling layering are the Bring to Front and Send to Back commands in the Item menu.

The Bring to Front and Send to Back commands function as sweeping controls, moving a selected object all the way to the back or all the way to the front layer. You can also take a step-by-step approach and use the Bring Forward or Send Backward commands to move an item forward or backward just one layer at a time.

▼ ▼

Tip: Grab Down Deep. If you've ever struggled to get ahold of an item that's buried three levels deep underneath other items, you'll be happy to know that you can select page items that are covered up by other page items. You don't need to drag all of the items placed in front out of the way. Hold down the Control-Alt-Shift keys while clicking with either the Item or Content tool. One click selects the object one layer down, the second click selects the object on the next layer down, and so on. Note that you don't have to click directly on the hidden object itself; getting close is what matters.

▼ ▼

Grouping Objects

If you'd like to handle a number of items as a group, instead of one at a time, here's the good news: You can select multiple items on a page and move or modify them together. And here's even better news: those items can be grouped together to act as a single object, which makes it even easier to position and move a group of objects on the page with the Item tool, and you can still get in and modify single elements of the group using the Content tool.

Here's what you do.

1. Using the Item tool, select the items you want grouped. You can hold down the Shift key to select multiple items or you can drag a marquee over or around the objects. (Any object that touches the marquee is selected.)

2. Select "Group" from the Item menu (or type Control-G).

It's that easy. When the group is selected with the Item tool, a dotted line shows the bounding box of the grouped objects (see Figure 1-14).

To ungroup a bunch of objects, select the grouped object with the Item tool and select "Ungroup" from the Item menu (or type Control-U).

Figure 1-14
Grouped objects

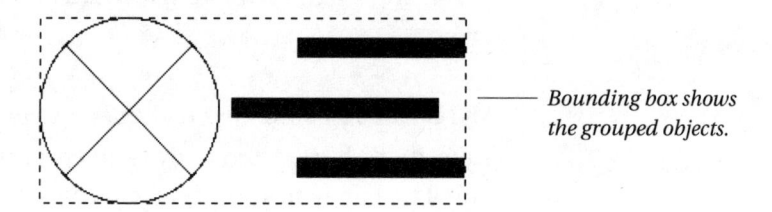

Bounding box shows the grouped objects.

▼▼▼▼▼▼▼▼▼▼▼▼▼▼▼▼▼▼▼▼▼▼▼▼▼

Tip: Multilevel Grouping. Not only can you group multiple objects, but you can group multiple groups, or groups and single objects. This means that you can build levels of grouped objects. For example, on a catalog page you may have six picture boxes, each with a caption in a text box. You can group each caption box with its picture box, then select these six grouped objects and group them together. Later, if you ungroup the six objects, each picture box is still grouped with its caption box.

▼▼▼▼▼▼▼▼▼▼▼▼▼▼▼▼▼▼▼▼▼▼▼▼▼

Modifying Grouped Objects

As we mentioned above, once you have grouped a set of objects, you can still modify each one of them using the Content tool. Just select the element and change it. Each item can be rotated, resized, or edited just as usual. To move a single object in a grouped selection, hold down the Control key to get a temporary

Item tool, then move the object where you want it and release the Control key.

QuarkXPress lets you do some nifty things with grouped items. If you select "Modify" from the Item menu (or type Control-M, or double-click on the group with the Item tool), QuarkXPress gives you a specifications dialog box for the group. This only works for a simple group, not for a group of groups. If every object in a group is the same type of object (all rules, or all text boxes, etc.), it gives you a modified specifications dialog box for that type of object. The Origin Across and Down values are the measurements for the upper-left corner of the group, rather than any one object within the group.

If you change a value in one of these composite specifications dialog boxes, you change that value in every one of the objects in the group. For example, if you specify a background color to the grouped objects, the background color is applied to all of the boxes in the group. If you apply a Picture Rotation value of 20 degrees to a group of picture boxes, the contents in each of the picture boxes are rotated within their box (see Chapter 6, *Pictures*).

You also can change several specifications for a group of mixed-type objects. For example, you can specify "Suppress Printout" for a group, and each of the objects in the group is assigned "Suppress Printout." If you later ungroup the objects, the settings you made while they were grouped remain.

Note that if you have any lines (rules) in the group, changing the background color of the group affects the color of the line itself.

▼ ▼

Tip: Modifying Frames for Groups. If your grouped objects don't contain any other grouped objects, you can modify each and every frame in the group by selecting "Frames" from the Item menu (or typing Control-B). You can't select this when there are grouped groups.

▼▼▼▼▼▼▼▼▼▼▼▼▼▼▼▼▼▼▼▼▼▼▼▼▼▼▼

Tip: Watch Out for What You Group. We love the ability to drag a marquee out with the Item tool in order to select multiple objects. It's fast, it's effective, and it picks up everything in its path. Sometimes it even picks up things you don't want it to pick up. For example, let's say you have an automatic text box on your page and you place some picture boxes on it. If you drag a marquee across the page to select the picture boxes, chances are you'll select the text box, too. You may not notice this at first, but if you start dragging the group off into a library or someplace else, you'll be dragging the text box along for the ride. This spells havoc (press Control-Z quick to undo the last action).

So, just a quick lesson from people who've been there: watch out for what you select and group. And if you do select more than you want, remember that you can deselect items by holding down the Shift key and clicking on them. (The same technique works for adding more items to a selection.)

▼▼▼▼▼▼▼▼▼▼▼▼▼▼▼▼▼▼▼▼▼▼▼▼▼▼▼

Constraining

We talked a little about the parent and child box constraint relationships earlier in this section. Let's be clear here, for those not familiar with this feature. We're not referring to the type of constraining that people usually talk about (and that we've mentioned earlier in this book), which refers to holding down the Shift key to constrain the movement of an object to a 45- or 90-degree angle. This is a different sort of constraint.

When David thinks about parent and child box constraints, he thinks of a baby's playpen (probably some leftover childhood trauma, but he doesn't want to get into it). A playpen is basically a box that is a structure in its own right. However, you can place objects (or babies) into it, and they can't get out unless you physically take them out.

Similarly, a parent box is a text or picture box that has certain structural constraints so that any items created or placed inside its boundaries ("child" items) can't easily get outside those boundaries. For example, imagine a text box that was specified as a parent box. It acts as a normal text box. However, when you draw a line inside it using one of the Line tools, that line cannot be moved or resized to extend outside the text box. The only way you can get it out is to cut it and paste it elsewhere.

We know it sounds awful, but as we said, there *are* some great applications. For example, building a table by adding vertical and horizontal rules to a text box is aided if those rules don't slip away when you move the box (child items move with their parents). Also, if you have a specific area in which all items must remain, creating a parental constraint ensures that you don't accidentally mess up your specs when your eyes are bleary at three in the morning.

You can create parent and child box constraints in two ways: automatic constraints and manual constraints. Let's look at each of these in turn.

Automatic constraints. With automatic constraints turned on, all picture and text boxes act as parent constraint boxes. You can turn automatic constraints on and off by clicking the Auto Constraint button in the General Preferences dialog box. You can turn on "Auto Constrain" while you create boxes specified to act as parent boxes and child items, and then turn it off to create "normal" boxes and items. This means that when you turn "Auto Constraint" off, the parent boxes act only as parent boxes to the child items that you created while "Auto Constraint" was on.

Note that the parent box and the child items are grouped when you select them with the Item tool. To unconstrain these items, see "Manual constraints," below.

Manual constraints. If you prefer, you can apply your own parent and child box constraints to a set of objects by manually constraining them. It's easy to do.

1. Make sure the page elements you want to be child items are totally within the boundaries of your parent box.

2. Make sure the soon-to-be parent box is behind each of the objects that are soon-to-be-constrained. Parent boxes

must be on a lower layer than their children. You can think of the playpen analogy: The playpen must be under—and surround—the child.

3. Group the child and parent objects and boxes together (see "Grouping," above).

4. Select "Constrain" from the Item menu.

Those objects that are on top of the parent box and in that group are constrained to the boundaries of the parent box.

You can deconstrain this group of objects by clicking on the parent/child group with the Item tool and selecting either "Unconstrain" or "Ungroup" from the Item menu. "Unconstrain" removes the constraints, but leaves the items grouped. "Ungroup" removes both the grouping and constraining specifications (you cannot have parent/child constraints without grouping).

Aligning and Distributing Objects

The Space/Align feature lets you line up a bunch of page items or distribute them evenly across a given space. We didn't know how badly we needed it until we started using it. Now we use it all the time.

Both alignment and distribution are covered in the same feature: the Space/Align function in the Item menu. Selecting this function brings up the Space/Align Items dialog box (see Figure 1-15). This dialog box is broken down into Horizontal and Vertical sections, and you can use one or the other—or both—by clicking in their respective check boxes.

Because the controls are the same in each area (except that you can select "Top Edges" and "Bottom Edges" in the Vertical

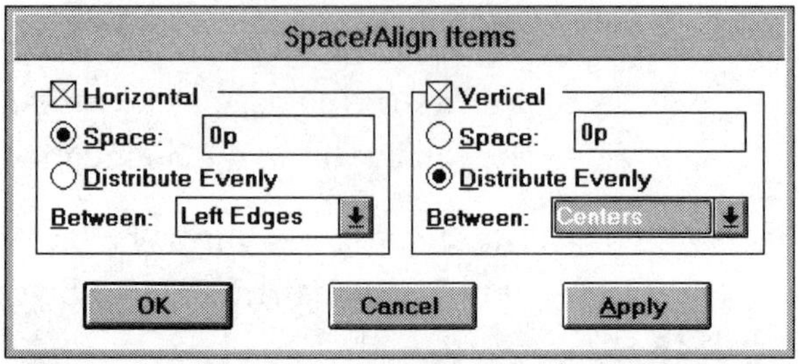

Figure 1-15
Space/Align items dialog box

section items rather than "Left Edges" and "Right Edges" in the Horizontal section), we discuss the basics of each feature just once (see Figure 1-16 for examples of alignment and distribution). The controls that appear in the Horizontal and Vertical areas are Between, Space, and Distribute Evenly.

Between. So, you want to align or distribute two or more objects. But do you want to base this function on the centers of the objects, the left edges, or the right edges? Or do you want to base the movement on the edges of the items themselves? You can do any one of these by selecting the option from the Between pop-up menu. As we mentioned above, "Left Edges" and "Right Edges" change to "Top Edges" and "Bottom Edges," depending on whether you're in the Horizontal or Vertical section of the dialog box.

The concept of aligning or distributing objects based on "Item" is sometimes confusing to people. "Item" refers to the bounding box of the page element. For example, horizontally aligning two text boxes based on "Item" results in the right side of one box being aligned with the left side of the second. Note

Figure 1-16
Alignment and distribution

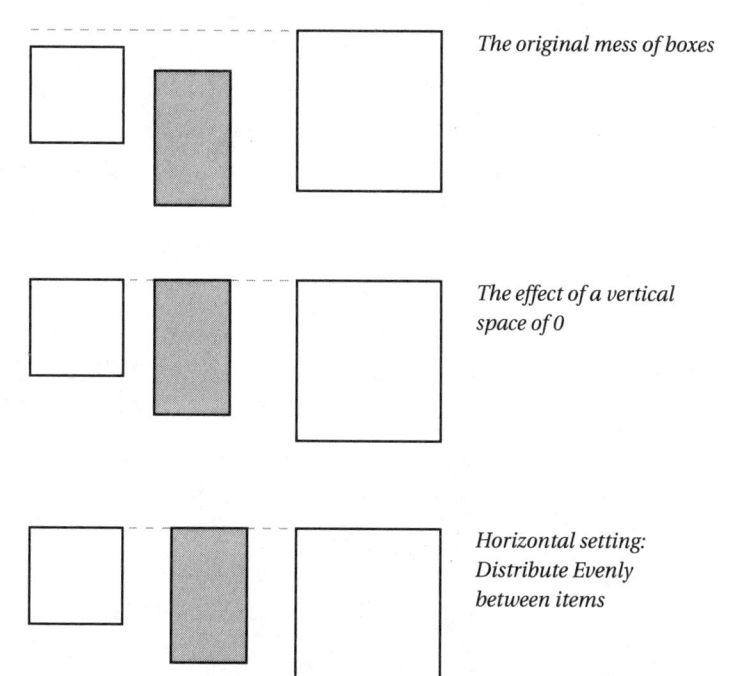

The original mess of boxes

The effect of a vertical space of 0

Horizontal setting: Distribute Evenly between items

that we said this is based on the bounding box of the object, which is the smallest rectangle that can enclose the entire object. This may result in alignment that you might not expect, especially when you're working with oddly shaped polygonal picture boxes.

Space. Enabling the Space value lets you align objects. The value in the Space field determines how far apart the objects should be. For example, let's say you are horizontally aligning two boxes and you have "Centers" selected in the Between pop-up menu. If you specify "0p" (zero picas) as the Space value, the center of the first box is centered exactly on the center of the second box. If you specify "5p" as the Space value, the center of the first box is placed 5 picas away from the center of the second box.

But which box moves? The topmost or leftmost items are stationary; they are the reference points for alignment. Other page elements move to align with them, even if those objects are locked.

As we said, we use alignment all the time. If we have four text boxes that we want to line up on their left edges, we no longer have to select each one to make sure their horizontal positioning is equal. Now, we just select them all and align their left edges with the Space value set to zero. Similarly, if we have multiple objects on the page and want to center all of them on top of each other, we can apply both a vertical and a horizontal alignment to them, with "Centers" selected in the Between pop-up menu.

Distribute Evenly. Instead of aligning objects, you can distribute them across an area. For example, if you have three picture boxes, you can move the center box so that the space between the center of the first box and the middle box is the same as the space between the middle box and the last box. We find distribution very helpful when we have a number of items that are all the same size, but are scattered around the page.

"Distribute Evenly" always takes the leftmost and rightmost, or the top and bottom, page elements that you have selected and uses them as the distribution boundaries. In other words, those objects don't move, while all of the other objects that you selected for distribution do move, including locked items.

Note that the Between pop-up menu has an effect on how page items are distributed. For example, QuarkXPress can distribute the items by their centers, left edges, right edges, and so on. The method that you use should be determined by the context.

Getting Around Your Document

One of the first things you'll notice about QuarkXPress is the pasteboard—an area that surrounds each of the pages in a document. This wide perimeter has many uses, including bleeding objects off a page and temporarily storing boxes and lines. We also find it useful just for giving a better view of the page and how it will print.

However, unless you happen to work on an enormous screen, you never get to see much of the pasteboard—much less your entire page—at one time. Let's look at how you can move around to see different parts of a page, and different pages, within your document.

Scrolling

The first step in moving within your document is *scrolling*. Scrolling refers to using the horizontal and vertical scroll bars on the right and bottom sides of the document window to move your page (see Figure 1-17). If you click in the arrow at the top of the vertical scroll bar, you move a bit "up" your page (closer to the top). If you click in the left arrow in the horizontal scroll bar, you move to the left on your page, and so on. We find that many people never get past this elementary level of scrolling. This is conceivably the slowest method you could use. We implore you to look at our alternatives, instead.

You can shift large distances in your document by moving the little white box in the scroll bars up and down. Just drag the box along the bar. Clicking in the area above the white box moves you up one screen; clicking below the box moves you

Figure 1-17
The document window

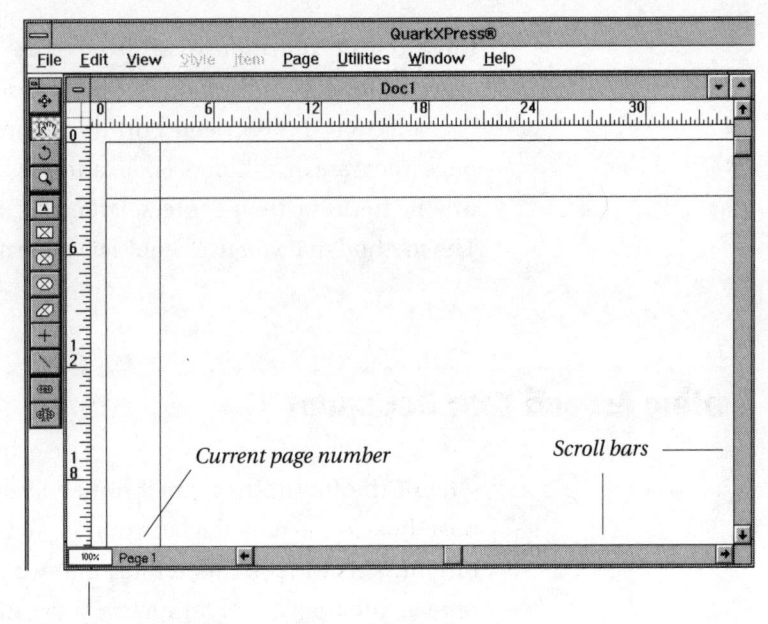

Current page number
Scroll bars
View percentage field

down one screen, and so on. You also can use keystroke commands to move around the screen vertically. Table 1-4 shows you how.

Table 1-4
Moving around within your document

To move	Type
Up one screen	Page up
Down one screen	Page down
Start of document	Home
End of document	End
First page	Shift-Home
Last page	Shift-End
Next page	Shift-Page down
Previous page	Shift-Page up

NEW IN 3.3
See page 565

If you do use the scroll bar arrows to get around, you definitely want to examine the Scroll Speed feature in the Application Preferences dialog box (accessed via the Preference command under the Edit menu). This feature lets you control how far each click in a scroll bar arrow takes you. For example, if you have the Scroll Speed set to "Fast," then one click in an arrow may move you an entire screen or more. If you have it set to "Slow", a click may only move the screen 1 or 2 points.

▼▼▼▼▼▼▼▼▼▼▼▼▼▼▼▼▼▼▼▼▼▼▼▼

Tip: "Live" Scrolling. When you drag the white box along the scroll bar, it's often difficult to tell how far you've gone on the page. This is because the vertical scroll bar represents the entire length of your document and the horizontal scroll bar represents the full length of the pasteboard. If you have multipage spreads in your document, the pasteboard can be very large (see more on spreads in Chapter 2, *Document Construction*). But if you hold down the Alt key while you drag the white scroll bar box, the screen scrolls *with you,* so you can see how far you're going (this is called *live scrolling*).

You can enable live scrolling on a permanent basis by placing a check mark in the Live Scroll check box in the Application Preferences dialog box.

▼▼▼▼▼▼▼▼▼▼▼▼▼▼▼▼▼▼▼▼▼▼▼▼

See page 565

Tip: Use the Grabber Hand. You have the option of turning your cursor into a Grabber hand that lets you move your document around the screen in any direction. Just hold down the Alt key, click someplace on the page, and drag. The document moves—relative to the screen, which scrolls automatically—where you move the Grabber hand. If you move the Grabber hand to the left, the screen scrolls to the left (so you see farther to the right). We think it's one of the greatest methods for getting around the page.

▼▼▼▼▼▼▼▼▼▼▼▼▼▼▼▼▼▼▼▼▼▼▼▼

Tip: Adjusting Your Pasteboard. The Application Preferences dialog box lets you modify the width of your pasteboard. You can make this change by entering another Pasteboard Width value in the Application Preferences dialog box (under the Edit menu). This value is specified in percentage of your page size. That is, 100 percent specifies that each side of the pasteboard should be the same size as a page. Thirty percent specifies a much narrower pasteboard. Note that the area above and below the page is unchangeable (and a little small for our tastes).

▼▼▼▼▼▼▼▼▼▼▼▼▼▼▼▼▼▼▼▼▼▼▼▼

Zooming

If you have a brand new, 90-inch monitor, you may not need to read this section. For the rest of us, zooming is a necessity of life. When you zoom in and out of a page, you are using an electronic magnifying glass, first enlarging a particular area of a page, and then reducing your screen view so that you are seeing the entire page or pages at once.

NEW IN 3.3
See page 561

QuarkXPress lets you magnify or reduce your screen view from 10 to 400 percent, in steps of .1 percent. You can jump between several preset views quickly by selecting them from the View menu or by using keystrokes. The menu lists scrolling values of 50 percent, 75 percent, Actual Size (100 percent), 200 percent, Thumbnails, and Fit in Window. This last item adjusts the zoom percentage to fit whatever size window you have open at the time. If you're working with facing pages, then the scale is set to fit a two-page spread in the window.

There are two basic keystroke-and-click combinations that you can use to zoom in and out. Clicking on your page with the right mouse button alternates between zooming out to "Fit in Window" and zooming in to "Actual Size." Holding down the Control key while you click on your page alternates your view between "Actual Size" and "200 percent." You also can type Control-0 (zero) to go to Fit in Window view, and Control-1 to go to "Actual Size."

Quark has placed a Zoom tool on the Tool palette for your quick zooming pleasure. Sorry, did we say "quick?" We hardly find clicking in the Tool palette, then on our document, then back in the Tool palette "quick." However, we're in luck. If you hold down the Shift key while pressing the right-hand mouse button, you get a Zoom In tool, and if you hold down both the Control and the Shift keys, you get a Zoom Out tool.

Each time you click on your page with the Zoom tool, Quark-XPress zooms in or out by a particular percentage. You can control the increments that it uses by changing the Zoom tool's default preferences (see " Changing Defaults," later in this chapter).

Another one of our favorite methods for zooming in and out is to adjust the View Percent field in the lower-left corner of the document window. Note that when you're in Actual Size, this field shows "100%." Whenever you zoom in or out, this field changes. Well, you can change it yourself by clicking in the field, typing a scaling percentage, and pressing Enter or Return.

But definitely our favorite zooming technique is to hold down the Shift key (to get the Zoom tool) and drag a marquee with the right mouse button around a specific area. When you let go of the mouse button, QuarkXPress zooms into that area at the precise percentage necessary to fit it on your screen. That is, if you're at "Actual Size" and drag a marquee around one word, QuarkXPress zooms in to 400 percent and centers that word on your screen. You can use this to zoom out, too, by dragging a marquee that's larger than your screen (the screen scrolls along as you drag the marquee), but we don't find this as useful.

▼ ▼

Tip: Fitting More in Your Window. Here's a quick tip for zooming in and out. If you select "Fit in Window" (or type Control-zero) from the View menu, QuarkXPress fits the current page to the window. However, if you hold down the Control key while selecting "Fit in Window" from the View menu, it zooms to fit the entire width of the pasteboard into the window. We don't often use this, but when we do, it's a lifesaver.

▼ ▼

Moving from Page to Page

In the last section, we talked about moving within your page via scrolling and zooming. Because every page in your document sits on one big pasteboard, these same techniques work for moving within your document. That is, you can scroll from one page to another using the scroll bars and the Grabber hand, and so on. But let's be frank: this is not the fastest way to get around. It might help in moving around a two-page spread, but not for moving around a 200-page book. Instead, there are ways to move by whole pages at a time or simply jump to the page that you want.

You can move one page forward or backward by typing Shift-Page Up or Shift-Page Down. You may find yourself wanting to jump to the very beginning or the very end of your document. Just press the Control-Page Up or Control-Page Down key combinations. These keystrokes move you to the top of the first or last page in your document. If you're trying to get to a page somewhere in the middle of your document, there are two methods to get there quickly.

- Select "Go to" from the Page menu (or better yet, type Control-J).
- Double-click the page icon in the Document Layout palette.

Note that for any of the keystrokes we've outlined here, there is a menu item in the Page menu. We think working with a mouse and menus is fast, but there is no doubt that once you start working with keystrokes, moving around your document becomes lightning fast.

Manipulating Your Document

Okay, now that we've covered how you can move within your document, let's talk about how you can insert, delete, and move pages within your document. There are three good ways to handle these tasks in QuarkXPress: menu items, thumbnails, and the Document Layout palette. Let's look at each one of these.

Menu Manipulations

As we said much earlier in this chapter, the Page menu holds QuarkXPress's page manipulation tools. In this section we're primarily interested in the first three menu items: Insert, Delete, and Move. We're holding off on a discussion of inserting pages until the next chapter (see "Making Pages" in Chapter 2, *Document Construction*), so we'll talk about the last two.

When you choose "Delete" from the Page menu, Quark-XPress displays the Delete dialog box. This is a simple dialog box asking you which page or pages to delete. If you only want to delete one, just type it in the left field. If you want to delete consecutive pages, then type the end of the the page range in the Thru: field.

▼▼▼▼▼▼▼▼▼▼▼▼▼▼▼▼▼▼▼▼▼▼▼▼▼▼

Tip: Deleting to the End. We sometimes find ourselves wanting to delete from page such-and-such to the end of the document. But this is a hassle if you don't know the page number of the last page. Instead, you can type "end" in the Thru: field.

▼▼▼▼▼▼▼▼▼▼▼▼▼▼▼▼▼▼▼▼▼▼▼▼▼▼

If you want to move a page or a range of pages, you can select the Move item from the Page menu. Here you have the dialog box, in which you can specify the page or pages to move, and where to move them (see Figure 1-18). For example, if you want to move pages 15 through 21 to after the last page in your document, you can type 15 in the first field, 21 in the second field, and click "At End of Document." You also can specify a move to before or after a specific page.

Figure 1-18
The Move Pages dialog

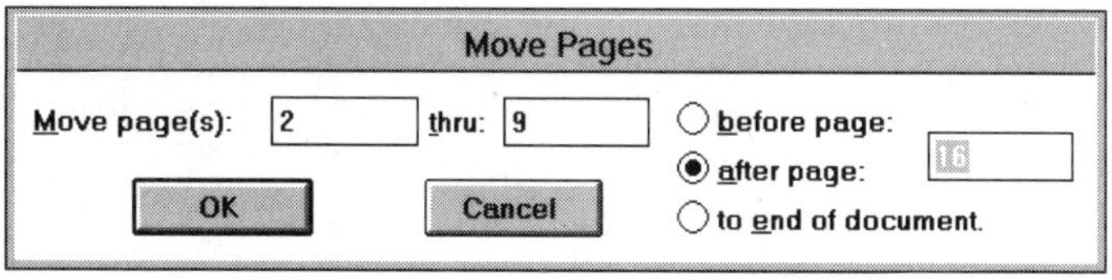

Thumbnails

QuarkXPress includes a View mode called "Thumbnails." You access it in the same way you select any other specific percentage scaling view: from the View menu (or by typing "Thumb" into the Percentage Scaling field in the lower-left corner of the document window). Although you can use this feature to view your document as thumbnails (like looking at it in 10-percent viewing mode), "Thumbnails" is actually more useful as a tool for moving pages.

To move a page in Thumbnails mode, simply select the page and drag it where you want it. While moving a page around in Thumbnails mode, you'll find the cursor turning into two different icons. The first icon looks like a redundant minipage. If you release the mouse button with this icon displayed, the page is moved, but it's added as a spread; that is, the rest of the pages won't shuffle and reflow (see "Multiple Page Spreads" in Chapter 2, *Document Construction*).

The second icon, an arrow, appears when you move the cursor directly to the left of or under another page. This arrow means that the page will be placed directly before or under a specific page, indicated by whether the arrow points up or down. Letting go of the mouse button when you see this arrow cursor reflows the pages in the document. This is the same as moving pages using "Move" from the Page menu.

▼ ▼

Tip: Moving and Deleting Multiple Pages. It's easy to select more than one page at a time while in "Thumbnails," or to delete or move pages while in the Document Layout palette (more on the latter in the next section). If the pages are consecutive (from page 4 through 9, for example), just hold down the Shift key while you select each page, or click on the first page in the range, hold down the Shift key, and click on the last page in the range. Every page is then selected between the two (this is just like selecting text).

You can select nonconsecutive pages (such as pages 1, 3, and 9), while in Thumbnails mode or in the Document Layout palette by holding down the Control key while clicking on each page.

▼ ▼

Document Layout Palette

See page 572

The Document Layout palette is one of the key elements in working efficiently with multipage documents. You can move pages, delete them, insert new ones, create and apply master pages, and more, with a quick drag of an icon. Let's look at how you can use this palette to delete and move pages.

To open the Document Layout palette, select "Show Document Layout" from the View menu (see Figure 1-19). For our purposes right now, you only need to think about two areas in

QUARKXPRESS BASICS 65

Figure 1-19
The Document Layout palette

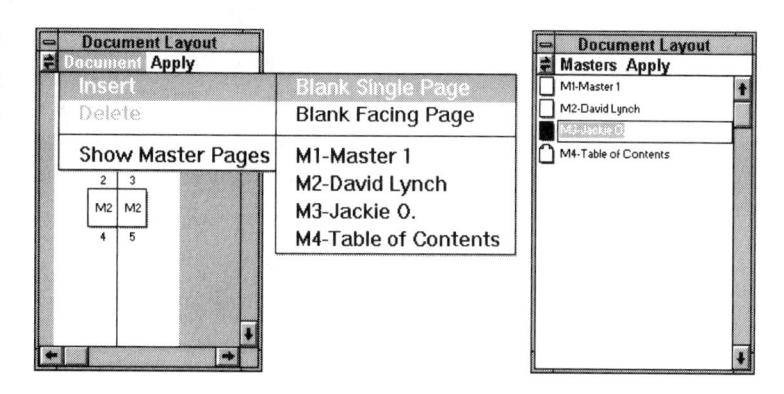

the palette: the page icons at the bottom, and the pop-up Document and Apply menus. We'll get into more advanced uses (applying master pages, for instance) in Chapter 2, *Document Construction*.

Moving pages within the Document Layout palette is just like moving them in Thumbnails mode, except that you can't see what's on the pages. Simply select the page or pages that you want to move and drag them to their destination. QuarkXPress uses the same icons here as in Thumbnails mode; that is, the little page icon means that you're creating a spread, and the right and down arrow icons mean that you're moving the pages into the flow (the other pages displace to accommodate this page).

Deleting a page with the Document Layout palette is simple: Just select the page and choose "Delete" from the pop-up menu. However, note that you cannot undo your actions and retrieve a page that you threw away in QuarkXPress. QuarkXPress displays an alert box every time you try to delete a page, asking you to confirm your decision.

Moving Items Between Documents

But you don't have to stop at moving items and pages just within your document. You can move them from one document to another faster than you can say, "Why can't I open more than one document at a time with PageMaker?"

To move a page item from one document to another, you must have both documents open and visible on your screen. This is sometimes difficult on small screens. You can usually resize one or both screens by dragging the corners or sides of each document window or by selecting "Tile" from the Windows menu to automatically resize each window to fit on the screen. Then, select the item you want to move with the Item tool (or just hold down the Control key to get the Item tool temporarily) and drag it across.

If you pause between the document windows, the first document may start to scroll. Don't worry, it's just QuarkXPress not realizing that you want to move it all the way into the second document. Just move the item a little further and the scrolling should stop. Once you release the mouse, the item is copied over into the new document. Note that we say "copied." The item is not actually moved, rather it is copied from one into the other. If you want to get rid of it in the first document, just delete it (Backspace, Delete, or Control-K).

Of course, there is always the old standby method for getting items from one document to another: Copy and Paste. Here, you want to make sure that you have the Item tool selected while in both documents, or else QuarkXPress won't know that you want to copy or paste the item itself.

Moving Pages Between Documents

You can actually drag a page from one document into another, as long as both documents are in Thumbnails mode. This is especially handy if you like to see the pages that you're copying before you copy them. Still, we'd like to see a Get Document feature that would let us import pages from another QuarkXPress document without having to actually open the document.

▼▼▼▼▼▼▼▼▼▼▼▼▼▼▼▼▼▼▼▼▼▼▼▼▼▼▼▼▼▼▼▼▼▼

Linking

We need to introduce a concept here that is crucial to working with text boxes: *linking*. Links, sometimes known as chains, are the connections between text boxes that allow text to flow from one into the other. You can have as many text boxes linked up as you like. There are two ways to link text boxes together: have QuarkXPress do it for you automatically or do it yourself manually.

We cover automatic text links in Chapter 2, *Document Construction*. We cover manual linking here.

Linking Text Boxes

Let's say you have two text boxes. The text in the first box is overflowing (a little box with an "x" in the lower-right corner indicates a text overflow), so you want to link it to the second box. First, choose the Linking tool from the Tool palette (it's the one that looks like three links in a chain). Next, click on the first text box and then on the second text box. When you click on the first text box, a flashing dotted line should appear around it. Then, when you select the second text box, an arrow should connect from the first text box to the second. We call this the *text link arrow*. This happens even if the two text boxes are on different pages.

That's it. The boxes are now linked, and text flows between them. If you want to link another box to your text chain, just follow the same procedure: click on the second text box, then on the third, and so on. Note that you cannot link a box to another box that already contains text.

If you want to add a text box to the middle of a text chain, first click on a box that is already linked, and then click on the text box you want to add. The text now flows from the original chain, through your added text box, and back to the original chain (see Figure 1-20).

Unlinking Text Boxes

If you want to remove a link between two text boxes, use the Unlinking tool from the Tool palette. The process is simple. Let's say you have a link between two text boxes that you want to sever. First, click on one of the text boxes with the Unlinking tool. As soon as you click on it, you should see the gray arrow linking the two boxes. Then click on either the arrowhead or the tailfeathers of this text-link arrow. The arrow disappears, and the link is gone.

If other page items are on top of the text-link arrow's arrowhead and tailfeathers, you may not be able to click on it. This always seems to happen at 1 A.M., after everything else has gone

Figure 1-20

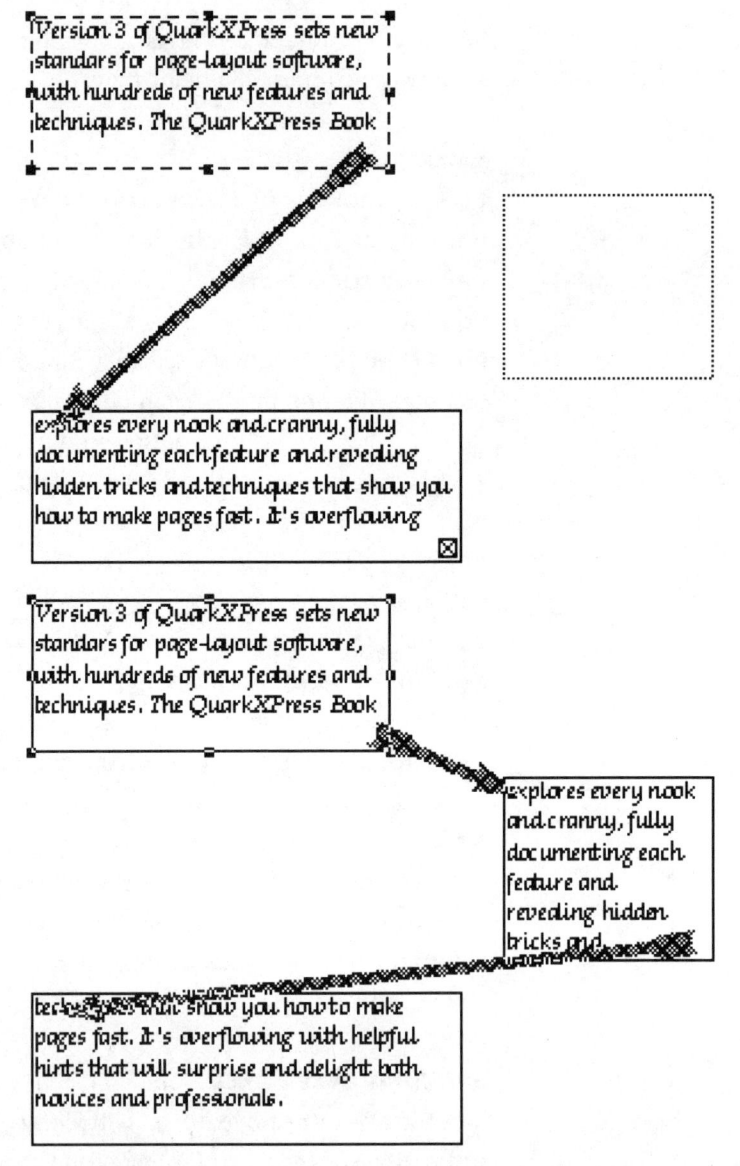

Linked text boxes

wrong on the project, and this is the last straw. Nonetheless, the way we solve this problem is to rearrange the layers using "Move to Front" and "Move to Back" or to temporarily shift the obstructing objects in order to get to one of the two.

Another problem some people encounter is that they can click and click on the arrowhead or tailfeather, but can't make it disappear. Quark has made it difficult to click those items, so that you don't accidentally click the wrong text-link arrow. Try placing the cursor right over the very tip of the arrow or the point where the two tailfeathers meet.

▼▼▼▼▼▼▼▼▼▼▼▼▼▼▼▼▼▼▼▼▼▼▼▼▼▼

Tip: Unlinking a Text Box from the Middle of a Chain. If you unlink a text box from the middle of a chain by clicking the arrowhead or tailfeathers with the Unlinking tool, the entire text chain is broken at that point. Instead, you can tell QuarkXPress to remove a text box from the text chain without breaking the rest of the flow by selecting the Unlinking tool, then holding down the Shift key while clicking on the box you want to remove.

▼▼▼▼▼▼▼▼▼▼▼▼▼▼▼▼▼▼▼▼▼▼▼▼▼▼▼▼▼▼

Guides and Rulers

When you are working on your document, you usually have rulers on the top and the left of the window. This not only gives you a perspective on where you are on the page, but it's a great visual aid in selecting coordinates. Let's say you want to change the size of a picture box by dragging a corner handle. If you're visually inclined, you may not want to bother with referring to the Measurements palette while you drag. Instead, if you watch the rulers, you'll see that gray lines show the left, right, top, and bottom edges as it moves. For example, if you want to visually place a box at the 2-inch mark (as opposed to using the Measurements palette), you can follow the gray lines in the rulers as you drag the box. When the gray line is over the 2-inch mark, the box is truly at 2 inches, even when you're at a view other than 100 percent, or if you've changed the Points/Inch value.

You can turn the rulers on and off by selecting "Show" or "Hide Rulers" from the View menu, or by typing Control-R. The only time you really need to turn the rulers off, though, is when you want to get a slightly larger view of the page. Otherwise, just leave them on.

▼▼▼▼▼▼▼▼▼▼▼▼▼▼▼▼▼▼▼▼▼▼▼▼▼▼

Tip: Adjusting your rulers. The zero point of a ruler doesn't have to be set at the upper-right corner of the page. You can, in fact, set the rulers' origin to anywhere you want. To change the origin of the rulers, click in the upper left corner of the rulers (that little box where the horizontal and vertical rulers meet) and drag the cursor to where you want the zero point. When you let go of the mouse button, the origin is shifted. To reset the rulers to where they were originally, double-click in the ruler-origin box.

This tip especially comes in handy when you try to print using Manual Tiling (see Chapter 10, *Printing*).

▼ ▼

You can specify which measurement system you want to use in your rulers in the General Preferences dialog box (via the Preferences command under the Edit menu, or type Control-Y). The vertical and horizontal rulers don't have to use the same measurement system. For example, you can set "Horizontal Measure" to inches and "Vertical Measure" to picas. This just confuses us, so we generally keep both measurement systems the same (we always use picas).

The values you choose in the General Preferences dialog box are not only used on the rulers, but also throughout the Measurements palette and Item Specifications dialog box. For example, if you change the "Vertical Measure" to ciceros, then every vertical measurement shows up in ciceros and points. You can still type in measurements using other units (see Table 1-2, earlier in this chapter), but QuarkXPress always converts them.

Guides

NEW IN 3.3

See page 563

Back in the good old days, before we started laying out pages by sitting in front of little plastic boxes, no one worked without guides. We had blueline guides on pasteup boards, straightedge guides on drafting tables for making sure we were aligning items correctly, and transparent rulers to ensure that we were measuring type and rules correctly. We certainly didn't throw any of that away when we bought our PCs—they still come in handy often. However, QuarkXPress gives us all of those tools electronically.

You can add a vertical or a horizontal guide to your page by clicking in one of the rulers and dragging it out onto the page. Note that the guide runs the length of the page from top to bottom or from side to side. However, guides won't cross over a spread (see "Tip: Longer Guides," below). Once you've placed a guide on your page, if you have the Item tool selected, you can move a guide by clicking on it anywhere you want. Of course, to click on the guide it must be visible, so you may need to have the Guides control in the Preferences dialog box (Control-Y) set to "In Front."

The Measurements palette displays the coordinate of where the guide is while the guide is moving. Unfortunately, once you let go of the guide, there is no way to find out the measurement of where it sits on the page without "grabbing" it again. Also, you can't create or manipulate guides while in Thumbnail view.

To remove a guide from your page, grab it in the page margin area or anyplace where there are no other objects and drag it out of the window (either back into a ruler, or off to the right or bottom of the window).

▼ ▼

Tip: Longer Guides. As we noted above, if you drag a guide onto a page, the guide reaches from one side of the page to the other and doesn't cross over a spread, or even onto the pasteboard. You can make a longer guide that reaches over both of these areas by dragging a guide onto the pasteboard, letting go, and then moving it onto the page. Another method is to click and drag out a guide and then let go while the mouse cursor is over the pasteboard.

▼ ▼

Guides don't print, so it doesn't matter where you place them on your page. However, you may want to adjust the guides to fall in front of or behind opaque text or picture boxes. You can do this by changing the Guides setting in the General Preferences dialog box. Your two choices are "Behind" and "In Front."

Snap to Guides

One of the most important values of guides is that picture and text boxes can snap to them. All guides have this feature, including margin and column guides (we'll talk more about them in Chapter 2, *Document Construction*). You can turn "Snap to Guides" on and off by selecting it in the View menu. For example, if you have five picture boxes that you want to align, you can pull out a guide to the position you want, and—if "Snap to

Guides" is enabled in the View menu—as the picture boxes are moved next to the guides, they snap to that exact line.

On the other hand, there are times when you probably want to disable "Snap to Guides"—so just select it again from the View menu. For example, if you are working with a line very close to a column guide, it may snap to the guide when you don't want it to. Just turn it off. Generally, however, we leave this feature on.

The distance at which a guide pulls an item in, snapping it to the guide position, is determined by The Snap Distance field in the General Preferences dialog box. The default value is 6 points.

▼▼▼▼▼▼▼▼▼▼▼▼▼▼▼▼▼▼▼▼▼▼▼▼▼▼▼▼▼▼▼▼▼▼▼▼▼

Frames

There are times when you want to put a picture on your wall with a frame, and there are times when you just tape it up frameless. When you're making pages, there are times when you want a frame around a text or picture box, and there are times when you don't. QuarkXPress lets you have your choice. All picture and text boxes default to a frame of width 0 (zero), which means there's no frame at all. You can add a frame to any picture or text box by selecting it and choosing "Frame" from the Item menu (or typing Control-B).

The Frame Specifications dialog box contains fields and pop-up menus that let you specify the weight, color, shade, and line style of your frame (see Figure 1-21). Color, style, and shade are self-explanatory, but we need to talk a little about frame thickness.

Frame Weight

Quark calls the thickness of a frame its "width." We're used to calling it the "weight." No matter what you call it, it's the thickness of the frame. And in a similar manner to lines, if the line weight is not thick enough, the frame style may not show up properly (a triple line set to .5 point comes out looking just like a single half-point line).

Frames can grow from the box edge in or the box edge out; that is, a 10-point frame is measured from the edge of the box

Figure 1-21
Frame Specifications dialog box

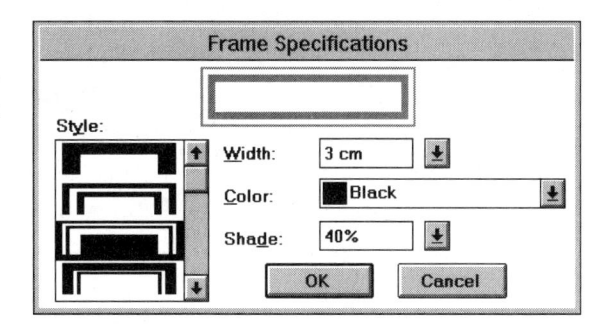

either out or in. This is different from lines, whose weight is measured from their center (a 10-point line falls 5 points on one side of the line and 5 points on the other).

You can control which side of the box edge the frame falls on with the Framing pop-up menu in the General Preferences dialog box (accessed via the Preference command under the Edit menu, or type Control-Y). Choosing "Inside" from this menu places frames on the inside of a box; "Outside" places them on the outside.

Note that you can create a frame on a box while in the Inside mode, then change the mode to Outside. Subsequent frames are built on the outside of boxes (or vice versa). Existing boxes don't change when you change the preferences.

Libraries

QuarkXPress lets you keep libraries full of items: picture boxes, text boxes, lines, groups of objects, and so on. These libraries are saved as external files on a disk that you can move from one place to another. For example, while writing this book, we placed each piece of artwork, grouped with figure numbers, captions, and callouts, in a library. The artwork was later taken out of the library by the production team and placed on the QuarkXPress pages. This increased the chance that nothing too weird would happen when we were making pages, and decreased the time it took to produce a chapter.

Note that a library holds a page item, plus its contents. For example, you could place a text box with a particular headline in a particular style in a library. However, picture boxes in libraries don't necessarily fully contain their pictures. If a picture is in an EPSF, TIFF, or PCX format, the library only remembers the link to the external file, rather than the file itself. So, although our artwork could be stored in a library, we still had to move many of our EPSF and TIFF files from disk to disk (if you are lost, don't worry; we talk about all these issues in Chapter 6, *Pictures*).

You can have up to seven libraries open at a time, and each library can hold up to 2,000 entries. You can even label each library entry for quick access. Let's look at how all of this is done.

Manipulating Libraries

See page 549

To open a library, select "Library" from the Utilities menu. QuarkXPress brings up a dialog box asking you to find the library you want. If you want to create a new library, you can click "Create." Once you choose a library, QuarkXPress brings it up on your screen as a palette.

You also can expand the Library palette by dragging out any side or corner. Note that this type of zooming doesn't have anything to do with a percentage scaling view. To automatically expand the palette to fill the screen, click the control box at the upper right corner, and then select Maximize from the dropdown menu. To decrease the library palette back to "normal" size, select Restore from the control box.

Adding and Moving Library Entries

You'll hardly believe how easy it is to add and remove library entries. To add a page item to an open library, just click on the item with the Item tool (or hold down the Control key to get a temporary Item tool), and drag the item into the library. As you drag into the library, your mouse cursor turns into a pair of glasses (don't ask us why; all the librarians we know wear contacts), and two triangular arrows point to your position in the library. When you let go of the mouse button, the item you're dragging is placed in the library where these pointers are indicating. You can position your page item anywhere in the library by dragging it into place.

You also can add an item to a library by using Cut or Copy and Paste. You need to use the Item tool to cut or copy an item from the page, but you can use either the Item or the Content tool to paste it in a library. Just click in the position where you want the item to go, then type Control-V (or select Paste from the Edit menu of the Library window). When picking a place to paste the item, click between two items, so that you can see the positioning arrows. If you click on an item in the library before pasting, you are telling QuarkXPress to replace that item with this new one.

After you add an item to a library, then you can see a thumbnail-size representation of it (see Figure 1-22). Note that this representation is highlighted, and you won't be able to do any work on your page until you click someplace other than the library. For example, a common mistake is to type the Page-Up or Page-Down keys while an item is selected in the Library. Nothing happens! You must first activate the document window again by clicking in it (or closing the library).

You can move an item in a library from one position to another by clicking on it and dragging it to a new position. If you have more items in your library than what fits in the palette, you may have some difficulty, because the library doesn't automatically scroll as you drag. We use one of two methods to get around this. First, you can cut and paste items as we described above. Second, you can use the Maximize and Restore commands in the library window's control box (upper-left corner) to expand the size (maximize), reposition the item, and then rezoom the box down to a small palette (restore).

Removing Library Items

To take an item from an open library and place it on a page, just click on it with either the Item or the Content tool and drag it out onto your page. This doesn't remove the item from the library; it just makes a copy of it for your page. If you want to delete an item from a library, click on it, then select "Delete" from the Edit menu of the Library window (or press the Delete key). You also

Figure 1-22
Adding an item to a library

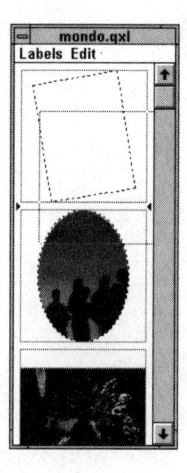

Each item is reduced to a thumbnail representation.

can use Cut from the Edit menu (Control-X), which removes the item and places it on the Clipboard. (You can see what's on the Clipboard by selecting "Show Clipboard" from the Edit menu.)

Labeling Library Items

Imagine having 150 different items in a library and trying to find just the ones that are pictures of baby seals. Remember that all you can see on screen is a thumbnail representation of the items. Luckily, you have labeled each library item with a foolproof system, and you are just a pop-up menu item away from finding those baby seals.

Every item in a library may be labeled either for identification purposes or to categorize items (or both). With your library items labeled, you can access the library items by a single label, multiple labels, and more.

To assign a label to a library item, double-click on its thumbnail representation. Up comes the Library Entry dialog box (see Figure 1-23). There is only one field in this dialog box for you to type the label in. Note that after you add one label to an item, the drop-down menu in this dialog box is enabled. This drop-down menu lists each of the previous labels you've assigned (see "Tip: Grouping Library Items").

After you have labeled items in your library, you can select from among them with the drop-down menu at the top of the Library palette (see Figure 1-24). This acts as a kind of electronic card catalog. There are always two items in this drop-down

Figure 1-23
The Library Entry dialog box

menu: All and Unlabeled. Selecting "All" shows you every item in the library. Selecting "Unlabeled" displays only the items that have not yet been labeled. Any other labels that you have assigned to library items also appear on this drop-down menu. If you select one of these, you can see any item (or items) that has been assigned that label.

If you select a second label from the drop-down menu, that label is added to the category you're already looking at. The labels in use appear with a check mark before the label name. You can deselect one label category by rechoosing it from the drop-down menu (that is, these labels in the drop-down menu act as on-and-off toggle switches). You can deselect all the subcategories by choosing "All" from the drop-down menu.

▼ ▼

Tip: Grouping Library Items. As we mentioned above, you can group library items together (this isn't the same as grouping items on the page). You do this by giving them the same label—effectively categorizing them. For example, if you have a group of lines that you use a often for one magazine, you might label them all "Mag Lines." Then, when you need one, you simply pull down the Library palette's drop-down menu and select that label. However, if each one of the item's labels isn't exactly the same, QuarkXPress won't know to group them together. Instead of typing the same label over and over again for each item, you can just type it once. Then use the drop-down menu in the Library Entry dialog box to choose that label each time you want to assign it to an item within the library. This is faster, and you avoid typos.

▼ ▼

Figure 1-24
Selecting a subcategory in the library

Saving Libraries

No matter how hard you try, you won't find a command to save the library file. This can be disconcerting, to say the least. What happens to all those items if you can't save them?

QuarkXPress normally saves a library only when you quit the program or close your current document. This is generally unacceptable, because people work for long periods of time without quitting or closing a document (during the production of the Macintosh version of this book one person lost over an hour's worth of work because of a system crash before the library was saved).

Fortunately, there's an Auto Library Save option in the Application Preferences dialog box, which makes QuarkXPress save a library every time you place a new item in it. This may slow down your work a little if you're adding a number of items, but it could also save you lots of time if something should go wrong.

▼▼▼▼▼▼▼▼▼▼▼▼▼▼▼▼▼▼▼▼▼▼▼▼▼▼▼▼▼▼▼▼▼▼

XTensions

Here's an aspect of QuarkXPress that we think is so hot and amazing that we couldn't think of a nasty thing to say about it even if we tried. Quark has built in a system so that programmers can write add-on modules (XTensions) to work with QuarkXPress. There are over 100 developers around the world creating these XTensions. Some cost $5,000 or $10,000 and are designed for a limited market, such as large newspapers. Others are free, and can (and should) be used by anyone using QuarkXPress. Appendix E, *Resources*, gives more information about how to get your hands on XTensions.

We'll be talking about various XTensions throughout the book, so it'll behoove you to know how to deal with them. In order to use an XTension, all you have to do is place it in the same subdirectory as QuarkXPress. When you start up QuarkXPress the XTension does its thing, whatever that may be. Usually, XTensions add an item to a menu, or even add a whole new menu. Most XTensions add items to the Utilities menu, because they are utilities.

Changing Defaults

QuarkXPress gives you plenty of options for customizing the internal default settings. A default setting is a value or a way of doing something that QuarkXPress uses unless you specifically choose something else. For example, a default setting for picture 'and text boxes is that they are created with no frame around them (see "Frames," earlier in this chapter). But you can change default settings. You can modify QuarkXPress so that every text box you create is framed automatically with a 2-point line.

Default settings range from how guides are displayed on the screen to how QuarkXPress builds small caps characters. There are four basic dialog boxes that let you specify your default settings preferences: Application Preferences, General Preferences, Typographic Preferences, and Tool Preferences. Each of these dialog boxes can be accessed through the Preferences submenu under the Edit menu.

We talk about "Typographic Preferences" in Chapter 4, *Type and Typography*, and we cover several items from the General

Preferences dialog box throughout the rest of the book, so we'll cover the "missing" areas in a quick rundown here.

Application Preferences

NEW IN 3.3
See page 564

Any selections you make in this dialog box are application-wide; that is, they aren't just for the document you have open. Let's jump in and discuss each element.

Guide Colors. The controls in the upper-left corner of the Application Preferences dialog box let you change the colors of QuarkXPress's three types of guide lines: margin, ruler, and grid. The margin guides are the lines that show where the page margins are. As discussed in this chapter, the ruler guides are the guides you can pull out onto the page, and the grid guides are the lines that the program displays when you have "Show Baseline Grid" enabled (see Chapter 4, *Type and Typography*).

Live Scroll. Steve, our editor, keeps telling us not to be redundant in our writing. And since we already gave our *shpiel* about Live Scroll earlier in this chapter, we'll just say, "Yes, this is a great feature, but nowhere near as cool as the Page Grabber hand."

Page Grabber hand. See "Scrolling" earlier in this chapter.

Auto Library Save. As we said earlier in this chapter, libraries are generally saved only when you close them. Enabling "Auto Library Save" makes QuarkXPress save the library every time you add an item to it. This slows down production time a little, but it's worthwhile as a safety measure.

Low Resolution TIFF. When you have "Low Resolution TIFF" checked, imported TIFF images are shown on the screen at half the resolution of your monitor (unless you hold down the Shift key while importing them; see Chapter 8, *Modifying Images*). If you uncheck this item, QuarkXPress toggles the settings: TIFF images are brought in at the resolution of your monitor (screen redraw takes longer) unless the Shift key is held down.

256 Levels of Gray. Here's another control over gray-scale images. If you have a monitor capable of displaying 256 levels of gray and you're working with 8-bit (256 levels of gray) gray-scale images, you may want to see the detail in those images better by displaying all 256 levels of gray. You can do this by enabling the 256 Levels of Gray feature in the Application Preferences dialog box. When this is turned off, QuarkXPress only shows you grayscale images in 16 levels of gray (4-bit). Note that Super VGA adapters (256 colors) and SVGA adapters extended via Sierra HiColor technology (about 32,000 colors) can display only 64 and 32 levels of gray, respectively.

Once again, it's a time versus quality issue. Turning this feature off speeds up screen redraw. Turning it on usually results in a better image (especially on a 24-bit color display).

Of course, if you don't have an 8-bit image, you can't display it in this 8-bit mode anyway. Note that this feature doesn't affect the images themselves or how they print—just how they're displayed on the screen.

Display DPI Value. Due to the wide variation in dots-per-inch resolution of PC displays, the Actual Size view selection of many DTP programs is anything but actual size. Here's where you can adjust for this in QuarkXPress. Use a ruler to see whether the inch marks of the QuarkXPress on-screen rulers are truly an inch apart. If they're more than an inch apart, decrease the Display DPI Value until they equal an inch. Do the reverse calibration if the inch-marks are too close together.

Or, to get a rough estimate of your screen's resolution, divide your monitor's horizontal resolution by the width of the display (not including any black areas that surround the display). For example, David's monitor (an NEC 4FG) has a horizontal measure of about 10.625 inches, and has a horizontal resolution of 1024 (in the mode he uses it, anyway, with a Matrox Impression-S board). Dividing 1024 by 10.625 results in a dpi of about 96.3. That's the number he puts in his Application Preferences dialog box.

Scroll Speed. Here's another control over how QuarkXPress reacts when you do something. In this case, it's how fast QuarkXPress scrolls when you use the scroll bars. Note that the Scroll Speed control is originally set to be pretty slow. Increasing the speed (by clicking the right arrow) can make a drastic difference in how quickly you can make your pages (although if you're using a slow machine, this won't speed up your redraw time).

Trap. We hate to keep putting this off, but we're postponing the discussion of the Trap section of the Application Preferences dialog box until Chapter 9, *Color*. Don't worry, it'll be worth the wait.

Pasteboard Width. See "Tip: Adjusting your Pasteboard," earlier in this chapter.

Reg. Marks Offset. We don't know about you, but if we were operating a two-ton paper-cutting machine on a tight schedule, we wouldn't always make cuts within three or four points (.055 inch) of accuracy. That's what QuarkXPress is asking your printer to do when it prints its registration marks only 6 points from the edge of the page (see Chapter 10, *Printing*). However, you can adjust how far out you want the registration marks to print with the Reg. Marks Offset control. We generally set this at about 12 to 18 points.

General Preferences

Of all the default preferences in the General Preferences dialog box (see Figure 1-25), only two are *not* described elsewhere in this book: Points/Inch and Ciceros/cm. Here's a list of where you can find information on the other 14 defaults.

Horizontal Measure and Vertical Measure. See "Guides and Rulers," earlier in this chapter.

Auto Page Insertion. See "Automatic Page Insertion," in Chapter 2, *Document Construction*.

Framing. See "Frames," earlier in this chapter.

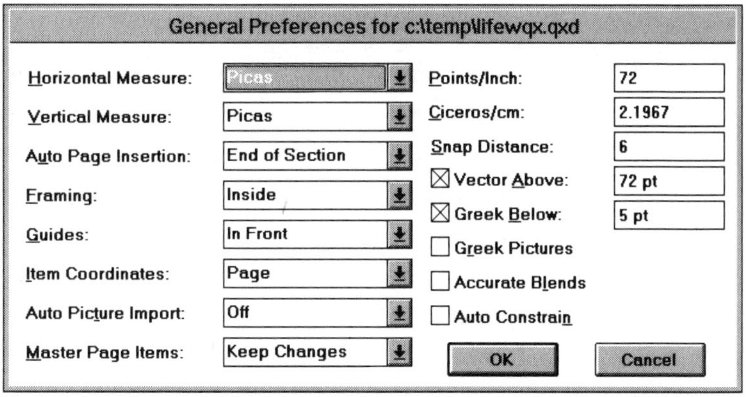

Figure 1-25
The General Preferences dialog box

General Preferences for c:\temp\lifewqx.qxd

Horizontal Measure:	Picas	Points/Inch:	72
Vertical Measure:	Picas	Ciceros/cm:	2.1967
Auto Page Insertion:	End of Section	Snap Distance:	6
Framing:	Inside	☒ Vector Above:	72 pt
Guides:	In Front	☒ Greek Below:	5 pt
Item Coordinates:	Page	☐ Greek Pictures	
Auto Picture Import:	Off	☐ Accurate Blends	
Master Page Items:	Keep Changes	☐ Auto Constrain	

[OK] [Cancel]

Guides and Item Coordinates. See "Guides and Rulers," earlier in this chapter.

Item Coordinates. See "Facing Pages" in Chapter 2, *Document Construction*.

Auto Picture Import. See "Picture Usage," in Chapter 6, *Pictures*.

Master Page Items. See "Changes to Document Pages" in Chapter 2, *Document Construction*.

Vector Above. See "Type Rendering," in Chapter 4, *Type and Typography*.

Greek Below. See "Text Greeking," in Chapter 4, *Type and Typography*.

Picture Greeking . See "Greeking and Suppression," in Chapter 6, *Pictures*.

Accurate Blends. See "Blends" in Chapter 9, *Color*.

Auto Constrain. See "Constraining," earlier in this chapter.

Points/Inch. Somebody, sometime, somewhere along the line, decided that PostScript should measure 72 points to an inch. However, as it turns out, the printers and graphic designers have always measured just over 72 points to the inch. QuarkXPress, being the power-rich program that it is, gives you the choice of how you want to measure points. If you have a burning need to work in a traditional measurement setting, you could change the value of the Points/Inch field in the General Preferences dialog box to 72.27 (the value used by almost all of the traditional typesetting and graphic arts systems). We tend toward forward progress and think that people should just throw out their old rulers and embrace a new standard. Thus, we leave it at 72 points per inch.

Ciceros/cm. If you're like us (Americanus stupidus), you'll need to be told that a cicero is a measurement in the Didot system, used primarily in France and other continental European countries. QuarkXPress gives you the option of changing the number of ciceros per centimeter. Just as a pica equals 12 points, the cicero equals 12 points. The difference? Differently sized points. A Didot point equals .01483 inch instead of the American-British .01383 inch. Anyway, the only really important note is that QuarkXPress defaults to 2.1967 ciceros per centimeter. This is close enough to a traditional cicero (you can do the math). Note that this control doesn't change the points-per-inch value; if you're working in any measurement system other than ciceros, just ignore this control.

Tool Preferences

You may find yourself making the same change or changes repeatedly to a type of page item; for example, you always change the text inset for text boxes from 1 to 0 (zero) points, or always change your lines to .25-point thickness after drawing them. These item attributes, as well as most other attributes for page items, are defaults that you have some say in.

You can use the Tool Preferences dialog box to change the default settings for any of the item-creation tools on the Tool palette, plus the Zoom tool (see Figure 1-26). To change a default for an item-creation tool (the tools that create picture boxes, text boxes, or lines), select the tool's icon in the dialog box, and then

Figure 1-26
Tool preferences dialog box

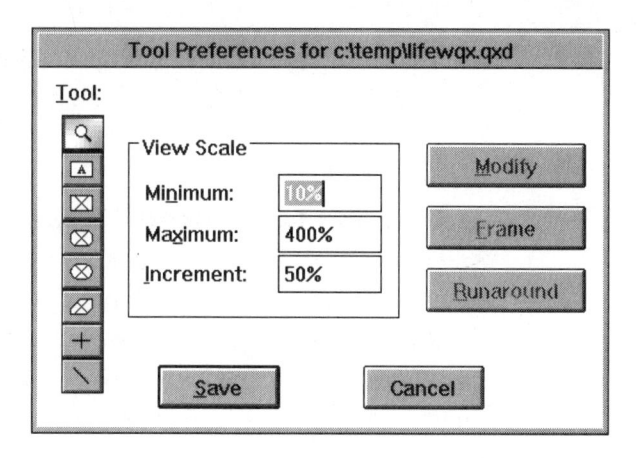

click one of the three buttons to change some aspect of that tool: Modify, Frame, or Runaround.

Modify. This button brings up the Item Specifications dialog box for the particular tool. As we discussed earlier in this chapter, a picture box has a different specifications dialog box than a text box, and so on. You can change any value in this dialog box that is not grayed out. For example, you can change the default corner radius of a rounded-corner rectangle picture box, but you can't change its default width or height. We rarely want our picture boxes to have a colored background, so we have changed our picture box tools' defaults so that the "Background Color" is set to "None."

Frame. You can specify an automatic frame for text or picture boxes by clicking the Frame button. Let's say you specify a 1-point single-line frame for the Polygon Picture Box tool. After you click OK, every polygonal picture box you make has that frame. You don't have to keep the frame if you later don't want it. Just remove it as you would any other frame: change it's width to 0. But this is the default setting for creating new ones.

Runaround. You also can change the text runaround value for boxes made with a tool. For example, you can set the Text Box tool to make text boxes that have no runaround. Note that you can set any runaround that you normally could for a box or line, except that you cannot set a picture box to Manual Image Runaround mode.

▼▼▼▼▼▼▼▼▼▼▼▼▼▼▼▼▼▼▼▼▼▼▼▼▼▼

Tip: Get to Those Tool Preferences Quickly. As you can probably tell, we do almost anything to avoid actually making a selection from a menu. We just find other methods are faster for us, and they should be for you, too. For example, you can jump to the Tool Preferences dialog box by double-clicking a tool in the Tool palette. This automatically highlights the tool you chose, and you're ready to make your change. Don't forget that you can type the first letter of the button's name rather than clicking on the button. For example you can type "R" to activate the Runaround button, and so on.

▼▼▼▼▼▼▼▼▼▼▼▼▼▼▼▼▼▼▼▼▼▼▼▼▼▼

Tip: Document Defaults Versus Program Defaults. There's an important difference between changing your default preferences when you've got a document open and when you don't. If you have a document open when you change a default preference, that change is specific to that document. If no documents are open when you set a default preference, then you are setting new defaults for the whole program, and that change is made to every new document you create from then on.

For example, if you set the increments on the Zoom tool to 100 percent while a document is open, the preference is logged for that document only. If you set it while no documents are open, that setting is made for every new document you create. However, documents that were created using the original setting keep their defaults.

This doesn't apply to the Application Preferences, though. These are always application-wide defaults.

XPress Preferences

As we just mentioned, any preferences you change are saved in the document (if one is open) and (if one is not) in a file called XPRESS.PRF that resides in the same subdirectory as QuarkXPress. This file, typically called the XPress Preferences file, also contains information about kerning and tracking tables, hyphenation exceptions, and auxiliary dictionaries. We cover what all those are and how to use them in Chapter 4, *Type and Typography*, but it's important for you to know about the XPress Preferences file up here in front.

Any changes you make to the kerning tables, tracking tables, and the hyphenation exceptions are saved in both the document (if one is open) *and* the XPress Preferences file. That means that these preferences act as both document-wide and application-wide preferences. For example, if you change a kerning table while a document is open, then save that file and bring it to another machine with a different copy of QuarkXPress, that machine alerts you that something is different (the tables in the Preferences file are different from those in the document). It then asks you whether you want to use the information that was stored with the document or not (see Figure 1-27). If you respond that you don't want to use the document's original information, QuarkXPress reflows your pages using this new QuarkXPress's information. If you respond that you do want to use the document's original information, it is used and continues to be saved right along with that file.

Figure 1-27
When document settings are different from application settings

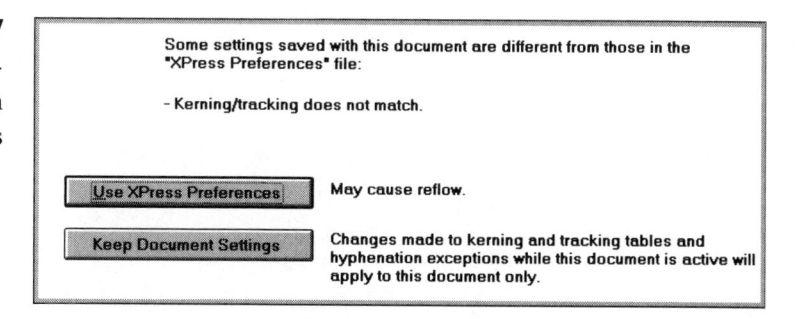

This means that when you send your QuarkXPress documents to a service bureau, you don't necessarily need to include the XPress Preferences file. The service bureau just tells the program to use the document's information, and no text reflow occurs.

If you've created custom information for a document, you may not want that information to be used in the next document you create. In that case, after you save and close that first document you can reset kerning or tracking tables, or clear out the hyphenation exceptions dictionary. If you don't clear and reset these controls, XPress Preferences file remembers them, and they are used for each document that you create (see "Tip: Single Document Preferences," below).

▼ ▼

Tip: Resetting and Switching Preferences. If you delete the XPress Preferences file (or move it out of the QuarkXPress subdirectory), then QuarkXPress creates a clean, new one for you. This is a great method for starting over from scratch with the default tracking and kerning tables, and with no items in hyphenation exceptions.

If you have two or more XPress Preferences files with varying information, you can move them in and out of your QuarkXPress subdirectory with the File Manager. However, you do have to quit and relaunch QuarkXPress for the new items to take effect.

▼ ▼

Tip: Single Document Preferences. There are a few select times that you might find yourself wanting an XPress Preferences setting set only for a single document. You can do this with a little work. First, close all open documents. Then, change something that QuarkXPress saves in its XPress Preferences file. For example, you can change a kerning pair in the Kerning Editor. Next, open the document again. QuarkXPress asks you if you want to use the document preferences or the XPress Preferences; choose document preferences.

Finally, make any changes you want to that document, including changes to hyphenation exceptions, tracking tables, and kerning pairs. When you save and close that file, the changes you've made are made only to that file's preferences. The general XPress Preferences remain the same.

Finally, close all documents again, and reset the preferences back to what they were (e.g., take out that kerning pair change you made).

Moving On

You now know the basics of how QuarkXPress relates to you, and the general concepts of how you can use its tools to make your pages. If you weren't familiar with these tools before, a little practice will turn you into a pro in no time. If you were familiar with them, we hope you have increased your arsenal of high-caliber techniques. Either way, you should now be ready to move into the next chapter, in which we move away from a free-form, throw-it-all-on-a-page style of working and introduce you to systematic methods of building documents.

CHAPTER 2

DOCUMENT CONSTRUCTION

Document design is a contradictory process. A good design requires order and regularity so that the document is readable. But it also needs a dose of freedom and creativity so that it's interesting to look at. How do you resolve that contradiction? Start your documents with an orderly foundation; then you're free to place text and graphics creatively upon that foundation, without generating a mess.

This chapter is about starting that design process: building an infrastructure for your document. We call this *document construction*. It's just like the construction of a building. First you decide on the building's specifications—how tall and wide, and so on. Next, you lay a foundation and build structural supports.

In QuarkXPress it's very similar. First we decide on the specifications of the document—how tall, how wide, whether it's double or single sided, and so on. Next, we build the structures of the page—repeating page elements, page numbering, and text flow. If you don't take these steps first, the foundation of your work will be unreliable—and your building might just fall down.

Step with us into the building mode. The first stop is opening a new document.

Building a New Document

When you open QuarkXPress under the program defaults, you'll see a blank screen underneath the menu bar, with the Tool and Measurements palettes showing. The first step in creating a new document is to choose "New" from the File menu (or type Control-N). This brings up the New dialog box, shown in Figure 2-1. It is here that you take the first steps in determining a document's page dimensions, page margins, the number of columns, the spacing between columns, and whether the pages are laid out facing each other or not.

Figure 2-1
New dialog box

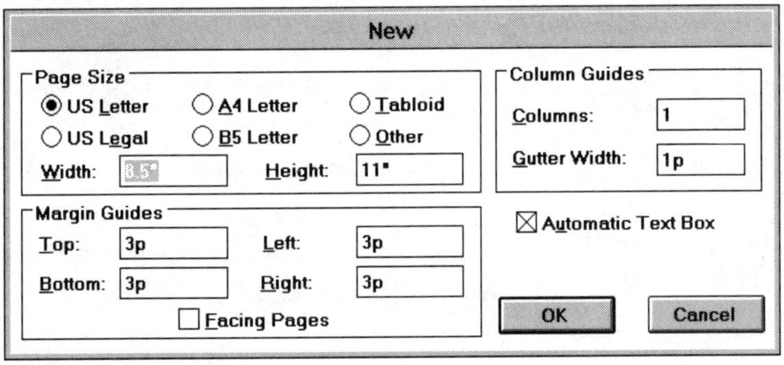

The New dialog box is "Checkpoint Charlie" for entering the new document zone (walls may crumble, but metaphors remain). Note that there is nothing in the New dialog box that locks you in; you can make changes to these settings at any time within a document, even after you've worked on it a lot.

Let's take a look at each of this dialog box's items in detail.

Page Size

When you make your pass through the New dialog box on the way to creating a document, you have the opportunity to determine the dimensions of its pages. The default setting—the one QuarkXPress chooses for you if you make no change—is a standard, 8.5-by-11 inch page. You can choose among five preset choices or choose a custom-size page. Table 2-1 shows the measurements for each of the preset choices in three common measurement units.

Table 2.1
Preset Page Sizes

Name	In Inches	In Picas/Points	In Millimeters
US Letter	8.5 by 11	51p by 66p	216 by 279.4
US Legal	8.5 by 14	51p by 84p	216 by 355.6
A4 Letter	8.27 by 11.69	49p7.3 by 70p1.9	210 by 297
B4 Letter	6.93 by 9.84	41p6.9 by 59p.7	176 by 250
Tabloid	11 by 17	66p by 102p	279.4 by 431.8

Choosing "Other" lets you create any page size from 1 by 1 inch to 48 by 48 inches. You also can select another page size by simply typing the page dimensions into the Width and Height fields. Note that if you're using one of the preset radio button choices, these fields show the measurements for those pages.

▼ ▼

Tip: Page Size is Not Paper Size. "Page Size" in the New dialog box refers to the size of the pages you want as your finished output—not to the size of the paper going through your printer. These may or may not be the same. In the Page Size area, type in the page dimensions of the actual piece you want to produce. For example, if you want to create a book page 7 by 9 inches, enter these values in the Width and Height fields, even if you're outputting to a laser printer capable of only letter-size pages.

▼ ▼

Margin Guides

The Margin Guides area allows you to specify the margin sizes on all four sides of a page. When you work with facing pages (see below), "Left" and "Right" change to "Inside" and "Outside." These margin guides can be used to define the column area. This column area is often called the live area (see Figure 2-2). The term "live area" may be slightly misleading, however, because everything that's on a page prints out, whether it's inside the margin guides or outside—or even partially on the page and partially off it.

Like almost every other measurement in QuarkXPress, you can type the Margin Guide values in inches, in picas, or in any

Figure 2-2
The column, or "live" area

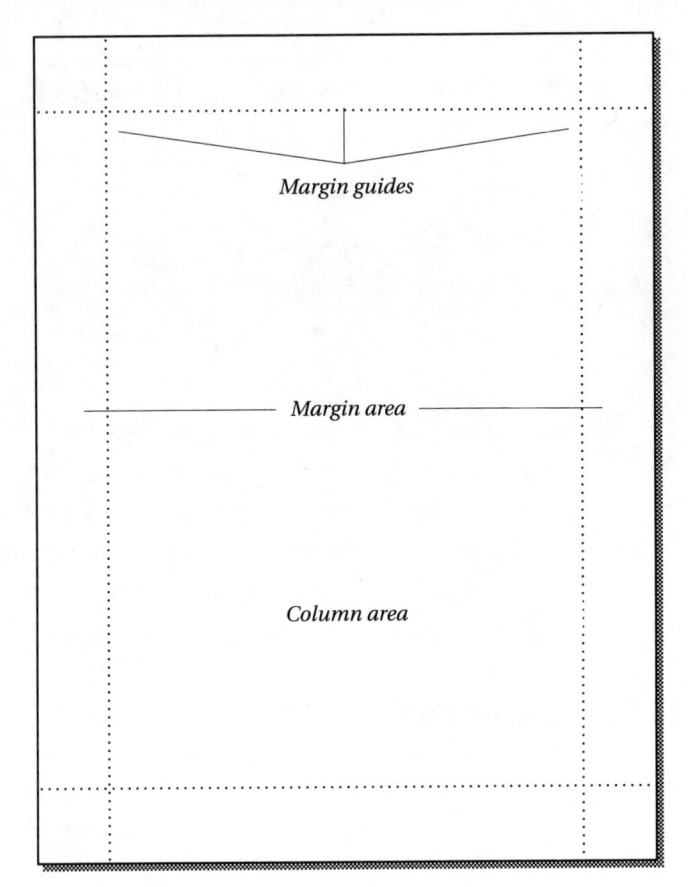

Margin guides

Margin area

Column area

other measurement units. However, there are some qualities about margin guides that are less universal. Although margin guides resemble ruler guides both in form and in function, once you place margin guides you cannot change their position by dragging them. We explain these kinds of modifications in "Making Pages," later in this chapter.

All pages in your document don't have to have the same margins; however, they do until you create multiple master pages, because you can only change margin guides on master pages. Once again, we defer discussion of this process until later in the chapter. For now, let's just concentrate on building one simple document.

Facing Pages

Although the Facing Pages feature is located in the Margins area of the New dialog box, it deserves some special attention. At this stage in the game, you have two choices for your document: single-sided or facing pages.

Single-sided pages. Single-sided pages are what most people generate from desktop-publishing equipment. For example, handbills, flyers, posters, letters, memos, or one-page forms are all single sided. In QuarkXPress, a normal, single-sided document looks like a series of pages, each positioned directly underneath the next (see Figure 2-3).

Facing pages. Facing pages are radically different in form and function from single-sided pages. Whereas nonfacing pages are destined to be single, facing pages are always married to another page (well, almost always). These two pages are adjacent to each other. For example, pick up a book. Open it in the middle. The left page (the verso) faces the right page (the recto). In many books (like the one you're looking at), the left and right pages are almost exactly the same. However, most books have a page with a slightly larger inside margin (binding margin) than they do an outside margin. This is to offset the amount of the page "lost" in the binding.

QuarkXPress displays facing pages directly next to each other on the screen (see Figure 2-4). For example, moving from page 2 to page 3, you must scroll "across" rather than "down." Note that page 2 is always a left page, and page 3 is always a right page. Even numbers fall on the left; odd numbers fall on the right.

If you select "Facing Pages" in the New dialog box, QuarkXPress sets up two master pages: a left page and a right page. These can be almost completely different from each another. Later in the chapter we'll see how.

Column Guides

There's another kind of automatic guide you can place on a page: *column guides*. The area within the margin guides can be subdivided into columns by selecting a value larger than 1 for the Columns field in the New dialog box. For example, if you want a page that ordinarily has three columns of text on it, you can specify a value of 3 (see Figure 2-5).

Figure 2-3
Single-sided pages

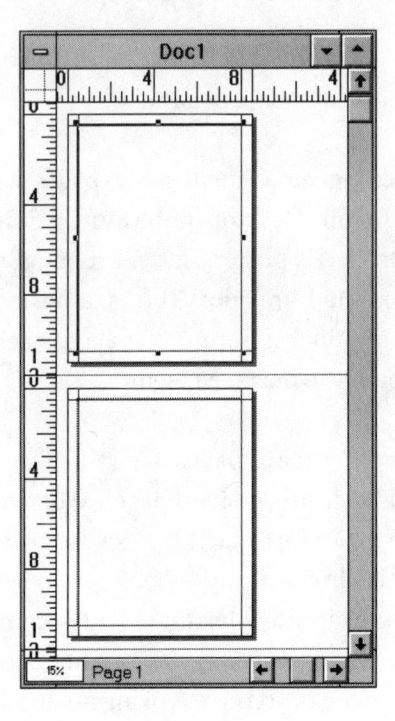

Your next decision is the amount of gutter space. This is a different "gutter" than people sometimes use to refer to the inside page margin. In QuarkXPress, the *gutter* is the blank space between columns.

Note that column guides don't print out; nor do they limit what you can do on the page. They are simply part of the general infrastructure of the document and are meant to be guides. Not only can you change these guides at any time, but you can disregard them entirely.

Perhaps the best way to think about column guides is the concept of the page grid. Unfortunately, QuarkXPress can't automatically create a true horizontal and vertical grid for your page. However, it gives you the tools to make one yourself. Column guides are the first part of that procedure: They allow you to place columns of space on a page. When you have "Snap to Guides" selected on the View menu, items such as text boxes and lines snap to your column guides (see Chapter 1, *QuarkXPress Basics*).

Figure 2-4
Facing pages

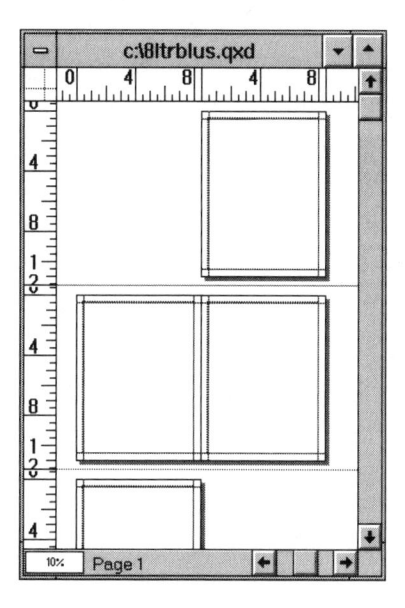

Automatic Text Box

Here's a relatively easy choice: Do you want your first page and all subsequent pages you add to have a text box already placed on them? If so, just check this box. The text box fills the page to the margin guides. This is clearly the way to go if you're working with documents, such as books or flyers, that are mostly text.

Figure 2-5
Column guides

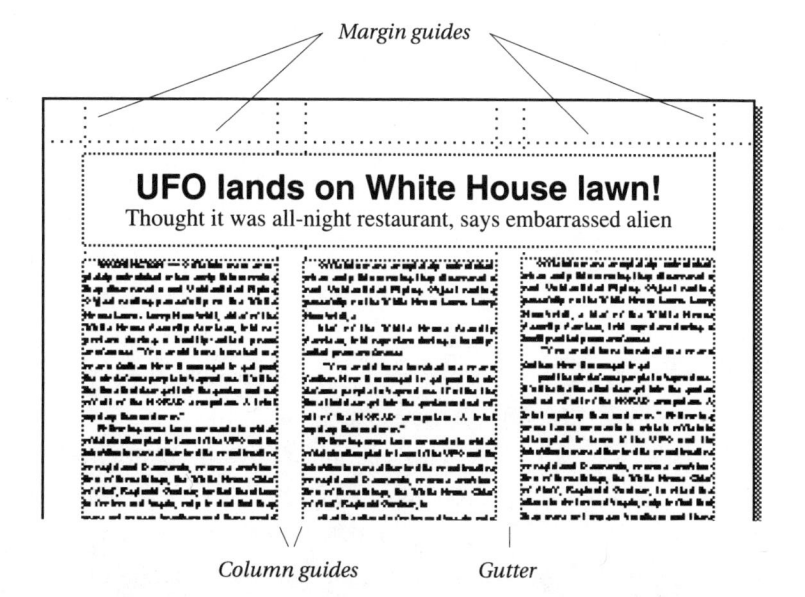

Margin guides

Column guides   *Gutter*

If you do select "Automatic Text Box," the text box that QuarkXPress makes for you is set to the same number of columns and gutter size that you specified in the Column Guides area.

▼▼▼▼▼▼▼▼▼▼▼▼▼▼▼▼▼▼▼▼▼▼▼▼▼▼▼

Tip: Check That New Dialog Box. QuarkXPress remembers what you selected in the New dialog box for the last document and gives you the same settings the next time you start on a new document. This can be helpful, or it can be a drag. You'll read this throughout the book: Verify each dialog box as you go. Don't just assume that you want every default setting. Pay attention to those details and you'll rarely go wrong.

▼▼▼▼▼▼▼▼▼▼▼▼▼▼▼▼▼▼▼▼▼▼▼▼▼▼▼

Master Pages: Elementary

The second stage of building a document is creating master pages. This is, along with style sheets (see Chapter 4, *Type and Typography*), one of the most commonly neglected elements in QuarkXPress. Unfortunately (for those who neglect it), master pages are also one of the most powerful features in the program. If you don't use master pages, you may be missing out on a great way to increase your efficiency.

Master pages are the best way to manage repeating elements common to a number of pages in your document. For example, if you want a page number (folio) to go on every page in your document, you have two choices. First, you could place a text box on every page. Or better, you could simply put one text box on a master page and then assign that master page to your document pages. It's not just page numbers, either. Master pages are also great for headers, footers, borders, repeating graphics, or any other item that you want to show up on many different pages.

The reason that master pages are so powerful is not just that you can quickly format a bunch of pages by assigning a master page to them, but that you can also go back later and change the master page, effecting a change on every page that is based on it. In fact, QuarkXPress not only lets you go back and change master pages, but it offers more flexibility in master page creation than any other Windows publishing program. However, if you use other page-layout software, you should note that QuarkXPress's master pages differ drastically from the competition's.

How PageMaker Does It

For example, it's common to describe master pages in PageMaker by using a metaphor of transparent "underlays" beneath each page. You create and edit the document on your document pages, and the master page underlay displays and prints beneath it. You can "slide out" this master page underlay at any time, change the page formatting, and then slide it back in.

In programs like PageMaker, you can choose to base document pages on master pages, or not—simply by turning the master on or off for specific pages. However, you cannot change any master page elements locally within actual document pages, because although they display and print there, they really exist only on the underlay—which is untouchable unless you slide them out. Also, you can't choose to use particular elements on a master page; everything on the master page is either turned on or off.

How QuarkXPress Does It

The master pages in QuarkXPress are totally different. Master page elements (the boxes and lines on QuarkXPress's master pages) show up on your document's pages not as view-only elements sitting on an underlay, but as real elements that you can edit just like any other page element. If you don't want a certain element of the master page on one page, you can simply select it and delete it. If you want to change it for that page, you can select it and change it. This sort of change is called local formatting.

You can base a document page on either a standard or a blank master page (the latter is the QuarkXPress equivalent of turning a master page "off"). Plus, you can have up to 127 different master pages in a document, so you can base different document pages on different master pages. This is very useful if your document comprises multiple sections that require different looks.

Before we get too far in-depth with master pages, let's look at the basics. Working with master pages isn't complicated if you take it step by step.

Your First Master Page

Two things happen simultaneously when you click OK in the New dialog box: QuarkXPress builds a master page called Master A and creates the first page of your document for you to work on. The master page and the document page are almost identical. If you specified "Facing Pages" in the New dialog box, QuarkXPress still only creates a single document page, but it makes two master pages: a left page called L-Master 1 and a right page called R-Master 1.

You can move between viewing the master pages of a document and the document itself using two methods: the Document Layout palette and the Display menu.

NEW IN 3.3
See page 572

Document Layout palette. To see a list of master pages, click the Document menu at the top of Document Layout palette and drag down to select the Show Master Pages command. The master page icons will appear in the palette window. To jump to the master page you want to view, simply double-click on its icon (see Figure 2-6).

Display menu. You can choose either your document or your master pages by selecting one of them from the Display submenu under the Page menu (see Figure 2-7).

You can tell whether you're looking at a document page or a master page by three tell-tale signs.

- A page number indicator in the lower-left corner of the document window tells you that you are looking at a document page.

- An automatic text-link icon is always in the upper-left corner of a master page. (We discuss this in the next section.)

DOCUMENT CONSTRUCTION **101**

Figure 2-6
Viewing a master page

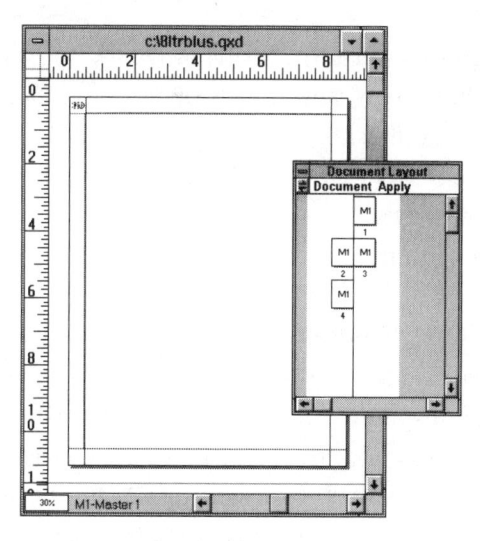

Figure 2-7
Selecting a page to look at

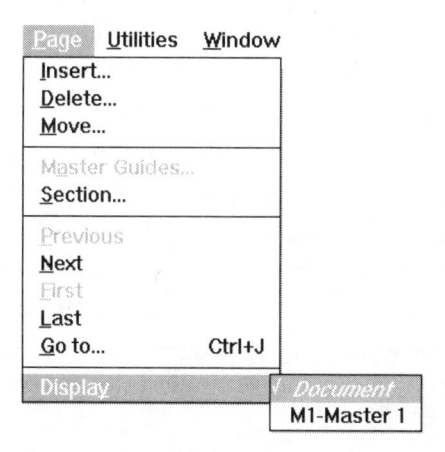

- While viewing a master page, you can't perform certain functions that are usually available. For example, the Go To (Control-J) feature is disabled, as well as "Insert."

▼▼▼▼▼▼▼▼▼▼▼▼▼▼▼▼▼▼▼▼▼▼▼▼▼▼▼▼▼▼▼
Parts of a Master Page

Although master pages look similar to normal document pages, there are some basic differences you need to know. These differences include the master guides, the automatic text link icon, and the automatic text link box. Note that "automatic text link icon" is our term for what Quark refers to as both the "Intact Chain Icon" and the "Broken Chain Icon." Similarly, our term "automatic text link box" is referred to as "automatic text box" in the Quark manuals. We think our terminology is more descriptive, so that's what we use. If you like Quark's, then do a mental substitution.

Master Guides

We said above that you could change the margins and column guides after you set them in the New dialog box. The Master Guides dialog box is the place to do it. The Master Guides dialog box is available by selecting "Master Guides" from the Page menu (see Figure 2-8) when displaying a master page.

When you use the Master Guides dialog box to change the margin guides or the column guides, only the master page that you have open changes. However, after you learn about multiple master pages later on in this chapter, you'll see that you can have a different set of margins and columns for each master page in your document.

Figure 2-8
The Master Guides dialog box

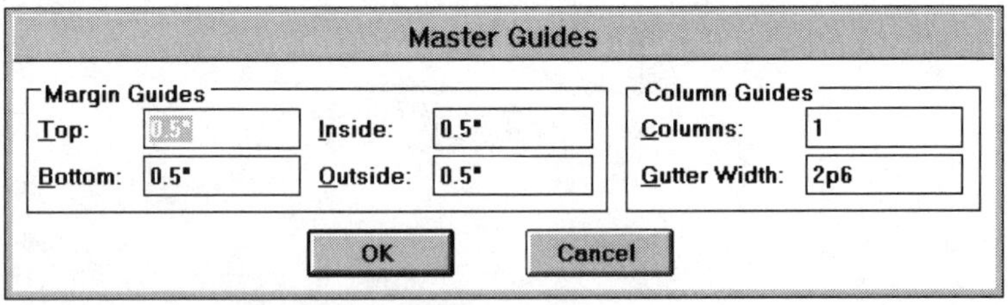

Automatic Text Link Icon

The automatic text link icon is the little picture of a chain link in the upper-left corner of every master page. It is the gateway to QuarkXPress's automatic text linking feature. This feature allows QuarkXPress to automatically link together text boxes that lie on each page. This process also can be accomplished manually, but it is much slower. The automatic text link icon works in conjunction with the automatic text link box, which we discuss soon.

The automatic text link icon is either broken (disabled) or linked (enabled). You can use the Linking and Unlinking tools while viewing your master pages to switch the automatic linking on and off (see below).

Automatic Text Link Box

The automatic text link box is a text box that is linked through QuarkXPress's automatic linking mechanism. Automatic linking is the way that QuarkXPress links pages of text together. We know this sounds confusing, so let's look at an example.

Picture a one-page document with only one master page, Master A. If your text fills and overflows the text box on the first page, you can add a page by selecting "Insert Page" from the Page menu. If your Master A has an automatic text link box on it, then the overflow text automatically flows onto the newly added page. If there is no automatic text link box on the master page, then QuarkXPress does not link your first page text box to anything, and you have to link things manually (see Chapter 1, *QuarkXPress Basics*).

There are two ways to get automatic text link boxes on your master page.

- **Automatic Text Box.** If you select "Automatic Text Box" in the New dialog box, QuarkXPress places a text box on your first document page and also on Master A. The text box on the master page is automatically assigned to be an automatic text link box.

- **Linking to the chain.** You can create your own automatic text link box by drawing a text box on your master page and then linking it to the automatic text link icon. First, select the Linking tool. Second, click on the automatic text link icon in the upper-left corner of the page and then on the text box you want automatically linked (see Figure 2-9).

An automatic text link box is a special-case text box. It is reserved solely for text that is typed in document pages, so you cannot type any text in it while on the master page. This is different from other boxes that are on the master page, which can

Figure 2-9
Creating an automatic text link box

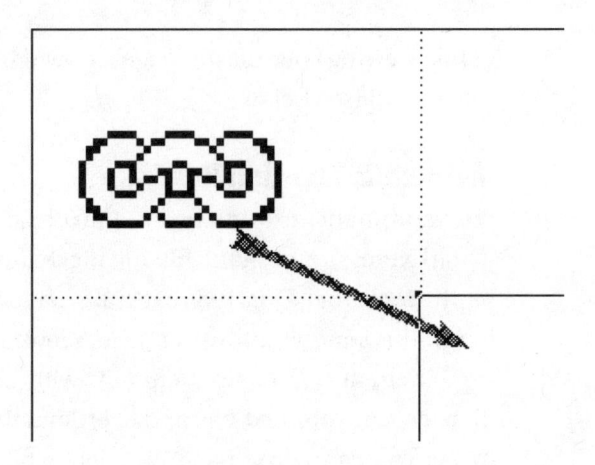

contain text or graphics. We'll look at why you would want to use these other types a little later on.

Modifying Automatic Text Link Boxes

While you cannot type in automatic text link boxes on a master page, you can apply many formatting specifications to them. For example, you can specify the number of columns, width, height, background color, and frame. While QuarkXPress originally places automatic text link boxes so that they fill the area outlined by the margin guides, you can move and resize them to suit your needs.

▼▼▼▼▼▼▼▼▼▼▼▼▼▼▼▼▼▼▼▼▼▼▼▼

Tip: Assigning a Startup Font. As we just said, you can't actually type in automatic text link boxes while on a master page. However, you *can* assign character formatting to the box. Just select the text box with the Content tool and specify the font, size, style, and so on. Then, when you return to the document page, the text you type in that box appears in the font, size, and style that you chose. Text that is imported into that box does not necessarily appear in that font, however.

▼▼▼▼▼▼▼▼▼▼▼▼▼▼▼▼▼▼▼▼▼▼▼▼

Creating Multiple Automatic Text Link Boxes

You can actually have any number of automatic text link boxes on a master page. What you have to do is link them all in the order in which you want text to flow into them. You define the first box as automatic, using the procedures described above. Then you click in succession with the Linking tool on the boxes you want to define as automatic text link boxes. This defines them as part of the automatic text chain. You'll see the linking arrows shoot out with each new link that you create. To continue the link from a left master to a right master, click on the right master's automatic text link icon and then on the right master's automatic text box.

Unlinking Automatic Text Link Boxes

The easiest way to discard an automatic text link box while either on a document page or on the master page is to delete it (Control-K, or Backspace). But if you want to keep the box and simply negate its definition as an automatic text link box, you can do that using the Unlinking tool. First, click on the automatic text link icon with the Unlinking tool, thereby showing the linking arrow. Next, click on the tail of the linking arrow to break the chain and turn the box into a "normal" master page text box. In the case of multiple, successively linked boxes, the automatic linking is broken wherever you've broken the chain, though any other links you've created among those boxes remain.

▼ ▼

Tip: Make Sure that You're Working with the Correct Pointer. It's very easy to attempt linking and unlinking, only to find nothing happening—no arrows popping up between boxes or changing course. When this happens, remember that you can't tighten a screw with a ball-peen hammer: You must use the right tool for the right job! Hold down the Alt key as you select the Linking or Unlinking tools (as your operation requires), so that they remain selected and therefore provide you with the correct pointer, without which you can't conduct these operations.

▼ ▼

Tip: Use Step and Repeat to Copy Page Geometry. Remember, there's no need to recreate boxes and graphic elements for the right side of a master page if you've already created the left side. Simply duplicate the items and drag them to the opposite page: Select each item to duplicate and use the Duplicate or Step and Repeat features (under the Item menu) to create copies. A "Step and Repeat" with a vertical offset of 0 (zero) ensures that the copies are at precisely the same vertical position on a page as the original. Remember that you can hold down the Shift key as you drag copies with the Item tool to constrain movement horizontally or vertically. After you move the items, change the text content and the character and paragraph formatting as is appropriate to your right master formatting plans.

What to Put on a Master Page

Although your creativity in formatting master pages is unlimited, the most common uses for master pages are for headers and footers. These typically contain such information as publication name, chapter or section title, author's name, date or number of the issue, and page numbering. These items are perfect for master pages because creating them for every page in your document would be a chore that Hercules would shudder at and Job would give up on.

- Headers are repeating sections at the tops of pages, usually in the margin area.

- Footers are headers that fall at the bottoms of pages.

- You can also have a hybrid header or footer that appears in the side margins of pages. Far less common than headers and footers, they are usually reserved for wide margins since you don't want them abutting regular text. In bound documents, they most often appear on the outside margin of each page, so that they don't disappear into the binding. We don't really have a name for these; in the Macintosh edition of this book we called them *siders*, but—to tell you the truth—we hate that term.

If you're used to working with a dedicated word-processing program, you know that the way to create and edit headers and footers is to call up a special window and type into it, thereafter choosing to hide or show the header/footer on scrolling pages, as the particular program allows. There is no way to automatically hide headers and footers in QuarkXPress. You create them directly on your master pages as standard text or picture boxes, and they show up everywhere you go. Figure 2-10 shows a page with headers and footers.

Figure 2-10
Headers and footers

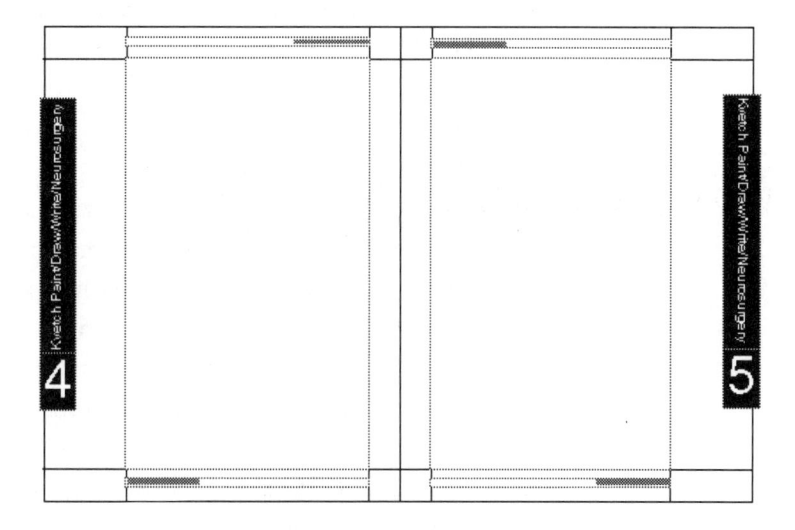

Automatic Page Numbering

Part of building a firm infrastructure for your document is to make your document work for you rather than to have you working for your document. A perfect example of this is page numbering. We have a confession to make. Before we knew better, we would type "1" on the first page, "2" on the second page, and so on. When we deleted or added pages, we just took the time to renumber every page. That seemed reasonable enough. What else could we do?

QuarkXPress lets you set up automatic page numbering for an entire document. You don't actually type any number on the master page. What you type is the Current Box Page Number character (Control-3). This gives you a "number placeholder." This placeholder is replaced by the page number when you are looking at the document in Document view. In master pages, the page number placeholder looks like this: <#>.

The number appears in whatever font, size, and style you choose on the master page. For example, if you make the <#>

character 9-point Trump-Mediaeval, all the page numbers come out in that style.

Remember, the Current Box Page Number character is simply a character that you type, manipulate, or delete using keyboard commands. You also can type it alongside other text, to form text blocks that read, "Page <#>" or "If you wanted to find pg. <#>, you found it."

These page numbers change as you add, delete, and move pages. For example, if you move page 23 to be your new page 10, every page in the document changes its numbering accordingly. Also, if you change the page numbering scheme to Roman numerals or whatever (see "Sections," later in this chapter), QuarkXPress automatically changes that style on every page containing a Current Box Page Number character.

Graphics and Master Pages

You can do anything with a graphic on a master page that you can do on a regular document page, including defining it for text runarounds. You can be subtle and put a small graphic in your header or footer, or you can put a great big graphic in the background of every page (see Figure 2-11).

Remember, when formatting master pages with graphics—whether as backgrounds or for runaround effects—that what you place on the master page appears on every page of the document that is based on that master page. If you only want a graphic on a few pages in your document, you're better off either handling such things on a page-by-page basis in the regular document view or creating different master pages to hold different graphics.

Changing Master Page Items

After you have created your master page, you can manipulate the text and picture boxes in either master page or document view. The view you're in when you make a change determines what effect the change has on your document.

Figure 2-11
Placing a graphic on your master page

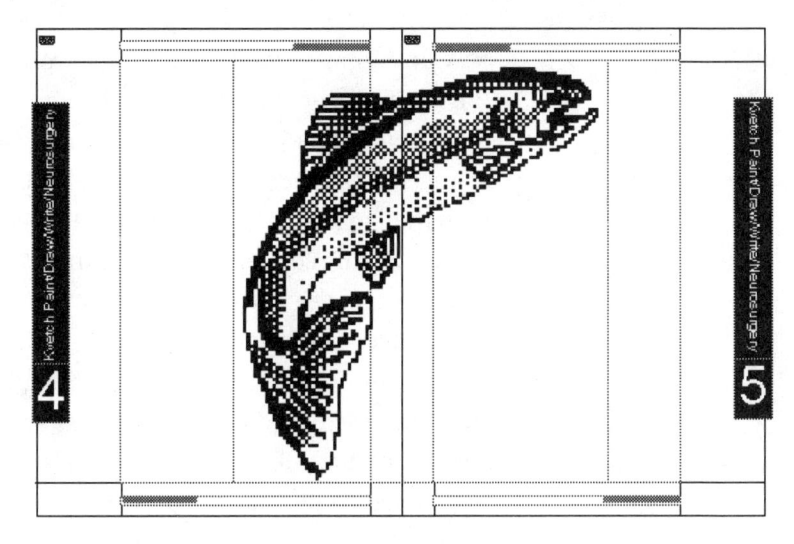

Changes to Document Pages

If you make a change to a master page item (a picture or text box, or a rule, that comes from the master page) when you're on an actual document page, the change affects only that actual page; that is, the master page itself is not affected by the local page formatting. However, as we'll see in the next section, any local changes you make to master page items can have a drastic effect on how those items act later when changing or reapplying master pages.

Changes on Master Pages

If you are in master page view when you make a change to a master page item, the change is reflected on every page in your document that is based on that master page—unless that item has been changed locally on a page while in document view.

For example, let's say you have a header with the name of the document and the page number. You have created a 30-page document based on this master page, so each page has that header on it. If you change the header so that it reads differently, that change shows up on all 30 pages. However, if you changed the header on page 10 while in document view before reworking the header on the master page, the header on every page except page 10 is changed. Page 10 remains unchanged because your local page change overrides the master page for that text box.

Continuing with this example, if you delete the header from the master page, the header is deleted from every page of the document, as long as no local page changes were made. But if a change had already been made locally to the header on page 10, then that header on page 10 is not deleted.

Taking this concept one step farther, if you actually delete a master page, the master items that appear on document pages are deleted, too, unless you have locally modified them in some way. For example, if you have a picture box on a master page, and page 3 is based on that master page, then the picture box appears on page 3. Unless you modify that picture box in some way, deleting the master page removes the picture box from page 3. This makes some sense if you think about it for a while, even though it's often frustrating.

Master Pages Preferences

The determining factor for what happens to master page items that have been modified locally (while in document view) is the Master Page Items feature in the General Preferences dialog box, accessed via the Preferences menu under the Edit menu. You have two choices: Delete Changes and Keep Changes.

Delete Changes. If "Master Page Items" is set to "Delete Changes," every master item on a page is deleted and replaced with new master items—even if changes have been made locally. If you have made changes, this is a great way to "reset" the page: reapply a master page to a document page while "Delete Changes" is set in the General Preferences dialog box. All of the locally modified items are deleted and reset back to the original master items.

Keep Changes. The alternative to deleting locally modified master items is keeping them. When "Keep Changes" is selected in the Preferences dialog box, QuarkXPress skips over any master items that you have modified (changed their position, size, shape, font, text, and so on). This is the default setting when you start a document. Again, this is only relevant when reapplying a master page.

Master Pages: Advanced

If you've come this far, you've learned the hardest aspects of QuarkXPress's master pages. We're calling this the advanced section not because it's more complex or difficult, but because it represents a higher level of control by offering additional options.

- Creating new master pages
- Creating new master pages based on existing ones
- Naming and ordering master pages
- Applying master pages to document pages
- Deleting master pages

There are many ways to use multiple master pages. For example, most books are separated into several sections, including front matter, body text, and index. Each section is paginated and formatted differently from the body, with different (or no) headers or footers. You can create a master page for each of these sections. Multiple master pages are almost required for magazine production, where you may have a plethora of different sections: departments and columns, regular article pages, photo features, full-page ads, and small-ad sections, to name a few.

Multiple master pages are accessible primarily through the Document Layout palette. We introduced the Document Layout palette in Chapter 1, *QuarkXPress Basics*. Now we're going to concentrate on how you can use it to work with your master pages.

Document Layout Palette

See page 572

The Document Layout palette for the facing-pages document in Figure 2-12 looks deceptively simple: two drop-down menus (Document and Apply) and the document layout area. There's more under the hood though, since this palette serves for managing both document pages and master pages.

Figure 2-12
Document layout palettes for single-sided and facing-pages documents

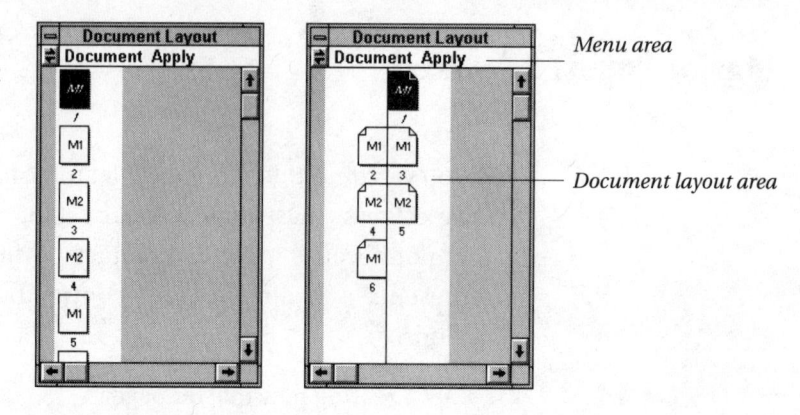

Menu area

Document layout area

Document menu. At the upper left of the Document Layout palette is the Document menu. This is used for creating and deleting both document and master pages. Click and hold down the mouse button on the Document menu and you'll see three commands: Insert, Delete, and Show Master Pages (or Show Document Pages, if Show Master Pages was previously selected). This last command gives a dual purpose to the Document Control palette. Select Show Document Pages, and the document layout area below the palette menu bar displays document icons arranged to show your document layout; select Show Master Pages, and the document layout area displays a column of page icons that represents your master pages.

To create a new master page, click on the Document menu and drag along the drop-down menu to select the Show Master Pages command. You'll see that the Document menu has changed its name to the Masters menu, so click on the Masters menu and then on the Insert command. A pop-up list appears with the names of master pages (see Figure 2-13), so just drag down and select the one you want. If you're in hurry, clicking the small icon to the left of the Document/Masters menu toggles between document or master page view.

Similarly, you can delete a master page by first selecting the icon of the master page you want to delete and then selecting the Delete command from the Masters menu. Remember, once you delete a master or document page, it is deleted forever. This action is not reversible with Undo (Control-Z) so make sure you really want to do it.

DOCUMENT CONSTRUCTION   **113**

Figure 2-13
Creating a new master page

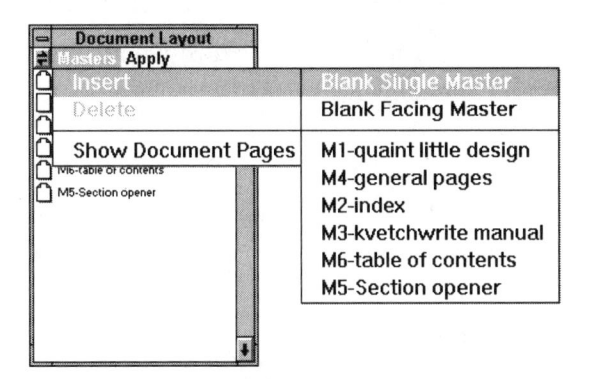

```
Document Layout
Masters  Apply
  Insert        ▶  Blank Single Master
  Delete           Blank Facing Master
  Show Document Pages  M1-quaint little design
  M6-table of contents  M4-general pages
  M5-Section opener     M2-index
                        M3-kvetchwrite manual
                        M6-table of contents
                        M5-Section opener
```

▼▼▼▼▼▼▼▼▼▼▼▼▼▼▼▼▼▼▼▼▼▼▼▼▼

Tip: Retrieving Document Layout Deletions. If you've deleted a master page from the Document Layout palette, the only way to get it back is to select "Revert to Saved" from the File menu. This, of course, only works if you've saved your document recently. Bear in mind that this method wipes out all changes you've made since your last save, so pause a moment and reflect before you jump into this last resort.

▼▼▼▼▼▼▼▼▼▼▼▼▼▼▼▼▼▼▼▼▼▼▼▼▼

If you have more than two or three master pages, Quark-XPress lets you change the order in which their icons appear in the list. Just click on a master page icon and drag it up or down to where you want it. The cursor will appear as a small downward-, left-, or right-pointing insertion pointer when you're at an appropriate drop spot, so just release the mouse button to leave the master page at its new position to left, right, above, or below an existing master page. Note that the second master page you create is called "Master 2," even if you place the icon in the master page selection list before Master 1.

Master pages name field. You can assign a new name to each master page by first clicking on a master page icon in the document layout area. The name following the icon becomes a temporary field, and you can replace the name "Master 1" (or whatever) with any name you care to type. You can type up to three characters before a hyphen, and then up to 60 more. If you don't type a hyphen, QuarkXPress assigns a prefix of "M1-" or something. The name you assign is the name that appears in master page scroll lists and menus throughout the program. The prefix (the characters before the hyphen) shows up in the Document Layout palette icons.

▼▼▼▼▼▼▼▼▼▼▼▼▼▼▼▼▼▼▼▼▼▼▼▼▼▼▼

Tip: Master Pages Naming Conventions. Note that although you can name a master page anything you like, QuarkXPress displays page icons with only the letter "M" followed by a number (M1, M2, M3, and so on). We find that it helps to name master pages with a letter or number as a prefix so we can keep them in order easily. For example, if Master 1 is a master page for the table of contents, we might change the label to "A-TOC." Your next master page may be called "B-Front Matter," and so on.

To get a listing of all the master pages' names, select "Insert" from the Page menu, and while holding the mouse button down, create a screen dump (type Alt-Print Screen). You can then print out this screen dump as a reference guide.

▼▼▼▼▼▼▼▼▼▼▼▼▼▼▼▼▼▼▼▼▼▼▼▼▼▼▼

Document layout area. The largest area in the Document Layout palette is the *document layout area*. This shows icons of the document's pages, which are numbered and positioned in the order of their actual appearance in the document (see Chapter 1, *QuarkXPress Basics* for more on this area). Each page icon on the palette displays the master page that it is based on. When you first open a new document, only one page is visible, and it is based on Master 1.

Basing a New Master Page on Another

If you need a new master page but don't want to format it from scratch, you can base it on another master page that carries at least some of the formatting you wish to retain. You do this by first creating a new master page as described above and selecting its icon in the document layout area. Then click the Apply command in the Document Layout palette and select the name of the particular master page whose formatting you wish to copy. An alert box will pop up asking you if it's "OK to completely replace 'Master 2' with 'Master 1'?" (Your master page names may vary). Click OK to commit yourself to the change.

Master 2 now contains all of the elements and formatting from Master 1. Go in and make your changes to customize Master 2 to your needs.

Applying Master Pages to Document Pages

You can also apply the formatting of any master page to an existing document page, whether that page was based on a master page or not. It's a maneuver similar to the one described above for applying the formatting of one master page to that of another.

1. Select the Show Document Pages icon from the Masters menu if the document pages aren't displayed in the document layout area.

2. Select the page icon to which you want to apply a master page format. (To select more than one icon, hold down the Shift key while you click the first and last page icons if they're consecutive. If they're not consecutive, hold down the Control key).

3. Click the Apply command and drag down the list of master page names. You can release the mouse button as soon as the page name is highlighted.

The document page assumes the formatting of that master page. Unmodified master items (from the old master page) are deleted. Items that have been modified may or may not be deleted, depending on your Preferences settings (see "Changing Master Page Items," above).

Making Pages

In Chapter 1, *QuarkXPress Basics*, we discussed moving pages around and deleting them. Clearly, that was slightly premature since we had yet explained adding new pages to a document. We cover that procedure here.

There are two ways to add pages to your document: the Insert Pages dialog box and the Document Layout palette.

Insert Pages

The first way you can add pages to your document is by selecting "Insert" from the Pages menu. This brings up the Insert Pages dialog box (see Figure 2-14). This dialog box is almost entirely self-explanatory, but we'll cover it piece by piece just to be sure.

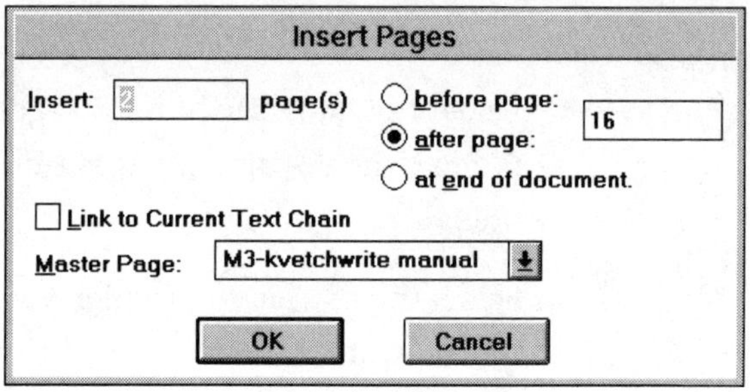

Figure 2-14
The Insert Pages dialog box

You can type the number of pages you want to add in the Insert field and then select where you want those pages to be added. You have three choices: before a page, after a page, and at the end of the document. The first two choices require that you choose a page that the page(s) should be added before or after; the third requires no additional number, as it places the pages after the last page in the document.

Before you hit OK, though, you need to think about two other things in this dialog box: the Link to Current Text Chain check box and the Master Page specification. Let's look at these in reverse order.

Master Page specification. You can choose which master page you want these pages to be based on by selecting one from the Master Page drop-down menu of the Insert Pages dialog box. Or if you like, you can base the pages-to-be on blank single-sided or facing-page pages (labeled as Blank Single or Blank Facing Page in the Master Page menu; you can choose the latter only if you're working with a facing-page document).

Link to Current Text Chain. If a text box is selected on your page, and the master page you are basing your inserted pages on has an automatic text link box, then you have the option of automatically linking the inserted pages with the text box you have selected. This is a potentially confusing concept, so let's look at it carefully.

Let's say you have a text box on a page overflowing with text. Let's also say that your master page "3-FeatureOpener" has an enabled automatic text link box (linked to the automatic text link icon).

1. Select the text box on the document page.

2. Select "Insert" from the Page menu.

3. Add a page based on master page 3-FeatureOpener at the end of the document.

If you click "Link to Current Text Chain" in the Insert Pages dialog box, then the text from your document page text box automatically links to your inserted pages. If you do not select "Link to Current Text Chain," then the pages are still added, but there is no link between your text box and the text boxes on those pages. You can, however, link them up manually using the Link tool.

Document Layout Insertions

The second method for inserting pages is to use the the Document Layout palette. Adding pages is accomplished with the Insert command. Click "Insert" (make sure that document page icons are displayed in the layout area) and drag along the drop-down list to select a master page. Then, move the cursor down to the layout area into the position you want (before a page, after a page, at the end of a document, or as a page in a spread).

The cursor changes into an insertion pointer (a left-, right-, or downward-pointing arrow or a document icon) at the points where you can appropriately insert a page, either to the left or the right or above or below an existing page. Just click once when you hit the spot. If you don't want the page based on a master page, just select the Blank Single Page or Blank Facing Page master page choices from the Insert command's drop-down list (as mentioned above, you can only select Blank Facing Page if you are working with a facing-page document).

Although Quark's documentation says that you can add multiple pages by holding down the Control key while you select a page from the Insert drop-down menu, it's actually not true. Instead, if you want to add more than one page at a time or want to add pages that are linked to the current text chain, then you must hold down the Control key when you click where you want your pages in the Document Layout palette. For example, if you want to add four pages after page 2, first select the master page that you want the pages based on from the Insert drop-down menu, then hold down the Control key while clicking in the space after page 2. After you click, QuarkXPress gives you the Insert Pages dialog box. You can select the appropriate items, such as number of pages, as described above.

Modifying Your Pages

Fortunately for desktop publishers, it is possible to change the foundation of a document significantly more easily than a construction worker can change the foundation of a building. Not only can you modify your master pages in many ways, as we've seen, but you can modify the underlying page sizes, margins, column guides, and more. Let's look at each of these controls.

Changing Page Size

Even after you click OK in the New dialog box and begin adding pages to a document, you can still change the page size in the Document Setup dialog box (choose "Document Setup" from the File menu; see Figure 2-15). Note that this dialog box bears a striking resemblance to a portion of the New dialog box. The rules are just the same (see "Page Size," above).

Your only real limitation in modifying page size is the size of any objects you have already placed on the page. QuarkXPress won't let you make a page so small that page elements would

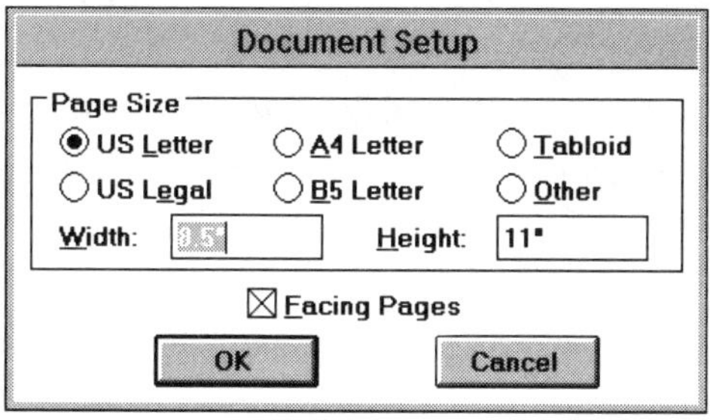

Figure 2-15
The Document Setup dialog box

"fall off" the pasteboard (the size of the pasteboard surrounding each page is based on the size of your document page). If this is a limiting factor, you may be able to work around the problem by adjusting the width of the pasteboard (see "Tip: Adjusting Your Pasteboard," in Chapter 1, *QuarkXPress Basics*).

Changing Facing Pages

You can change one other page feature with the Document Setup dialog box: facing pages. If you originally specified your document as single-sided, you can change it to a facing-page document by clicking the Facing Pages item in the Document Setup dialog box. Facing-page documents can have facing master pages (the facing-page icon is enabled in the Document Layout palette). However, you cannot change a facing-page document to a single-sided document if you have any facing master pages.

If you need to change a facing-page document to a single-sided document, first delete all of the facing master pages by using the Delete command in the Document Layout palette and then go to the Document Setup dialog box and deselect "Facing Pages."

Changing Margins

As we mentioned above, every page in your document has the same margins until you create multiple master pages, each with different margins. When you first open a master page, its margin guides are set to the values you specified in the New dialog box. You can change these margins by selecting "Master Guides" from the Page menu. Remember that the Master Guides menu item is available only when a master page is being displayed.

▼▼▼▼▼▼▼▼▼▼▼▼▼▼▼▼▼▼▼▼▼▼▼▼▼

Tip: Ignoring the Guides. Even without creating and applying different master pages, you can get "de facto" different margins within a document, since margin guides are only that—guides. If you want, you can simply ignore them. Draw out or resize a text or graphics box so that it is bigger or smaller than the margin-defined area, creating a custom "active area" for your page elements. But unless you're dealing with one-page documents, it's really best to handle multiple margin definitions by going ahead and changing the Master Guides settings.

▼▼▼▼▼▼▼▼▼▼▼▼▼▼▼▼▼▼▼▼▼▼▼▼▼

Changing Column Guides

Migrants from PageMaker should be aware that QuarkXPress's column guides cannot be repositioned by dragging them with the mouse. Instead, you change the Column Guides settings in the Master Guides dialog box. QuarkXPress lets you have a different number of columns and varied gutter sizes for each master page. If you don't want to have column guides on a page, type "1" in the Columns field.

▼▼▼▼▼▼▼▼▼▼▼▼▼▼▼▼▼▼▼▼▼▼▼▼▼

Tip: Snap to Guides for Box Fitting. We often find it more helpful to draw separate text boxes for each column rather than to use one large text box separated into columns. Column and margin guides make this process easy. If you have "Snap to Guides" turned on (under the View menu), you can quickly draw a text box that fills one column. This text box can be duplicated, then positioned in the next column, and so on, until each column is created. Bob sometimes decides he doesn't want the column guides cluttering up the page after he's drawn these text boxes, so he simply removes them from the master page using "Master Guides." David, having lived with clutter most of his life, just leaves the guides where they are.

Automatic Page Insertion

Importing a long text document can be a harrowing experience when you're working with automatically linked text boxes. Where does the rest of the text go when the first text box is filled? QuarkXPress lets you control this through the Auto Page Insertion pop-up menu in the General Preferences dialog box (accessed via the Preferences command under the Edit menu). You have four choices: "End of Story," "End of Section," "End of Document," and "Off." The default setting (the way it's set up if you don't change anything) is "End of Section."

End of Story. With this option enabled, QuarkXPress inserts new pages right after the page containing the last text box in a story, and those pages bear the master page formatting of the page that held that box. If, for instance, your story starts on page 1 and jumps to page 5, any text overflow from the page 5 text box causes pages to be inserted following page 5, not page 1.

End of Section. Under this option, pages are inserted following the last page in a section (see "Sections and Page Numbering," later in this chapter). Additional pages bear the master page formatting of the last page in that section. Thus, if your page 1 story jumps to page 5, and page 5 is part of a section that ends with page 8, new pages inserted because of text overflow appear right after page 8.

End of Document. This option causes pages to be inserted after the last page of the document, regardless of its length and despite any sections you might have set up. Inserted pages bear the master page formatting of the last page of the document.

If you have only one story and one section in a document, then all three of these settings mean the same thing.

Off. When "Auto Page Insertion" is set to "Off," QuarkXPress never adds pages automatically. Instead, you must add pages manually (see "Making Pages," earlier in this chapter).

Text Linking

Remember, the Automatic Page Insertion feature only works if your master page has an automatic text link box. That makes sense, because otherwise pages are inserted based on text flowing through the automatic text chain. You cannot have automatic page insertion without an automatic text link, and you cannot have that without an automatic text link box.

Multiple Page Spreads

When the rest of the world thought that facing-page spreads were pretty nifty, Quark came along and added the capability to build three-page spreads. In fact, you can quickly and easily build four-page, five-page, or any-number-page spreads, as long as the combined width of the spread doesn't exceed 48 inches.

Once again, this is a job for the Document Layout palette. Spreads can be created in both facing-pages and single-sided documents by dragging a page icon to the right side of a right page or to the left side of a left page (single-sided documents, for this purpose, are made entirely of right pages). The pasteboard (represented by the dark gray area in the palette) automatically expands to accommodate the pages. Figure 2-16 shows an example of creating a three-page spread in a facing-page document.

Note that dragging a page to the left of a right page or to the right of a left page may result in reshuffling the file rather than building a spread.

Sections and Page Numbering

Earlier in this chapter, we discussed how to apply automatic page numbers to your document's master pages. Here we talk about how to customize those page numbers and how to create multiple sections within a single document.

Figure 2-16
A three-page spread

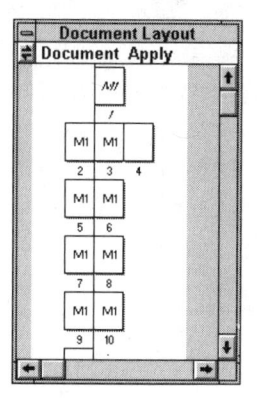

Ordinarily, a QuarkXPress document has one section. Page numbers start with the Arabic numeral 1 and go up consecutively, page by page. However, you can change the starting page number, the style of page numbers, and add multiple sections that each have their own page-numbering styles.

Changing Your Page Numbering

Let's say you're producing a book, and each chapter is saved in a separate QuarkXPress file. If the first chapter ends on page 32, you can tell QuarkXPress to start the page numbers in chapter two at page 33, and so on.

1. Go to the first page of the document (the one on which you want to change the numbering).

2. Select the Section item from the Page menu.

3. Enable the Section Start feature by clicking in the box (an "X" should appear).

4. Type the number at which you'd like your document to start, and click OK (see Figure 2-17).

The first page of a new section always has an asterisk after its name. It doesn't print out and is just a sign on the screen indicating that this is a section beginning.

▼ ▼

Tip: Get to That Section Quickly. You also can get to the Section dialog box quickly by clicking on the page icon for the first page

Figure 2-17
Setting up a new section

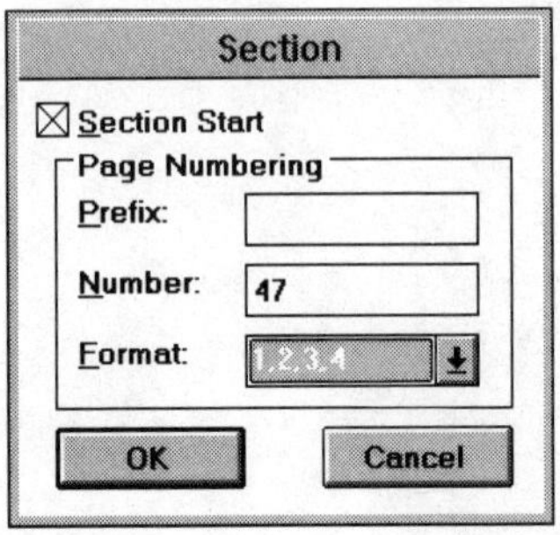

in the section and then clicking once the page number under the icon in the Document Layout palette.

▼ ▼

Changing the Page-Numbering Style

QuarkXPress lets you choose among five formats for numbering pages.

- Arabic numerals (1, 2, 3, 4, etc.)
- Uppercase Roman numerals (I, II, III, IV, etc.)
- Lowercase Roman numerals (i, ii, iii, iv, etc.)
- Capital letters (A, B, C, D, etc.)
- Lowercase letters (a, b, c, d, etc.)

You can change the numbering style for a section by going to the first page in a section, selecting "Section" from the Page menu, and choosing a numbering format from the Format pop-up menu.

Prefixes

The automatic page numbers can contain more than just a number in the five formats listed above. You also can include a prefix of up to four letters or numbers to the page number. For example, you may want the page numbers in a book appendix to read A-1, A-2, and so on. The "A-" is a prefix to the Arabic numerals. You can type this sort of prefix in the Prefix field of the Section dialog box.

Automatic "Continued…" Pagination

In magazines and newspapers, where stories can jump from page 6 to page 96, it is often helpful to have a "Continued on Page X" message at the bottom of the column from which text is jumping and a "Continued from Page X" message at the top of the column to which it is jumping. These are sometimes called jump lines. QuarkXPress can't automate creation of the lines, but it can automate the placement and revision of the page numbers in them. This is useful because you may change links, or insert or delete new pages, and such actions could change the page numbers referred to. In such cases you won't have to go through and manually update the numbers.

To Create a "Continued on…" Message

It's easy to create these jump lines (see Figure 2-18).

1. Make a text box the same width as the column or text box it concerns and move it on top of that text box. If this new text box is set behind the original text box, you can select "Bring to Front" from the Item menu.

2. Be sure the new box's runaround is set to "Item" (see Chapter 7, *Where Text Meets Graphics*). This ensures that your jump line has its own space and isn't jumbled in on top of the other text.

Figure 2-18
Jump lines

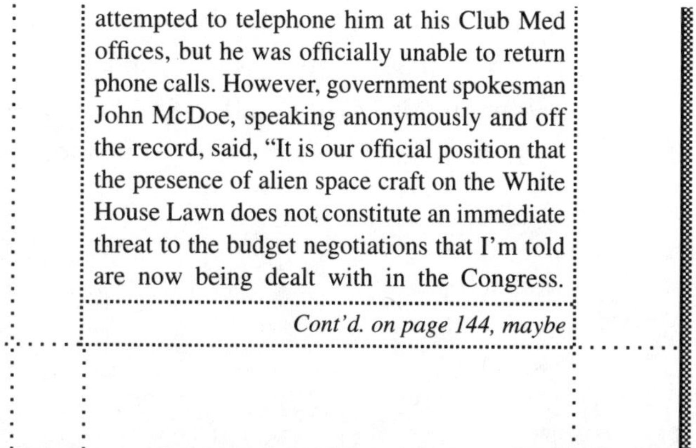

attempted to telephone him at his Club Med offices, but he was officially unable to return phone calls. However, government spokesman John McDoe, speaking anonymously and off the record, said, "It is our official position that the presence of alien space craft on the White House Lawn does not constitute an immediate threat to the budget negotiations that I'm told are now being dealt with in the Congress.

Cont'd. on page 144, maybe

3. Type the text of your jump line (for example, "Continued on"), and when you come to placement of the page number, type Control-4. This is the Next Text Box Page Number character. If you haven't yet linked the text box to a text box on another page, the character will look like this: <None>.

If your text links change, pages get shuffled, or an act of god is invoked, QuarkXPress always knows where your text is going and updates the Next Box Page Number. Nonetheless, these jump lines can sometimes get confused. When QuarkXPress sees one of these jump lines, it looks at any text box that is behind the jump line. If there is more than one text box that is behind the jump line text box, QuarkXPress chooses the one that is "closest" to it; in other words, the text box that is on the next layer down.

To Create a "Continued from..." Message

You can create a "Continued from" jump line by following the same procedures for creating a "Continued to..." text box, but place it at the top of the column concerned. When you come to the page number, type Control-2, for the Previous Box Page Number character, which shows the page number of the previous text box in the chain. This number is also automatically updated as necessary.

Your messages don't have to read "Continued on/from..." You can type any words you want. For instance, "Started on page <None>" or even "If you really care about finishing this story, you'll have to flip past the bulk of this magazine and go all the way to page <None>, where you'll find it buried among the facial cream ads." What matters is that you type the relevant placeholder character somewhere in your message text box.

Crop Marks and Print-Area Considerations

Crop marks, sometimes called trim marks, sit off the four corners of a page or page spread, indicating page edges. We'll hold off discussing them until Chapter 10, *Printing*. However, a couple of things are worth considering now. The two decisions you need to make are whether or not you want crop marks, and whether you want QuarkXPress to make your crop marks automatically or you want to make them yourself.

To Crop or...

The decision of whether to crop or not depends on the sort of document you are producing and on the output device you are using. If you're producing 8.5-by-11-inch or 8.5-by-14-inch letters, memos, reports, flyers, or newsletters on your laser printer for mass reproduction based on those printouts, you don't need trim marks (you won't be cutting the pages). If you're producing document pages that are smaller than the surrounding physical media on which they print—for example, printing to a roll-fed imagesetter—you'll need crop marks so that your lithographer knows exactly what to work with.

Who Crops What

Normally we just let QuarkXPress make the crop marks at the edges of our document pages, but we have run into at least two situations where we want to create them ourselves. These situations break down into multiple-up copies and special services.

Multiple-up copies. When we use QuarkXPress to design and create business cards, we might step-and-repeat the final version two, four, or even eight times to create multiple-up copies on one letter-size page. Each one of these cards needs its own trim marks, and this is a situation where QuarkXPress cannot place them for us (see Figure 2-19).

Special service. If we don't want the registration marks or QuarkXPress's job information for some reason, then we have to make

Figure 2-19
Multiple-up copies

our own crop marks. Note that crop marks should be a minimum of 6 points long, and preferably 1 to 2 picas from the actual page boundary. The Reg. Marks Offset field of the Application Preferences dialog box lets you set how far you want the automatic registration and crop marks from the boundary (See "Application Preferences" in Chapter 1, *QuarkXPress Basics*).

Foundations

You are now ready to build your pages with the understanding and confidence that you have a strong infrastructure to hold up the document. You can use the tools discussed in Chapter 1, *QuarkXPress Basics*, to build text and picture boxes on your master and document pages. Next we'll talk about how to fill those boxes with text and pictures.

CHAPTER 3

WORD PROCESSING

Whether you write your stories on a typewriter, a word processor, or in wet cement, you can't set type in QuarkXPress until you get the words into the program. In the early days of desktop publishing, that usually meant typing them into a word-processing program, fiddling around and revising until deadline time, and then importing the text files into a page-layout program. QuarkXPress, however, has a capable word processor built right in, so you can easily create and edit even the most complicated documents using just QuarkXPress.

However, it's not always as easy as it sounds. In complex documents, QuarkXPress can become so slow that even a moderately skilled typist can get ahead of it.

In this chapter, we'll examine the strengths and weaknesses of writing in QuarkXPress, including its powerful Find/Change feature and its spell checker. We'll also give you some tips for overcoming QuarkXPress's occasional sluggishness.

Entering Text

The most basic aspect of entering text into a QuarkXPress document is making sure that what you type shows up where you want it. QuarkXPress novices often become flustered when they open a document and start typing, only to find that nothing is happening. That's because to enter text in a text box, you must use the Content tool and must select a text box.

So remember, before you can type anything, click on the Content tool (if it isn't already selected), and then click on the box where you want your text to appear.

Tip: Where Did the Rest of My Page Go? QuarkXPress novices, and even experienced users, often get a rude shock when working on complicated page layouts because of a feature of the Content tool. Whenever you select a text (or picture) box, any other page elements that overlap that box are hidden. This feature can be useful because it lets you edit the contents of a box free of any distractions caused by other page elements. However, the sudden disappearance of many or most of the elements on a page can panic even experienced users, particularly if they've turned off the guides display, which also hides the borders of any non-selected boxes.

But of course these "vanished" elements are not lost and can be quickly brought back to view by deselecting the box you're editing or switching to the Item tool.

Selecting and Navigating

As we mentioned in the Preface, you should be familiar with the basic mouse and editing techniques used by almost every Windows application. QuarkXPress adds many extras to the standard Windows way of moving the insertion point and selecting text. Like most Windows programs, QuarkXPress gives you the flexibility of having more than one method for performing the same action; in the case of selecting and navigating, you can use either the mouse or the keyboard.

Using the Mouse

As with any Windows program, you can select a range of text by dragging the pointer diagonally up or down a text column, or you can select a word by double-clicking on it. But QuarkXPress has additional multiple-click selections (see Table 3-1). If you triple-click, you can select a line of text. Quadruple-clicking selects a paragraph, and quintuple-clicking selects all the text in the active box's text chain (If you can quickly click five times in a row at 9 A.M., you're better than we are; we just type Control-A).

Table 3-1
Effects of multiple clicks in text

To Select	Click
A word and contiguous punctuation	Twice
A line	Three times
A paragraph	Four times
An entire story	Five times

▼ ▼

Tip: Extend by Word. If you continue to press down on the mouse button after your final click, you can extend your selection by dragging. If you've selected a word by double-clicking, you can drag to select more text, word by word. If you've selected a paragraph with four clicks, you can similarly drag to increase your selection, paragraph by paragraph.

▼ ▼

If you hold down the Shift key and click anywhere in your text chain, all the text from the previous location of the insertion point to the location of your click is selected.

Note that if you select a range of text in a text box, then deselect the box and edit other boxes, QuarkXPress remembers the selection. When you select the text box again, the same text is automatically selected.

Using the Keyboard

You can use the keyboard to duplicate most of the selections you can make with the mouse. You can also do many things with the keyboard that are not possible with the mouse alone (see Table 3-2).

Table 3-2
Keyboard text editing

To move to the	Type
Previous character	Left Arrow
Next character	Right Arrow
Previous line	Up Arrow
Next line	Down Arrow
Previous word	Control-Left Arrow
Next word	Control-Right Arrow
Start of line	Control-Alt-Left Arrow
End of line	Control-Alt-Right Arrow
Start of story	Control-Alt-Up Arrow
End of story	Control-Alt-Down Arrow

Holding down the Shift key in combination with any of the keyboard movement commands selects all text between the insertion point's original location and the location to which the key combination sends it. Again, to select all of the text in a story, type Control-A.

The ability to quickly jump to the beginning or end of a story by using Control-Alt-Up Arrow or Control-Alt-Down Arrow is especially handy, as it can save you a lot of scrolling if you forget the exact page on which a story starts or finishes.

▼▼▼▼▼▼▼▼▼▼▼▼▼▼▼▼▼▼▼▼▼▼▼▼▼▼

Tip: The Lazy Man's Way to Follow a Text Chain. QuarkXPress has a simple feature that can help if you need to follow a story through your document, but you don't need to remember exactly the page to or from which the text chain is jumping. All you have to do is position the insertion point at the beginning or end of the story's text box on the current page. If you're at the beginning of the text box, use the Left Arrow key to move the insertion out of the current box to the previous box in the chain. Similarly, if you're at the end of the box, use the Right Arrow key to jump the insertion point to the next box in the text chain.

As soon as you move the insertion point out of the current box, QuarkXPress follows it, scrolling automatically to the page containing the text box to which you've moved the insertion point. If possible, QuarkXPress even nicely centers the box in the document window.

▼▼▼▼▼▼▼▼▼▼▼▼▼▼▼▼▼▼▼▼▼▼▼▼▼▼

Deleting Text

There are a number of ways to delete text in QuarkXPress (see Table 3-3). You can, of course, use the Delete key to remove a text selection or to delete text to the right of the insertion point one character at a time. And like most programs, the Backspace key deletes the character to the left of the insertion point. Similarly, Control-Delete gets rid of the entire word to the right of the insertion point, and Control-Backspace removes the word to the left of the insertion point.

Table 3-3
Keyboard deletions

To delete the	Type
Previous character	Backspace
Next character	Delete
Previous word	Control-Backspace
Next word	Control-Delete
Any selected text	Delete or Backspace

Finding and Changing

QuarkXPress's powerful Find/Change feature is one of the reasons many desktop publishers prefer to use QuarkXPress as their word processor. You can use the Find/Change feature either to look for and change occurrences of any text you specify, regardless of attributes such as font, style, point size, and so on, or it can look for and change these attributes, with no regard to the actual words being modified. It can also look for and change only occurrences of specified text with specified attributes.

As you read about the various options that can be set for the Find/Change dialog box, remember that you can change its defaults by opening it and modifying it with no document open.

Where QuarkXPress Looks

QuarkXPress can check either the entire text chain connected to the active text box or look for and change text everywhere in a document. If you have a text box selected, QuarkXPress searches through the story from the location of the insertion point to the end of the story.

To search an entire story, you must either have the insertion point at the very beginning of the story (press Control-Alt-Up Arrow) or hold down the Control key the first time you click on the Find button. When you hold down the Control key, it changes the Find button to a Find First button that looks for the first instance of the text in the story.

To have QuarkXPress check all the text in the document, choose the Find/Change command, and select the Document check box in the Find/Change dialog box. QuarkXPress can reliably search all of a document's text only if no text boxes are selected. If you currently are displaying a document's master pages, this check box will be labelled "Masters," and you can use it to search all the document's master pages.

Specifying Text

To simply change all occurrences of text, regardless of attributes, you can use the Find/Change dialog box as it first appears when you select the Find/Change command from the Edit menu (see Figure 3-1). Enter the text you want QuarkXPress to find in the Find What field, then enter the new text you want in the Change To field. You can type up to eighty characters in each field.

Figure 3-1
The Find/Change dialog box

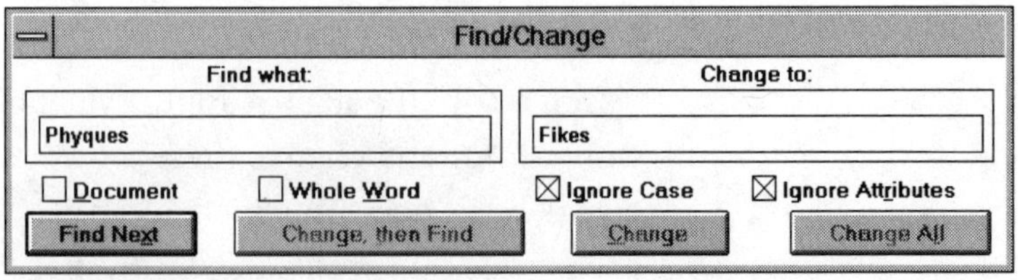

Special characters. You can enter certain special characters in the Find What and Change To fields by typing a special code starting with a backslash. For example, if you want to search for all of the new-paragraph characters in a document (what you get when you press Return at the end of a paragraph), you select the Find What field and type \p.

Table 3-4 shows characters you can enter in these fields and how to type them.

Table 3-4
Special characters in the Find/Change dialog box

To enter this character in a field...	Type this...
Tab	\t
New paragraph	\p
New line	\n
New column	\c
New box	\b
Previous box page number	\2
Current box page number	\3
Next box page number	\4
Wild card (single character)	\?
Backslash	\\

You can use the wild card character to represent any character. This is useful if you're looking for a word you may have spelled different ways, such as "EPS" and "EPSF." Instead of running two search operations to find all occurrences of this word, you could simply type "EPS\?" in the Find What field. Note that the wild card character can only be used in the Find What field.

To use the backslash character itself in the Find What or Change To text box, type the backslash twice.

Whole Word. Next to the Document check box you'll find another one labelled "Whole Word." Checking this box means that QuarkXPress only finds occurrences of the text in the Find What field if it's not bounded by other text or numerals. So a Whole Word search for "ten" would find the word "ten" when it's bounded by spaces, punctuation, or special characters such as new line or paragraph marks. It would not find "often," "tenuous," or "contentious." If you don't have "Whole Word" selected, QuarkXPress will find every occurrence of the text you entered, even if it's embedded in other text.

Ignore Case. If the Ignore Case box is checked, QuarkXPress finds all occurrences of the text in the Find What field, regardless of whether the capitalization of the text found in the document exactly matches what you typed into the Find What field. For example, if you entered "Help," QuarkXPress would find "Help," "HELP," and "help."

When "Ignore Case" is checked, QuarkXPress determines the capitalization it uses when it changes text based on how the text it finds in the document is capitalized. If the found text begins with an initial capital, QuarkXPress similarly capitalizes the first letter of the text in the Change To field when it's used at that location.

Similarly, if the found text is in all capitals, or all lowercase, QuarkXPress applies the same capitalization to the replacement text. If the found text doesn't match any of the above three cases, QuarkXPress capitalizes the replacement text exactly as you entered it into the Change To field.

For example, let's say you are searching for all examples of "QuarkXPress" and want to make sure the internal capitals are proper. If you leave Ignore Case on, and the program finds "quarkxpress," it does not capitalize the proper characters. Turn Ignore Case off, and QuarkXPress replaces it with "QuarkXPress," properly capitalized as you entered it.

Specifying Attributes

The Ignore Attributes box in the Find/Change dialog box lets you specify whether you want QuarkXPress only to look for and replace text, regardless of formatting attributes (font, size, style) or whether you want it to include attribute information in the criteria it uses for searching and changing. When the box is checked, QuarkXPress looks for all occurrences of the Find What text no matter how it's formatted and replaces it with the Change To text, without making any changes to the character formatting at that location in the document.

When you deselect the Ignore Attributes box, the Find/Change dialog box expands (see Figure 3-2). In addition to text fields under the Find What and Change To headings, there are areas for specifying font, size, and style under each heading.

What to Find, What to Change

Notice that there's a check box next to the name of each area under the Find What and Change To headings. By checking and unchecking these boxes, and by modifying what's inside each area, you tell QuarkXPress just what attributes you're looking

Figure 3-2

The Find/Change attributes dialog box

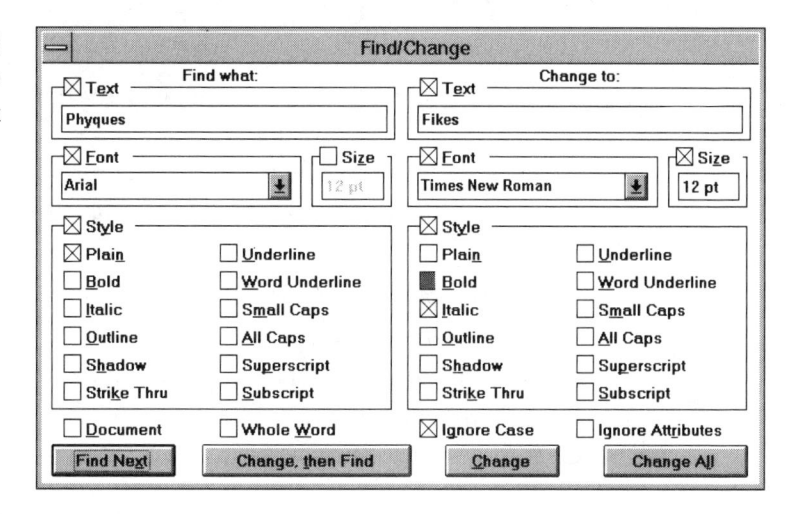

for and what you want them changed to. There is no need for parallels between what you specify in the Find What side and the Change To side. In fact, such "asymmetrical" searches offer some of the most intriguing possibilities for finding and changing.

For example, you can easily add the bold style to every instance of the word "bold." If you're editing a revision of a document, you can indicate possible deletions by applying the strike-through style. Then, if the deletions are approved, use the Find/Change command to remove them quickly (search for strike-through and replace with no text). You could also find all occurrences of a company name and apply a special typeface or style to it.

The Text, Font, and Size areas are simple to use. If you want to specify something, make sure the area's box is checked. Then, you simply enter the text or point size in the appropriate fields and use the pop-up font menu to select the font to be found or changed. In the Find What side, the Font menu lists only the fonts actually used in the current document; on the Change To side, it lists all fonts currently available.

If the document uses fonts that are currently not open in your system, QuarkXPress will list them in the Find What side (enclosed in curly brackets), along with a number assigned by QuarkXPress. You can then use the Find/Change command to change the unavailable fonts to ones that are currently available (though you can expect the whole document to reflow, since the character widths vary so much between fonts).

Finding and Changing Character Styles

Specifying the many character styles available in QuarkXPress is a bit more complicated when you're using the Find/Change dialog box. The check boxes next to most of the Style choices can be checked, unchecked, or grayed. Click an unchecked box once to make it gray, twice to check it, and a third time to uncheck it again (see Figure 3-3).

A checked box on the Find What side means that you want

Figure 3-3
Check boxes in the Find/Change dialog box

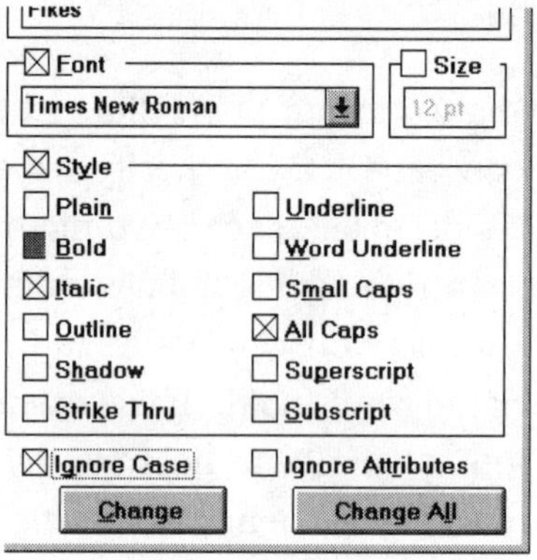

QuarkXPress to find text containing that style. An unchecked box means you don't want it to find text with that style. A gray box means that it doesn't matter if the text contains that style; you want QuarkXPress to find text either way.

Similarly, checking a Style box on the Change To side means you want QuarkXPress to apply that style when it changes the text it finds. An unchecked box means you don't want that style to be present in the changed text, and if it's there, QuarkXPress removes it. A gray box means that QuarkXPress doesn't do anything to that style. If it's already there, it stays there; if it's not, QuarkXPress doesn't add it.

If you check the Plain style box, all of the other style boxes will be unchecked. The styles listed under Plain (Bold, Italic, Outline, Shadow, and Strike Through) may be checked, unchecked, or grayed in any combination, but the styles on the right side of the Style lists operate as pairs. A word can't have both the Underline and Word Underline styles simultaneously. So checking on one unchecks the other and graying one automatically makes the other gray as well. Small Caps/All Caps and Superscript/Subscript have the same relationship.

Going to It

Now that you know how to specify what you want to find, what you want to change, and how to tell QuarkXPress where to search, you can use the four buttons at the bottom of the dialog box to begin finding and changing. When you first specify your Find/Change criteria, all buttons except "Find Next" are grayed out (see Figure 3-4). Click "Find Next," and QuarkXPress searches for the next occurrence of text matching your specifications in the current story or document. If you've selected the Document search option and you've not selected any text boxes, then the "Find Next" button actually finds the first occurrence of your Find What entry.

Figure 3-4
The Find/Change control buttons

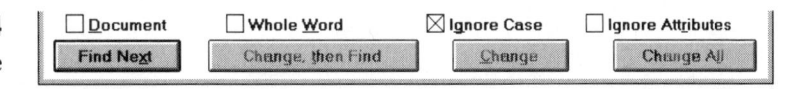

If your text insertion point happens to be somewhere in the middle of a story, but you want to search the story from the beginning, hold down the Control key. The Find Next button changes into a Find First button, which automatically searches the story from its beginning. However, if you choose to search, QuarkXPress flips to the page and text box displaying the found text and selects the text.

You then have a choice. Clicking "Find Next" again takes you to the next occurrence of text meeting your specifications, without changing the currently selected text. Clicking "Change, then Find" changes the selection as specified in the Change To side of the dialog box. QuarkXPress then looks for the next occurrence of matching text. The Change button changes the selected text and leaves it selected, and the Change All button causes Quark-XPress to search for and automatically change all occurrences in the story or document.

▼▼▼▼▼▼▼▼▼▼▼▼▼▼▼▼▼▼▼▼▼▼▼▼▼▼▼

Tip: Seeing Text as It Is Found. If you are one of the unlucky sods who has a small screen attached to your machine (or work on a laptop computer), you'll find that the Find/Change dialog box fills almost the entire screen when you are searching for or replacing attributes. Thus, when you click "Find Next," you can't see what the program found. However, you can reduce the size of the dialog box considerably by pressing F3, or if you have lots of time to kill, clicking the control box at the upper-left corner of the Find/Change dialog box and selecting Condense (see Figure 3-5). The reduced view shows only the buttons you need to navigate and change what you've specified. Pressing F3 again takes you back to the larger dialog box.

Figure 3-5
Shrinking the Find/Change dialog box

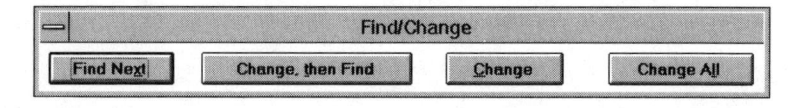

▼▼▼▼▼▼▼▼▼▼▼▼▼▼▼▼▼▼▼▼▼▼▼▼▼▼▼▼▼

Spell-Checking

Of course, once your text is written or imported into QuarkXPress, you don't want to print it without first running it through QuarkXPress's spell-checker. QuarkXPress comes with an 80,000-word dictionary, and you can create your own auxiliary dictionaries as well (see "Auxiliary Dictionaries," later in this chapter). The Check Spelling command is on the Utilities menu and allows you to check a selected word, a story, or an entire document (see Figure 3-6).

Checking a Word

To check a word, select it and choose "Word" from the Check Spelling hierarchical menu (or type Control-W). The Check Word dialog box appears (see Figure 3-7), listing all words in the

Figure 3-6
The Check Spelling hierarchical menu

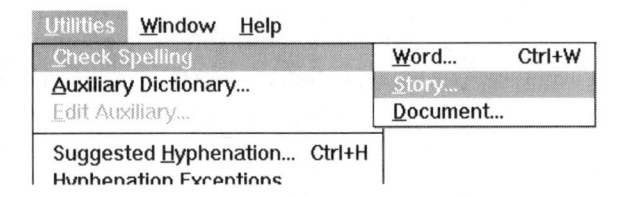

Figure 3-7
Checking a word

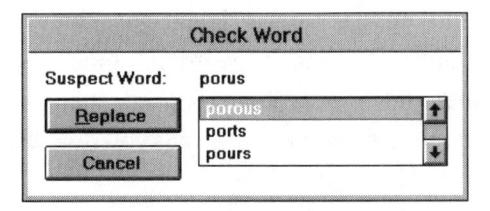

QuarkXPress dictionary (and the open auxiliary dictionary, if any) that resemble the word you selected. QuarkXPress calls this the *suspect word*. If the suspect word appears in a dictionary, it will appear in the scrolling list and be selected automatically. This means that, as far as QuarkXPress is concerned, the word is spelled correctly, and you can click the Cancel button and continue.

If the suspect word doesn't appear in an active dictionary, you can scroll through the list of words and select a replacement. Click on the word in the list, then click the Replace button. The new spelling replaces the word in your story, and the Check Word box closes.

If QuarkXPress can't find any words that approximate the suspect word, it displays the message, "No similar words found." Click the Cancel button to close the Check Word dialog box.

Checking a Story

To check a story, select the story's text box (any box in a linked chain will do) and make sure the Content tool is active. Select "Story" from the Check Spelling hierarchical menu (or type Control-Alt-W). The Word Count dialog box appears, showing running totals as QuarkXPress scans the story, counting the total number of words, the total number of unique words (each word counted once, no matter how many times it occurs), and the number of suspect words—ones that QuarkXPress can't find in its dictionary or in an open auxiliary dictionary.

When QuarkXPress is finished counting, click the OK button. This returns you to your document if no suspect words have been found. If they have been, the button brings up the Check Story dialog box (see Figure 3-8). This dialog box displays suspect words one at a time, in the order they occur in the story. As each word appears in the dialog box, QuarkXPress scrolls the document window to the word and highlights it, so you can see it in the context in which it is used. If a suspect word is used more than once, QuarkXPress tells you how many times.

Figure 3-8
The Check Story dialog box

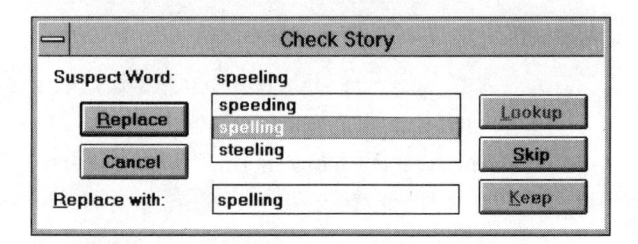

Changing the Spelling. If you know the correct spelling for a suspect word, you can enter it in the Replace With field, then click the Replace button to have the new spelling replace the one in your document. If you want QuarkXPress to look for possible spellings in its dictionary or in an open auxiliary dictionary, click the Lookup button (or press Alt-L). QuarkXPress displays a list of possible alternatives in the scrolling text field. You can select a spelling by clicking on it, then clicking the Replace button. The new spelling replaces the suspect word in your document, and QuarkXPress moves on to the next suspect word in the story. If there are no more suspect words, the Check Story dialog box closes.

Note that if QuarkXPress finds more than one occurrence of a suspect word, it will replace every occurrence of the word with the new spelling you choose.

Skipping and keeping. To go to the next suspect word without changing the spelling of the current one, click the Skip button (Alt-S). To add the current suspect word to an auxiliary dictionary, click the Keep button (Alt-K). This button is only active when an auxiliary dictionary is open (see "Auxiliary Dictionaries," later in this chapter).

Checking a Document/Master Page

You can check all of the text in an entire document by selecting the Document command from the Check Spelling hierarchical menu. QuarkXPress counts and checks all of the words in your current document, from the first page to the last page. It displays the Word Count dialog box, then lets you change suspect words through a Check Document dialog box, which is identical in layout and function to the Check Story dialog box.

Similarly, when master pages are displayed, the Document command on the menu becomes "Masters." By selecting this command, you can check all of the text on every master page in your document, using a Check Masters dialog box that works the same as the Check Story and Check Document dialog boxes.

▼ ▼

Tip: Getting a Word Count. You can get an accurate word count in a story or document by performing a spell-check. Actually, you don't even need to spell-check the entire document or story; just start the spell check going and QuarkXPress provides you with a dialog box that tells you how many words there are, as well as how many unique and suspect words. The first number is the one that we find helpful.

▼ ▼

Auxiliary Dictionaries

You can't add words to or edit QuarkXPress's standard dictionary. You can, however, create and use auxiliary dictionaries so that QuarkXPress's spell-checker takes into account specialized words that aren't in the standard dictionary. Note that you can have only one auxiliary dictionary open at one time for each document.

Creating or opening an auxiliary dictionary. To open an existing auxiliary dictionary or to create a new one, select the Auxiliary Dictionary command from the Utilities menu. This opens the

Auxiliary Dictionary dialog box, which is a standard file-opening dialog box. You can locate a dictionary by looking through the subdirectories on your mounted drives. Select it and then click the Open button.

You can also create a new auxiliary dictionary by clicking the New button, which brings up a file-saving dialog box that lets you specify the name and location of the new dictionary. Enter the name of the new dictionary in the text field and click on the Create button.

Remembering dictionaries. If you open or create an auxiliary dictionary with a document open, QuarkXPress automatically associates the document with the dictionary. Whenever you open the document, QuarkXPress also opens the dictionary, until you either close the dictionary or open a different one. You can also open a dictionary with no documents open at all; this dictionary will be applied to all documents you create subsequently. However, QuarkXPress may not be able to find an auxiliary dictionary if you move either the dictionary or a document associated with it, in which case, you'll receive an error message when you try to spell-check your document (just relink with the dictionary by opening it again, or close it by selecting Aux Dictionary and then clicking Close).

Adding and removing words. When you create an auxiliary dictionary, it contains no words. You can add words to the dictionary by using the Keep button when you're spell checking. This button adds the current suspect word to your auxiliary dictionary. Another way to add words is to use the Edit Auxiliary item on the Utilities menu. This feature is available only when there's an open auxiliary dictionary.

When you select "Edit Auxiliary," a simple dialog box appears with a scrolling list of all the words in the currently open dictionary (see Figure 3-9). To add a new word, enter it in the text field and click the Add button or press Enter (Return). Words added to the dictionary cannot contain any spaces or punctuation (not even hyphens). To remove a word from the dictionary, scroll

Figure 3-9
The Edit Auxiliary Dictionary dialog box

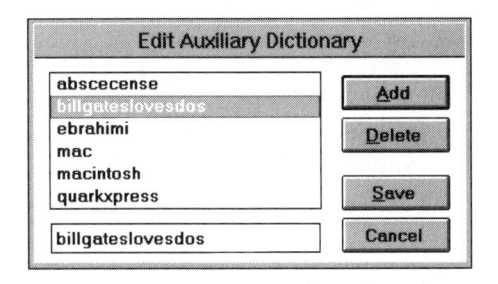

through the list until you find the word. Select it by clicking on it, then click the Delete button.

▼▼▼▼▼▼▼▼▼▼▼▼▼▼▼▼▼▼▼▼▼▼▼▼▼▼▼

Tip: Editing Dictionaries the Fast Way. For major auxiliary dictionary editing, you can avoid the Edit Auxiliary Dictionary dialog box and edit the dictionary as a text file right in QuarkXPress. You might, for example, want to quickly enter a batch of words from a technical dictionary. To do this, open a new QuarkXPress document and use the Get Text command under the file menu to load the QuarkXPress auxiliary dictionary file you'd like to edit. The dictionary will appear as a simple list of words, with each word on a line by itself. Simply enter a new word and press the Enter key. When you're finished, select "Save Text" from the File menu and enter the dictionary's correct name in the Save Text dialog box. Also, from the Save File as Type drop-down list box, make sure "ASCII Text" is the current choice. QuarkXPress saves the auxiliary dictionary file in the proper text format.

▼▼▼▼▼▼▼▼▼▼▼▼▼▼▼▼▼▼▼▼▼▼▼▼▼▼▼

Tip: Editing Dictionaries in a Word Processor. Even though the auxiliary dictionaries are simple text files, editing them with DOS and Windows word processors is problematic at best. This is because the line breaks are not really PC (that's "politically correct") due to QuarkXPress's Macintosh origins. On the PC, word processors actually use two invisible characters (carriage return and line feed) to mark paragraph ends. Mac word processors just use carriage returns, and that's how the auxiliary dictionaries are set up, even in QuarkXPress for Windows. When imported into most word processors as plain text, the missing line feed causes the entries to run together so they don't appear on separate lines. Even if you manage to import an auxiliary dictionary so that the entries appear as an editable list (one entry per line), saving the dictionary as plain text often places a carriage return *and* a line feed code at the end of each entry. QuarkXPress then complains of a "damaged" auxiliary dictionary file the next time you spell check with the edited file, and it might even attempt to ruin your day by crashing.

If you want to edit auxiliary dictionaries with a word processor, you can follow this workaround.

1. Open the auxiliary dictionary in the word processor so that each word comes out on a separate line. Some word processors may not be able to do this. You can achieve this in Microsoft Word for Windows by opening the file as "DOS Text with Layout."

2. Make your changes, additions, deletions, and so on.

3. Save the file as text only.

4. Import the file into a QuarkXPress text box and delete any blank lines at the end of the document. There's usually at least one for some reason (maybe we're dense, but we can't figure it out).

5. Save all of the text as a text file with the file name extension ".qdt".

The file is now ready to be an auxiliary dictionary. Personally, we prefer previous the tip; it's cleaner making the changes in QuarkXPress.

▼ ▼

Tip: Adding Your Microsoft Word Dictionary. The user dictionaries that Microsoft Word for Windows creates are text files as well, and like QuarkXPress dictionaries, they have one word per line. They have .DIC file name extensions, such as CUSTOM.DIC. Since a Word dictionary is a text file (plain ol' ordinary ASCII text), you can import it into a QuarkXPress text box, remove any extra blank lines, and then save it out again as a .QDT file that you can use as an auxiliary dictionary. You can also combine Word's and QuarkXPress' dictionaries in the same text box before you save them as a single .QDT file.

When Not to Use QuarkXPress

While QuarkXPress does have powerful word-processing features, as we've seen in the preceding sections of this chapter, there are reasons why you may not want to use it for most of the word processing in your documents. The main reason to use QuarkXPress is that you never have to worry about losing any formatting information when importing and exporting text. If your text stays in QuarkXPress, that isn't a problem.

But there are good reasons to consider editing and writing your text outside QuarkXPress. First of all, word-processing programs tend to be much less expensive than QuarkXPress. If you're in a big office or workgroup, it may make more financial sense to do basic text entry on word processors, rather than a powerhouse page-layout program like QuarkXPress.

Another reason is that—powerful as QuarkXPress may be—it doesn't offer features available in the most powerful word processors, such as outlining or automatic numbering of paragraphs. If you're working on a long, complicated document with sections that might require constant rearranging and reorganizing, you probably need the organizational power of a good outlining feature like the one in Microsoft Word. Since Word's style sheets work well with QuarkXPress's, Word is usually considered the best word processor to use with QuarkXPress (see Chapter 5, *Copy Flow*).

Slow Going

Perhaps the most important reason to consider doing your word processing in a program other than QuarkXPress is speed—or rather the lack of it. Sometimes writing and editing text in QuarkXPress can seem to slow to a crawl. Entering text becomes so sluggish that the program can't keep up with even a moderate typist, and worse still, some typed characters seem to fall into a black hole while they're waiting to appear on the screen. So your normally excellent typing can suddenly appear riddled with typos.

Why does this happen? First, QuarkXPress often has to jump all over the document as you type, unlike a word processor, which simply scrolls top to bottom. Secondly, QuarkXPress has to do much more work than a typical word processor whenever it must reflow text. If you have specified complicated hyphenation and justification settings, if you've set the automatic kerning threshold so that it's active for most of the text in a story, or if you've applied a lot of kerning or tracking effects, QuarkXPress has to perform extra calculations in order to determine where line breaks should fall whenever it reflows text. If you're working on a long story that goes through several pages of linked boxes with many runarounds caused by other page elements, this complexity also adds to the computations that QuarkXPress must perform whenever you change or add text. So you can often get the feeling that you're physically pushing a heavy load of text along a tortuous path as you type. Here are a few suggestions for working around the problem of sluggish text entry in QuarkXPress.

▼ ▼

Tip: Use a Text-Editing Windows Accessory. Veteran QuarkXPress users have discovered that, while characters may be lost when typing into a QuarkXPress story, type pasted in from the Windows Clipboard never gets lost or damaged. One way to get text into the Clipboard quickly is to type it in a simple text-editing accessory such as Windows Notebook (included with Windows) or a word processor (if memory allows), such as Windows Write, and then copy and paste it into QuarkXPress. There are several notepad programs on the market, but you should be able to make do with the Windows Notepad accessory (see Figure 3-10) and certainly Windows Write, both of which are normally installed in the Accessories group in Program Manager.

The disadvantage of working this way is that the text you paste from the Clipboard is pure, unformatted text. You must apply any formatting attributes after you've pasted it into QuarkXPress.

▼ ▼

Figure 3-10
The Windows Notepad
text-editing accessory

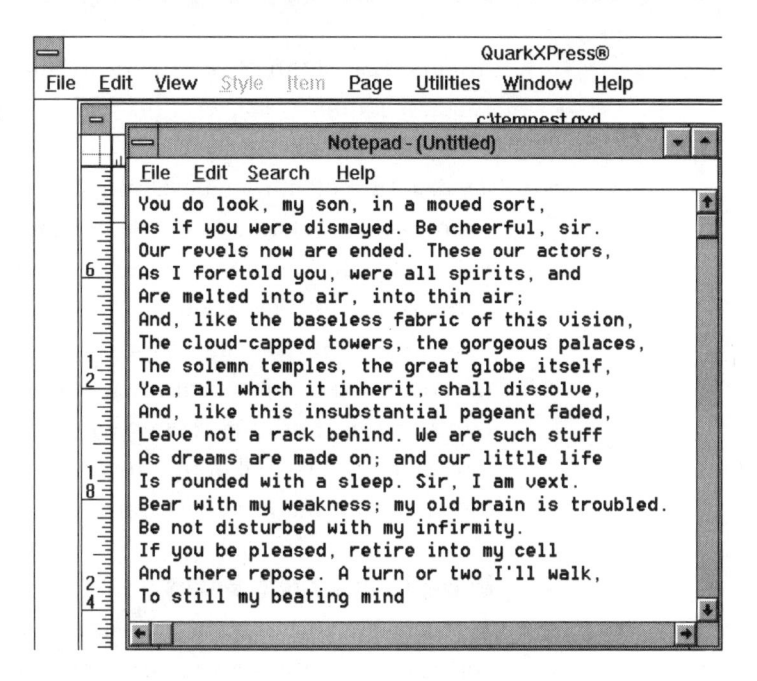

Modifying Preferences and Settings

You can quickly modify some of the things that affect the speed with which you can enter or edit text in QuarkXPress.

Hyphenation. Turn off hyphenation as much as possible in your document. If QuarkXPress doesn't have to determine if and where it should hyphenate a word whenever it breaks a line, it will be able to incorporate new or changed text into a story more quickly. Simply edit all of the H&J settings used in your document, turning off hyphenation (see Chapter 4, *Type and Typography*). Turn hyphenation back on when you're ready to proof or print your document.

If you're using style sheets, you can streamline this process a bit. Instead of editing your H&J settings each time you want to turn hyphenation on or off, you can create a special hyphenation setting with hyphenation off, called NoHyphens, for example. If you've based most of the styles in your document on the Normal style, all you have to do is edit the Normal style and select the NoHyphens setting to turn off hyphenation in all styles based on Normal. To turn hyphenation back on, just reselect Normal's original H&J setting (we discuss style sheets in more detail in Chapter 5, *Copy Flow*).

Kerning. Turn off automatic kerning in your document. Go to the Typographic Preferences dialog box for your document (available from the Edit menu) to make sure the Auto Kern Above check box is not checked.

Note that the two suggestions above affect where line breaks fall and how text will appear when printed. You should make certain to return both the H&J and kerning settings to those you intend to use for final output before you check your document for widows, orphans, or loose lines.

Using Dummy Text Boxes

The problem with using a text-editing utility to type text is that you can't include any character formatting attributes. And if you modify the settings of your QuarkXPress document to speed things up, you may forget to change them back and end up printing a document with incorrect hyphenation and kerning. Moreover, if you have complicated layouts, entering text into QuarkXPress will still be sluggish, even if you have turned off hyphenation and kerning, as QuarkXPress must still reflow the entire story as you enter or change text.

Another solution to the text-entry problem is to create a text box in the pasteboard area of the page where you want to enter or change text. If you simply need to add text to the page, type the text into the box on the pasteboard area, copy or cut it, and then paste it into the correct location in the story's text box on the page.

If you need to edit text that's already there, as well as add text, select the text to be modified from the page and then copy and paste it into the box on the pasteboard. Make all of the necessary edits there, then copy or cut the revised text and paste it back to the same location on the page. Since QuarkXPress remembers the last selection you made in any text box, all you need to do is select the story's box on the page. It won't be necessary to reselect the text that you originally copied out. QuarkXPress does that for you automatically.

▼ ▼

Tip: Use a Dummy Document. If you must make many changes to a story, you may find it cumbersome to create boxes on each page's pasteboard area as described above. Another solution is to make a new document with a simple page layout, copy the entire story to be edited over to the dummy document, make all of your changes there, then copy the story back to your original document.

1. Open the document containing the story that needs editing.

2. Create a new, blank document using the New command from the File menu.

3. Using the Content tool, select a text box in the original document that contains part of the story to be edited.

4. Type Control-A (or click five times) to select all of the story in the text chain and type Control-C to copy it.

5. Make the window for the new, blank document active. Select the default text box on the first page and press Control-V to paste the entire story into it.

6. Make all of your edits in the new document. Since there is only the simplest of layouts—a single rectangular box on each page—delays in reflowing text as you edit are minimal.

7. After you've made your corrections, press Control-A to select all of the text in the new document and press Control-C to copy it.

8. Activate the window for the original document. Click in a text box belonging to the edited story. QuarkXPress should automatically highlight the entire story, just as it was the last time you selected the text box. If it doesn't, be sure to type Control-A to select the entire story again.

9. Press Control-V to paste the edited story back into its proper location in the original document. Because you had the original story selected in the last step, the Paste command replaces the entire story with the modified story.

There's one caveat to observe with this technique. Copying and pasting text brings over all of the styles contained in the text to the new document, except for any that are already there. If you're starting a new, blank document, this means that the Normal style will already be present (along with any other default styles you may have defined) and may not match the Normal style in your original document. If you apply the Normal style to any text in the new, dummy document, it may not have the formatting attributes you want, and it will retain these attributes even after you paste the story back into the original document, where you'll have to remove and then re-apply the Normal style to make sure that paragraph has the correct formatting applied.

There are two ways to avoid this headache. The simplest is to remember not to mess around with styles when you're editing text in a dummy document. If you must work with styles when you're editing a story in a dummy document, save your original document with another name (perhaps even as a template). Then delete all of the document pages, create a simple, new blank page, and use this new document as the dummy document into which you paste and edit text from your original. Bear in mind that you may have to repeat this process every time you make significant changes to the styles in your original document.

Watching Your Words

By following the tips in this chapter, you may not be able to have QuarkXPress write your documents for you, but you'll be able to get the very most out of the program's advanced word-processing features.

Next we'll see how you can take those blocks of plain text that you've created and turn them into type using QuarkXPress's extensive typographic controls.

CHAPTER 4

TYPE AND TYPOGRAPHY

In the 90s, thanks to the ubiquity of graphical computing, type is *in*. Fancy fonts will soon appear in the Sharper Image catalog, and people of taste will chatter about the latest faces over cocktails or high tea. In the typical emotional blackmail of TV ads, a guy like Dave will always be saying to a guy like Bob, "Face up to it, Bob! Your layout's a flop 'cause your *font* is flat."

Plus, you won't want to be caught dead using any page-layout program other than QuarkXPress, not if you're truly font-cool. That's because no other desktop-publishing application handles typesetting as powerfully as QuarkXPress. In this chapter we discuss the many typographic controls that QuarkXPress puts at your fingertips. We're going to start with the basics: fonts and typographic principles. However, professionals should at least skim over this section. (The fundamentals of fonts are rarely taught, and many people find themselves in deep…uh…water at some point because of it.)

Next, we discuss control of both character- and paragraph-level formatting, including—among many other items—kerning and tracking, hyphenation and justification, and typographic special effects.

If you're reading this book from cover to cover, expect to spend a while on this chapter. We have much to discuss, and we think you'll find it rewarding.

Fonts

People have been throwing the word "font" around loosely for so long that it now has several meanings. Historically, it refers to a set of characters in a given typeface and size. Typefaces are the general appearance of the character set. For example, Helvetica is a typeface, while 14-point Helvetica is a font.

However, for the sake of simplicity, we're following the path that has become popularized over the past few years, defining both typeface and font as synonyms: a font or a typeface is a set of characters that shares a particular look. For example, the text you're reading is one particular font or typeface, while the headings for each section are in a different font or typeface. Some technically inclined people use the word *font* for the actual computer file used to generate type on screen or paper.

Typefaces can be found cast in metal, carved from wood, or imaged on photographic negatives. In the case of computer typesetting, typefaces are represented digitally. That is, you can't see the typeface until you tell the computer to process the digital information and image a character to either the screen or onto paper or film. As it turns out, earlier versions of Windows were built in such a way that they imaged fonts to the screen in a different way than they printed them. That's less of problem these days thanks to built-in Windows TrueType screen font generation, and screen font generation provided by Adobe Type Manager (ATM). Basically, what you see on the screen will be almost exactly what you get on paper.

Adobe Type Manager and TrueType

Since we're still at the beginning of the chapter, we're going to act as if you aren't using Windows TrueType or Adobe Type Manager (ATM) on your computer. However, consider it homework to start using TrueType or ATM before you get to the end of this chapter. Why should you use them? Primarily because they make the fonts you see on the screen bear a much greater resemblance to those you get from your printer—at any size. Figure 4-1 shows the difference between type on a Windows screen with and without ATM or TrueType.

Figure 4-1
Screen type with and without TrueType or ATM

Wiz ATM

Wizzout ATM

Screen Fonts

Let's start simple: At the most basic level, Windows images fonts on the screen using screen fonts. These fonts are collections of bitmapped images—one bitmapped image for each character at each size (if you don't know the differences between bitmapped and outline graphics, take a quick peek at that section at the beginning of Chapter 6, *Pictures*).

When you press a key on the keyboard, the computer goes to the font file, extracts that character at the size nearest to the one you want, then scales the image to create the specified size. For example, if you specify that you want to type in 17-point Goudy, the computer gets the nearest screen font it has, let's say 12-point Goudy, and then scales it up. One look at Figure 4-2 and you can see this is an ugly way to do things. But, until a couple of years ago, it was the only way to do things.

Printer Fonts

If screen fonts image on the screen, then printer fonts must image on printers. That's just the way of the world. Whereas the screen font is bitmapped, the TrueType or PostScript printer font is made up of outlined characters that can be scaled, rotated, and skewed in all sorts of ways without the ugly extrapolation encountered on the screen.

Fortunately, Windows TrueType and ATM use printer fonts to create on-screen type, eliminating screen/printer font schizophrenia, since the same font-scaling technique is applied to

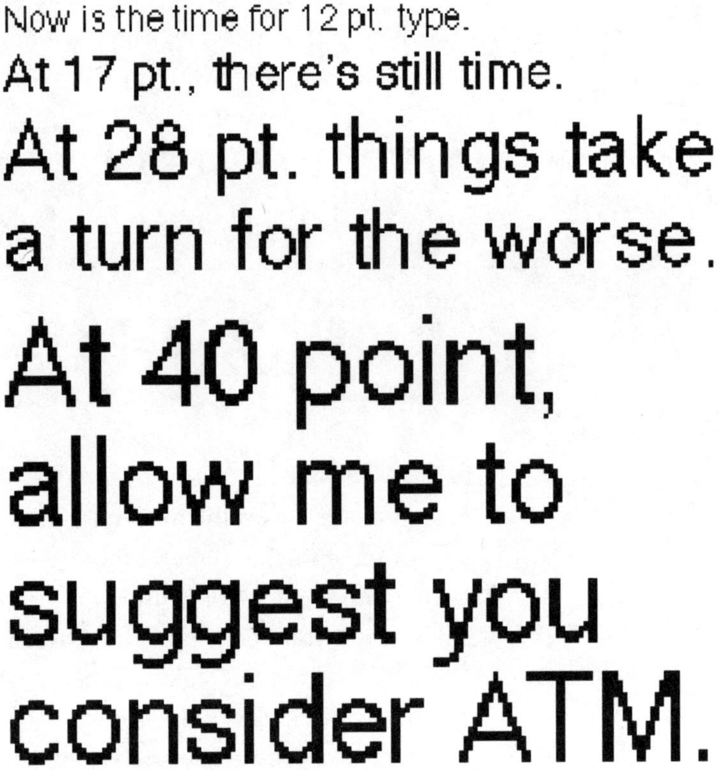

Figure 4-2
Extrapolating various sizes from bitmapped information

Now is the time for 12 pt. type.

At 17 pt., there's still time.

At 28 pt. things take a turn for the worse.

At 40 point, allow me to suggest you consider ATM.

screen and printer fonts. We'll talk more about this process, called *rendering*, in "Type Rendering," below.

You should note that there are presently two types of outline fonts to use with QuarkXPress for Windows: TrueType and PostScript Type 1. Hair-splitting debates still rage over which format is "better," and we leave that question to the font technologists. For us, the Type 1 format has the widest font selection and works best with high-resolution imagesetters. The following section tells more of the TrueType story.

Type 1 vs. TrueType

In 1990, when Microsoft decided to build font scaling into Windows, they steered clear of Adobe Systems' ATM and formed a joint licensing agreement with Apple Computer. The deal: Microsoft got Apple's TrueType scalable font technology, and Apple got Microsoft's newly acquired PostScript clone software, called TrueImage. Together, Apple and Microsoft pledged to forge an "open" scalable font technology, making an end run around Adobe, who'd kept tight control over their Type 1 PostScript font technology. Font and printer vendors who felt squeezed out of the action by Adobe's tight policies rallied to the TrueType/TrueImage cause. Apple added TrueType font scaling to their Macintosh System 7, and months later, Microsoft did the same with Windows 3.1.

Several other things happened, though. Under pressure, Adobe published the secrets of their Type 1 font format and became even better at producing fonts, graphics software, and printer controllers. On the other hand, after floundering around with TrueImage for over a year, Microsoft kicked it out the door and left further development to third parties. Of the early TrueImage devotees, it seems that LaserMaster made the best go of it by substantially improving TrueImage and renaming their version TruePage. Apple, meanwhile, dropped immediate plans for TrueImage, made up with Adobe, and now continues to license Adobe PostScript for their line of PostScript-based LaserWriters and plans to integrate ATM into Macintosh System 7.

As we suggested above, while typographers quibble over which format—TrueType or Type 1—has the most potential for type design, you face a simpler decision. Do you plan to use a PostScript-based imagesetter to produce the final version of your document? If so, avoid TrueType. As a general rule, at least for now, PostScript imagesetters can't handle TrueType fonts very well. Most service bureaus feel that they've barely gotten things smoothed out for Type 1 fonts and Windows. The looks on their faces when you march in with a TrueType job would unsettle most souls, so don't even think of it, stick with Type 1. And if you really want to use a TrueType font, you can convert it to Type 1 first, using a program such as FontMonger.

Fonts and Windows

NEW IN 3.3

See page 579

The problem is that PostScript wasn't originally part of Microsoft's plan for world conquest. In fact, they still probably wish it and Adobe would go away. This becomes obvious (aside from historical evidence) when you peel through the sublayers of Windows itself. You'll notice that Windows has built-in utilities for installing and removing TrueType or Hewlett-Packard LaserJet fonts, but there's *nothing* built-in to help you manage PostScript fonts. On top of that, QuarkXPress also handles PostScript fonts differently than most other Windows applications. Let's take a look at how you can work with fonts in Windows; first TrueType, then PostScript.

Managing TrueType

TrueType is Microsoft's favored child, so in contrast to handling PostScript fonts, installing and uninstalling TrueType fonts is a breeze. The Fonts dialog box of the Windows Control Panel provides an easy way to add or remove TrueType fonts. Click the Add button, select one or several fonts, and then click OK. The fonts are then available both for your screen and for your printer, without restarting Windows. You will, however, need to quit and restart QuarkXPress before font deletions or additions appear in any menus. Still, this is much simpler than managing PostScript fonts (see below). The TrueType font metrics are all contained within the outline fonts themselves.

As we said, we think that you shouldn't really be using TrueType fonts if you're doing professional graphic design and are working with an imagesetter. If you decide that you're in this group and would prefer *not* to use TrueType, you can perform this simple trick.

1. Open the Fonts utility in the Control Panel.

2. Click the TrueType button.

3. Deselect the Enable TrueType option.

4. Restart Windows.

This turns TrueType off throughout the system and prevents you from selecting most of the TrueType fonts while in QuarkXPress (they just don't show up in the menus). This is important because otherwise QuarkXPress won't tell you if a font is TrueType or Type 1.

On the other hand, if you want to take your chances with TrueType, you can simply leave the function enabled.

Managing PostScript Fonts

The first thing you need to know about PostScript fonts is that you need to use ATM to work with them in QuarkXPress. The next thing you need to know is how to install them. To use PostScript fonts with Windows you must install them twice, once for Windows (for printing), and once for ATM (for screen display). ATM can combine these actions into a single step (see "Tip: Install ATM last," below). You can install fonts with Windows using the font installation utility that came with your fonts or a third-party utility. These utilities copy the PostScript font metrics and outline font files to your hard disk, and then add some font reference information to the Windows WIN.INI system configuration file. Windows uses the WIN.INI file font references to locate the font metrics and outline font files so that applications can actually use the fonts and automatically download them to the printer, if necessary.

For ATM, you install fonts via the ATM Control Panel, which was automatically installed in the Windows "Main" program group when you installed ATM. Although Windows doesn't have a PostScript font manager that displays installed and uninstalled fonts in handy lists so you can add or remove the ones you want, ATM can perform this task to some degree (see Figure 4-3; also, see "Tip: Use FontMinder," below). Fortunately, Windows and ATM will share the same font files; they just use them in different ways.

Okay, given that you can install PostScript fonts for Windows (WIN.INI font references), for ATM, or for both, here are a few of the implications concerning QuarkXPress:

- If you want to use a PostScript font with QuarkXPress you must install it for ATM, which means you must install ATM. If you only install the font for Windows (using the font

Figure 4-3
The ATM Add Fonts dialog box

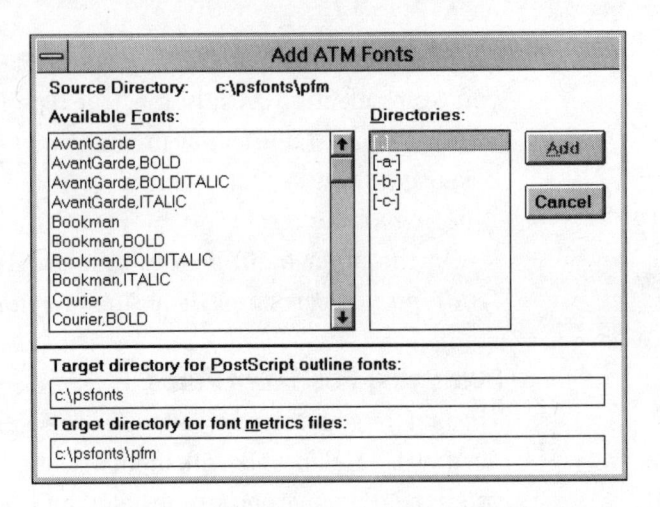

[Add ATM Fonts dialog box showing Source Directory c:\psfonts\pfm, Available Fonts list including AvantGarde, AvantGarde,BOLD, AvantGarde,BOLDITALIC, AvantGarde,ITALIC, Bookman, Bookman,BOLD, Bookman,BOLDITALIC, Bookman,ITALIC, Courier, Courier,BOLD; Directories list with [-a-], [-b-], [-c-]; Add and Cancel buttons; Target directory for PostScript outline fonts: c:\psfonts; Target directory for font metrics files: c:\psfonts\pfm]

vendor's installation utility) and not for ATM, the font won't appear in any of QuarkXPress's font menus. QuarkXPress is a bit weird in this respect because most other Windows programs, like Word for Windows, can access the PostScript fonts if they're installed for Windows but not ATM; you just won't get smooth type on screen.

- If you install a PostScript font for ATM but don't install it for Windows, QuarkXPress will at least recognize the font and let you use it on screen, but the font won't print. That's no big deal if you don't use a PostScript printer to proof your pages (but you should be doing this anyway if you're going to a PostScript imagesetter later).

Fortunately, ATM 2.0 makes PostScript font installation for Windows a bit simpler, since any font that you install for ATM will also automatically install itself for Windows in one step instead of two. However, this feature gets a bit unreliable when you're up around 200 fonts.

▼ ▼

Tip: Install ATM last. If you're installing ATM and PostScript fonts for the first time, install your fonts for Windows first (using the font vendor's font installer) then install ATM. That way, the ATM installer will grab the PostScript font information from Windows and automatically install it for ATM. Bob is so lazy, in fact, that if he has added a few more fonts to Windows, he simply re-installs

ATM to automatically install them, instead of manually adding the new fonts to ATM.

▼ ▼

WIN.INI Revealed

Sooner or later something funny will happen to your Windows font setup, especially when you're adding fonts frequently or changing printers. Fonts may seem to disappear, or they may print out as Courier. That means it's time to look into your WIN.INI file. It's like looking under the hood of your car, only slightly less greasy.

The WIN.INI file (pronounced "win inny") contains one or more sections of PostScript font references. It's located in your Windows subdirectory. Remember to always make a backup copy before you play around with it. You can use the Windows Notepad accessory to examine or edit the WIN.INI, since it easily handles text-only (plain ASCII) files, like WIN.INI. However, we often use the SYSEDIT program included with Windows; it opens the WIN.INI file automatically.

Here's what a PostScript font reference section looks like in WIN.INI (the paragraph marks are inserted to show the hard line breaks; you don't need to type the character).

```
[PostScript,LPT1]¶
softfonts=8¶
softfont1=c:\psfonts\pfm\ab_____.pfm,c:\psfonts\ab_____.pfb¶
softfont2=c:\psfonts\pfm\abflf___.pfm,c:\psfonts\abflf___.pfb¶
softfont3=c:\psfonts\pfm\ae_____.pfm,c:\psfonts\ae_____.pfb¶
softfont4=c:\psfonts\pfm\agd_____.pfm,c:\psfonts\agd_____.pfb¶
softfont5=c:\psfonts\pfm\agdo____.pfm,c:\psfonts\agdo____.pfb¶
softfont6=c:\psfonts\pfm\agw_____.pfm,c:\psfonts\agw_____.pfb¶
softfont7=c:\psfonts\pfm\agwo____.pfm¶
softfont8=c:\psfonts\pfm\alflf___.pfm¶
```

The font listings under the "softfonts=8" heading are pointers to two types of PostScript printer files: Printer Font Metrics (PFM) files and outline fonts. Soft font number one, for example, first lists the disk location of the font's font metrics file, followed (after the comma) by the actual outline printer font (ending in .PFB, in this case, though it can vary). The "softfonts=n" statement simply indicates the total number of softfonts installed. If you're having trouble, it's worth checking to see if this number matches what's in the list of softfonts. By the way, David's WIN.INI file doesn't look like this at all because he uses a LaserMaster Unity 1000. This sort of printer doesn't require the same sort of listings in the WIN.INI file.

Most Windows applications—QuarkXPress excluded—need the font's PFM file reference in WIN.INI in order to use the font. The second part of the entry—the outline font reference—is optional. If it's included, then Windows will automatically download the font when it's required. If the outline font reference isn't added, as in softfont entries 7 and 8 in the sample reference above, then Windows won't automatically download the font. We cover this even further in Chapter 10, *Printing*.

If you have additional PostScript printers installed on other printer ports, then your WIN.INI file will have a font reference section for each port. For example, if you also had a printer installed on your PC's LPT2: (parallel) port, you'd have another section labeled [PostScript,LPT2], dealing with PostScript fonts on LPT2:. A printer port in Windows doesn't really have to exist, by the way. The port FILE:, which is used to create PostScript print files, will also have a section head of its own. We cover PostScript print files in Chapter 10, *Printing*.

Since Windows manages PostScript fonts on a port-by-port basis, you'll run into a problem when you try to switch printer ports. Here's a common situation: All of your fonts were printing fine on LPT1:, but when you changed your printer default to LPT2:, your fonts stopped printing. Check your WIN.INI file, and you'll see the reason. Windows added a new section, [PostScript,LPT2], but it didn't add any font references, hence no fonts. Since, unlike other applications, QuarkXPress relies on ATM for it's font information, you'll still get your fonts, on screen at least. But for other applications, you'll essentially have no fonts to work with. You can solve the problem by copying all of the font references from the [PostScript,LPT1] section and pasting them under the [PostScript,LPT2] section. Then save WIN.INI as a text-only file and restart Windows for the changes to take effect.

▼ ▼

Tip: Update Your Port. When you change your PostScript printer connection from LPT1: to LPT2:, COM1:, or to FILE:, etc., you'll need to update font references for that port. You can edit your WIN.INI file as described above, or you can try the Lazy Bob technique and use ATM (Adobe Type Manager) to quickly update the font references for the newly selected port. After selecting the new port in the Printers Control Panel, open the ATM Control Panel, and from the Installed ATM Fonts list, select all of the fonts you want installed for the newly selected port or ports. Once the fonts are selected, simply click the Add button. Then quit ATM and restart Windows. You should now have a font selection for the new port.

This technique will create an extra ATM icon in the Main program group, so simply delete one of them. It's also a bit unreliable if you have more than 200 fonts installed.

▼ ▼

Tip: Use FontMinder. If you use lots of fonts—say, over 50—then you should seriously think about getting FontMinder from Ares Software. You may never fiddle with you WIN.INI file again.

When you have hundreds of fonts installed for Windows, you're in danger of expanding the size of your WIN.INI file beyond its 64K limit. Plus, it's a chore to scroll through a hundred fonts when a particular project may only call for a dozen fonts.

With FontMinder, you can create smaller groups of Type 1 or TrueType fonts and quickly install or uninstall the groups as you need them. It's all handled via FontMinder's handy point-and-click interface. Keep in mind that the outline font files themselves aren't affected, only the font references in the WIN.INI and ATM.INI system configuration files (where ATM keeps its font references). Prior to FontMinder, we kept multiple copies of WIN.INI containing different PostScript font references on hand. Now we all use FontMinder.

Formatting Text in QuarkXPress

Let's be clear here: We're not going to transform you into an amazing typographer in the course of one chapter. We may not even make a dent in the enormous learning curve that everyone must go through to learn about type, but we will give you the information you need to use QuarkXPress as a powerful tool when you do know what you want. We will also try to point out some important issues in desktop typography.

We're going to spend the rest of this chapter talking about QuarkXPress's basic font manipulation tools and then move into more complex issues of typography and how to make your type look great.

Tip: Use the Content Tool. The very first thing you need to know about the control of type in QuarkXPress is that you must have selected both the Content tool and the text box that contains the text you want to change. If you want to make a character-based change, you must select those characters you want to alter. If you want to make a paragraph-based change, you can select the entire paragraph (four mouse clicks) or a portion of the paragraph. You can even have the cursor located anywhere within the paragraph. Just remember: If you want to change the contents of a text box, use the Content tool.

Character Formatting

There are two types of typographic controls: character-based and paragraph-based. The character-based controls let you change the character formatting; the paragraph-based controls let you change the paragraph formatting. It's as simple as that. Let's talk about character formatting first.

The character-based controls are those that affect only the text characters that you select. If you have selected only one word in a sentence and apply a character style to it, that word and *only* that word is changed.

Character styles include typeface, size, kerning, color, and a whole slew of other things. Let's look at each character-formatting control, how you can use it, and why you'd want to.

Selecting a Typeface

Picking a typeface is a very personal thing, fraught with implication and the anxiety of decision. If someone tells you he wants a document set in the 10-point Courier typewriter face, it may be better just to stay quiet. However, once the choice has been made, there are a number of ways to select the typeface. Let's look at each of them here.

The Style menu. Almost every typographic control can be accessed through an item on the Style menu. When you have selected the text you want to change, you can select the typeface name from the Font submenu.

The Measurements palette. If the Measurements palette is closer within reach, or if you would rather avoid hierarchical submenus, you can select a typeface from the Measurements palette instead. Here you have two methods of selection.

- You can click the arrow button to bring up a menu of fonts. It is often quicker to select from this menu than from the Style menu.

- You can type the name of the typeface you want by clicking to the left of the first character of the typeface name shown in the Measurements palette (or typing Control-Alt-Shift-M), then typing a few characters of the typeface name you want. As soon as QuarkXPress recognizes the name, it types the rest of it for you. For example, if you want to change from Helvetica to Avant Garde, click just to the left of the "H" and type "Ava." By the time you type these three letters, chances are it will recognize Avant Garde (as long as you have that font installed). This is clearly a boon to desktop publishers who have many fonts and are tired of scrolling down a list for five minutes just to select Zapf Dingbats.

You can use these two methods together to select a typeface from the Measurements palette. For example, if you're looking for Zapf Dingbats but can't remember how "Zapf" is spelled, you can simply type "Z" and then click on the arrow button. You are transported directly to the end of the list as opposed to the beginning.

Character Attributes dialog box. The Character Attributes dialog box is the Style menu and half the Measurements palette rolled into one; it's also a simple keystroke away (Control-Shift-D). Here you can change the typeface using the same methods described in "The Measurements palette," above.

Find/Change and Font Usage dialog boxes. Let's say you have half your document in Helvetica and you want to change that copy to Futura. You can use the Find/Change or the Font Usage dialog boxes to search for and replace all instances of characters set in the Helvetica font with Futura. We discussed the Find/Change dialog box in some detail back in Chapter 3, *Word Processing*, and we'll discuss the Font Usage feature later in this chapter.

Font Size

See page 559

Changing the size of the typeface is as easy as...well, just about as easy as changing the typeface itself. In fact, you use the same options for changing the type size as we described above: Style menu, Measurements palette, Character Attributes dialog box, and the Find/Change or Font Usage dialog boxes. In addition, you can use a set of keystrokes to make your selected text larger or smaller (see Table 4-1).

Table 4-1	Pressing...	Does the following...
Font-sizing keystrokes	Control-Shift-Period	Increases point size through a preset range
	Control-Shift-Comma	Decreases point size through a preset range
	Control-Alt-Shift-Period	Increases point size in 1-point increments
	Control-Alt-Shift-Comma	Decreases point size in 1-point increments

The preset range mentioned in Table 4-1 is the same range listed on the Size menu: 7, 9, 10, 12, 14, 18, 24, 36, 48, 60, 72, 96, 120, 144, 168, and 192 points. When you increase through the preset range with a keystroke, your character size jumps from one to the next on this list.

▼ ▼

Tip: Precision Font Sizing. If you aren't satisfied with the preset font sizes, you can type in your own—in .001-point increments—in the Font Size dialog box. You can get to this dialog box by selecting "Other" from the Size submenu or by typing Control-Shift-\ (backslash).

▼ ▼

Type Styles

QuarkXPress has 13 built-in attributes that you assign at a character level. Figure 4-4 gives samples of each of these, plus examples of how to use them.

These type attributes can be assigned to selected text in four ways that are similar to how you assign typefaces and type size.

Style menu. You can select a type style from the Type Style submenu under the Style menu (see Figure 4-5).

Measurements palette. Each of the type styles is displayed by an icon in the Measurements palette (see Figure 4-6). The icons either display a sample of the style or give a graphic representation of it. For example, Superscript is shown by the numeral 2 over an up arrow. To select a type style, just click on the icon. The icon acts as a toggle switch, so to turn the style off you simply

Figure 4-4
Type styles

> Plain text
> **Boldface**
> *Italics*
> Outline
> Shadow
> S̶t̶r̶i̶k̶e̶-̶t̶h̶r̶o̶u̶g̶h̶
> Underlined (everything)
> Word underlining
> LARGE & SMALL CAPS
> ALL CAPS
> Su^{per}script (baseline shown as dotted line)
> Sub$_{script}$
> Superior char^{acters}

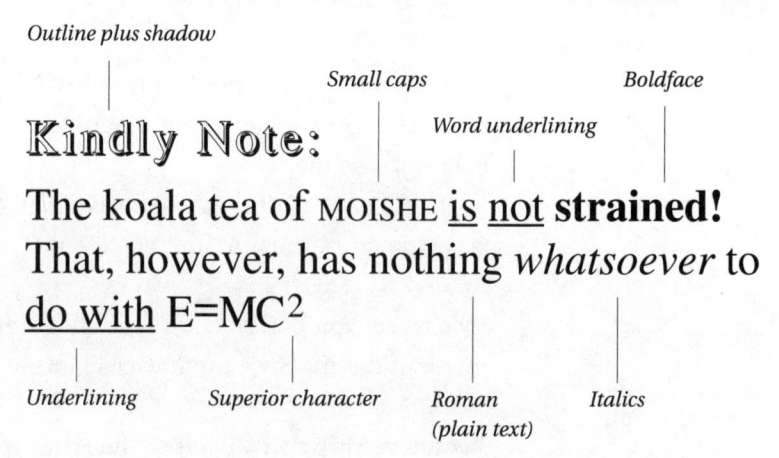

Outline plus shadow — *Small caps* — *Word underlining* — *Boldface*

Kindly Note: The koala tea of MOISHE is not **strained!** That, however, has nothing *whatsoever* to do with E=MC^2

Underlining — *Superior character* — *Roman (plain text)* — *Italics*

click on it again. If you have several type styles selected, you can quickly rid yourself of them by clicking on the "P" (for Plain).

Keystrokes. Each type style can be selected by a keystroke, as shown in Table 4-2. Once again, the styles are toggled on and off

Figure 4-5
The Type Style submenu

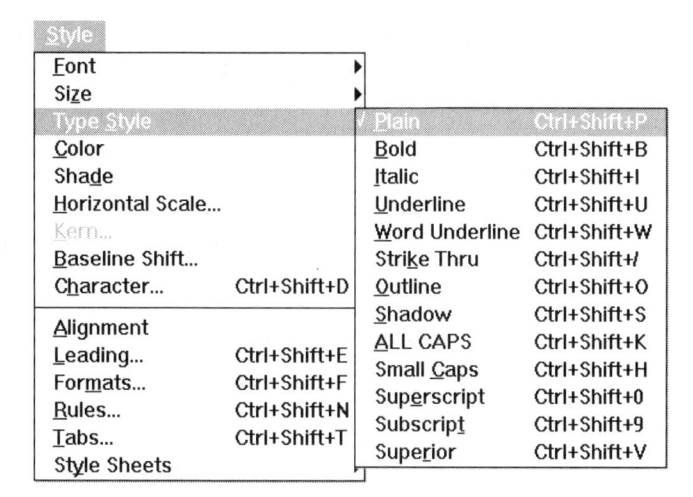

Style			
Font	▶		
Size	▶		
Type Style		✓ Plain	Ctrl+Shift+P
Color		Bold	Ctrl+Shift+B
Shade		Italic	Ctrl+Shift+I
Horizontal Scale...		Underline	Ctrl+Shift+U
Kern...		Word Underline	Ctrl+Shift+W
Baseline Shift...		Strike Thru	Ctrl+Shift+/
Character...	Ctrl+Shift+D	Outline	Ctrl+Shift+O
		Shadow	Ctrl+Shift+S
Alignment		ALL CAPS	Ctrl+Shift+K
Leading...	Ctrl+Shift+E	Small Caps	Ctrl+Shift+H
Formats...	Ctrl+Shift+F	Superscript	Ctrl+Shift+0
Rules...	Ctrl+Shift+N	Subscript	Ctrl+Shift+9
Tabs...	Ctrl+Shift+T	Superior	Ctrl+Shift+V
Style Sheets			

with each keystroke. We find keystrokes especially useful while typing directly into QuarkXPress; we can enter text and change styles while never taking our hands from the keyboard.

Character Attributes. Type styles in the Character Attributes dialog box (Control-Shift-D) are turned on and off by checking boxes. These attribute check boxes can be in one of three states: on, off, or indeterminate.

- **On.** An "X" in the check box means the style is selected for the entire piece of selected text.

Figure 4-6
Measurement palette type styles

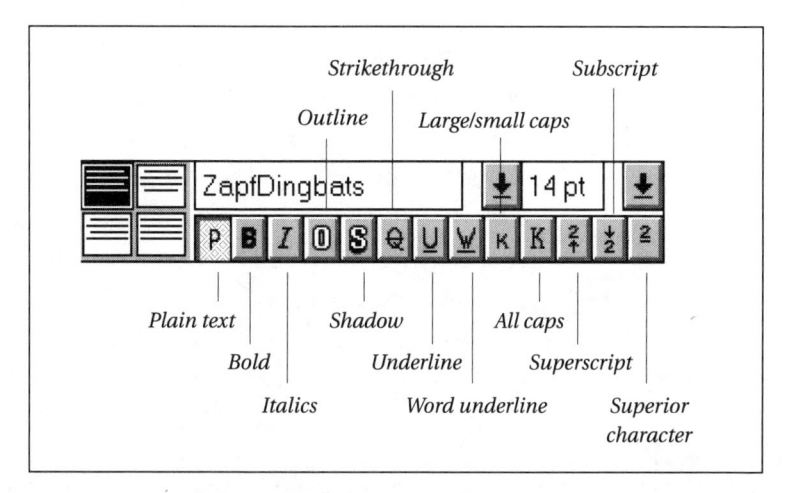

Strikethrough
Outline
Large/small caps
Subscript

Plain text
Bold
Italics
Shadow
Underline
Word underline
All caps
Superscript
Superior character

- **Off.** If the check box is blank, that style is not applied to any of the selected text.

- **Indeterminate.** A check box shaded gray means that some of the characters have that type style and others don't. Click a gray box again, and it is turned on. A second click turns it off.

Table 4-2
Type styles

Type...	To get...	Example
Control-Shift-P	Plain text	Ecce Eduardus Ursus
Control-Shift-B	Bold	**Ecce Eduardus Ursus**
Control-Shift-I	Italic	*Ecce Eduardus Ursus*
Control-Shift-U	Underline	Ecce Eduardus Ursus
Control-Shift-W	Word underline	Ecce Eduardus Ursus
Control-Shift-/	Strikethrough	Ecce Eduardus Ursus
Control-Shift-•	Outline	Ecce Eduardus Ursus
Control-Shift-S	Shadow	Ecce Eduardus Ursus
Control-Shift-K	All caps	ECCE EDUARDUS URSUS
Control-Shift-H	Small caps	ECCE EDUARDUS URSUS
Control-Shift-0	Superscript	Ecce Eduardus Ursus
Control-Shift-9	Subscript	Ecce Eduardus Ursus
Control-Shift-V	Superior	Ecce Eduardus Ursus

Note that these three states are also used to display the type style in the Measurements palette. However, instead of an "X," the Measurements palette uses a reversed box.

Styling by Attributes Versus Font Choice

Windows 3.1 automatically organizes installed TrueType and PostScript typefaces into families, typically consisting of the bold, italic, and bold italic fonts of a given face. For example, say you're working with the Bodoni font and want to italicize some selected text. Simply choose "Italic" as a style. Note that the bold, italic, and bold italic versions of a typeface are actually entirely separate faces from the "base" or "Roman" font.

Some typefaces have more than the standard four styles, which can cause some confusion if you're not familiar with the face. The Adobe Minion font package, for example, includes Regular, Semi-bold, Bold, and Black font weights. Selecting the "bold" style for Minion Regular yields Minion Semi-bold on your page and screen. To step up to Minion Bold, you must select Minion Bold by name from the font list. And as you can probably guess by now, selecting the bold style for Minion Bold doesn't yield Minion Black, either. Indeed, an emboldened Minion Bold will appear bolder on screen, but it will simply print out as Minion Bold with extra space between the characters in order to approximate the on-screen super-bold spacing—hardly something you want.

Remember that the Type Style selections you make are preserved when you change the text's font. But in our example, text highlighted in Minion Bold will loose its bold format when you change a paragraph's font to, say, Times. That's because the Minion Bold selection was a font change, not a style selection.

Color and Shade

You can quickly and easily change the color or the tint (shade) of a piece of text. First, select the text and then select either the color from the Color submenu or the tint value from the Shade submenu under the Style menu. The default color palette contains nine colors (see Chapter 9, *Color*, for information about adding and editing colors in this list). The default shades are 10-percent tints; you can assign a specific tint value by selecting "Other" in the submenu.

Tip: Reversed Type. There is no specific command for reversed type—typically white-on-black type—as there is in PageMaker. But that doesn't mean you can't achieve that effect. Simply select the text and choose "White" from the Color submenu or from the Character Attributes dialog box (Control-Shift-D). If you want the reversed type on a black background, either place a black box behind it or color the text box's background under the Text Box Specifications dialog box (Control-M).

Horizontal Scale

NEW IN 3.3

See page 581

Imagine the characters in a typeface as being rubber and stretchable. Now imagine stretching a typeface that took hundreds of hours to laboriously design at a specific width to 60 percent of its size, warping the characters into something they were never meant to be. Now imagine the designer's face.

Okay, you get the idea: typefaces were designed to be a specific width and shouldn't be messed with unless you have some really good reasons. What are some good reasons? The best reason of all is that you want the typeface to look that way. If you're responsible for the typographic design, then you can make any choice you want. Note that we're not talking about using a 70-percent compression of Helvetica because you don't feel like buying another package from Adobe. We are talking about using an 85-percent compression of Cheltenham because it looks cool.

Another good reason to play with the horizontal scaling is if you need to make some body copy fit a particular space. Here, we're talking about changing the horizontal scaling of the text two or three percent wider or narrower, not 10 or 20 percent. We'd be surprised if anyone other than the designer could see the difference of a few percent, especially at small sizes. Scaling Times Bold to 50 percent of its size to make it fit as a headline is a bad idea (see Figure 4-7).

If you want to play with the horizontal scaling of your type, you can do so by using the Horizontal Scale feature found under the Style menu. Entering values under 100 percent will squeeze the text narrower; values over 100 percent will stretch it wider. Note that you don't have to type a percent sign; just the number will do.

You can also alter horizontal scaling through keystrokes: Control-] (close square bracket) makes selected text wider in

Figure 4-7
Horizontal scaling of type

Got a problem?   20 pt. Helvetica Compressed Bold
Check your compression.

Got a problem?   20 pt. Helvetica (horizontal scaling: 60%)
Check your compression.

Got a problem?   20 pt. Helvetica bold (horizontal scaling: 60%)
Check your compression.

Times bold with horizontal scaling of 50% — word spaces not scaled

Rats! Squashed again!

Times bold with horizontal scaling of 50% — word spaces also scaled

Squashed! Rats again!

5-percent increments; Control-[(open square bracket) makes the selected text narrower in 5-percent increments. We remember the difference in an obscure way: The key on the left means narrow (or less) and the key on the right means wider (or more).

Kerning and Tracking

There are times in life when those little letters on a page are just too far apart or too close together. The problem might occur between two characters in 120-point display type or throughout an entire typeface. Whatever the case, QuarkXPress can control it through the use of kerning and tracking. They're similar, but let's look at them one at a time.

▼▼▼▼▼▼▼▼▼▼▼▼▼▼▼▼▼▼▼▼▼▼▼▼▼▼▼▼

NEW IN 3.3

See page 581

Tip: Know Your Ems and Ens. Many typographic controls are specified in units of measure called *ems* and *ens*. These units are not nearly as confusing as some people make them out to be. An em, in QuarkXPress, is equal to the width of two zeros side by side in the font size you're working in. This is usually close to the font size itself. Therefore, an em space in 60-point type is approximately 60 points wide. An en space is half of an em space, so it would be about 30 points wide. This is a weird way of doing things (normally an em would be just the same as the point size), but it's the Quark Way, so we follow it.

If you're typing along and decide to change point size, then the size of the em and en units changes as well. This can be a great aid. For example, if you change the size of a word after painstakingly manually kerning it, your kerning does not get lost or jumbled. The kerning was specified in ems, and therefore is scaled along with the type.

Note that because QuarkXPress figures its em spaces weirdly, an em space and an em dash are not the same width. Oh well.

▼▼▼▼▼▼▼▼▼▼▼▼▼▼▼▼▼▼▼▼▼▼▼▼▼▼▼▼

Kerning

NEW IN 3.3

See page 592

Adjusting space between character pairs is referred to as *kerning*. You'll sometimes find kerning defined purely as the removal of such space. In QuarkXPress, kerning can be the removal or addition of space—moving two characters closer together or farther apart. Figure 4-8 shows some examples of type, first unkerned and then kerned. The problem is made obvious here: too much space between characters can make words look uneven or unnatural.

QuarkXPress supports two kinds of kerning: automatic and manual.

Automatic. When we say automatic, we mean automatic: All you have to do is turn the function on, and QuarkXPress makes use of the font's built-in kerning pairs. It's up to font vendors to determine how many—and what—kerning pairs to include with a font and what values to assign them. Most fonts come with anywhere between 100 and 500 such pairs.

Figure 4-8
Kerned and
unkerned type

No automatic or manual kerning

DAVID WAVES!

Auto-kerning on; no manual kerning

DAVID WAVES!

Manual kerning applied to all character pairs

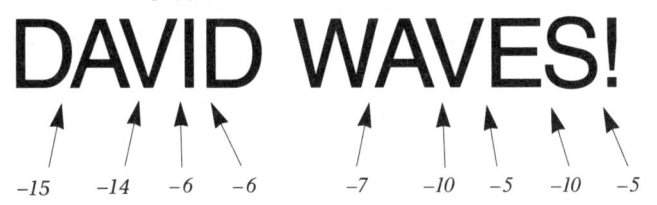

DAVID WAVES!

–15   –14   –6   –6   –7   –10   –5   –10   –5

There's almost no good reason to turn off automatic kerning, but if you want to, the switch is in the Typographic Preferences dialog box under the Edit menu. There is, however, very good reason to make judicious use of automatic kerning. The issue is speed; the more kerning pairs in a font, the slower it will display and print. Because of this, and because you really don't need kerning enabled for text smaller than 5 or 6 points, "Typographic Preferences" also allows you to set the smallest point size to which automatic kerning will be applied. We usually keep it set to 6 points (we can easily see the difference between kerned and unkerned text blocks at 7 points). If you're picky about your body copy and you're printing fine type to a high-resolution imagesetter, you may want to lower this value to 4 or 5 points.

Manual. Figure 4-8 showed a word in three renditions: with no kerning, with automatic kerning, and with manual kerning in addition to automatic kerning. The last looks the best, doesn't it?

Manual kerning in QuarkXPress is the adjustment of space between character pairs on a case-by-case basis. You make each adjustment in increments of em spaces (see "Tip: Know Your Ems and Ens," above). Why anyone would want to kern to a precision of 1/20,000 of an em space is beyond us, but QuarkXPress lets you do just that.

Manual kerning is usually reserved for larger type sizes for two reasons. First, it's harder to see poorly kerned pairs in smaller point sizes, so people say, "Why bother?" Secondly, you wouldn't want to meticulously kern pairs through a sizable amount of body text in the 8- to 14-point range. It would take forever; leave kerning of small type sizes to automatic kerning. If you don't like the built-in kerning pairs in a font, you can change them (see "Kerning and Tracking Tables," below).

▼▼▼▼▼▼▼▼▼▼▼▼▼▼▼▼▼▼▼▼▼▼▼▼▼▼▼

Tip: What To Do with These Numbers. We're going to throw a bunch of numbers at you like 1/20 em, but the important thing to remember is how the type looks, not the numbers that get you there. When we're working in QuarkXPress, we never think, "Oh, we're going to change the kerning 1/20 em." We just say, "Oh, let's see how adding some kerning here would look." Focus on the methods, and you'll get the feel for it pretty quickly.

▼▼▼▼▼▼▼▼▼▼▼▼▼▼▼▼▼▼▼▼▼▼▼▼▼▼▼

Manual kerning is a character-level attribute, but with a distinct difference from other character styles. Instead of selecting the text you want to change, you only place the cursor between two of the characters before applying kerning (see Figure 4-9). If you select one or more characters, you apply tracking rather than kerning (see "Tracking," below). You can then control the space between the characters in four different ways.

Kern menu item. You can also select the Kern feature from the Style menu, which brings up the Kern dialog box. Whole number values typed in here represent units of 1/200 em. For example, typing in 10 adds 10/200 (1/20) em of space and typing -.1 removes 1/2000 em of space (the minus sign—a hyphen—before the value makes a negative value). You can enter kerning and tracking values up to plus or minus 500 units.

Figure 4-9
Cursor placement for kerning

Manual kerning — correct cursor placement

Hey! K|ern me!

Incorrect cursor placement for manual kerning, but right for tracking

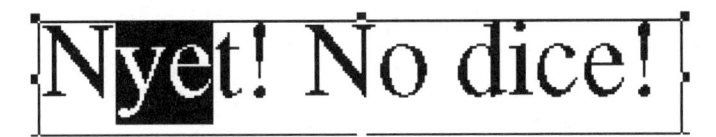

N|ye|t! No dice!

Character Attributes. Changing the kerning value between two characters by using the Character Attributes dialog box (Control-Shift-D) works just fine, but it's probably the slowest method you could use.

Measurements palette. The Measurements palette contains a left arrow and a right arrow that control tracking and kerning in text (they mean something different for pictures). Table 4-3 gives you a rundown on how to use them.

Table 4-3
Kerning control with Measurements palette

Clicking on...	While holding...	Does this...
Right arrow		Increases space 10 units (1/20 em)
Right arrow	Control key	Increases space 1 unit (1/200 em)
Left arrow		Decreases space 10 units (1/20 em)
Left arrow	Control key	Decreases space 1 unit (1/200 em)

Keystrokes. David hates to take his hands off the keyboard while he's working. He asks, "Why should I, when I can do just about everything I need through keystrokes?" He's got a point there. Table 4-4 shows the keystrokes you can use to control kerning.

Table 4-4
Kerning keystrokes

Holding down...	Results in...
Control-Shift-}	Increases space 10 units (1/20 em)
Control-Alt-Shift-}	Increases space 1 unit (1/200 em)
Control-Shift-{	Decreases space 10 units (1/20 em)
Control-Alt-Shift-{	Decreases space 1 unit (1/200 em)

No matter which method you use to kern, you can see the kerning value in the Measurements palette (just to the right of the left and right arrows), in the Kern dialog box, and in the Character Attributes dialog box.

▼ ▼

Tip: Kerning the Kerned. What shows up as the kern value when you want to kern a pair that is already kerned through automatic kerning? Nothing. You'll still find a zero in the Kern Amount field. QuarkXPress regards the values applied in automatic kerning as the "norm," so you don't have to worry about them.

However, if you have applied manual kerning to a pair of characters while "automatic kerning" was switched one way (on or off), and then later you switch it the other way, your kerning values may fly way off track.

▼ ▼

Tracking

In QuarkXPress two different functions are referred to as "tracking." They're similar, but we need to break them down for clarity. The first is a character-level attribute, and we're going to talk about it here. The second is a font-level attribute (changing this value changes the font as a whole, rather than just a selected set of characters), and we'll discuss it in great detail later in this chapter.

Tracking, as a character-level attribute, is the adjustment of space between a range of characters. It's sometimes called track kerning or kern tracking, though we think the best name for it is *range kerning*. The idea is simple: You can add or subtract space between many pairs of characters all at one time by using tracking controls (see Figure 4-10 for examples of tracking). These controls are so similar to the kerning controls that we're not even going to waste time and paper going into much depth.

You can control tracking by selecting a range of type and, using the Measurements palette, the Track feature from the Style menu, the Character Attributes dialog box, or the same keystrokes as kerning. The reason all the controls are virtually the same is that QuarkXPress "decides" for you whether to kern or

Figure 4-10
Tracking text

Tracking: +7

Art directors *everywhere* were ignoring me until I realized what I needed:

Much tighter tracking!
Tracking: –12

Tracking: 0. The art director threatens to fire you because this copy takes up three lines.

Hey, look, duuuuuude, you're, like, crowding into my space!

Problem solved! Tracking: –4

Hey, look, duuuuuude, you're, like, crowding into my space!

track, based on what is selected in the text box. In fact, these controls have the same functions. One is applied to a single pair of characters; the other is applied to several or many pairs.

▼ ▼

Tip: Tracking and the Single Word. The way tracking works, technically, is by adding or subtracting space to the right of each selected character. If you want to track a single word and don't want the space after the last character adjusted, you should select only the characters up to the last letter, not the entire word. For example, if you want to apply a -10 unit track to the word "obfuscation," without changing the space after the "n," you would only select the letters "obfuscatio" and apply tracking.

▼ ▼

Note that kerning and tracking are totally separate items, even though they seem to be the same. One result of this is that kerning and tracking are cumulative. For example, if you kern a character pair -10 units and apply tracking of -10 units to those characters, the space between them ends up 20 units smaller than normal.

▼ ▼

Tip: When To Track. Ah, we hear the reader sighing, "But what about some real-world tips?" Okay, let's throw some rules out for you.

- If you're setting text in all capital letters, add between 5 and 10 units of space by tracking the word. Remember not to add the tracking to the last character of the word, or else the space character will be affected, too.

- Printing white text on a black background often requires a little extra tracking, too. We don't need to get into the scientific reasons for this; just try it and see.

- Larger type needs to be tracked tighter (negative tracking values). Often, the larger the tighter, though there are aesthetic limits to this rule. Advertising headline copy is often tracked until the characters just "kiss." You can automate this feature by setting up dynamic tracking tables, which we'll discuss later in this chapter.

- A condensed typeface, such as Futura Condensed, could usually do with a little tighter tracking. Sometimes we'll add as little as -1 unit to a text block to make it hold together better.

Remember, however, that no matter how solid a rule, you are obliged to break it if the finished design will be better.

▼ ▼

Baseline Shift

The final character attribute that we discuss here is baseline shift. The baseline is the line—if you will—on which the type sits. For example, each line of text you're reading is made of characters sitting on a baseline. You can shift a character or group of characters above or below the baseline using the Baseline Shift feature under the Style menu. The baseline shift is specified in points; negative values shift the character down, positive values shift it up. You can enter any value up to three times the font size you're using; for example, you could shift a character off the baseline by 30 points in either direction if that character were 10-point type.

Note that baseline shift is similar to kerning and tracking in an important way: Even though you specify values in points rather than ems, the value of the baseline shift will change as the font size changes. For example, if you specify a 4-point baseline shift for some 15-point type, when you double the font size to 30 points, the shifted character is "reshifted" to 8 points (2×4).

The truth of the matter is that you can and will use the superscript and subscript type styles for almost every instance of raising or lowering a character. So what's the advantage of having a separate Baseline Shift control? Figure 4-11 shows several examples of how you might use baseline shift in your text.

Figure 4-11
Baseline Shift

I DON'T NEED NO BASELINE SHIFT.
I FEEL A NEED FOR A SUPERSCRIPT.
ME, I'D RATHER BE A SUPERIOR CHARACTER.
OY. I'M FEELIN' KINDA UNSTABLE, WHAT WITH ALL THIS BASELINE SHIFTING GOING ON.
We're having our ups and downs today!

▼▼▼▼▼▼▼▼▼▼▼▼▼▼▼▼▼▼▼▼▼▼▼▼▼▼▼▼▼▼▼▼▼

Paragraph Formatting

Character formatting is all very well and good, but when it comes to how text flows in a column, it don't make Bo Diddley squat. To handle text flow on a paragraph level, we move to paragraph formatting. These controls include indents, leading, tabs, and hyphenation and justification, as well as some esoteric functions such as "Keep with Next ¶" and a widow and orphan control. We'll discuss each of these features and more. In addition, as usual, we'll give you lots of examples so you can see what we're talking about.

The central headquarters of paragraph formatting is the Paragraph Formats dialog box, accessed via the Formats command under the Style menu (see Figure 4-12). Let's discuss each feature in this dialog box in turn, branching off on tangents when we need to.

Figure 4-12
The Paragraph Formats dialog box

Alignment

Why not start with the most bold and blatant paragraph attribute—its alignment. Most people are familiar with the four horizontal alignment options: left-aligned, right-aligned, justified, and centered. We will discuss each of these first, then move on to a less-known feature: vertical alignment.

Horizontal Alignment

New in 3.3
See page 584

If you've been involved with desktop typography long enough (a day or two), you'll know that different sources have many names for the same thing. For example, what QuarkXPress calls "left-aligned," others may call "left-justified," "flush-left," or "ragged-right." We're not going to start naming names, but QuarkXPress's terms are simpler and make more sense. For one thing, "justified" means only one thing: text fitting flush left and right. "Fully justified" is redundant, and "left-justified" is, well, it just isn't. Figure 4-13 shows some examples of text with various horizontal alignments.

Figure 4-13
Horizontal alignment

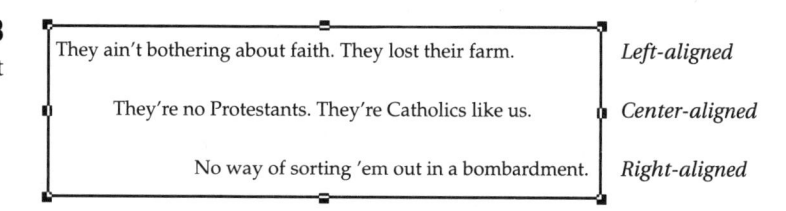

> They ain't bothering about faith. They lost their farm. — *Left-aligned*
>
> They're no Protestants. They're Catholics like us. — *Center-aligned*
>
> No way of sorting 'em out in a bombardment. — *Right-aligned*

You can specify alignment for a paragraph using any of four methods.

Paragraph Formats. As we said above, the Paragraph Formats dialog box is always an option when you're changing paragraph formats. The alignment control is a pop-up menu item (see Figure 4-14).

Figure 4-14
Alignment control in the Paragraph Formats dialog box

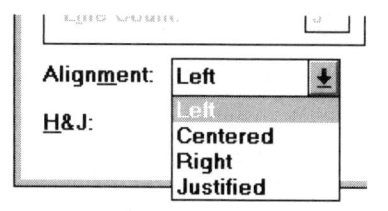

Style menu. You can also select the horizontal alignment you want from a submenu labeled "Alignment" under the Style menu.

Keystrokes. Note that the Alignment submenu lists a keystroke for each style. These are easy to remember since they rely on a first-letter mnemonic ("L" for left, "R" for right, and so on).

Measurements palette. Perhaps the easiest alignment method of all is to use the Measurements palette. When you have an insertion point in a paragraph, QuarkXPress displays four icons representing the four horizontal alignment selections (see Figure 4-15). To change a paragraph's alignment, just click on the icon you want.

Figure 4-15
Horizontal alignment in the Measurements palette

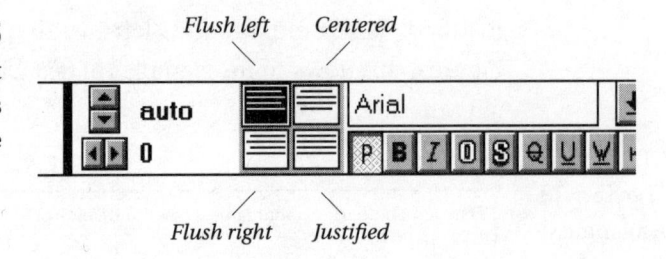

Flush left   Centered   Flush right   Justified

While left-aligned, right-aligned, and centered paragraphs are relatively straightforward, justified text is more complicated. However, we're putting off talking about justification and hyphenation until later in this chapter.

Vertical Alignment

Vertical alignment is not really a paragraph attribute, but rather an attribute of each text box. Nonetheless, as we're talking about alignment, we might as well bring this into the discussion.

Just as horizontal alignment is the horizontal placement of the text within a column, vertical alignment is the vertical placement of the text within its box. You can specify attributes similar to those used in horizontal alignment: top, bottom, center, and justified. The only place you can change this setting is in the Text Box Specifications dialog box (Control-M). Here you're presented with a pop-up menu for each selection (see Figure 4-16).

Let's look briefly at each of the alignment possibilities.

Top. This is the default setting for text boxes. It's what you're probably used to if you use QuarkXPress regularly. The text starts at the top of the text box, and as you type, fills the box. Exactly where the text starts depends on the first baseline control (discussed later in the chapter).

Bottom. By specifying "Bottom," you force the first line of text to be placed at the bottom of the box. Then, as text flows into the

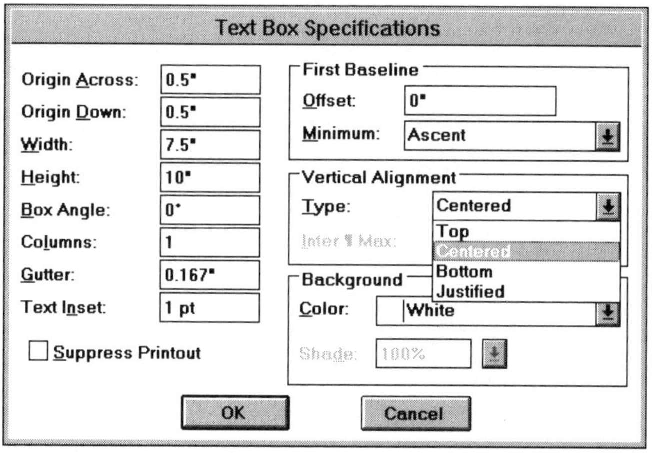

Figure 4-16
Vertical alignment in the Text Box Specifications dialog box

text box, each line pushes the type higher in the box. The last line of text in the box is always flush with the bottom of the box. Note that it is the bottom of the descender that is flush with the bottom of the box, rather than the baseline.

Center. When "Vertical Alignment" is set to "Center," the text within the text box is vertically centered. That sounds trite, but we can't explain it any better than that. See Figure 4-17 for an example of this effect.

▼ ▼

Tip: Centering Text. Horizontal or vertical center alignment may not result in text that looks perfectly centered. Why? These are two reasons. First, the mathematical horizontal centering of text may not look as "right" as an optical centering, especially if you have punctuation before or after the text. You can use invisible characters (colored white) or altered indentation (see "Indents," below) to change the way the text looks (see Figure 4-18). Remember, what looks right is more "right" than what the computer says.

▼ ▼

In the case of vertical centering, text in all capitals or text in fonts such as Zapf Dingbats may not be centered correctly in the box. The reason for this is that QuarkXPress does not actually find the center of the characters you've typed. Rather, it uses the full height of the font—ascent and descent combined—to calculate

Figure 4-17
Vertical alignment

Gray line represents a text box

> Installing **KvetchWrite** is the absolute living essence of simplicity.
>
> First, except on old S-100 systems, you will need to reformat your hard disk. As you know, this is a short and simple procedure that anyone can do.
>
> Next, remove Disk 27 from its fireproof container. If you forget the

Vertical alignment: justified

> Installing **KvetchWrite** is the absolute living essence of simplicity.
> First, except on old S-100 systems, you will need to reformat your hard disk. As you know, this is a short and simple procedure that anyone can do.
> Next, remove Disk 27 from its fireproof container. If you forget the

Vertical alignment: bottom

> Installing **KvetchWrite** is the absolute living essence of simplicity.
> First, except on old S-100 systems, you will need to reformat your hard disk. As you know, this is a short and simple procedure that anyone can do.
> Next, remove Disk 27 from its fireproof container. If you forget the

Vertical alignment: top

> Installing **KvetchWrite** is the absolute living essence of simplicity.
> First, except on old S-100 systems, you will need to reformat your hard disk. As you know, this is a short and simple procedure that anyone can do.
> Next, remove Disk 27 from its fireproof container. If you forget the

Vertical alignment: centered

proper placement. We suggest using baseline shift to move the characters around until they look the way you'd like them to.

Justified. Here vertical justification means that the text will be flush with the top and the bottom of the box. QuarkXPress puts

Figure 4-18
When centering is not centered

"Take your little brother swimming with a brick."

This is not visually centered because of the quotation marks.

"Take your little brother swimming with a brick."

This is adjusted by placing invisible punctuation on each line.

the first line of the text box at the top, the last line at the bottom, and then adds or deletes space between interior lines. Leading settings are overridden when necessary.

Many people think that vertical justification is the greatest thing since the transistor. Our response is: If you set up your leading grids and text boxes correctly, you shouldn't need to have some computer going through your drawers, shuffling lines around. We wouldn't want a computer to marry our daughters (if we had any), and we don't want a computer changing our leading and paragraph spacing.

No matter how picky we are about correctly setting up our documents, we do admit that there are times when vertical justification comes in handy. For example, many newspapers use this feature to consistently "bottom out" their columns.

You can specify a maximum distance between paragraphs in a vertically justified text box by changing the Inter ¶ Max value in the Text Box Specifications dialog box. A setting of "0" (zero), which is the default, tells QuarkXPress to distribute all space evenly by adding interline spacing (leading)—between both lines and paragraphs. A setting higher than 0 lets the program add extra space between paragraphs rather than changing your leading. Figure 4-19 shows some examples of vertically justified text with different Inter ¶ Max settings.

▼▼

Indents

Horizontal alignment depends entirely on where the left and right margins are set. In a column of text, the margins are usually

Figure 4-19
Varying the
Inter ¶ Max setting

> Ior, auritulus cinereus ille annosus Raili, solus in silvae angulo quodam carduoso stabat, pedibus late divaricatis, capite deflexo de rerum natura meditans.
>
> "Cur?" cogitabat, modo "quemadmodum?" Itaque Puo appropinquante Ior paulisper a meditatione desistere gavisus est ut maeste "Ut vales?" ei diceret.

All text in the examples is 10/11. Inter ¶ Max setting here is 0p. The leading is ignored completely.

Gray line represents the edge of the text box.

> Ior, auritulus cinereus ille annosus Raili, solus in silvae angulo quodam carduoso stabat, pedibus late divaricatis, capite deflexo de rerum natura meditans.
>
> "Cur?" cogitabat, modo "quemadmodum?"
>
> Itaque Puo appropinquante Ior paulisper a meditatione desistere gavisus est ut maeste "Ut vales?" ei diceret.

Inter ¶ Max setting is 4 pt. The leading is adjusted slightly, while space is added between paragraphs.

> Ior, auritulus cinereus ille annosus Raili, solus in silvae angulo quodam carduoso stabat, pedibus late divaricatis, capite deflexo de rerum natura meditans.
>
> "Cur?" cogitabat, modo "quemadmodum?"
>
> Itaque Puo appropinquante Ior paulisper a meditatione desistere gavisus est ut maeste "Ut vales?" ei diceret.

Inter ¶ Max setting is 1 pica. The leading is back to normal, and space is added only between paragraphs.

at the edges of the text box. However, you may want the first line of every paragraph to be indented slightly, or you might want the left or right margin to be moved in from the edge of the text box. You control each of these margins by changing the values for the paragraph indents.

▼▼▼▼▼▼▼▼▼▼▼▼▼▼▼▼▼▼▼▼▼▼

Tip: Watch the Text Inset. The default text inset for text boxes is 1 point, so your text is indented one point from each side of the box automatically. Make sure to change the text inset value in the

Text Box Specifications dialog box (Control-M) if you don't want the 1-point indent.

▼ ▼

QuarkXPress lets you change three indenting values: left indent, right indent, and first-line indent. All three controls are located in the Paragraph Formats dialog box (Control-Shift-F; see Figure 4-20). We'll discuss each one and then talk about how you can use them for special typographic effects.

Figure 4-20
Right, left and first-line indents

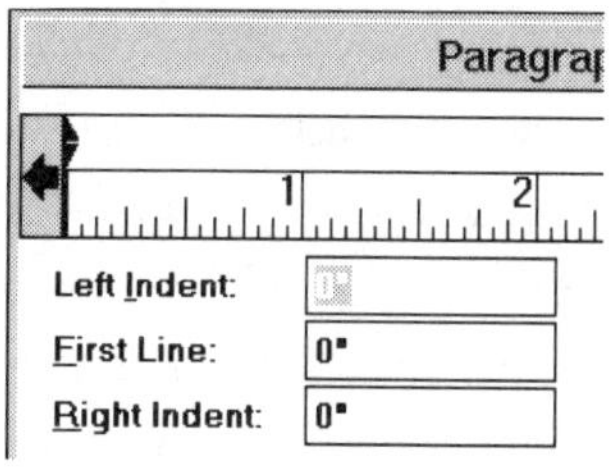

Left Indent. The Left Indent control specifies how far the selected paragraph will sit from the left side of the text box or column guide. The left indent does not take the Text Inset settings into account (see Chapter 1, *QuarkXPress Basics*), so you should add those in yourself. For example, if you want your paragraph to be indented exactly 3 picas from the side of the text box, and your Text Inset setting is 4 points, then your left indent should be 2p8 (3 picas minus 4 points).

Right Indent. The Right Indent control specifies just the opposite of "Left Indent"; in other words, how far the right edge of the paragraph is positioned from the right edge of the text box or column guide. For example, if you change the right indent to .5 inch, you can imagine an invisible line being drawn one-half inch from the right column guide. The text cannot move farther to the right than this line (see Figure 4-21.)

First Line. Whatever you do, wherever you go, don't type five spaces to indent the first line of each paragraph. If you must, use a tab. If you want to avoid the problem in the first place, use a first-line

Figure 4-21
Right indent

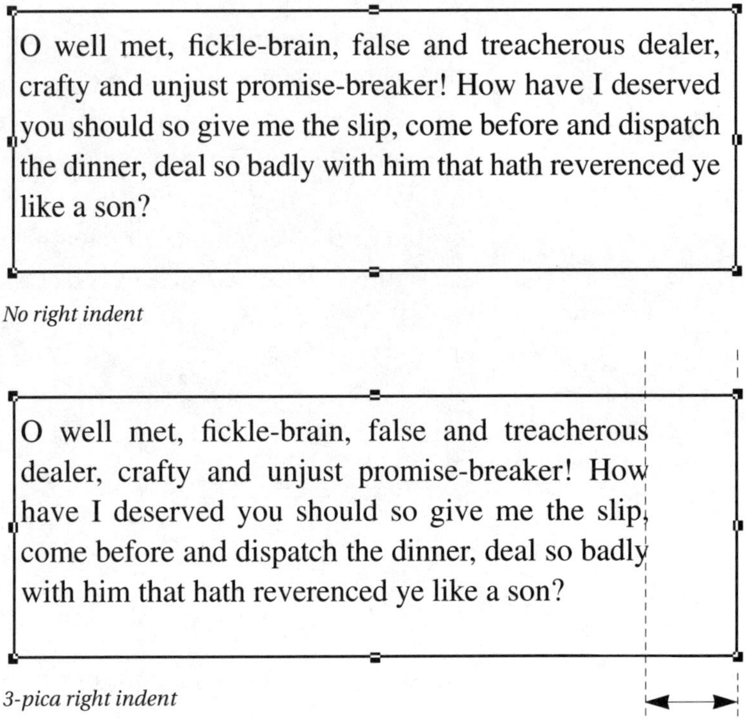

> O well met, fickle-brain, false and treacherous dealer, crafty and unjust promise-breaker! How have I deserved you should so give me the slip, come before and dispatch the dinner, deal so badly with him that hath reverenced ye like a son?

No right indent

> O well met, fickle-brain, false and treacherous dealer, crafty and unjust promise-breaker! How have I deserved you should so give me the slip, come before and dispatch the dinner, deal so badly with him that hath reverenced ye like a son?

3-pica right indent

indent. The First Line indent feature does exactly what it sounds like it would do: indents only the first line of each paragraph.

The size of your indent depends primarily on your design and the typeface you are working with. If you are working with a typeface with a large x-height (the height of the lowercase "x" in comparison with the height of the capital letters), you should use a larger first-line indent than if you are working with a low x-height typeface.

▼▼▼▼▼▼▼▼▼▼▼▼▼▼▼▼▼▼▼▼▼▼

Tip: Hanging Indents. You can use "Left Indent" and "First Line" to create hanging indents (used for bullet lists and the like) by typing a negative number as the first-line indent. We often use 1p6 (one and a half picas) for a left indent and -1p6 for a first-line indent. This places our first character (a bullet) at the zero mark and the subsequent lines at the 1p6 mark (see Figure 4-22). Typing a tab after the bullet causes QuarkXPress to skip over to the 1p6 mark whether or not we have a tab stop there (we'll discuss tabs and tab stops later in this chapter).

▼▼▼▼▼▼▼▼▼▼▼▼▼▼▼▼▼▼▼▼▼▼

Figure 4-22
Hanging indents

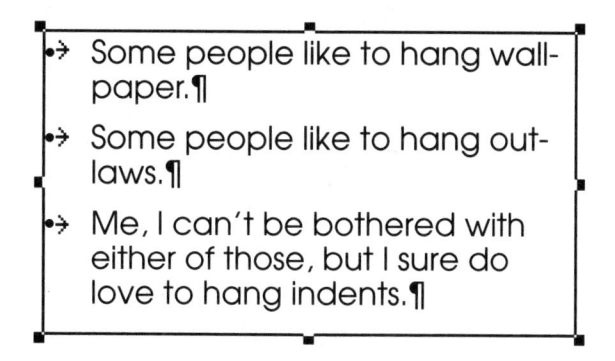

> •→ Some people like to hang wall-paper.¶
>
> •→ Some people like to hang outlaws.¶
>
> •→ Me, I can't be bothered with either of those, but I sure do love to hang indents.¶

Note that you don't have to specify any of the indents by typing numbers. While the Paragraph Formats dialog box is open, you are shown a ruler along the top of the dialog box (see Figure 4-23). This ruler contains three triangle markers in it: two on the left and one on the right. You can move these icons by clicking and dragging them along the ruler.

Figure 4-23
The text ruler associated with the Paragraph Formats dialog box

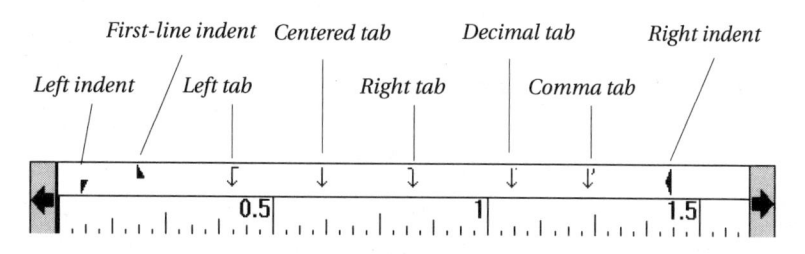

First-line indent   Centered tab   Decimal tab   Right indent
Left indent   Left tab   Right tab   Comma tab

The right triangle is the right indent. The bottom-left triangle is the left margin. The top-left triangle is the first-line indent. While moving these triangles around, the first-line indent moves with the left indent. This is the same as Microsoft Word and other programs (though those programs let you move the left indent independently by holding down the Shift key). For example, if you set a 1/4-inch first-line indent, and then move the left margin triangle to 1/2 inch, the first-line indent moves with it to the 3/4-inch point (1/2 inch plus 1/4 inch).

Leading

If we could get any one concept across to you in this chapter, we'd want it to be: Don't follow the defaults. By not following default values, you are forced to pay attention to how the type looks, rather than letting the computer do it for you. There is perhaps no better example of why this is important than leading.

Leading (pronounced "ledding") is the space between lines of text. The name originates from setting lead strips or blocks between lines (slugs) of metal type. QuarkXPress gives you considerable control over leading values for each paragraph, or it can "fly on automatic," specifying leading for you.

In this section we discuss the two modes and three methods for specifying leading. Pay close attention to the words "color" and "readability" in this section; they're the reasons we bother to be so meticulous.

Specifying Leading

Although QuarkXPress lets you use any measurement system you want, leading is traditionally measured in points. When talking type, most typesetters and designers say things like, "Helvetica 10 on 12," and write it out as "10/12." Designers who have grown accustomed to digital equipment (in other words, just about everybody), would say that 10/12 means setting 10-point type so that the baseline of one line is 12 points from the baseline of the next line (see Figure 4-24).

Leading is a paragraph-level attribute. That is, each paragraph can have its own leading value, but you can't change leading within a paragraph. You specify your leading in one of three places: the Paragraph Formats dialog box (Control-Shift-F), the Leading dialog box (Control-Shift-E), or the Measurements

Figure 4-24
Specifying leading

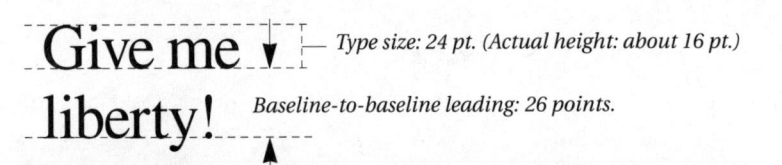

Type size: 24 pt. (Actual height: about 16 pt.)

Baseline-to-baseline leading: 26 points.

palette. Whereas in the first two dialog boxes you can type in only the leading value (more on this below), in the Measurements palette, you can change leading in two ways (see Figure 4-25).

- You can select the leading value and replace it with the value you want.

- Clicking the up and down arrows next to the leading value increases or decreases the leading value in 1-point increments.

Figure 4-25
Leading in the Measurements palette

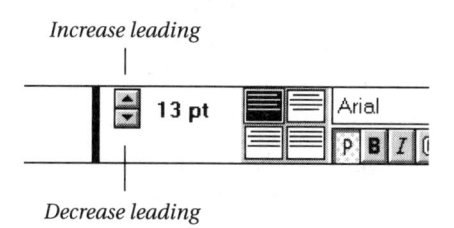

Increase leading

Decrease leading

You can also use shortcuts to change a paragraph's leading. Table 4-5 shows the four keystrokes.

Table 4-5
Leading keystrokes

Typing...	Results in...
Control-Shift-'	Increases leading in 1-point increments
Control-Alt-Shift-'	Increases leading in .1-point increments
Control-Shift-;	Decreases leading in 1-point increments
Control-Alt-Shift-;	Decreases leading in .1-point increments

QuarkXPress lets you specify leading values in three ways: absolutely, automatically, and relatively. Let's look at these.

Absolute. Setting your leading in an absolute form makes your leading as steadfast as Gibraltar. If you specify 14-point leading, you get 14-point leading—no matter what size text the paragraph contains. If your type is bigger than your leading, the type will overprint on preceding lines. When, as in the example given above, someone talks about 10/12 type, this is what they're talking about.

QuarkXPress lets you type any absolute leading value between .001 and 1,080 points.

Automatic. "Auto leading" sets leading as a percentage of the largest font size on a given line. This percentage is usually 20 percent greater than the font size. For example, if the largest font size on a given line is 10 points, then your leading will be set to 12 points (10 plus 20 percent of 10). If you change the font size to 12 points, then the leading changes to 14.4 points. Note that if you change only one character on a line to a larger font size, then that line alone will have a different leading value, even though "Auto Leading" is a paragraph-wide feature (see Figure 4-26).

"Auto leading" is built into QuarkXPress; it's the default setting of any new text box. However, to choose it specifically, you can type in either the word "Auto" or the number 0 as the leading value.

You can change the automatic-leading percentage value in the Typographic Preferences dialog box (accessed via the Preferences command under the Edit menu, or by typing Control-Alt-Y). There are two things you should note about this method, though. First, the change is document-wide; you can't change the automatic-leading percentage for only one paragraph or text box. Second, you must specify clearly what the automatic-leading measurements are; that is, if you want a percent, you must type a percent sign. This is important because you can specify the automatic leading to be a relative leading value (more on relative values in a moment).

To be honest with you, we use automatic leading when we're typing up grocery shopping lists. But when we're working on a project professionally, we define it for ourselves using absolute or relative leading.

Figure 4-26
The effects of Auto leading

Using Auto leading can result in irregular leading within a paragraph.

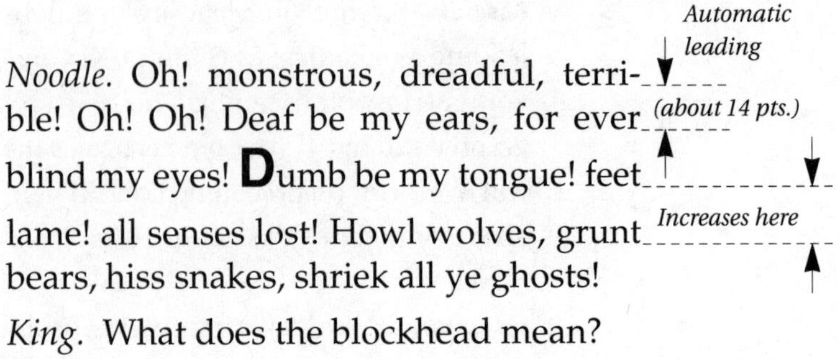

Noodle. Oh! monstrous, dreadful, terrible! Oh! Oh! Deaf be my ears, for ever blind my eyes! **D**umb be my tongue! feet lame! all senses lost! Howl wolves, grunt bears, hiss snakes, shriek all ye ghosts!

King. What does the blockhead mean?

Automatic leading (about 14 pts.)

Increases here

Relative. Whereas automatic leading generally determines the leading value based on a percentage of font size, relative leading determines leading by an absolute value. You specify relative leading by including the characters + or - (plus or minus/hyphen) before your leading value. For example, applying a leading value of +3 to 12-point type would result in 12/15 leading. If you changed the font size to 22 point, you would get 22/25 leading (22 plus 3).

By typing a negative relative value, you can tighten up the leading. However, you have a limit: The height of a capital on the lower line cannot move higher than the baseline of the upper line.

We often use relative leading when we are specifying leading as "solid"—that is, when the leading equals the point size. Instead of keying in 30-point leading for 30-point type, we simply type +0. Then, if (or when) we change the font size, the leading changes with it.

Leading Modes

When specifying leading in QuarkXPress, you can work in one of two leading modes: word processing and typesetting. You can select which mode to use in the Typographic Preferences dialog box (under the Preferences submenu under the Edit menu). Selecting one or the other determines the method QuarkXPress uses to measure leading.

Word processing. Let's be straight here. Even if you are using QuarkXPress only as a word processor, you shouldn't use Word Processing mode. There's just no point to it. Selecting Word Processing mode makes QuarkXPress use an ascent-to-ascent measurement. Ascent-to-ascent means that the leading value you specify is measured from the top of a capital letter on one line to the top of a capital letter on the next line. The only reason Quark included this feature was because many word-processing programs use this method. But you shouldn't, because the leading will change depending on the typeface you're using.

Typesetting. As we noted above, the proper way to specify leading is to measure from the baseline of one line to the baseline of the next. QuarkXPress calls this *Typesetting* mode. Make sure to enable that mode, then leave it alone.

▼▼▼▼▼▼▼▼▼▼▼▼▼▼▼▼▼▼▼▼▼▼▼▼▼▼

Tip: When Black and White Is Colorful. When designers and typesetters talk about the *color* of a page or the color of type, they probably don't mean red, green, or blue. They're referring to the degree of darkness or lightness that the text projects, which is also called its *weight*. The color of text is directly related to the typeface, the letter spacing, word spacing, and leading. Other design elements, such as drop caps, graphic elements, or pullquotes, can have a significant effect on the color or weight of a page. It's usually a good practice to maintain an even and balanced color throughout your page, unless you're trying to pull the viewer's eye (as opposed to pulling the viewer's leg) to one area or another (see Figure 4-27).

One way to see the color of a page or a block of type is to hold the printed page at some distance and squint severely. You can also turn the page over and hold it up to light, so you can see the text blocks without being distracted by the text itself.

▼▼▼▼▼▼▼▼▼▼▼▼▼▼▼▼▼▼▼▼▼▼▼▼▼▼

Tip: Leading Tips. Here are a few tips and tricks for adjusting your leading. Remember, though, that ultimately it is how easily the text reads and how comfortable the color looks that counts. Figure 4-28 shows some samples for each of these suggestions.

- Increase the leading as you increase the line length. Solid leading may read fine with a line containing five words, but it would be awful for a line containing 20 words.

- Generally use some extra leading for sans serif or bold type. It needs the extra room.

- Note the x-height of your typeface. Fonts with a small x-height can often be set tighter than those with a large x-height.

- Set display or headline type tightly. Large type can, and should, be set tightly, using either +0 relative leading or even absolute leading smaller than the point size you're using.

Figure 4-27
The color, or weight, of text blocks

Eduardus ursus, amicis suis agnomine "Winnie ille Pu"—aut breviter "Pu"—notus, die quodam canticum semihiantibus labellis superbe eliquans

New Century Schoolbook 10/11

Eduardus ursus, amicis suis agnomine "Winnie ille Pu"—aut breviter "Pu"—notus, die quodam canticum semihiantibus labellis superbe eliquans

Times-Roman 10/13

Eduardus ursus, amicis suis agnomine "Winnie ille Pu"—aut breviter "Pu"—notus, die quodam canticum semihiantibus labellis

Palatino, 0 tracking

Eduardus ursus, amicis suis agnomine "Winnie ille Pu"—aut breviter "Pu"—notus, die quodam canticum semihiantibus labellis superbe

Franklin Gothic, 0 tracking

Eduardus ursus, amicis suis agnomine "Winnie ille Pu"—aut breviter "Pu"—notus, die quodam canticum semihiantibus labellis superbe eliquans

Franklin Gothic Condensed Bold, 0 tracking

Eduardus ursus, amicis suis agnomine "Winnie ille Pu"—aut breviter "Pu"—notus, die quodam canticum semihiantibus labellis

New Century Schoolbook Bold 10/11

Eduardus ursus, amicis suis agnomine "Winnie ille Pu"—aut breviter "Pu"—notus, die quodam canticum semihiantibus labellis superbe

Helvetica 10/13

Eduardus ursus, amicis suis agnomine "Winnie ille Pu"—aut breviter "Pu"—notus, die quodam canticum semihiantibus labellis superbe eliquans

Palatino, -10 tracking

Eduardus ursus, amicis suis agnomine "Winnie ille Pu"—aut breviter "Pu"—notus, die quodam canticum semihiantibus labellis superbe eliquans

Franklin Gothic, -10 tracking

Eduardus ursus, amicis suis agnomine "Winnie ille Pu"—aut breviter "Pu"—notus, die quodam canticum semihiantibus labellis superbe eliquans

Franklin Gothic Condensed Bold, -10 tracking

- When using tight leading, be careful not to let the ascenders of one line touch the descenders of the line above.

A corollary tip to all of these: Break the rules if it makes the design look better!

Figure 4-28
Leading techniques

Look, s'pose some general or king is bone stupid and leads his men up a creek, then those men've got to be fearless, there's another virtue for you. S'pose he's stingy and hires too few soldiers, then they got to be a crowd of Hercule's. And s'pose he's slapdash and don't give a bugger, then they got to be clever as monkeys else their number's up.

9/9.5

The longer a line, the more leading you need.

9/11

Look, s'pose some general or king is bone stupid and leads his men up a creek, then those men've got to be fearless, there's another virtue for you. S'pose he's stingy and hires too few soldiers, then they got to be a crowd of Hercule's. And s'pose he's slapdash and don't give a bugger, then they got to be clever as monkeys else their number's up.

The misery of this one woman surges through my heart and marrow, and you grid imperturbed over the fate of thousands!

9/11.5

The misery of this one woman surges through my heart and marrow, and you grid imperturbed over the fate of thousands!

9/9.5

Fonts with small x-heights can be set tighter.

The best thing since sliced bread

36/31

Display type can be set tightly.

Cagney Jads

48/39

Watch out for your ascenders and descenders.

Space Before and Space After

Not only can you place interline space with leading, you can add space between each paragraph by using the Space Before and Space After attributes. You can find both of these controls in the Paragraph Formats dialog box (Control-Shift-F).

While it is entirely your prerogative to use both the Space Before and Space After attributes, you normally will need to use only one or the other. Think about it: If you add equal space before and space after a paragraph, it doubles the amount of space between each paragraph. Whichever you use is immaterial. David always uses "Space Before," and Bob likes "Space After." Each requires a slightly different way of thinking, but the concepts are ultimately the same.

We've seen more than one designer become flustered when applying "Space Before" to the first paragraph in a text box. Nothing happens. Remember that "Space Before" has no effect on the first paragraph in a text box. To add space before the first paragraph in a text box, use the First Baseline placement control (see "First Baseline," below).

Tip: Adding Extra Space. Let's see if we can pound this idea into your head as strongly as we did with "Don't use multiple spaces between words or punctuation." Don't ever use an extra carriage return to add space between paragraphs. Not only will you offend the people at Quark who spent long hours implementing the Space Before and Space After features, but you will—nine out of 10 times—mess yourself up with extra blank paragraphs hanging out at tops of columns or in other places where you don't want them. If you want a full line of space between paragraphs, apply it through "Space Before" or "Space After" in the Paragraph Formats dialog box.

First Baseline

The first line of a text box is always a tricky one for perfectionists. How far away from the top edge of the text box should the line sit? And how to get it there? With some programs this can take some heavy-duty fiddling. Fortunately, Quark has implemented First Baseline control in the Text Box Specifications dialog box (Control-M).

The key issue to remember here is that QuarkXPress places the first line of the text box according to one of three values: the size of the type, the Text Inset value, or the First Baseline Offset value. This is potentially confusing, so let's take it slowly. First, QuarkXPress compares the three values (type size, "Text Inset", and "First Baseline Offset"). If the size of the type is larger than either the First Baseline Offset value or the Text Inset value, then the first baseline is measured down from the Text Inset value. If the First Baseline Offset value is larger than both the type and the Text Inset value, then it is used as the first line's placement.

When the Text Inset is the value used, rather than the First Baseline Offset value, then a fourth factor is brought into the equation: the Minimum setting. The Minimum setting specifies where the top of the text is. You can choose three values for the Minimum setting: Cap Height, Cap + Accent, and Ascent (see Figure 4-29).

For example, if your text box has a text inset of 6 points and a first baseline offset of 3 picas (36 points), QuarkXPress places the first line 36 points down from the top edge of the box. On the other hand, if the type changes to 60 points, then QuarkXPress ignores the First Baseline Offset value and places the top of the text (as determined by the Minimum setting) at the Text Inset value.

Tabs

If you've ever typed on a typewriter, you've probably encountered tabs. A tab is a jump-to marker. For example, if you're typing

Figure 4-29
First baseline settings:
Minimum and Offset

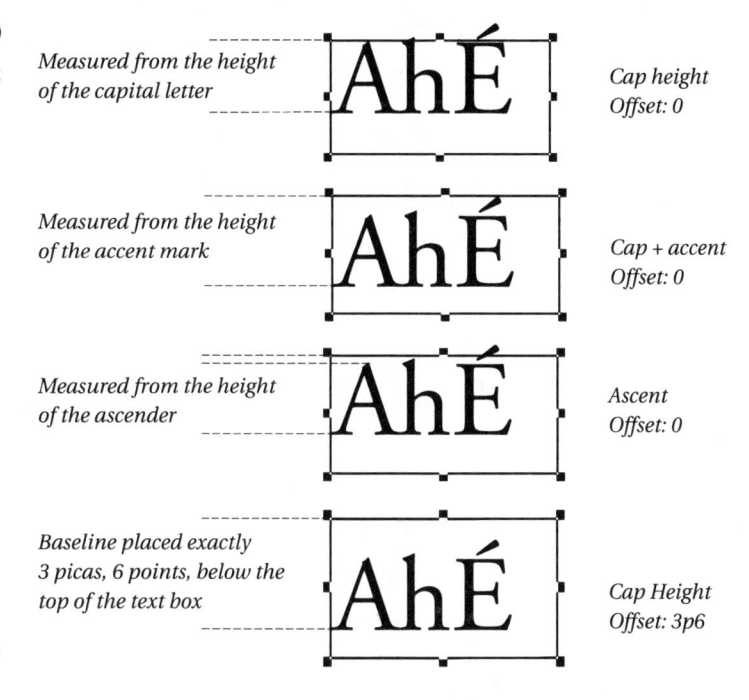

Measured from the height of the capital letter

AhÉ

*Cap height
Offset: 0*

Measured from the height of the accent mark

AhÉ

*Cap + accent
Offset: 0*

Measured from the height of the ascender

AhÉ

*Ascent
Offset: 0*

Baseline placed exactly 3 picas, 6 points, below the top of the text box

AhÉ

*Cap Height
Offset: 3p6*

along and press the tab key, the text cursor jumps to the next tab stop along the line. You can place these tab stops anywhere you like across the text column; they are paragraph-specific, so each paragraph can have a different set of tab stops.

If you don't specify your own tab stops, QuarkXPress sets default stops every 1/2 inch across the text box. If you are setting up a table and you want to place tabs between each column, follow the same rule as for spaces: Don't place multiple tabs in a row to make your columns align. Set one tab stop for each column. Then just press Tab once to jump from column to column.

QuarkXPress lets you set six types of tab stops using two different methods. Let's look at the types of tabs first.

- **Left tab.** This is the type of tab you're used to from typewriters. The text after the tab continues on as left-aligned.

- **Right tab.** Tabbing to a right tab stop causes the following text to be right-aligned; that is, it will be flush right against the tab stop.

- **Center tab.** Text typed after a center tab will center on the tab stop.

- **Decimal tab.** This is a specialized type of tab. It acts as a right tab until it encounters a decimal point (period). From that character on, it acts as a left tab (also, see "Tip: Hanging Tabs," below).

- **Comma tab.** If you're reading this in Europe or anyplace else where it's common to type a decimal using a comma rather than a period (as we usually do here in North America), you'll probably use the new Comma tab stop. It acts just like the decimal tab stop, except that it uses a comma.

- **Align On tab.** Actually, tab stops aren't limited to the period or comma characters. You can align tabbed text at any character by choosing Align On from the Alignment pop-up menu in the Paragraph Tabs dialog box. When this tab stop style is selected, QuarkXPress adds a small text field in which you can type the character to which you want the tabbed text to align. The default character is a period. If you change it to a dollar sign, the tabs line up at that dollar sign (see Figure 4-30).

Figure 4-30
Align On tab

> **Public Contributions to the Chavez Museum of Private Art**
>
> *"All of the art for some of the people."*
>
> ALL FIGURES IN MILLIONS
>
> Los Angeles . . . . US$45
>
> Toronto . . . . CAN$23.3
>
> Sydney . . . . AU$3
>
> Orange County . . . . US$0.3

Align On tab stop set to "$"

▼ ▼

Tip: Hanging Tabs. There's another QuarkXPress tab trick you'll love, if you ever need to create balance sheets. The decimal tab doesn't just line up decimals. In fact, QuarkXPress thinks of any non-number that falls after a number to be a "decimal point" and aligns to it. For example, if you type '<tab>94c2.44' on a line with a decimal tab, QuarkXPress aligns the "c" rather than the period. We thought this was a bug, until we realized how handy it could be. For example, if you are lining up numbers in a column, the negative-value parentheses hang outside of the column. You can even create hanging footnotes, as long as they're not numbers (see Figure 4-31).

Figure 4-31
Hanging tabs

Grazing Goose Records
"It's a cadillac, dear."

Securities	$223
Properties	152[A]
Cash	(148)[B]
Shoebox fund	33

[A] This month's rent is paid
[B] We owe that guy for the pizzas

▼ ▼

The easiest and most precise way to place your tab stops is through the Paragraph Tabs dialog box, which you can find by selecting "Tabs" under the Style menu or by typing Control-Shift-T. When this dialog box is open, you can move it around to place its ruler bar at the bottom of the box across your text, for visual reference. You can place a tab stop by first selecting the kind of tab stop you want from the Alignment choices, and then either clicking in the ruler area or typing a tab stop value into the Position box. If you choose the latter and simply type in the value, you must click either the Apply button or OK to make the tab stop appear in the ruler bar (see Figure 4-32).

Figure 4-32
The Paragraph Tabs dialog box

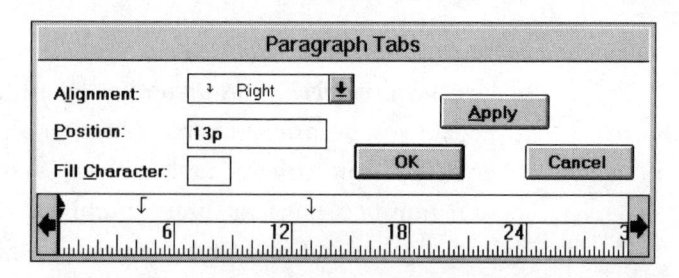

You can also add a leader to each tab stop. A leader fills the tab space with a repeated character, such as a period or a dash (see Figure 4-33). To add a leader to a tab stop that has not been created yet, set the alignment of the tab, type the leader character into the Fill Character field (we prefer the word "leader" to "fill character"), and then place the tab stop. To add a leader to a tab stop that has already been placed, click on the tab stop icon, type the leader in the appropriate box, and then click the Apply button. If you want to place more than one tab with a leader, you must click the Apply button for each one. When you have placed the tabs you want, click OK to save the changes to that paragraph. The second method for applying tabs is through the Paragraph Formats dialog box. However, in this instance, you can create only left tab stops and must place them by clicking in the text box ruler; in other words, it's really a very limited way to apply tabs to a paragraph.

New in 3.3 — See page 579

Figure 4-33
Tab leaders

Period used as leader character (18 pt. — same as other type on the line).

Moishe is ....not strange.
Oh yes . . . . he is too.

Tab character selected; reduced to 10 pt.; tracking value of 100 applied.

It droppeth ----------------as the purple
rain from ®®®®®®®®®® Hollywood

Other characters used as tab leaders.
In the second line, the point size of the tab itself is reduced to 10 pt.

You can go back and edit the tabs by dragging the tab icons along the ruler in either the Paragraph Tabs or the Paragraph

Formats dialog boxes. Note that you cannot type a new value for a tab stop in the Position box (this just adds a new tab rather than moving the old one). You can rid yourself of an unwanted tab, by the way, by clicking on the tab's icon in the ruler and dragging it out of the ruler boundaries. A click in the ruler with the Control key held down erases all of the tab stops for that paragraph.

Right Indent Tab

Trying to set a tab stop exactly at the right margin can be very frustrating. Even worse, if your right margin or the size of your text box changes, your tab stop doesn't follow along. Now you can type Shift-Tab to insert a Right indent tab. This type of tab acts as though you've placed a right tab stop flush with the right margin of your paragraph. Plus, it adjusts as you adjust the margin or the text box. (We can hear the handful of people who 'get it' sighing appreciatively in the background. Those of you who don't, just try it once and you'll understand.)

The Right indent tab acts just like a tab (you can even search for it the same way, using "\t"), though there's no way to set its own leader (what QuarkXPress calls a "Fill Character"). It picks up the same leader as the last tab in the paragraph. Note that you won't see a tab stop in the Tab dialog box's ruler: It's always set to the right margin, wherever that is. Also, you should note that Shift-Tab jumps past all other tab stops in that paragraph.

Figure 4-34 shows examples of each of these types of tabs in a common example—a table.

▼ ▼

Tip: Don't Use Space Where You Really Want Tabs. Have you ever tried to align multiple columns using spaces? If you have, you have probably experienced frustration like no other frustration known to desktop publishers. We call it the "it-works-on-a-typewriter" syndrome. It's true; you can line up columns on a typewriter. But you shouldn't in desktop publishing. The reason has to do with fonts.

On most standard typewriters, the font you're using is a monospaced font. That means each and every character in the font is the same width. However, most typefaces are not monospaced. Therefore, you cannot rely on an equal number of

Figure 4-34
Using tabs

Acme Digital Frammis Corp.
"Have a *wonderful* day!"
1990 Customer Dissatisfaction as a Function of Product Color

Product Color	Units Sold	Unit Price	Dissatisfaction Index*
Moon Maid	2001	$ 12.95	6.77
Stuck Pig	5877	19.95	13.32
Curmudgeon	31	6.88	57.91
Haggis	3	129.97	3244.36

* Parts per million

Left tab   Centered tab   Decimal tab   Right tab

characters always being an equal distance. Figure 4-35 shows this phenomenon clearly. So, don't use multiple spaces when you're trying to align columns. In fact, don't use multiple spaces ever. Use tabs.

Figure 4-35
Using spaces for alignment

Take one	from column "a"	and one	from column "b"
but here	you actually	have four	columns see?

Aligned with spaces (bad)

Take one	from column "a"	and one	from column "b"
but here	you actually	have four	columns see?

Aligned with tabs (good)

Hyphenation and Justification

There are few items more dear to a typesetter's heart than hyphenation and justification—often called simply *H&J*. Proper hyphenation and justification of a document is often the single most important factor in the appearance of a document. And if your H&J is bad...well, there's little that anyone can do (see Figure 4-36).

Figure 4-36
Hyphenation and justification can make the difference

Doing a good job with the program involves knowing a little something about good hyphenation and justification settings. If y'ain't got the good settings, you don't got the good-looking type, either. This paragraph, for example, is simply atrocious.

Doing an *especially* good job with the program involves taking the time to learn about its hyphenation and justification controls. You'll be glad you did.

QuarkXPress has some very powerful controls over how it hyphenates and justifies text in a column. However, this is once more a situation where you won't want to follow along with its default settings. Let's take a look at what hyphenation and justification is all about, and then get into the details of how you can make it work for you.

The Basics of H&J

Although hyphenation and justification are entirely separate functions, they almost always go together—almost always.

The idea behind both hyphenation and justification is to make text fit into a given space and still make it look as good as possible. It turns out that there are three basic ways to fit text without distorting it too much: controlling the spacing between each of the letters, controlling the spacing between the words, and breaking the words at a line break by hyphenating. Any one of these, if performed in excess, looks awful. However, it is possible to mix them together in proper measure for a pleasing result.

▼▼▼▼▼▼▼▼▼▼▼▼▼▼▼▼▼▼▼▼▼▼▼▼▼

Tip: Check for Rivers. Often the first problem that arises when people set their text to justified alignment is that their documents start looking like a flood just hit; all these rivers of space are flowing around little islands of words. Too much space between words is disturbing to the eye. We told you in "Tip: When Black and White are Colorful," above, that turning the page over and holding it up to the light is a good way to check the color of a text block. It's also a great way to check for rivers in your text. This way your eye isn't tricked into actually looking at the words—just the spaces.

▼▼▼▼▼▼▼▼▼▼▼▼▼▼▼▼▼▼▼▼▼▼▼▼▼

Although you can't adjust the algorithms that QuarkXPress uses for H&J, you can change many variables that help in its decision making. These values make up the Edit Hyphenation & Justification dialog box, found by first selecting H&Js from the Edit menu, and then clicking the Edit button (see Figure 4-37).

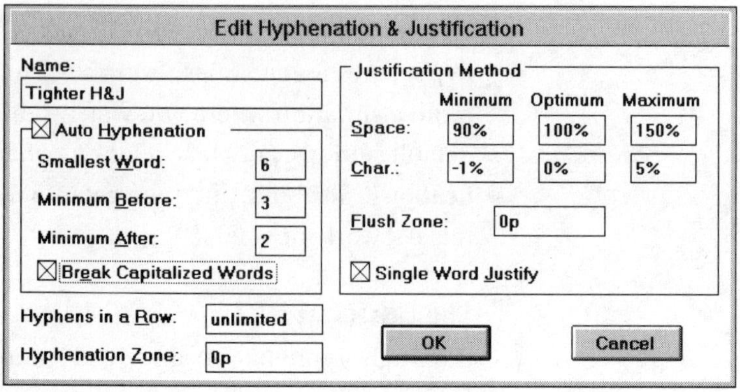

Figure 4-37
The Edit Hyphenation & Justification dialog box

Let's divide the controls in this dialog box into two groups and discuss them one at a time.

Auto Hyphenation

QuarkXPress can automatically hyphenate words at the end of a line, breaking them into syllables according to an internal algorithm. When you first start up the program, Auto Hyphenation is turned off, and QuarkXPress won't hyphenate any words unless you include hyphens or discretionary hyphens (see "Formatting Characters," below). You can turn Auto Hyphenation on by clicking in the Auto Hyphenation check box in the Edit Hyphenation & Justification dialog box. When you enable hyphenation, several items turn from gray to black. These features are the basic controls over QuarkXPress's internal hyphenating algorithms. Let's look at them one at a time.

Smallest Word. When QuarkXPress is attempting to hyphenate a line of text, it must decide what words are eligible for hyphenation. You can quickly discard most of the smaller words by specifying the smallest word QuarkXPress considers. For example, you might not want the word "many" to hyphenate at the end of a line. By setting the Smallest Word value to "5" or higher, you tell QuarkXPress to ignore this word, as well as any other word with fewer than five letters. The minimum Smallest Word setting is 3 characters.

Minimum Before. The Minimum Before value specifies the number of letters in a word that must come before a hyphen break. Depending on your tastes and your pickiness level, you might set this value to "2" or "3." Otherwise, words like "tsetse" (as in "fly") might break after the first "t." The smallest Minimum Before setting is 1 character.

Minimum After. The Minimum After value specifies the number of letters in a word that must come after a hyphen break. Again, this value is based on aesthetics. Some people don't mind if the "ly" in "truly" sits all by itself on a line. (*The New York Times* breaks "doesn't" after the "s.") For most quality work, however, you would want a minimum setting of "3." You can enter as few as two characters for your Minimum After setting.

Break capitalized words. The Break Capitalized Words control is self-explanatory. You can tell QuarkXPress to either break capitalized words or not to. The feature is there for those people who think that names should never be broken. We're picky, but not that picky.

Hyphens in a Row. One area in which we are that picky is the number of hyphens we allow in a row. For most work, we hate to see more than a single hyphen in a row down a justified column of text. QuarkXPress defaults to "unlimited," which is the same as typing 0 (zero). If you're creating newspapers, this might be appropriate. If you're making art books, be a bit more careful with your hyphens.

Hyphenation Zone. Another way to limit the number of hyphens in a section of text is the Hyphenation Zone setting. While relatively simple in function, this feature is one of the more complex to understand fully (it was for us, anyway). The idea is that there is an invisible zone along the right margin of each block of text. If QuarkXPress is trying to break a word at the end of a line, it looks to see where the hyphenation zone is. If the word before the potentially hyphenated word falls inside the hyphenation zone, then QuarkXPress just gives up and pushes the word onto the next line (it does not hyphenate it). If the prior word does not fall within the hyphenation zone, then QuarkXPress hyphenates the word.

Normally, the Hyphenation Zone value is set to 0 (zero) picas. This setting specifies no hyphenation zone, so all lines can have hyphenation (up to the limit of the Hyphens in a Row value).

For example, if the words "robinus christophorus" came at the end of a line and QuarkXPress was about to hyphenate "christophorus," it would first look at the word "robinus" to see if any part of it fell inside the hyphenation zone. If it did, QuarkXPress would not hyphenate "christophorus" at all; if it didn't,

QuarkXPress would use its standard hyphenation algorithms to break "christophorus" appropriately.

Justification

As we mentioned above, justifying text is the process of adding or subtracting space throughout a line of text to keep it flush on the left and the right. You can alter several of the parameters Quark-XPress uses for determining justification by changing values found in the Edit Hyphenation & Justification dialog box. These values are controlled in three different areas: "Word Spacing," "Character Spacing," and the "Flush Zone." Let's look at each of these.

Word Spacing. As we describe above in "Character Formatting," word spacing describes the amount of space between words. In the case of justification, it describes the spectrum of how large or how small the spaces between words can be. In the Space fields, you can specify Minimum, Maximum, and Optimum percentages of a normal space character. For example, a minimum value of 80 percent allows a space between words that is 80 percent of a normal space.

We almost always specify a tight minimum and maximum, such as 90 percent and 130 percent, with an optimum value of 100 percent. We do this because we'd rather have tightly spaced lines than loose lines. (Depending on the typeface, we might even set "Optimum" to around 95 percent.)

Character Spacing. In the Char: fields, you can also set Minimum, Maximum, and Optimum percentages for the widths of characters. The percentages are based on the width of an en space (see "Formatting Characters," below). Whereas 100 percent was normal width for "Word Spacing," 0 (zero) percent is the normal width for "Character Spacing," and should almost always be used for the Optimum setting.

We generally don't give QuarkXPress much freedom in adjusting the tightness of characters because we think the typeface designer probably knows more than we do about how the characters should be spaced (and certainly more than QuarkXPress does). For example, we might set "Minimum" to -1 percent, "Maximum" to 2 percent, and "Optimum" to 0 (zero) percent. But here, again, is an area where you need to print out a few text blocks, preferably on an imagesetter or whatever your final output device will be, look at the color of the type, and decide for yourself.

Flush Zone. If you thought the Hyphenation Zone setting was obscure, you just hadn't heard about Flush Zone yet. The Flush Zone setting does one thing, but it does it very well: It determines whether the last line of a paragraph gets force-justified or not. The value you type in the field is the distance from the right margin that QuarkXPress checks. If the end of the line falls into that zone, the whole line gets justified.

Single Word Justify. This checkbox lets you tell QuarkXPress whether you want a word that falls on a justified line by itself to be force justified. Newspapers will probably leave this on. Art directors of fancy foreign magazines might insist that it be turned off. Personally, we don't like what the word looks like either way, and we'd just as soon have the sentence rewritten, or play with other formatting to reflow the paragraph. Note that this feature doesn't apply to the last line of a paragraph; you still need to use the Hyphenation Zone feature (see above).

Setting Your Own H&J

Different paragraphs in your document may need different hyphenation and justification settings. For example, you may want each paragraph on one page to hyphenate regularly, but on another page to remain unhyphenated. You can use QuarkXPress's H&Js feature to set up multiple H&J settings to be applied later at a paragraph level.

Creating an H&J Setting

When you select "H&Js" from the Edit menu, the H&Js for Document dialog box appears (see Figure 4-38). You can add, delete, edit, duplicate, or append H&J settings. The list on the left side of the dialog box shows the names of each H&J setting. A new document contains only one setting: Standard. This is the default setting for all text paragraphs.

Figure 4-38
The H&Js for Document dialog box

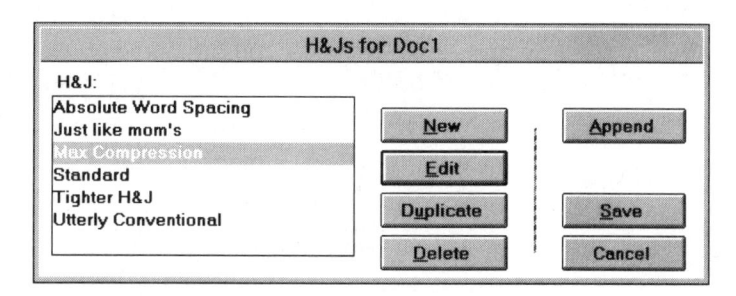

You can add a new H&J setting in two ways.

- Click on the New button to open a new H&J setting. Change the hyphenation and justification parameters as described above, then give the setting a name. When you are done, click on OK. The Edit H&Js dialog box you see when you click "New" is a duplicate of the Standard setting.

- Click on a setting (such as "Standard") first and then on the Duplicate button. You can then edit a duplicate of the setting you first clicked on. This is helpful for basing one H&J setting on another.

New in 3.3
See page 583

To delete a setting, first click on its name, then click the Delete button. If you have set up H&J settings in a different document, you can append them to your current document's list by clicking the Append button and then selecting the document to import from. If the names of any appended H&J settings are the same as settings in your open document, they are not imported.

Applying an H&J Setting

Once you have created more than one H&J setting, you can choose which setting to use on a paragraph level by using the

Paragraph Formats dialog box. With the cursor in a paragraph, or with multiple paragraphs selected, you can select an H&J setting from the pop-up menu in the Paragraph Formats dialog box (see Figure 4-39). Note that QuarkXPress also takes the Hyphenation Exceptions that you've created into account when breaking words (see "Hyphenation," later in this chapter).

Figure 4-39
Applying an H&J setting

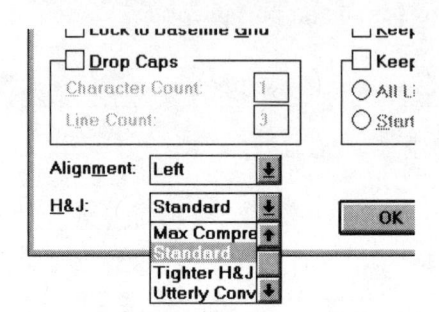

▼ ▼

Tip: Tighter and Looser H&Js. David almost always works with a minimum of three H&J settings in his document: Standard, Tighter, and Looser. First, he edits the Standard H&J setting, turning on "Auto Hyphenation", and tightening up the character and word spacing parameters. The Tighter and Looser settings are for specialty cases. If a line looks better with slightly tighter than normal H&Js, then he applies "Tighter." If the Standard settings are too limiting for a paragraph, and having looser spacing wouldn't hurt it, then he applies "Looser."

One of the most important things to remember when fooling around with these types of settings is the color of the page. If setting a tighter H&J makes one text block look significantly darker than the rest of the page, you may need to alter the paragraph manually rather than letting the H&J settings do it for you.

▼ ▼

Widow and Orphan Control

We mean no disrespect to widows and orphans, but when it comes to typesetting, we must carefully control them, stamping out their very existence when we have the chance.

If you know what we're talking about already, bear with us or skip this paragraph (or test whether you can remember which is the widow and which is the orphan). A *widow* is the last line of a paragraph that ends up all by itself at the top of a column or a page. An *orphan* is the first line of a paragraph that lands all by itself at the bottom of a column or page. David likes the following mnemonic device: widows sounds like "windows," which are high up (top of the page), whereas orphans make him think of tiny Oliver (who was small, and thus, at the bottom of the page).

Typesetters sometimes also refer to a line of text comprised of only one word as either a widow or an orphan. To avoid the confusion, in our office we prefer the word "runt."

All typographic widows and orphans are bad, but certain kinds are really bad—for example, a widow line that consists of only one word, or even the last part of a hyphenated word. Another related typographic horror is the subhead that stands alone with its following paragraph on the next page.

Fortunately, QuarkXPress has a set of controls that can help prevent widows and orphans from sneaking into your document. The controls are the Keep With Next ¶ and Keeps Lines Together features; you can find them in the Paragraph Formats dialog box (Control-Shift-F). Let's look at each of these.

Keep With Next

See page 583

The Keep With Next ¶ feature is perfect for ensuring that headings and the paragraphs that follow them are always kept together. If the paragraph is pushed onto a new column, a new page, or below an obstructing object, the heading follows right along (see Figure 4-40).

You may want to keep paragraphs together even in cases not involving subheads. For example, entries in a table or list that shouldn't be broken could each be set to "Keep with Next ¶."

Keep Lines Together

The Keep Lines Together feature is the primary control over widows and orphans for your paragraphs. When you click on the Keep Lines Together check box in the Paragraph Formats dialog

Figure 4-40
Keep With
Next ¶ feature

Mephisto Du übersinnlicher sinnlicher Freier, Ein Mägdelein nasführet dich. **Faust** Du Spottgeburt von Dreck und Feurer! **Mephisto**	Und die Physiognomie versteht sie meisterlinch: In meiner Gegenwart wird's ihr, sie weiß nicht wie, Mein Mäskchen da weissagt ver- borgnen Sinn;

This paragraph style does not have Keep With Next ¶ set

Mephisto Du übersinnlicher sinnlicher Freier, Ein Mägdelein nasführet dich. **Faust** Du Spottgeburt von Dreck und Feurer!	**Mephisto** Und die Physiognomie versteht sie meisterlinch: In meiner Gegenwart wird's ihr, sie weiß nicht wie, Mein Mäskchen da weissagt ver- borgnen Sinn;

This paragraph style does have Keep With Next ¶ set

box, QuarkXPress activates the control parameters options in this area (see Figure 4-41). Let's look at these controls one at a time.

All Lines in ¶. You can keep every line in a paragraph together by selecting the All Lines in ¶ button. For example, if a paragraph is broken onto two pages, enabling "All Lines in ¶" results in that entire paragraph being pushed onto the next page to keep it together. However, if you specify "All Lines in ¶" to a text block larger than your column, QuarkXPress simply breaks the paragraph, ignoring this control.

Start. You don't have to specify that all lines in a paragraph should be kept together. Instead, you can control the number of lines

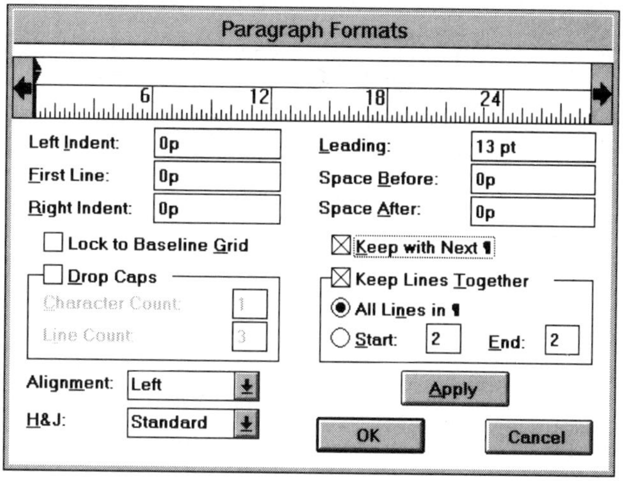

Figure 4-41
Keep Lines Together feature

[Paragraph Formats dialog box]

that should be kept together at the beginning and at the end of the paragraph.

The value you type in the Start field determines the minimum number of lines that QuarkXPress allows at the beginning of a paragraph. For example, specifying a two line Start value causes paragraphs that fall at the end of a page to maintain at least two lines on the first page before it breaks. If at least two lines of that paragraph cannot be placed on the page, then the entire paragraph is pushed over to the next page.

The Start feature is set up to eliminate orphans in your documents. If you don't want any single lines sitting at the bottom of a page, you can specify a value of 2 for the Start control (some designers insist that even two lines alone at the bottom of a page are ugly and may want to adjust the Start value to 3 or greater).

End. The value specified in the End field determines the minimum number of lines that QuarkXPress allows to fall alone at the top of a column or after an obstruction. A value of 2 or greater rids you of unwanted widowed paragraphs (if a widow occurs, QuarkXPress "pulls" a line off the first page onto the second page or column).

▼ ▼

Tip: Other Orphan and Widow Controls. It's all very well and good to let QuarkXPress avoid widows and orphans for you, but for most documents you still need to painstakingly peruse each page, making adjustments as you go. You have many other tools to help you avoid widows and orphans. Here are some of our favorites.

- Adjust tracking by a very small amount over a large range of text. Nobody can tell if you've applied a -0.1 tracking to a paragraph or a page, but it might be enough to pull a widow back.

- Adjust horizontal scaling by a small amount, such as 99.5 percent or 100.5 percent.

- Make sure "Auto Hyphenation" and "Auto Kern Above" are on. Kerning can make a load of difference over a large area of text. And remember that you can set up different hyphenation and justification settings for each paragraph. You might apply a tighter or a looser setting for a range of paragraphs.

If none of these techniques work for you, don't forget you can always just rewrite a sentence or two (if it's yours to rewrite). A quick rewrite of a sentence can fix up just about any problem.

Baseline Grid

In typography, the smallest change can make the biggest difference in a piece's impact. For example, look at a high-quality magazine page that has multiple columns. Chances are that each line matches up with a line in the next column. Now look at a crummy newsletter. Place a rule across a page and you'll see lines of text all over the place. What's missing is an underlying baseline grid. You can create a grid and lock each line of text to it with QuarkXPress's Baseline Grid feature.

Each document has its own Baseline Grid setting, which is pervasive throughout every page. However, whether a block of text actually locks to that grid is determined on a paragraph level. You can set the Baseline Grid value for the document in the Typographic Preferences dialog box (from the Preferences submenu under the Edit menu, or just type Control-Alt-Y). You have two controls over the Baseline Grid: the Start value and the Increment value. The Start value determines where this grid begins on the page, measured from the top of the page. Set it to start at the first baseline of your body copy.

The Increment value determines the distance from one horizontal grid line to the next. Generally, this value is the same as the leading in the majority of your body copy. For example, if your body copy has a leading of 13 points, then you should type "13 pt" as your Increment value.

To lock a paragraph to the baseline grid that you have established, click the Baseline Grid checkbox in the Paragraph Formats dialog box (Control-Shift-F). Note that the baseline grid overrides paragraph leading; if your paragraph has a leading of 10 points, when you enable "Baseline Grid," each line snaps to the Increment value (13 points, in the example above). If your paragraph has a leading larger than the Increment value, each line snaps to the next grid value. In other words, your leading never gets tighter, but it can get very loose. If your Increment value is 13 points and your leading is 14 points, each line snaps to the following grid line, resulting in a 26-point leading.

There is no doubt that a careful study and practice of baseline grids can make your document better looking. However, you can get the same quality from being careful with your leading and text box placement.

Maintain Leading

If you don't use baseline grids, but still want to maintain consistent leading on your page, you might want to look closely at the Maintain Leading feature. This feature—which we usually just leave turned on in the Typographic Preferences dialog box—ensures that each line in a text box is placed according to its leading value when another object (such as a picture box or a line) obstructs the text and moves text lines around.

When Maintain Leading is turned off, two things happen. First, the line of text following an obstruction abuts the bottom of that obstruction (unless the obstruction's text runaround is larger than 0 points). Second, the rest of the lines of text in that text box fall on a different leading grid than do those above the obstruction. This is much easier to see than to read (or write) about, so check out Figure 4-42. This feature has no bearing on paragraphs that are already set to Lock to Baseline Grid.

Figure 4-42
Maintain Leading

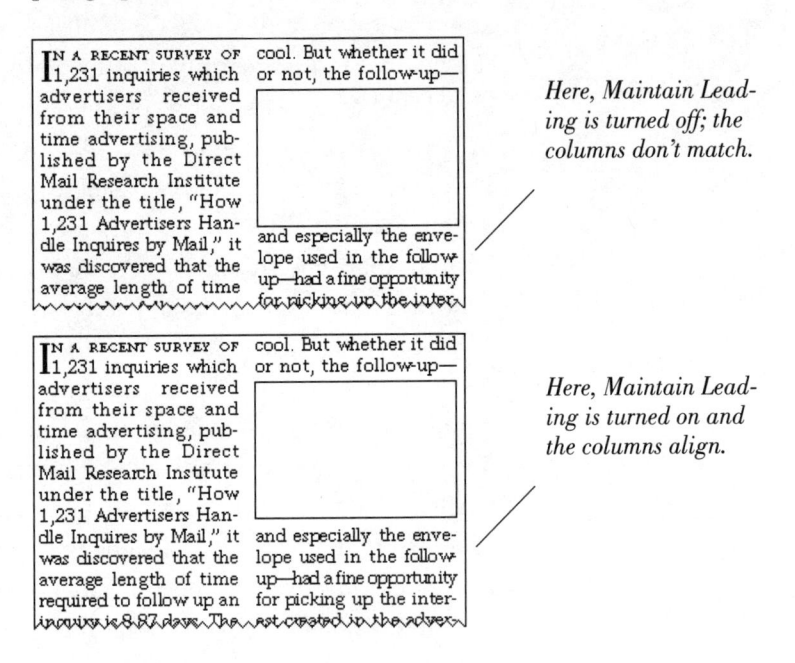

Here, Maintain Leading is turned off; the columns don't match.

Here, Maintain Leading is turned on and the columns align.

Fine-Tuning Type

Almost everything we've talked about in this chapter has been at a character or paragraph level. Here we're going to talk about making typographic adjustments on a document level. You have control over several areas at a document level, including how superscript, subscript, superior, and small caps characters are "built," and which words will hyphenate. You can also create custom automatic tracking and kerning tables, and run through an automatic check for typographic "problem areas."

Let's look at how you can use each of these controls in your documents.

Typographic Preferences

By selecting "Typographic" under the hierarchical Preferences submenu (under the Edit menu), you can alter QuarkXPress's default settings for superscript, subscript, superior, and small caps characters (see Figure 4-43). We talk about these items here, as well as the Character Widths setting. You can find a discussion of baseline grid and of leading preferences in "Leading," earlier in this chapter.

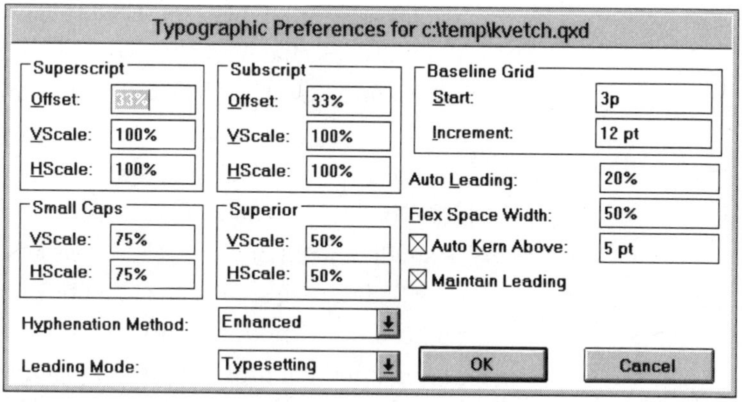

Figure 4-43
The Typographic Preferences dialog box

Superscript and Subscript. Few people ever bother to get into the nitty-gritty of type styles, but the controls are here if you ever want them. Both the Superscript and the Subscript controls are the same: Offset, VScale, and HScale.

- **Offset.** You can determine how far from the baseline your superscript or subscript characters should move by altering the Offset amount. You specify "Offset" as a percentage of the text size. For example, if the offset for "Subscript" were set to 50 percent, then a subscript character would move 9 points down for 18-point type.

- **VScale and HScale.** These terms are short for "Vertical Scale" and "Horizontal Scale," which are responsible for how tall and how wide the super- or subscript text is. The controls default to 100 percent, which we find much too large. We generally set both to a value between 70 and 80 percent, so that a superscript or subscript character doesn't stand out too much against the rest of the text.

Superior. You don't have to worry about the offset for superior characters because they are automatically set to be flush with a capital letter in that font. So the only modifications you can make here are to the vertical and horizontal scaling of the character. This is clearly an area of aesthetic choice. We tend to like the 50-percent default that QuarkXPress gives us.

Small Caps. You can also set the vertical and horizontal scaling of all small caps characters in a document. Though it would be nice to be able to set the characteristics of small caps on a paragraph or story level, these controls are usually good enough.

There are times when adjustable small caps are even better than traditional small caps (fonts designed especially to be used as small caps). For example, we know a designer who recently specified that all small caps in a book's body copy should be 9.5 points tall. The body text was 10-point Palatino, so the company producing the templates just changed the small caps specifications to 95 percent in the horizontal and vertical directions (95 percent of 10-point type is 9.5-point type). A traditional small cap would not achieve this effect.

Flex Space Width. When you type Control-Shift-5 you get what's called a *flex space*. This is just like a spaceband (what you get when you press the space bar), but you can specify how wide you want it to be (it flexes to your will). Also, this space is a fixed width; it won't change width, even in justified text. The control for this character's width is in the Typographic Preferences dialog box (Control-Alt-Y). The percentage is based on the width of an en space. Therefore, the default value, 50 percent, is half an en space. 200 percent makes the flex space an em space. However, note that em or en spaces created with the Flex Space feature probably won't be the same widths as em or en dashes in a font (see "Tip: Know Your Ems and Ens," earlier in this chapter). Also note that when you change the width of a flex space in the Typographic Preferences dialog box, QuarkXPress changes the widths of all flex spaces throughout that document.

Enhanced hyphenation. If you've never used QuarkXPress before and don't plan on converting old Mac QuarkXPress (pre-1991) files to the PC, just leave this control in the Typographic Preferences dialog box set to "Enhanced." This way QuarkXPress can use its better hyphenation scheme on your documents. However, if you convert a Macintosh QuarkXPress 3.0 (or earlier) document and it's imperative that the line breaks stay exactly the same, you may want to switch this feature to standard hyphenation for that document.

Kerning and Tracking Tables

As we noted earlier in this chapter, most fonts include built-in kerning tables of 100 to 500 pairs. However, you can modify these pairs or add your own by using Quark's Kern/Track Editor XTension (it's free and comes with QuarkXPress, as a file named KTEDIT.XXT). You must make sure that this XTension is located in the same subdirectory as your copy of QuarkXPress.

Modifying tracking and kerning tables is different from many of QuarkXPress's typographic controls in that it is font-specific. For example, if you alter the kerning table for Avant Garde, those changes will be in effect whenever you use Avant Garde in any QuarkXPress document.

The modifications you make are stored in the XPress Preferences file and in your document files, so you aren't really altering the font itself. As we said back in Chapter 1, *QuarkXPress Basics*, when you create a kerning table (or a tracking table or hyphenation exceptions) while in a document, the information is stored in two places: in XPress Preferences (XPRESS.PRF) and within the file itself.

Kerning Tables

To modify a font's kerning table, choose Kerning Table Edit from the Utilities menu. This brings up the Kerning Table Edit dialog box, which presents a scrolling list of available fonts (see Figure 4-44). The list lets you choose Plain, Bold, Italic, and Bold Italic variants of each installed font.

Figure 4-44
The Kerning Table Edit dialog box

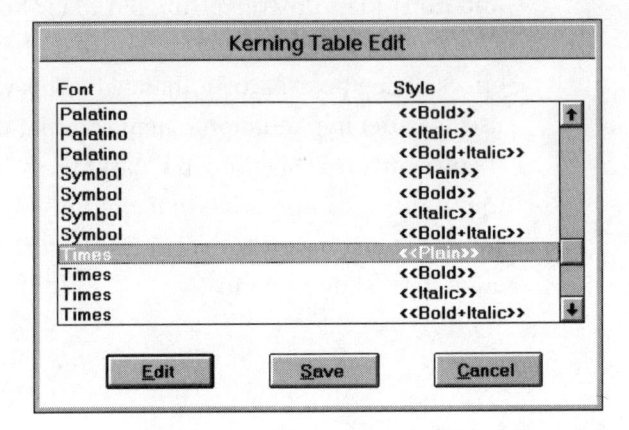

Just as we warned you in the earlier section "Styling by Attributes Versus Font Choice," not all fonts have these four variants, but the Kerning Table Edit dialog box will list them as if they do. Using Adobe's Minion Bold again as an example, there is no bold variant of Minion Bold, but you'll find it listed anyway as Minion Bold <<bold>> (the bold variant of Minion Regular is Minion Semibold). According to Quark you simply have to be aware of that and ignore variants that you know aren't there.

You have to edit kerning tables for one font at a time. This means that you cannot edit Palatino in its Plain style and expect all the Bold, Italic, and Bold Italic variants to be altered as well.

After selecting a font from the list, click OK to move to the Kerning Values dialog box (see Figure 4-45). Here you can edit an existing pair, add a new pair to the list, or delete a pair. You can also import and export lists of these kerning pairs in a text file format. Let's look at how each of these operations is performed.

New in 3.3
See page 592

Adding a pair. You can add a new kerning pair to QuarkXPress's list in three steps.

Figure 4-45
The Kerning Values dialog box

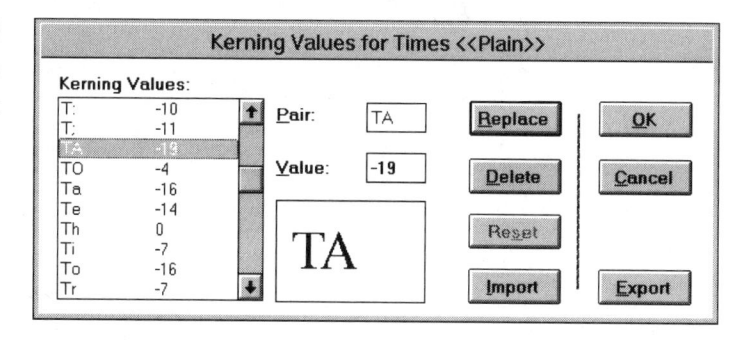

1. Type the two characters in the Pair field.

2. Type a kerning amount into the Value field. This value is specified in 200ths of an em (see "Tip: Know Your Ems and Ens," earlier in this chapter). You can see a graphic representation of the kerned pair in the window below the Value field.

3. Click the Add button.

That's all there is to it.

Editing a pair. You can adjust kerning pairs that you have created or that come predefined in the font by clicking on a pair in the Kerning Values table and then modifying the value in the Value field. You see the results of the adjustment in the window beneath the Value box. Once you have set the value you want, click the Add button to add it back to the table.

Deleting or resetting a pair. If you don't like a kerning pair that you added, or you want to remove one that was built in, simply select the pair from the list and click the Delete button. If you have altered a kerning pair and want to reset it back to its original value, click on the pair and then on the Reset button.

Import/Export. There are those who know kerning pairs so well that they'd rather just type up a bunch of them in a text-editing program and then import them all at once into QuarkXPress. You can do this by creating a text-only file within any text editor (such as Microsoft Word, WordPerfect, or Windows Write) in the following format.

1. Type the kerning pair (the two letters).

2. Type a space.

3. Type the kerning value in QuarkXPress's kerning units (1/200 of an em). Negative numbers mean negative kerning.

4. Save the list as a text-only file, using a .KRN filename extension.

5. In the "Kerning Values for…" dialog box (accessed via the Edit button in the Kerning Table Edit dialog box) click the Import button to bring this text file in.

If you want to edit the kerning values that are already built into the font, you can first export those values by clicking the Export button, then editing and re-importing them.

▼▼▼▼▼▼▼▼▼▼▼▼▼▼▼▼▼▼▼▼▼▼▼▼▼

Tip: Quick Kerning for Families. Applying kerning pairs to a number of faces can be very time-consuming and tiresome. You can speed up this process by using the Import feature to apply the same kerning tables to several typefaces. Once you've imported the kerning tables, you can go back and edit them to adjust for specifics of that typeface.

▼▼▼▼▼▼▼▼▼▼▼▼▼▼▼▼▼▼▼▼▼▼▼▼▼▼▼▼▼▼

Tracking Tables

Most fonts need to have tighter tracking applied to them in larger point sizes. In the past, we were used to changing the tracking for various display fonts because font vendors do not build supplemental tracking values into their fonts. Fonts come with only one tracking value: the normal font letter spacing, as determined by the type designer. However, QuarkXPress lets you create custom tracking tables for each font you use (see Figure 4-46).

A tracking table tells QuarkXPress how much tracking to apply at various sizes of a font. This, too, is part of the Kern/Track

Figure 4-46
The Tracking Edit dialog box

Editor XTension that comes with QuarkXPress, and you must have this XTension file in the same subdirectory as your copy of QuarkXPress for it to work.

Here's an example to illustrate this feature. Let's say you're creating a template for a new magazine. You've decided to use Futura Bold for your headers, which are at a number of different sizes. You know that your largest header is 60 points with -20 tracking and your smallest header is 12 points with no tracking. Here's what you do.

1. Select "Tracking Edit" from the Utilities menu.

2. Choose the font that you want to edit—in this case Futura—and click the Edit button. The tracking table is applied to all four basic style variations (Plain, Bold, Italic, and Bold Italic) that apply to that font.

3. You see the Tracking Values dialog box (see Figure 4-47). The vertical axis represents tracking values from -100 to 100 in increments of 1/200 em. The horizontal axis represents type sizes from 0 to 250 points. The farther to the right on the grid, the larger the type. The default setting is a horizontal bar at the zero tracking level. In other words, all point sizes have a zero tracking value.

4. Click on the line at the far left axis. As you hold down the mouse button, you can see the graph values shown in the dialog box. Note that clicking on the graph places a new

Figure 4-47
A tracking table graph

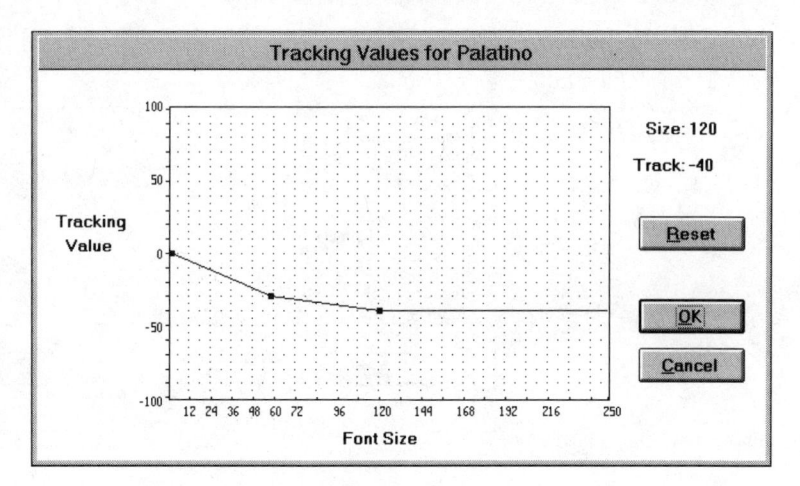

[Screenshot: Tracking Values for Palatino dialog showing a graph of Tracking Value vs. Font Size, with Size: 120, Track: -40, and Reset, OK, Cancel buttons]

point on it. You can have up to four corner points on each graph. This first point is the anchor at the zero tracking level.

5. Click on the line at the 60-point size and drag the graph line down to the -20 tracking level. If we saved this now, whenever you used Futura Bold all point sizes larger than 12 points would have negative tracking applied to them.

6. You can add a third control handle at the 14-point type size and set it to zero tracking. Now all type larger than 14 points has tracking applied.

7. To save your changes, click OK. Then, if you're finished with your tracking table edits, click Save.

While editing a font's tracking table, you can start over by clicking the Reset button. You can always go back (even after you've saved), and click the Reset button to get the horizontal graph back.

Note that these tracking values are only applied to a font when "Auto Kern Above" is turned on. In fact, the tracking tables only apply to font sizes above the automatic kerning limit, which has been entered in the Auto Kern Above value field in the Typographic Preferences dialog box.

Hyphenation

QuarkXPress gives you two other tools for controlling hyphenation: Hyphenation Exceptions and Suggested Hyphenation. Let's look briefly at each of these.

Suggested Hyphenation

The entire life's work of the Suggested Hyphenation feature is to help you figure out how QuarkXPress is going to hyphenate a word. First, select a word or place the cursor somewhere within or immediately to the right of a word. Then select the Suggested Hyphenation command from the Utilities menu (or type Control-H). In the Suggested Hyphenation dialog box that appears, QuarkXPress shows you how it would hyphenate the word (see Figure 4-48).

Figure 4-48
Suggested hyphenation

Suggested Hyphenation
cur-mud-geon-ly
[OK]

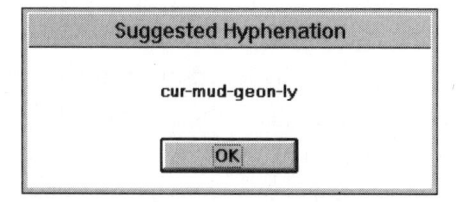

QuarkXPress uses an algorithm to hyphenate words. The algorithm takes many things into account, including the parameters set within the Edit Hyphenation & Justification dialog box, such as the number of entries in "Break Capitalized Words," "Minimum Before," and so on. For example, when "Minimum After" is set to "3," the word "wildly" does not appear hyphenated in the Suggested Hyphenation dialog box. However, if you change "Minimum After" to "2," it does.

Hyphenation Exceptions

You can control the hyphenation fate of particular words by setting your own specific hyphenation in the Hyphenation Exceptions dialog box, which you access by selecting "Hyphenation Exceptions" from the Utilities menu (see Figure 4-49). You can then add or delete words at will from the Hyphenation Exception list.

Figure 4-49
The Hyphenation Exceptions dialog box

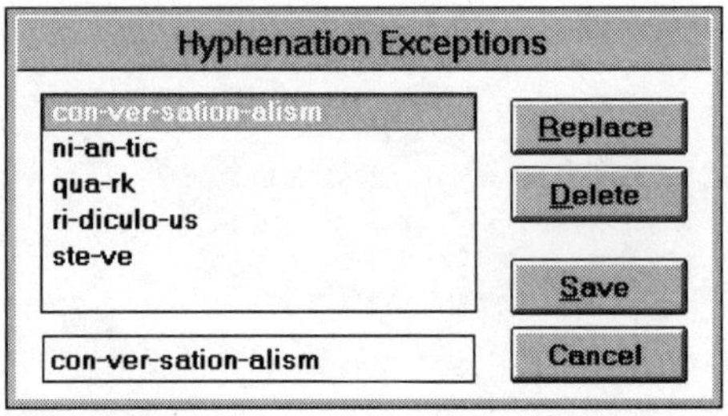

When you first open the dialog box, it is empty. To add a word, just type it in the available space, including hyphens where you want them. If you don't want a word to hyphenate, don't put any hyphens in it.

Once you've created some hyphenation exceptions, you can edit them by clicking on them, making the necessary changes, and then clicking the Replace button (note that the Add button changes to a Replace button in this case). You can also delete items on the list by selecting them and clicking the Delete button.

Hyphenation exceptions are stored in the XPress Preferences file and in your document. The changes you make are global: They affect each and every document on that machine when you create or open them.

▼ ▼

Tip: Watch Those Hyphens. There's nothing like giving your document a good once over before you print it out. One of the things you want to look for is a badly hyphenated word. Remember that QuarkXPress uses an algorithm to hyphenate words rather than a look-up dictionary like some other programs. Because of this, it can hyphenate more words than other programs, but it doesn't always do it right. For example, QuarkXPress hyphenates the word "Transeurope" normally as "Transeur-ope" rather than "Trans-europe." If you find these problem words, you can either change them manually (by adding discretionary hyphens) or make a global change using "Hyphenation Exceptions."

Special Characters

If you're using QuarkXPress to type letters to your mother, you probably don't need this section. If you're doing just about anything else with it, stand by.

When you look at your keyboard, you see about a hundred characters represented on the keys. What you don't see are the hundreds of special characters you can access with just a few keystrokes. In this section we look at some of those characters, including the invisible "utility" characters, dingbats, math symbols, and special punctuation. By no means do you have to memorize most of these; instead, you may want to refer back to the tables we've included when you're working on documents.

Formatting Characters

The first set of characters we look at are invisible characters that are used for special formatting in your document. Several of these characters are visible when you select "Show/Hide Invisibles" from the View menu (or type Control-I). However, a few are not; you just have to remember where you put them. Let's take a look at these characters (see Table 4-6 for more information on each character).

Enter (often labeled "Return"). Sometimes known as a "carriage return" or a "hard return," this is the key to press when you're at the end of a paragraph. In fact, the carriage return character delineates paragraphs from each other. Most people don't think of the Enter key as a character, but you can actually see it and select it with "Show/Hide Invisibles" turned on.

QuarkXPress is great at wrapping characters onto the next line, so don't press Enter after each line as you would on a typewriter. Also, don't press Return twice in a row to add extra space between paragraphs. Instead, use "Space Before" and "Space After" (see "Space Before and Space After," above).

Note that the Enter key on your keyboard's numeric keypad is different from the Enter immediately to the right of the letters (we'll see how a little later).

Table 4-6
Invisible formatting characters

Name	Keystroke
Return	Enter (or Return)
Soft Return (new-line)	Shift-Enter
Tab	Tab
Indent here	Control-\
Discretionary new line	Control-Enter
Discretionary hyphen	Control-Hyphen
Nonbreaking hyphen	Control-Shift-Hyphen
Nonbreaking space	Control-Spacebar
New column	Enter (on numeric keypad)
New box	Shift-Enter (on numeric keypad)
En space	Control-Shift-6
Nonbreaking en space	Control-Alt-Shift-6
Flex space	Control-Shift-5
Nonbreaking flex space	Control-Alt-Shift-5
Current page number	Control-3
Previous text box page number	Control-2
Next text box page number	Control-4

Soft Return. Holding down the Shift key while typing the Enter key results in a soft return, often called simply the "new line" character. A soft return forces a new line without starting a new paragraph with all of its attendant attributes—space before and after, first line indent, paragraph rules, and so on. For example, we use soft returns for tabular text or for forcing a line break in justified text. This is a character that takes some getting used to, but we recommend you play with it until you do, because it really comes in handy.

Tab. People also rarely think about the Tab key as inserting a separate character, but that's just what it does. We talked somewhat about tabs in "Tabs," above, so we just want to say that you should really understand your tabbing and never (never) use the Spacebar to align columns.

Indent Here. QuarkXPress has an invisible formatting character, Control-\ (backslash) called "Indent Here." Typing this character

New in 3.3
See page 579

causes the rest of the lines in a paragraph to indent over to that character. We find this feature particularly useful for hanging punctuation or inline graphics, drop caps, or headings (see Figure 4-50).

Figure 4-50
The Indent Here character

> How do I love thee? Let me count the ways: ¶
>
> 1) ▲This is the first one. I can't remember quite what it is, but I'm sure I mean well.¶
>
> 2) ▲Here's the second one. Hmmm. Can't quite ▲remember it, either, but now at the ▲very least I know exactly how to ↵ use the Indent Here character.
>
> *Arrows indicate positions of Indent Here characters*

H▼ow do I love thee? Well, don't you think that's a bit of an impertinent question? I mean, if I'd asked *you* that, you'd have every right to throw me out. I mean, such nerve . . .

▼"We, the curmudgeonly, having solemnly sworn to

Discretionary New Line. You can place the discretionary new line character, a Control-Return, within a word to suggest places to break the word if QuarkXPress needs to. For example, if you type an en dash and feel comfortable about the surrounding words breaking at a line end, you can type a Control-Return after the en dash (en dashes won't break without this). If QuarkXPress determines that it needs to break the line at this point, it does. If it doesn't need to break the line there, it doesn't break it (and the character, being invisible, has no other effect on your text). Figure 4-51 shows an example of this character in action.

Figure 4-51
The discretionary new-line character

Whilst riding the
Schenectady–to–Albany Express,
the train ran out of room.

En dashes in the text cause the line to break.

Whilst riding the Schenectady–to–
Albany Express, the train ran out of

Discretionary new line character here allows the line to break differently.

Discretionary hyphen. The discretionary hyphen character (Control-Hyphen) acts in the same manner as the discretionary new line character, but if the line needs to break at that point, QuarkXPress adds a hyphen at the break. This is the only way to manually suggest hyphenation for a particular word.

Discretionary hyphens also play another role in QuarkXPress. If you place a discretionary hyphen before a word, that word will never hyphenate at the end of a line. In other words, the discretionary hyphen can also turn off hyphenation for a single word.

▼▼▼▼▼▼▼▼▼▼▼▼▼▼▼▼▼▼▼▼▼▼▼▼

Tip: Adding Hyphenation. When you need to add your own hyphenation to some text, don't go in and add regular hyphens. Why? What happens if the text has to reflow for some reason (like when you add a word)? All of a sudden you have hyphens scattered throughout your text (see Figure 4-52). Instead, use discretionary hyphens (Control-Hyphen). These turn into hyphens at the ends of lines if they need to, but "disappear" when they're not needed (even Find/Change ignores the character).

▼▼▼▼▼▼▼▼▼▼▼▼▼▼▼▼▼▼▼▼▼▼▼▼

Nonbreaking hyphen. You will probably come upon a word that should be hyphenated, but shouldn't be broken at the end of a line. A nonbreaking hyphen is placed within text by typing Control-Shift-Hyphen.

Nonbreaking space. A nonbreaking space looks just like a normal space character. However, it will never break at the end of a

Figure 4-51
Reflowed hyphens

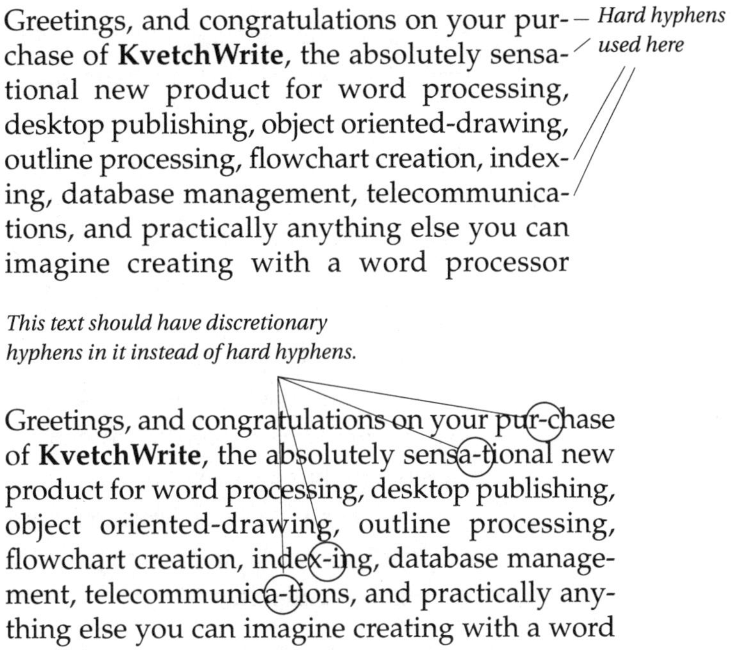

Greetings, and congratulations on your purchase of **KvetchWrite**, the absolutely sensational new product for word processing, desktop publishing, object oriented-drawing, outline processing, flowchart creation, indexing, database management, telecommunications, and practically anything else you can imagine creating with a word processor

— Hard hyphens used here

This text should have discretionary hyphens in it instead of hard hyphens.

Greetings, and congratulations on your pur-chase of **KvetchWrite**, the absolutely sensa-tional new product for word processing, desktop publishing, object oriented-drawing, outline processing, flowchart creation, index-ing, database manage-ment, telecommunica-tions, and practically any-thing else you can imagine creating with a word

line. A great use for this is in company names that include spaces, but shouldn't be broken over several lines (unless absolutely necessary).

New Column and New Box. If your text box contains multiple columns or is linked to other text boxes, you can use the New Column and New Box characters to force text to jump from one column or text box to the next. Typing Enter from your keyboard's numeric key pad forces a text jump to the next column. If the character is placed in the last (or only) column of a text box, it will force a jump to the next linked text box. Otherwise, typing Shift-Enter (keypad) forces a jump to the next linked text box.

En space. As we mentioned earlier in the chapter, an en is half an em, which—to QuarkXPress—equals the width of two zeros. With a quick calculation we find that an en space must equal the width of one zero. Typing Control-Shift-6 results in an en space, which acts just like a space character. Control-Alt-Shift-6 gives you an en space that doesn't break at the end of a line. Note that because of the way QuarkXPress defines an en, an en space is rarely the same width as an en dash.

Flex space. This character's default width is half an en space, but as we saw in the Typographic Preferences section earlier in the chapter, you can adjust its width in the Typographic Preferences dialog box.

Page numbers. QuarkXPress lets you use three characters to display page numbering (see Table 4-7). As we noted in Chapter 2, *Document Construction*, these characters are not only page-dependent, but also text box-dependent. For example, you can place a text box with the Next Text Box character (Control-4) on top of a linked text box, and the page number registers the link of the text box under it.

Table 4-7
Page numbering characters

Type...	To get the page number of...
Control-2	The previous text box
Control-3	The current text box
Control-4	The next text box

Punctuation and Symbols

A typographer shouldn't feel limited using Windows. The typefaces from the major vendors (Adobe, Bitstream, Monotype, and so on) are loaded with the characters you need to create excellent type, including proper quotation marks, ligatures, and em dashes. If you aren't already a typographer, you'll want to pay careful attention to the tips and examples we show. Using some simple techniques may make the difference between a piece that looks like it was desktop published (in the worst sense of the phrase) and a piece that is professional.

We can't discuss every special character that appears in a font, but we'll hit on a few of the important ones. Table 4-8 shows how to type each of these, plus a good number of additional characters; Appendix C, *ANSI Codes*, describes even more.

Table 4-8
Special punctuation and symbols in most fonts

Name	Looks like	Keys to press
Opening double quote	"	Alt-Shift-[
Closing double quote	"	Alt-Shift-]
Opening single quote	'	Alt-[
Closing single quote	'	Alt-]
Em dash	—	Control-Shift-=
Non-breaking em dash	—	Control-Alt-Shift-=
En dash	–	Control-=
Bullet	•	Alt-Shift-8
Copyright	©	Alt-Shift-c
Registered	®	Alt-Shift-r
Section	§	Alt-Shift-6
Paragraph	¶	Alt-Shift-7

Em and en dashes. An em dash, typed with an Control-Shift-=, should be used instead of double hyphens to indicate a pause or semi-parenthetical. For example, don't do this: "There entered villainous-looking scoundrels--eight of them." An em dash is named for its length (one em).

An en dash (Control-=) should generally be used for duration and distance, replacing the word "to"—as in "June 1–3," and "the New York–Philadelphia leg of the trip." It's half as long as an em dash, so it doesn't stand out quite as much.

Note that QuarkXPress will break a line after an em dash in wraparound text, but not an en dash. You can make a nonbreaking em dash by typing Control-Alt-Shift-=.

Ligatures. Ligatures are to type what diphthongs are to language. That is, they slur characters together by connecting them. Whereas many classic typefaces would contain up to ten ligatures, most typefaces for Windows include two basic ligatures, but alas, they're not included in the Windows character set. We publishers simply didn't howl loud enough to be heard by Microsoft. And the fact is, most people don't bother to use them, for some obscure reason. It's a pity, because they really can help a piece of text look great. Your best option for using ligatures for the "fi" and the "fl" combinations is to buy a font for which an expert set is available. Expert sets contain additional typographic characters, including "fi," "fl," "ffi," and other ligatures which you *can* access from Windows. Although using ligatures may make your type look nicer, they may make your life harder. For example, QuarkXPress for Windows doesn't presently understand words with ligatures in them; those words come up as "wrong" during spell checking, they hyphenate improperly, and are difficult to search for. Perhaps these problems will change with time, but for now, working with ligatures is a trade-off.

▼ ▼

Tip: Finding and Replacing Ligatures. We often hold off to the last minute to find the "fi" and "fl" combinations in our documents before replacing them with the proper ligatures. If you use ligatures, make sure you're careful about replacing them. Especially make sure you turn off "Ignore Case" in the Find/Change dialog box. If you don't, capitalized "Fi" or "Fl" combinations get changed, too! Remember that your search-and-replace strategy must also change the character combination's font to the expert set font containing the ligatures.

▼ ▼

NEW IN 3.3

See page 569

Quotation Marks. The first tip-off that someone is green behind the ears in desktop publishing is his or her use of straight quotes instead of proper "printer's quotes." Straight quotes, which are what you get when you press the ' and " keys, can be used for notation of measurements (inches and feet) or for special typographic effects (some fonts' straight quotes look great in headline type). Plus, many people who use the straight quotes as measurement symbols make them italic, more like the characters in the Symbol font. Printer's quotes, or curly quotes, should be used for English/American quotations.

Registration, copyright, and trademark. The registration, copyright, and trademark characters are found in the Alt-Shift-R and Alt-Shift-C keys, and the ANSI character code 0153. We have only one thing to say about using these characters: Be careful with your sizing and positioning. We recommend immediately assigning

Figure 4-53
Special symbols

KvetchWrite™ is a product of No Accounting For Taste, Eh?®
Documentation © Copyright 1990 No Class Productions.

Trademark and registration characters re-done as superior characters:

KvetchWrite!™ is a product of No Accounting For Taste, Eh?®
Documentation © Copyright 1990 No Class Productions.

Registration mark kerned +12 to give it a little room to breathe.

the superior type style to the character, then determining whether it should be kerned or not (see Figure 4-53).

▼▼▼▼▼▼▼▼▼▼▼▼▼▼▼▼▼▼▼▼▼▼▼▼

Tip: Character Mapping. Anyone who can remember every character in a font, including all special symbols and characters, is no one to borrow money from. We can never remember most of the characters we need, so we use the Windows Character Map accessory in the Accessories application group (see Figure 4-54). The Character Map accessory presents a table of characters for any font you choose. Simply double-click on the character you want (or click once and then click the Select button). The character appears in the Character to Copy box, along with any other characters you may select. To enter the selected characters into QuarkXPress, click the Copy button, switch to your QuarkXPress document, place your insertion point, and Paste (Control-V).

Figure 4-54
The Windows Character Map accessory

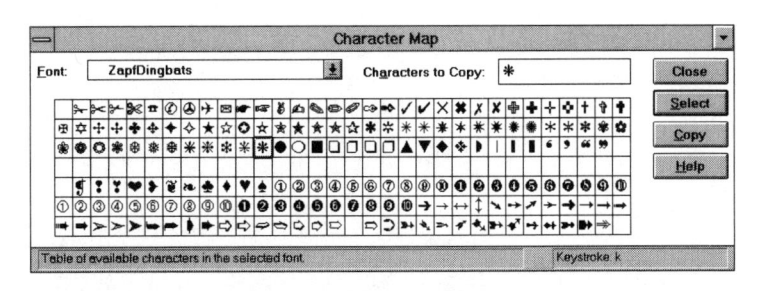

Another way to type in a character not found on your keyboard is to enter its Windows ANSI code. First, you need the code, which you can find in Appendix C, *ANSI Codes,* at the back of the this book, or in your Windows 3.1 manual. Notice that they're all 4-digit codes, each beginning with zero. To enter a code, hold down the Alt key while you key in the code on your keyboard's numeric keypad.

▼▼▼▼▼▼▼▼▼▼▼▼▼▼▼▼▼▼▼▼▼▼▼

Foreign Punctuation and Accents

Working in a foreign language is really a trip. Foreign languages have a different word for everything. Many foreign languages, such as French and Spanish, contain accented characters that are built into fonts from the major type vendors. For example, you can type without moving to some other obscure font. Either use Windows Character Map accessory to select and paste in the character or enter the character's Windows ANSI character code, as discussed above.

▼▼▼▼▼▼▼▼▼▼▼▼▼▼▼▼▼▼▼▼▼▼▼

NEW IN 3.3

See page 581

Tip: Get it Right for Overseas. We, in the United States, grew up with the ethnocentric viewpoint that the way we write and typeset is the way everybody does it. Not so. For example, double quotation marks are used in America where single quotation marks are used in Britain. In other European countries, our quotation marks are replaced with guillemets (« and »). The Spanish language sets a question or an exclamation point at both the beginning (upside down) and at the end of a sentence. Figure 4-55 shows examples of each of these styles.

Figure 4-55
Foreign punctuation

¡Mi llama se llama Spot! ——— *Spanish inverted exclamation and question marks*

¿Dónde está la casa de Pépe?

Il dit «La fromage, ça va bien?» ——— *European guillemots*

"He said, 'totally, dude' and walked off into the sunset."   'He said, "totally, dude" and walked off into the sunset.' ——— *American (left) and British (right) quotation marks*

Other languages, such as Hebrew, Farsi, Russian, and Greek, must be typed using a font specific to that language, and may require specialized software.

▼▼▼▼▼▼▼▼▼▼▼▼▼▼▼▼▼▼▼▼▼▼▼▼▼▼

Math Symbols and the Symbol Font

QuarkXPress is the wrong program in which to produce a mathematics textbook. You can use utilities such as MathType for Windows or Word for Windows' equation editor to help you create equations. But if you don't have either of these, you can still do a pretty good job in QuarkXPress, as long as you don't have to produce 2,000 different equations in a document. The key, besides the typesetting control, is the symbols themselves. Most typefaces come with a wide variety of built-in math symbols. Appendix C, *ANSI Codes*, provides a list of the most common ones and how to type them.

If you want to typeset an equation of any complexity (such as multiplication), you will want to learn about the Symbol font. The Symbol font is a Greek and math font that comes with Windows (in TrueType format), and is also built into most PostScript printers. It includes characters such as a true multiplication sign (×), which you can create by typing Alt + 0180 (on the numeric keypad). Or you can use the Windows Character Map accessory mentioned earlier to examine and enter the other characters in this typeface. (In a normal Windows font, like Times, the multiplication sign uses ANSI code 0215, division 0247.)

▼▼▼▼▼▼▼▼▼▼▼▼▼▼▼▼▼▼▼▼▼▼▼▼▼▼

Tip: One-stroke, One-character Font Change. QuarkXPress has so many keystrokes and shortcuts that we can never remember them all. Here are two that Bob uses all the time, but David always forgets about: typing Control-Shift-Q sets the next character you type in the Symbol font and typing Control-Shift-Z sets it in Zapf Dingbats. After you type the character, QuarkXPress automatically reverts back to the typeface you were in.

▼▼▼▼▼▼▼▼▼▼▼▼▼▼▼▼▼▼▼▼▼▼▼▼▼▼

Dingbats

Letters, numbers, and symbols do not a funky design make. Often you need Dingbats. Dingbats, or pi fonts, are collections of interesting and useful shapes, pictures, graphics, and so on. The most popular desktop-publishing dingbat font by far is Zapf Dingbats, which is included in almost all PostScript laser printers. Appendix C, *ANSI Codes*, shows a listing of the Zapf Dingbats typeface and how to type them.

Other examples of dingbat or pi fonts are Carta, Morbats, and Pi (see Figure 4-56 for some examples of Carta).

Figure 4-56
Some other dingbats

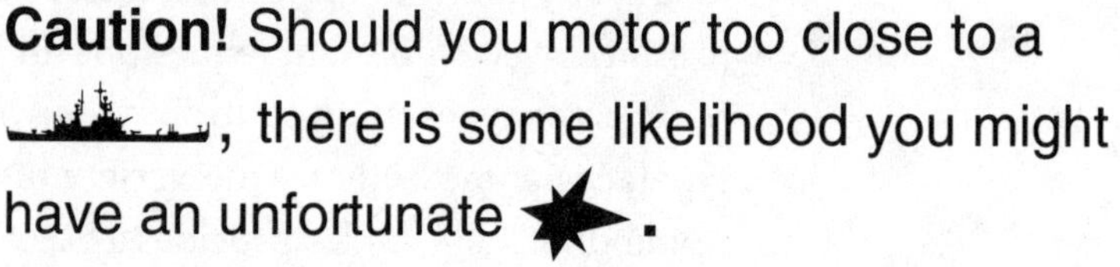

Caution! Should you motor too close to a ⛴, there is some likelihood you might have an unfortunate ✹.

Two symbols from the Carta font.

You can use these fonts for fun, but you'll more likely want to use them in a functional way. Most people use them for bullets (those round Alt-Shift-8 bullets get tiring to look at pretty quickly). David's favorite use for this function is the lowercase "v" from Zapf Dingbats (❖).

You can also use these characters as graphics on your page. Don't forget you can shade and color type to act as a background or foreground graphic.

▼ ▼

Tip: Ballot Boxes and Custom Dingbats. Up until now, the best way to create blank "ballot" boxes has been to type either a Zapf Dingbats lowercase "n" and set it to outline style or use the TrueType Wingdings font that comes with Windows. (Wingdings has an assortment of ballot boxes, including a checked-off one. You can even convert TrueType Dingdings to Type 1 format, as we discussed earlier.) The problem with the first method is that imagesetting the outline often results in a hairline that is too thin to reproduce well. The only problem with the second method is that it costs something to convert it. Nonetheless, QuarkXPress gives us a better option.

1. Create a picture box of any size.
2. Give the picture box a border frame (Control-B); we like to use .5 points.
3. Using the Item tool, cut the box to the Windows Clipboard.
4. Using the Content tool, select where in the text you want the box to go, and then paste the box in.
5. Resize it to suit your needs.

You can make box characters this way, as well as any polygon, or anything else you can create within the application. Also, by importing a graphic into the picture box before you cut and paste it, you can create your own custom dingbats (see Figure 4-58).

Figure 4-58
Custom dingbats

And re*mem*ber! 👷 The *"cornier"* your Presentation, the less likely it is to be *Taken Seriously!*

Custom dingbat created by placing an EPS (Encapsulated PostScript) file within an anchored picture box. Picture box has been resized, and its baseline shifted, until the block of text looked appropriately corny.

☐ *Ballot box made with an outlined Zapf Dingbat ("n")*

☐ *Ballot box made with an anchored (square) picture box having a 0.5-pt. frame.*

▼▼▼▼▼▼▼▼▼▼▼▼▼▼▼▼▼▼▼▼▼▼▼▼▼▼▼

Mismatched Character Sets

The letter *"T"* you enter into your word processor remains a *"T"* when you move the text into QuarkXPress. That's because most of the characters you see on your keyboard use standard character identification codes. All computer characters are saved as codes, and most systems use ASCII (American Standard Code for Information Interchange) for these common keyboard characters. ASCII uses 128 codes (0-127, requiring seven bits of information). The letter "A" uses code 65, for example, and the $ symbol uses code 36, in almost every program.

This poses a problem for publishing types, because there's no additional room for special typographic characters among those 128 codes. Fortunately, since PCs, Macs, and other systems use 8 bits, not just 7, to code characters, we actually have 256 possible character codes. Although people often refer to the entire set of 256 codes as "ASCII," only the first 128 are standard ASCII.

To add the extra characters, individual vendors have developed or adopted new character sets that assign the extra foreign-language, graphics, or typographic characters to the codes above 127. Naturally, they all do it differently, so that the same code doesn't usually produce the same character when you transfer a document between software applications or between different computer systems. The extended character set of Word Perfect for DOS, for example, doesn't match the Windows ANSI character set, nor does the Macintosh character set. As a result, fl ligatures, for example, simply disappear or turn into bullets when text containing such characters are imported into a Windows program (which lacks them) or when you're opening a Macintosh QuarkXPress document in the Windows version. QuarkXPress and other programs attempt to "remap" these extended ASCII characters in order to fix up the mismatch, but we've never seen a program that does it perfectly.

For short documents it's usually quicker to just manually reenter the en dash, em dash, quotation mark, trademark symbol, or whatever characters lost their way in the transfer. In some cases, a simple find-and-change operation can replace the incorrect character for the right one, provided that the "incorrect" character isn't used in other contexts within the text. For ambiguous character set mismatches in long documents, Bob has occasionally gone back to the original document and tagged some of the problem characters. All instances of the trademark symbol, for example, can be changed into a standard ASCII tag, like @T. Once transferred into QuarkXPress, you can then use find and change to substitute the trademark symbol for @T.

One possible solution to this chronic character mismatch problem lies with UNICODE, an international standard character set that codes characters in 16 bits instead of 8, resulting in 65,000 character codes compared to the current 256. With that kind of room, each character has a unique ID to settle into for all time; no need to shuffle them around according to a vendor's whim. Microsoft is building UNICODE into Windows NT, an advanced multitasking operating system. However, there are still problems: even UNICODE may not handle ligatures properly!

Typographic Special Effects

QuarkXPress is not a special-effects program, such as Adobe TypeAlign or Bitstream Makeup. But this doesn't mean that it can't give you the power to create many exciting effects with your type. In this section, we're going to look at a few of the possibilities, like drop caps, rotated text, shadowed type, and type as a picture. But we can't cover everything that you can do. This, especially, is an area in which to play around.

Chapter 7, *Where Text Meets Graphics*, covers a few other special effects that you can create using QuarkXPress, such as text runaround.

Fractions

Desktop publishing isn't so young that it doesn't have some hallowed traditions. One of the most hallowed is groaning in pain at the mention of creating fractions. But as with most traditions, you shouldn't let that frighten you. The "fraction problem" in desktop publishing arises because most Windows fonts do not come with a large enough set of prebuilt fraction characters. The ½, ¼, and ¾ *are* included in the Windows character set (ANSI codes 0189, 0188, and 0190, respectively), however, and you can enter them via the Windows Character Map or via Windows ANSI codes, as discussed earlier.

You can create your own fractions five different ways. Let's take a look at each of these and discuss why you'd want to use some and avoid others.

Pseudo-fractions. You can create pseudo-fractions by just typing in numbers separated by a slash. Let's be frank: They look awful and are considered bad form. But in some cases, such as simple word-processed documents or manuscript text, they're perfectly acceptable. Opinion varies on how best to type these characters, especially when you have a fraction following a number. We generally like to add a hyphen between a number and its fraction. For example, one and one half would be typed "1-1/2."

Don't try to use the "fraction bar" character instead of the regular slash for this kind of fraction. It almost always bumps into the second number and looks *shmatta* (like junk).

Proper fractions. You can create proper fractions—such as 1/8, 3/16, or 29/32— by applying specific character-level formatting to each character in the fraction. The following example shows you how.

1. Type the pseudo-fraction, such as 3/8. In this case, you should use the fraction bar character (Alt-0164 on the numeric keypad) rather than the normal slash character.

2. Select the numerator—in this case, the 3—and set it to "Superior."

3. Select the denominator—in this case, the 8—and change its size to match the numerator. You can figure out the size by checking the Superior settings in the Typographic Preferences dialog box. For example, at the default Superior settings of 50 percent, you would need to change a 12-point denominator to 6 points.

4. Kern the fractions as desired. The spaces between the numerator and the fraction bar, and the fraction bar and the denominator, almost always need to be tightened up.

You can change the size of the numerator by changing the Superior settings in the Typographic Preferences dialog box. But remember to reset your denominator to the proper point size. Differently sized numbers in a fraction look very weird.

When a proper fraction follows a number, you probably don't want any sort of hyphen or even a space (see Figure 4-59).

Figure 4-59
Fractions

A pseudo-fraction

They tell me getting there is 3/8 of the fun.

A pseudo-fraction, followed by one created via the method noted in the text (see "Proper Fractions")

I went to see *8-1/2* but only stayed for ¾ of it.

A real fraction from the typeface.

About ¼ of the time, I won't even give him a dime.

Stacked fractions. QuarkXPress also lets you create stacked fractions, such as ¼ and ¾. Here's a quick formula for making them.

1. Type the numerator and the denominator, separated by an underline (Shift-Hyphen).

2. Change the point size of these three characters to 40 percent of the original size. For example, 12-point type gets changed to 4.8-point type.

3. Select the numerator and the underline and apply a baseline shift equal to the point size (40 percent of the original).

4. Leave the numerator and underline highlighted and apply -90 units of tracking.

5. At your discretion, apply extra kerning between the characters to achieve a more precise look. You may want to zoom to 400% or print a test sheet.

You may need to adjust the numbers we provide for different typefaces and number combinations. Note that this method of creating stacked fractions works only when both numbers are single digits.

Fonts and utilities. Some fonts, such as EmDash's Fraction Fonts, consist entirely of fractions. Usually, these fonts are set in Times or Helvetica, so unless you're using those typefaces, they won't perfectly match your text.

You can also create your own fraction fonts with a utility program such as Fontographer, Publisher's Type Foundry, Font-Monger or even the CorelDRAW draw program in conjunction with its WFN BOSS utility. This strategy allows you to use any font that you're already using to generate custom fraction characters.

Initial Caps

Initial caps are enlarged characters at the start of a paragraph. Initial caps lend a dramatic effect to chapter or section openings. There are four basic types of initial caps: raised, dropped, hanging, and contoured. Each of these styles is fairly easy to create with QuarkXPress' automatic drop caps and the Indent Here character (Control-\).

Let's look at several initial caps to see how they are made.

Standard raised caps. Raised caps can be created as simply as enlarging the first letter of the paragraph (see Figure 4-60). It's important to use absolute leading, not Auto, when creating standard raised caps. If you don't, the first paragraph's leading gets thrown way off.

Figure 4-60
Standard raised caps

Unaccustomed as I am to public speaking . . . but that never did prevent me from running off endlessly at the mouth . . . you, sir! Stop that hideous snoring! But I digress . . .

14-pt. copy with a 30-pt. cap

Hung raised caps. A spin-off of the standard raised cap is the hung raised cap (see Figure 4-61). You can hang the letter "off the side

Figure 4-61
Hung raised caps

Unaccustomed as I am to public speaking . . . but that never did prevent me from running off endlessly at the mouth . . . you, sir! Stop that hideous snoring! But I digress . . .

14 pt. copy with a 30 pt. cap. Indent Here character has been placed to the immediate right of the raised cap.

of the column" by placing an Indent Here character after it or by creating a hanging indent with indents and tabs. The rest of the text block's lines indent up to that point.

Standard drop caps. QuarkXPress includes a feature that lets you make drop caps quickly and painlessly. The Drop Caps control is located in the Paragraph Formats dialog box (see Figure 4-62). To create a drop cap in a paragraph, just place the text cursor in the paragraph and enable "Drop Caps" by clicking in its check box. You can then modify two parameters for this feature: "Character Count" and "Line Count."

Figure 4-62
Standard drop caps

Let it never be said that the Koala tea of Moishe is not strained. Should this be said, it is entirely possible that the very fabric of civilization would fall utterly into the hands of the

Note what happens in the Measurements palette when you place the cursor at the very beginning of such a text box or select (highlight) the drop cap. If you call up the "Font Size" dialog, it will also show "100%".

The character count is the number of characters that are made to drop. The line count is the number of lines that they drop. For example, specifying "3" in "Character Count" and "4" in "Line Count" would make the first three characters of the paragraph large enough to drop four lines down. You don't have to worry about sizing the character, aligning it, or specifying the space between the drop cap and the rest of the text. In this example, the baseline of the drop cap aligns with the fourth line down, and the ascent of the drop cap aligns with the first line's ascent. Note that some fonts have ascents that are taller than their capital letters. This may make the process slightly more difficult, depending on the effect you're trying to achieve.

Note that you can change the amount of space between the initial cap and the text that is flowing around it by kerning the space directly after the drop cap character.

Hanging drop caps. This effect is achieved the same way as the hanging raised caps: just place an Indent Here character (Control-\) directly after the dropped character (see Figure 4-63). You can adjust the spacing between the drop cap and the following text by adjusting the kerning value between the drop cap and the next character (in this case, the Indent Here character).

Figure 4-63
Hanging drop caps

3-line drop cap with indent-to-here character placed here, creating hanging drop cap.

L et it never be said that the Koala tea of Moishe is not strained. Should this be said, it is entirely possible that the very fabric of civilization would fall utterly into the hands

Scaled drop caps. You have one hidden feature on drop cap characters and drop cap characters only: percentage scaling. After creating a standard drop cap (as described above), you can select the drop cap character(s) and change the point size to a percentage of the original drop cap size. For example, Figure 4-64 shows a paragraph first with a standard drop cap, and then with the drop cap scaled to 150 percent. You can change the percentage of the drop cap character(s) to anything you want, and the baseline will always align with the Line Count line.

Anchored raised caps. Another way to make a raised cap is to create it in a separate text box, then anchor that box to the beginning of the paragraph (we discuss anchored text and picture boxes in Chapter 7, *Where Text Meets Graphics*). The raised cap in Figure 4-65 is

Figure 4-64
Scaled drop caps

The same, with the capital "L" enlarged to 150% of its normal size:

Let it never be said that the Koala tea of Moishe is not strained. Should this be said, it is entirely possible that the very fabric of civilization would fall utterly into the

The Measurements palette reflects the change — again as a percentage of the normal drop cap size (not in points).

actually a separate text box containing a large capital letter on a tinted background. The character is centered horizontally and vertically within the frame. We also applied other formatting to the initial cap, such as kerning and baseline shift.

Figure 4-65
Anchored raised caps

We fully recognize that the message "Now formatting your hard disk. Have an *exceedingly* nice day," appearing during the **KvetchPaint** installation, is a bit alarming. Rest assured that it is a harmless prank by one of our programmers — who is, you can also rest assured, no longer with us. As soon as we can break the encryption he used, we will certainly eliminate this silly

Anchored drop caps. After creating an anchored raised cap, you can make it "drop" by selecting "Ascent" in the Anchored Text Box Specifications dialog box (select the anchored box and type Control-M, or double-click on the anchored box). Figure 4-66 shows an example of this, along with an anchored drop cap that has been "hung."

Wraparound drop caps. When using letters such as "W" or "A," you may want to wrap the paragraph text block around the letter (see Figure 4-67). There is no way to do this using automatic features, but you can still do it manually, as follows:

Figure 4-66
Anchored drop caps

We fully recognize that the message "Now formatting your hard disk. Have an *exceedingly* nice day," appearing during the **KvetchPaint** installation, is a bit alarming. Rest assured that it is a harmless prank by one of our programmers — who is, you can also rest assured, no longer with us. As soon as we can break the encryption he used, we will certainly eliminate

Figure 4-67
Wraparound drop caps

As literally dozens screamed with the blood lust and *ennui* to which the Romans of those times were so often given, without fear an unrepenting Androgynous strode onto the filthy floor of the Desultorium, there to meet his fate before the sinister person of GLUTEUS MAXIMUS, vice-tonsil of Rome, one of the meanest guys ever to pack iron in the Big SPQR.

1. Copy the first letter of the paragraph into a new, smaller text box.

2. Size the initial letter approximately to fit the number of lines you want.

3. Set both the background and the runaround of your text box to "None."

4. Place your initial cap text box over your paragraph text box. The paragraph should not reflow if you've set "Runaround" to "None."

5. Draw a line or a polygon around the initial cap, creating a border where you want the text to wrap.

6. If you drew a line, change its shade to 0 (zero) percent.

7. Make sure the wraparound object is on top of the paragraph, but under the initial cap.

This is only one of many variations on a theme for creating wraparound drop caps. Another is to use an initial cap brought in from a draw or illustration program (as any sort of graphic file).

You can then use QuarkXPress's automatic runaround or manual runaround features to control the text runaround (we discuss text runaround in detail in Chapter 7, *Where Text Meets Graphics*).

Illuminated caps. We've just seen the use of graphics "disguised" as text. Figure 4-68 shows a graphic as text, but with no disguise at all. This fancy illuminated capital letter was found in an art book, scanned, and brought into a picture box as a TIFF image.

Figure 4-68
Illuminated caps

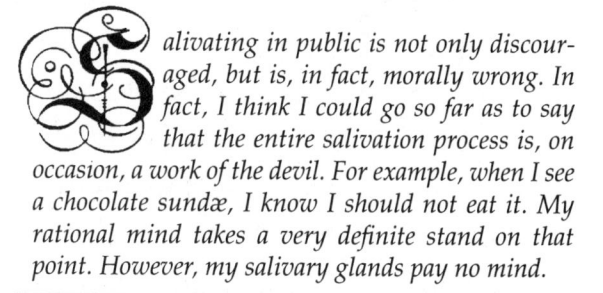

S alivating in public is not only discouraged, but is, in fact, morally wrong. In fact, I think I could go so far as to say that the entire salivation process is, on occasion, a work of the devil. For example, when I see a chocolate sundæ, I know I should not eat it. My rational mind takes a very definite stand on that point. However, my salivary glands pay no mind.

Mixed font caps. We've already cautioned you about using too many fonts on a page. But if there was ever a time to break the rules, it's with initial caps (see Figure 4-69). If you want your initial caps in a different font, simply change the font for those characters. However, note that when you change the initial cap's typeface, the character may not align properly with the rest of the text.

Figure 4-69
Mixed font initial caps

Zapf Chancery   Adobe Garamond

S conce, call you it? So you would leave battering, so I would rather have it a head. And you use these blows long, I must get a sconce for my head, and ensconce it too, or else I shall seek my wit in my shoulders. But, I pray, sir, why am I beaten?

Multiple initial caps. "Character Count" in the Drop Caps feature lets you drop up to eight letters in your paragraph. So a drop cap could be a drop word, if you like (see Figure 4-70).

Figure 4-70
Multiple initial caps

5-character drop cap. Horizontal scaling of 75%; font size changed from 100% to 87.5%

Comma scaled down to 75% of normal font size, not 87.5% (it's less obtrusive that way).

What, gone in chafing, and clapped to the doors? Now I am every way shut out for a very bench-whistler; neither shall I have entertainment here or at home. I were best to go try some other friends, and ask counsel what to do.

Playing with initial caps. Like we said, initial caps are great opportunities to play and come up with creative ideas. Can you re-create the initial cap examples in Figure 4-71?

Figure 4-71
More initial caps

A POOR MAN IS OBSERVED STARING in admiration at the large and ornate tombstone of the richest man in town. He shakes his head slowly and mutters, "Now, that's what I call living!"

Of course, the last time I went to one of those big banquets, I lost my wallet. I went up to the microphone and announced "Ladies and gentlemen, I have lost my wallet, with eight hundred dollars in it. Whoever finds it will get a reward of fifty dollars!"

Then a voice from the back of the room yelled out, "I'll give seventy-five!"

Shadowed Type Alternatives

Applying the Shadow type style to any range of selected type creates a generic shadow that cannot be customized. For example, you cannot change its thickness, shade, or offset. Although this is a perfectly nice shadow effect and is useful for many purposes, you may occasionally want more control over your shadows.

You can have total control over your shadows by using duplicate text boxes. Here's one way to do it (see Figure 4-72).

1. Create a text box with a line of text in it.

2. Duplicate the text box (Control-D).

3. Select the text within the second text box and modify it (change its color or tint, etc.).

4. Send the second text box to the back (choose "Send to Back" under the Item menu).

5. Change the Runaround of the first (top) box to "None." This automatically changes the background to None (transparent), as well.

You can then move the second text box around until you have it placed where you want it. You might also want to group the two text boxes together in order to move them as if they were one item.

Figure 4-72
Alternative shadows

Introducing

KvetchWRITE

"You've tried the best, now try the rest!"

THREE

Text Handling

The focus of this chapter—and this book, for that matter—is high-quality printed output. However, before you can get there you often spend lot of time staring at a computer screen. Let's look at two more functions that QuarkXPress offers for handling type: Text Greeking and Vector Above.

Text Greeking

After all this talk about making text look better on the screen and on your printed output, you probably need a relief from type. Let's talk about how to make type go away.

Designers have long worked with a concept known as greeking. Greeking is a method of drawing gray bars to represent blocks of text, rather than taking the time to image them all on the screen. QuarkXPress can greek text under a specific size limit, which you define in the General Preferences dialog box (Control-Y). The default value for text greeking is 7 points; you can set it from 2 to 720 points.

Unless you really want to see every character of every word at every size, there's hardly any reason to turn off text greeking. However, depending on your page design, you may want to adjust the Greek Below values at different times.

Tip: Checking Your Layout. When we need to get an idea of how a page's design and balance is looking, we often set our minimum text greeking size to a size large enough to include everything on our page, except headlines or display type. This way we can see the page itself without being bothered by either the text redraw or the particulars in the text.

Vector Above

Maybe it's because we're at the end of a very long chapter; or maybe it's because we think there are parts of Windows (especially parts that are left over from earlier versions of the operating system) that should just disappear. But whatever the case, we feel pretty strongly about a certain feature in QuarkXPress called *Vector Above*. This feature is a simple option in the General Preferences dialog box. It lets you tell Windows when you want any bitmapped fonts you're working with to automatically switch over to a standard outline (vector) font. For example, let's say you're working with some bitmapped font that you found on some bulletin board system somewhere. There's no printer font for the font, just the bitmapped screen font. And let's say you have Vector Above set to 36 points. If you select some text, set it to that bitmapped typeface, and then set it to over 36 points, QuarkXPress automatically replaces the bitmapped font with some outline font.

If we really cared about this feature, we'd dig deep to discover what outline font Windows and QuarkXPress uses. However, we don't care because we'd never use this feature. First, we don't typically use bitmapped fonts in QuarkXPress. Second, if we *do* use a bitmapped font, we want it to stay that font, not change into something else. Perhaps we're missing the point here; if you know why anyone would want to use this feature, please let us know. Meanwhile, we just leave it turned off (or set to a very high point size, such as 700 points). Remember, these sorts of general preferences can be set for a particular document, or—if you set them while no documents are open—for every new document you create.

Putting It Together

If you got through this entire chapter and are still not too bleary-eyed to read this, you must really be a QuarkXPress die-hard. After having learned about QuarkXPress's word-processing capabilities in the last chapter and what you can do to those words in this chapter, you're ready to move on to the theory and practice of style sheets and copy flow. You don't need to know everything that's in Chapter 5, *Copy Flow*, to work with type in QuarkXPress, but we think it's a good idea to learn it. There's working with type, and then there's working hard at type. We're trying to get your work to be as easy as possible, and that's what we cover in the next chapter.

CHAPTER 5

COPY FLOW

In the last chapter, you saw the beautiful things you can do with type in QuarkXPress. But a beautiful document isn't worth much if it isn't finished on time. Fortunately, QuarkXPress is also designed to help you format your document text and to make necessary changes quickly and accurately.

In the development of a publication, copy is almost never static. For any number of reasons, you may have to make drastic changes in the formatting or content of the copy (usually at or beyond the last minute). Your success in meeting deadlines (and getting paid) can often depend on how carefully you've anticipated such changes. If you don't plan from the very beginning to manage the flow of your document's copy, it will surely end up managing you, and in ways you won't appreciate.

Managing Copy

QuarkXPress has two very powerful tools for automating the formatting and management of your document's copy: Style Sheets and XPress Tags. Use these tools wisely, and you'll soon make your copy jump through hoops at the snap of your fingers (or the click of your mouse). Use them poorly, or not at all, and you'll be the one jumping through the hoops, probably at three in the morning before a major job is due. In this chapter we explain how to make the best use of these features. The key is learning to work smart.

Working Smart

Simply put, there are two ways to handle your copy in QuarkXPress: the dumb way and the smart way. What's the main difference between the two? Working the smart way, you make the computer do your work as much as possible. Working the dumb way, you take it upon yourself to do the kind of mindless, repetitive tasks computers were meant to do—in this case the repetitive formatting and reformatting of copy.

It takes a bit more time at first to set up a document to take advantage of QuarkXPress's automation, but it is well worth it if you ever need to make even the simplest document-wide text-formatting change. Of course, if you're the type of person who always gets everything right the first time, you'll never, ever need to change any formatting once you've entered it, so you may not find this chapter of much use. The rest of you should pay careful attention.

The dumb way. The dumb way to format your copy is the way you most likely learned earliest; by selecting text and directly applying various characteristics. Should a paragraph be centered? Go to the Style menu and center it. Need to change the typeface? Go to the Font menu and do it.

"What's so dumb about that?" you may ask. It's not that there's anything inherently wrong with applying formatting directly to your copy; it's just that by doing so, you doom yourself to performing the same selections and modifications over and over again whenever another text element needs the same formatting, and whenever you need to make major changes to your document. For instance, if the paragraphs you centered need to be flush left, you must select and change each paragraph individually.

Another way of working dumb is to carefully format your text in QuarkXPress, and then, when heavy editing is required, export the copy to a word processor, edit it, then re-import it into QuarkXPress. Suddenly you may notice that you've lost most of your special QuarkXPress formatting (such as horizontal scaling, superior characters, kerning, etc.), and it's time for another long, painstaking formatting pass through your document.

The smart way. The smart way to handle your copy is to take the time to be lazy. Make QuarkXPress's features work for you. Whenever you create a new paragraph format, for any reason at all, assign a style to the format. The next time you need to make another such paragraph, you can simply apply the appropriate style, and QuarkXPress will instantly apply the correct formatting.

If you've been religious about creating and applying styles for all of your document's paragraphs, you can then make sweeping formatting changes throughout your document with only a few keystrokes. Also, be sure to use XPress Tags in exporting your text. This will keep your formatting information intact, even if you must send stories out to be edited in a Macintosh or DOS program. The following sections reveal the best ways to work smart with QuarkXPress.

Style Sheets—What They Are, and Why You Need Them

A Style Sheet is simply the name QuarkXPress gives to a collection of formatting attributes applied to a paragraph. For every paragraph in your document, QuarkXPress keeps track of the information you've specified for fonts, type style and size, leading, alignment, indents, and much more.

Warning: A Style Is a Style Sheet Is a Style

For some reason, Quark decided not to follow accepted terminology when it named its Style Sheet feature. It is commonly understood in desktop publishing that the group of formatting attributes for a particular type of paragraph is called a *style*. Furthermore, the list of all the styles in a document is called a *style sheet*. In QuarkXPress, each paragraph has its own Style Sheet and the collection of these is simply referred to as the Style

Sheets. Generally, we'll use the more commonly accepted terminology, since the usual distinction between style sheets and styles is a useful one. However, when you see the term Style Sheet with initial caps, we are referring to that particular feature of QuarkXPress.

And Now, Back to the Show

Whether you've actually used style sheets before or not, you already think in terms of styles as you create a document. Every time you decide that a particular paragraph needs to be formatted differently from those around it—even if the change is something as simple as centering a heading—you're thinking in styles.

QuarkXPress's Style Sheets let you assign a unique name to any group of formatting attributes for a particular type of paragraph. You can create a style name for titles, for different levels of subheads, for footnotes, or for any type of paragraph. Once you've defined a style, you can quickly apply it, with all its attributes, to any paragraph, saving yourself many trips to QuarkXPress's Style menu.

Even better, whenever you make a change to a particular attribute within a style, those changes are automatically applied to every paragraph that's tagged with that style. So if you've had the foresight to define and use styles conscientiously when creating your documents, you won't be fazed by last-minute requests to change the size, font, and alignment of every picture caption in a book. Because you've had the foresight to create a "caption" style that is applied to every caption in your book, you need only change the attributes of that style to change the style of every caption. Otherwise, you're in for a long, tedious stretch of hunting down and manually changing every caption in your book.

Tagging

We've mentioned that you must give a style a name. Another word for a style name is a *tag*. Here's how it works: If you know that you'll need two kinds of subheads in your document, you can make styles named, for example, SubheadA and SubheadB, and apply them to the appropriate paragraphs. The process is called *tagging*. It's important to remember that there's a difference between a style's name (its tag), and a style's formatting. Once you've tagged a paragraph with a style, you can change the style's formatting to anything you like.

As you work on a document, be sure to tag each paragraph by clicking in it with the Content tool and choosing a style from the Style Sheets menu (see Figure 5-1). After a paragraph is tagged, you can easily change its appearance by modifying its style. Therefore, when you begin to work on a document, it's not really that important what formatting is associated with each style, since you can always change the formatting later. Once you've tagged all the paragraphs in your text, you can experiment by modifying the formatting of their styles at your leisure.

Figure 5-1
The Style Sheets menu and palette

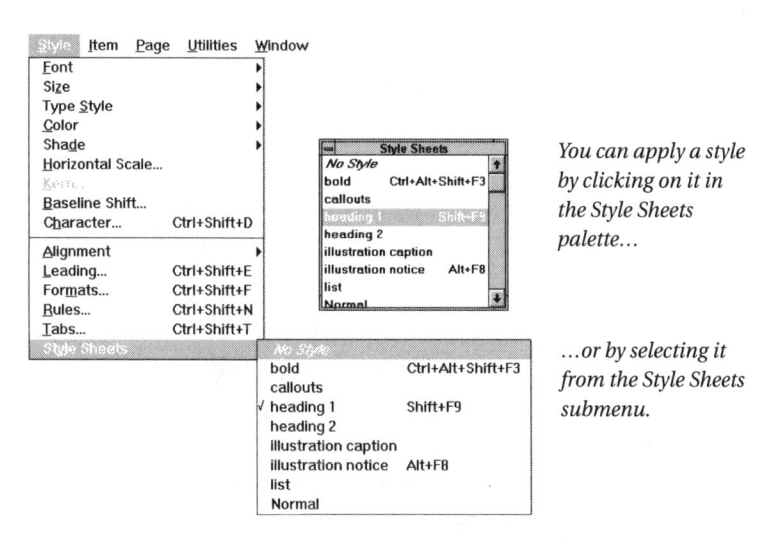

You can apply a style by clicking on it in the Style Sheets palette...

...or by selecting it from the Style Sheets submenu.

Local Formatting Versus Style Formatting

NEW IN 3.3

See page 584

Another point to remember about QuarkXPress styles is that the character formatting contained in a style is applied to an entire paragraph. If the style calls for Times Roman, the entire paragraph will be in Times Roman. You can override the style's font for specific text within the paragraph. This "local" or "hard" formatting will remain, even if you apply a different font to the paragraph's style or apply a different style to the paragraph. (But if a paragraph has the QuarkXPress option No Style applied to it, all local formatting will be wiped out when you apply a style to it. See "Normal Style and No Style," later in this chapter.)

Local formatting is the only way to format *part* of a paragraph; QuarkXPress doesn't have styles that can be applied to selected characters. Some programs, such as FrameMaker and the DOS version of Microsoft Word, have both paragraph and character styles. This can be extremely useful for applying specific formatting to elements within a paragraph, such as bold, run-in heads at the beginning of a paragraph.

Unfortunately, there is one instance in which QuarkXPress will lose track of local formatting. If you apply a style to a paragraph that contains the same formatting information as you've used in local formatting and then apply a style with different formatting, your original local formatting will be lost.

For instance, assume you have a paragraph whose style calls for plain text (that is, neither bold nor italic) and have made a few words in the paragraph bold. Now you apply a style that makes all of the text bold, and then apply a style that isn't bold. All of the text in the paragraph will no longer be bold, including the text to which you originally applied the bold formatting. This doesn't just apply to making text bold or italic, but to any local formatting that can also belong to a style.

It seems that QuarkXPress simply says to itself, "Aha, this text which once contained local formatting should now have the same formatting as all of the text around it. So I don't have to remember the local formatting anymore." And it doesn't (see Figure 5-2).

Defining Styles

To create or edit styles, use the Style Sheets command on the Edit menu. This calls up the Style Sheets dialog box (see Figure 5-3). If you call up this dialog box when a document is open, you'll see all the styles for that document. You can use this dialog box to create, edit, and delete styles, and, by using the Append button, import the style sheet of another QuarkXPress document. If you use this dialog box with no open documents, you'll be able to edit and add to QuarkXPress's default style sheet list, which will be automatically included in all new documents.

COPY FLOW   **265**

Figure 5-2
How QuarkXPress loses local formatting

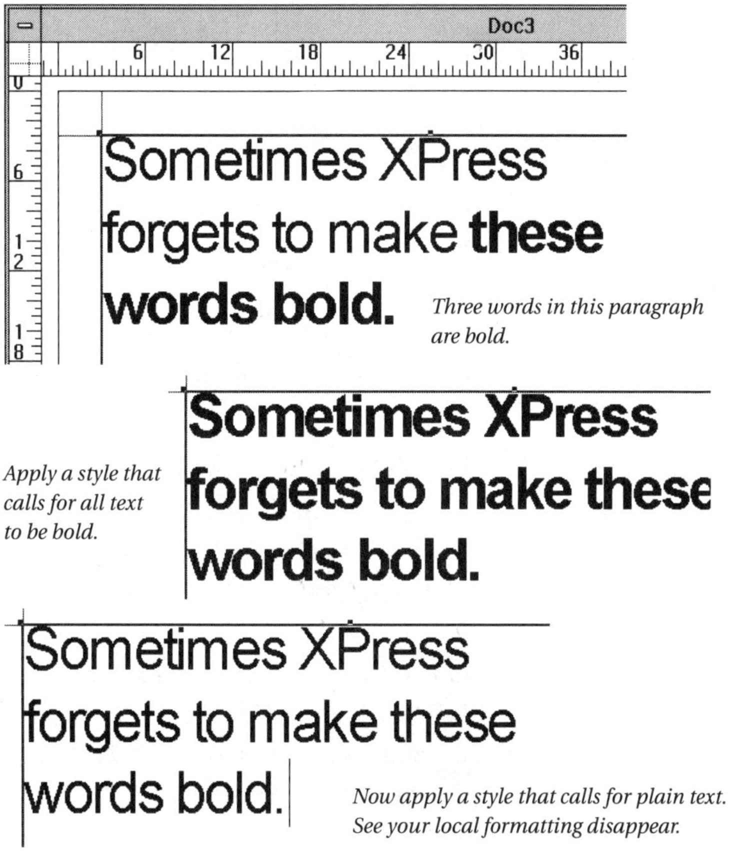

Sometimes XPress forgets to make **these words bold.** *Three words in this paragraph are bold.*

Apply a style that calls for all text to be bold.

Sometimes XPress forgets to make these words bold.

Sometimes XPress forgets to make these words bold. *Now apply a style that calls for plain text. See your local formatting disappear.*

Figure 5-3
The Style Sheets dialog box

Style Sheets for Doc1

Style Sheet:
callouts
heading 1
heading 2
illustration notice
list
math stuff
Normal

New | Append
Edit
Duplicate | Save
Delete | Cancel

(Symbol) (10 pt) (+Bold) (Red) (Shade: 100%) (Track Amount: 10) (Horiz. Scale: 100%)
(Alignment: Left) (No Drop Cap) (Left Indent: 2p) (First Line: -1p) (Right Indent: 0p)
(Leading: 14 pt) (Space Before: 0p) (Space After: 0p)

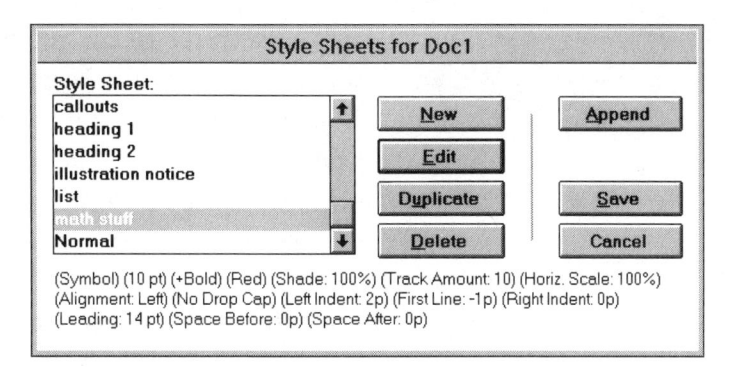

Creating a New Style

NEW IN 3.3

See page 584

To create a new style sheet, click the New button in the Style Sheets dialog box. The Edit Style Sheet dialog box appears (see Figure 5-4). In the Name field, enter the name of the new style you want to create. If you want to define a keystroke combination that will automatically apply the style, click in the Keyboard

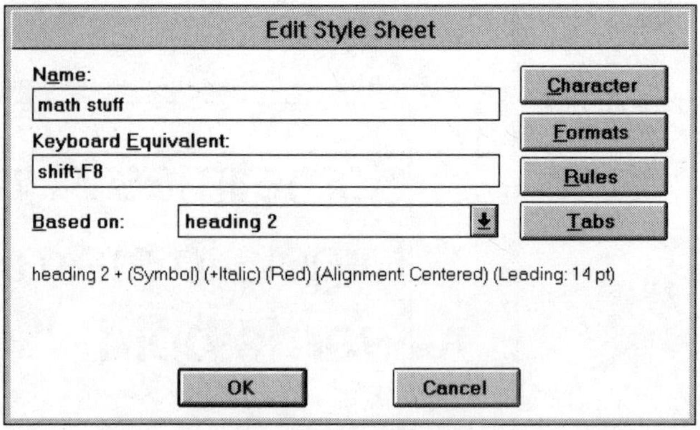

Figure 5-4
The Edit Style Sheet dialog box

[Edit Style Sheet dialog box showing:
Name: math stuff
Keyboard Equivalent: shift-F8
Based on: heading 2
heading 2 + (Symbol) (+Italic) (Red) (Alignment: Centered) (Leading: 14 pt)
Buttons: Character, Formats, Rules, Tabs, OK, Cancel]

Equivalent field and press the key combination you want. It's often a good idea to use a keypad key in combination with the Control key, because keystrokes defined this way won't conflict with any other QuarkXPress or Windows key commands.

▼▼▼▼▼▼▼▼▼▼▼▼▼▼▼▼▼▼▼▼▼▼▼▼▼

Tip: Keys You Can Use for Style Shortcuts. You can use only certain keys for applying styles—the function keys (F1 through F12) and the numbers on the numeric keypad. In combination with the Control, Shift, and Alt keys, which provides for a lot of shortcuts. The F1 key is reserved for the Help command, and the F10 key is reserved for selecting the QuarkXPress menu bar for keystroke (instead of mouse) menu selection. You should avoid using the Alt key in combination with the keypad, since Windows also uses those combinations to let you enter characters via Windows ANSI codes (see Appendix C, *ANSI Codes*, and "Punctuation and Symbols" in Chapter 4, *Type and Typography*). Also, some keystrokes that include the Alt key are reserved for other things (Alt-F4 is reserved, and so on). We suggest you just forget about the Alt key when choosing keystrokes for style sheets.

There's no way to print a list of what keystrokes go with what styles (see "Tip: Printing Your Style Sheet"), so we just print a screen shot of the Style Sheets submenu and tape it to our wall. If you have a really long style sheet, you may have to take a couple of screen shots.

▼▼▼▼▼▼▼▼▼▼▼▼▼▼▼▼▼▼▼▼▼▼▼▼▼

Once you've named a style, you can define it by clicking the Character, Formats, Rules, or Tabs buttons. These buttons call up dialog boxes with the same names as those available from the Style menu for text. You can use these boxes to define your new style, just as you would to format any paragraph of text.

When you're finished defining the style, click OK, and you return to the Style Sheets dialog box. Click the Save button. Hold the mouse button down when you select "Style Sheets" under the Style menu, and you'll see your new style listed and ready to be applied. Or select the Show Style Sheets command from the view menu in order to display the Style Sheets palette.

Normal Style and No Style

Every QuarkXPress document has a default style—the Normal style. This is the style that is automatically applied to all of the text in a document if you don't specifically apply a style. You can edit the Normal style just like any other.

"No Style" is different. Applying "No Style" removes all style information from a paragraph. All of the formatting is then treated as local, hard formatting. Normally, local formatting doesn't change when you apply a style to a paragraph. However, if the paragraph has "No Style" applied to it, applying a style overrides all local formatting.

Appending Styles

The Append button in the Style Sheets dialog box (brought up by choosing "Style Sheets" from the Edit menu) lets you import styles from one QuarkXPress document into another. Clicking the Append button brings up a standard directory dialog box, which you can use to choose the file whose styles you want to import.

Another way to move styles from one QuarkXPress document to another is to copy text containing those styles. You can either use the Copy and Paste commands or simply drag a box containing the text from document to document.

It's important to remember that you can only import styles that don't have the same names as ones already used in your document. So if you already have a style named "Body Text" in a document, you can't import the Body Text style from another document. QuarkXPress simply ignores the styles with matching names and imports the styles whose names don't match any already in the document.

Furthermore, when you bring in text that has the same style names as existing styles, but different formatting, QuarkXPress does an odd thing. It brings in the text with its source formatting intact, but as local, hard formatting. The style name is still there, but it doesn't do you any good. You have to apply "No Style," then reapply the style, losing *all* local formatting in the process.

For example, let's assume that the Normal style in the original document calls for 12-point Helvetica, and the Normal style in the target document is set for 10-point Palatino. If you move text from the originating document to the target, any "Normal" text you bring over won't change to 10-point Palatino. It remains 12-point Helvetica (local, hard formatting). Even though these paragraphs are tagged with the Normal style, you have to re-apply the tag by applying "No Style" and then Normal again in order for the correct formatting to appear.

▼▼▼▼▼▼▼▼▼▼▼▼▼▼▼▼▼▼▼▼▼▼▼▼▼▼

Tip: Macro Styles. Style sheets are powerful, but we don't always find them accessible enough. So we've created macros using Windows Recorder or other Windows macro programs to automate two actions for which QuarkXPress doesn't provide keyboard shortcuts.

- Selecting "No Style" from the Style Sheet submenu.

- Opening the Style Sheets palette.

▼▼▼▼▼▼▼▼▼▼▼▼▼▼▼▼▼▼▼▼▼▼▼▼▼▼

Tip: Creating Styles by Example. Instead of using the Edit Style Sheet dialog box to define the format of a style, you can create a style based on an existing paragraph in your document (see Figure 5-5). This way you can format a paragraph just the way you want it, and then create a style that has all of those attributes.

To create a style based on an existing paragraph's formatting, position the insertion point anywhere in the paragraph, then create a new style. When you get to the Edit Style Sheet dialog

Figure 5-5
Creating a style by example

Place the insertion point in a paragraph.

Silicon Mirage

The art and science of virtual reality

When you click on the New button from the Style Sheets dialog box, you'll see an Edit Style Sheet dialog box listing all the attributes of the selected paragraph.

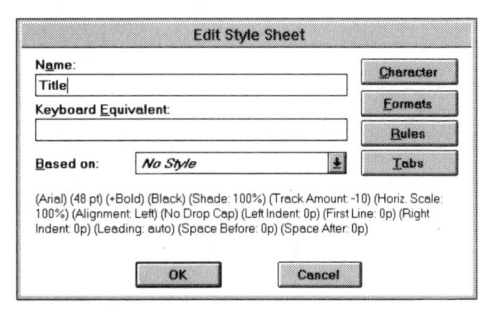

box, you'll see all of the formatting that's applied to the current paragraph listed at the bottom of the box. All you have to do is name the new style, click OK, and save your changes.

▼ ▼

Basing One Style on Another

A powerful feature of QuarkXPress's Style Sheets is the ability to base one style on another. By basing many styles on, say, the Normal style, you can quickly change many elements in your document by simply changing the Normal style.

For example, let's say you want all of your subheads to be the same as the Normal style, only in bold and larger type. By basing the subhead style on the Normal style you can ensure that every change you make to the Normal style is instantly reflected in the subhead style. If you change the Normal style's font from Helvetica to Franklin Gothic, the font of the subheads based on the Normal style automatically changes from Helvetica to Franklin Gothic as well. The subheads retain their larger size and boldness, however.

To base one style on another, use the pop-up Based On menu in the Edit Style Sheet dialog box to select the style upon which you want to base your new style (in this case, Normal). Next, use the buttons in the dialog box to change only those attributes you want to be different in the new style (in this case, increasing the type size and making it bold). Notice that the text at the bottom of the Edit Styles dialog box shows the style that your new style is based on, along with all the additional formatting you've applied to the new Style Sheet.

If you plan your style sheets carefully, you can use this based-on feature to create nested hierarchies of styles based upon one another, so that a simple change made to one style is applied to all of the styles that are based on it, and the styles that are based on those, ad infinitum. This "ripple effect" is a great time-saver, so it's well worth your while to carefully plan your styles to take greatest advantage of this effect.

▼▼▼▼▼▼▼▼▼▼▼▼▼▼▼▼▼▼▼▼▼▼▼▼▼

Tip: Copy Styles from One Paragraph to Another. In addition to using the Style Sheets menu and keyboard shortcuts to apply a style to a paragraph, you can also use a neat shortcut to copy formats from one paragraph to another. Click in the paragraph whose format you want to change. Then Shift-Alt-click on any other paragraph whose format you want to copy. Not only is the paragraph's style copied, but any local changes to the paragraph's formatting (margins, tabs, leading, etc.) are also applied to the destination paragraph. No local character formatting in the destination paragraph is changed.

▼▼▼▼▼▼▼▼▼▼▼▼▼▼▼▼▼▼▼▼▼▼▼▼▼▼▼▼▼

Style Palette

To save you from constantly having to open the Style menu for the Style Sheets list, you can apply, edit, and view style sheets on the fly by using the Style Sheets palette. The palette lists all the style sheets in your document (if you have lots of styles, you can make the palette larger or just scroll through them), along with their keyboard shortcuts if they have any.

The beauty of this floating palette is that you can put it right next to your text box while you work. To apply any style to a paragraph, just put the text cursor somewhere in that paragraph and click on the desired style in the palette. To apply No Style to a paragraph, just click on "No Style" in the palette. As you move through your text, the style sheet for each paragraph is highlighted in the Style Sheets palette; you can quickly see the styles that are applied. This is especially helpful if local formatting overrides styles or if you have two styles that are similar and you want to know if a paragraph is tagged with one or the other.

To edit a style, click on that style in the palette while holding down the Control key. This brings up the Style Sheets dialog box with the style highlighted. Just click Edit, or type Return or Enter to edit that style sheet.

▼▼▼▼▼▼▼▼▼▼▼▼▼▼▼▼▼▼▼▼▼▼▼▼

Tip: Creating New Styles. Note that because Control-clicking on a style in the Style Sheets palette brings you to the Style Sheets dialog box, you can quickly create a new style by clicking the New or Duplicate buttons instead of the Edit button. This is faster than selecting Style Sheets from the Edit menu.

▼▼▼▼▼▼▼▼▼▼▼▼▼▼▼▼▼▼▼▼▼▼▼▼

Tip: Totally Overriding Local Formatting. Any paragraph that has "No Style" applied to it loses all local formatting (including bold and italic) when it's tagged with another style. This, more often than not, is a pain in the butt and causes much confusion. However, there are some powerful uses for this feature, such as stripping out all local formatting that some dumbbell put in for no good reason. Always on the lookout for a faster way to do something, we were pleased to find that we could apply "No Style" to a paragraph and then apply a style sheet in one stroke by Shift-clicking on the style.

▼▼▼▼▼▼▼▼▼▼▼▼▼▼▼▼▼▼▼▼▼▼▼▼

Tip: Use Search and Replace to Fake Character Styles. Although QuarkXPress doesn't have character styles, it is possible to use the search-and-replace feature to achieve some of the functions of character styles. If you regularly use text with specific local formatting within your paragraphs—with a specific font, size, and weight—the Find/Change command can save you a lot of keystrokes. Use it to replace a unique, easily applied style (such as outline or shadow) with the more complex formatting you intend, which would require multiple keystrokes or trips to the Style menu (such as 12-point New Baskerville Bold).

1. In your word processor, assign a seldom-used character style, such as underline, outline, or shadow, to the text to which you want to apply your special local formatting.

2. Bring the text into QuarkXPress.

3. Select the Find/Change command from the Edit menu. Deselect the Ignore Attributes check box by clicking in it. Click the appropriate boxes to replace the style you originally applied with the new formatting you want.

4. Click the Change All button.

Unfortunately, you can't use this method to apply QuarkXPress's more sophisticated typographic controls, such as tracking or horizontal scaling.

▼▼▼▼▼▼▼▼▼▼▼▼▼▼▼▼▼▼▼▼▼▼▼▼▼▼▼

Tip: Start a Style at the Top. If you want a paragraph style that tells the paragraph to always start at the top of a column, you can define its style sheet to have a "Space Before" value as big as the column is tall. That is, if the column is 30 picas tall, just set the Space Before value for the style sheet to 30 picas.

▼▼▼▼▼▼▼▼▼▼▼▼▼▼▼▼▼▼▼▼▼▼▼▼▼▼▼

Combining Paragraphs For Run-in Heads

Another way to fake character styles—this time to create run-in heads—is to combine paragraphs. If you have two consecutive paragraphs with different text formats and you combine them by deleting the carriage return that separates them, the text within the new paragraph will retain the formatting of the paragraph it originally belonged to. For example, you could create a head using a paragraph style calling for 14-point Futura Bold, and follow it with a body paragraph whose style calls for 12-point Garamond. By deleting the return after the Futura Bold paragraph, you end up with the Futura Bold text as a run-in head for the body text set in Garamond.

Note that if you put some special character or series of characters at the end of heads that you want to be run-in, you can use the Find dialog box (Control-F) to remove the carriage returns. (Remember: \p is the code for carriage returns in the Find/Change dialog box.)

There are a few drawbacks to this paragraph combination trick, however. You must be aware that you're basically fooling QuarkXPress. When you combine two paragraphs, QuarkXPress applies all the settings for the first paragraph to the new, combined paragraph. QuarkXPress also applies the style for the first paragraph to the new paragraph. So in our example, QuarkXPress thinks that the 14-point Futura Bold is the default font for the entire new paragraph, even though part of it appears as 12-point Garamond. QuarkXPress doesn't consider the Garamond formatting to be local, hard formatting, and if you apply a new style to this paragraph, both the Futura and Garamond will be changed to the font called for in the new style.

Since the fake character styles created by this technique are rather fragile, you should probably not use this technique unless you're certain that you won't have to ever change the style that's applied to the combined paragraph.

Importing Text

New in 3.3

See page 576

An important part of controlling the flow of copy is getting your copy into QuarkXPress in the first place. You do this with the Get Text command in the File menu. In order to access this command, you must have the Content tool selected and a text box active. To bring text into the active text box, follow the steps below.

1. Position the insertion point where you want the text to be brought into the text box.

2. Choose "Get Text" from the File menu (Control-E).

3. When the Get Text dialog box appears (it looks very similar to a standard Windows directory dialog box), select

one of the files listed. It displays all files that are in a word-processing format that QuarkXPress can import.

4. You can either double-click the file you want, or single-click it to select the file and either press Return or click the Open button.

If you'd like QuarkXPress to automatically convert straight double and single quotes (" and ') to curly double and single quotes (", ", ', and '), and to convert double hyphens (--) to true em dashes (—), check the Convert Quotes box in the Get Text dialog box.

If you're importing a Microsoft Word file and want Quark-XPress to include the file's style sheets, check the Include Style Sheets box. Also, if you're importing an ASCII (text) file that uses XPress Tags to contain formatting and style sheet information, you must also be sure to check the Include Style Sheets box (more on XPress Tags later).

What Filters Are, and How To Use Them

QuarkXPress uses files called *filters* to contain the information that it uses to convert text to and from word-processing formats. The formats QuarkXPress can understand are Microsoft Word for Windows versions 1.x and 2.x, Windows Write, WordPerfect 5.1 and WordPerfect for Windows, Ami Pro 2.0, XyWrite 3.0 Plus, Rich Text Format (RTF), ASCII text, and ASCII text using XPress Tags. In order for QuarkXPress to understand these file formats, you must have the appropriate filter (in the form of a Quark XTension) in the same subdirectory with QuarkXPress. If you don't need a particular filter XTension, move it out of that subdirectory so the program will load faster.

When It Is Okay To Use QuarkXPress As Your Word Processor

As we saw in Chapter 3, *Word Processing*, QuarkXPress has very powerful word-processing features. Its search-and-replace function, in particular, is far more powerful than that found in many word processors. For small documents, you can easily dispense with the fairly standard desktop-publishing procedure of writing your text in a word processor and then importing it. Instead, you can simply use QuarkXPress to create your text as well as flow it into pages.

However, there is a pitfall. With medium-size and long documents that have long text chains flowing through complicated multipage layouts, writing and even heavy-duty editing can become very slow, even on a fast computer. QuarkXPress reflows its text almost every time a line wraps. If you're a fast typist, you may find yourself having to deliberately slow down to prevent characters you've typed from getting lost as they slowly make their way into QuarkXPress. If you run into this frustrating problem, you should consider exporting your text to a word processor, editing it there, and then re-importing it to QuarkXPress (see "Exporting Text," below).

What Word Processor to Use?

Although QuarkXPress can import formatted text from several word processors, it currently can correctly interpret only the style sheets of Microsoft Word files and files saved in RTF. Since style sheets are so important to the proper management of your copy, Word automatically becomes the best word processor for working with QuarkXPress. (Unless you decide to work exclusively with XPress Tags, which can be used, albeit awkwardly, by any word processor that can import and export ASCII files—that is to say, nearly all word processors).

Another plus for Word is that QuarkXPress will correctly import pictures contained in Word files as inline graphics.

How QuarkXPress Works with Word

Importing a Microsoft Word document into QuarkXPress may not go as smoothly as you hoped, however. Let's take a quick look at the three primary formatting areas and how QuarkXPress handles them with Word documents: character formatting, paragraph formatting, and style sheets.

Character formatting. QuarkXPress can import a great deal of Word's own formatting. Almost every character attribute available in Word can be carried over into QuarkXPress. QuarkXPress ignores the values you've entered for super- and subscripts; instead, it applies the values you've specified for them within your QuarkXPress document (in Typographic Preferences). One of the settings it doesn't seem to bring in is expanded and condensed type. Perhaps a later version of the filter will perform this properly.

Paragraph formatting. For paragraph formats, QuarkXPress brings in most available Word settings, except that only the top rule set for bordered paragraphs will be imported (though QuarkXPress does a good job of interpreting the correct size and weight of rules). QuarkXPress ignores any values you've set for space between rules and their paragraphs. Any of Word's attributes that can be applied to styles can be successfully imported as styles by QuarkXPress, with the exceptions noted above.

Style sheets. When you bring a Word document into QuarkXPress, and you've checked the Include Style Sheets box, QuarkXPress takes into its own Style Sheet every style you've *used* in the Word document, *not* every style in the Word document. In other words, if you've defined a style in Word, but haven't applied it to any text, then that Word style won't show up in QuarkXPress. If you import a Word document that was saved as RTF, QuarkXPress includes *every* defined style from the Word style sheet, even those styles that were not used in the particular document.

If you import a Word file that has styles with the same name as styles already in the QuarkXPress document, those Word styles won't be imported, and the style already within QuarkXPress will be applied instead. The QuarkXPress styles predominate. However, any local formatting you've applied in the Word document will be imported.

This ability to replace Word styles with QuarkXPress styles is very important, since you can use Word's style sheets to tag paragraphs with style names and have QuarkXPress apply the appropriate formatting as soon as you import the text. The

QuarkXPress styles take over from the Word styles with the same names, so you can create styles in QuarkXPress using all of its sophisticated formatting and be secure in the knowledge that none of that style sheet formatting will be lost if you ever have to export the text back to Word for editing: The QuarkXPress formatting will be waiting patiently for the copy's return.

▼ ▼

Tip: Don't Worry About Word Styles. Remember that QuarkXPress overrides Microsoft Word's formatting for style sheets; that is, if your Microsoft Word document's Normal style is 18-point Helvetica and your QuarkXPress document's Normal style is 12-point Palatino, the imported text that is tagged as Normal appears in Palatino (as you'd want). The implication of this is that you never really have to worry about what the styles look like in Word. For example, in this book, our Microsoft Word text was all in Helvetica and Courier, but when we imported the text files into QuarkXPress, they came out in the fonts you're reading (Utopia and Futura).

▼ ▼

How QuarkXPress Works with WordPerfect

If your Microsoft Word documents don't flow into QuarkXPress as smoothly as you'd like, don't hold your breath when working with WordPerfect. Although many people use this program, Quark's filter doesn't handle WordPerfect files as well as we'd hoped. Here are the basics.

Character formatting. The good news is that almost all of WordPerfect's character formatting is imported correctly. Bolds come in bold, italics come in italic, and so on. Also, redlining (revision marks) are handled appropriately. That is, any deleted text gets deleted on import, and any added text gets added. However, where QuarkXPress doesn't have the same formatting, it ignores it. For example, double underlining doesn't import.

Nor have we been able to get fonts to import correctly. Any files with multiple fonts in them get screwed up pretty badly.

This bug will most likely get ironed out in the not-too-distant future, so you'll just have to try it yourself to see what works.

Paragraph formatting. Paragraph formatting also works as well as can be expected, with a few glitches here and there. For example, decimal and right tab stops don't appear to import correctly, but again that could simply be a bug that will soon be fixed.

Style sheets. Style sheets, one of our favorite power tools in desktop publishing, pose the biggest problem with the current WordPerfect import filter. The problem isn't entirely QuarkXPress's, of course; WordPerfect just doesn't have robust enough style sheets for QuarkXPress to grab hold of. Therefore, QuarkXPress imports WordPerfect files with all the paragraphs tagged properly, but doesn't appear to bring the style formatting with it.

For example, if you import a file with three paragraphs in it, each styled differently, QuarkXPress brings the name of the style in and appends it to the style sheet. However, the style is "hollow." That is, it has no formatting to it. Rather, it is the same as the Normal style. This won't do you much good if you are trying to import defined style sheets, but it's quite reasonable if the styles have already been defined in your QuarkXPress document.

Exporting Text

After you go through all the trouble of bringing copy into QuarkXPress and formatting it, why would you want to then export it? Aside from administrative reasons (backups, etc.), there are two major situations in which exporting text is important.

If you encounter sluggishness when working with text in QuarkXPress, consider exporting your text into a word processor, editing it there, and then re-importing it back into QuarkXPress.

Moreover, if you work in a busy workgroup-publishing environment, you may find it absolutely necessary to extract text from QuarkXPress so that editors can work on it while you continue to refine a newsletter's or magazine's layout.

How to Export Text

Exporting text from QuarkXPress is basically the opposite of importing it.

1. With the Content tool, select a text box containing the story you want to export.

2. Choose "Save Text" from the File menu. The Save Text dialog box appears.

3. Enter the name you'd like the exported text to be saved under. Select either the Entire Story or Selected Text button.

4. Use the Save File as Type: pop-up menu to choose the format for the exported file. The formats listed in the menu will depend on which filter XTensions you have in the QuarkXPress subdirectory.

5. Press Return or click OK.

Pitfalls

The most important consideration when taking text out of QuarkXPress and then bringing it back in is how to accomplish it without losing the formatting you've applied within QuarkXPress. No current word processor can handle horizontal scaling, for instance, and such formatting could easily be lost during the export/re-import process. There are ways to keep this formatting intact no matter where your QuarkXPress text ends up, however, by using style sheets or XPress Tags.

Exporting to WinWord

One solution is to export to Microsoft Word for Windows, in either native format (.DOC) or Rich Text Format (.RTF). Word files made from QuarkXPress contain style sheet information, and as mentioned above, the appropriate formatting will be applied automatically when you bring the text back into QuarkXPress. But using Word is only a partial solution to the formatting problem, since only formatting that's applied to an entire paragraph can be stored in style sheets. Some special local formatting to individual characters or words (such as superior type, tracking, kerning, or scaling) is lost during the export/re-import process, even if you use Word and take full advantage of style sheets. Other text formatting, like sub- or superscript, is retained. In a nutshell, the current import/export filters are far from perfect.

▼ ▼

Tip: Exporting Styles. We often use QuarkXPress's Export feature to export all of our styles to Microsoft Word. This saves us from having to recreate every style name on Microsoft Word's style sheet. To do this, create a little one-line paragraph for each style. Apply the style, then export that text in Rich Text Format (RTF). When you open the file in Word, all of the styles are there.

▼ ▼

Tip: Printing Your Style Sheet. We can't find any way to print out a list of every style on our style sheet along with descriptions from QuarkXPress. However, if you export the styles as described in the last tip, you can print out the styles from Word. When you've opened your Microsoft Word document with each of the styles, select the Print command under the File menu (or type Control-Shift-F12), select "Styles" from the pop-up Print selection box, then click OK to print out the list of style definitions.

▼ ▼

A Solution: XPress Tags

There is a solution to the problem of losing formatting when exporting and re-importing text. Export the file in the special ASCII format called XPress Tags. XPress Tags uses special—and complicated—coding that can record every single one of QuarkXPress's text formatting attributes, from style sheets to local formatting (see Figure 5-6).

You may find an ASCII file with XPress Tags confusing to look at, with its many arcane numbers and codes. However, there are several reasons why XPress Tags is the best format to use when you need to edit and then re-import copy.

COPY FLOW 281

Figure 5-6
XPress Tags

When you save this file in XPress Tags format...

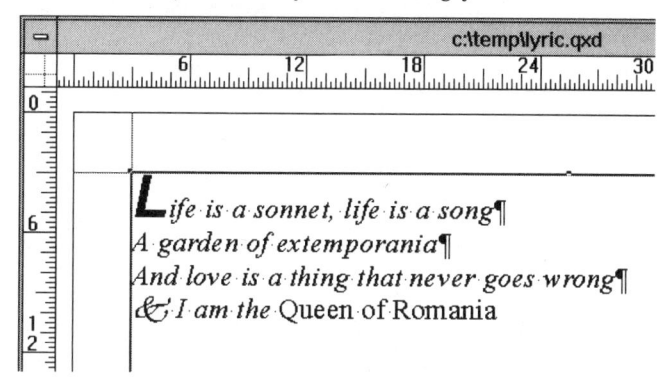

Life is a sonnet, life is a song¶
A garden of extemporania¶
And love is a thing that never goes wrong¶
& I am the Queen of Romania

...the text file looks like this:

```
<v1.60><e1>
@list=[S"",""]<*L*h"Standard"*kn0*kt0*ra0*rb0*d0*p(0,0,0,0,0,0,
g,"U.S. English")*t(0,0," "):
Ps100t0h100z12k0b0c"Black"f"Arial">
@list:<*p(0,0,0,20,0,0,g,"U.S. English")Blz36>L<Bz18f"Times
New Roman">ife is a sonnet, life is a song
A garden of extemporania
<k-10>A<k0>nd love is a thing that never goes wrong
<f"Wingdings">k<f"Times New Roman"> I am the <lk-7>
Q<k0>ueen of <k-10>Ro<k0>mania
```

Why Use XPress Tags?

Not only do files using XPress Tags contain all of a story's QuarkXPress formatting, but because ASCII is a universal file format, these files can be edited by virtually any word processor—Mac, MS-DOS, or UNIX. Although the coding may appear daunting if you're used to the WYSIWYG world of Windows, professional typesetters have been working with code-based systems for years, and tagged files can be easily integrated into such an environment.

So if you find yourself regularly needing to export QuarkXPress stories with sophisticated text formatting, XPress Tags is clearly the way to go. While it may take a while to get used to editing an XPress Tags file, it's a lot less work than reformatting your copy painstakingly each time you bring it back into your QuarkXPress document. We've included a comprehensive list of the codes used in XPress Tags in Appendix D, *XPress Tags*.

Note that when you export a text file with XPress Tags (from the Save Text item in the File menu), the file is saved with a .XTG extension. However, the file really is just a text file. To open an .XTG file in a word-processing program, just rename the file to have a .TXT extension, or (even easier) tell your word processor to "see" files of all types (*.*).

▼▼▼▼▼▼▼▼▼▼▼▼▼▼▼▼▼▼▼▼▼▼▼▼▼▼

Tip: Automate Your Copy Processing with XPress Tags. Once you're familiar with the coding format used by XPress Tags, you can easily set up a macro to apply formatting codes in your word processor. If you're ambitious and handy with database programs, you can design a report format that creates a file that incorporates XPress Tags, and which you can then bring into QuarkXPress fully formatted.

▼▼▼▼▼▼▼▼▼▼▼▼▼▼▼▼▼▼▼▼▼▼▼▼▼▼

Tip: Importing Text from Ventura Publisher. XPress Tags uses almost the same coding format as that powerhouse of DOS-based desktop publishing, Ventura Publisher. That's right, if you take a tagged, coded ASCII file from Ventura Publisher, you can import that file into QuarkXPress using the XPress Tags filter. You won't get the proper formatting, and you certainly won't get page layout, but you will save yourself a bundle of time in applying style sheets!

The trick is to alter the tags slightly before importing the file. Here's what you do.

1. Open the Ventura text document in a word processor or import it as straight ASCII text into a QuarkXPress text box.

2. Search for all instances of " = " (there's a space on either side of that equal sign) and replace it with ": " (that's a colon followed by a space).

3. Save that document as ASCII text again.

4. Import it into a QuarkXPress text box with the Include Style Sheets checkbox on.

When you import the file, all of the style sheet names are automatically brought into the QuarkXPress document. However, if you've already created style sheets with the same names as the Ventura document, then QuarkXPress will use the style definitions that you've created in QuarkXPress.

You can also perform a reverse procedure to bring formatted text from QuarkXPress to Ventura.

Getting Your Stories Straight

Once you've taken advantage of some, if not all, of these QuarkXPress features, you may still find it necessary to burn the midnight oil making last-minute changes. But at least you'll have the full power of QuarkXPress on your side—not buried within a user's guide. Get to know styles, import and export filters, and especially XPress Tags, and you can go a long way toward being lazy: making your computer do the work, rather than having to do it yourself.

CHAPTER 6

PICTURES

There's little doubt that proper use of typography can work miracles, but it's rare that all text and no pictures can attract a reader's attention and pull a dull document up to stardom (David even complained when his new copy of *Moby Dick* wasn't illustrated). Certainly, less sensational material, like textbooks, manuals, company newsletters, financial reports, and so on, quickly become more enjoyable and informative when accompanied by the right selection of graphics and images.

Although so far we've talked only about rudimentary graphic elements like rules, arrows, circles, and squares, QuarkXPress offers much, much more, as you'll see below. For starters, you can bring line-art and photographic images onto your QuarkXPress pages from a wide variety of sources. Once they are on the page, you can rotate, crop, scale, skew, slice, and dice them practically any way you want. In fact, you can probably do more with graphics in QuarkXPress than you can with any other page-layout program. Here are the three basic steps of importing pictures into your documents.

1. Create a picture box. Make sure you have the Content tool selected.

2. Bring in a picture either by pasting from the Windows Clipboard or by using the Get Picture feature (similar to the Place command in other programs).

3. Manipulate the image until you like the way it looks on the page.

But what types of pictures are available for use? And how do you accomplish the desired look? In this chapter we explore the full range of possibilities for bringing graphics in from other applications and manipulating them on the page. In Chapter 8, *Modifying Images*, we'll talk about some of the effects you can achieve by modifying graphics once they're on the page.

First, let's take a close look at the different types of pictures you can use with QuarkXPress for Windows.

Graphic File Formats

If there is a question we're asked more often than "Why won't my file print?" it's "what's the difference between all those different graphic formats?" The question refers to a host of formats with names such as EPS, EPSF, EPSP, TIFF, PCX, BMP, WMF, GEM, compressed TIFF, CGM, and CDR. No one can be blamed for being confused when faced with such a list! Some of these formats are different names for the same thing, others are subtly different, and a few represent totally, to-the-core different concepts.

The fundamental question when considering a graphic file is whether it is a bitmapped or object-oriented file.

Bitmaps

Bitmapped images are the most common type of file format. When you use a scanner and scanning software, you are generating a bitmapped image. When you use an image-editing and painting program such as Publishers PaintBrush, Microsoft Windows Paint, Aldus PhotoStyler, or Micrografx Picture Publisher, you are working with and generating bitmapped images. When you capture a screen shot to disk, you're capturing a bitmapped graphic. However, no matter how ubiquitous bitmapped images are, you are still strictly limited in the ways you can use them.

Bitmapped images are just that: images made of mapped bits. A *bit* is a small piece of information. To begin with, let's think of it as a single pixel (or dot), which can be turned on or off. When you look very closely at the screen of a black-and-white computer, you can see that the screen image is made up of thousands of these tiny bits. Some are turned on (black), and some are turned off (white). The map is the computer's internal blueprint of what the image looks like: "bit number 1 is on, bit number 2 is off," and so on (see Figure 6-1).

Figure 6-1
Each pixel sits on the grid

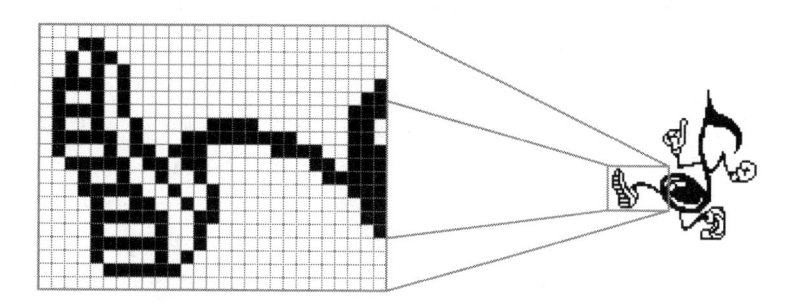

There are three primary pieces of information that are relevant to any bitmapped image: its size, resolution, and pixel depth.

Size. The bitmap is a rectangular area that describes every dot (pixel) in the image. This area is broken down into a grid of many square pixels. Each pixel is whole—not fractured. You can describe the size of the gridded area in several ways, but it is most often specified in the number of squares or pixels per side, or in inches per side.

Resolution. The resolution of the bitmapped image is usually defined as the number of pixels, or squares, per inch on the grid (of course, this is different in countries using the metric system).

A low-resolution bitmapped image may have 72 pixels per inch (called *dots per inch*, or *dpi*). A picture described using only 72 dots per inch looks very rough. Such low-resolution images are often called *jaggy*. A higher resolution bitmapped image may be 300 dots per inch or above (many slide scanners scan images at over 4,000 dpi). These images, when printed, are much crisper and cleaner, with fewer jaggies (see Figure 6-2).

Figure 6-2
Low-resolution versus high-resolution bitmapped line art

72 dpi   300 dpi

Pixel depth. Each pixel, then, is specified as a color. The range of colors available is determined by the type of bitmapped image it is (see "File Types," below). In the simplest bitmapped images, each pixel is defined as either black or white. These are called bilevel or 1-bit images because each pixel is described with one bit of information, and as we mentioned above, that one bit can be either on or off (1 or 0). Bilevel images are flat; they have no depth. More complex bitmapped images are *deep*, because they contain pixels that are defined with multiple bits, enabling them to describe many levels of gray or color. For example, an 8-bit image can describe up to 256 shades of gray for each pixel (those of us in the Northwest, having to look at gray a great deal, can identify and name most of those shades). A 24-bit image can describe over 16 million colors (see Figure 6-3).

Manipulating bitmapped images. The limitations inherent in bitmapped images become most clear when you manipulate the picture in some way, such as enlarging it significantly. The key is that the picture's resolution is related directly to its size. If you double the size of a bitmap, you cut its resolution in half; if you reduce the size of the picture to one-quarter, you multiply its resolution by four. For example, a 72-dpi, 1-bit graphic, when

Figure 6-3
The number of bits determines the number of gray levels

1-bit (2 shades)

4-bit (16 shades)

enlarged to 200 percent, becomes a twice-as-rough 36-dpi image. However, when reduced to 50 percent, it becomes a more detailed 144-dpi image (see Figure 6-4).

A gray-scale or color image, when enlarged, becomes "pixelated," rather than looking "rougher." You begin to see each square pixel and its tonal value (see Figure 6-5).

Object-Oriented Graphics

Instead of describing a picture dot by dot, object-oriented files specify each object in a picture as a mathematical formula, based on a coordinate system. Therefore, whereas a bitmapped picture could take an enormous amount of space describing one circle, an object-oriented file could describe it in one line: Draw a circle of this size with a center at x,y. The computer knows what a circle is and how to create it. Different object-oriented formats can describe different things, but most can easily specify objects such as lines, curves, and type, as well as attributes such as shading and object-rotation angles.

Figure 6-4
Bitmap scaling and resolution

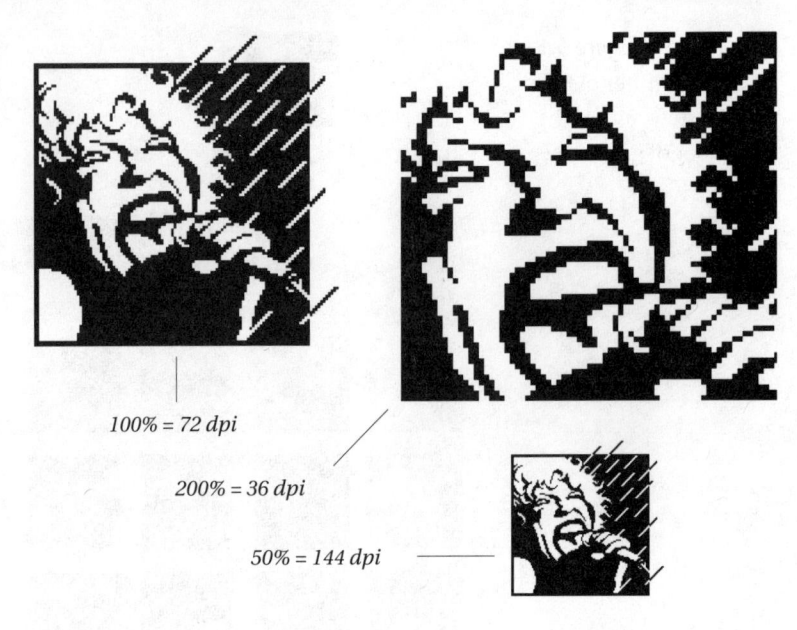

100% = 72 dpi

200% = 36 dpi

50% = 144 dpi

Figure 6-5
Pixelation from enlarging a gray-scale image

72 dpi, 4-bit grayscale TIFF at 100%

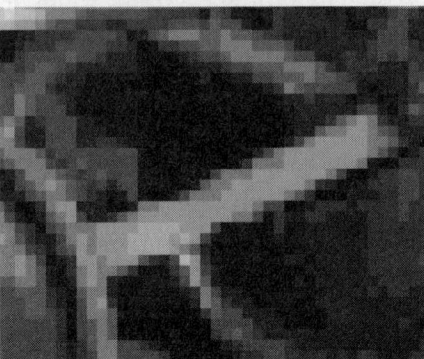

72 dpi, 4-bit grayscale TIFF at 400%

Most object-oriented graphics can also contain bitmapped graphics as objects in their own right, though you may or may not be able to edit those bitmaps with a paint program. These files are almost always created by an application such as Micrografx Designer, Aldus FreeHand, CorelDRAW, or Adobe Illustrator.

The magic of object-oriented graphics is that you can stretch them, rotate them, twist them into a pastry, and print them on various resolution printers without worrying about how smooth the lines will print. When you print on a 300-dpi, plain-paper laser printer, you get a full 300 dpi, and when you print to film with a 3,000-dpi printer, you get beautifully smooth lines at 3,000 dots per inch. There is no inherent limit of information for the picture, as there is in bitmaps (see Figure 6-6). Theoretically, there are no inherent limits to the number of gray levels in an object-oriented picture. Realistically, however, each format has upper limits.

Figure 6-6
Object-oriented graphics versus bitmapped images

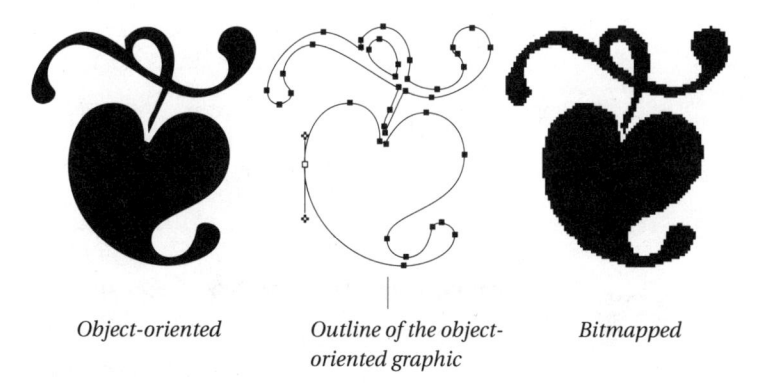

Object-oriented   *Outline of the object-oriented graphic*   *Bitmapped*

File Types

See page 594

When we talk about file types in this book, we're talking about two things: how the information is formatted within the file and how the file is saved to disk. The common usage of file type—such as Windows Paint or Publishers PaintBrush PCX format—refers to the way in which the information is formatted. Then there is the way you should name files when you save them to disk; we typically give every file an actual, technical, three-letter name extension indicating the file type. For instance, files generally referred to as Tagged Image File Format (TIFF) files are given a .TIF filename extension. For the sake of simplicity, we use the terms type and format interchangeably.

It's up to you and your colleagues to name your files using the proper filename extension. Otherwise, there's no way to tell which graphics file format it's written in, which means more trial and error when comes to importing the file into QuarkXPress. It's important to understand and identify file types for the discussion below, where we cover the main graphic file formats used with QuarkXPress (see Table 6-1).

Table 6-1
QuarkXPress's graphic file format support

File Type	Extension
Bitmap	.bmp, .dib, .rle
CompuServe GIF	.gif
Computer Graphics Metafile	.cgm
Encapsulated PostScript	.eps
Hewlett-Packard Graphics Language (HPGL)	.plt
Macintosh PICT	.pct
Micrografx Designer	.drw
Paintbrush	.pcx
Scitex CT	.ct
Tagged Image File Format (TIFF)	.tif
Windows Metafile	.wmf

New in 3.3
See page 599

Encapsulated PostScript/EPSF. Encapsulated PostScript format (EPSF or EPS) is certainly the most reliable format for putting images on paper or film. PostScript is a powerful, object-oriented page-description language, though its files may contain noneditable bitmaps as well. Although it has built-in font-handling features, it ultimately treats type as a graphic made of lines and curves. This makes working with fonts in a PostScript environment a joy, with many possibilities. It is easy to create a PostScript file, but to print it out you must have a PostScript-compatible printer. With non-PostScript printers, QuarkXPress just prints the low-resolution screen representation of an EPS graphic.

EPS images come in two basic varieties: EPS without a preview ("generic EPS") and EPS with a preview. The preview-enclosed feature in many EPS files allows you to bring that file into Quark-

XPress and see a low-resolution representation of the image on the screen. When the file is printed to a PostScript printer, however, the bitmap is ignored and the underlying PostScript is used. If a preview image is not available, then you just see a big gray box on the screen, which may contain some basic information, such as the file's name.

On the PC, the preview image is a low-resolution bitmapped image much like a TIFF file (see below) that sits at the beginning of the graphic file. You can see this header info (along with the PostScript definition of the graphic) by opening the file with a word processor, but it won't do you much good, as the graphic is encoded. EPS previews on the Macintosh are handled differently, making it necessary to use some sort of translation program to convert files (or else you may not see the preview correctly).

Tagged Image File Format. The Tagged Image File Format (TIFF or .TIF) is a form of bitmap, and the most widely used on microcomputers. A TIFF file can be created at any size and any resolution and can include gray-scale or color information. It is important to remember, especially when we move into image-editing and color-separation work in later chapters, that these images are still just big bitmaps, and therefore only contain a finite amount of information.

Nonetheless, because of the flexibility of TIFF files, most scanning and image-editing programs such as PhotoStyler, Hewlett-Packard DeskScan, Picture Publisher, and ImageIn can save and open the TIFF format.

TIFF files can seem simple until you really need to work with them in a variety of environments. As it turns out, there are several different TIFF formats, including uncompressed, several types of compressed TIFF , TIFF-5, and the newly introduced TIFF-6, including a CMYK variant. TIFF files are also generally handled differently between the Macintosh and the PC, so be careful and do some testing in advance if you plan to move graphic files between platforms.

PCX. Whereas TIFF is a trade standard, PCX is owned and controlled by ZSoft Corporation, the developers of Publishers Paintbrush. It's a grand-daddy of bitmapped formats, predating Windows 1.0 when it hit the streets as part of PC Paintbrush. The current version supports 24-bit color and 256-color palette color (indexed to 24-bit color palette), up from earlier 4- and 16-color versions. Since a variety of palette-color techniques have been applied to PCX over the ages, files from earlier programs can have some serious color-mismatch problems. But if you're satisfied with the results of importing the PCX images you've been provided, then go for it. If not, see if your source can provide files in TIFF, which is a more open and flexible standard. We typically recommend using TIFF.

Computer Graphics Metafile. It's not often you meet a truly international graphics standard, but here it is: CGM, an object-oriented standard certified by the American National Standards Committee and the International Standards Organization. Primarily used in CAD, you'll also find it hanging around most desktop publishing and graphics programs. It's been a relatively convenient format to use with nonPostScript printers, which can't print EPS files. If you're working on part of a government contract or international project, for example, CGM may be the preferred format, for compatibility's sake.

Quark uses a filter XTension for CGM, so if you want to import this type of picture, you must have the filter in your QuarkXPress directory when you start the program. When you select a CGM file from the Get Picture dialog box, the CGM Format Graphic Filter dialog box appears, with a few import options to consider; let's look at each of them (see Figure 6-7).

- **Force Vector Fonts.** If you import the CGM file and the type looks really bad, try reimporting it with "Force Vector Fonts" turned on. The poor quality of the fonts may be caused by bitmapped fonts in the picture, and this option converts them to vector format. They scale better, but may loose some subtlety in the translation (CGM lacks the high level of font support you find in PostScript and

Figure 6-7
The CGM import filter

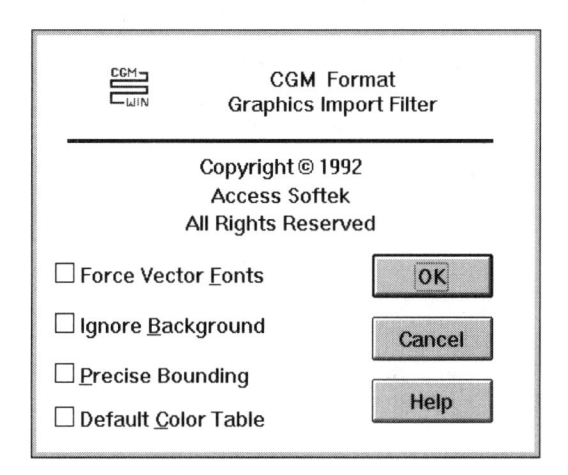

[Dialog box: CGM Format Graphics Import Filter. Copyright © 1992 Access Softek, All Rights Reserved. Options: Force Vector Fonts, Ignore Background, Precise Bounding, Default Color Table. Buttons: OK, Cancel, Help.]

Encapsulated PostScript, so don't expect the same results). The truth of the matter is that if you have bitmapped fonts in the graphics, changing them to "Vector Fonts" isn't going to help matters much. They'll probably still look as ugly as can be.

- **Ignore Background.** In some CGM images, the background appears opaque when you import it into a QuarkXPress picture box. Turning on the Ignore Background option renders the picture's background transparent, which is probably closer to what you want.

- **Precise Bounding.** "Precise Bounding" performs both of the above functions automatically. Plus, it trims the picture's boundaries to that of the visible image, eliminating any invisible border. This is especially helpful if you're trying to scale the image or fit it to the picture box's size.

- **Default Color Table.** Here's a basic one: turn on the "Default Color Table" option if you're importing a picture that was created in Harvard Graphics—simple as that.

Micrografx Designer. QuarkXPress also reads native Micrografx Designer files (.DRW). These files fall into the object-oriented format category. The truth is that we tend to export Designer documents (and other object-oriented graphics) as EPS files, rather than rely on this QuarkXPress filter. However, if you're printing on a nonPostScript printer like a LaserJet then this filter is a good option.

Like the CGM filter mentioned above, this import filter XTension must be in your QuarkXPress directory when you start the program. The Force Vector Fonts and Ignore Background options in the DRW Graphics Import Filter dialog box function as they do in the CGM import filter.

Hewlett-Packard Graphic Language (HPGL). A command language for driving pen plotters (those feverish little robots that actually draw on paper with colored pens), HPGL has long provided one of the only avenues for exchanging engineering drawings between programs. Although many engineering design and drafting programs like the venerable AutoCad now support PostScript, HPGL still serves at least a fall-back role. You simply print your CAD drawing to a pen plotter, but capture the HPGL pen plotter commands as a "plotter" file (it usually has a .PLT file extension). You can then import the .PLT file directly into QuarkXPress or into many desktop drawing programs.

The HPGL Graphics Import Filter dialog box lets you choose between four plotting dimensions: A (letter size), B (tabloid size), A3, and A4 (see Figure 6-8). Letter size works for most purposes, unless you're really creating pages with tabloid-size industrial drawings. HPGL files also retain plotter pen selection, and the PLT filter lets you adjust the color for up to six pens. As a vector format, HPGL is crude compared to PostScript and handles text poorly. We suggest you stay away from this if you're trying to do nice work.

Graphics Interchange Format (GIF). A bitmap format, GIF is the "house brand" image file format of the CompuServe on-line information service. Most image-editing programs can now import and export GIF image files. Unlike TIFF, which can record 24-or 32-bit images, GIF supports 24-bit color via its 256-color palette, meaning that a single image can contain only 256 colors, selected from a 24-bit range (16 million colors). Indexed color *can* be a problem, since GIF and other indexed-color formats sometimes get

Figure 6-8
The HPGL Graphics Import Filter dialog box

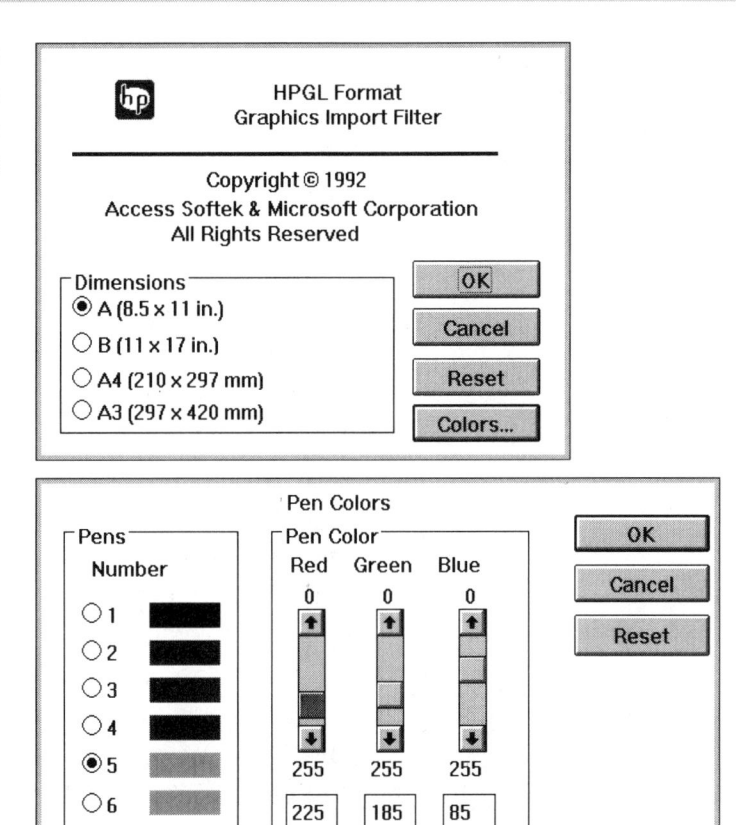

their color pointers (the index) rearranged. The result? Image colors that change unexpectedly. Still, if you're given GIF files to work with and they seem OK, then keep your life simple and use this filter. Otherwise, convert them to TIFF.

Windows Bitmap. Windows Bitmap (.BMP) is the bitmap format native to Windows Paint, but isn't usually encountered outside of Windows and OS/2 Presentation Manager. You can store a 1-, 4-, 8-, or 24-bit image. We still prefer TIFF, given its compatibility across different computer systems, including Macintoshes and UNIX workstations.

Windows Metafile (WMF). Closely tied to graphics technology underlying Windows, WMF is a reliable object-oriented format to use in Windows. It's the only object-oriented format that seems to work reliably, in our experience, with the Windows Clipboard when cutting and pasting images between Windows applications. Like Windows itself, WMF can handle 24-bit color or indexed palette color.

Macintosh PICT. The PICT (QuickDraw Picture) format was a part of the original Mac system, but it was first made easy to use with MacDraw. It tackles graphic images on an object level rather than a bitmap level. However, a PICT file can contain bitmaps either along with object-oriented drawings or as its only object.

Ultimately, the biggest problem with the PICT format is its unreliability in several respects. For example, line widths can change when moving a picture from one program to another, and text spacing can change, sometimes drastically. Also, printing to high-resolution printers (1,200+ dpi) can be spotty. Remember that when you print a PICT to a PostScript imagesetter, the computer has to convert from one object-oriented language to another. Similarly, when you move a PICT image from the Macintosh to the PC, it must be translated somehow. We trust these conversions about as far as we can throw them. So, even though PICT is the primary format on the Macintosh for printing to non-PostScript devices, we just tell the graphic arts community, "Just say no to PICT."

Scitex CT. Scitex Corporation has developed several graphic file formats for describing bitmapped images on their high-end systems. Over the past year or so, these formats have crept into the personal computer market. Typically, people don't use these formats unless they're dealing with a service bureau that is using a Scitex scanner or imagesetter.

QuarkXPress can import both Scitex CT (continuous tone) and LW (line work) files. However, it can only perform a color separation on CT files. Note that when we say CT files, we are actually referring to CT HandShake files. We know of at least one guy who got burned because he asked a color house for CT files and got Scitex's proprietary format instead of the open-format CT HandShake files.

Importing Pictures into QuarkXPress

NEW IN 3.3

See page 592

Now that we know the types of pictures we are dealing with, let's look at how we'll deal with them. As we mentioned, the first step in importing a graphic from another application is to create a picture box within your QuarkXPress document. This is covered in Chapter 1, *QuarkXPress Basics*, in the discussion of rectangles, ovals, and polygons. When you have an empty picture box on your page, you can see an "X" in the middle of it. At this point, you're ready to bring a picture into the box.

Note that we're bringing a picture into the box, rather than replacing the box or even "melding" the two together. The picture box is one entity and the picture is another. You might think of the box as a window frame through which you can see the picture. You can manipulate the picture box, the picture, or both.

The two primary ways to bring a picture in are pasting from the Clipboard and using the Get Picture feature. In order for either of these methods to work, you must have the Content tool selected. This, of course, makes some inherent sense: If you're trying to manipulate (in this case, import) the contents of a picture box, you want to use the Content tool.

The Clipboard

Windows has a storage area called the *Clipboard* that lets you take information from one place and put it in another. Whenever you cut, copy, or paste, you're using the Clipboard. Thus, you can cut or copy a picture from one application into the Clipboard and then paste it from the Clipboard into another application.

The problem with cutting and pasting is that the Windows Clipboard handles only certain types of picture formats. Furthermore, the Clipboard is a loosely defined entity, so program developers don't implement it in a standardized way. Frankly, we're never sure if the picture we copy from one program will be in that same format when we paste it into another application. If you are trying to bring an outline illustration over from Aldus FreeHand, for instance, you cannot simply cut and paste because outside applications (for example, QuarkXPress) don't understand FreeHand's outline format. They do, usually, understand the WMF (Windows Metafile) graphics file format, and Windows Bitmap (BMP). Don't count on copying an EPS image from another application and pasting it into QuarkXPress. At best, you end up with a WMF, if QuarkXPress even lets you complete the operation.

Okay, you made us say it: Especially with graphics, *import*, don't paste. That way you'll avoid the unpredictability of the Windows Clipboard. That's not to say it won't be handy in a few circumstances, but you'd better be willing to experiment.

Get Picture

New in 3.3
See page 590

When creating most of your high-quality documents, you will be working with EPSF and high-resolution TIFF images. These, of course, output as fine line art, or as gray-scale or color halftones for photographs, with smooth edges at any resolution, and—for EPS pictures—clean and dependable type at any size. With the possible exception of importing small pictures or type directly from an illustration program, you should use "Get Picture" from the File menu, rather than copying and pasting via the Windows Clipboard. "Get Picture" assumes that a file has already been created and is located on disk somewhere.

With your picture box created and the Content tool selected, you can select "Get Picture" from the File menu (or be like the pros and use Control-E). A directory dialog box appears, allowing you to find the file that you wish to import. Remember your retrieval shortcuts here: use Up and Down arrows to move up and down the list, tab or control buttons to move between directory, disk volume, and file list boxes, and press Enter or double-click on a list box item to open it.

Once the file is selected in the dialog box, click the OK button or just double-click on the file name. Note that some of the QuarkXPress import filters (DRW, HPGL, and CGM) display dialog boxes that provide the import options. For the other file formats, the lower left corner of the document window changes to show the percentage completion of the import operation. If you're importing a 3MB file on your 8-MHz 286, you can see how quickly (slowly) it is processing (perhaps this is the best time of the day to go out for an espresso).

▼ ▼

Tip: Grab That Pencil. You will undoubtedly find yourself in a situation at some point where you want to manually re-import a picture or import a new picture into an already used picture box. Problem: You lose the specifications for the original picture box (scaling, offset, rotation, and so on). This is a case where you can use the most technologically advanced tools available to humankind, but all you really need is a simple notepad and a pencil. Just jot down the specs for the previous picture (nice of QuarkXPress to show them to you in the Measurements palette), then, after you bring the new picture in, retype the original specs (remember, if you have multiple changes to the picture box, it's usually quicker to make them in the Picture Box Specifications dialog box—Control-M—all at once).

▼ ▼

Object Linking and Embedding

Bill Gates, chairman of Microsoft, has a vision: Applications shouldn't be isolated like islands or nation states. They should unite, with open borders and common data currency; programs should even be able to share features. Gates sees the Windows desktop of the future as one giant application. At present, the humble glue propping up that lofty vision is Object Linking and Embedding, known commonly by its acronym OLE (pronounced olé, like the cheer people use at bull fights and out-of-control tapas bars). OLE manifests itself in QuarkXPress in the Paste, Paste Special, and Paste Link commands under the Edit menu, and as the Insert Object keyboard command (Control-Shift-I).

Vision aside, what does OLE actually do? In a nutshell, OLE lets you start one application from within another, as though the second application were part of the first application. Let's say you've linked or embedded a drawing from CorelDRAW into QuarkXPress. With OLE, you can simply double-click on the drawing in QuarkXPress, and Windows automatically takes you to CorelDRAW, with the graphic already loaded for editing. That's definitely more efficient than good old-fashioned Windows Clipboard copying and pasting.

In a normal copy-and-paste operation, you'd select a graphic in Corel and copy it to the Windows Clipboard. Then you'd switch to QuarkXPress and paste it into a picture frame. (Chances are it would come across as a Windows Metafile, by default.) If you later look at the graphic you pasted into Quark-XPress and decide to change it, you'd have to switch back to the draw program, edit the graphic there, and repeat the copy-and-paste process. There's no connection between the two programs, and QuarkXPress has no idea where the graphic (the object) came from.

With OLE, the two programs *are* connected, via the object, which unlike a standard Clipboard object, knows darn well where it came from, and more. But OLE doesn't work with just any old Windows program; applications must be specially programmed to handle OLE, which is part of Windows 3.1 and Windows for Workgroups, but not Windows 3.0.

Let's look at how OLE works and why you would (or, rather, wouldn't) want to use it.

Servers and clients. It takes two to tango, and that means two kinds of OLE programs: OLE servers and OLE clients. A program that can offer an object for use by other programs is called the OLE *server* application. A program that can use an OLE object is called a *client* application. An application can be a client or server, or both. QuarkXPress is strictly a client. On the other hand, Corel-DRAW 3.0 is both an OLE server and a client application.

Linking and Embedding

As OLE's full name suggests, you can either *link* or *embed* an object from one application to, or into, another.

Linking. When you link an object, only a representation of the object passes from the server to the client, say from CorelDRAW to QuarkXPress. The object itself stays with CorelDRAW, but CorelDRAW remains aware that the object is currently being used in QuarkXPress. You simply copy the object in CorelDRAW to the Clipboard and then paste it into a QuarkXPress picture frame using either the Paste Link command under the Edit menu or the Paste Link button in the Paste Special dialog box (both methods seem to produce the same results).

Embedding. When you *embed* a picture, however, the CorelDRAW object—the drawing itself, not just a representation—is stored with (embedded in) the QuarkXPress document. The object also contains instructions for launching CorelDRAW (in our example) from within QuarkXPress. You can embed an object using either the Paste command under the Edit menu or the Paste command in the Paste Special dialog box.

Another way to embed an object is via the Insert Object command (Control-Shift-Insert). It differs from Paste and Paste Special in several ways. First, it bypasses the Windows Clipboard. Because of this more direct connection, you can force QuarkXPress to update the object by issuing a command from the server application, which we'll illustrate below. Secondly, because it bypasses the Clipboard, the embedding process is a bit different from what we describe above.

Here's an example of how you'd use Insert Object with CorelDRAW. First of all, since we're talking "embedded," CorelDRAW doesn't have to be running when you invoke Insert Object. Create your picture box and select it with the Content tool. Next, press Control-Shift-I. The Insert Object dialog box appears on screen, listing all OLE server applications and other available objects.

Not all of the objects listed in the Insert Object dialog box work properly with QuarkXPress, but many of them do (you just have to test them to see). Familiar objects, such as "CorelDRAW! Graphic," generally work as well as any. Select "CorelDRAW! Graphic" and click OK (or double-click the selection). CorelDRAW loads and opens a blank drawing named "XPRESS01." This blank document is now embedded in QuarkXPress, and an update link now exists between the two programs. You can draw whatever you want onto that page, and when you leave CorelDRAW, QuarkXPress automatically brings the picture in.

Here's an important part to remember: the Insert Object procedure closes any drawing you've already loaded in CorelDRAW, politely asking you to save (if you hadn't yet). If you have a finished drawing that you want to embed, use the Import command under CorelDRAW's File menu to get the drawing onto "XPRESS0001." *Don't* use the Open command. Opening a drawing breaks the update link.

Whether you start a new drawing from scratch, or Import one, you can quickly update the embedded version in QuarkXPress by selecting the Update command in CorelDRAW's File menu when an update link exists.

When push comes to shove, whether you link or embed, the end result is the same; you can quickly edit the object from within QuarkXPress. Double-click on the linked or embedded object, whether it's a CorelDRAW drawing or an Excel table, and you're automatically switched to CorelDRAW or Excel (or whatever), where you can edit the object. When you're finished editing, you can quickly switch back to QuarkXPress and update the object to reflect the changes you made.

Using OLE with QuarkXPress. Here are some important implications of using OLE, especially with QuarkXPress.

- If you use object *linking*, both the server and the client application must be running at the same time. Your system must therefore have enough memory to run both applications.

- If you use object *embedding*, the server application automatically launches itself when needed and doesn't have to be running ahead of time. To edit and update the object in QuarkXPress, both applications have to be running, so you still need enough RAM.

- QuarkXPress expects to find a linked object at the disk location where it was first linked. If you rename it or move it to a different disk or subdirectory, the link will break. Obviously, linking is not the way to go if you're planning to send a QuarkXPress document to a service bureau or to a different computer in your company.

- OLE is a disk hog. In our experience, a document with graphics installed via OLE can easily swell to twice the size of the same document with the same graphics imported via the Get Picture command.

- In QuarkXPress, OLE only works for bringing in graphics and spreadsheet charts and tables. Text "objects" from word processors are not supported (this would be cool, but once you start thinking about it, it really would become a massive problem).

- **New in 3.3** *See page 597* — Graphics brought into a QuarkXPress document via OLE don't appear in the QuarkXPress Picture Usage dialog box—a bummer, in our minds. Objects that are *linked*, though, *do* appear listed in the Links dialog box, accessed via the Links command under the Edit menu. You can view a document's linked objects and update or change a link. But the Links dialog box doesn't list which page an object is on, unlike the Picture Usage dialog box, nor does it have a Show Me command, so it's not as useful for image management.

▼ ▼

Tip: If You Must Paste. We mentioned it above, but we'll spell it out here: the QuarkXPress Paste command automatically becomes an Embed command when you paste something that was copied to the Clipboard from an OLE server, such as CorelDRAW. But what if you just want a good, old-fashioned, uncomplicated Paste? No problem. Skip the Paste command and use "Paste Special" instead. In the Paste Special dialog box you see a list of Data Types. For a CorelDRAW object you see two types: "Corel-DRAW Object" and "Picture." Choose "Picture" instead of "CorelDRAW Object," and click the Paste command. The Paste Link command should be grayed out if you've selected "Picture" as the data type. Double-click the pasted drawing; nothing should happen.

▼ ▼

The truth about OLE. We think OLE in QuarkXPress is problematic at best—the kind of thing that a lot of people may think they want to use because it seems like it would simplify everything. But it doesn't. It just makes a document more difficult to manage. In most cases, at least for graphics, you'd be better off putting your time and energy into using better image-management techniques.

Why do we think such thoughts? First of all, OLE is new and unpredictable. It's tacked onto QuarkXPress almost as an afterthought. It's barely mentioned in the Reference Manual, and incompletely documented in the OLE.WRI "read me" file in your QuarkXPress directory. Plus, because of the way OLE works, the image that gets printed may not be what you expect. Typically, if the image looks okay on the screen, there's a reasonable chance it'll print okay. But using the screen display for an indicator makes us nervous. We'd rather just not use it at all unless we have to (for example, if we need an image from some application, such as Excel, that can't export the information in a format that QuarkXPress can import with Get Picture).

To us, OLE will make more sense in QuarkXPress when it functions reliably over high-speed networks. Then it will provide the glue to effectively let workgroup members use different software on different computer stations, but still blend their tasks into a single collaborative document. But for now, it's better to keep your distance.

What Happened to My Picture?

When you import a picture, you may not see exactly what you were expecting or wanting in the picture box. It may be that you see only a gray box with some type, or that the image is misplaced, or even that you can't see it at all. Remember the First Rule of Computer Anomaly: Don't Panic.

Can't see the picture at all. The first thing to check for is whether or not the big "X" is still in the picture box; if it is, then "Get Picture" failed to retrieve the picture. Try again.

If what you see is just a blank frame, then the picture is probably somewhere in the box but you can't see it yet. The Get Picture feature automatically places the image in the upper-left corner of the bounding box of the frame. Note that we say the "bounding box" and not the box itself. The bounding box is the smallest rectangle that completely surrounds the frame. It's what you see when you are looking at your frame with "Reshape Polygon" (under the Item menu) off (see Figure 6-9). If you have an oval or a polygonal box, and the image is rather small, then you may have to move the object into the frame (see "Moving Your Pictures Around," later in this chapter).

Figure 6-9
Bounding box of a polygon

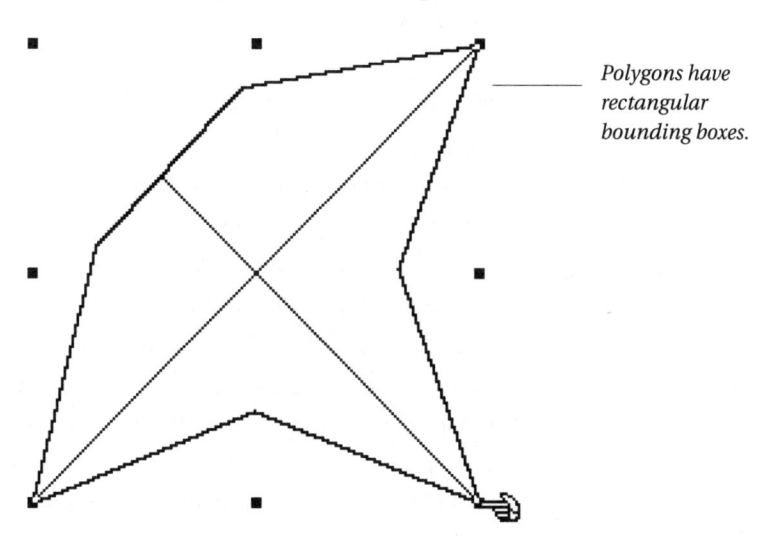

Polygons have rectangular bounding boxes.

There's no picture—just a gray box. If the image you imported was an EPS file with no image attached for a screen representation, then QuarkXPress represents the image as a gray box with the note "PostScript Picture" and the name of the file directly in the center of the gray box. This gray box shows the bounding box of the image, as defined in the header of the EPS document.

Another cause of the gray box effect is looking at a complex picture from too far back. That is, when you look at the page from "Fit in Window" (under the View menu), it looks like a muddled gray box, but when you go to "Actual Size," it looks like what you were hoping for.

The third cause of the gray box effect is that the picture you imported was, in fact, a gray box. If this is the case, we can only suggest that you think about whether or not you really consider a gray box an exciting enough graphic for your publication.

Working with Your Picture

Now that you have brought something (which may or may not look like the graphic you wanted) into the picture box, you can manipulate it in more ways than you ever could in other page-makeup programs.

Moving Your Picture Around

In Chapter 1, *QuarkXPress Basics*, you learned about moving your picture and text boxes around on the page. You can also move the picture itself within the picture box. You may want to do this for two reasons: for picture placement and for cropping a portion of the image. Several methods for moving your image within (or even outside of) the box follow. Remember that even though the picture is inside the frame, they are two different entities, and you can move and manipulate them using different tools.

Centering. Often the first thing you'll want to do with a picture, whether or not you can see it on screen, is to center it within the picture box. Designers and computer hackers alike have muddled through various tricks to center graphics perfectly within boxes, with varying degrees of success. We suggest you just type Control-Shift-M and let QuarkXPress do it for you. QuarkXPress centers the picture within its bounding box—that is, its lower-left and upper-right corners. Therefore, pictures that are oddly shaped (for example, an L-shaped picture; see Figure 6-10) may not be centered exactly where you'd expect them to be at first glance.

Moving the picture. If you want the image somewhere other than in the upper-left corner or in the center, you can use the Con-

Figure 6-10
Centering an oddly-shaped graphic

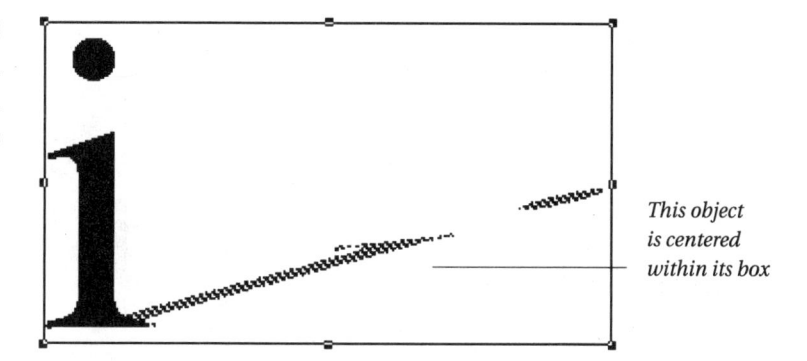

This object is centered within its box

tent tool (which switches to a Grabber hand when placed over the picture box) to move the picture around. Anyone who has ever done this can tell you that if the image is a large one, it can take quite some time for the picture to respond to the hand movements. You may want to zoom in for precision alignment when you get close to where you want it, but remember that what you're looking at is still only a low-resolution (36- or 72-dpi) rendition of the real picture, which may be slightly off in a few details.

If you know exactly how far you want to move the picture, you can type in the offset amounts in either the Measurements palette or in the Picture Box Specifications dialog box (type Control-M or hold down the Control key while double-clicking on the picture). This method is a real godsend when precision is the key, but there are some pitfalls to look out for. One such pitfall is expecting to know where the graphic image is either by the screen representation or the original placement (thinking it's up against the left edge of your box). In the first case, remember that you're looking at only a 72-dpi image, and in the second case, remember that an EPS image almost always has some white space surrounding it. Therefore, when you import it, the image itself is slightly farther to the right than the left edge of the picture box. Until QuarkXPress is released on a Display Post-Script system, when working with this method you're probably better off printing the page and then measuring how far you want the image to be moved (see Figure 6-11).

Figure 6-11
Minor picture offsetting within the box

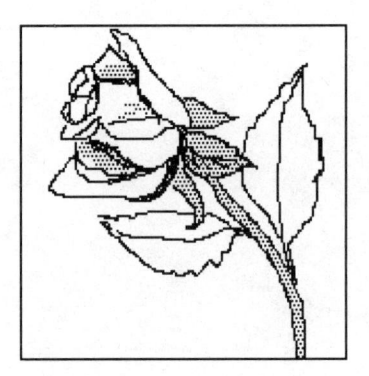

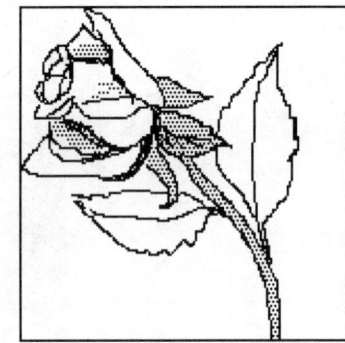

Original object (with no offset)   *Moved horizontally*

▼▼▼▼▼▼▼▼▼▼▼▼▼▼▼▼▼▼▼▼▼▼▼▼

Tip: Minimoves. When you have the Content tool selected and have selected a picture box, you can "nudge" the picture within the box in tiny increments by pressing the cursor arrows on your keyboard. Each click moves the image one point in that direction. Holding down the Alt key while pressing an arrow key moves the picture in one-tenth-of-a-point (.1-point) increments.

▼▼▼▼▼▼▼▼▼▼▼▼▼▼▼▼▼▼▼▼▼▼▼▼

Cropping. If you only want a portion of the picture, then you can "cut out" the unwanted areas by reducing the size of the box and moving the picture so that you see only the area you want (see Figure 6-12). However, there are those who crop out 90 percent of the image in order to use one flower in a bouquet, then duplicate that image 12 times and wonder why their file doesn't print (don't laugh too loudly; we've seen highly paid professionals do this!). Remember that QuarkXPress doesn't get rid of or forget the parts of the picture that aren't shown. That's why you can always go back and change your cropping or picture specifications. But the upshot of this is that it still has to process the entire image, which can take quite some time. So remember to use cropping judiciously. If you want only a small portion of the file, then use

Figure 6-12
Edge of a picture box cropping a picture

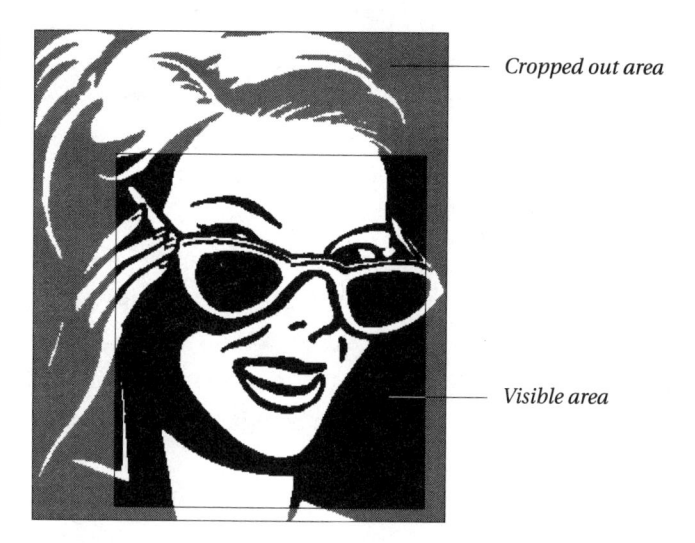

Cropped out area

Visible area

an editing program such as Publishers PaintBrush or PhotoStyler to cut out the other parts before you import the image.

▼ ▼

Tip: Precision Placement. One way to achieve better precision in placing EPS graphics from CorelDRAW or Designer is to build crop marks around the image before importing it into QuarkXPress. Once you import it, you can adjust the placement of the picture so that the crop marks lie just outside the picture box frame.

▼ ▼

Resizing your picture. After placing the graphic image where you want it, you may want to scale it to some desired size. QuarkXPress allows you to resize the image within the picture box, stretching or compressing it horizontally and/or vertically. Most often we find ourselves wanting to enlarge or reduce the picture the same amount in both directions in order to best fit the available space.

If the picture box you created is just the size you want your picture to be, you can quickly and automatically resize the picture to fit the box by pressing Control-Shift-F. However, because this usually stretches the picture disproportionately (adjusting the horizontal and vertical sizing measures differently in order to fill the box), you probably want to press Control-Shift-Alt-F (that's a handful!), which makes the picture as large as it can be within the box without distorting it. Note that if you've rotated or skewed the picture first (see "Rotating, Skewing, and Distorting" below), autoresizing may not work exactly as you'd expect it to.

David almost never uses the simple and quick keystroke method, however, preferring to type the particular percentages he wants into the Measurements palette or into the Picture Box Specifications dialog box (Control-M). Of course, you can use a combination of these two methods, or even use a third: resizing the picture box.

Usually when you resize the picture box, it has no effect on the image which is in it, other than possibly cropping out areas of the picture. However, if you hold down the Control key while resizing, the image resizes along with the box (see Figure 6-13). As usual, holding down the Shift key constrains the picture box (and image) to a square or circle; holding down the Alt key along with the Control and Shift keys constrains the picture box (and image) to its proper proportions.

Figure 6-13
Resizing a picture by dragging the picture box handles

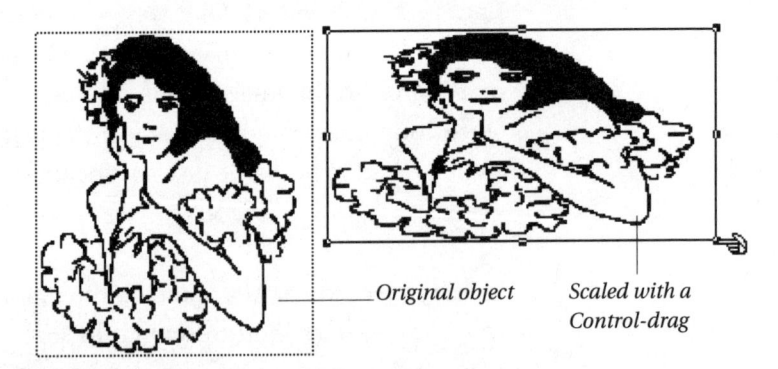

Original object

Scaled with a Control-drag

Resizing for better print quality. As we mentioned earlier, changing the size of a bitmapped image can significantly alter its appearance, either for the better or for the much worse. In general, reducing the size of a bitmapped image, especially if it's a low-resolution graphic, improves its output quality by effectively increasing its resolution (a 72-dpi image printed at 50 percent becomes a 144-dpi image). However, sometimes even a slight reduction can make a big difference.

Bilevel images that contain repeating patterns to produce a gray shade, for instance, can come out in plaid patterns when printed (see Figure 6-14). This is due to the incongruity between the resolution of the image and the resolution of the printer, and can be easily rectified by slightly scaling the image by a specific percent. The appropriate reduction can be determined by the following equation.

```
Picture resolution / Output resolution × Any
    whole number = Scaling percentage
```

You can use the chart in Table 6-2 to determine the best reduction for you, or you can create your own chart using the equation above. Let's walk through an example slowly. You have a 200-dpi bitmapped image that you want to reduce to about 35 percent, and you plan to print on a 600-dpi printer. If you divide the picture resolution by the output resolution, you get .333. In this case, the best whole number multiplier is one hundred, resulting in a 33.3-percent scaling. If you multiply by 110, you get 36.7 percent. Reducing to 35 percent may pattern, but either 33 or 36.7 percent probably won't.

Figure 6-14
Patterning due to nonintegral scaling

Table 6-2
Integral scaling for bitmapped images

When printer resolution is...	Scale 72-dpi images to any of...
1270 or 2540	34.02%
	56.69
	79.37
	96.38
	102.05
	119.06

	Scale 72-dpi images to any of...
300 or 600	12.00%
	24.00
	48.00
	72.00
	96.00
	120.00

	Scale 300-dpi images to any of...
1270 or 2540	23.62%
	47.24
	70.87
	94.49
	118.11
	141.73

Rotating, Skewing, and Distorting

QuarkXPress has such amazing graphic manipulation tools that you may never need to use an illustration program to distort images again. For example, let's look at two other modification techniques: rotating and skewing.

Rotation. QuarkXPress lets you easily rotate your imported pictures to a degree unheard of (and certainly rarely needed): one-thousandth of a degree. Once again, you are able to set the rotation of the image in several ways.

The first question you want to ask yourself is whether you want to rotate the frame, and along with it, the image, or just rotate the image itself inside the frame. You can accomplish either of these actions by typing in the rotation angle in the appropriate place in the Measurements palette or the Picture Box Specifications dialog box (see Figure 6-15).

Figure 6-15

The Picture Box Specifications dialog box and the Measurements palette

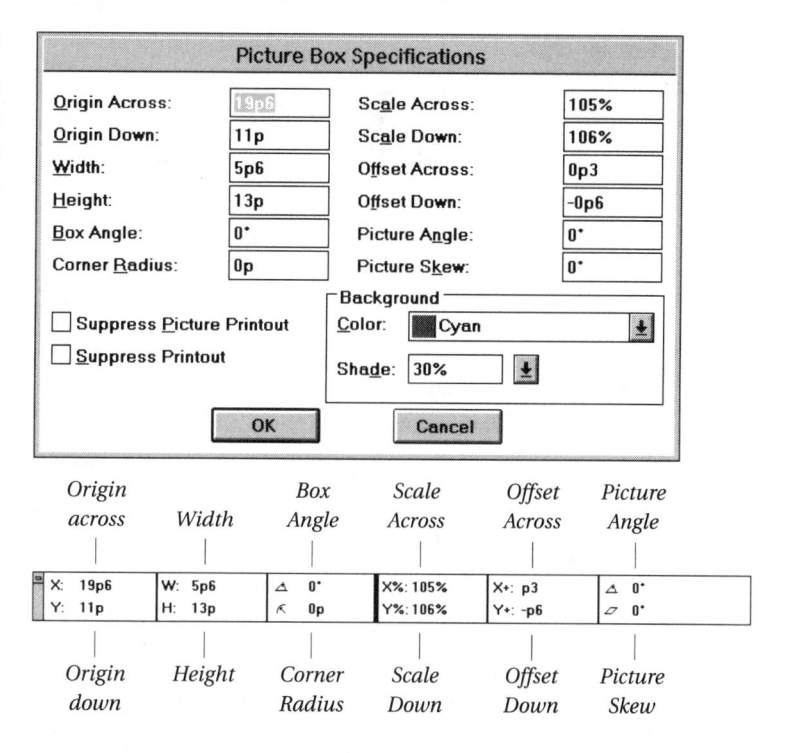

Picture Box Specifications		
Origin Across: 19p6	Scale Across: 105%	
Origin Down: 11p	Scale Down: 106%	
Width: 5p6	Offset Across: 0p3	
Height: 13p	Offset Down: -0p6	
Box Angle: 0°	Picture Angle: 0°	
Corner Radius: 0p	Picture Skew: 0°	

Background
Color: Cyan
Shade: 30%

☐ Suppress Picture Printout
☐ Suppress Printout

[OK] [Cancel]

Origin across — *Width* — *Box Angle* — *Scale Across* — *Offset Across* — *Picture Angle*

X: 19p6   W: 5p6   △ 0°   X%: 105%   X+: p3   △ 0°
Y: 11p   H: 13p   ⟨ 0p   Y%: 106%   Y+: -p6   ⟨⟩ 0°

Origin down — *Height* — *Corner Radius* — *Scale Down* — *Offset Down* — *Picture Skew*

▼▼▼▼▼▼▼▼▼▼▼▼▼▼▼▼▼▼▼▼▼▼▼▼▼

Tip: Rotating Your Picture Boxes. Rotating the frame rotates the image, too. The quickest way to "straighten out" your image is to rotate it back by the same amount. If you rotate your box 28 degrees but you want the picture to be straight, then rotate the image -28 degrees.

▼▼▼▼▼▼▼▼▼▼▼▼▼▼▼▼▼▼▼▼▼▼▼▼▼

NEW IN 3.3

See page 555

Skewing. Technically, skewing is the process of rotating the two axes differently, or rotating one and not the other. That is, if you rotate just the y-axis (vertical axis) of the coordinate system to the right, everything you print out is "obliqued" (see Figure 6-16). Quark-XPress allows you to skew only in the horizontal direction (rotating the y-axis), which is not a hindrance, as vertical skewing (or "shearing" as it is often referred to) is rarely required. Clearly, skewing an item is not needed every day, but it can be of great use in certain situations, enabling you to create interesting effects.

Figure 6-16
Skewing rotates the vertical axis

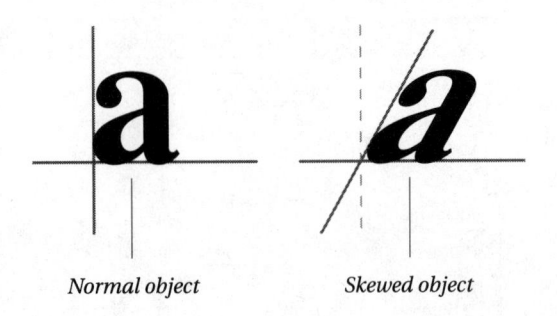

Normal object   *Skewed object*

You usually use only one of these effects at a time, perhaps in conjunction with scaling (resizing), but using all three together can make a graphic look quite unusual (see Figure 6-17).

One of the great advantages of these features is that they're not incremental. Unlike CorelDRAW or Aldus FreeHand, when you've rotated something 60 degrees, you just type 55 degrees rather than adjusting -5 degrees to change that rotation to 55 degrees. This makes it incredibly easy to get back to where you started with an image when you've distorted it beyond recognition: Just reset the scaling to 100 percent and the rotation and skewing to 0 degrees.

▼ ▼

Tip: Faking Perspective. To make a picture look like it's lying horizontally, change the picture rotation to -15 degrees, the picture skew to 45 degrees, and the vertical scaling to 70 percent (see Figure 6-18).

▼ ▼

Tip: Making Multiple Changes to Your Picture. If you know you are going to make multiple changes to your graphic image—changing the skewing, rotation, scaling, and offset, for example—you can speed up your formatting by making those changes in the Picture Box Specifications dialog box (press Control-M or Control-double-click on the object) so QuarkXPress processes all changes at once rather than one at a time.

PICTURES 317

Figure 6-17
Using all of the tools

Actual size

Scale across: 84%
Scale down: 149%

Across: 84%
Down: 149%
Rotate –30 degrees

Scale across: 300%
Scale down: 75%

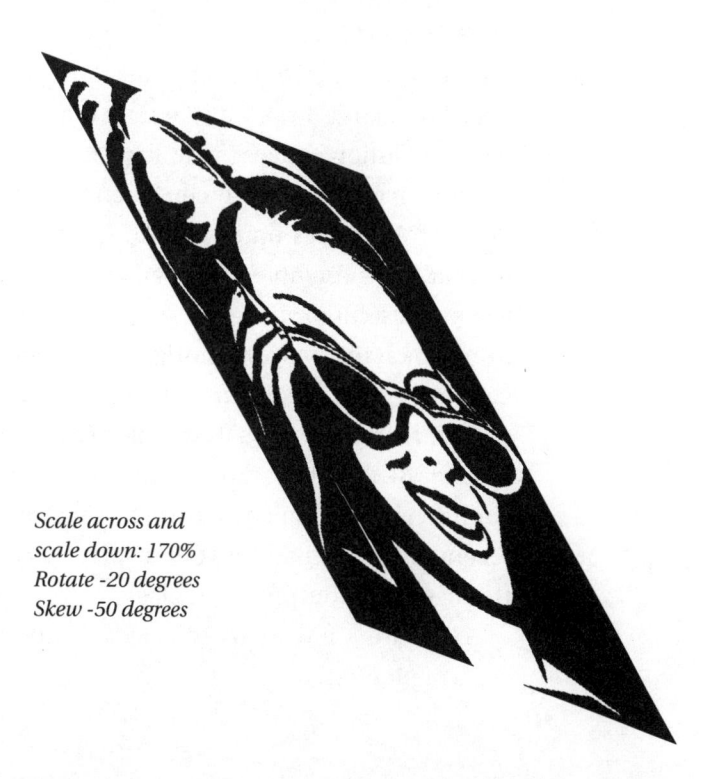

*Scale across and
scale down: 170%
Rotate -20 degrees
Skew -50 degrees*

Figure 6-18
Pseudo-perspective

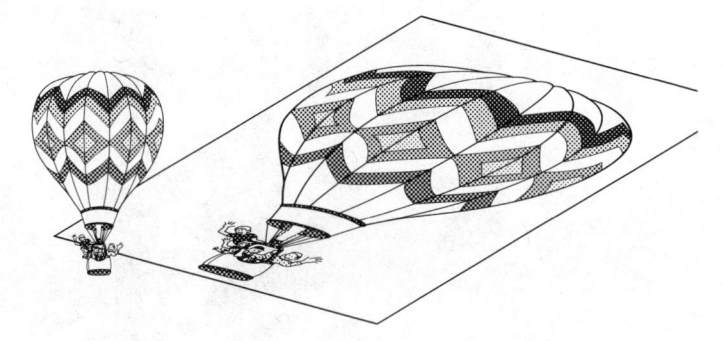

▼▼▼▼▼▼▼▼▼▼▼▼▼▼▼▼▼▼▼▼▼▼▼▼▼▼▼▼▼▼▼▼▼▼
Picture Management

Possibly the worst nightmare of a desktop publisher is arriving at the local service bureau to pick up 300 pages of film negative output, only to see that every illustration has come out as a low-resolution bitmap. Throwing away a thousand dollars is one way to learn some basics of picture management. Reading this section is another.

To Represent

The verb "to represent" means to stand in place for or to act as a placeholder. It is important to note that QuarkXPress represents high-resolution images (including TIFF, PCX, and EPSF) as low-resolution pictures on the screen when you import them using "Get Picture." When it's time to print, QuarkXPress searches for the original high-resolution image and uses it to automatically replace the low-resolution image. It looks first in the disk subdirectory from which the image was originally imported, then in the same subdirectory as the document you're printing, and finally in the subdirectory where you've installed QuarkXPress. If QuarkXPress is successful in this search, your output will look beautiful. If it cannot find the original, it uses the bitmapped 36- or 72-dpi representation (or whatever your display resolution) for printing. In this case, your output will look ugly.

Here are a few items to keep in mind when you use these sorts of pictures.

- Don't trash your file after importing it, assuming that it's placed for all time.

- Don't import your picture and then move the picture file into another subdirectory titled PICTURES (though doing the reverse of this is probably all right).

- Do be sure you know where your picture files are located.

- Do keep your picture files together if possible, to avoid confusion if you need to move your document someplace (like a service bureau).

- If you send your document to a service bureau (or anywhere else, for that matter), put the document and its high-resolution (EPSF, TIFF, or PCX) pictures together in the same disk subdirectory.

Picture Usage

Submitted for your approval: You've just completed a 600-page document with CorelDRAW illustrations on every page. The day before sending it to the imagesetter, you realize that you have to make changes to every other picture. Tearing your hair out in clumps, you stay up all night changing all of the pictures and recreating new EPS documents to replace the old ones. But now it's dawn, and you have to send it off or risk ruining the whole office's schedule. How will you re-import all of those graphics in time? What about replacing, rotating, and skewing them to the correct positions? What will you do? What *will* you do?

Fortunately, you remembered to bring along your copy of QuarkXPress, which can automatically re-import every image that has changed since the last time you saved the document. QuarkXPress keeps a running tally of all the pictures that you bring into a document, including the time when they were last modified. If you have "Auto Picture Import" set to On in the General Preferences dialog box, each time you open the document, QuarkXPress checks to see if any of the files have been modified.

If they have, QuarkXPress brings the new copy in transparently and seamlessly. You won't even know that anything has changed.

Clearly, not knowing what QuarkXPress is doing behind the scenes is sometimes disconcerting or frustrating. You have another option here, which is to set your document preference to "On (verify)." With this selected, QuarkXPress checks for modified or missing files, and if it finds any, asks you whether you want to re-import them. As with all QuarkXPress features, there is no one "right" way to set up your documents; in some situations you want verifiable auto-importing and in others you don't want any at all.

NEW IN 3.3

See page 597

No matter how you set the Auto Picture Import feature, you can always see a list of the pictures you have imported into your QuarkXPress document. Note that we said "imported." This does not include graphics that you have pasted in from the Clipboard or via OLE. The menu item to access this information is "Picture Usage" under the Utilities menu. The Picture Usage dialog box lists the pictures used, where they were originally found (their disk subdirectory path, starting from the disk volume and moving subdirectory by subdirectory down to the file in typical DOS fashion), the page number of the document where the picture is located, and the status of the picture—OK, modified, or missing (see Figure 6-19).

Figure 6-19
The Picture Usage dialog box

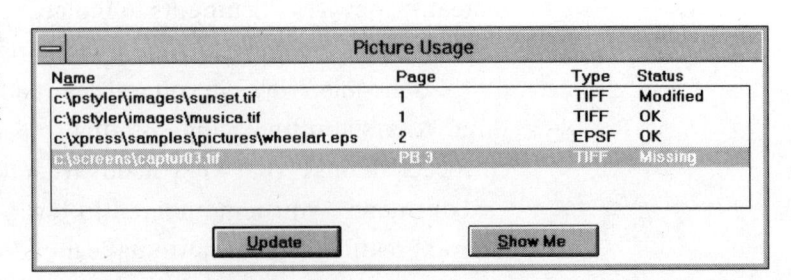

Name	Page	Type	Status
c:\pstyler\images\sunset.tif	1	TIFF	Modified
c:\pstyler\images\musica.tif	1	TIFF	OK
c:\xpress\samples\pictures\wheelart.eps	2	EPSF	OK
c:\screens\captur03.tif	PB 3	TIFF	Missing

OK. This is what you always hope for, especially before printing. QuarkXPress first looks for the picture file in the same place from which the file was imported, then in the same folder as the document, and finally in the QuarkXPress folder. If it finds it in any of these places, you receive the OK notation.

Modified. If the file has been changed in any way since you imported it, you see the Modified notice in the status column. You have two options at this point.

- You can ignore the "problem." Remember that because QuarkXPress uses the external file for printing, the document prints with the updated version rather than the original. In other words, it probably prints the way you want it to, as long as you want the modifications that were made to the picture.

- You can update the image. All this really means is that you bring in a new representation image for your document. This approach may help you avoid the annoying dialog box at print time, "Some pictures have been modified or missing." To update the file, just select the name and click the Update button.

Missing. If QuarkXPress cannot find a file with the same name anywhere it looks, it tells you that the file is missing. Again, you have two options.

- You can ignore it. This method is appropriate if you are trying to get some wild artsy effect using low-resolution printing, but is inappropriate for anyone trying to achieve a normal, good-looking, high-resolution print.

- You can update the image. If the picture has just been moved to another folder, you can update the link by selecting the file and clicking "Update." Here, you're not just bringing in a new representation, but actually relinking the "missing" picture with the document.

See page 590

"Picture Usage" is also valuable when you want to jump to a particular image and aren't sure where it is. For example, if you have many figures on many pages and want to go to the page that contains Figure 28-b, you can select that item in the Picture Usage dialog box and click the Show Me button. This results in the document displaying the appropriate page and highlighting the picture box that contains that figure. This also works for graphics that have been anchored to text and have flowed to unknown places.

The characters "PB" appearing next to the page number in the Picture Usage dialog box signifies that the picture is on the pasteboard as opposed to on the page itself.

▼ ▼

Tip: Relinking with a New Picture. When you update an image in the Picture Usage dialog box, you don't have to relink with the same picture. You can relink with any other picture, and that image comes in using the same picture specifications as the original (scaling, skewing, and so on).

▼ ▼

Greeking and Suppression

There are times when we'd really rather not see all of those pictures. Perhaps the screen redraw or printing time is too long. Or perhaps we want to use the picture for placement only in the electronic document and don't want it to print out. Or perhaps we just hate the pictures. Whatever the case, QuarkXPress has a solution for you.

Picture greeking. With "Greek Pictures," you can basically replace pictures with a gray box. The primary benefit of doing this is to speed up screen redraws: It takes much longer to redraw a detailed picture than it does to drop in a gray box where the image should be. Another benefit is found when designing your pages. Sometimes having greeked-in type and pictures allows you to see the page layout—including its balance and overall tone—better than if you are looking at "the real thing."

To greek the pictures in your documents, click on the Greek Pictures item in the General Preferences dialog box (use Control-Y for a shortcut to this dialog box). Note that with this option selected, all picture frames except for empty and selected frames are greeked. Selecting a frame with either the Item or the Content tool ungreeks the picture.

PICTURES 323

Suppression of pictures. In the instances when you want the picture on the screen but not on your printouts, you can select "Suppress Picture Printout" in the Picture Box Specifications dialog box (type Control-M, double-click using the Item tool, or go the easy route: Select "Modify" from the Item menu). You can also select "Suppress Picture Frame" in this dialog box, which suppresses both the picture contents and the frame itself.

New in 3.3
See page 591

Page as Picture

David recently worked on a book that required importing illustrations that had been created in QuarkXPress into PageMaker (horrors!). This is not an uncommon practice, of course; there are many times when you'd like to move text or graphics from QuarkXPress into other applications, or even to bring a page of a QuarkXPress document into another QuarkXPress document as a picture. You can take care of these situations with the Save Page as EPS feature.

Selecting "Save Page as EPS" from the File menu brings up a dialog box in which you can select a page of your document and save it as a separate EPS file. You can adjust the scaling of the page (for example, make the page 25 percent of full size) and choose between a color or a black-and-white screen image (or no screen image at all). There are two other issues that you should be aware of when saving a page as EPS: OPI and page size.

Using OPI

The OPI (Open Prepress Interface) method is based on postseparating full-color pages that include color, bitmapped images—especially scanned images. For example, you can import a single, low-resolution color TIFF file into a QuarkXPress document, save that page as an EPS, and separate it on a high-end color system, such as Hell or Crosfield. The low-resolution image is replaced in the EPS by OPI comments that indicate the file name and where the separation program can find it.

As it turns out, however, the OPI method also works very well for separating pages to an imagesetter such as the Linotronic 330 or the Agfa SelectSet 5000. You can export an EPS file with OPI comments in it and print that EPS file with Aldus PrePrint directly to the imagesetter. Aldus PrePrint "strips in" the high-resolution color image at print time, where the OPI comments tell it to.

This is nice for a couple of reasons. First, Aldus PrePrint has much better registration marks than QuarkXPress (unless you've built your own; see "Tip: Better Registration Marks," in Chapter 10, *Printing*). Secondly, it's often nice to have the option to move a small EPS page file around separately from the large TIFF files. (In a DCS image, when you make a PostScript dump or save the page as EPS, the image is encapsulated with it.) A third reason for using OPI and Aldus PrePrint is that you don't have to separate each TIFF image until you want to print it.

If you're saving the page as EPS in order to color-separate it on an OPI-specified system, you have three further options, in the OPI drop-down list: Include Images, Omit TIFF, and Omit TIFF & EPS.

Include Images. The default selection, "Include Images," simply means business as usual. QuarkXPress does not include OPI comments in the generated EPS files, but it does include the TIFF or EPS pictures that were placed on the page.

Omit TIFF. This is the basic setting for OPI comments. If you choose "Omit TIFF," any TIFF files placed on the page are excluded from the generated EPS file, and QuarkXPress includes OPI comments instructing the OPI system where to look for the high-resolution image files.

Omit TIFF & EPS. To tell you the truth, we don't know of any OPI system that requires you to use this last option, "Omit TIFF & EPS." Nonetheless, you can check with your OPI system operator to be sure. This option assumes that the OPI system substitutes both high-resolution TIFF and EPS files for the low-resolution versions you see on your screen.

Page Size

The page size of the generated EPS file is displayed in the dialog box so that you know how large the bounding box of the EPS image is. You can adjust this by changing the scaling. Remember that because this is PostScript, you can scale your EPS page down to 10 percent, bring it into another program, scale it back up to original size, and you won't lose any quality in your output (though your screen image may look awful).

Why would you care? The only two reasons we can think of are scaling to fit the needed size and attempting to save disk space. The latter is based on the fact that the smaller the percentage you specify, the smaller the preview TIFF has to be. We've seen a 20-percent difference in file size by adjusting this. However, we typically don't care that much about this factor, so we just leave it at 100 percent. By the way, the preview image of the EPS file is saved at the same resolution as your monitor.

Figure 6-20 shows a sample of a QuarkXPress page that was saved and brought back into another QuarkXPress document.

Figure 6-20
QuarkXPress page as EPS document

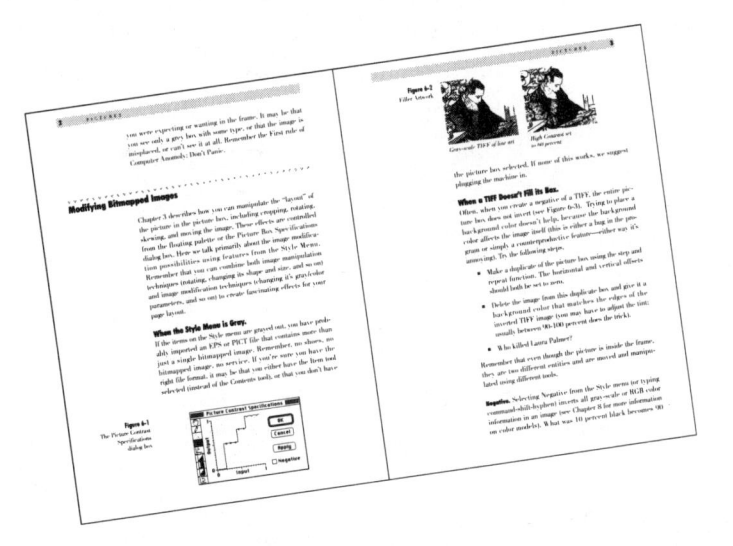

A word of warning here about EPS files from QuarkXPress: We don't mean to be pessimistic when we say that it would be foolish to save a full-color QuarkXPress page as EPS, export to Illustrator, save, then place on a PageMaker page, and only then send it through SpectreSeps PM for final color separations and expect it to work. Each of these programs was written by a different group of people, and consequently handles color, type, and graphic elements differently. Even though, theoretically, the above process should work (PostScript is PostScript, right?), there is almost no way that it ever would (if you can do it, send us a copy!). So, be careful and prudent when you combine programs; PostScript is not as stable as it sometimes seems, especially when pushed to the limit.

▼ ▼

Tip: Suppressing Pictures in EPS Pages. There are times when you don't want to see a graphic or have it print, but you still want it in the proper place in the document. For example, you've got a low-resolution scan set up for the text runaround, and you create an EPS file of the QuarkXPress page, placing the higher-resolution scan in another program. Creating an EPSF file of a page with a graphic that has been suppressed does not suppress the screen image of that graphic (although it still suppresses the printing of the picture). If you don't want to see the screen placement picture, you can cover it with another picture box (a rectangle or a polygon perhaps) with the background color set to 0-percent black (nontransparent) before creating the EPS file.

▼ ▼

CHAPTER 7

WHERE TEXT MEETS GRAPHICS

Putting text and graphics together on the page is perhaps the most daunting of design tasks. Done right, text and graphics enhance each other and create a natural visual flow on the page. Done recklessly, the result is about as aesthetically pleasing as a demolition derby. QuarkXPress offers more ways to position text around graphics than any other page-layout program. The technology itself won't make you a good designer, but if you know what you're doing, you'll be able to do it more easily. In Quark-XPress, putting text and graphics together on a page can yield four results.

- They can be positioned so that they don't interact at all.

- They can intrude on one another, with either the picture or the text prevailing (the text flows on top of the graphic or the graphic sits on top of the text).

- They can bump into one another with the text keeping its distance (called *text runaround*).

- One can become embedded in the other and move wherever the other goes.

QuarkXPress allows for each of these possibilities with features such as transparent boxes, text runaround, and anchored boxes. In this chapter, we look at each of these features and how they affect your pages.

Transparency

The concept of transparency was introduced in Chapter 1, *QuarkXPress Basics*, when we talked about layering objects in QuarkXPress. The point we want to stress here is that QuarkXPress lets you treat transparency and text runaround separately.

To make a text or picture box transparent, give it a background color of "None" in the Text or Picture Box Specifications dialog box (double-click on the box with the Item tool, or select it with either the Content or Item tool and press Control-M).

If one transparent picture box sits on top of another picture box, you can see the second picture box in back (unless there's a picture in the way). On the other hand, if a transparent picture box sits on top of a text box, the text can do two things: it may freak out and flow around the picture or the picture box, or it may sit there quietly and be trounced on (in which case you're able to see the text behind the picture box).

Text Runaround

You can control text flow around a graphic element using the Runaround Specifications dialog box, which is found by selecting a text or picture box and choosing "Runaround" from the Item menu (or typing Control-T). Text runaround is an attribute of a particular text or picture box. You must apply the runaround setting to the box around which the text should flow. For example, if you want text to wrap around a picture box, you should apply a runaround setting to the picture box.

Figure 7-1 shows the Runaround Specifications dialog box for a picture box. Note that each picture or text box has its own text runaround specification. The Runaround Specifications dialog box gives you four text runaround options for picture boxes and two options for text boxes. Text boxes have the option of either "None" or "Item." Picture box options are "None," "Item," "Auto Image," and "Manual Image." Let's look at each one of these options in detail, as they can give you radically different effects.

Figure 7-1
The Runaround Specifications dialog box

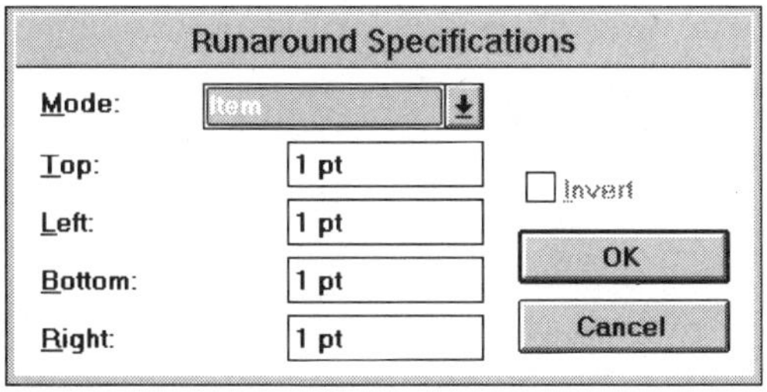

None

When you specify "None" as the Text Runaround mode, text that is "behind" a picture box flows normally. No text is offset, nothing is different. You may not be able to see much of the text behind the picture, but hey, that may be your design choice (see Figure 7–2). This option is available for both picture and text boxes.

Figure 7-2
Text Runaround Mode: None

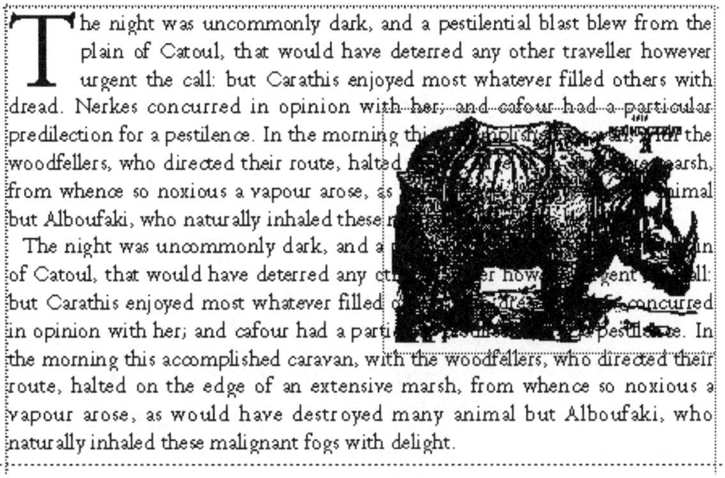

The night was uncommonly dark, and a pestilential blast blew from the plain of Catoul, that would have deterred any other traveller however urgent the call: but Carathis enjoyed most whatever filled others with dread. Nerkes concurred in opinion with her, and cafour had a particular predilection for a pestilence. In the morning this accomplished caravan, with the woodfellers, who directed their route, halted on the edge of an extensive marsh, from whence so noxious a vapour arose, as would have destroyed many animal but Alboufaki, who naturally inhaled these malignant fogs with delight.
   The night was uncommonly dark, and a pestilential blast blew from the plain of Catoul, that would have deterred any other traveller however urgent the call: but Carathis enjoyed most whatever filled others with dread. Nerkes concurred in opinion with her; and cafour had a particular predilection for a pestilence. In the morning this accomplished caravan, with the woodfellers, who directed their route, halted on the edge of an extensive marsh, from whence so noxious a vapour arose, as would have destroyed many animal but Alboufaki, who naturally inhaled these malignant fogs with delight.

Item

The Item runaround specification is also available for both text and picture boxes. The key here is to remember that "Item" refers to the box itself; it doesn't matter what's in the box. Any text that bumps into it flows around the edges of the box (see Figure 7-3). When you have "Item" specified in the Mode pop-up menu, you can change how far away the text should flow from the box on each of its four sides. This distance is called the *text outset*.

Figure 7-3
Text Runaround Mode: Item

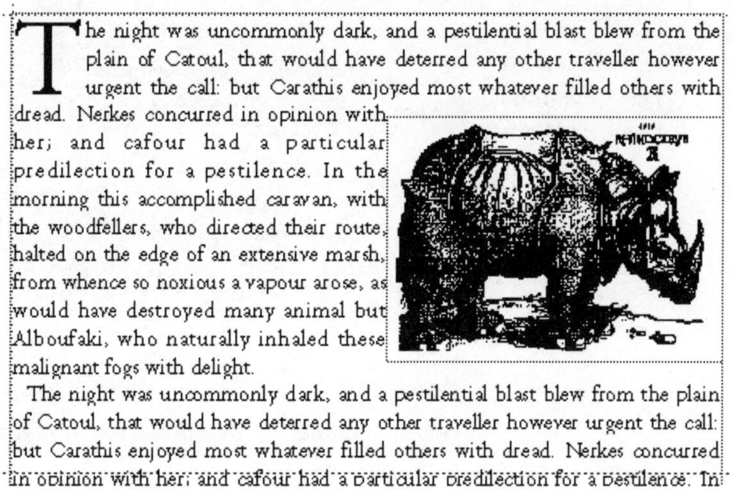

The night was uncommonly dark, and a pestilential blast blew from the plain of Catoul, that would have deterred any other traveller however urgent the call: but Carathis enjoyed most whatever filled others with dread. Nerkes concurred in opinion with her; and cafour had a particular predilection for a pestilence. In the morning this accomplished caravan, with the woodfellers, who directed their route, halted on the edge of an extensive marsh, from whence so noxious a vapour arose, as would have destroyed many animal but Alboufaki, who naturally inhaled these malignant fogs with delight.
  The night was uncommonly dark, and a pestilential blast blew from the plain of Catoul, that would have deterred any other traveller however urgent the call: but Carathis enjoyed most whatever filled others with dread. Nerkes concurred in opinion with her; and cafour had a particular predilection for a pestilence. In

Auto Image

The Auto Image Text Runaround mode is available only for picture boxes (that's why the word "image" is in the title). You can specify the text offset for the runaround, and QuarkXPress automatically determines where the image is and how the text should flow around it (see Figure 7-4).

The image is defined by its screen representation; if you have an EPS picture with a TIFF screen representation, QuarkXPress uses the low-resolution bitmapped image to figure out where the text should run around. If the EPS picture has no screen representation and you see only a gray box, QuarkXPress cannot figure out what the image looks like "inside" the gray box. In this case, it just uses the gray rectangle as the runaround boundary.

Although TIFF images are defined by a rectangle, QuarkXPress treats white space as "blank" space; if you have either a black-

Figure 7-4
Text Runaround Mode:
Auto Image

The night was uncommonly dark, and a pestilential blast blew from the plain of Catoul, that would have deterred any other traveller however urgent the call: but Carathis enjoyed most whatever filled others with dread. Nerkes concurred in opinion with her, and cafour had a particular predilection for a pestilence. In the morning this accomplished caravan, with the woodfellers, who directed their route, halted on the edge of an extensive marsh, from whence so noxious a vapour arose, as would have destroyed many animal but Alboufaki, who naturally inhaled these malignant fogs with delight.

The night was uncommonly dark, and a pestilential blast blew from the plain of Catoul, that would have deterred any other traveller however urgent the call: but Carathis enjoyed most whatever filled others with dread. Nerkes concurred in opinion with her, and cafour had a particular predilection for a pestilence. In

and-white or a gray-scale TIFF image with a lot of white space around the edges, QuarkXPress "sees" the boundary of the non-white image. However, even a single gray pixel apart from the main image can cause havoc with text runaround because QuarkXPress sets the text to run around that pixel, too (see Figure 7-5). Sometimes increasing the contrast of an image can help remove unwanted stray pixels (see Chapter 8, *Modifying Images*).

Figure 7-5
Misplaced pixels in a TIFF file

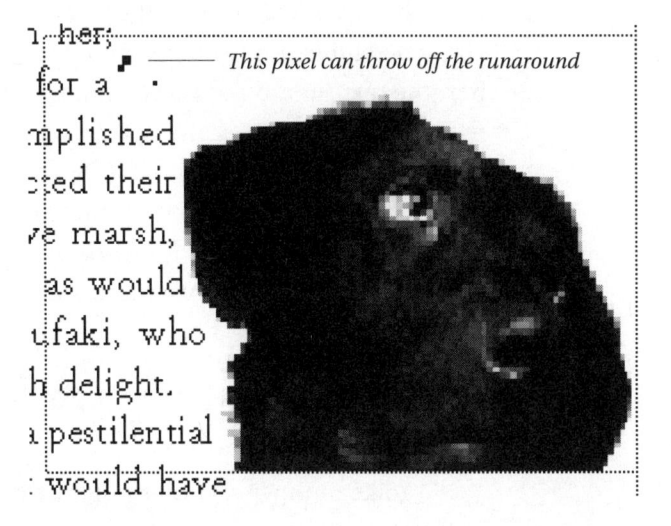

This pixel can throw off the runaround

Manual Image

The Manual Image Text Runaround feature is one of the coolest features in the program. It lets you specify exactly where you

NEW IN 3.3

See page 557

want a runaround to be using a text runaround polygonal boundary. These polygons are similar to the polygonal picture boxes we discussed in Chapter 1, *QuarkXPress Basics*, except that they are used only for text runaround purposes. Figure 7-6 shows an image with a manually set text runaround. Note the handles and dotted line specifying the corners and segments of the text runaround polygon.

Figure 7-6
Text Runaround Mode: Manual Image

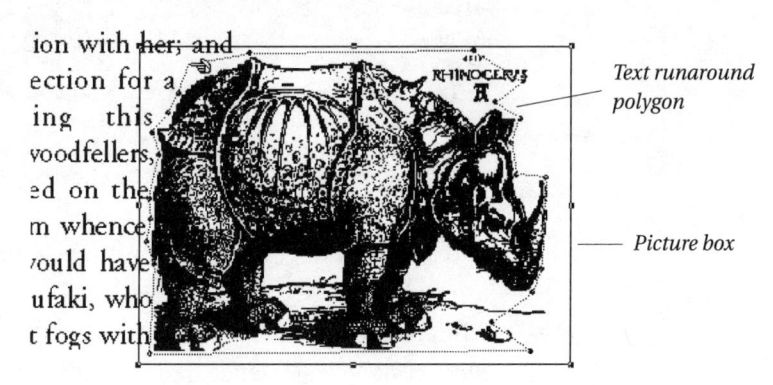

Text runaround polygon

Picture box

It's important to remember here that QuarkXPress is creating a new polygon that specifies the text runaround path. This polygon is tied inherently to the picture box. If you move the picture box, the text runaround polygon moves, too. However, you can resize or reshape either the polygon or the picture box without affecting the other.

For those of you who were in such a hurry to get into the book that you skipped Chapter 1, *QuarkXPress Basics*, here is a quick rundown of the necessary concepts and tools for working with polygons.

- Polygons are made up of segments joined by corner points.

- You can move a corner point by clicking on it and dragging it.

- You can also move a segment line of a polygon by clicking on it and dragging it. This moves the corner points at both ends of the segment.

- Moving corners or line segments while holding down the Shift key constrains the movement to 0, 90, or 45 degrees.

- You can add a corner point by holding down the Control key and clicking on a line where you want the corner point. When you hold down the Control key, the cursor turns into a hollow circle.

- You can delete a corner point by holding down the Control key and clicking on it.

- On text runaround polygons, you can delete the entire polygon by holding down the Shift and Control keys and clicking on the polygon. This deletes just the text runaround polygon, but not the picture box or the picture itself. The picture box then has no runaround assigned to it.

When you specify "Manual Image" for a picture box's runaround specification, QuarkXPress gives you the text runaround polygon that it uses internally for the Auto Image specification. You can then alter the polygon using the techniques outlined above so that the text runaround meets your design needs. Don't worry about getting it perfect the first time; you can always go back and change it.

Note that even though the text runaround polygon and the picture box are linked together when you move them, the picture box in no way restrains the movement of the polygon. For example, corner points and segments can be placed inside or outside the picture box (see Figure 7-7). In fact, you can use the Content tool to drag a picture and its text runaround polygon anywhere you want on the page (the picture "disappears" outside the picture box, but the text runaround polygon is still visible and active).

▼▼▼▼▼▼▼▼▼▼▼▼▼▼▼▼▼▼▼▼▼▼▼▼▼▼

Tip: Speed up Polygon Editing. Every time you change a corner or a line segment of a text runaround polygon, QuarkXPress redraws the polygon and recomposes the text to go around it. This quickly becomes tedious. You can delay reflowing the text until you've finished editing by holding down the Spacebar. When

Figure 7-7
The polygon is not restrained by the picture box

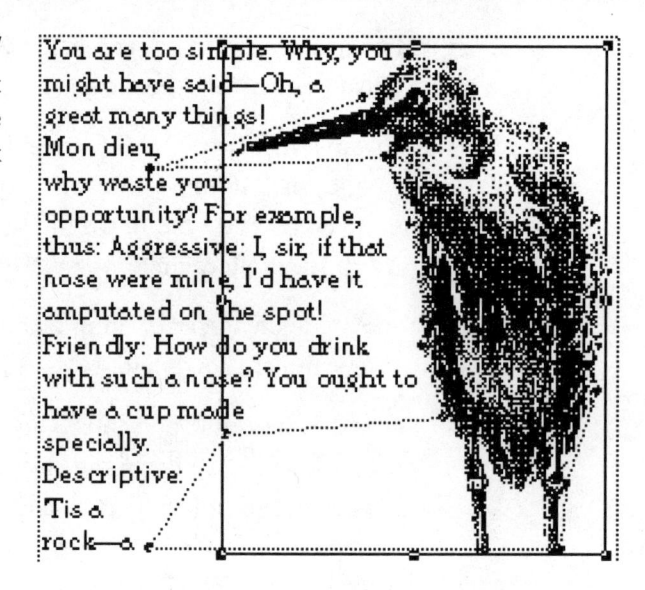

You are too simple. Why, you might have said—Oh, a great many things! Mon dieu, why waste your opportunity? For example, thus: Aggressive: I, sir, if that nose were mine, I'd have it amputated on the spot! Friendly: How do you drink with such a nose? You ought to have a cup made specially. Descriptive: 'Tis a rock—a

you're finished, just let go of the Spacebar, and QuarkXPress reflows the text.

▼▼▼▼▼▼▼▼▼▼▼▼▼▼▼▼▼▼▼▼▼▼▼

Tip: Picture Wrap with No Picture. After you have built a text runaround polygon around a graphic image, you can delete the picture, and the polygon remains. Remember to delete the picture while the Content tool is selected or else you delete the picture box (and the picture and the polygon with it), instead of just the contents of the box.

▼▼▼▼▼▼▼▼▼▼▼▼▼▼▼▼▼▼▼▼▼▼▼

Tip: Polygons from Empty Boxes. If a picture box is empty when you apply Manual Image text runaround, the text runaround polygon is created in the shape of the picture box itself. We find this handy for creating quick, custom text runaround paths that don't necessarily have anything to do with a graphic. It's useful, for example, to force a block of text to justify at an angle or wrap around a large drop cap (see Figure 7-8).

▼▼▼▼▼▼▼▼▼▼▼▼▼▼▼▼▼▼▼▼▼▼▼

Inverting the Text Wrap

Each of the text runaround types we've discussed is based on wrapping text around the outside of an object or polygon. The text flows on one side of the object only—on whichever side is

Figure 7-8

Text runaround polygons with no images attached

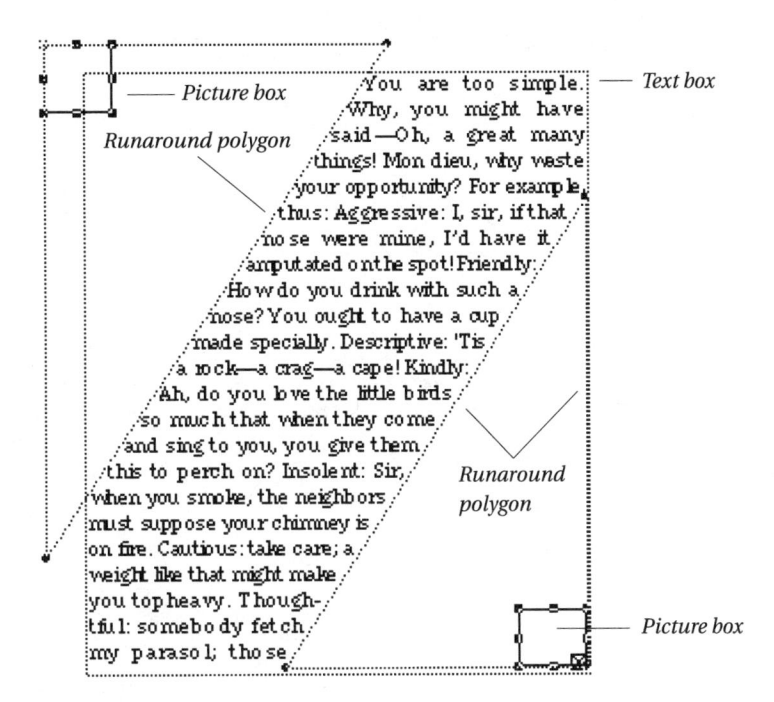

Picture box
Runaround polygon
Text box

You are too simple. Why, you might have said—Oh, a great many things! Mon dieu, why waste your opportunity? For example, thus: Aggressive: I, sir, if that nose were mine, I'd have it amputated on the spot! Friendly: How do you drink with such a nose? You ought to have a cup made specially. Descriptive: 'Tis a rock—a crag—a cape! Kindly: Ah, do you love the little birds so much that when they come and sing to you, you give them this to perch on? Insolent: Sir, when you smoke, the neighbors must suppose your chimney is on fire. Cautious: take care; a weight like that might make you topheavy. Thoughtful: somebody fetch my parasol; those

Runaround polygon
Picture box

wider and fits more text. However, you can also flow text inside a text runaround polygon (see Figure 7-9). This is called inverting the text wrap.

The trick in understanding how to invert the runaround quickly and easily is to remember that text flows where it has the most space to flow. First, select the picture box and give it a Manual Image text runaround (Control-T). Before you click OK in the Runaround Specifications dialog box, click the Invert button to make it possible to invert the runaround. When you click OK, your text may or may not run inside the text runaround polygon. If there is more space for the text to run outside the picture box, it does that.

To ensure that the text runs on the inside of the text runaround polygon, first confirm that the Invert button is checked. Then, resize the picture box (not necessarily the runaround polygon) so that the text has little or no room to flow around it.

Figure 7-9
Text flowing inside a text runaround polygon

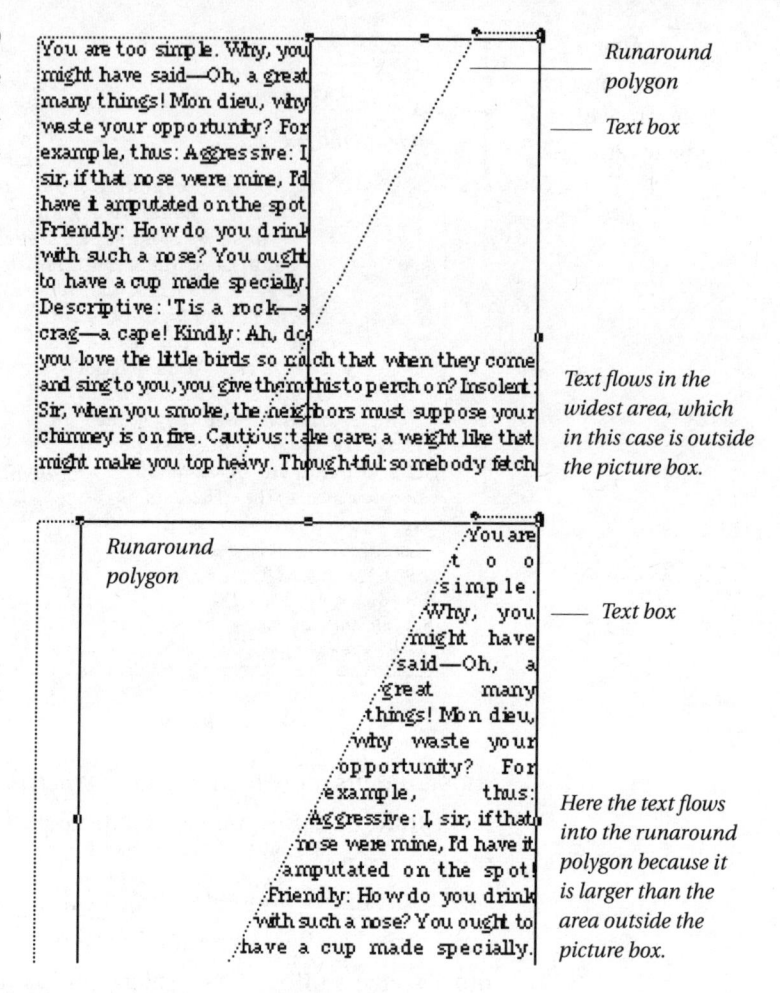

You are too simple. Why, you might have said—Oh, a great many things! Mon dieu, why waste your opportunity? For example, thus: Aggressive: I sir, if that nose were mine, I'd have it amputated on the spot. Friendly: How do you drink with such a nose? You ought to have a cup made specially. Descriptive: 'Tis a rock—a crag—a cape! Kindly: Ah, do you love the little birds so much that when they come and sing to you, you give them this to perch on? Insolent: Sir, when you smoke, the neighbors must suppose your chimney is on fire. Cautious: take care; a weight like that might make you top heavy. Thoughtful: somebody fetch

Runaround polygon

Text box

Text flows in the widest area, which in this case is outside the picture box.

Runaround polygon

You are too simple. Why, you might have said—Oh, a great many things! Mon dieu, why waste your opportunity? For example, thus: Aggressive: I, sir, if that nose were mine, I'd have it amputated on the spot! Friendly: How do you drink with such a nose? You ought to have a cup made specially.

Text box

Here the text flows into the runaround polygon because it is larger than the area outside the picture box.

▼▼▼▼▼▼▼▼▼▼▼▼▼▼▼▼▼▼▼▼▼▼▼▼▼

Tip: Disappearing Runaround Text. Remember that text runaround is based entirely on box layering. A picture box must be on top of a text box in order for Auto or Manual Image text runaround to have any effect. One problem many seasoned veterans of QuarkXPress have is that they forget they can assign a runaround to a picture box, while the box still has an opaque background. If you assign a text runaround and find that you can't see the text behind the picture box, make sure your box has a background color of "None."

▼▼▼▼▼▼▼▼▼▼▼▼▼▼▼▼▼▼▼▼▼▼▼▼▼

Tip: Full Wrapp'n'. We find that, occasionally, we'd like to have text wrap around both sides of a slender graphic extending down the middle of the text. The problem is that QuarkXPress wraps text only on one side or the other of a graphic, but not around both sides. We have a couple of ways to get around this, but—to tell you the truth—none of them is really that great. The best way (in our humble opinion) is just to tell your designer to design it differently! Barring that, you could try a method that uses a bunch of one-line-high text boxes.

1. Your text box should be only one column wide, with a graphic somewhere in the middle of it.

2. The graphic should have its runaround set to "None."

3. Make the text box end just above the graphic.

4. Put a new text box below the graphic, reaching down to the bottom of the column.

5. Link the top text box to the bottom one.

6. Make a single text box that is the height of one line of text. For example, if your text is 12/14, make a 14-point tall text box. Set the runaround to "None." This box should go just below the top text box (overlapping the graphic slightly).

7. Duplicate this box several times using Step and Repeat so that there are two stacks of text boxes reaching from the original, top text box to the new bottom one.

8. Link all of the text boxes together using the Link tool (remember that you can hold down the Alt key when you select the tool to keep it selected beyond one use). The Links should run from the top box to the first row of line-high text boxes, skipping over the graphic, to the next row, and so on. Ultimately, you'll have a bunch of linked text boxes with the graphic in the middle of the two columns.

9. Adjust the width of the line-high text boxes so that the graphic can be seen in the middle (you might want to bring the graphic to the front, too).

You can make life easier by selecting the Show Baseline Grid command from the View menu when you draw the line-high text boxes. This horizontal grid of handy "snap-to" guide lines makes it easy to create and adjust the series of text boxes you need.

If this tip sounds overly complex, it's only because it's really a kludge. However, after trying it once or twice, we find that we can do a half-page column in about five minutes.

Anchored Boxes

You probably don't think we can come up with a decent encore after those cool, manual-image text runaround polygons. Well, here's another cool effect: anchored boxes. Many programs let you paste graphic images directly into text. These are usually called *inline graphics*. QuarkXPress takes the concept of inline graphics one step farther by letting you paste either a picture or a text box directly into the flow of text. These picture or text boxes become *anchored* to the point where they have been pasted. In other words, as you type, they flow along with the text in the same position.

Anchored boxes can be used in many situations, such as placing small pictures in text as icons, creating picture drop caps, and allowing tables and figures to keep their place in text. Let's look at how these anchored boxes are created and how to work with them.

Turning a Box into a Character

We like to think of anchored boxes as turning a picture or a text box into a character that can be manipulated in a text block. This proves to be a useful model for working with anchored boxes. There are two steps involved in turning a picture or text box into an anchored box character.

1. Cut or Copy. The first step in creating an anchored box is to cut or copy the picture or text box using the Item tool. Click on the picture or text box and select Cut or Copy from the Edit menu (or type Control-X or Control-C). Because you're using the Item tool rather than the Con-

tent tool, the box itself is being cut or copied rather than just its contents.

2. Paste. The second step is to paste the box into the text using the Content tool. Select the text box and place the cursor where you want your anchored text box to sit, then select Paste from the Edit menu (or type Control-V). Because you're using the Content tool, the box is pasted in as a character in the text block rather than a separate box.

What you can't do. QuarkXPress prohibits you from making certain objects into anchored boxes. First of all, you cannot anchor a group of objects. Second, anchored boxes are just that: boxes. Therefore, you cannot anchor something that can't be defined as a box, like a line. And even though QuarkXPress calls polygons and ovals "boxes," it doesn't really let you anchor them (it turns them into rectangular picture boxes). A third function that the program won't allow is anchoring text boxes that have anchored boxes within them.

Plus, although there's lots of cool stuff you can do with anchored boxes, there's some stuff you simply can't do. For example, you cannot select and drag an anchored box to a new location. Nor can you rotate anchored boxes (unless you rotate the text box that they are pasted into). You can only resize anchored boxes using the sizing handles on the right and bottom sides.

Finally, one limitation that drives people crazy: You can't change the runaround specifications for an anchored box. The text runaround for an anchored box is determined primarily by its alignment within the text box (see "Alignment," below). If you want to adjust the text outset, you need to adjust it before you cut or copy it (note that as QuarkXPress stands right now, it only reads the text outset for "Top" and ignores the outsets for "Left," "Bottom," and "Right" when setting text around anchored boxes). Another prohibited function is text linking: You cannot link to or from an anchored text box; text within anchored boxes is self-contained, not chained to other boxes.

Modifying Anchored Boxes

But don't let all these "no-can-do's" dishearten you. There's still lots you can do.

The root of every change you can make with anchored boxes is the Anchored Box Specifications dialog box (there is one for picture boxes and another for text boxes; see Figure 7-10). Selecting the anchored box with either the Item or the Content tool and choosing "Modify" from the Item menu (or typing Control-M, or double-clicking the box with the Item tool) brings up the appropriate dialog box for the type of box that is anchored.

Figure 7-10
The Anchored Box Specifications dialog boxes

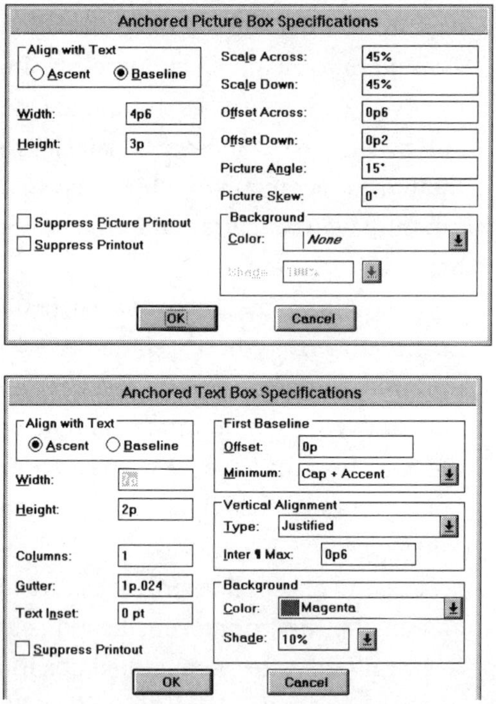

Resizing. You can resize anchored boxes either by dragging one of the three handles or by specifying a width or height in the Anchored Box Specifications dialog box or the Measurements palette. Remember that anchored picture boxes are just like normal picture boxes in most ways. For example, you can scale both the picture box and its contents by holding down the Control key while dragging one of the three control handles.

Contents modification. Both anchored text boxes and picture boxes are fully functional; you can edit, import, or reformat the contents of any anchored box. To alter the contents of an anchored box, you must use the Content tool, just as if you were altering a normal box.

▼ ▼

Tip: Blend in Anchored Boxes. Note that the background color for an anchored box is not necessarily equal to the text box in which it is located. For example, if your text box is set to 10-percent gray, and you anchor an opaque picture box into it, the anchored picture box most likely doesn't match its surroundings. If you can think of a better word than "tacky" to describe this, let us know. Be sure to specify "None" for the background in anchored boxes.

▼ ▼

Alignment. You can align an anchored box in two ways: "Ascent" or "Baseline." When you specify an anchored box to align by "Ascent," the top of the box aligns with the ascender of the tallest font in that text line. The rest of the figure drops down, and text wraps around it. This is most commonly used for creating drop-cap-like initial characters.

When you specify an anchored box to align by "Baseline," the bottom of the box aligns with the baseline of the line it's on. This is very helpful if the anchored box is within a line of text and is acting as if it were a special text character. How the text in previous lines accommodates this baseline alignment depends on the leading in the paragraph. If you specify absolute leading, the anchored box may overlap the text above it (see Figure 7-11). If you are using automatic or relative leading, the space between lines is widened to accommodate a larger anchored box. Again, the model of the anchored box as text character is particularly fitting, since these are the exact effects you would achieve by using an oversized character in a text block (see Chapter 4, *Type and Typography*).

When using a baseline-aligned anchored box that acts as a character within a line, we recommend that you use absolute leading for your paragraph. Otherwise, all hell can break loose,

Figure 7-11
Auto leading for anchored boxes

Set anchored boxes to Auto leading to prevent the graphic from overlapping text.

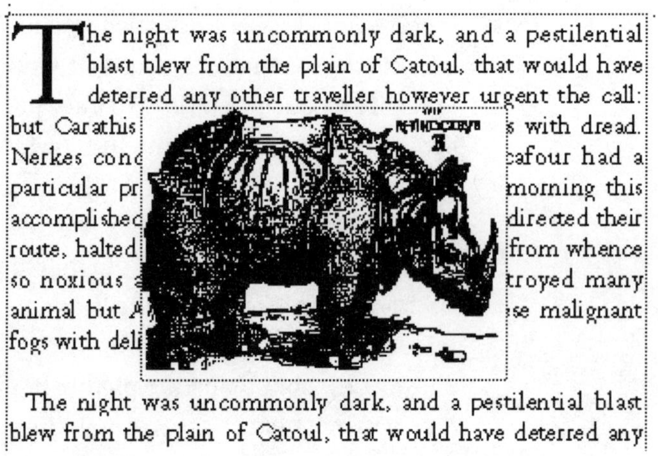

> The night was uncommonly dark, and a pestilential blast blew from the plain of Catoul, that would have deterred any other traveller however urgent the call: but Carathis   s with dread. Nerkes con   cafour had a particular pr   morning this accomplished   directed their route, halted   from whence so noxious   royed many animal but A   se malignant fogs with del
>
> The night was uncommonly dark, and a pestilential blast blew from the plain of Catoul, that would have deterred any

Absolute leading

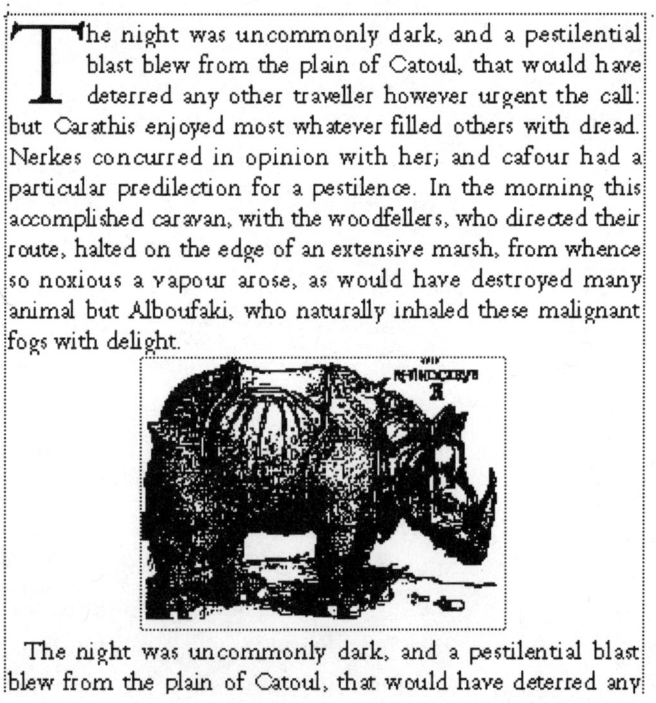

> The night was uncommonly dark, and a pestilential blast blew from the plain of Catoul, that would have deterred any other traveller however urgent the call: but Carathis enjoyed most whatever filled others with dread. Nerkes concurred in opinion with her; and cafour had a particular predilection for a pestilence. In the morning this accomplished caravan, with the woodfellers, who directed their route, halted on the edge of an extensive marsh, from whence so noxious a vapour arose, as would have destroyed many animal but Alboufaki, who naturally inhaled these malignant fogs with delight.
>
> The night was uncommonly dark, and a pestilential blast blew from the plain of Catoul, that would have deterred any

Auto leading

and text is shoved all over the place (however, see "Tip: Anchored Figures on Their Own Line," below).

You can choose the anchored box's alignment in two places: the Anchored Box Specifications dialog box or the Measurements palette. To change the alignment using the Measurements palette, click on one of two icons on the far left of the palette. The top icon represents "Ascent," and the bottom icon represents "Baseline."

▼▼▼▼▼▼▼▼▼▼▼▼▼▼▼▼▼▼▼▼▼▼▼▼▼▼

Tip: Anchored Figures on Their Own Line.
You might use an anchored box within a line of text for a symbol, complex dingbat, or company logo, but more frequently you'll use it as a single "character" within its own paragraph. You can quickly get your page into a muddle unless you're careful with paragraph leading. We know we said we hated automatic leading and that you should never use it, but here's an exception. Setting the paragraph that contains the anchored box to "Auto Leading" ensures that there is enough space above the image so that it doesn't overlap any text. The anchored box's alignment should be set to "Baseline," too (see Figure 7-12).

▼▼▼▼▼▼▼▼▼▼▼▼▼▼▼▼▼▼▼▼▼▼▼▼▼▼

Figure 7-12
Anchored box alignment

Upwards and onwards, into the breach of contract he jumped, pen in hand and gas pedal under foot, ☞ whizzing along the Los Angeles freeways and bylaws.

Aligned by baseline. Text has absolute leading.

Upwards and onwards, into the breach of contract he jumped, pen in hand and gas pedal under foot, ☞ whizzing along the Los Angeles freeways and bylaws.

Also aligned by baseline. Text has automatic leading.

Tip: Aligning Text in Anchored Boxes. If you're trying to align the baselines of text in an anchored text box with text that surrounds it, you need to make sure of three things.

- The leading in the anchored text box and the surrounding text box must be equal.

- The anchored text box must be set to 0 (zero) text outset in the Runaround Specifications dialog box. Note that this is not the same as selecting "None." Because you cannot specify runaround for a box once it's anchored, you should set this before you cut and paste it.

- The anchored text box must have a text inset of 0 (zero). You enter this value into "Text Inset" in the Anchored Text Box Specifications dialog box (Control-M or double-click with the Item tool).

▼▼▼▼▼▼▼▼▼▼▼▼▼▼▼▼▼▼▼▼▼▼▼▼▼

Tip: Anchored Boxes as Initial Caps.

NEW IN 3.3
See page 589

In Chapter 4, *Type and Typography*, we implied that you could use anchored boxes as initial drop caps simply by pasting them in as the first character of a paragraph and setting their alignment to "Ascent." However, you may run into a problem. At the time of this writing, there is a bug in QuarkXPress that still has not been fixed. The bug is that if your paragraph has any sort of left indent, some text lines that wrap around the anchored box are indented from the anchored box itself (see Figure 7-13).

Figure 7-13
Anchored boxes can cause problems

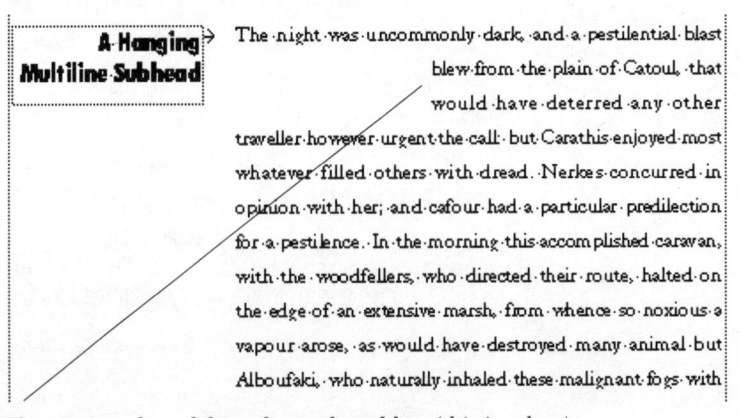

The text is indented from the anchored box (this is a bug)

You have four choices for fixing this problem.

- Don't use left-indented text.

- Don't use anchored boxes for left-indented text.

- Use the Indent Here character (Control-\). This works only if your anchored box is supposed to be hanging in the margin.

- Write a postcard to Quark telling them to fix this problem.

▼▼▼▼▼▼▼▼▼▼▼▼▼▼▼▼▼▼▼▼▼▼▼▼▼▼▼

Working with Anchored Boxes

David had a professor once who maintained that when someone reaches perfection, the skies open and he or she is lifted into the heavens in perfect bliss. Given that you're reading this book, you probably haven't reached that pinnacle yet. So what happens if you don't place the anchored box perfectly where it should be? Or what if you decide to change your mind and delete the anchored box?

Don't worry, we've got answers for all of that (even though the skies aren't opening here, either).

Moving anchored boxes. As we said earlier, you cannot move an anchored box by just dragging it around, as you would any other box. Using the model that once an anchored box is placed in a text block it behaves like a text character, you can move the anchored box "character" by cutting and pasting it with the Content tool.

Deleting anchored boxes. We'll say it just one more time: Anchored boxes are just like text characters. Do you delete text characters with the Delete command from the Item menu (or type Control-K)? No, a character is not an item; it's a character and should be treated as one. If you want to stamp out the measly existence of an anchored box, place the cursor to the right of it and press the Backspace key—or before it and press Delete or Shift-Backspace.

Also, once you've turned a box into a character to anchor it, you can't just cut it and paste it somewhere else as with a stand-alone graphic.

Tip: Getting an Anchored Box out Again. We like to say, "There's always a workaround." As it happens, there are actually two ways to get an anchored box out as a standalone graphic. The first way is to select it with either the Content or the Item tool (we mean click on the box rather than drag over it like a character) and select "Duplicate" from the Item menu (Control-D). This makes a copy of the box, but in standard (nonanchored) form. The second method is to select the anchored box with the Item tool, copy it, and then paste it elsewhere (while still using the Item tool). This is the one instance where it does no good to think of the anchored box as a character. Oh well, models can't always be perfect.

Anchored Rules

While it's true that you cannot paste rules (lines) into text to anchor them, you can actually produce anchored rules using a different method. You can set anchored rules through paragraph-level formatting in text, and build them into style sheets. Unlike so many other features in QuarkXPress, you can only set anchored paragraph rules in one way. Unfortunately, these rules can only be horizontal (see "Tip: Vertical Rules," later in this chapter).

Rule Above/Rule Below

The one way to set anchored paragraph rules is via the Paragraph Rules dialog box. While your text cursor is in a paragraph or highlighting it, you can select "Rules" from the Style menu (or type Control-Shift-N). You then have the choice—place a rule above the paragraph, below it, or both. When you select one of these rule positions, QuarkXPress expands the dialog box to give you more choices (see Figure 7-14).

The expanded Paragraph Rules dialog box gives you many options over the placement, size, and style of your horizontal rule. Let's look at each element of the dialog box.

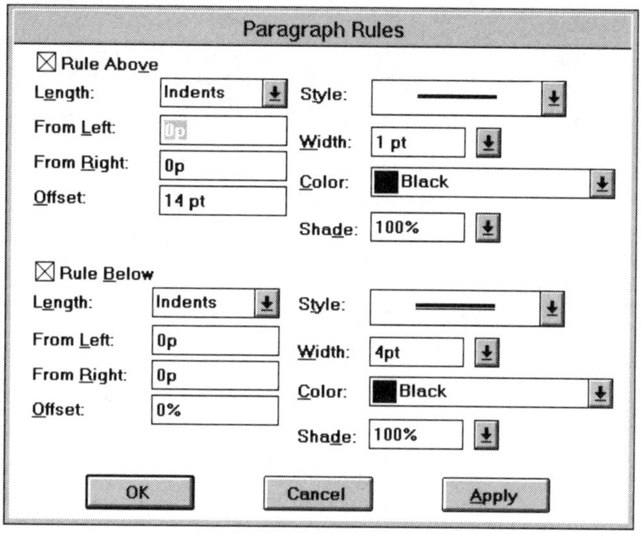

Figure 7-14
The Paragraph Rules dialog box

On the right side of the Paragraph Rules dialog box, you can choose the line style, width (thickness), color, and shade for the rule using the pop-up menus. You can also type in your own value for the Width and Shade fields to the thousandth of a point or tenth of a percent.

The line styles available are the same styles available for all lines (see Chapter 1, *QuarkXPress Basics*).

Length. You can specify the length of the rule and its horizontal position using the Length pop-up menu and the From Left and From Right controls. You first need to decide whether you want the rule to stretch from the left indent of the paragraph to the right indent (select "Indent" in the Length pop-up menu) or only to stretch as far as the text (select "Text" in the Length pop-up menu). Figure 7-15 shows examples of these settings.

Horizontal offsets. Offsets from the left and right are the next considerations in determining the length of the rule. You can specify how far from the left or right the rule should start (or end) by typing a measurement into the From Left and/or the From Right fields. Your only limitation in offsetting the rule is that the rule cannot go outside the text box. If your paragraph is set to a left indent of 1p6, the minimum left offset you can type is -1p6.

Figure 7-15
The Length setting in "Rule Above/Rule Below"

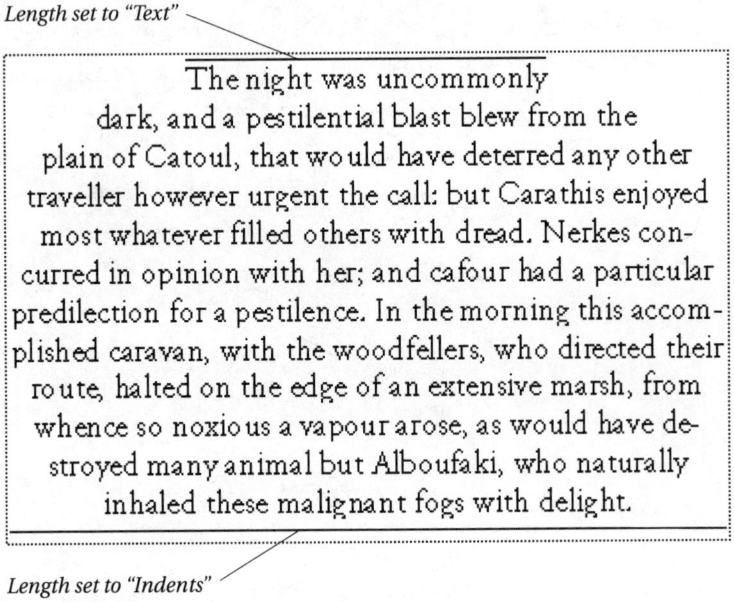

Length set to "Text"

> The night was uncommonly dark, and a pestilential blast blew from the plain of Catoul, that would have deterred any other traveller however urgent the call: but Carathis enjoyed most whatever filled others with dread. Nerkes concurred in opinion with her; and cafour had a particular predilection for a pestilence. In the morning this accomplished caravan, with the woodfellers, who directed their route, halted on the edge of an extensive marsh, from whence so noxious a vapour arose, as would have destroyed many animal but Alboufaki, who naturally inhaled these malignant fogs with delight.

Length set to "Indents"

Vertical position. The third specification you can make for an anchored paragraph rule is its vertical position relative to the paragraph to which it is attached. This concept is a little tricky, and Quark's documentation doesn't do a lot to help clarify the idea. Let's break it down into pieces.

The vertical positioning of the rule is set in the Offset field. We don't like the word "offset," as it confuses the issue. We prefer the term "positioning," so that's what we'll use. Just remember that these values go in the Offset field. You can specify positioning with either an absolute measurement or a percentage. QuarkXPress handles each of these very differently.

Let's take absolute positioning first. An absolute measurement for a rule above is measured from the baseline of the first line in the paragraph to the bottom of the rule. An absolute measurement for a rule below is measured from the baseline of the last line in the paragraph to the top of the rule (see Figure 7-16).

Specifying the vertical position of a rule by percentage is slightly more complex. The first thing to remember is that the percentage you are specifying is a percentage of the space between the paragraphs. This space is measured from the descenders of the last line of a paragraph to the ascenders of the first line of the next paragraph.

Figure 7-16
Vertical positioning of rules

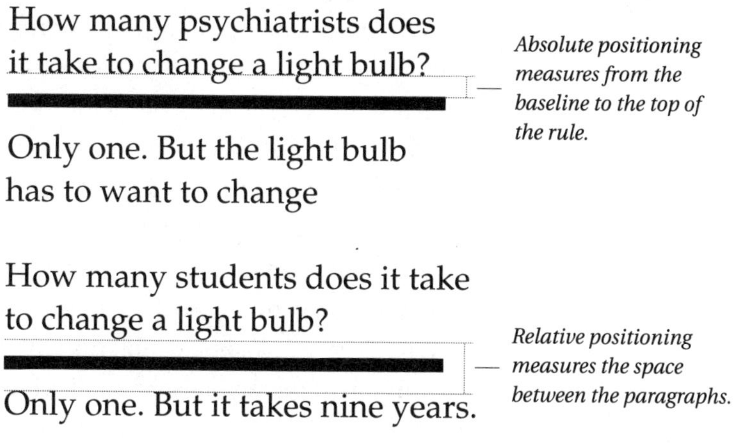

How many psychiatrists does it take to change a light bulb?

Absolute positioning measures from the baseline to the top of the rule.

Only one. But the light bulb has to want to change

How many students does it take to change a light bulb?

Relative positioning measures the space between the paragraphs.

Only one. But it takes nine years.

Let's look at an example. If you position a rule below a paragraph to 60 percent, QuarkXPress measures the distance between the two paragraphs (descender to ascender) and places the center of the rule 60 percent of that distance down.

From there on, though, the process gets mighty confusing. QuarkXPress for Windows doesn't appear to follow the same rules as the Macintosh version. Whether or not this is a bug, we're going to report it as we see it at print time. You have two choices: You can read the next paragraph or skip it (we wrote it, and we'd *still* skip it!).

Assuming, for example, that you're using a "rule below" at 0 percent, the rule grows *down* from the bottom of the paragraph as you increase its weight. At 100 percent, the rule grows *up* from the top of next paragraph. At 50 percent, the midpoint of the rule coincides with the midpoint between the two paragraphs and grows up and down equally from its midpoint. At 25 percent, the rule grows up and down proportionally from its quarter point. That means that a point ¼ of the way down from the top of the rule coincides with a point ¼ of the way between the two paragraphs. Another way of stating this relationship is that at a point 25 percent of the distance between the two paragraphs, 25 percent of the rule grows upward, and 75 percent of it grows downward. The same holds true for any percentage you choose, although it reverses once you get past 50 percent. At 75 percent, for example, 25 percent of the rule extends down from the 75-

percent point between the two paragraphs, and 75 percent extends up. There may be order in this scheme, but, whew! It takes too much arithmetic to determine how much space there is between the text and the actual top edge of the rule.

To us, percentage-based positioning is equivalent to automatic leading: We don't like it or its kind. We don't think it should be run out of town, because there's always a place for that kind of feature, but in general, we don't like to use it.

Why? There are some problems with percentage-based rules (in addition to the mental gymnastics required). For example, if a paragraph is specced to have a rule 30 percent above it, the rule doesn't show up if that paragraph sits at the top of a text box. A paragraph with a rule set some percentage below it won't appear if that paragraph is the last paragraph in the text box. It is nice that positioning a rule based on a percentage ensures that the rule doesn't overlap any text (it pushes the paragraphs away from each other if it needs to). Overall, we would rather have complete control over where the rule falls and feel sure that the rule is there no matter what happens to the paragraph.

▼ ▼

Tip: Reversed Type in Rules. This is one of the oldest tricks in the book. You can make reversed type that is anchored to text by assigning a thick rule above or below a paragraph and setting the type in the paragraph to white. You need to specify a vertical positioning for the rule so that it "overlaps" its own line. Out of habit, we always use a rule above about four or five points larger than the text size and specify a -2- or -3-point offset (vertical position). You can use this same technique to create multiple-tinted tables (see Figure 7-17).

▼ ▼

Tip: Vertical Rules. Nope, there's no way to cajole, coerce, or configure QuarkXPress to paste or place an anchored vertical line in a text block. Or is there? We work around this problem with the following technique:

1. Create a picture box as thin or thick as you want your rule.

2. Give the picture box the background color you want the rule to be (for example, 80-percent magenta).

Figure 7-17
Type in a rule

Wednesday, 1855		
Spread	750	1000
Full page	600	800
Half page	400	500
Quarter page	275	375
Spot	175	250
Fido	100	102

— Rule Above with -5-point offset

⟩ These are rules, too!

3. Copy and paste this empty picture box into the text block as described in "Anchored Graphics," above. You'll probably want to paste it either at the beginning of a paragraph or on a line on its own.

4. Set the anchored box to Ascent alignment and the text in the text box to absolute leading, so it wraps around the picture box/rule.

Figure 7-18 shows a sample vertical rule made using this method. Note that in this example, the rule appears as if it is set off from the left text margin. Actually, the text is set off from the rule using a 9-point tab and then an Indent Here character. The picture box/rule is the first character in the paragraph.

Figure 7-18
Anchored vertical rule

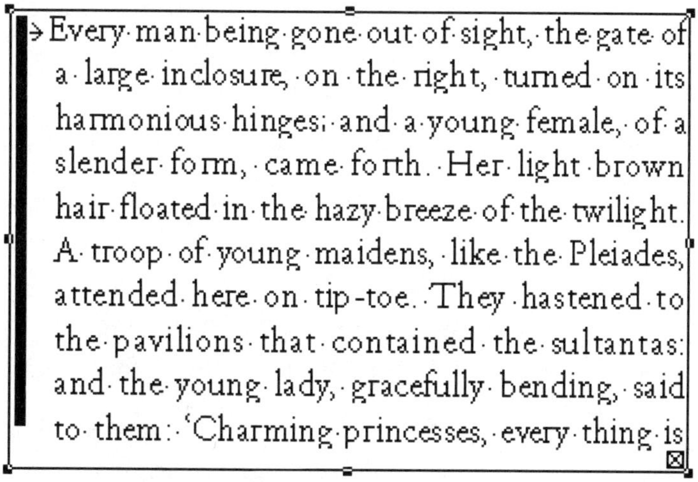

> Every man being gone out of sight, the gate of a large inclosure, on the right, turned on its harmonious hinges; and a young female, of a slender form, came forth. Her light brown hair floated in the hazy breeze of the twilight. A troop of young maidens, like the Pleiades, attended here on tip-toe. They hastened to the pavilions that contained the sultantas; and the young lady, gracefully bending, said to them: 'Charming princesses, every thing is

▼▼▼▼▼▼▼▼▼▼▼▼▼▼▼▼▼▼▼▼▼▼▼▼▼▼

Tip: Return of Vertical Rules. If you need a vertical rule thinner than 1 point, you're out of luck with the last tip. The minimum thickness of a picture box is 1 point. It's obviously time to resort to drastic measures: Build the rule in a drawing program and then import it into a picture box before anchoring it in a text box. If you need to lengthen or shorten the rule, just change the vertical scaling of the picture.

▼▼▼▼▼▼▼▼▼▼▼▼▼▼▼▼▼▼▼▼▼▼▼▼▼▼

Tip: Vertical Rules Strike Back. Here's an easy way to use the Rules command to create vertical rules that move along with a paragraph, as shown in Figure 7-19. The secret of this trick is to fool QuarkXPress into making a vertical rule out of a horizontal paragraph rule that's much, much thicker than it is long. Here's what you do.

Figure 7-19
More vertical rules

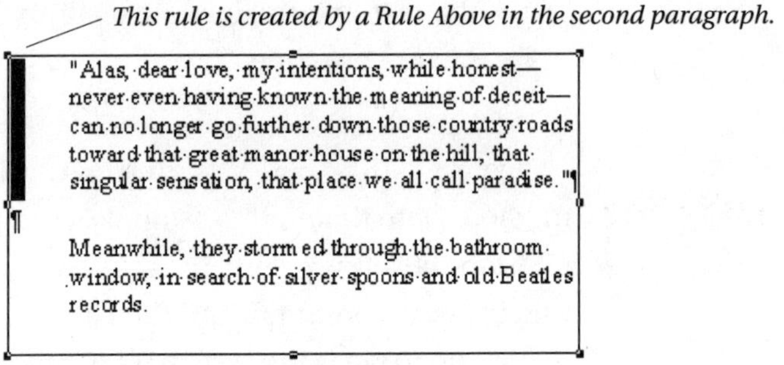

This rule is created by a Rule Above in the second paragraph.

"Alas, dear love, my intentions, while honest—never even having known the meaning of deceit—can no longer go further down those country roads toward that great manor house on the hill, that singular sensation, that place we all call paradise."

Meanwhile, they stormed through the bathroom window, in search of silver spoons and old Beatles records.

1. Give the paragraph a left indent wide enough for the thickness of the rule that you want, plus some extra thickness for white space.

2. Add a second paragraph below the first, with no left indent.

3. Use Paragraph Rules (Control-Shift-N) to set a rule above the second paragraph. Set the rule's offset equal to the distance between the baseline of the first line of the second paragraph and the last line of the first. If you set your offset using percentages, this trick won't work.

4. Set the width of the rule equal to the depth of the paragraph above. So if the paragraph above contains five lines with 10-point leading, set the rule's width to 50 points.

Now you can experiment with the three following methods for setting the width of the vertical rule.

1. Set the length of the rule equal to the paragraph's indents, then specify a large right offset.

2. Even better, set the length to Indents, then go to the Paragraph Format dialog box and drag the right indent triangle in the ruler over to the left until you have a very skinny paragraph. Clicking Alt-Apply will let you see the effect of your dragging on the width of the vertical rule. As the right indent gets wider, the rule gets narrower.

3. Set the length to "Text" and type a period, hyphen, or em dash in the second paragraph. The rule instantly becomes as wide as the character. You can then make the character white, or 0 percent black, so it won't print. This also works with the Tab character.

Poking and Prodding

Where text meets graphics: Like we said, it's a wild, woolly frontier just waiting to be mastered. We've explored how different boxes and page elements can interact, but these are mysterious regions where there is no substitute for poking and prodding about on your own.

The next two chapters deal with a few of the more detail-oriented features in QuarkXPress: modifying bitmapped images and working in color. After reading those, you'll be able to create any page known to humankind (and a few that aren't).

CHAPTER 8

IMAGE MODIFICATION

Once your graphics are on the page, there's one more set of QuarkXPress features to consider: image modification. It's not the kind of image modification you find in *Vogue* or *Gentleman's Quarterly*. We're all familiar with that kind (Bob keeps a Nehru jacket and gold chains in his closet for such emergencies, and David has a chest full of white socks). No, we're chiefly concerned here with gray-scale images, such as scanned photos. Given the vagaries of the printing process, it seems there's no end to the amount of tweaking such images require. Fortunately, you can do some of that last-minute fine-tuning right in QuarkXPress.

In Chapter 6, *Pictures*, we discussed several graphic file formats, how to bring them into your QuarkXPress documents, and how to do basic manipulations with them, such as rotating, skewing, and scaling. In this chapter, we look at how you can use QuarkXPress in place of other image-editing software to modify the imported image itself. Bear in mind that we're not talking about image editing. You can't actually change the contents of imported graphics in QuarkXPress. You can, however, change some of their overall parameters, such as contrast, color, and halftone screen.

We begin this chapter by examining the types of images we can modify, and then we move into how to modify them. Much of this is potentially confusing, but bear with us, read carefully, and you'll be an inexorable image modifier faster than you can say "phylogeny recapitulates ontogeny."

The Picture File

In this chapter, we are only concerned with bitmapped images. Bitmapped images, as far as QuarkXPress is concerned, are black-and-white, gray-scale, or color, and are found in TIFF, PCX, GIFF, Windows bitmap, and some Macintosh PICT files. Due to the nature of object-oriented EPSF files, QuarkXPress can import them (see Chapter 6, *Pictures*) but does not allow any modifications, such as contrast control, to be performed on them. We typically use TIFF files whenever possible, though Windows Paintbrush files are fine for small black-and-white images.

Bitmapped Images

You may want to take this opportunity to refresh your memory from Chapter 6, *Pictures*, about bitmapped images and the particular file types of PCX and TIFF. Here are the highlights.

- Bitmapped images are simply rectangular grids of pixels (dots).

- The resolution of the image is the number of these dots per inch.

- Each pixel is assigned to be black, white, a level of gray, or a color. This color is represented by a number; for example, black might be 256 in a 256-gray-level file.

- Scaling the image has a direct effect on the resolution of the image. Enlarging the picture to 200 percent cuts the resolution in half, which may result in jaggies or pixelation. Reducing the image to 50 percent doubles the resolution, which may improve image quality (see Figure 8-1).

- A TIFF file can be a rectangle of any size with any number of dots per inch, and each pixel can have any level of gray or color, which is definable by the color models described in Chapter 9, *Color*. TIFF files are said to be "deep" if they contain four or more gray levels (more than 2 bits per sample point).

Figure 8-1
Resolution and scaling with a bitmapped image

50%

100%

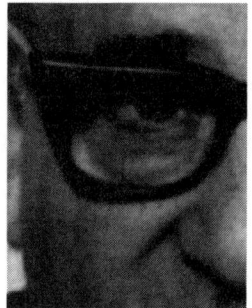

300%

Modifying Images

It is rare that a scanned image prints the way you want it to without some modification. You may also want to apply image-modification techniques to synthetic pictures created with a paint program. QuarkXPress lets you alter an image in several ways. Here's what you can do.

- Replace its contrast curve with preset, high-contrast, or posterized effects.

- Apply a custom gamma curve.

- Invert the image.

- Change the picture's on-screen or printed resolution.

- Apply a color or tint to the picture.

- Change the picture's halftoning parameters.

Each of these features is not only related, but interdependent on the others. Let's take a look at these controls and how you can use them to your benefit.

Welcome to the world of image modification!

Importing High-Resolution TIFF Graphics

The first alteration you can make to your file is to upgrade or downgrade high-resolution TIFF files. This control is available only when you first import the picture (see "Get Picture" in Chapter 6, *Pictures*), so we had better cover it quickly before we move on.

New in 3.3

See page 566

Upgrading screen quality. QuarkXPress normally brings in a screen representation of a high-resolution TIFF or PCX file at one half of your screen resolution. This low-resolution screen image provides for a relatively quick screen refresh rate (when, for example, you move around the page). However, the image on the screen may look rougher than you'd like. You can double the screen resolution by holding down the Shift key while clicking the OK button in the Get Picture dialog box. This won't have any effect on your printed output, but do note that this may slow down your screen redraws (those of you who have 66-MHz, 486-based PCs can stop chuckling). Note, however, that using the high-resolution preview can double or triple the size of your document file, compared to using the low-resolution preview.

Changing TIFF types. If you are heavily into image editing and control, you will undoubtedly want to change the TIFF type of an image at some point. Following are two tricks for changing the type at importation.

- Holding down the Alt key when clicking Open in the Get Picture dialog box changes a TIFF line-art (one-bit) image into an 8-bit gray-scale image.

- Holding down the Control key when clicking Open in the Get Picture dialog box changes TIFF gray-scale images to line art (1-bit) and TIFF color images to gray scale.

The Style Menu

Chapter 6, *Pictures*, describes how you can manipulate the "layout" of the picture in the picture box, including cropping, rotating, skewing, and moving the image. These effects are controlled from the floating palette or the Picture Box Specifications dialog box. Here we talk primarily about the image modification possibilities using features from the Style menu. Remember that you can combine both image-manipulation techniques (rotating, changing shape and size, and so on) and image-modification techniques (changing gray/color parameters and so on) to create fascinating effects for your page layout.

Tip: When the Style Menu Is Gray. If all of the items on the Style menu are grayed out, you have probably imported an EPS file. Or, if only some of the items on the Style menu are grayed out, it could be that the graphic file type that you've imported can't be styled in the way you want. Table 8-1 shows what sort of image manipulation you can do to different file types.

Remember, no shirt, no shoes, no bitmapped image, no service, no exceptions. If you're sure you have the right file format, it may be that you either have the Item tool selected (instead of the Content tool) or that you don't have the picture box selected. If none of this works, we suggest plugging in the machine.

Color. We cover color fully in Chapter 9, *Color*. So at this point, suffice it to say that changing the color of the image using Quark-XPress's color feature effectively replaces all black pixels with ones of a particular color. For example, if you have a black-and-white image and you change the color to red, you then have a red-and-white image. Contrary to some forms of logic, selecting "White" from the menu does not have the same effect as reversing the image; It just makes all pixels in the image white, and believe us, there are easier ways of making white boxes!

Table 8-1
What you can do to what

Picture Type	Color	Shade	Negative	Contrast	Screen
.BMP, .DIB, .GIF, .PCX, .RLE					
Line art	yes	yes	yes	no	yes
Gray scale	yes	yes	yes	yes	yes
Color	no	no	yes	no	no
.CGM, .DRW, .PCT, .PLT, .WMF					
Line art	yes	yes	yes	no	yes
Gray scale	yes	yes	yes	yes	yes
Color	no	no	yes	no	no
.EPS					
All types	no	no	no	no	no
.CT, .TIF					
Line art	yes	yes	yes	no	yes
Gray scale	yes	yes	yes	yes	yes
Color	no	no	yes	no	no

▼▼▼▼▼▼▼▼▼▼▼▼▼▼▼▼▼▼▼▼▼▼▼▼▼

Tip: Making Your Gray-Scale Picture "Transparent." The simple answer to "how do I make my gray-scale TIFFs transparent?" is that you can't. Gray-scale TIFFs are not and cannot be transparent. The reason for this is that every pixel has been assigned a gray level (whereas, in black-and-white, 1-bit TIFFs, the "white" pixels are transparent). However, you can fake a transparent look in some situations by importing the picture into a polygon that just wraps around the edges of the graphic. The best way we've found to do this is to import a graphic into a rectangular picture box, trace the edges using the Polygon Picture Box tool, then cut the graphic out of the first box and into the new picture box (see Figure 8-2).

▼▼▼▼▼▼▼▼▼▼▼▼▼▼▼▼▼▼▼▼▼▼▼▼▼

Shade. In the same spirit as changing each pixel's color, you can change the gray value for each pixel in the image. The method varies depending on whether you're working with flat or deep bitmapped images. With flat, bilevel bitmapped images, you can select one of the percentages from 10 percent to 100 percent from the hierarchical menu, or choose "Other" and type in a tint value

Figure 8-2

Making a fake transparent gray-scale TIFF

happiness runs in a circular motion; life is like a little boat upon the sea; everything is a part of everything anyway; you can have everything if you let yourself be; happiness runs in a circular motion; life is like a boat upon the sea; every   of everything anyw   thing if you let yours   s in a circular m   little boat upon the s   part of everythin   an have everything y u   be; happiness run in a c   motion; life is like a li le boat upon the sea; everything is   part of everything anyway; you can ave every

in 1-percent increments. This alters the printed output—every place there was a black pixel in your graphic, a gray pixel prints.

While the present-day Macintosh version of QuarkXPress doesn't let you adjust the shading of a gray-scale image via the Shade item on the Style menu, the Windows product does. We don't know why there's a difference. Perhaps it's just those wacky software engineers having fun with us. So, while in the Macintosh version you must adjust shading by using the Other Contrast dialog box (see "Other Contrast," below), here in the Windows version, you can simply select a percentage from the hierarchical menu (though, of course, you have even more control over shading in the Other Contrast dialog box).

Negative. Selecting "Negative" from the Style menu (or typing Control-Shift-Hyphen) inverts all black-and-white, gray-scale, or RGB color information in an image (see Chapter 9, *Color*, for more information on color models). Each color becomes its chromatic opposite on the color wheel. For example, green becomes magenta.

Contrast

The Style menu also has the ability to change the contrast of gray-scale images. If you are working with 1-bit (black-and-white) or color pictures, these elements are inaccessible.

Contrast refers to the relationships among the tonal values of a picture. A high-contrast picture divides up the gray shades into a few sharply distinct tones; a low-contrast picture has little differentiation between tones and looks grayed-out. You should try to strike some balance between these two, though you may want to create an unnatural-looking image by altering the contrast controls drastically.

The basic concept to remember regarding contrast controls is "input/output." David likes to think of these controls as a machine into which he is inserting his TIFF or PCX images and out of which comes what is going to print on the page. Other people sometimes think of this process as that of a filter through which the image is poured each time the page gets printed. Remember, though, that neither you nor QuarkXPress actually alters the picture file itself; you only alter the "filter" or the "machine." Let's look at the controls QuarkXPress offers.

Normal Contrast. This filter "leaves well enough alone" and doesn't affect the image at all. This is the default setting for every gray-scale and color picture you import.

High Contrast. Selecting "High Contrast" from the Style menu has the immediate effect of making your gray-scale pictures look like they were badly scanned at a 1-bit (black-and-white) setting. The literal effect of this filter is to change all values under 30 percent gray to white, and all gray values 30 percent or above to black. Why Quark chose the 30-percent mark is beyond us; it makes for some really ugly images. We'll look at how to change this "break point" later in this chapter.

Posterized. Whereas the High Contrast setting breaks down the image into only two gray values—0 percent and 100 percent—"Posterized" divides the tonal values into six levels of grays : 0, 20, 40, 60, 80, and 100 percent. Gray levels in the original picture are mapped to these levels based on what they're closest to (for example, a 36-percent gray maps to the 40-percent level). Posterization is a common technique in image editing, though it should be used carefully (see Figure 8-3).

Figure 8-3
Posterization of a gray-scale TIFF image

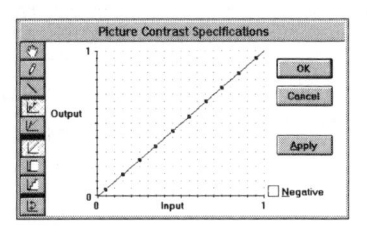

Normal contrast
Normal screen

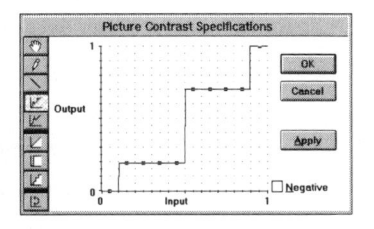

Standard posterization setting
Normal screen

Other Contrast. The ultimate contrast control within QuarkXPress comes from the Picture Contrast Specifications dialog box, which you can access by selecting "Other Contrast" from the Style menu. This dialog box shows you the mechanism (or filter) through which you are putting the picture. If you select "Other Contrast" after selecting "High Contrast" or "Posterize" from the Style menu, you see the contrast curve for those items. Otherwise, with "Normal Contrast" selected, you see a 45-degree line on the graph (see Figure 8-4).

Looking carefully at the graph, we see that the axes are labeled Input and Output, and each is defined from zero (per-

Figure 8-4
The Picture Contrast Specifications dialog

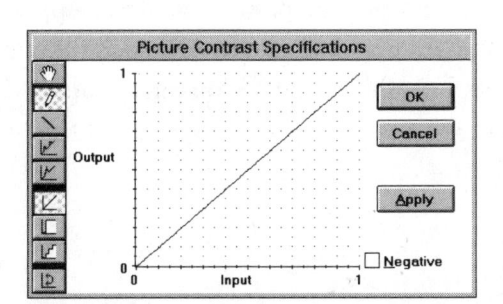

cent) to 1 (100 percent). Tick marks on the axes are shown in increments of 5 and 10 percent.

The basic 45-degree, Normal Contrast line defines a filter that doesn't change gray levels. For example, a gray level of 20 percent in the input picture is mapped (output) to 20 percent, 40 percent to 40 percent, and so on. By changing this line, we can change the mapping of the gray levels, affecting the contrast and shading of the printed picture.

Following are some basic tips and tricks to help you when you're modifying images using the Picture Contrast Specifications dialog box.

▼ ▼

Tip: Applying Your Changes. The Apply button is one of the all-time most helpful features that we've ever had the pleasure to use, especially on a large screen (anything larger than 9 inches). You can move the Picture Contrast Specifications dialog box out of the way of the picture you're working on by selecting the top portion of the dialog box and dragging. You can then make changes to the curve and click the Apply button (or type Alt-A) to see the change take place. If you don't like that effect, change the curve again. Selecting OK puts the most recent change into effect, but clicking Cancel (or pressing the Escape key) cancels any changes you've made.

▼ ▼

Tip: Continuous Apply. You can also hold down the Control key and click Apply for a continuous apply. (The Apply button changes to the Auto button while you're pressing the Control key.) This feature applies every change you make right after you make it. Sometimes it'll slow you down, but use it once and you'll find yourself becoming addicted to it. Clicking the Auto button turns off continuous apply. Remember: Applying a change does not make it permanent; that only happens when you click OK or press Return (and even then you can go back and change it if you want!).

▼ ▼

Picture Contrast Specifications Dialog Box

As we mentioned above, the Picture Contrast Specifications dialog box (Control-Shift-C) is the representation of the overall contrast filter through which the picture is processed. The nine tools in this dialog box enable you to create all sorts of filters for gray-scale images. These controls still aren't anywhere near the caliber of programs like PhotoStyler or Image-In, which are designed for the purpose of image editing, but they do give you a good bit of control.

You can use the tools to change the contrast curve into either a straight line or a curve. By definition, any contrast curve that is not a straight line is a gamma curve. There's nothing mysterious about a gamma curve; it's simply a curve with a fancy name.

Why would you want to apply a gamma curve to an image? The immediate answer is so that you can create really far-out and wild images (see Figure 8-5). However, perhaps more importantly, you can use gamma curves to correct for poorly scanned images or to boost certain tonal values in a picture. Let's look at how this is done.

Figure 8-5
Gamma curves in action

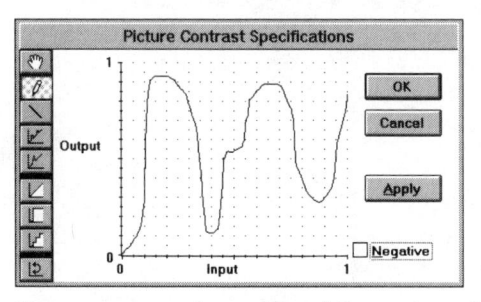

Gamma curves can be used for subtle or not-so-subtle contrast modifications.

Hand tool. You can use the Hand tool to move the curve (or straight line) on the contrast graph by selecting it, positioning it over the graph, and dragging with the mouse. The Hand tool is the easiest way to make adjustments to the contrast curve as a whole. For an example, see "Tip: Adjusting the Break Point on a High-Contrast Image" below.

Pencil tool. If you've ever used the CorelDRAW drawing program or Aldus PhotoStyler, you're already familiar with the freehand Pencil tool. By selecting this tool and dragging over the curve, you can make both large and small adjustments. With the Pencil tool, you can draw smooth gamma curves that adjust for problems in the original scan (see Figure 8-6). Or you can draw wild and bizarre roller-coaster curves that map the gray levels in weird ways. You can also make small corrections in the curve by carefully drawing over areas (see "Tip: Correcting Errors in the Curve," below). Remember, though, that you don't need to have a perfectly smooth curve all of the time; slight bumps and dips have little effect on the final output.

Figure 8-6
Gamma curve created with the Pencil tool

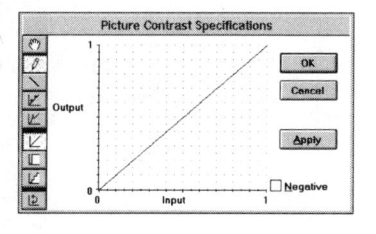

Default settings

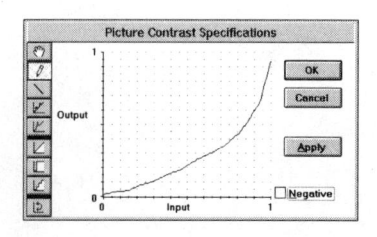

With a gamma contrast curve

Straight Line tool. If you can't figure out that the Straight Line tool draws straight lines, we wish you the best of luck with the program. However, the purpose of these straight lines is not so obvious. Think of the slope of a line in the same way you think of the steepness of a hill. A large slope steepens very quickly; a small slope steepens slowly. You can draw steep and gentle slopes easily with the Straight Line tool.

The steeper the slope, the higher contrast the image has. The gentler the slope, the less contrast; that is, the "grayer" the picture looks. However, remember that by using the straight line rather than a curved line, you are always losing tonal values. A steep, contrasted line loses the highlights and the shadows; a flat, low-contrast line loses midtones (see Figure 8-7).

Figure 8-7
Linear image adjustment

Linear adjustments result in noticeable loss of tonal values.

Posterizer tool. As we described earlier, posterization is the act of cutting out or dividing an image's gray or color levels into a few basic tonal values. By selecting "Posterize" in the Style menu, QuarkXPress divides the gray or color levels into six tonal values. When you select the Posterizer tool, QuarkXPress adds handle points to your line or curve at 10-percent increments. By moving these handles, you flatten and move that entire 10-percent area. By lining up multiple handles, you can easily create posterized effects with any number of levels up to ten (see Figure 8-8).

Figure 8-8
The Posterizer tool

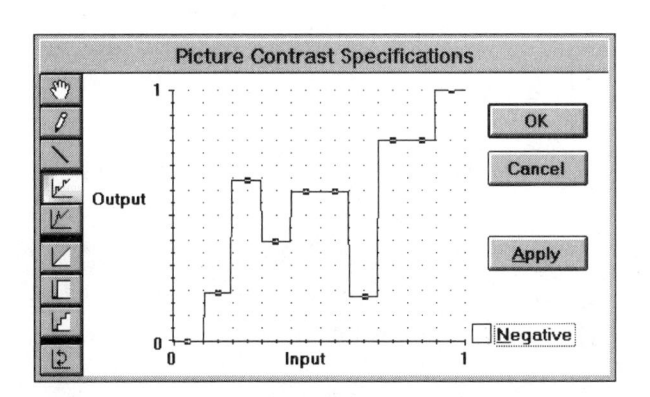

Spike tool. Whereas the Posterizer tool places handles between the 10-percent marks and levels out (flattens) that 10-percent area, the Spike tool places handles directly on the 10-percent marks and has no affect on the area between the handles other than to adjust the lines to keep them contiguous. Spiking a line is good for boosting particular tonal values; for example, if you wanted a 60-percent gray area to appear black, you could spike it up to 100 percent. Similarly, if you wanted to drop out all dark areas, you might use this tool. We usually use the Spike tool for drastic changes in the image, but sometimes it's just the thing for a quick minor adjustment. Also, if you are uncomfortable with the Pencil tool, you can approximate the curve path you want by clicking on the Spike tool and adjusting the spike handles.

Normal Contrast tool. Clicking on the Normal Contrast tool reverts the contrast curve back to its initial 45-degree straight line.

High Contrast tool. Clicking on the High Contrast tool switches the curve to the standard bilevel high-contrast setting as described above. The break point is set to 30 percent.

Posterizer tool. When you click on this tool, the curve you're working on switches to the standard posterized curve. Tints under 10 percent go to white, those over 90 percent go to black, and other tints round off to the nearest 20 percent. You can then use the Posterizer tool (or any other tool) to adjust further.

Inversion tool and Negative check box. Although the Inversion tool and the Negative check box do exactly the same thing in the Windows edition of QuarkXPress (they're slightly different in the Macintosh version, but only in color images), Quark has kindly given us both options for inverting gray-scale images. By clicking on either of these options, you can fully invert all gray-scale files; where there was white, there is black, where there was 20 percent black, there is 80 percent black, and so on. Plus, both of these functions have the same effect as selecting the Negative option in the Style menu (see "Negative," above).

▼▼▼▼▼▼▼▼▼▼▼▼▼▼▼▼▼▼▼▼▼▼▼▼▼▼

Tip: Adjusting the Break Point on a High-Contrast Image. As we described above, the cutoff point on a high-contrast image is 30 percent, which does hardly anyone any good. Using the Hand tool in the Other Contrast dialog box, you can adjust this point horizontally to anywhere on the scale. Try moving the vertical line over to around 60 percent. This cuts out most of the lower gray values and gives you a clean and recognizable image for many gray-scale or color pictures (see Figure 8-9). This is also of great help when working with line art that was scanned as a gray-scale image. By adjusting the cutoff point, you can alter the line thicknesses in the artwork.

Figure 8-9
Adjusting the high-contrast break point for a gray-scale image

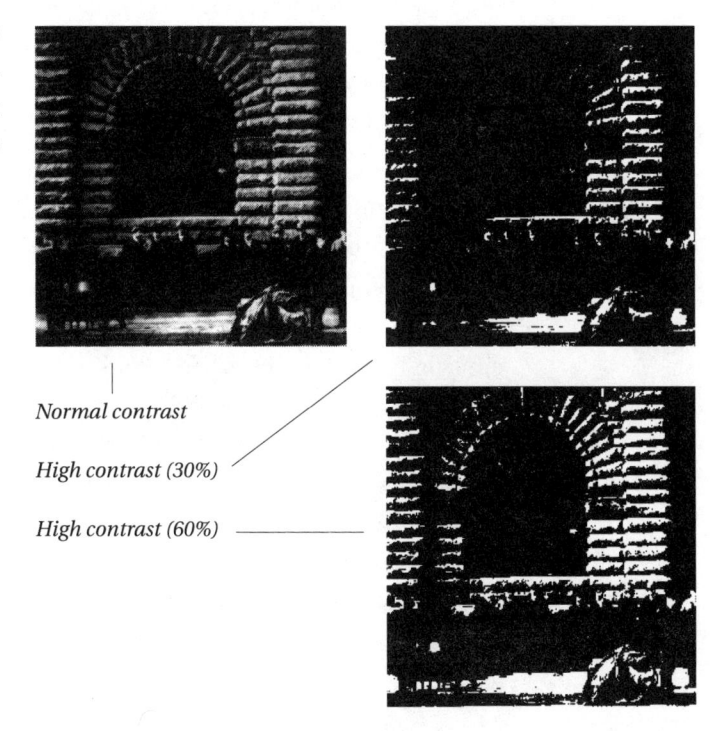

Normal contrast

High contrast (30%)

High contrast (60%)

▼▼▼▼▼▼▼▼▼▼▼▼▼▼▼▼▼▼▼▼▼▼▼▼▼▼

Tip: Correcting Errors in the Curve. You can make changes to the contrast filter at any time. This means that if you are using the Pencil tool and can't keep your hand steady, you can smooth out the curve by going back over the rough parts after you've finished the basic line. It also means that if you hit OK and then decide that the image looks like crud, you can type Control-Z to Undo Item

Change, or just select "Normal Contrast" from the Style menu to get back to the picture's original state (at time of importing).

Halftones

Let's face it. Every high-resolution imagesetter on the market prints in only black and white. And almost every low-resolution laser printer prints in only black and white. There's clearly a lot to be said for black and white. What we need to realize, however, is that black and white is not gray. Real laser printers don't print gray (at least not the ones we're going to discuss).

So how do we get a picture with grays into the computer and out onto paper? The answer is halftones. The magic of halftoning is that different levels of gray are represented by different size spots, which, when printed closely together, fool the eye into seeing the tint we want.

Take a look at any photograph in a newspaper; it's easy to see the halftoning. Notice that the spacing of the spots doesn't change; only their size changes. There are large spots in dark areas, small spots in light areas. Let's take a look at the elements that make up digital halftones.

Dots. A laser printer prints pages by placing black dots on a white page (remember, this is the simple approach, and we're not getting into film negs and whatnot yet). Each and every dot on a 300-dpi printer is going to be $1/300$ of an inch in diameter (or thereabouts). That's pretty small, but it's still 8.5 times larger than what you can achieve on a Linotronic 300 ($1/2540$ of an inch, which is almost too small for the human eye to see). The primary factor concerning the size of the dot is the resolution of the printer (how many dots per inch it can print).

Spots. As was said before, a halftone is made up of spots of varying sizes. On a black-and-white laser printer or imagesetter, these spots are created by bunching together anywhere between one and 65,000 printer dots. The spots can be of different shapes, and to be redundant over and over again, different sizes. We look at several different types of spots later in the chapter.

Screen frequency. In the traditional halftoning process, a mesh screen is placed in front of the photograph to create the desired effect of spots (albeit rather square ones) all in rows. Keeping this process in mind can help you understand this concept. The screen frequency of a halftone is set by the mesh screen and is defined as the number of these rows per inch. The lower the screen frequency, the coarser the image looks. The higher the screen frequency, the finer the image looks (see Figure 8-10).

Figure 8-10
Various screen frequencies

20 lpi   *75 lpi*   *120 lpi*

To complicate issues a bit, the screen frequency of a halftone is often called its *line screen*. Whatever you call it, it's specified in the number of lines per inch (lpi). See Table 8-2 for information about when to use a particular line screen.

Table 8-2
When to use a screen frequency

Output	Lines per inch
Photocopier	50-90 lpi
Newspaper quality	60-85 lpi
Quick printer	85-110 lpi
Direct-mail pieces	110-150 lpi
Magazine quality	133-185 lpi
Art book	185-300 lpi

▼▼▼▼▼▼▼▼▼▼▼▼▼▼▼▼▼▼▼▼▼▼▼▼▼▼▼

Tip: Gray Levels in Your Halftones. Picture this: Each spot is made up of tiny dots, and different gray levels are achieved by turning various dots on and off (at a 10-percent tint, 10 percent of the dots within a spot's cell are turned on). Okay, now remember that the lower the screen frequency, the bigger the spot and the more dots used per spot. The higher the frequency, the fewer dots are used. Thus, the higher the screen frequency, the fewer possibilities for levels of gray there are.

To find out how many levels of gray you can achieve, divide the resolution by the screen frequency, square it, and add one. For example, you can get 92 levels of gray when you print a 133-line screen at 1,270 dpi ($(1270/133)^2+1$), but only 6 levels of gray when you print a 133-line screen at 300 dpi ($(300/133)^2+1$). The output is clearly posterized. To get 92 levels of gray on a 300-dpi laser printer, you would need to print at 30 lines per inch—pretty coarse. It's an unfortunate fact, but this is one of the inherent trade-offs of digital halftoning.

▼▼▼▼▼▼▼▼▼▼▼▼▼▼▼▼▼▼▼▼▼▼▼▼▼▼▼

Angle. The halftone screen does not have to be horizontal or vertical. It can rotate to other angles as well (see Figure 8-11), which can be of great use in both special effects halftoning and color separation (see Chapter 10, *Printing*). For reference sake, 0 (zero) and 180 degrees are horizontal, 90 and 270 degrees are vertical (some types of spots look the same in all four of these, and others look very different at each angle). A 45-degree angle is used most commonly, primarily because it is the least distracting to the eye. Remember that changing the angle of the halftone screen doesn't change the angle of the picture itself!

Making Halftones Work for You

Once again, just to be clear: Any graphic image that contains gray requires halftoning. Even a simple box with a 10-percent tint comes out as a halftone. There's no other way to render grays on a black-and-white output device or a printing press with black ink. With bitmapped images, QuarkXPress lets you change the parameters of the halftones: spot type, line screen, and angle.

IMAGE MODIFICATION **373**

Figure 8-11
Rotating the halftone screen to 0, 30, and 45 degree angles

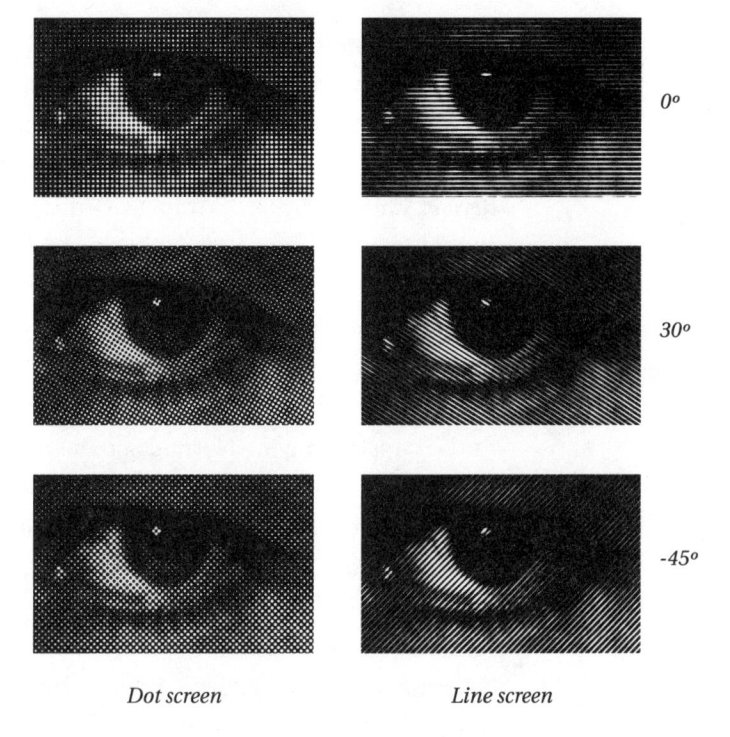

0°

30°

-45°

Dot screen   Line screen

The first four items in the screen section of the Style menu (see Figure 8-12) are preset combinations for you to choose. By choosing the fifth item, "Other Screen," you access the Picture Screening Specifications dialog box, which allows you to input your own choices, giving you the greatest amount of flexibility.

Figure 8-12
Halftoning control in the Style menu

| Style | Item | Page | Utilities | Window |

Color
Shade
Negative   Ctrl+Shift+–

Normal Contrast   Ctrl+Shift+N
High Contrast   Ctrl+Shift+H
Posterized   Ctrl+Shift+P
√ Other Contrast...   Ctrl+Shift+C

√ Normal Screen
  60-lpi Line Screen/0°
  30-lpi Line Screen/45°
  20-lpi Dot Screen/45°
  Other Screen...   Ctrl+Shift+S

Preset Screen Combinations

Let's look at QuarkXPress preset screen frequency and angle combinations first. Figure 8-13 shows a sample picture for each setting.

Normal Screen. Normal, in this case, means default. This is the setting all pictures automatically print with unless you specifically change them. The spot is a round dot (see further description of the round dot shape below), the angle is 45 degrees, and the screen frequency is whatever you chose in the Printer Setup dialog box (move like the pros: Type Control-Alt-P). In most cases you will find yourself using the Normal Screen setting.

60-Line line screen, 0° setting. Why conform to "Normal Screen" when you have a choice like this? This screen setting uses a line screen—lines rather than dots. We often call this a "straight-line screen" just to differentiate from screen frequency, which, as mentioned above, is also sometimes specified as the "line screen." This particular straight-line screen is set at a screen frequency of 60 lines per inch (lpi), each line being set to a 0 (zero) degree angle (horizontal). Printing at 60 lpi is coarse enough for the eye to see each line easily, but fine enough so that a casual observer won't notice it immediately. Nonetheless, the picture definitely looks different than if you use a round spot.

30-Line line screen, 45° setting. We're now in the realm of a very coarse straight-line screen. If you look too closely at this picture you won't even be able to tell what it is. This is a popular screen for special effects, though an angle of -45 (or 315) degrees is often used instead (we discuss how to change the angle below). Because it's easy to see where the lines in the straight-line screen get fatter and thinner, the eye holds longer on how the image was created than what the image is itself.

20-Line dot screen, 45° setting. Here's another potentially confusing term. Here we have a "dot screen," which just means a spot that is round (the dots that make up the spot haven't changed any). A screen frequency this low can really only be used for special

IMAGE MODIFICATION **375**

Figure 8-13
The halftoning presets

Normal Screen

60-Line Line Screen/0°

30-Line Line Screen/45°

20-Line Dot Screen/45°

effects, unless you're printing on a billboard or other signage that won't be viewed up close.

Other Screen Option

We now come to the powerhouse behind QuarkXPress's screen features. Using the Other Screen feature under the Style menu (Control-Shift-S), we can choose between five screen patterns and select any screen frequency or angle we like—well, almost any. Because of limitations in PostScript and the laser printer hardware, there are certain screen frequencies and angles that cannot be achieved (see the book *Real World PostScript*, listed in Appendix E, *Resources*, for a detailed discussion of this problem). When this occurs, the printed output is as close as possible to what you requested.

Following is an in-depth description of these settings.

Screen. David's dream is to print out a halftone image at a screen frequency of 1 lpi—with each spot having a diameter of one inch. He doesn't have a particular reason for this; he just thinks it would be neat. Unfortunately, PostScript won't presently handle anything below 8 lpi, and QuarkXPress won't accept any value under 15. The upper range of 400 lpi is less of an inconvenience, though you may never have the urge to approach either of these limits. Select the screen frequency you want by typing it in, or type "0" (zero) or "default" to defer to the setting that is assigned in the Printer Setup dialog box.

Angle. We discussed angles several sections ago, and we'll discuss them again in Chapter 10, *Printing*, when we talk about color separations, so we won't discuss them here. Just type in a number between 0 (zero) and 360 (or 0 to -360 if you think backwards). Once upon a time when you specified a particular angle, the angle would not rotate along with a page printed transversely (see Chapter 10, *Printing*). This caused much consternation for people using coarse screens. We're happy to say that this is no longer the case, and when you specify an angle, you get that angle no matter how you print it.

Pattern. Pattern refers to the spot shape. You have five shapes to choose from (see Figure 8-14).

Figure 8-14
Various halftone spot shapes (patterns)

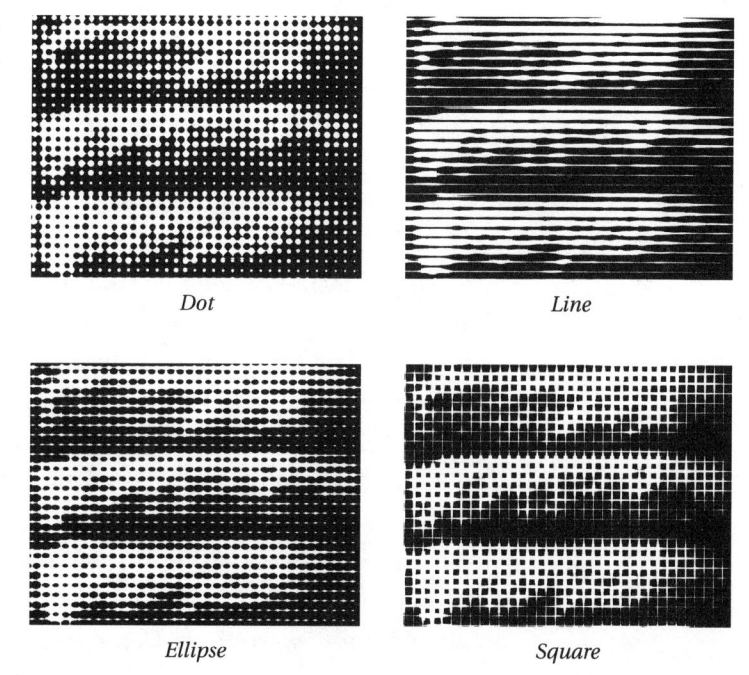

Dot

Line

Ellipse

Square

- **Dot pattern.** This is the round spot that you see in almost all PostScript output. At low tint values, it's a round black spot that gets larger until nearly 50 percent, at which point it converts to a square, then inverts to a progressively smaller white spot for higher tint levels.

- **Line.** Straight-line screens seem to go in and out of fashion, but they're always good for waking up your audience, and if you use too low a line screen, making eyeballs fall out. The line is thick at high tint values and thin for low values.

- **Ellipse.** No, this is not a traditional elliptical spot. Printers have used elliptical spots for years and customers have grown accustomed to asking for them by this name, even though the shape of the spot is more of a rounded-corner diamond. The spot that QuarkXPress creates is an oval. We haven't found any good use for this.

- **Square.** Here's another funky special-effect spot that may come in handy some day. Each of the spots is square; low tint values are little squares, high values are big squares. Try some really coarse screen frequencies for this one.

- **Ordered Dither.** This spot shape is actually an attempt to go beyond traditional halftoning. It's more of a dither pattern optimized for printing on 300-dpi laser printers. Because the dithered pattern adjusts to the resolution of the laser printer, you shouldn't use this if you're planning on printing to an imagesetter (you'd get a dither at over 1,000 dots per inch, which could not be reproduced). The Ordered Dither pattern is also not optimal for offset printing.

    When should you use this? Quark maintains that you should use it when you are printing to a laser printer for making multiple copies on a photocopier. But don't even bother if you have a PostScript printer; it looks terrible. Well, we guess it's nice to have the option.

Display Halftoning option. In most programs on the PC, you cannot see the halftoning settings you choose until you print out a page. However, QuarkXPress can display a representation of the halftone if you click on the Display Halftoning check box. How well it displays the halftone type depends primarily on the resolution of your screen. You almost never need this to be turned on, unless you're working with low screen frequencies for special effects. Once again, it's sometimes nice just to have the option.

Many Colorful Shades of Gray

We've taken a pretty good look at the options you have for working with images in your QuarkXPress documents, from rotating them to changing their halftone spot shape. Next we go to the world of color and discuss how to bring color onto your pages. Finally, we'll move on to what is perhaps the culmination of all we have learned in this book: printing our documents.

CHAPTER 9

COLOR

Dave's poor dog. His 10-inch schnoz may inhale rhapsodies of aromas we'll never dream of, but alas, the splendor of sunset through broken clouds will never be his. However, unlike dogs, few people are totally color blind. We're surrounded by color, at least until the lights go out. It affects our moods and thoughts, and gains our attention almost instantly, along with our pleasure or revulsion. With today's automatic cameras, almost anyone can catch a piece of the color world around them, but getting color into your documents is nowhere near as simple.

The good news is that QuarkXPress probably has the best color-handling features of any desktop publishing program. The bad news is that you still have to know quite a bit about color and color printing in order to get good results. The complicated issues in desktop color range from specifying the color you want, to getting that color to print out on either a color or—more likely—a black-and-white laser printer, to producing separated film ready for offset printing. Desktop color has come a long way in the last year, and at the time of this writing, it's finally becoming satisfactory for a production environment. In another year, everything may change, and achieving quality color from your PC may be as easy as turning on the computer; but for now, we have some work cut out for us.

We begin this chapter with an overview of some basic theories of color, including the various color models (ways in which you specify color on the computer). This leads us into the color components of QuarkXPress's feature set, including building a color palette and building traps for better print quality. Although we discuss the fundamentals of color separation here, we cover the area of actually generating color separations of your documents later, in Chapter 10, *Printing*.

Welcome to the wild and weird world of color!

What You See and What You Get

Before we even begin talking desktop color, it's important for you to know that the color you see on the screen is almost never what you get out of your color printer or slide recorder, much less what you can expect to see from a printing press. Why? The primary reason is the difference in medium. Colors are displayed on the screen by lighting up phosphors that emit colored light, which then enters your eyes. This is significantly different from color printed material, which depends on other light sources to reflect off of it into your eyes. If you use a different method of showing color, you see different colors.

Pantone colors are a great example of this. Take a Pantone swatch book and pick a color. Hold that color up to the screen next to QuarkXPress's Pantone color simulation. Chances are it is a totally different color. Even color proofs created from your final film aren't completely reliable (though they're the best predictor you can hope for). What comes off press may look different.

Another reason for the difference in color correspondence is that representing four process color plates with three colors (red, green, and blue) just doesn't work. The eye sees and processes the two types differently.

Want more reasons? Okay, how about the monitors and imaging devices themselves? Take a color document on your color PC and bring it to someone else's computer; it almost undoubtedly looks different, especially if the monitor is a different brand. Take that a step farther and image the document using a high-end slide recorder. The device uses light, just like your monitor, but the colors you get are very different from what you see on your computer.

Some monitors are better than others at displaying certain colors, and a monitor with a 24-bit color card is one step more accurate than an 8-bit video card. Some companies, such as Radius, sell monitor calibration systems to adjust the screen colors so that they more closely match your printed output. However, many of the best calibration systems are cost-prohibitive for most people.

See Appendix G

Whatever you use, remember that what you see is rarely what you get. The solution to this uncertainty is to specify your colors from a swatch book. Look at the book, see what color you want, and spec it. If possible, create your own swatch book and print it from your final output device—offset press, color printer, slide recorder, whatever. If you're printing process color, spec your colors from a process swatch book, such as Trumatch. If you're printing PMS colors, use a PMS book.

▼▼▼▼▼▼▼▼▼▼▼▼▼▼▼▼▼▼▼▼▼▼▼▼▼

Tip: Taking a Color Reality Check. Russell Brown, senior art director at Adobe Systems, has some interesting things to say about working in color. To begin with, here are some questions to ask yourself before you consider working in color.

- Do I really want to do my own production?
- Will I save time?
- Will I save money?
- Am I using color as a design solution?
- Am I crazy?

Clearly, the last question is the most relevant one. Jumping into desktop color is like roller skating on the seven hills of San Francisco: If you don't really know what you're doing, it'll get ugly.

▼▼▼▼▼▼▼▼▼▼▼▼▼▼▼▼▼▼▼▼▼▼▼▼▼▼

Tip: Color on Monochrome Monitors. Quark has decided that, for the time being, color should be shown on monochrome screens by its tint value rather than its brightness. What this means is that if you specify a 100-percent yellow, you see 100-percent black. When printing, you can set the colors to print as various shades of gray, but on screen it always looks black.

If you're using a monochrome monitor, try tinting every color, and when you're ready to print, go back and change them to solids.

▼▼▼▼▼▼▼▼▼▼▼▼▼▼▼▼▼▼▼▼▼▼▼▼▼▼▼▼▼▼▼

Describing Color

In a perfect world, you should be able to say, "I want this object to be burnt sienna," and your computer, service bureau, and lithographer should know exactly the color you mean. Outside of picking Crayola crayon colors, however, this just can't be done. Everyone from scientists to artists to computer programmers has been trying for centuries to come up with a general model for specifying and recreating colors. In the past 50 years alone, these color models have been created: HSB, NTSC, CMYK, YIQ, CIE, PAL, HSL, RGB, CCIR, RS-170, and HSI, among others. (And we thought that Windows graphic file format names were far-out!)

QuarkXPress presently handles three color models and three color matching systems (we describe the difference later): RGB, CMYK, HSB, Focoltone, TruMatch, and Pantone. Because these color models are intimately connected with printing and other reproduction methods, we first discuss the particulars of printing color, then move into each color model in turn.

Spot Versus Process Colors

When dealing with color, either on or off the desktop, you need to understand the differences between *process* and *spot* color. Both are commonly used in the printing process. Both can give you a wide variety of colors. But they are hardly interchangeable.

Depending on your final output device, you may also be dealing with composite colors. Let's look at each of these, one at a time.

Process color. Look at any color magazine or junk mail you've received lately. If you look closely at a color photograph or a tinted color box, you'll probably see lots of little dots making up the color. These are *color halftones* (see Chapter 8, *Modifying Images*, for further information on halftones) made up of one to four colors: cyan, magenta, yellow, and black. We talk about this color model (CMYK) later; what's important here is that you see that many, many colors are represented by overlapping the four basic colors. The eye blends these colors together so that ultimately you see the color you're supposed to.

Cyan, magenta, yellow, and black are the process colors. The method of separating the millions of colors into four colors is referred to as creating *process color separations*. Each separation (or plate) is a piece of film or paper that contains artwork for only one of the colors. Your lithographer can take the four pieces of film, burn metal plates from each of the four pieces, and use those four plates on a four-color press.

Don't get us wrong: process color is not just for full-color photographs or images. If you're printing a four-color job, you can use each of the process colors separately or together to create colored type, rules, or tint blocks on the page. These items appear as solid colors to the untrained eye, but they are actually made from "tint builds" of the process colors.

Spot color. If you are printing only a small number of colors (three or fewer), you probably want to use *spot* colors. The idea behind spot colors is that the printing ink (or light source, if you're going to color slides) is just the color you want, which makes it unnecessary to build a color using the four process colors. With spot color, for example, if you want some teal blue type, you print it on a plate (often called an overlay) that is separate from the black plate. Your lithographer prints that type using teal blue ink—probably a PMS ink (see "Pantone," below) like PMS 3135 or 211—and then switches to black to print the rest of the job.

Once again, the difference between process and spot colors is that process colors are built using four separate inks printed on top of each other, while spot colors are printed using just one colored ink (the color you specify). In either case, your lithographer runs the page through the press once for each color's plate, or uses a multicolor press that prints the colors successively on a single pass.

Mixing the two color types together. There is no reason why you can't use both spot and process colors together in a document, if you've got the budget for a five- or six-color print job. Some lithographers have five- or six-color presses, which can print the four process colors along with one or two spot colors.

Composite color. If your final output is created on a film recorder (slides or transparencies) or a color printer, you may well encounter what we call *composite color*. Composite color is color that falls between spot colors and process colors. For example, most film recorders print using the RGB model (we cover this model later), whether your color is specified as CMYK or RGB or anything else QuarkXPress allows. Similarly, the QMS ColorScript 100 represents both spot and process colors using either an RGB or a CMYK ribbon, depending on the type you have loaded.

The key here is that the colors you specify are represented using some color model that you may not have intended. If you know that you are printing on such a device, you should refer to the service bureau and/or the owner's manual for tips on how to work best with that device.

Color Models

See page 602

Before we jump into how to specify the colors you want, let's talk about each of the color models that QuarkXPress handles and what each is good for.

RGB. Color models are broken down into two classes: additive and subtractive systems. An *additive* color system is counter-intuitive to most people: The more color you add to an object, the closer you get to white. In the case of the RGB model, adding 100 percent of red, green, and blue to an area results in pure white. If you have a color television or a color monitor on your computer, you have already had a great deal of experience with the RGB model. These pieces of equipment describe colors by "turning on" red, green, and blue phosphors on the screen. Various colors are created by mixing these three colors together.

- Black: zero percent of all three colors
- Yellow: red + green
- Magenta: red + blue
- Cyan: green + blue

Color TIFF files, such as color scans of natural images, are usually saved using RGB specs, occasionally in CMYK. Most slide recorders image film using RGB.

CMY. *Subtractive* colors, on the other hand, become more white as you subtract color from them, and get darker as you add more color. This is analogous to painting on a white piece of paper. CMY is a subtractive color model: the more cyan, magenta, and yellow you add together, the closer you get to black.

The connection between RGB and CMY is interesting: They are exact opposites of each other. In other words, you can take an RGB color and mathematically invert each of the RGB values and get the same color in the CMY model. If this doesn't come intuitively to you (it doesn't to us), don't worry. The theory behind this is much less important than what it implies.

The implication of RGB and CMY having an inverse relationship is that colors in either model should be easy to convert. This is true. They are easy to convert. The problem is that the CMY model has few practical applications because cyan, magenta, and yellow don't really add up to make black in the real world. Inks are imperfect, so they actually make a muddy brown. Thus, lithographers over the years have learned that they must add a black element to the printing process.

CMYK. The color model that results when black is added to the CMY model is called CMYK. Where RGB is a standard for phosphorous screens, CMYK is the standard in the printing world and the basis of color separations. It breaks every color down into four colors: cyan, magenta, yellow, and black ("K" is used in the acronym rather than "B" to avoid confusion with "blue"). However, the conversion between RGB and CMYK is nowhere near as precise as one could hope. In fact, different programs use different conversion algorithms, so an RGB color from QuarkXPress prints differently than it would from another application.

You can describe many colors using this method. The following is how Quark describes a few, to the nearest percent:

- Red: 99.6 percent magenta, 99.8 percent yellow
- Green: 77.3 percent cyan, 100 percent yellow
- Blue: 99.6 percent cyan, 95.7 percent magenta

Almost every full-color job that gets printed on paper uses the CMYK process.

HSB. Rather than breaking a color down into subparts, the HSB model describes a color by its hue, saturation, and brightness. The hue is basically its position in a color spectrum, which starts at red, moves through magenta to blue, through green to yellow, and then through orange back to red. The saturation of the color can be described as the amount of color in it, or conversely, the amount of white in it. A light pink, for example, has a lower saturation than a bright red. The color's brightness reflects the amount of black in it. Thus, that same bright red would, with a lower brightness, change from a vibrant red to a dark, dull, reddish-black.

You could also say that mixing a color (hue) with white produces a tint (a degree of saturation). Mixing it with black produces a tone (a degree of brightness).

HSB is not easy to understand intuitively, especially when it comes to specifying colors. For example, here are the hue values for the same colors specified above.

- Red: 0

- Green: 21,845 (QuarkXPress specifies this as 33.3 percent)

- Blue: 43,690 (QuarkXPress specifies this as 66.7 percent)

You may find HSB speccing useful if you're creating slides on a film recorder or the like, but it's not of much use for print publishing.

Pantone. Pantone Inc.'s, sole purpose in life (and business) is to develop, maintain, and protect the sanctity of the Pantone Color Matching System (PMS for short).

Printers and designers alike love the PMS system for its great simplicity in communicating color. As a designer, you can look in a Pantone-approved color swatch book, pick a color, then communicate that color's number to your printer. He or she, in turn, can pull out the Pantone color mixing guidelines, find that color's "recipe," and dutifully create the ink for you. Almost all spot color printing is done with PMS inks.

Bear in mind that you can simulate many PMS inks using combinations of process inks. Some simulations are better than others. A pale blue is fairly easy to simulate with process inks, for instance; a rich, creamy, slate blue is almost impossible; and you'll never get anything approaching copper or gold with CMYK.

Pantone, knowing a good thing when it sees it, has licensed its color library to Quark so that you can specify PMS colors from within QuarkXPress (notice that there are even process equivalents for the Pantone colors). However, the color you see on the screen may have little correlation to what the actual PMS color is on paper. A computer screen is no substitute for a swatch book (we talk more about this later).

There are three problems with PMS color.

- Only certain colors are defined and numbered. If you want a color that is slightly lighter than one described, but not as light as the next lightest color in the Pantone book, you have to tell your lithographer to tweak the ink mixture.

- Color specification books are never fully accurate or alike. David works with a Pantone book that is almost totally different from his printer's, due mostly to the difference in the age of the books, the ink types, and the paper types the books are printed on.

- We've never met anyone who actually understood the PMS color numbering scheme. For example, PMS 485 and PMS 1795 are very similar, though every number in between is totally different.

On the other hand, some designers use Pantone colors to avoid some pitfalls that process colors create. For example, the Understanding Company's road maps are often designed and printed using one to five different Pantone colors in various tints and combinations. This minimizes both the potential moiré patterning (see Chapter 10, *Printing*) and the possible loss of detail in small, colored type.

Remember that the Pantone system is really designed for color matching rather than describing a color abstractly as other color models do.

Focoltone. Developed in Wales, the Focoltone matching system is used widely in Europe, though very little in North America. After buying the rather expensive Focoltone cross-referenced swatch books, you have to wade through them to find the color you want (you have a choice of only 763 colors). These are similar to the Pantone books, which are also in disarray (at least from a user's standpoint). We can't explain Focoltone's numbering system or color sequence to you, because we just can't figure them out.

Trumatch. Trumatch was built by people who know and use color from the desktop (especially color from QuarkXPress, as it turns out). This is more important than it might seem. Creating tint builds from the desktop has a particular advantage over having a printer build tints traditionally: We can specify (and a properly calibrated imagesetter can provide us with) a tint value of any percentage, not just in 5- or 10-percent increments. The folks at

Trumatch took advantage of this and created a very slick, very easy-to-use system with over 2,000 evenly gradated colors.

The Trumatch swatch books tuck this information away, so we want to explain the Trumatch system here. The colors in the swatch book (and in the Trumatch color selector in the Edit Color dialog box) are arranged in the colors of the spectrum: from red through yellow to green through blue to violet and back to red. The first number in a Trumatch code indicates a color's hue (its place on the spectrum). These numbers go from 1 to 50.

The second item in a color's Trumatch code indicates its tint (its value strength from "a"—saturated, 100-percent value strength—to "h"—faded, unsaturated, 5-percent value strength). The third item, a number, indicates the color's brightness (the amount of black). Black is always added in 6-percent increments. The brightness code ranges from 1 (6 percent black) to 7 (42 percent black). If there's no black in a color, this third code is left off.

So, why is this so great? Well, first of all, you can quickly make decisions on the relativity of two colors. For example, you can say, "No, I want this color to be a little darker and a little more green." When you go back to the Edit Color dialog box, you can quickly find a color that suits your desires. Compare this with the Pantone or Focoltone matching systems and you'll understand. Trumatch gives us hope that there really is a positive evolution in electronic publishing.

The key thing to remember when speccing spot colors is that you should probably use a PMS swatch book. When speccing process colors (tint builds), you should probably use a Trumatch swatch book.

Specifying Color

We've discussed applying colors to objects in previous chapters. Here, we discuss how to create colors in QuarkXPress over and above the nine that come as default settings.

The Color List

Before you can use a color in QuarkXPress, you have to create it so that it appears in your document's color list. QuarkXPress allows up to 127 different colors on this list, including the six colors that must be present: Cyan, Magenta, Yellow, Black, White, and Registration (we talk about this last "color" later in this chapter). You can access this list through the Colors dialog box via the Edit menu. From there, you can add, delete, and modify colors.

The Colors dialog box (see Figure 9-1) is made up of the color list (you can scroll through them if there are more than eight entries), plus several buttons to manipulate them. Let's discuss each feature, step by step.

Figure 9-1
The Colors dialog box

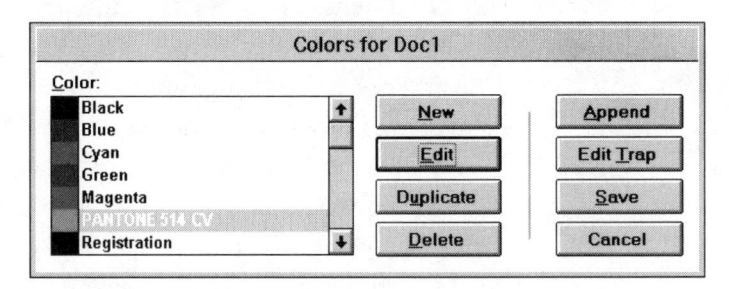

▼ ▼

Tip: Making Your Colors Stick Around. You can alter the default color list—the list which all new documents open with—by adding, deleting, and modifying colors while no document is open. These changes stick around forever, or at least until you either change them again or reinstall QuarkXPress. Note that changes to the default color list don't appear in previously created documents. Changing the color list while a document is still open changes only that document's list and does not affect any other document.

▼ ▼

New

Clicking the New button brings you to the Edit Color dialog box (see Figure 9-2). The name that you type in the Name box appears on the Color scroll list, the Colors palette, and the color lists in other menus throughout the program.

Figure 9-2
The Edit Color dialog box

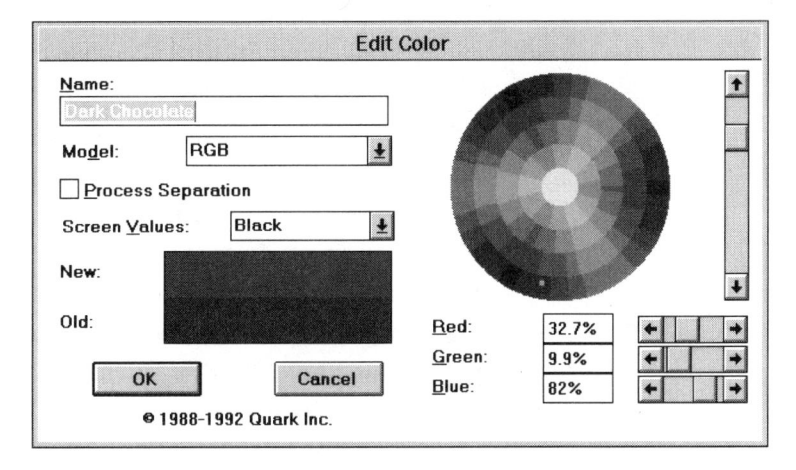

You can call your color anything you want. For example, when David is working with process colors, he usually defines the color he wants using CMYK (see how to do this under "The Right Way," below), then names it something like "10c80m0y20k." It's a bit cryptic at first, but he seems to like it. Bob, on the other hand, likes to call the color by some name; for example, he might have a palette full of "fuchsias," "royal blues," and so forth.

If you use Bob's way for spot color, you'll want to be sure you know what the corresponding color is in your color swatch book. For example, if you use the name "Copper," you'll want to remember that it represents PMS 876 so that you can communicate this color identifier to your printer. If you use the name "PMS 876," on the other hand, that's what prints out on the edge of the sheet when you pull spot-color overlays. Otherwise, "Copper" would print out.

You also have two other decisions to make: the color model to use and whether the color is a spot color or if it will be separated into process colors at print time. To make the color a spot color, leave "Process Separation" off in the Edit Color dialog box. To make the color separate onto the four process plates, just turn the checkbox on. Note that you can create a Pantone color—which usually would be specified as a spot color—as a process color, thereby forcing it to separate into four plates at print time. What results is a process simulation of the Pantone color.

Similarly, you could create a CMYK color that would print as a spot color on its own plate, simply by leaving "Process Separation" off. The first example has some usefulness; the second has almost none.

You can specify a color in three ways.

The wrong way. You can use the mouse to click on an area of the color wheel when you're specifying colors in RGB or HSB color space. Note that the farther towards the center of the circle you go, the less saturated the colors are. In the center, all colors have zero saturation; they're white. You can choose a pink color by clicking in the red area (near the label "R") and then moving the pointer left until you find a saturation level you like. When you have the general hue and level of saturation you want, you can specify the level of brightness by using the scroll bar to the right of the wheel. The lower the box goes in the scroll bar, the darker the image becomes (remember, the lower the brightness, the higher the concentration of black).

This is the wrong way, because what you see on the screen probably has no relation to what you actually get on paper or film. We should add a caveat here, though. We call this method the wrong way only because amateurs and professionals alike are easily fooled into believing that what they see on the screen is what they're going to get off the press. They (we know you wouldn't) use this method to create process-separating colors, but they shouldn't.

You can, however, use this color-picking method for coming up with spot colors, if you're careful. For example, in a job we finished recently, we knew we wanted a greenish background printed with a Pantone color, but we didn't know which one. So we picked a color that looked about right on the screen and set it to a nonseparating spot color called Kelly Green. We then discussed the color choice with our lithographer and decided on a Pantone ink. This is a fine way of working with color. But, as we've said, it's too often used wrongly.

The right way. You can type in the value for each aspect of the model you're working with. When you are working in RGB, QuarkXPress shows you the percentages of red, green, and blue in the lower-right corner of the dialog box. When working in CMYK, QuarkXPress displays the cyan, magenta, yellow, and black values. As an alternative to typing in your own percentages in these boxes, you can use the scroll bars to raise or lower the values.

This is the right way, because what you specify is close to what you get. Don't get us wrong: It's not *easier* this way by any means. You need to have a color swatch book for the color model you're working with, so that you can find the color you want in the swatch book and then type the values in. It's a hassle, but it works.

Another right way. Because Pantone colors are based on a matching system, you can also use a swatch book to determine a PMS color. When you have Pantone selected as the color model, you can select the color by either clicking on the color in the Pantone Color Selector box (see Figure 9-3) or by typing the desired PMS number into the Pantone No. box. When you type the number in, QuarkXPress automatically jumps to that color. In fact, if you type "312," it'll jump to that number, then when you type another "5" it'll jump to PMS 3125.

The same thing works with Trumatch, which is the best process color swatch book we've seen. However, we often just read the CMYK values from the swatch book and type them directly into the CMYK fields in QuarkXPress, rather than use the Trumatch code. Either way works just fine.

But remember two things when working with Pantone colors. First of all, never trust the screen to give you an accurate representation of the color, and second, even your swatch book may be "wrong" due to fading, a bad batch of ink, or some other act of god.

▼ ▼

Tip: Make Your Pantones Look Right. If you're working with spot colors, you can change the color specs for any Pantone color to make it look better on screen or on a color printer. The color specs have no effect when you print the spot overlays; they come out black, as they should.

Figure 9-3
The Pantone and Trumatch Color Selector boxes

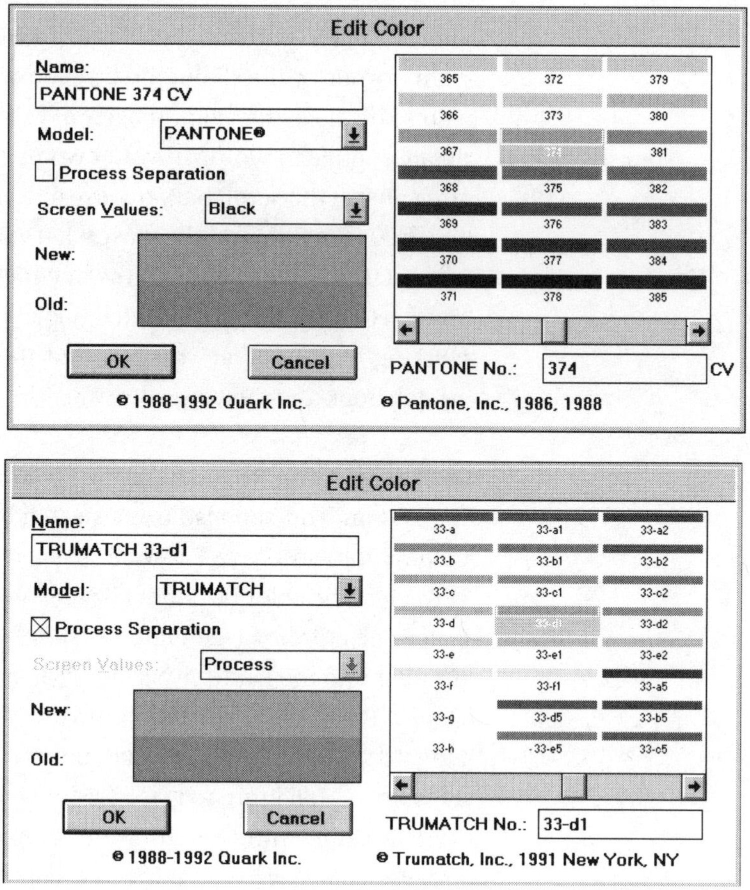

▼ ▼

Tip: Multiple Models. We include this tip with a caveat: It's fun and somewhat educational to play with color on the screen, but as we've said repeatedly, it often has little relationship to what you see on the final output.

Sometimes you get a color just the way you want it in RGB, except that you want a slightly darker tone. At this point, you can switch to the HSB model by clicking the appropriate button and then simply lowering the brightness level slightly. The same applies for any combination of models. For example, start with a Pantone color, then get the CMYK values for it by clicking the CMYK button, alter it, then translate to RGB for further changes. Every color model can be translated into the others.

▼ ▼

The final element in the Edit Color dialog box is the New/Old preview. When you are creating a new color, the lower half of this rectangle remains white (blank) since there is no "old" color to show. When you specify a color using one of the methods described above, the upper rectangle shows what that color looks like. You can specify a color, look at this preview window, then change the specifications and actually see the change in the way the color looks.

When you have the color the way you like it, clicking OK closes this dialog box and adds your color to the Color list.

▼ ▼

Tip: Color Tricks the Eye. Placing a colored object next to another differently colored object makes both colors look different than if you had just one color alone. Similarly, a color can look totally different if you place it on a black background rather than on a white one. These facts should influence how you work in two ways. First, when you're selecting colors from a swatch book, isolate the colors from their neighbors. We like to do this by placing a piece of paper with a hole cut out of it in front of a color we're considering. Second, after you've created the colors you're going to work with in your document, try them out with each other. You may find that you'll want to go back and edit them in order to create the effect you really want.

▼ ▼

Edit

Once you have a color on the color list, you can edit it by clicking on that color's name in the Color scroll list, then clicking "Edit" (or just double-clicking on the color's name). In the default color list (the one that's there when you first open QuarkXPress), you can edit four of the colors: Red, Green, Blue, and Registration. The other six colors, which include the four process colors, plus white and black, cannot be edited. When you edit a color, you see the same Edit Color dialog box as described above, but with several basic differences.

- The name of the color already appears in the Name box. If you change the name, the color's new name appears in the Color scroll list, and the color of each object you painted with the previous name changes to reflect the color of the new name.

- Both the upper and lower halves of the New/Old preview rectangle fill with the color. When you change the color specifications using the methods described above, only the upper half—the New preview—changes. In this way, you can quickly see a representation of the old versus the new color.

- The choice of color model is set to the model used to create or edit the color. For example, if the color was last modified using CMYK, it appears based on the CMYK model.

- The color's RGB and process color breakdown specifications are displayed by selecting the various color models and viewing the percentage values on the lower right of the Edit Color dialog box.

You can change any of the color's specifications using the same methods described above. When you like the new color, click OK to display these changes to the color scroll list.

- Click the Process Separations check box if your new color should print as a process color separation.

- If your newly specified color is a spot color (that is, if you *didn't* click the Process Separations option box), the Screen Values pop-up menu lets you specify a screen angle for halftones or tints in that color. Your choices are limited to the halftone angle setting for the Black, Yellow, Magenta, or Cyan colors; if you pick Yellow, your spot color's tints print out at the same halftone angle as the process color Yellow, usually 90 degrees. We talk more about color separations in Chapter 10, *Printing*.

▼ ▼

Tip: Returning to Your Origins. While editing any color, you can quickly revert back to the original color in two ways. The first way is to press Cancel and then Edit again (this just cancels the work you did). The better and faster way is simply to click on the Old color in the Old/New color area. That resets the color, but doesn't reset any other setting in the Edit Color dialog box.

▼ ▼

Duplicate

Let's say you love the color blue. We do. You want a new blue color that's really close to the one that is in the color palette, but you don't want to change the one already there. Click on the color Blue, then on "Duplicate." This opens the Edit Color dialog box, just as if you were editing the color, but the name of the color is changed to "Copy of..." In this case, "Copy of Blue." As long as you don't change the name of your new color back to its original (or any other color already specified), you can change the specifications, and save it to the color list without replacing the original color.

Unfortunately, QuarkXPress won't allow you to replace a color on the color list with another of the same name. In other words, if you want to replace all instances of Blue with Red, you must go in, edit Blue, and then change its name.

Delete

Is this button self-explanatory enough? Click on the color you most hate, then click "Delete." It's gone. Gone almost forever. See "Tip: Recovering from Color Boo-Boos," below, to see how to retrieve it. Note that you cannot delete the four process colors, or Black, White, or Registration. Also note that when you delete a color that has already been used within your document, Quark-XPress asks you if you really want to delete it. If you say OK, then objects of that color are changed to Black.

Append

When you click the Append button, QuarkXPress lets you find another QuarkXPress file. Then, when you click Open, that document's colors are added to your color palette. Note that colors with the same names as colors that you already have are not appended. We think this is unfortunate; you should at least have the option.

▼ ▼

Tip: One More Way to Append a Color. If you want just one or two colors from another file, and don't want to append the entire list, you can copy and paste, or drag across an object filled with that color from another document. The color and its specifications come across too, and are added to the color palette and the color list.

▼ ▼

Tip: Libraries of Colors. Here's one more way to save your colors so that you can bring them into a new document. Place an object (even just a picture box with a colored background) in a Library file. David has a Library file named "DVDSCOLR.QXL" into which he places colors he knows he'll use in various documents, but which he doesn't want to place in the default color palette. When he wants a particular color, he opens the library, pulls that color's object out onto the document page, and then deletes it. The object is gone, but the color stays in the color palette. Within the Library file, you can group your colors into types such as "Warm Colors," "Cool Colors," or "Newsletter Colors" using the Library's labeling feature.

▼ ▼

Edit Trap

Selecting the Edit Trap option in the Colors dialog box brings up the Trap Specifications dialog box. Trapping is a whole other *mishegoss* (Yiddish for "craziness"), so we'll put it off for now and discuss it at some length later in this chapter.

Save

When you are finished with adding, deleting, or editing your colors, you can click Save to save those changes to your document's color palette. Remember that even when you save the changes you can still come back and edit them later. These changes apply only to the document's color palette, not the default color palette.

▼ ▼

Tip: Adding Document Colors to the Default Palette. Frequently you'll find that you want to add a color that you have created in a document to the default color palette. Unfortunately, there's no easy way to transfer the color. We suggest Uncle Izzy's Notepad Method: Open the color using the Edit button, write the CMYK or Pantone values on your handy-dandy notepad, close the color, the color palette, and all of your documents, and then add the color back into the color palette with no documents open. Boring procedure. But it works.

▼ ▼

Cancel

Almost every dialog box in QuarkXPress has a Cancel button. This one works the same as all the rest: It cancels your entries without saving any changes.

▼ ▼

Tip: Recovering from Color Boo-Boos. We've found that working with the color palette can seem intimidating to some people. It always seems as if something could go terribly wrong somehow. What if you delete a color by accident? Or change a color that should remain the same? Or create some really obscure colors, then remember that you don't have a document open and saving them would save the entire list to the default palette? Whatever you do, don't panic. Remember your friendly neighborhood error-catcher buttons: Cancel and Revert.

You can click Cancel anytime before clicking Save, and all of your changes are…well, canceled. This goes for both the Color scroll list and the Edit Color dialog box. On the other hand, don't accidentally click this after spending an hour perfecting a color, or else your work is lost. If you have clicked Save but then decide you want to go back to the way colors looked before, you can select "Revert to Saved" from the file menu. Note that this reverts the entire file, not just the colors, back to the version last saved.

▼ ▼

Special Colors

QuarkXPress has two special "colors" that aren't really colors. They are "Registration," which we have mentioned before, and

"Indeterminate," which you'll see when dealing with trapping, later in this chapter.

Registration

This "noncolor" appears in the Color scroll list and on all color selection lists throughout the menus. When you color an object or type with this, it appears on every color separation plate you print. It's especially nice for job identification marks and for registration or crop marks (if you are creating your own, rather than letting the program do it for you; see Chapter 10, *Printing*, for more information on these special marks).

For example, David often prefers to bypass QuarkXPress's regular crop mark feature and draws his own crop marks in the border around the finished piece. Then he colors these "Registration," and they print out on every piece of film that comes out for that job. Note you can do the same thing by hanging pictures off the edge of the page (see "Tip: Additional Job Information" in Chapter 10, *Printing*).

▼▼▼▼▼▼▼▼▼▼▼▼▼▼▼▼▼▼▼▼▼▼▼▼

Tip: Editing the Registration Color. You can use the Edit feature described earlier to change the on-screen color of "Registration" to anything you like. Because "Registration" is originally black, the Edit Color dialog box appears with the brightness scroll bar down to zero. Just raise the brightness to the level you want and then change the color.

No matter what color you specify, it always prints out on every plate. Changing the color changes nothing but the screen representation for that color.

▼▼▼▼▼▼▼▼▼▼▼▼▼▼▼▼▼▼▼▼▼▼▼▼

Tip: Unique Registration Colors. Use a color that is distinctly different from anything else in the document you're creating. That way you always know at a glance what's normal black stuff and what is colored "Registration."

▼▼▼▼▼▼▼▼▼▼▼▼▼▼▼▼▼▼▼▼▼▼▼▼

Indeterminate

When QuarkXPress looks at a selection and finds that either several colors are specified within that selection or that it's a color picture, it calls this an Indeterminate colored background. This is not something you can change in any way. It's just a definition that the program uses to tell you there are several colors in the selection. Note that this "color" is found only in the Edit Trap dialog box (see "Trapping," later in this chapter).

Colors Palette

Just like style sheets, you can apply and edit colors with a click, using the Colors palette (see Figure 9-4). This floating palette contains a list of every available color, along with a tint-percentage control and three icons. These icons change, depending on what object you have selected. When you select a text box, the icons represent frame color, text color, and background color for that box. When you select a line, two icons gray out, and only the line color remains.

New in 3.3
See page 598

To apply a color to an object, first click on the correct icon for what you want to change, then click on the desired color in the color list. If you want a tint of that color, first change the percentage in the upper-right corner, then type Return or Enter to apply the change (you can also just click somewhere other than on the palette). For example, let's say you want to change one word in a text box to 30 percent cyan. First, select the word in the text box. Second, click on the center icon in the Colors palette, which represents text. Third, click on Cyan in the colors list. Fourth, change the percentage to 30 and press Enter. It's funny, but those four steps are often much faster than selecting a color and tint from the *Style* menu.

Note that you can change the color of a text or picture box frame, even if the box doesn't have a frame. If you later add a frame, it will be the color you designated.

You can also edit or create new colors by Control-clicking on a color in the Colors palette. This brings up the Colors dialog box, in which you can edit, duplicate, append, or delete colors (see "Edit," earlier in this chapter). This is also the fastest way to the Edit Trap dialog box.

Figure 9-4
The Colors palette

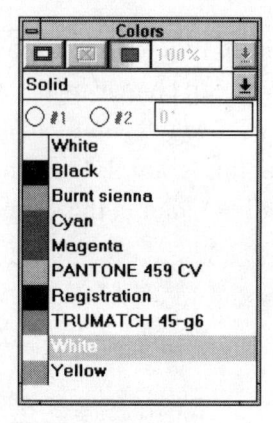

Color Blends

NEW IN 3.3

See page 599

The Colors palette is also the home of the Linear Blend feature. Linear blends are often called vignettes, fountains, or graduated fills, but the concept is always the same: a background in a text or picture box can blend from one color to another (see Figure 9-5). Unlike some other programs that create graduated fills, Quark-XPress blends any combination of spot colors, process colors, white, black, or registration.

Creating a blend is easy. Just follow these steps.

1. Select the text or picture box to which you want to apply the blend.

2. Click on the background icon in the Colors palette, if it's not already selected.

3. Select Linear Blend from the pop-up menu in the Colors palette.

4. Make sure button #1 is selected, then click on the beginning color of the blend (you can adjust the tint level, too).

5. Click button #2 and select the ending color of the blend (and adjust the tint, if necessary).

6. Specify the angle of the blend. Zero degrees (the default value) puts color #1 on the left and color #2 on the right. Increasing the value rotates the blend counter-clockwise (so at 75 degrees, color #1 is almost at the bottom of your box).

Figure 9-5
Color blends

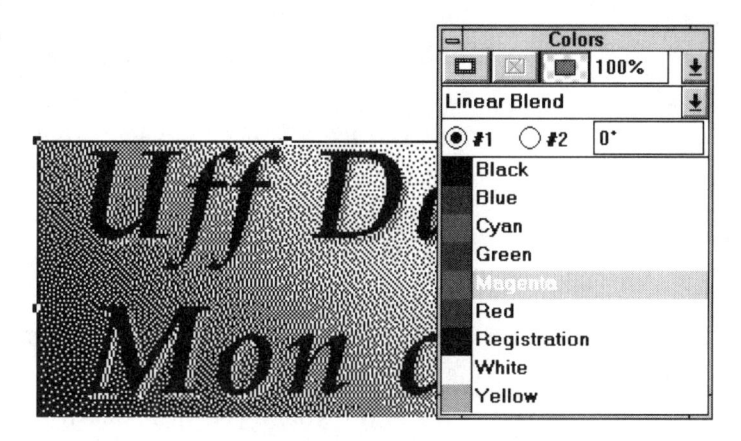

That's it. If you don't see the blend on your screen, it means one of two things. First, you performed this procedure incorrectly. Second, you have the Contents tool selected. When the Contents tool is selected, the active item (the text or picture box you have selected) shows you only the beginning color of the blend. This is so screen redraw can take place quickly and efficiently. To see the blend, either deselect the active picture or text box or select the Item tool.

If you want to change one of the colors of the blend, simply click radio button #1 or #2, then select the color, change its tint, or adjust the angle.

A warning for those placing blends behind gray-scale TIFFs: Our experience has shown that this usually results in something that looks as pleasant as a baboon's behind. Proceed at your own risk.

▼▼▼▼▼▼▼▼▼▼▼▼▼▼▼▼▼▼▼▼▼▼▼▼▼▼▼▼▼▼▼▼▼▼

Trapping

Nothing is perfect, not even obscenely expensive printing presses. When your print job is flying through those presses, each color being added one at a time, the paper may shift slightly. Depending on the press, this could be an offset of anywhere between .003 and .0625 inches (.2 to 4.5 points). If two colors abut each other on your artwork and this shift occurs, then the two colors may be moved apart slightly, resulting in a white "unprinted" space. It may seem like a .003-inch space would look like a small crack in a large sidewalk, but we assure you, it could easily appear to be a chasm. What can you do? Fill in these potential chasms with traps and overprints.

The concept and practice of traps and overprints contain several potential pitfalls for the inexperienced. Up until now, most designers just let their lithographers and strippers handle it. There is a school of thought that says we should still let them handle it. But you know these desktop publishers; they always want to be in control of everything. The problem is that designers weren't trained to do trapping! Let's look carefully at what it's all about.

Overprinting. Picture the letter "Q" colored magenta on a cyan background. Normally, when creating color separations, the cyan plate (we talk more about color separations and plates in Chapter 10, *Printing*) has a white "Q" knocked out of it, exactly where the magenta "Q" prints. This way the cyan and the magenta don't mix (see Figure 9-6). You can, however, set the magenta to overprint on the cyan. This results in the "Q" not being knocked out of the cyan; the two colors overprint in that area, resulting in a purple "Q" on a cyan background.

Trapping. A *trap* is created by very slightly overprinting two colors where they abut. Then, if—or when—the paper shifts in the printing press, the space "between" the colors is filled in with the additional trap color (see Figure 9-7). The trap can be created using two methods: choking or spreading. *Choking* refers to the background area getting smaller. *Spreading* refers to the foreground object (in the above example, the "Q") getting slightly larger.

Simple idea, right? But not necessarily a simple process when you're just beginning. First, you should know that only PostScript printers can handle trapping. If you're using a PCL or other non-PostScript printer, you're out of luck. There are two ways to

Figure 9-6
Knocking out and overprinting

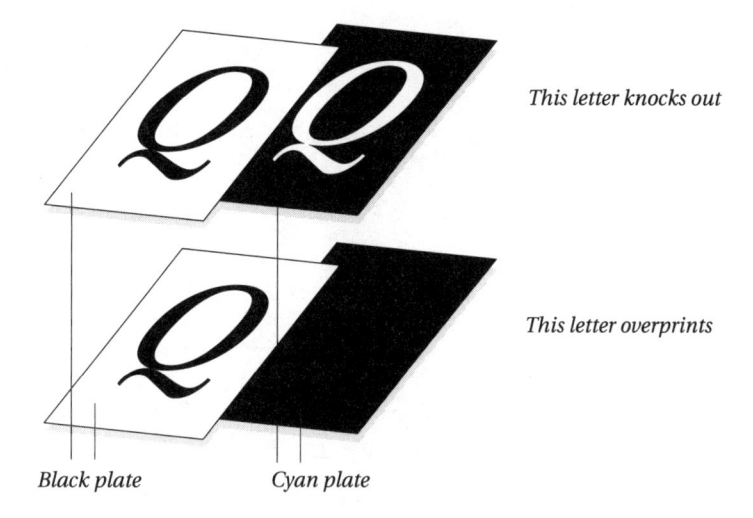

This letter knocks out

This letter overprints

Black plate   Cyan plate

control trapping in QuarkXPress: the Trap Specifications dialog box and the Trap Information palette. Let's look at each of these.

Edit Trap

The Trap Specifications dialog box lets you specify trapping in your documents at a color level (see Figure 9-8). You get to this dialog box by clicking the Edit Trap button in the Colors dialog box. When we say "at a color level," we mean that you are creating trapping and overprinting parameters for pairs of colors: the foreground and the background color. For example, picture some red type on top of a blue area. The blue is the background color; the red is the foreground color.

You can edit the trapping and overprinting parameters for background/foreground pairs by selecting the foreground color from the Color scroll list and clicking on "Edit Trap." You are then shown the Trap Specifications dialog box for that color. The list on the left side of the dialog box is the pairing list: each of the colors is a potential background color.

Note that the color Indeterminate is listed. This "color" refers to three cases: a color picture in the background, a background where several different colors are present, or an item only partially covering a background color (when Ignore White is turned off; see "Auto Trap Preferences," later in this chapter). If you leave this set to "Automatic," QuarkXPress doesn't include trapping at all in these circumstances.

Figure 9-7
Trapping two colored objects

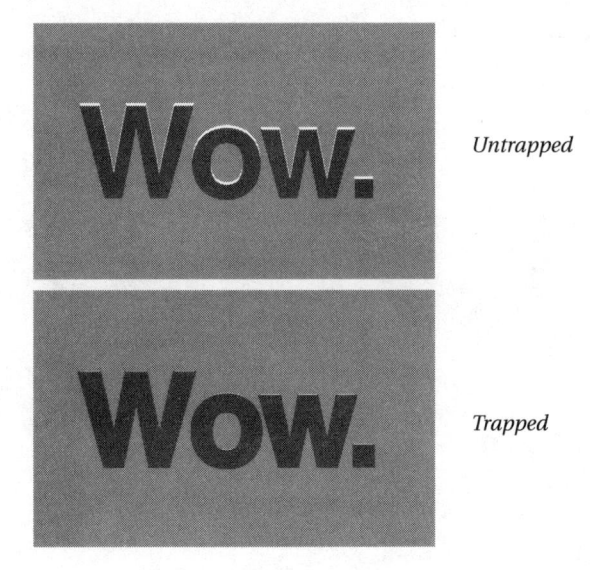

Untrapped

Trapped

You can edit one, some, or all foreground/background pairs with three buttons: Automatic, Overprint, and Trap. Remember that you can edit more than one color pair at a time by holding down the Shift or the Control key while clicking on background colors.

Automatic. When you first open the Trap Specifications dialog box for a color, each of the colors on the background list is set to Automatic trapping. Values for Automatic trapping are entered in the Application Preferences dialog box under the Edit menu (see "Auto Trap Preferences," later in this chapter). If you change the trapping parameters with the tools described below, you can change a color pair back to "Automatic" by clicking this Automatic button. "Automatic" refers to the following built-in trapping algorithm.

Figure 9-8
The Trap Specifications dialog box

- Translate each color to its CMYK values.

- Note the black content of each color.

- If the foreground color has less black, spread it so that it slightly "overlaps" the background color.

- If the background color has less black, then choke it, so that it slightly "underlaps" the foreground color.

- If neither color contains black, don't trap.

This algorithm is based on the rule that in trapping, lighter colors should encroach on darker ones. That way the dark element defines the edge, and the lighter color overlapping doesn't affect that definition (see Figure 9-9).

Figure 9-9
Trapping from light into dark

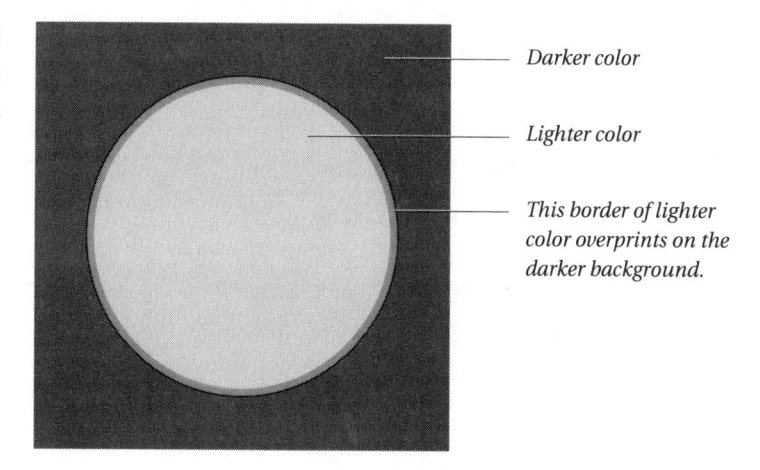

Darker color

Lighter color

This border of lighter color overprints on the darker background.

If the foreground color is black and its shading is set to 95 percent or greater, the automatic trapping algorithm sets black to fully overprint the color beneath it. In all other situations, though, the amount of trapping that the automatic algorithm uses depends on the settings you enter in the Auto Amount field in the Trap section of the Application Preferences dialog box.

To get technical for a moment, the way QuarkXPress determines the size of the automatic trap (using the proportional method) is by subtracting the two darkness values and multiplying that value by the Auto Amount value. Note that we use the word "darkness" here rather than "blackness." QuarkXPress is programmed to look at the luminance of the color, not just the amount of black in it. For example, if the background color has a luminance value of 80, the foreground object has a value of 20, and the Auto Amount is 1 point, then the foreground is spread by .4 point (.8 - .2 = .6 × 1 point = .6 point). Note that you can't really tell what the darkness value is; only QuarkXPress knows that!

If we're going to be opinionated here, we should tell you that we don't think using the Automatic trapping feature is a good idea. Why? Again, it comes down to control. We don't like the computer to make decisions for us on items such as trapping. Trapping is a delicate control and is often determined by the printing press, the paper, and ink the lithographer will use. Check with your printer first.

All in all, adjusting these settings can generally help when you're working with automatic trapping, but they're still not going to make your document look as good as just using common sense and manual trapping.

▼ ▼

Tip: Trapping Small Type. You can run into trouble when you're using small type, especially serif type, in a color document. Since the type is so fine—especially the serifs—even a small amount of trapping can clog it up (see "Tip: Trapping Tiny Objects," below). The counters can fill in, and the serifs can get clunky (see Figure 9-10). Bear this in mind when you're setting up your trapping preferences and when you're specifying colors for type.

▼ ▼

Overprint. As we described above, telling QuarkXPress to overprint a color pair has the effect of printing the background color with no knocked-out white space. The foreground color fully overlaps the background color.

There are a few very important times when you'll want to overprint colors. If you overprint red on blue, for instance, you get purple, which is probably not what you intended. The most important of these times, perhaps, is printing fine black lines or type on a colored background. In fact, almost any time you have a black foreground object, it should overprint the background.

Figure 9-10
Trapping small type

Monsieur de Bergerac
Untrapped

Monsieur de Bergerac
Trapped

To set a color pair to "Overprint," select the background color from the list and click the Overprint button.

▼▼▼▼▼▼▼▼▼▼▼▼▼▼▼▼▼▼▼▼▼▼▼▼▼▼▼▼▼

Tip: Overprinting Black. There are times when we want black to overprint and times when we don't. To give ourselves the option, we added a color to our color palette called "OverprintBlack," which is a duplicate of the color black. We then edited the trapping specifications for each of the blacks: Black always knocks out and sometimes traps, and "OverprintBlack" always overprints.

A large black box printing over a multicolored background may look mottled if it overprints, so we'd use black. However, fine black type over the same background probably looks just fine, so we'd use "OverprintBlack."

▼▼▼▼▼▼▼▼▼▼▼▼▼▼▼▼▼▼▼▼▼▼▼▼▼▼▼▼▼

Tip: Four-Color Black. Even better, you can create a much richer black color by defining a separate black in your color list that contains a bit of other process colors in it. The standard rich black that color strippers use is 100 percent black along with 40 percent cyan. Bob sometimes likes to get complicated, though, and adds 20 to 30 percent each of magenta and yellow. When a plain black (100 percent K) object overlaps colored objects, it can look mottled. Adding color to your blacks solves the problem.

This trick works not only for achieving richer black off a printing press, but also better blacks from a thermal color printer. However, if the thermal color printer is your final destination, you might boost the additional colors to between 50 and 100 percent each.

Note, though, that you should think carefully about how you apply this rich black. A potential problem lurks behind this technique (see the next tip).

▼ ▼

Tip: Knockout Lettering from Rich Black. Rich black is all very well and good, but when you have text or an object knocking out the rich black, any misregistration on the press results in the cyan (or other colors) peeking out horribly from behind the black. The engineers at Quark have built a very cool internal solution to this problem.

QuarkXPress checks to see if an object is knocking out a rich black. If it is, it only spreads the cyan, magenta, and yellow plates of that rich black color, leaving the black plate alone. You need this kind of help most when you're placing a white object (such as white, reversed text) over a rich black. QuarkXPress handles this trapping for you automatically, spreading the cyan, magenta, and yellow plates by the amount specified in the Auto Amount field.

If you don't understand what we're talking about, try it yourself with proofs from a laser printer (but change the trap to something enormous like 3 points so that you can see what's going on).

▼ ▼

Trap. If you want to set your own specification for a trap, select the background color you want to apply the trap to, then type the amount of trap you want into the space provided. You can select any value between -36 and 36 points, in .001-point increments (why anyone would want a trap over 1 or 2 points is beyond us). A positive value spreads the foreground object (make it slightly larger by drawing a line around it). A negative value leaves the foreground object alone and chokes the background object. Don't select OK yet, though: you must first click the Trap button to activate the change (this last step has been the downfall of many a trapper).

The amount of trap you need depends a great deal on your lithographer. No printers worth their salt would say that their printing presses are dead on or that you don't need to build in any trapping. Chances are that a value between .2 points and 1 point is adequate. Just as a reference, for almost every color job we do, we set all trap values to .3 points.

One fine point on trapping: If you are familiar with trapping in illustration programs such as FreeHand or Illustrator, you know that when you apply a trapping stroke to an object, your trap is really only one half of that thickness (the stroke falls equally inside and outside the path). If you're in the habit of typing 2 points when you want a 1-point trap, break it when you use QuarkXPress. This program handles the conversion for you.

Trap Information Palette

While the Trap Specifications dialog box lets you set up trapping on a color level, the Trap Information palette gets more specific: It lets you trap a particular object to its background, rather than trapping one color in a document to another color. It's still not a perfect system (we discuss why in just a bit), but it's a big step in the right direction.

Unlike most palettes in QuarkXPress, where you have the option either to use them or to use menu items, the Trap Information palette is the only way that you can use object-by-object trapping. Let's take a gander at this palette's anatomy (see Figure 9-11).

Figure 9-11
Trap Information palette

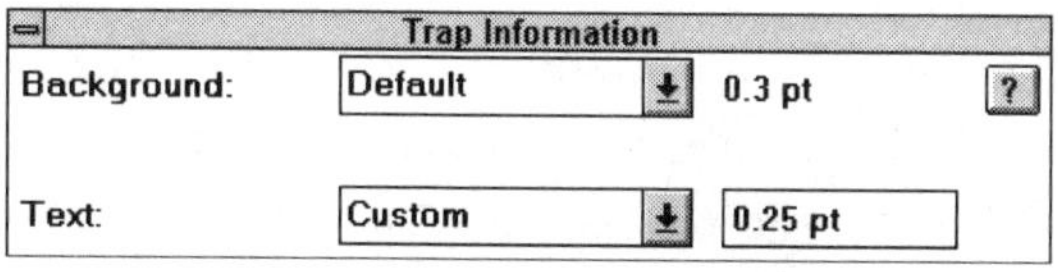

The Trap Information palette shows you the current trap information for a selected page object, gives you "reasons" for why it's trapping it that way, and lets you change that object's trap value. You can change the trap values depending on the object you have selected. For example, for a text box with no frame, you can adjust the trap for the background color of the box and the text in the box. For a box with a frame, you can set the trap for the inside of the frame (trapping to the background color of the box), and the outside of the frame (trapping to anything behind that box).

Unless you've changed the trap value, the Trap Information palette displays all objects at their Default trap. This means that the objects trap at the value set up in the Trap Specifications dialog box. QuarkXPress displays the trap value to the right of the word "Default" and then displays a gray button labeled with a question mark. If you click this button, QuarkXPress displays a message box explaining why it's trapping the object this way. For example, if you have a black line selected, the message might tell you that it's overprinting the black line because of the relationship between black and the background color. It doesn't usually go into much more detail than that, but it's better than just leaving you totally in the dark.

To change the trap value for part of an object (e.g., the inside frame of a picture box), you use the pop-up menu in the Trap Information palette. The menu is usually set to Default, but you can change this to Overprint, Knockout, Auto Amount (+), Auto Amount (–), or Custom. Overprint and Knockout are pretty self-explanatory. The two Auto Amount values use the value in the Auto Amount field of the Application Preferences dialog box (the value is either positive or negative, denoting a spread or a choke). When you select the last item, Custom, QuarkXPress gives you a field in which to type any trap value you want (from -36 to 36 points).

Note that text can be trapped character by character (see Figure 9-12), and one black object can be overprinted while some other black object knocks out (this kills the need for our tricky tip for a non-overprinting black).

Figure 9-12
Text trapped character by character

Saskatoon

Auto Trap Preferences

NEW IN 3.3

See page 602

The Trap section of the Application Preferences dialog box contains six controls: Auto Method, Auto Amount, Indeterminate, Overprint Limit, Ignore White, and Process Trap. These controls let you get pretty specific about how you want QuarkXPress's trapping to act. One thing to remember about these trap preferences, though, is that they are not saved within your documents;

if you move a file from one machine to another (let's say to your service bureau), they have to reset their trap preferences to match yours.

Auto Method. The Auto Method control is a two-item pop-up menu that determines how Automatic trapping should be handled. Your two choices are "Proportional" and "Absolute." The first choice, "Proportional," tells QuarkXPress to handle automatic trapping the way we described above: The width of the trap is determined by which color is darker and how much darker it is. The maximum trap amount is the value in the Auto Amount field.

The second choice, "Absolute," tells QuarkXPress to always use the same trapping value. This trapping amount is the value in the Auto Amount field. As far as we're concerned, there's rarely a reason to use Proportional trapping, so we always leave the Auto Method set to "Absolute." But then again, we try to avoid using automatic trapping as much as possible anyway (and we think you should, too).

Auto Amount. The value that you set in the Auto Amount field tells QuarkXPress the maximum value that Proportional automatic trapping can use, and the specific value that Absolute automatic trapping should use. The default value of .144 point (about two thousandths of an inch) seems a little small to us, so we usually change this to .25 or .3 point. However, remember to check with your lithographer first.

Indeterminate. The value that you set in the Indeterminate field sets the amount of trap that QuarkXPress uses for objects that are placed over indeterminate colors. Note that this is an absolute (not relative) value; any object that sits over an indeterminate color is trapped by this amount (unless you specifically change it in the Edit Trap dialog box or the Trap Information palette); it doesn't change depending on luminance or blackness.

If the foreground object overlaps two different colors, QuarkXPress checks to see what the differing trap values are set to. For example, a red circle placed half over a blue box and half over a green box is registered as having an Indeterminate background. But QuarkXPress checks to see what the red/blue and the red/green trapping values are set to. If they're both set to "Spread" or "Choke," QuarkXPress uses the smaller of the two values. If one is set to spread by some amount and the other is set to choke, then QuarkXPress uses the Indeterminate trapping specified in the Trap section of the Application Preferences dialog box.

Overprint Limit. Just because a color is set to overprint in the Trap Specifications dialog box doesn't mean that it'll really overprint. The key is this Overprint Limit value in the Application Preferences dialog box. QuarkXPress overprints the color Black and any other color that is set to overprint only when their tint levels are above the Overprint Limit. For example, let's say you have the color Green set to overprint. If you screen it back to 50 percent, QuarkXPress knocks out the color rather than overprinting it, because the tint falls below the Overprint Limit. Likewise, when the color Black is set to Automatic, it always overprints any color, as long as the black is above this Overprint Limit.

Of course, if you tell the object to overprint in the Trap Information palette, it will overprint no matter what the Overprint Limit says.

Ignore White. When a page item such as a picture box only partially overlaps another page item (see Figure 9-13), you have a say about what color is in the background—and not simply relegate it to "Indeterminate." When the Ignore White checkbox is turned on in the Application Preferences dialog box, QuarkXPress won't call a partial overlap "Indeterminate" because it ignores the white page background. If you turn this off, however, it "sees" the white background page and considers the mix of background colors to be "Indeterminate."

Process Trap. Take a look at the two process colors (foreground and background) listed in Table 9-1. If QuarkXPress merely spreads this foreground color (a yellow) into the background

COLOR PLATES **A**

Figure A
Process-color separations

Process-color image (four colors)

Cyan, 15 degrees

Magenta, 75 degrees

Yellow, zero degrees

Black, 45 degrees

Figure B
The elegant solution for shadow type with process colors

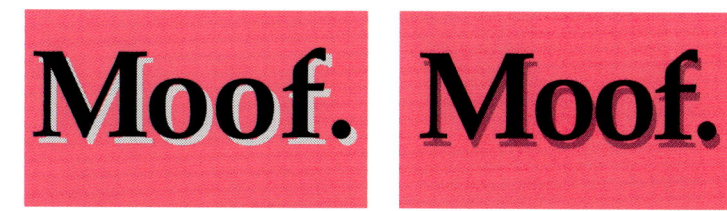

Normal shadow style applied (background color is 80-percent magenta)

Shadow is in separate text box (text color set to 30-percent black and 80-percent magenta)

B   COLOR PLATES

Figure C
Separations made with Photoshop and EfiColor

Scan was made on a Hewlett-Packard ScanJet IIc desktop flatbed scanner.

*Adobe Photoshop
(default separation settings)*

*EfiColor XTension
(Calibrated RGB profile)*

*EfiColor XTension
(ScanJet IIc profile)*

*EfiColor XTension
(Wrong profile; Solid Rendering)*

Figure D
A color swatch page from the TruMatch color selection book

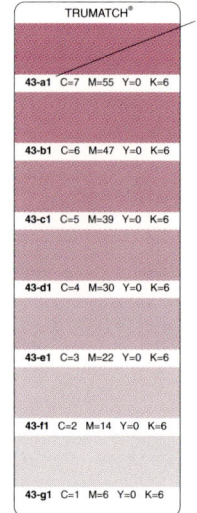

You can type this number directly in the Edit Colors dialog box with TruMatch selected. (Or you can type in the CMYK values.)

Figure E
Linear color blend between two process colors with an EPS image over it

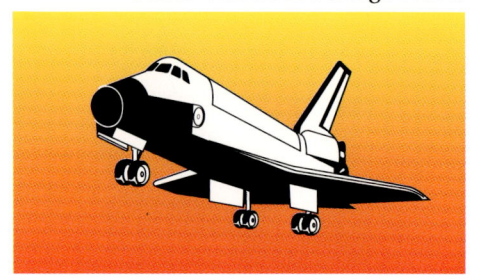

COLOR PLATES

Figure F
Rich black versus 100 percent black

100 percent black

Rich black (includes cyan and magenta)

Figure G
Trapping with process color on and off

These traps are much larger than you'd generally use.

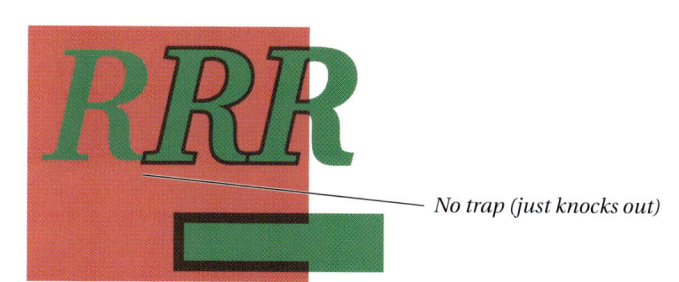

No trap (just knocks out)

Process Color turned on

Box spreads with Process Color turned off

Process Color turned off

Figure H
Blend inside one-bit image

D   COLOR PLATES

Figure I
EfiColor's gamut alarm

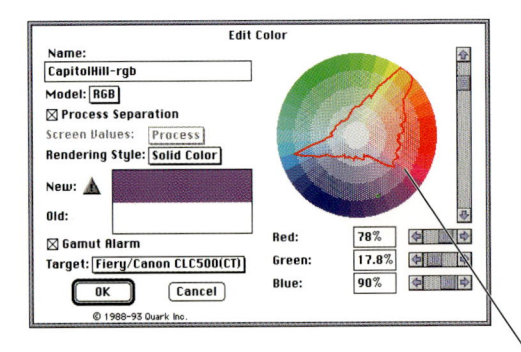

EfiColor's gamut alarm prompts you when a color cannot be printed on the target device.

Figure J
Modifying color images using Picture Contrast controls

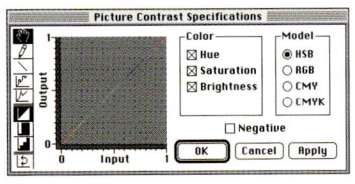

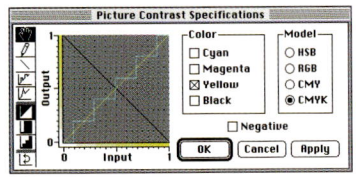

Figure 9-13
Ignore White

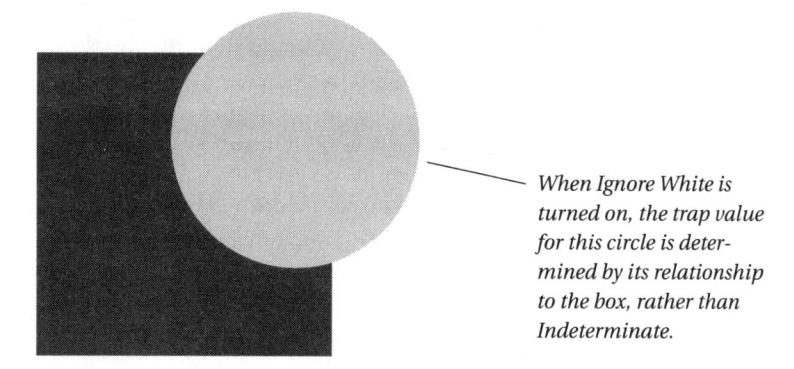

When Ignore White is turned on, the trap value for this circle is determined by its relationship to the box, rather than Indeterminate.

color (a muddy brown), the trap area doesn't mesh the two colors the way you want; the trap area is the same as the foreground color on each process color plate except for the cyan plate, on which the background shows through because the foreground has no cyan in it. Now you might say that for a quarter-point trap, who cares? No one will see it anyway. Think again. The greenish line that results stands out clearly.

Table 9-1
Color breakdown for trapping example

Color	Foreground box	Background box
cyan	0	30
magenta	20	50
yellow	100	90
black	5	0

However, when "Process Trap" is turned on, QuarkXPress spreads some process colors and chokes others. Here's how it works: Any process color in the foreground object that is darker than the same color in the background object is spread by half the trapping value (if you're using absolute automatic trapping, it's half the value in the Auto Amount field; otherwise it's half of the trapping value you specify). Any process color that's lighter is choked by half that value. In the example listed in Table 9-1, the cyan plate is choked by half the trapping value (let's say half of .25 point, or .125 point) because there is less cyan in the foreground box than in the background box. Magenta also chokes. However, the yellow and black plates spread by .125 point.

The result is a trap area as wide as the specified trapping value (in the example above, .25 point), centered on the edge of the foreground object, that has the darkest process colors of each of the objects.

If the overlapping process colors use Proportional Automatic trapping, then the situation is similar to the above explanation, except that QuarkXPress determines the amount of trapping by subtracting the darkness of the foreground object from the darkness of the background and multiplying the difference by the Auto Amount value you've entered in the Application Preferences dialog box.

If you don't understand this, read the last few paragraphs several times. If you still don't understand it, then give up and believe us when we tell you that it's a really good thing. Leave this control turned on.

A couple of notes on Process Trap. When all process colors in the foreground object are darker (or lighter), then QuarkXPress doesn't trap at all. This is because it doesn't need to. Also, Process Trap doesn't do anything for spot colors, again because it doesn't need to.

▼▼▼▼▼▼▼▼▼▼▼▼▼▼▼▼▼▼▼▼▼▼▼▼▼▼▼

Tip: Trapping Tiny Objects. All right, so this isn't really a tip. However, if you're getting heavy into trapping with QuarkXPress, we think you'd better know that the program often won't trap tiny objects; any text smaller than 24 points and any object that has a dimension of less than or equal to 10 points gets a special check to see if the shape of the object would be distorted or compromised by the trapping. QuarkXPress compares the darkness of the object on each color plate to the darkness of the background and spreads the object only if the darkness of the object is less than half the darkness of its background. Similarly, QuarkXPress only chokes the background when the darkness of the background is less than the darkness of the object.

▼▼▼▼▼▼▼▼▼▼▼▼▼▼▼▼▼▼▼▼▼▼▼▼▼▼▼

Color from Outside Sources

Up until now in this chapter we have concentrated our discussion on color items—text, boxes, rules, and so on—that are built entirely in QuarkXPress. But what about bringing color EPS graphics in from other programs? And although we discussed modifying color bitmapped images in Chapter 8, *Modifying Images*, what about being prepared for creating color separations? We address these points now.

Color TIFFs

QuarkXPress presently has no built-in method for creating separations from any file based on the RGB color model. It gladly prints a gray-scale representation of the entire picture, but when it comes to pulling it apart, it gives the big "no dice, dog lice." You can, however, separate color images that are specified in a CMYK model or use another application or XTension in conjunction with QuarkXPress. For example, color scans from desktop scanners are generally saved in an RGB format, so they can't be directly separated from QuarkXPress. However, if you convert the scan into a CMYK format, you can print the separations directly from QuarkXPress.

You have two choices for separating color bitmapped images: preseparating the picture or separating the entire file after you have the image placed. Although we really talk about color separation in detail in Chapter 10, *Printing*, let's explore these two methods briefly here.

Preseparating

Let's be clear about something right up front: As we go to press (November, 1992), color separation in desktop publishing is significantly better on the Macintosh than on the PC. We'd love to tell you that there are a number of programs that let you convert your RGB bitmapped images into CMYK files that QuarkXPress can separate, but the truth is that we can't even find one! Adobe Photoshop for Windows, which might well be released by the time you read this, should be able to perform this function. Aldus PhotoStyler probably will handle the conversion in the not-too-distant future, as well (right now it only separates into four distinct files, rather than a single CMYK file). But other than those programs, we can only recommend converting the files on another platform, such as Macintosh.

The Macintosh version of Adobe Photoshop allows you to separate a color bitmapped image and save it to disk as either a CMYK TIFF file or into what's called the *Desktop Color Separation* format (DCS). Let's look at each of these briefly.

See page 611

DCS. The DCS method is based on preseparating color images into five separate EPS files, which is why DCS is sometimes called PostScript-5 or EPS-5. Four of the files contain high-resolution information for each of the process colors. The fifth one includes a pointer to each of those other files and supplies a low-resolution representation of the image for placing on the page. This last file is the one that you import into your QuarkXPress document. When you go to print, QuarkXPress replaces this representation file (sometimes called the "main file") with the four high-resolution files. This means you can print the separations directly from QuarkXPress. This is great for situations where the color images are not huge and can transmit in a reasonable amount of time over a small bandwidth network such as AppleTalk.

▼ ▼

Tip: Making DCS Files on the Mac. We searched in vain through both Quark's and Adobe's documentation for instructions on how to create DCS files. Perhaps their feeling is that this is too technical for their readers. Let's look at the process, and then you can decide for yourself.

1. With your image opened in Adobe Photoshop, switch the viewing mode to "CMYK" (under the Mode menu).

2. Select "Save As…" from the File menu.

3. Select "EPS" from the File Format menu in the Save As dialog box.

4. Name the file and click OK.

5. Click the Five Separate Files checkbox to turn it on.

6. Click OK.

7. Import the master file into QuarkXPress. The master file is the file that contains the low-resolution representation of

the four-color image along with the pointers to the other files. Note that when you bring the five files over to the PC, you lose the screen representation.

8. Print your separations from QuarkXPress as described in Chapter 10, *Printing*.

If the name of the file is longer than six characters, you have to go through some hassle. Open the master file with a word processor. Right near the top of the file, you'll see some words like "%%CyanPlate: Dance.C %%MagentaPlate: Dance.M," and so on. The name after the colon is the pointer to the high-resolution image file. When you bring the files over to the PC, the names will probably be truncated or changed (you may have to change them yourself). Change the master file's pointers to the new names and save it again before importing it into QuarkXPress.

That's it. No fuss, no dishes to clean up, nothing. Of course, we've already said that color separation is not as easy as clicking a button. If you're looking for quality color, you had better really know Photoshop well enough to work with its undercolor removal and color correction settings. Remember that QuarkXPress cannot apply any image modification to the EPS files that you import. All of that must be done before importing the picture.

While this isn't too technical, we feel that it's kind of a pain. We prefer saving the file in CMYK TIFF format. But you never know when you'll need this information!

▼ ▼

CMYK TIFF. What we can't figure out is why people aren't jumping up and down with excitement over the CMYK TIFF format. The TIFF format was developed primarily by folks at Aldus, but it has always used an RGB color model. Now, Aldus has come up with a specification for a TIFF format based on CMYK values. It's been a long time coming, and we think it's the hot new thing in color prepress.

The good news is that QuarkXPress can separate a CMYK TIFF all by itself—just import the picture and print. The bad news is that not many programs create CMYK TIFFs yet. It's just too new. But the way this technology moves, by the time you read this, everything might support it. Right now, though, the only software packages we know of that can create CMYK TIFFs are the Macintosh versions of Adobe Photoshop 2.0, ColorStudio 1.5, and Aldus PrePrint 1.5.

Our suggestion is to bring an image (whether it be PICT or RGB TIFF or whatever) into Adobe Photoshop 2.0, covert it to CMYK (by changing modes), and then save as either EPS (to create a DCS file), or TIFF (to create a CMYK TIFF file). You can save the TIFF in a PC-compatible format and then move it over to the PC. The advantage of using CMYK TIFF is that you end up with a screen representation on the page, rather than a gray box.

Postseparating

The second method of separating color images relies on another program to separate your entire QuarkXPress document for you. You need not do anything special aside from properly importing your pictures and making sure you keep the files around so that the program or XTension can find them later.

The three methods that are currently available are Aldus PrePrint (on the Macintosh), Inset's HiJaak ColorSep, and Insight System's Publisher's Prism. Aldus PrePrint separates files that are saved with OPI comments (see "Using OPI" in Chapter 6, *Pictures*). HiJaak ColorSep and Insight Systems' Publisher's Prism separate full pages of PostScript. These separate color bitmap images, text, graphics, the works.

Which of these methods results in superior separations? Here we get to the aesthetics of color separation, and we wouldn't want to sway your opinion, which is the nice way of saying that, for once, we're not going to preach our opinions. Ultimately, we prefer going with a preseparated graphic image, using something like a CMYK TIFF.

Color EPS Files

We've avoided the subject of object-oriented graphic files for several chapters, but now it's time to delve back in. Designers frequently generate color artwork using draw programs such as

CorelDRAW, Adobe Illustrator, or Aldus FreeHand, saving it as encapsulated PostScript (EPS). QuarkXPress can not only import files from these programs, it can also generate color separations of them. Once again, the details of generating color separations (or "seps," as they're often called) are covered in Chapter 10, *Printing*. But while we're talking about color on the desktop, we need to cover some general information about using these programs with QuarkXPress. We tackle this discussion one color method at a time: first process color, and then spot color (we're including Pantone colors in the spot color discussion, though you can also create process simulations of Pantone inks).

Process color. QuarkXPress can create color separations of illustrations that contain process colors built in programs like CorelDRAW, Designer, FreeHand, or Illustrator. Period. All you have to do is specify your process colors in either application, save them as EPS, and import them into your QuarkXPress document using "Get Picture." Nice and easy.

Note that we say you must use "Get Picture." In fact, while we're on the subject, we should note that QuarkXPress may not be able to separate color EPS files from applications other than Illustrator and FreeHand. It depends entirely on whether those applications create EPS files according to Adobe's color specifications. So, while color separation sometimes works with OLE, we typically don't recommend this method.

See page 599

Spot color. The key to working with spot colors brought in from drawing programs is being careful with your color naming. Two scenarios should make our point clear to you.

First, let's say we've created a color illustration in CorelDRAW using process colors and one spot color, which we called "PANTONE Green CV." We exported our illustration as EPS and then imported it into a picture box in our QuarkXPress document. When we print color separations of this file, no PANTONE Green CV spot color plate appears. In fact, in this scenario, though we specified the color as a spot color in CorelDRAW, it separates as a process color in QuarkXPress.

Second scenario: let's say we've created a similar illustration in CorelDRAW (or Designer, for that matter), naming the one spot color the same thing. But this time, after we bring the picture into our QuarkXPress document, we create a new color in our QuarkXPress color palette called—guess what— "PANTONE Green CV." Now when we print our separations, the proper spot color plate appears, apart from the process color plates.

Obviously, the trick is to have spot colors with exactly the same names in both the illustration program and QuarkXPress. Whether or not the colors actually are defined the same is irrelevant for color separations to print correctly. The same goes for the Pantone colors. If you use a Pantone color in your CorelDRAW file, just make sure it's named the same thing in your QuarkXPress file and it'll print fine. Fortunately, all three applications name their Pantone colors the same.

Specifications in EPS Files

QuarkXPress prints exactly what is specified in every EPS file. In fact, QuarkXPress has no way to change them: encapsulated PostScript files are totally self-contained and cannot easily be modified by other programs. All halftoning information for objects and bitmapped images, all trapping and tinting information, and all color specifications are set in hard-packed mud (we like to think that you at least have a chance with hard-packed mud; "stone" is a bit too final).

This means that you must take a little more control into your own hands. You must specify your own trapping from within FreeHand or Illustrator and make sure that these EPS images contain traps for their surroundings in QuarkXPress documents. Luckily, all overprinting specified in Illustrator or FreeHand (or any other program that handles its color PostScript properly) is handled correctly when generating color separations from QuarkXPress. Conversely, if an object's color is not set to "Overprint," it knocks out any background colors or objects within QuarkXPress.

Note that QuarkXPress's trapping controls do not have any effect on colors or objects in EPS files. For example, if your EPS

See page 599

picture contains a spot color, PMS 345, and you have set up the equivalent spot color in QuarkXPress as described above, any trapping or overprinting assignments you make to PMS 345 in the Trap Specifications dialog box do not (and actually cannot) make any difference to the EPS file. They do, however, make all the difference to any objects created within QuarkXPress that are colored with PMS 345.

Deciding to Work in Color

We started this chapter with a comment from Russell Brown, so we think it's only fair to end with what he considers to be the most logical steps to successful color publishing.

1. Complete a black-and-white project with text only.

2. Complete a black-and-white project with text and graphics.

3. Complete a project with several spot colors.

4. Complete a project with process color tints.

5. Finally, attempt the use of color photography.

We couldn't agree more. A computer, no matter how powerful a tool, is still no substitute for experience. Work slowly and carefully, and in time, you too will become a raging color pro.

CHAPTER 10

PRINTING

Our coauthor, Bob, reacts harshly to advocates of today's "pepperless" office, given his Cajun heritage. But a "paperless" office, now that's another story. Silicon Valley ingenuity has outdone itself in Bob's eyes by evangelizing the thoroughly modern concept of "paperless" while enabling high-technology that actually helps us pump out more paper than ever before. "Paperless," alas, is at least 10 years away, when 10 dollars will by you a 2-pound computer with a built-in optical crystal drive for reading electronic books on the bus. As for "pepperless," that's David's idea of Matzoh Gumbo.

Ask anyone who's been involved with electronic publishing for a while if they have seen any sign of the paperless office. We have, and here's what it's like: the ratio of expended paper to normal refuse is such that we empty our small garbage cans every couple of weeks and the voluminous paper recycling boxes weekly. When it comes right down to it in our business, every piece of work that we do is based, ultimately, on a printed page or an imaged piece of film (which will probably be used to print on paper later).

How do we extract the digitized information on disk to print onto paper? Many people think the process is as easy as clicking the Print and OK buttons. In this chapter we discuss what's behind those two actions and go into some depth on how to get the most efficient and best quality print you can from your document. We also touch on tips for working with service bureaus and printers—both the mechanical and the human types.

Before we get into anything too complex, though, let's deal with two simple, yet crucial issues for most people's print jobs: PostScript and fonts.

PostScript

To put it simply, PostScript is what makes desktop publishing with QuarkXPress possible. PostScript is a page-description language—a bunch of commands that PostScript laser printers understand. When you tell QuarkXPress to print a page, it writes a program in PostScript describing the page and sends that program to the printer. The printer (or imagesetter), which has a PostScript interpreter inside it, interprets the PostScript describing the page and puts marks on the paper (or film) according to that description.

This chapter is dedicated, in part, to Chuck Geschke, John Warnock, and the other people who created PostScript. And we need to say one thing up front: We're not talking about PCL here. We're not talking about CORA or even SGML. These also are languages designed for putting marks on paper or film. In this chapter, however, we're talking about PostScript.

In other words, QuarkXPress has not been designed for the office automation market, so it doesn't handle PCL very well—and certainly not PCL fonts. If you're in the graphic arts industry, we can only suggest you go with the PostScript standard.

Fonts

Almost everyone uses QuarkXPress at some point to work with text. It's a given. When you work with text, you work with typefaces. Choosing a particular font was covered in Chapter 4, *Type and Typography*. Printing that font is covered here.

Fortunately, the dichotomy between screen fonts and printer fonts is largely history, thanks to TrueType and ATM. With either, screen fonts are automatically generated from the outline printer fonts you've installed for Windows. You needn't buy or manually generate separate screen fonts to match your printer fonts. Such unity of screen and printer was once only a dream; now we can take it for granted. In fact, we have no choice about it, since if we use PostScript fonts, QuarkXPress actually *requires* ATM, as we pointed out in Chapter 4, *Type and Typography*.

Printer Fonts

To repeat: The bitmapped type on your screen is created on the fly from your outline printer fonts. At print time, QuarkXPress automatically shifts gears from bitmapped screen type to outline fonts loaded in the printer. But to make this switch, it must be able to find the outline printer font—either in the printer's permanent memory or in a font file on disk, which it then downloads to the printer. If you're printing TrueType fonts on a PostScript desktop laser printer, Windows itself converts the TrueType fonts either to a Type 1 font or to a bitmap and sends that to the printer instead.

David thinks of downloading as sending the font file down the wire to the printer (especially because his printer sits down under his desk). Any way you think of it, the action is the same. First, QuarkXPress tries to find character-width, kerning, and other information about the outline font, which is contained in a Printer Font Metric (PFM) file accompanying PostScript Type 1 fonts, or in the TrueType printer font file itself. (Without a PFM file, Windows can't really use your Type 1 fonts.) Next, assuming that QuarkXPress can find the printer font, it downloads the font to the laser printer along with your document, if you've installed your fonts for automatic downloading, which we discuss below.

PostScript laser printers have memory allocated for font storage. However, printer models vary in their memory allocations—and thus, the number of fonts they can hold. For example, the old LaserWriters could only keep three or four fonts in memory at a time, while an Apple LaserWriter IINTX can keep about 12 or 13 fonts in memory. Exceeding the amount of memory available causes a PostScript error, which flushes your job and restarts the printer. (We talk about PostScript errors later in this chapter.)

We're not kidding when we say that QuarkXPress needs ATM in order to use PostScript fonts. Although with other Windows programs you don't strictly need the PostScript outline printer fonts to print using any font that is built into your printer, with QuarkXPress you do. That's because QuarkXPress gets its font information from ATM, not from Windows. If you don't install a font for ATM, it won't appear in QuarkXPress (as we discuss below). And you must have the outline font in order to install the font for ATM.

Most other Windows programs treat ATM as a luxury, not a necessity. For them, it's possible to install enough information about the font (just the metrics) so that a program can use it, without needing the outline itself, as is the case with built-in printer fonts. For example, all PostScript printers come with Times, Helvetica, Courier, and Symbol encoded directly into the printer's memory, so you normally wouldn't need a separate printer font to use these typefaces. But with QuarkXPress, you never know those fonts are there unless you install them for ATM, and for that, as we said above, you need the outline font.

Printing Ugly

Although you need the Type 1 outline font installed in ATM when you create the document, you might move the document to another PC that doesn't have the same fonts installed. Or your document might contain an EPS file with fonts that you haven't installed. When you have neither a printer font nor a printer-resident font available, QuarkXPress prints using the Courier typeface. We tend to break into hives at the sight of large areas of Courier. Perhaps Oscar Wilde said it best when he noted, "For those who like that kind of thing, that is the kind of thing they like."

More Font Downloading

Ordinarily, when your print job is done, the fonts that QuarkXPress automatically downloads are flushed out of the printer's memory. Then, the next time you print the document, QuarkXPress has to download the fonts all over again. Downloading one time may not seem to be a long process, but having to download the fonts repeatedly starts to make chess look like a fast sport.

But you don't have to wait. You can do something about your predicament. You can download the fonts yourself.

Manual downloading. You can download a typeface to your printer and make it stay there until you turn off the printer. There are several utilities that let you do this. Some, like Adobe's PCSEND (which comes free with Adobe fonts), runs in DOS and has a lean, mean command-line interface. Other programs, like PSPlot by Legend Communications and the WinPSX shareware utility, have menus to help you locate and download fonts.

Downloading a font manually is particularly helpful for typefaces that you use many times throughout the day. If Goudy is your corporate typeface, you can manually download it from one computer at the start of each day. And as long as no one resets the printer, you can use it to your heart's content from any of the computers hooked up to the network, without waiting for it to download each time.

Hard disk storage. If you have a hard disk connected to your printer, you have one more option: downloading a printer font to the printer's hard disk. Once you download a font this way, it stays there until you erase it (or drop the hard drive on the ground). Downloading utilities, such as Adobe's PCSEND or PSDOWN, have the extra features necessary for this task. If you have some odd sort of printer, you may have to get special software from the manufacturer.

Choosing a Printer

We're going to leave the choice of lithographers up to you. If it's MinutePress, good luck. If it's a really good printer, just listen to what they tell you and follow obediently. Instead, we want to talk here about what electronic-imaging device you use to output your document.

Clearly, the most important feature of a printer is its imaging resolution. Whereas many high-resolution imagesetters offer a variety of resolutions, most desktop laser printers are happy only when they're printing 300 dots per inch. Table 10-1 lists several printers with their resolutions.

Table 10-1
Resolution choices for some imaging devices

Device	Printing resolutions in dpi
Apple ImageWriter ii	72, 144
Desktop laser printers	300
Varityper VT-600	600
Linotronic 300/500	635, 1270, 2540
Compugraphic CG9400	1200, 2400
Linotronic 330/530	1270, 2540, 3386
Agfa Matrix SlideWriter	2000, 4000

We, like most people, use a desktop laser printer to print proof copies of our QuarkXPress documents before we send them to a service bureau to be imageset onto RC (resin coated) paper or film.

Printer Setup

New in 3.3

See page 611

Okay: you've got your document finished and you're ready to print. But wait! Don't forget to check the Printer Setup dialog box. Some people choose Printer Setup from the file menu, but when we're doing demos, we like to look like pros and confuse the audience by just typing Control-Alt-P (see Figure 10-1).

Figure 10-1
The Printer Setup dialog box

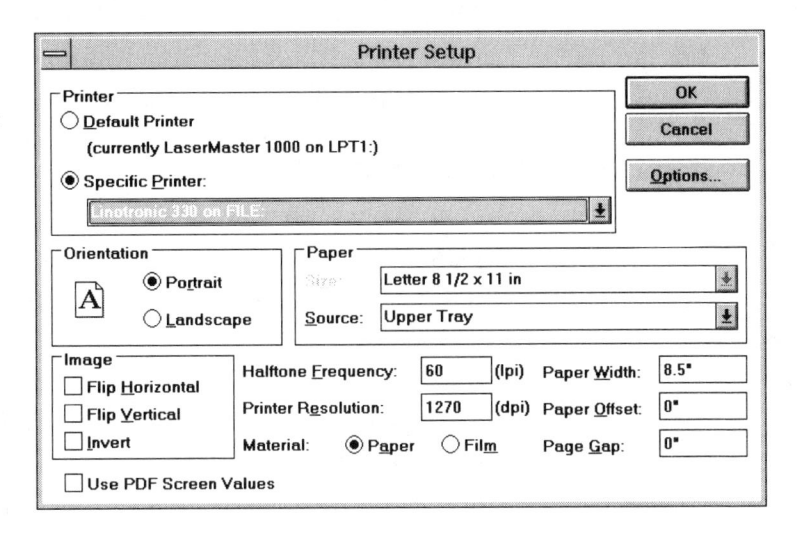

Although you can also access the Printer Setup Options dialog box through the Windows Control Panel, things work out a bit differently when you do so. When you open the Printer Setup Options dialog box from within QuarkXPress (from the File menu), any changes you make are saved with the document, but have no effect on other documents. On the other hand, when you open the Printer Setup Options dialog box from the Windows Printer Control Panel, any changes you make there stay in effect for every QuarkXPress document you try to print, *unless* you've already changed one of the options from within QuarkXPress. In the latter case, QuarkXPress overrides that particular Windows Control Panel setting.

The Printer Setup dialog box is divided into five areas: Printer, Orientation, Paper, Image, Roll-fed printer specifications, and Options. Let's take a look at each of these.

Printer

The first thing you need to do in the Printer Setup dialog box is tell QuarkXPress (and Windows) what printer you're printing to (or, to be a smidge more correct, "to which printer you are printing"). Your choices are simple: use the Default Printer option or choose one yourself.

Default Printer. This is the printer you've selected in the Windows Printer Control Panel as the default printer for all Windows applications. We typically set this to the printer we print most of our proofs to.

Specific Printer. When you want to print to a printer that is anything other than the default selection, select that printer from the Specific Printer pop-up menu. Specifying the printer lets QuarkXPress optimize the way it prints your document. If the printer you're using is not listed on the menu, you may have to install the printer driver for that printer (you do that through the Printers utility in the Windows Control Panel). If you still can't find the printer you're using, you can call your printer vendor to see if they have a Windows printer driver or a WPD (Windows Printer Description) file for you. Or if your printer is basically the same type of printer as one that's listed, go ahead and use the one that's there. For example, David prints to his Ricoh PC 6000/PS using Windows' Apple LaserWriter II selection because both printers are 300-dpi desktop laser printers of comparable speed, and so on. An Agfa Matrix SlideWriter slide recorder is not comparable to an Apple LaserWriter, so call Agfa first.

The Specific Printer selection becomes especially important when creating PostScript dumps, as we see later in this chapter.

Orientation

Remember back to the first day of high school when they had Orientation Day? The idea was to make sure you knew which way you were going while walking around the school grounds. Well, this orientation is sort of the same, but different. The idea is to make sure QuarkXPress knows which way you want your document to go while it's going through the printer. You have two choices: portrait and landscape. Luckily, these features have their own icons so that you don't have to think too hard about which one to choose. We've included some samples in Figure 10-2 so you can see what each option does.

▼▼▼▼▼▼▼▼▼▼▼▼▼▼▼▼▼▼▼▼▼▼▼▼▼▼

Tip: Save the RC Trees. When you're printing onto a roll-fed imagesetter (more on these later), you can save film or paper by

PRINTING

Figure 10-2
Tall versus Wide orientation.

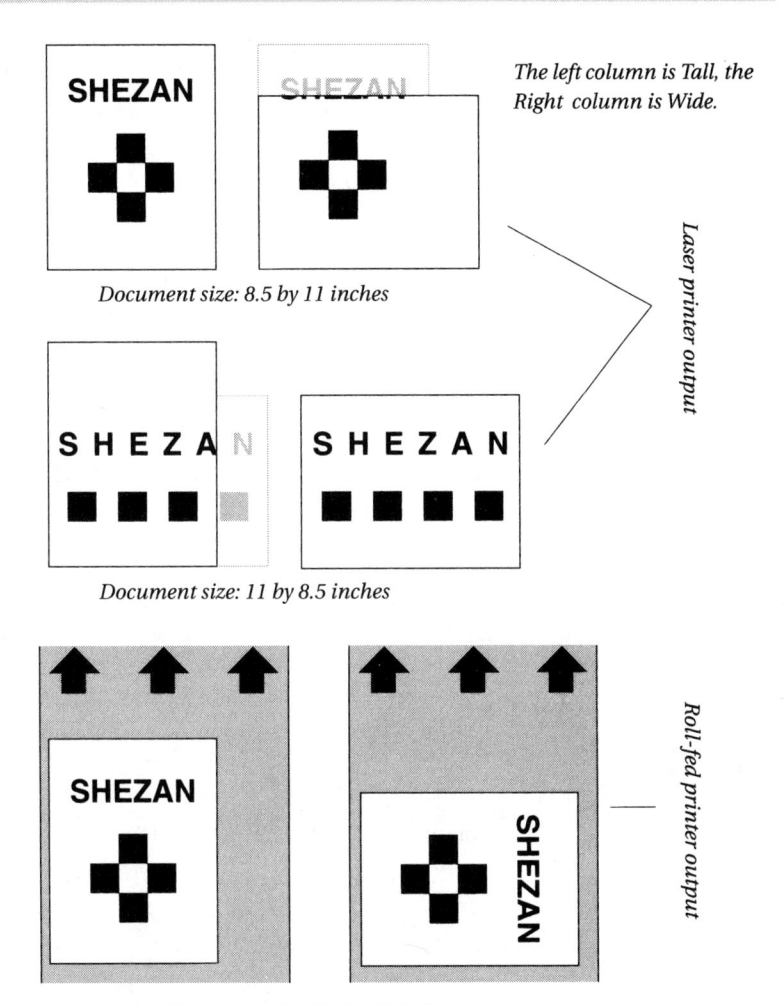

The left column is Tall, the Right column is Wide.

Document size: 8.5 by 11 inches

Document size: 11 by 8.5 inches

Laser printer output

Document size: 8.5 by 11 inches

Roll-fed printer output

printing your letter-size pages landscape rather than portrait. That way you only use around 8.5 inches on the roll rather than 11 inches. It may not seem like a great difference, but those three and a half inches really add up when you're printing a long document. For example, a hundred-page file saves an average of 300 inches of film or paper. Printing the pages landscape also makes it easy to cut them apart and stack them. Check with your service bureau to see if they'll give you a discount for the time and energy you've saved them.

▼ ▼

Paper

If you choose a non-roll-fed printer in the Printer section of the Printer Setup dialog box, QuarkXPress lets you set some parameters for the kind of paper you're printing on, and where that paper is coming from. The two controls in this section are Size and Paper Source.

Size. Contrary to popular belief, the paper size you choose in this area is not necessarily the page size of your document. It is the paper size onto which you want to print your document (see Table 10-2). For example, if your newsletter is set up on a regular 8.5-by-11-inch page, you can have it printed onto a tabloid-size area or onto an area as small as a Number 10 envelope.

Table 10-2
Paper sizes available in the Page Setup dialog box

Name	Inches
US Letter	8.5 by 11
US Legal	8.5 by 14
A4 Letter	8.3 by 11.7
B5 Letter	9.75 by 6.45
Tabloid	11 by 17
A3 Tabloid	11.7 by 16.5
Number 10 Envelope	3.8 by 9.1

The paper size you choose determines the printing area. So, if you choose B5 (182 x 257 mm) from the pull-down menu, but your document is actually larger than that size, your page is cropped down to 7.2 by 10.1 inches. Selecting a page size does not, however, determine where the automatic crop marks are placed (see "Registration Marks," later in this chapter).

In short, different printers have different page sizes available to them (the choices are determined by information in the printer description files or internally in QuarkXPress). Whatever the paper size you choose or the page size of your document (as determined in your Document Setup dialog box; see Chapter 2, *Document Construction*), the upper-left corner of your page is matched to the upper-left corner of the printed page. Confusing? Take a look at Figure 10-3 for a visual explanation.

Figure 10-3
Page size and paper size

Your printed page size is determined by the paper size you select. If you specify Number 10 envelope as the paper size, QuarkXPress only prints this much of your page.

Source. This feature specifies where you would like the printer to get its paper. Normally, you'd have this set to "Upper Tray." However, if you are using a printer that handles manual feed pages, you may want to select this option at various times—for example, when you print onto a single sheet of special stationery or onto an envelope.

When "Manual Feed" is selected, the printer waits for a designated time—usually 30 seconds or a minute—for you to properly place the sheet of paper at the manual feed slot. If you don't place the page in time, the PostScript interpreter returns a time-out error and flushes the rest of the print job.

Image

Okay, look. Unless you have been given permission from the highest authority at your service bureau, we suggest that you just ignore the controls in the Image section of the Printer Setup dialog box. You can do almost nothing other than get yourself into trouble. Nonetheless, out of sheer insistence on the part of our editor, we explain what this stuff does.

Flip Horizontal/Flip Vertical. We meld the two Flip options into one description, since they are really doing the same thing. Flipping an image is used primarily for creating either wrong- or right-reading film or film with emulsion side up or down. The differences? Let's look at what happens when you print onto film.

As the film moves through the imagesetter, the side of the film that is coated with a photographically sensitive emulsion is exposed to a beam of laser light. If you have neither "Flip Horizontal" nor "Flip Vertical" selected, the film is imaged wrong-reading, emulsion down (which is right-reading, emulsion up). This means that when you are holding the film so that the type and graphics look right ("right-reading"), the emulsion of the film is facing you. If you select either "Flip Horizontal" or "Flip Vertical," the film emerges right-reading, emulsion down. To look at it in a different way, this means that when you hold the film with the emulsion away from you, the text and graphics look correct ("right-reading"). See Figure 10-4 for a quick graphical reference.

If you want to know why you'd ever care whether the emulsion is up or down, check with your lithographer (and then talk to a screen printer; you'll see that they need different film output for similar yet different reasons). Typically, your service bureau can set this themselves, so you shouldn't have to set it.

Invert Image. Clicking on this feature inverts the entire page so that everything that is set to 100 percent black becomes 0 percent black (effectively, white). It is the same as selecting the Inversion tool from within the Contrast Specifications dialog box, except that it affects the entire print job. This is another feature that your service bureau can set themselves (and probably should), through either a hardware or a custom PostScript file.

▼ ▼

Tip: Negatives of Low Screen Frequency Halftones. If you are printing halftones or tints at very low screen frequency (anything coarse enough to actually see the spots), you should be aware of an important fact about "Invert Image." This feature does not actually invert pixels from black to white or white to black. It

Figure 10-4
The effects of "Flip Horizontal" and "Flip Vertical"

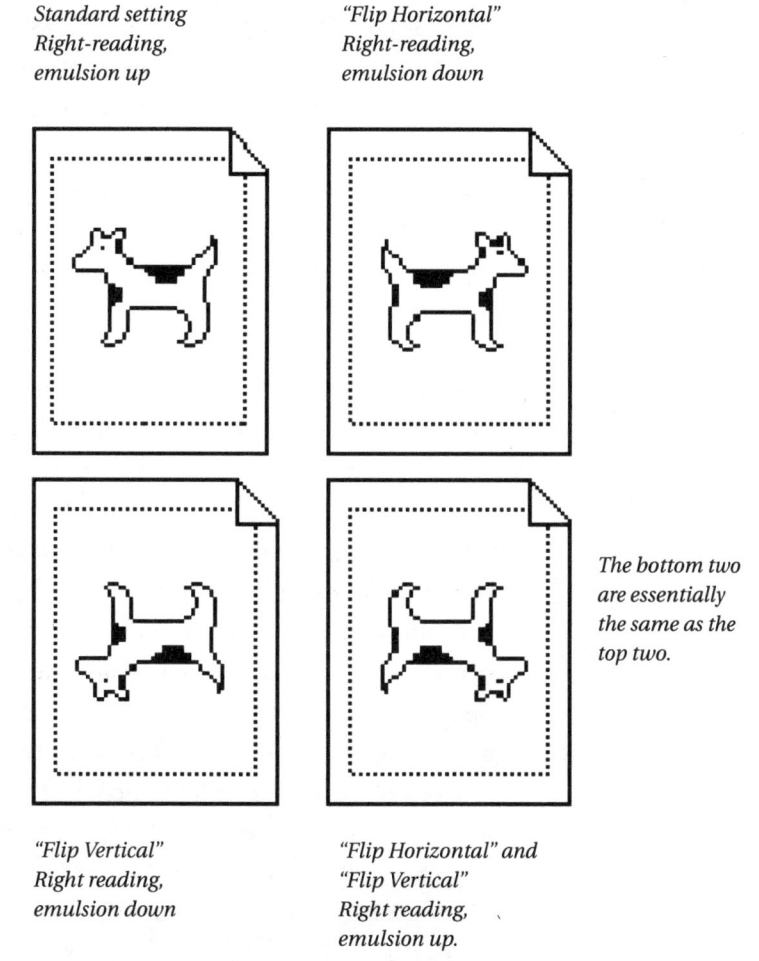

Standard setting Right-reading, emulsion up

"Flip Horizontal" Right-reading, emulsion down

"Flip Vertical" Right reading, emulsion down

"Flip Horizontal" and "Flip Vertical" Right reading, emulsion up.

The bottom two are essentially the same as the top two.

inverts gray levels. For example, a 70-percent black elliptical spot does not actually become a white elliptical spot 70 percent "large," but instead a white elliptical dot 30 percent large. It seems like a minor point, but it has caused enough difficulties around our offices. In cases like these, we now print to film positive and then take it to a stat house to get a negative shot of it.

▼ ▼

Roll-Fed Printer Specifications

Other than Halftone Frequency (which seems to have been placed in this area for the simple reason that no one could figure out a better place to put it), all of the features in this section of the Printer Setup dialog box apply only to—you guessed it—roll-fed printers. These are imagesetters such as those in the Linotronic, Compugraphic, and Varityper lines, that feed paper and film off rolls rather than one sheet at a time. The seven choices available to you when you have a roll-fed printer selected in the Printer Type menu are Halftone Frequency, Material, Resolution, Paper Width, Page Gap, Paper Offset, and Use PDF Screen Values.

Halftone Frequency. We talked at some length about halftones and halftone screens back in Chapter 8, *Modifying Images*. In the Printer Setup dialog box, this specification determines the halftone screen frequency of every tint in your document (except for those graphic images that you have set using the Other Screen features, and EPS graphics that have their screens specified internally). This includes gray boxes, tinted type, screened colors, and so on. The default value for the halftone screen (the one that QuarkXPress uses unless you specify something else) is 60 lines per inch. On a 300-dpi laser printer, this almost always gives you an actual screen frequency of 53 lpi. That's just the way it works. You can type your own setting from 15 to 400 lines per inch. Raising the screen frequency nets you "smoother" grays, but you'll find that you have fewer of them to work with.

You should note that changing the screen frequency in one document, saving the document, then opening a new document may retain the original screen frequency. Thus, it is advisable to always check the Printer Setup dialog box just to make sure you're getting a proper halftone screen (what if the last person to use the computer set it to a 15-lpi screen?).

▼ ▼

Tip: A Colorful Shade of Gray. A couple of caveats to this tip, before we really get to it: this is helpful primarily if you're printing proofs that won't be reproduced or if you don't need a wide spectrum of gray values in your output. That said, we think a great screen frequency to use for printing to a 300-dpi printer is 106. Go ahead and try it. We think you'll like the tone of the gray.

▼ ▼

Resolution. Don't change this number with the expectation that it has any major significance to how your job prints. It doesn't determine the resolution at which your job prints. However, bitmapped, 1-bit TIFF images that have a very high resolution may print significantly faster when you include the right printer resolution. For example, QuarkXPress internally reduces the resolution of a 600-dpi TIFF line art image when it prints to a 300-dpi printer. The printer doesn't need any more than 300 dots per inch anyway, and you save time because QuarkXPress only has to download half as much information (and the PostScript interpreter has to wade through only half as much).

Gray-scale halftones are "resolution reduced" to two times their screen frequency. For example, a gray-scale TIFF really needs only 266 dots per inch when printing at 133 lines per inch. So do yourself a favor and let QuarkXPress help you out: Type the correct printer resolution in this field.

Material. At last, a nice, easy specification that you hardly have to think about. Just click on "Paper" or "Film," depending on which you are printing to. What difference does it make? Well, the truth of the matter is that it usually doesn't make any difference whatsoever if you're using the default setup. However, if you turn on "Use Calibration" in the Print dialog box, QuarkXPress may print your document's gray levels differently depending on how you have this set. When it comes right down to it, we just leave this alone because QuarkXPress for Windows doesn't have a robust enough printer calibration control (at least not yet).

Paper Width. The Paper Width specification is not an actual control so much as a description of the device you'll be printing to. A Linotronic 330, for example, can image to 11.7 inches (79p2 or 79 picas, 2 points). A Compugraphic CG9400 images to 14 inches, and a Linotronic 500 images to 17.5 inches. Whatever the case, and whatever the measurement style, just replace the default number with the proper paper width.

David fondly recalls the time when he printed several pages with "Paper Width" set to 11p7 (11 picas, 7 points, or 139 points—1.93 inches), instead of 11.7 inches. Everything on each page was cut off at exactly 11p7 from the left edge. The rest of the page was blank. He wasn't happy, and has been studiously monitoring this feature ever since.

Paper Offset. This feature controls the placement of your document on the paper or film. The printer's default paper offset, even when set to zero, is actually enough so that you don't have to worry about changing the value of "Paper Offset" here. For example, on a Linotronic imagesetter, when "Paper Offset" is set to zero inches, the file is printed a quarter inch from the edge. If you want it farther from the edge, change this value.

However, the Paper Offset setting shouldn't exceed the document height subtracted from the paper width (that is, if you have a 10-inch tall document printing on 14-inch paper, your offset certainly should not be more than 4 inches, or else weirdness is sure to ensue).

Page Gap. The last roll-fed printer specification determines the amount of blank space between each page of the document as it prints out on the roll. Initially, this value is zero. We recommend changing it to at least .25 inch (1p6) so you can cut the pages apart easily. If you're printing spreads, this gap is placed between the spreads (more on printing spreads later), not between each page within the spread.

See page 611

Use PDF Screen Values. Printer Description Files (PDFs) are used on the Macintosh to provide printer calibration information to Mac applications. The Windows Printer Description files don't fulfill the same function, so Quark has built several PDFs right into QuarkXPress for Windows. We weren't able to test this feature ourselves, but Quark assures us that there's information in these descriptions that can enhance halftone printing on high-resolution imagesetters, and help solve other PostScript printing problems.

So, how do you know whether your printer or imagesetter is using an internal PDF? First of all, the Use PDF Screen Values option box in the Printer Setup dialog is active, not grayed-out. You'll also notice, at least with imagesetters, that the Size:

pop-up list is deactivated. That's because QuarkXPress is automatically using internal PDF information to calculate the paper size information.

Why would it do that? Because Microsoft's Windows 3.1 PostScript driver has made such a hash of custom page sizing, resolution control, and other aspects of high-resolution imagesetter printing that Quark has felt forced to make an end run around parts of the Windows PostScript driver and take direct control. See "Use the right driver" later in this chapter.

Options

The Printer Setup Options dialog box that opens when you click the Options button is the same for all Windows applications—Word for Windows, CorelDRAW, QuarkXPress, you name it (see Figure 10-5). You can also reach it via the Windows Printer Control Panel, whether you're using QuarkXPress or not. These options can be tricky because some of them duplicate (often in an inferior way) features found in QuarkXPress's Printer Setup and other dialog boxes. We've found that it's usually best to ignore any duplicate features. Some of the other options, especially the Advanced options we discuss below, are really great for configuring how your job prints. However, they're hardly self-evident, so we'll hack through all of it right here.

Figure 10-5
The Options dialog box

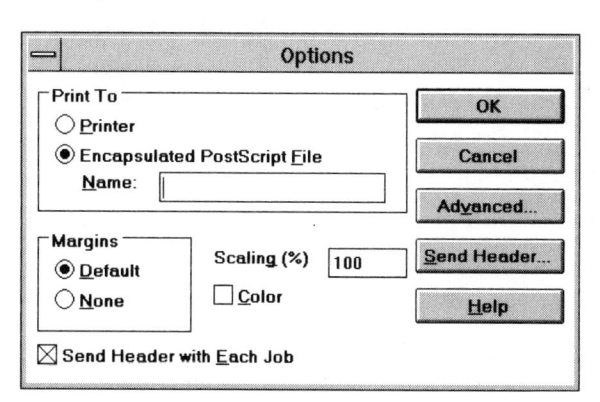

Print To. The very first option you get in the Options dialog box is where you want to print the document to. Perhaps not unexpectedly, this is also the very first option that you can totally ignore. Why? You've got two options in this area: Printer and

Encapsulated PostScript File. The Encapsulated PostScript File option is totally useless simply because QuarkXPress's Save Page as EPS command under the File menu does a much better job.

The main problem with the Option dialog box's Encapsulated PostScript File is that the resulting EPS file lacks a screen preview. With only a gray box to work with on screen you can't expect much in the way of fancy graphics placement. You'd have to print the page in order to see the effect of each move you make. We honestly can't think of a reason to use this feature with QuarkXPress, but we're open for suggestions. Instead, just leave this option set to Printer.

Margins. Curiously, the second option in the Option dialog box, Margins, is also just about totally useless for QuarkXPress users. Your options are Default and None.

If you're using a laser printer (you probably are), just keep the Margin option set to Default. Why? Because the Windows manual says to. Theoretically, you should select "None" if you want Windows to measure margins from the actual edge of the paper, while Default measures them from the edge of the actual printable area. You'd think that "None" would be the recommended choice, since I'm sure we'd all feel better knowing the margins we set in QuarkXPress really measure from the edge of the page. But no, the manual says use "Default." If you're a free thinker, go ahead, select "None"; it actually doesn't make any difference. That's how they do things down at Microsoft.

Scaling. The third option, Scaling, is the charm. Here's one that you can actually use! Changing this number affects the scaling of the document when you print. You can enter any whole number (no decimal points) between 10 and 400 percent. This is especially nice when printing proofs of a larger-format document, or when trying to create enormous posters by tiling them (you could create a 4-by-4-foot poster in QuarkXPress and then enlarge it to 400 percent so that when that last page printed out of your printer and you'd pasted all 414 pages together, you'd have a poster 16 feet square). Table 10-3 shows several page-size conversion settings.

Table 10-3
Converting page sizes

To print this size page	Onto this size page	Reduce/enlarge to
legal	letter	78%
tabloid	letter	64%
A4	letter	94%
letter	tabloid	128%

Color. This option is available only if you've chosen a color printer. If you decide that after spending $7,000 on a color PostScript printer you'd rather print your color work in gray scale anyway, simply click the Color check box so that the option is turned off. Your documents print in black and white.

Send Header with Each Job. Although normally you'd want to keep the Send Header with Each Job option turned on, there are times when you would want to turn it off (see "Tip: Manually Download PostScript Header," below). The "Header" this option refers to is a special PostScript file containing PostScript language programming routines that Windows needs to print properly on a PostScript printer. If the header isn't downloaded, the printer prints an error message when you try to print, telling you that the header isn't downloaded. When this happens, check that the Send Header with Each Job option is turned on, or manually download the header using the Send Header command button.

Send Header. Clicking the Send Header button doesn't automatically send Windows' PostScript header to your printer; it just opens the Send Header dialog box (see Figure 10-6). From there you decide whether to send the header to your printer or to a file. If you choose "Printer," the header is permanently downloaded to the assigned printer. Okay, so it's not really permanent. But it does last until you turn the printer off or it gets reset. On the other hand, if you choose File, you can send the header to a file (see "Tip: Automatically Download PostScript Header," below). Some print server software requires the header as a file, so this dialog box provides a way to obtain the Windows PostScript header file.

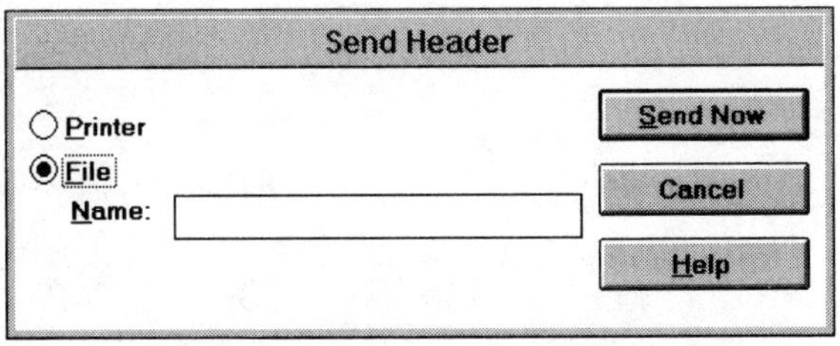

Figure 10-6
Send Header dialog box

Tip: Manually Download PostScript Header. Depending on the speed of your computer, printer, and printer connection, the PostScript header (about 11K of data) might need anywhere from 10 to 30 seconds to download along with your job. That seemingly feeble saving actually starts to matter after your fourth cup of coffee at two in the morning when you're trying to knock out "just one more proof" of an infinitely tweakable page. If those seconds matter, manually send the header to your printer using the Send Header command described above and then turn off the Send Header with Each Job option. Don't forget to manually download the header when you turn the printer on or reset it for any reason. Should you forget, a "header not downloaded" error message prints, instead of your page.

Tip: Automatically Download PostScript Header. If you find yourself manually downloading the PostScript header often, you might want to consider making a batch file that does this automatically. The easiest way to do this is to save the header to disk as described earlier and then add a line to your AUTOEXEC.BAT file. For example, if you save the header as C:\WINDOWS\HEADER.PS, you could add this line to your AUTOEXEC.BAT file: "copy c:\windows\header.ps lpt1:". Put it just before the line that says "win."

If your printer is turned off or restarted, you have to manually download the header again. Also, note that whenever the header is downloaded (either automatically or manually), the printer prints a page saying that the header has been downloaded. Now, we don't know about you, but this is really annoying to us. So we opened the header file with a word processor, went to the end of the file, and changed the header slightly.

1. Put a percentage sign at the beginning of the line (third to the end) that says "/Helvetica…"

2. Put a percentage sign at the beginning of the next line, too.

3. Put a carriage return between the word "showpage" and the word "quit" so that "quit" is on a line by itself, and "showpage" has a percent sign before it.

4. Save the file.

Now, when this header is downloaded to a virgin printer (one with no header in it, such as one that was just restarted), it won't print out a page.

▼▼▼▼▼▼▼▼▼▼▼▼▼▼▼▼▼▼▼▼▼▼▼▼▼▼

Advanced

Neither the QuarkXPress documentation nor the Windows 3.1 users guides document the labyrinth of technical details that you'll encounter when you click the Advanced option button. You'll find options for handling TrueType fonts, printer memory, additional printer effects, error messages, whew! So take our hands; we'll guide you through each of the options (see Figure 10-7).

TrueType fonts. The first section in the Advanced Options dialog box gives you options for using TrueType fonts with a PostScript printer. However, as we said back in Chapter 4, *Type and Typography*, we really can't condone you using TrueType fonts if you plan to print your document on a PostScript imagesetter. PostScript imagesetters are Adobe PostScript and Type 1 font territory. As such they just don't deal with TrueType fonts very well.

Possibly, though, you're content to use a desktop laser printer for your final pages. With 600-dpi machines going for under $5,000, such plain-paper printing is definitely an option for many types of documents. In that case, you might consider using TrueType fonts. Some printers, like the LaserMaster Unity 1000, are based on Microsoft's TrueImage PostScript-compatible interpreter, so they can handle downloadable TrueType fonts. For

Figure 10-7
The Advanced Options dialog box

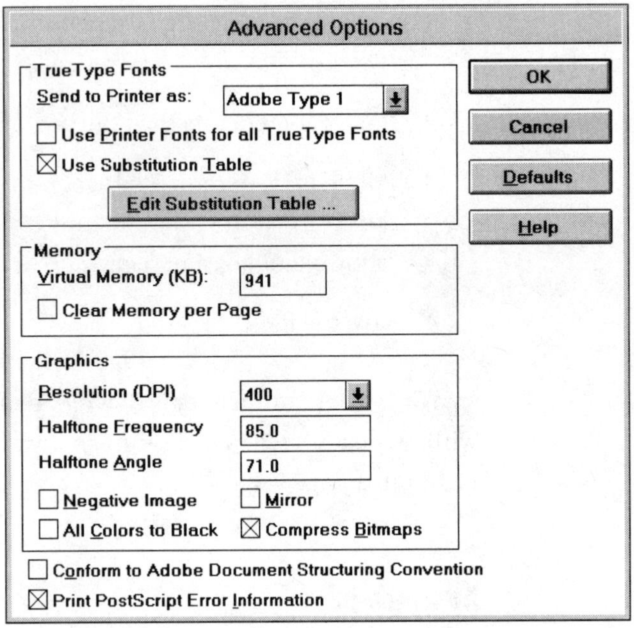

genuine PostScript and non-TrueImage PostScript compatible printers, Windows must play one or two little games to make TrueType fonts print.

Here are the options that Windows gives you if you do want to play with TrueType.

Send to Printer as. There are three possible choices in the Send to Printer as pop-up menu: Adobe Type 1, Bitmap (Type 3), and Native TrueType. Unless you have a TrueImage-based printer, chances are you'll see only the first two choices. That's because most PostScript-compatible printers lack the software to scale TrueType fonts, hence they can't handle the native format.

That leaves two other possibilities, neither ideal. If you select Adobe Type 1 from the pop-up menu, Windows automatically converts the TrueType font into Adobe Type 1 format and downloads the converted font to the printer. The printer can then scale the font. Windows' documentation claims that it performs this conversion only when the point size is 24 points or greater, and that for smaller type, Windows itself scales the outline font and sends the bitmap to the printer. However, in our own tests, we've observed that the TrueType font is always converted to Type 1 format, even for 4-point type.

Depending on the typeface and your degree of perfectionism, you may or may not find the quality of Windows' TrueType-to-Type 1 conversion acceptable. If you select the "Bitmap (Type 3)" option, Windows, as we mentioned above, scales the TrueType font, rasterizes it (turns it into a bitmap) and sends the bitmap to the printer as a Type 3 PostScript font. For really small point sizes, this works quickly and efficiently, but for large display type the bitmap fonts use lots of printer memory, which can overload it. In fact, the font can easily be four or five times as large as it would be if you had simply specced Type 1. The resolution of the bitmap fonts Windows automatically creates for a PostScript printer depends on your Graphics Resolution setting, which we discuss below. Because of this, we generally leave "Send to Printer as:" set to Type 1, when we use it at all.

Use Printer Fonts for all TrueType Fonts. When you turn on "Use Printer Fonts for all TrueType Fonts", Windows automatically substitutes one of your printer's built-in fonts for a particular TrueType font. This works fine if you're using a TrueType counterpart to one of the built-in printer fonts, in which case the font metrics should match. Times, which is built into virtually every PostScript printer, substitutes nicely for the Times New Roman TrueType font that ships with Windows. However, sometimes the printer font and the TrueType font have different metrics, and life gets a little screwy. We hate to think that Windows is doing substitution work for us; we always leave this turned off.

Note that if you do turn on this option, the Send to Printer as option is deactivated. You can't substitute for built-in fonts *and* send some fonts to the printer as Type 1, for example.

Use Substitution Table. The Use Substitution Table feature is the most versatile option in the TrueType Fonts section of the Advanced Options dialog box. It lets you substitute specific downloadable or built-in printer fonts for specific TrueType fonts. The font substitutions are managed via an editable font substitution table. Also, you can still select a Send to Printer as: option for TrueType fonts that lack an appropriate PostScript substitute.

The Edit Substitution Table button, which is activated only when you've selected the Use Substitution Table option, allows you to edit the fonts that are going to be substituted for specific Truetype fonts. When you click it, a dialog box opens up displaying two lists: TrueType fonts that are installed on your machine appear on the left, and PostScript fonts that are installed or built into your printer appear on the right. Click on a TrueType font, then select the appropriate PostScript substitute from the opposite list. If there isn't a good substitute, stick with the "Download as Soft Font" default choice. That font then downloads in the form you selected for the Send to Printer as option.

Memory

Printer memory is one of those things we tend to forget about until we run out of it. Then we wonder where we went wrong and start counting our downloadable fonts and guessing just how much printer memory we really *do* have. Windows provides you with two options to help you make the best of your printer memory: Virtual Memory and Clear Memory per Page.

Virtual Memory. Virtual memory is the memory your printer has in addition to what it uses as a page buffer and for PostScript work space. Usually it's used to store downloadable fonts. Increasing the amount of virtual memory from its modest default amount often speeds up your PostScript printing. That's because Windows uses the Virtual Memory figure to determine how many PostScript fonts it can automatically download without overloading the printer. Since Windows can't find out the printer memory itself, it's up to you to enter the right amount.

▼ ▼

Tip: Get Your Memory Straight. If you type a Virtual Memory value smaller than the amount you actually have in your printer, instead of letting fonts remain in memory to be used again, Windows starts flushing fonts and reloading them to save space it doesn't need to save—a real waste of time. Since the default setting for "Virtual Memory" is often lower than what your printer really has, send the TESTPS.TXT file (in the System subdirectory of your Windows subdirectory) to your printer using the DOS Copy command or a downloading utility. Your PostScript printer chugs out a short report showing the correct suggested VM setting for your printer.

By the way, David found out the hard way that if you're using a printer that automatically emulates either a PostScript, a PCL, or an HPGL printer, you may have to alter the TESTPS.TXT file slightly before you send it. Just put a line at the beginning of the file that reads: "%!PS-Adobe-3.0". That should do it.

▼ ▼

Clear Memory per Page. The second option in the Memory area of the Advanced Options dialog box is Clear Memory per Page. When you think a job won't print due to a memory shortage, try turning on this option. Checking this box forces Windows to flush all temporarily downloaded fonts from memory after printing each page. (Automatically downloaded fonts are "temporarily" downloaded, meaning that they're automatically flushed from memory at the initiation of a new print job. Manually downloaded fonts are usually "permanent," meaning that they stay resident until the printer is reset or turned off.) This option keeps the maximum amount of memory available for your print job, but it also slows down printing since more time is consumed temporarily downloading fonts for every page.

Graphics

The third section of the Advanced Options dialog box is called "Graphics." We don't mean to be too curt, but believe us when we say: Ignore everything in this section except for the first item, "Resolution." "Halftone Frequency," "Halftone Angle," "Negative Image," "Mirror," "All Colors to Black," and "Compress Bitmaps" do just about nothing, and are overridden by Quark-XPress's own settings.

"Resolution," however, does play a somewhat important role, especially in how Windows creates bitmapped images from TrueType fonts. It's easy to set; just select the proper resolution of the printer you're using. Typically, it's already set, so you don't have to worry about it much unless you're printing to a laser printer that has multiple options for resolution.

Conform to Adobe Document Structuring Convention

The last two items in this dialog box may have no effect on what you're doing...or they might make all the difference. The Conform to Adobe Document Structuring Convention option lets you tell Windows and QuarkXPress to output PostScript that includes lots of comments. These comments can be read by humans or some applications. The printer doesn't need them at all, so you don't have to worry about turning this on if you're just printing to a laser printer. However, if you're saving the PostScript to a file, this might be helpful. We typically don't turn it on unless we know that we really need to. Nonetheless, it doesn't add very much to the file, so it won't hurt to have it turned on.

Print PostScript Error Information

The Print PostScript Error Information option should almost always be turned on, in our opinion. That way, when your printer chokes on something in the PostScript code, it typically prints an error message instead of nothing at all. The message may make sense only to a PostScript programmer or to a product support specialist, but that's better than the mysterious disappearance of a file into the black hole of the printer.

On the other hand, if you're printing to an imagesetter, you may not want this feature to be turned on because it prints a page that may be expensive. For us, even this page is not entirely useless, however, as it can help us fix the problem faster (see "Troubleshooting," later in this chapter).

▼▼▼▼▼▼▼▼▼▼▼▼▼▼▼▼▼▼▼▼▼▼▼▼▼▼▼▼▼▼

Printing

Once you've got the proper values specified in the Printer Setup dialog box, you can move on to the actual Print dialog box, again found under the File menu (see Figure 10-8). Here you are confronted with even more buttons, controls, and special features designed to tweak your print job to the point of perfection.

Figure 10-8
The Print dialog box

Print
Printer: LaserMaster 1000 (LPT1:)
Copies: 1   Pages: ○ All ● From: [ ] To: [ ]
Cover Page: ● No ○ First Page ○ Last Page
Output: ● Normal ○ Rough ☐ Thumbnails
● All Pages ○ Odd Pages ○ Even Pages
☐ Back to Front ☐ Collate ☐ Spreads ☒ Blank Pages
☒ Registration Marks ● Centered ○ Off Center
OPI: [Include Images ▼] ☐ Calibrated Output
Tiling: ● Off ○ Manual ○ Auto. overlap: 3"
Color: ☐ Make Separations   Plate: [All Plates ▼]
☐ Print Colors as Grays
[OK] [Cancel] [Setup...]

In this section we take the dialog box apart and look at each feature to show how you can use it most effectively.

Printing Basics

NEW IN 3.3
See page 613

The first section in the Print dialog box is pretty standard, and you've seen the options before if you've printed from other Windows applications. Let's look at each item—Copies, Pages, and Cover Page—one at a time.

Copies. We might as well start with the simplest choice of all. How many copies of your document do you want to print? Let's say you choose to print a multiple-page document, specifying four copies. The first page prints four times, then the second page prints four times, and so on. In other words, you may have a good deal of collating to do later (see "Collate," below).

Pages. You can specify to print all pages in a document, or a range of pages. The values you type in for the From and To range must either be exactly the same as those in your document or be specified as absolutes. That is to say, if your document starts on page

23, you can't enter "1" in the From Page field; it must be either From Page 23 (or whatever page you want to start from) or From Page +1 (the plus character specifies an absolute page number). Similarly, if you are using page numbering in an alphabet system (such as a, b, c, etc.), or if you're using a prefix (see "Section and Page Numbering Systems" in Chapter 2, *Document Construction*), you have to type these sorts of numbers into the slots.

▼ ▼

Tip: From Beginning or End. If you want to print from the first page to a specified page, you can leave the From field empty in the Print dialog box. Similarly, if you leave the To field empty, QuarkXPress assumes you want to print to the end of the document.

▼ ▼

Cover Page. This feature is usually set to "No," and we almost never change it. But then again, we don't work in large workgroups. Each cover sheet includes the document's name, the application (QuarkXPress, in this case), the date and time you printed it, and the name of the printer. If you have several (or many) people printing to one printer, using cover sheets can be a real lifesaver. Not only does the cover page act as a label for each print job, but it separates each job so that one page from one document doesn't get mixed up with pages from the next document.

Note that you can set the cover page to print either before the first page or after the last page. Take your pick, depending on whether your printer dumps paper face up or face down. But, if you're in a workgroup situation, you probably want everybody to use the same setting to avoid confusion.

On the other hand, why use extra paper if you don't need to? If you're the only person using the printer, and you don't need to document each print cycle, just leave this feature off.

Output

The next section in the Print dialog box, Output, covers the details of how QuarkXPress prints your job: what style, more detailed page selection, what order the pages should print, and whether or not you want registration marks. Let's go over each one in order.

Normal. What can we say about "Normal?" It's normally how you'd want your normal documents to print out. This is the default setting in the Print dialog box, and the only time you change it is when you want special printing effects like those listed below. You get just what you created, no better, no worse.

Rough. If your document has many illustrations or special frames (from the Macintosh) in it, you may want to print your proof copies with "Rough" selected. This feature automatically replaces each picture in your document with a giant "X," and every complex frame with a double line of the same width (see Figure 10-9). Clearly, the pages print significantly faster than with "Normal."

Figure 10-9
Page printed with the Rough feature

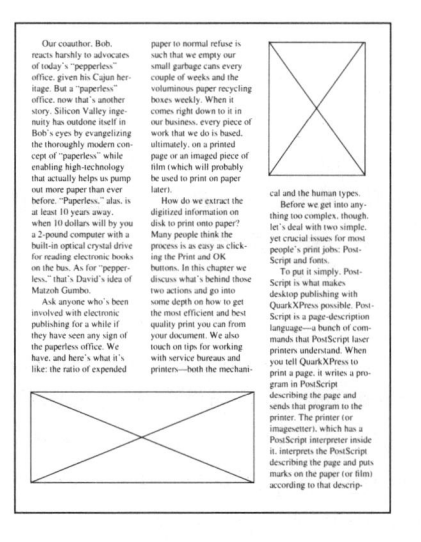

Thumbnails. Selecting "Thumbnails" shrinks each page of your document down to about 12.5 percent of its size and lines up the pages next to each other. It then fits as many as it can onto each printed page. This is great for an overview of your file, though the output you get is usually too small to really give you much of an idea of anything except general page geometry (see "Faster, Larger Thumbnails," below). Note that on PostScript printers, it takes just as long to print this one sheet of many pages as it does to print every page individually, so plan your time accordingly. If you just want to look over the pages, it is probably faster to see them on screen in Thumbnail view. Remember that you don't have to print all of your pages when you select "Thumbnail." We often find it helpful to just print one or two pages at a time to see how they look.

Tip: Faster, Larger Thumbnails. We find that the size "Thumbnails" usually gives us to be pretty useless; they're just too small! And if we have pictures on the pages, the job takes too long to print. So we use this feature in conjunction with two others: "Rough" and "Reduce or Enlarge." "Rough" is nearby in the Print dialog box. Just make sure this is checked, and your thumbnails print with "Xs" through the pictures and with simplified frames. The Reduce or Enlarge feature is found in the Printer Setup Options dialog box and is covered in that section above. Change "Enlarge" to 200 percent, and your thumbnails are printed at 24 percent instead of a little over 12 percent. This is just about the right size for most letter-size pages.

Tip: Two Thumbnails per Page. If you want your thumbnails much larger, you can up the scaling factor to 375 percent and turn the page landscape in the Printer Setup dialog box. With this value, you can get two letter- or legal-size pages on one page. You can get two tabloid-size pages on one letter-size landscape page with an enlargement of 300 percent. If your document is made of two-page spreads, you can print letter- and legal-size pages up to 400 percent (the maximum allowed for enlargement) and tabloid-size pages up to 350 percent.

All Pages. This is the default position for printing pages from QuarkXPress. It means "all pages that you have selected above." In other words, if you have selected a page range from 23 to 28, having "All Pages" selected won't counteract your desires; it just prints all those pages, as opposed to just the even- or odd-numbered ones.

Odd/Even Pages. These two choices are mutually exclusive. We sometimes joke about this feature when we're working on jobs with several strangely designed pages: "Just print the odd ones, and leave the rest." The only real value we've ever gotten out of this feature lies in the tip below, "Printing Double-Sided Documents."

▼ ▼

Tip: Printing Double-Sided Documents. You can print double-sided pages with the following technique. Note that you have to have an even number of pages in your document for this to work correctly.

1. Print all odd-numbered pages using the Odd Pages feature.

2. Place these pages back into the printer. Some laser printers require these to be face down, others face up. Test it first.

3. Select "Back to Front" (we discuss this feature in just a bit).

4. Print all even pages.

If everything is set up right, the second page should print on the back of the first, and so on. Check with your printer manufacturer before doing this, though. We've had no problems with Canon-engine printers, a few problems with the Ricoh engines, and Varityper technicians roll their eyes in horror at the idea of running a page through twice.

▼ ▼

Back to Front. The problem with talking about printing from QuarkXPress is that each PostScript printer model is slightly (or not-so-slightly) different from the next. For example, when you print a multiple-page document on your laser printer, does the first page come out face up or face down? Some printers do one, some the other, and some give you a choice. If the pages come out face up, you'll love the Back to Front feature. Selecting "Back to Front" prints the last page from your page selection first, then it prints "backwards" to the first page. The stack of pages that ends up in the output tray will be in proper order.

Note that you can't select this feature when you are printing spreads or thumbnails (if you want a good brain twister, try to think of how pages would print if you could select these together).

Collate. We said earlier that when you printed multiple copies of your document you would receive x number of the first page, then x number of the second page, and so on, leaving you to manually collate all of the copies. You can have QuarkXPress collate the pages for you, instead, so that the full document prints out once, then again, and again, and so on, by selecting the Collate feature.

The problem with "Collate" is that it takes much longer to print out your complete job. This is because the printer cannot "remember" what each page looked like after it goes on to the next page, and so it has to reprocess the entire document for each new copy. How long this takes depends on the number of fonts and pictures you use, among other things. On a long document, the time difference becomes a toss-up: Do you take the time to collate the pages yourself or have the printer take the time to process them?

Spreads. This is a powerful but potentially dangerous feature, so it should be used with some care. Selecting "Spreads" from the Print dialog box tells QuarkXPress to print a spread entirely on one page rather than as multiple pages. For example, printing a two-page, facing-pages spread with registration marks normally results in one page printing with its set of crop marks, then the next page, and so on. When "Spreads" is turned on, both pages abut and sit between the same crop marks. This is useful in a number of instances, perhaps the best of which is printing a spread that has text or a graphic across the page boundaries (see Figure 10-10).

However, there are two potential problems lurking behind the Spreads feature. The first has to do with printing costs. Let's say you're laying out a magazine with a standard facing-page format, except in the middle of the document you have a fold-out, resulting in two three-page spreads. You send the file off to be imageset, specifying that "Spreads" should be checked On. When you get the film or paper back you find everything worked just like you thought it would: two-page spreads spread across two pages, and the two three-page spreads spread all the way across three pages.

Figure 10-10
Printing spreads

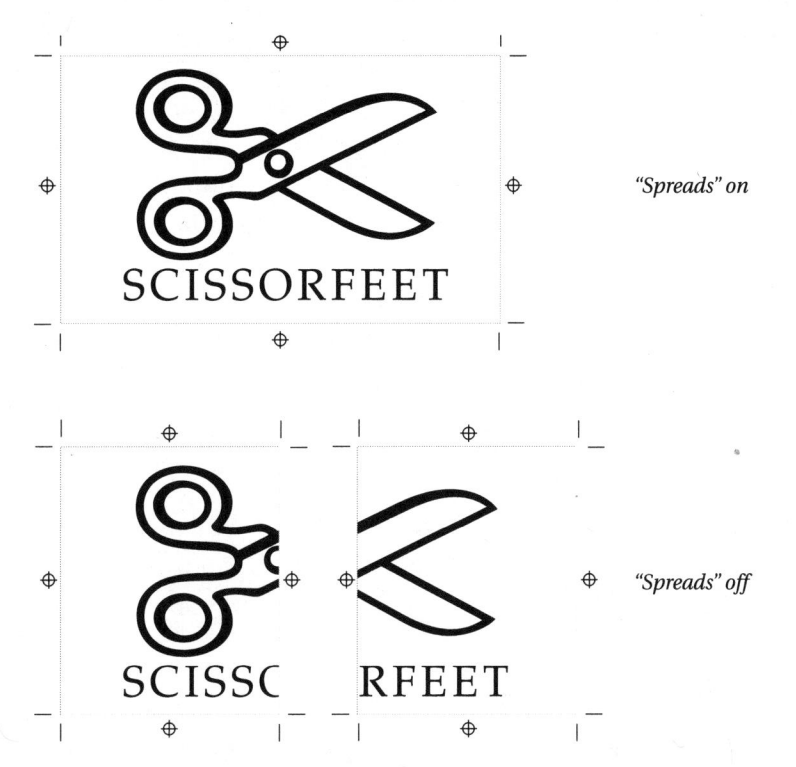

"Spreads" on

"Spreads" off

But when you get your bill, it's hundreds of dollars more than you expected. What happened? What went wrong? When you specify "Spreads," QuarkXPress tells the roll-fed imagesetter to advance the film the width of the widest spread in the page range specified. So in the example above, each two-page spread actually took three pages of film; hence it was much more expensive.

The second dangerous part of using Spreads is that it often causes a stripping nightmare for your printer. You should never, *never* use Spreads without consulting your printer first. For instance, if you printed the magazine pages described in the example described above with Spreads turned on, your printer (human lithographer) will attempt to smile while shoving all the film down your throat. Any money you had saved by using desktop publishing equipment would quickly be eaten up by the stripping department as they tried to pull apart the pages and put them in the proper order.

▼ ▼ ▼ ▼ ▼ ▼ ▼ ▼ ▼ ▼ ▼ ▼ ▼ ▼ ▼ ▼ ▼ ▼ ▼ ▼

Tip: Printing Spreads in a Document. Don't waste paper or film when you print contiguous spreads from a multiple-page document; if for no other reason, it's expensive. If you have a multiple-page spread crossing pages 45 through 47, have your service bureau print the pages from 1 through 44, and 48 through the end, as single pages, and then print the three-page spread on a separate pass (however, see the earlier warning about Spreads).

▼▼▼▼▼▼▼▼▼▼▼▼▼▼▼▼▼▼▼▼▼▼▼▼▼▼▼

Tip: Printing for Saddle-Stitched Binding. You can use the Spreads feature in conjunction with the Document Layout palette to "strip" together pages, which will be double-sided and saddle-stitch bound. We think this is one of the coolest things you can do with the Document Layout feature. Just follow these steps.

1. Create your document as usual, but with no facing pages (see Chapter 1, *QuarkXPress Basics*).

2. When you're finished, use the Document Layout palette to move the last page to the left of the first page. Then the second to last page (which has now become the last page) up to the right of the second page (which is now the third page). Then the next last page to the left of the next single page, and so on.

3. When you're done, every page should be paired with another page, and the last pages in the document should be the middle-most pages. For example, in an 8-page booklet, the final pages would end up being the spread between pages 4 and 5.

4. Make sure the Spreads feature is selected in the Print dialog box when you print the document page.

Note that this method won't work if you are using automatic page numbering (because you're moving pages around; for example, the final page ends up being page 1). Also, note that this should never be done without first consulting your printer. As we said in "Spreads," above, this kind of manipulation could be very dangerous to your bill.

If you're in need of more complex impositions, you might look into Aldus Presswise, Impostrip from Ultimate Systems, or DoubleUp from Legend Communications (see Appendix E, *Resources*).

▼▼▼▼▼▼▼▼▼▼▼▼▼▼▼▼▼▼▼▼▼▼▼▼▼▼

Blank Pages. We can't think of many reasons for printing totally blank pages—no header, no footer, no page number, nothin'—from a publication. As we write, our white paper recycling bin overfloweth. We go through so much paper that we feel guilty every time we drive through a forest (which is difficult to avoid in the Pacific Northwest). Therefore, whenever we have the chance to save a tree here and there, we jump at it. QuarkXPress is giving us just this chance with the inclusion of the Blank Pages control in the Print dialog box. When this is turned on (the default setting), QuarkXPress prints as it always has: every page, no matter what's on it (or isn't on it). When you turn "Blank Pages" off, QuarkXPress doesn't print a page if there isn't anything printable on it. This includes pages whose only objects are colored white, or are set to "Suppress Printout."

Registration Marks. In addition to the text and graphics of the pages themselves, your printer (we're talking about the human lithographer here) needs several pieces of information about your camera-ready work. One fact is where the sides of the printed page are. If you're printing multiple colors, another piece of information your printer needs is how each color plate aligns with the other (we talk about creating color separations later in this chapter). Additional job and page information may be helpful also. Selecting the Registration Marks feature answers all of these needs—QuarkXPress places crop marks, registration marks, and page information around your document (see Figure 10-11).

Crop marks specify the page boundaries of your document. They are placed slightly outside each of the four corners so that when the page is printed and cut to size, they will be cut away.

Registration marks are used primarily for color separation work, but you get them even if you just need crop marks on a

Figure 10-11
The Registration Marks feature

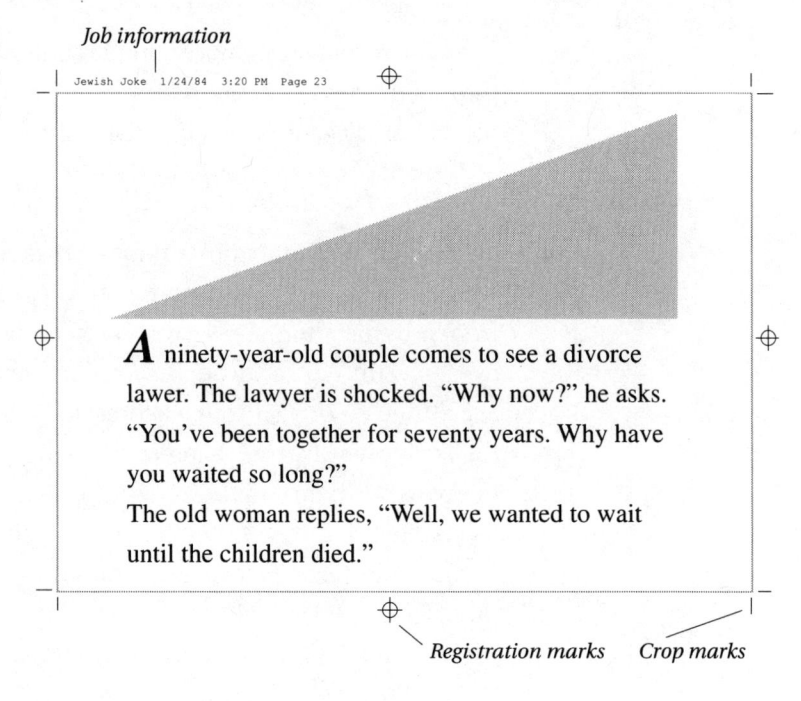

Job information

Jewish Joke 1/24/84 3:20 PM Page 23

A ninety-year-old couple comes to see a divorce lawyer. The lawyer is shocked. "Why now?" he asks. "You've been together for seventy years. Why have you waited so long?"

The old woman replies, "Well, we wanted to wait until the children died."

Registration marks   *Crop marks*

one-color job. These are used by your printer's stripper to perfectly align each color plate to the next (see "Tip: Better Registration Marks," below).

The page and job information that is printed in the upper-left corner of the page includes the file name, a page number, and a date and time stamp. If you want more job information than is listed here, see "Tip: Additional Job Information," below.

Centered/Off Center. This feature of the Print dialog box refers to the placement of registration marks and is available only when you have "Registration Marks" On. With "Centered" On, each registration mark is centered exactly in the center of each side of the printed page. This is where most strippers need it. Others, because of their pin-register systems, need the crop marks slightly off center. Ask your printer.

▼▼▼▼▼▼▼▼▼▼▼▼▼▼▼▼▼▼▼▼▼▼▼▼

Tip: Better Registration Marks. The registration marks that Quark-XPress creates for you are okay, but not great, and certainly not optimal from a stripper's point of view. This is how you can make a "better" registration mark directly in QuarkXPress (you can also make one in FreeHand or Illustrator and bring it in as EPS; see Figure 10-12).

Figure 10-12
A "better" registration mark

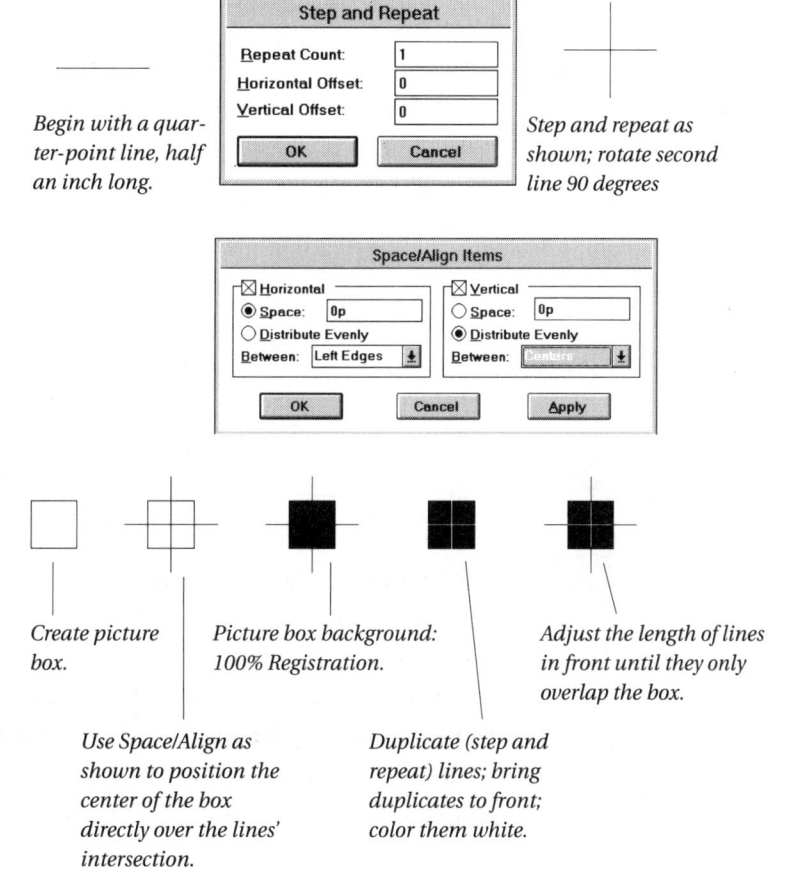

Begin with a quarter-point line, half an inch long.

Step and repeat as shown; rotate second line 90 degrees

Create picture box.

Picture box background: 100% Registration.

Adjust the length of lines in front until they only overlap the box.

Use Space/Align as shown to position the center of the box directly over the lines' intersection.

Duplicate (step and repeat) lines; bring duplicates to front; color them white.

1. Draw a line about .5 inch long. Set it to .25 points thickness, with Midpoints selected (in the Measurements palette).

2. Use the Step and Repeat feature from the Item menu to "clone" the line—creating one copy with no horizontal or vertical offset.

3. Make this second line perpendicular to the first by adding or subtracting 90 degrees from the line angle in the Measurements palette. Color the lines "Registration" (see Chapter 9, *Color*).

4. Draw a square picture box about .25 inch large (hold down the Shift key to maintain a square) and center it over the lines. You could center it either by using the Space/Align feature (see Chapter 1, *QuarkXPress Basics*) or by just aligning the box's handles directly over the lines. We prefer the latter, only because it's quicker for us.

5. Give the box a color of 100 percent "Registration."

6. Select the two lines and step and repeat both of them once with no offsets. Bring these lines to the front, if they're not already there.

7. Color the second set of lines white, and shorten them so that they overlap only the box.

The great benefit of this registration mark is that when you print to negatives, your printer can still align black crosshairs on a white background.

Going this route is clearly more work, as you need to build your page larger than necessary, then add your own crop marks and registration marks (and job info, if you want it), but it could be rewarding, depending on your situation.

▼▼▼▼▼▼▼▼▼▼▼▼▼▼▼▼▼▼▼▼▼▼▼▼▼▼

Tip: Additional Job Information. The pasteboard effect in Quark-XPress allows a great deal of flexibility to printing in the area "outside" the crop marks. We discussed bleeds in Chapter 1, *QuarkXPress Basics*, as items that are mostly on the page, but bleed slightly off it. But you can also create items that are mostly off the page, and only slightly on it. This is ideal for adding additional job information on your documents. As long as at least a bit of a picture or text box is on the page, it prints along with what's on the page.

Note that the page size that you have specified in the Printer Setup dialog box is the limiting factor to how far off the page you can print these notes. Anything outside these boundaries is simply cut off.

▼▼▼▼▼▼▼▼▼▼▼▼▼▼▼▼▼▼▼▼▼▼▼▼▼▼

Calibrated Output. According to Quark, when the Calibrated Output checkbox in the Print dialog box is turned on, QuarkXPress performs a dot gain adjustment if you're printing to a high resolution imagesetter. Unfortunately, as we go to press, we haven't had a chance to try out this feature or work out the details of how it works. Curiously, folks at Quark recommend leaving it off, turning it on only if you think that additional dot gain compensation is needed. The problem is that you can't control that dot gain yet. Well, perhaps in the next version it'll be useful.

Tiling

What's a person to do with a 36-by-36-inch document? Printing to paper or film is almost impossible (to be thorough we should mention it can be done through the Scitex VIP interface to an ELP printer or on Colossal System's giant 300-dpi electrostatic printer). You can, however, break each page down into smaller chunks that fit onto letter-size pages. Then you can assemble all of the pages together (keep your Scotch tape nearby). This process is called tiling, and is controlled in the Print dialog box. The three options for tiling are Manual, Auto, and Off.

Off. Off is off. No shirt, no shoes, no tiling. QuarkXPress just prints the upper-left corner of the page.

Auto. Selecting the Auto Tiling feature instructs QuarkXPress to decide on how much of your document to fit onto each printed page. You do have some semblance of control here: you can decide how much overlap you would like between pages. Remember that you have a minimum .25-inch border around each page (at least on most laser printers), so you'll probably want to set your overlap to at least a half inch to get a good fit. We generally use a value of 4 picas, just to be safe.

Note that QuarkXPress does not make an intelligent decision as to whether it would be more efficient to print the pages landscape or portrait, so you'll want to be careful to set this appropriately in the Printer Setup's Option dialog box (see Figure 10-13).

Figure 10-13
Tiling your document

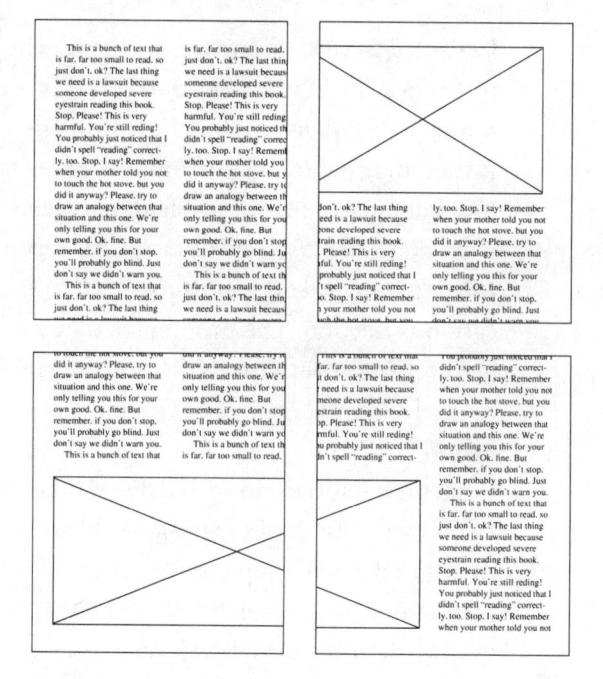

Manual. Most people seem to overlook the value of "Manual Tiling," skipping over it to "Auto Tiling." But there are times to trust a computer and times not to, and when it comes to breaking up our pages into manageable sizes, we generally prefer to make the choices ourselves.

When "Manual Tiling" is selected, QuarkXPress prints only as much of the page as fits on the page selected, starting at the ruler coordinate 0,0. You can then move the 0,0 coordinate to some other place on the page (see "Rulers" in Chapter 1, *QuarkXPress Basics*) and print the page again. In this way, you can manually perform the same task as "Auto Tiling" does, or you can be specific about what areas of the page you want to print. Note that if you have a six-page document and print using "Manual Tiling," you receive (for example) the upper-left corner of each of the six pages before the printer stops. If you want only one page or a smaller range of pages, use the From/To specifications at the top of the Print dialog box.

We should point out that where you place the 0,0 point is usually not where QuarkXPress starts printing. It actually tries to give you a little extra room so that the area you selected prints on the imaged area of the printer. For example, if you're printing to a desktop laser printer with "Larger Print Area" turned off, QuarkXPress actually moves your starting point a couple of picas up and to the left. This is another area where QuarkXPress tries to be helpful but ends up just being confusing and difficult to predict.

▼ ▼

Tip: Printer as Magnifying Glass. You can use "Manual Tiling" and "Enlarge" to blow up a particular area of the page for inspection (when 400 percent magnification on the screen still doesn't suit you). Change the enlargement factor in the Page Setup dialog box to 400 percent (or whatever you desire), then move the 0,0 point of the rulers to the area you want to inspect. Now print that page with "Manual Tiling" on. Voila! A super-size sectional.

▼ ▼

Print Status

NEW IN 3.3

See page 614

We don't know, but we have an inkling that "Print Status" is another feature that former PageMaker users talked Quark into throwing in so they'd feel more at home. The concept is as simple as its execution. Concept: We want QuarkXPress to show us its progress as it sends a print job to a PostScript printer. Execution: Hold down the Shift key while clicking OK in the Print dialog box (or pressing Enter). QuarkXPress not only tells you what page it's printing, but also what color plate, tile, and EPS/TIFF images it's working on (see Figure 10-14). Remember that no program can predict how long a page will take to print on a PostScript printer, so there's no way to show how much longer the print job will take. Instead, the status bar in the Print Status dialog box displays only the percentage of pages that have been printed (for example, if you have two pages in your document, the status bar is 50 percent full after the first page, even if the second page takes 10 times longer than the first one to print). Nonetheless, this is a nice intermediate step, and often makes us feel better when we're waiting for those long jobs to print.

Figure 10-14
Print Status dialog box

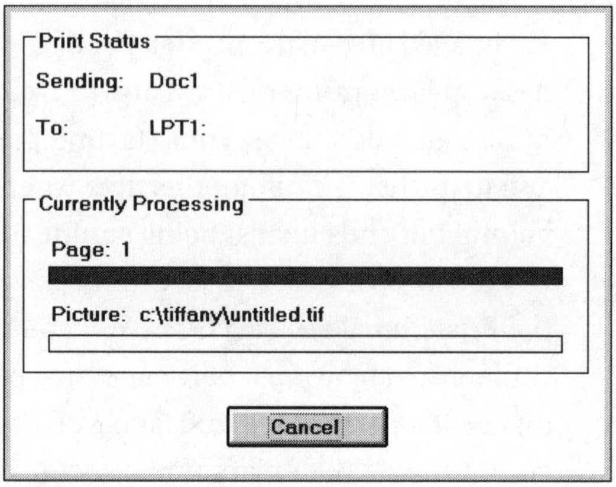

Color Separations

We come now to the last area of the Print dialog box, which, as a subject, deserves a whole section of the book to itself—color separations. The concept behind color separation is simple, and QuarkXPress does a good job of making the practice just as easy, but the truth is that this is a very complicated matter, which in the space of this book, we can only touch on briefly. Let's take a look at what color separation is all about, then move on to how QuarkXPress and various third-party products handle the process.

The Basics of Color Separation

A printing press can print only one color at a time. Even five- and six-color presses really print only one color at a time, attempting to give the paper (or whatever) a chance to dry between coats. As we discussed in Chapter 9, *Color*, those colors are almost always process colors (cyan, magenta, yellow, and black), or they may be spot colors, such as a Pantone inks. Colors that you specify in your QuarkXPress documents may look solid on the screen, but they need to be separated and printed onto individual plates for printing. If you print color separations for a job with only process colors, you output four pieces of film for every page of the document. Adding a spot color adds another plate to the lineup.

Print Colors as Grays

Before we go any farther, we should jump to the last, but certainly not least, item in the Print dialog box. This is the Print Colors as Grays feature. Be sure to click on this if you are proofing your color document on a black-and-white printer. This prints each color as a shade of gray rather than a solid black or white. You don't have too much control over which shades of gray go with which color, so subtle differences in colors (such as between a pink and a light green) may blend together as one shade of gray, but it's better than printing the file out as a page of solid black (see Figure 10-15).

Figure 10-15
Printing colors as grays

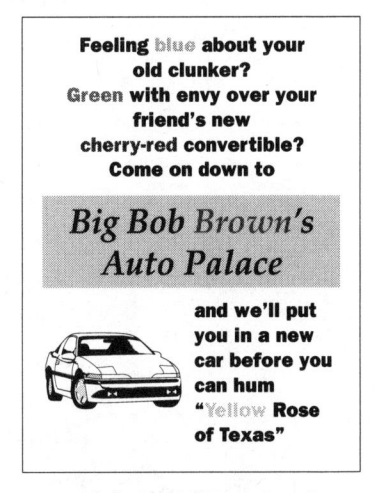

With "Print Colors as Grays" turned off

With "Print Colors as Grays" turned on

Another Look at Colors

If you haven't read Chapters 8 and 9, *Modifying Images* and *Color*, respectively, we recommend you go back and look them over before getting too in-depth with color separation. But given that you probably have as busy a schedule as we do, here's a quick rundown of the most important concepts.

- Process colors are colors that may look solid on the screen, but break down into varying tints of cyan, magenta, yellow, and black when printed as separations. We call these separating spot colors.

- Nonseparating spot colors are colors that don't separate at print time. Instead, they print on their own plates. These are typically Pantone (PMS) colors that are printed with PMS inks.

- The four process colors are printed as halftones (if you don't understand the fundamentals of halftoning, we *really* recommend you look at Chapter 8, *Image Modification*). By overlapping the screened tints, a multitude of colors is created.

Printing Color Separations

Let's start with the most basic method of printing color separations, and then move on to the more complicated concepts.

To print color separations, you check the Make Separations feature in the Print dialog box. This activates the Plates pop-up menu, giving you a choice of which color plates you want to print. By default, it's set to "All Plates," which includes the four process colors plus any nonseparating spot colors you have defined.

Even if you have "All Plates" selected, QuarkXPress prints plates only for the colors that are actually used in your document. If you create custom nonseparating spot colors, but don't actually use them in your document, they appear on the Plates menu. But don't worry; they don't print when you specify "All Plates." Note that if there's an EPS image on the page, however, QuarkXPress will probably print a plate for all four colors. Why? Because the program can't "see" into the encapsulated PostScript file in order to figure out what colors are actually being used. So it opts for the next best thing and prints a plate for each process color.

See page 599

We can't really call it a bug when the documentation says that it is supposed to work this way, but the fact that QuarkXPress prints a black plate when you select "All Plates" even when you don't have anything black on the page is really annoying, if not downright crazy. But that's the way it goes, and the only way around it is to print each separate plate one at a time, selecting only the plates that are actually necessary.

The Rosette

When the process color plates are laid down on top of each other, the halftones of each color mesh with each other in a subtle way. Each plate's halftone image is printed at a different angle, and possibly at a different screen frequency as well. The result is thousands of tiny rosette patterns (see Figure 10-16). If this process is done correctly, the colors blend together to form one smooth, clean color. If the angles or screen frequency are slightly off, or the registration (alignment) of the plates is wrong, then all sorts of chaos can ensue. Both of these problems can come about from errors on the lithographer's part, but more likely they are problems with your imagesetting process.

Figure 10-16
A simulated process color rosette

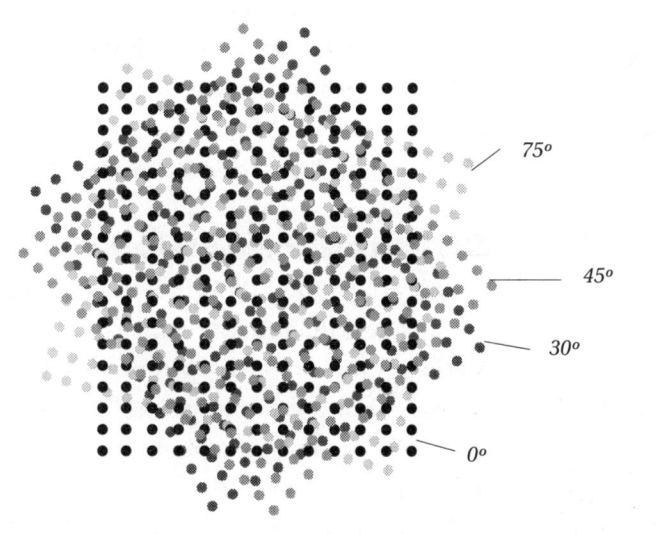

75º
45º
30º
0º

The most common effect of the above problems is a patterning in the color called a moiré pattern. There's almost no good way to describe a moiré pattern: it's best to just see a few of them. They might be pretty subtle, but it would behoove you to learn to identify them and learn how to make them go away. Figure 10-17 shows an outlandish example of this patterning caused by the screen frequency and angles being set completely wrong.

QuarkXPress uses the following angle values for process colors: black, 45 degrees; cyan, 75 degrees; magenta, 105 degrees; yellow, 90 degrees. These are pretty standard values, and they create a nice rosette, generally free of moiré patterns. However,

Figure 10-17
Moiré patterning

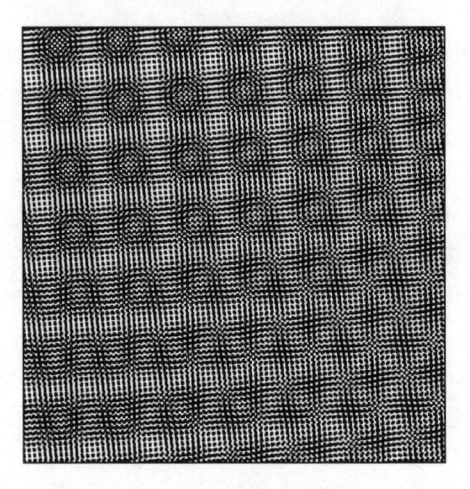

note that you may not get what QuarkXPress asks for when it comes to angles and screen frequencies. This is a problem between PostScript and the physical limitations of laser printers and imagesetters. For an in-depth discussion, see Chapter 10 on halftoning in *Real World PostScript*.

Dot Gain and Printer Calibration

It's easy to confuse the concepts of dot gain and printer calibration. They both have the same effect. To put it simply, both have to do with why the tint levels you specify in your files are not always what come out of the imagesetter or off the printing press. For example, you might specify a 40-percent magenta, and your final printed output will look like 60 percent. Don't kick yourself for typing 60 when you meant 40; remember that the problem could be in three places: dot gain, printer calibration, or your glasses might just be dirty. Let's look at each of these carefully and then explore what we can do about them.

Dot gain. Dot gain occurs while your artwork is actually on the press, and ink is flying about. The primary factors are the amount of ink on the press and the type of paper you're printing on (or, to be more specific, your lithographer is printing on). If there's too little ink on the press, your tints may print too lightly. If there's too much ink or if you're printing onto very absorbent paper, such as newsprint, your tints may print much too dark. A good lithographer can often control the ink problem, but the issue of what kind of paper you're printing on must be kept in mind while you're outputting your finished artwork.

Printer calibration. Just to be clear, we're talking here about imagesetter calibration. The idea is this: when the imagesetter's density knob is cranked up to high so type looks nice and black, and the film processor's chemicals haven't been flushed and replenished in two weeks, your delicate halftoned color separations are going to print less than optimally. All this equipment is so nifty that we sometimes forget that we're actually dealing with precision instruments designed to be able to produce very high-quality artwork. If you or your service bureau doesn't understand how to take care of the equipment, the artwork suffers.

We highly recommend that whoever is doing your imagesetting use a calibration utility such as Kodak's Precision Imagesetter Linearization Software or Technical Publishing Service's Color Calibration Software. Proper use of these sorts of programs keeps the output from the imagesetter relatively consistent on a day-to-day basis.

Glasses. The third possibility listed above is dirty glasses. In this busy world of contact lenses and corrective eye surgery, you have to stop yourself and ask: Why am I wearing these things, anyway? Then remember that if your computer explodes, the shattering glass will harmlessly bounce off those plastic lenses. But remember to keep them clean, or no matter what you do about dot gain and printer calibration, the colors will still look muddy.

▼ ▼

Tip: Laserchecking with LaserCheck. LaserCheck lets you print a document that was meant for an imagesetter on your desktop laser printer; you can actually set up the Printer Setup and Print dialog boxes just as though you were printing on an imagesetter, and your laser printer not only handles it correctly—with the help of LaserCheck—it tells you more than you'd ever want to know about the PostScript file it printed. We've found this handy for checking whether our tabloid-size pages were going to come out lengthwise or widthwise on the L330, and for seeing whether a file would just plain print. Generally, if it prints with Laser-Check, there's good chance it'll print on the imagesetter.

If it doesn't print on either, you might look into two PostScript error handlers: PinPointXT from the Cheshire Group and the Advanced PostScript Error Handler from Systems of Merritt (see Appendix E, *Resources*). David loves these, but he's a PostScript hacker and likes to muck about in moveto's and curveto's (PinPointXT is an XTension to QuarkXPress that requires much less knowledge of PostScript than most other error handlers). If you're not ready to jump into this sort of troubleshooting, perhaps you can talk your service bureau into it.

Working with a Service Bureau

The number of service bureaus with imagesetters has mushroomed over the past eight years, blossoming into many different varieties, from storefronts where you can rent a Mac or a PC to specialty services where you can send your files to be imageset on a number of medium- and high-end imagesetters. Alongside this growth, standard etiquette and rules spoken only in hushed voices (and usually after the customer has left the shop) have developed. In this section, we bring these rules out into the open and take you through, step by step, how best to send files to your service bureau and how to ensure that you'll receive the best quality output from them.

The first thing to remember when dealing with service bureaus is that they don't necessarily know their equipment or what's best for your file any better than you do. That's not to say that they are ignorant louts, but we are of the opinion that good service bureaus are few and far between, and you, the customer, have to be careful and know what you're doing.

The principal relationship we talk about in this section is that of you, the customer, sending your QuarkXPress files to a service bureau to be imageset. We'll talk first about sending the actual

QuarkXPress file, and then about sending a PostScript dump of the file.

Many of our suggestions may be totally wrong for the way your particular service bureau works, so take what works and leave the rest. Most prefer PostScript dumps of Windows documents, for instance, while a few opt for the QuarkXPress files themselves. Regrettably, most service bureaus favor the Macintosh; many don't even have PCs connected to their imagesetters. These factors clearly define how you must work.

Tip: Does Your Service Bureau Have a Densitometer? A densitometer is another piece of expensive equipment that you may not wish to spring for. Generally, you shouldn't have to; it's the responsibility of the service bureau to check their output regularly (at least daily) to make sure the density of their paper or film is correct and that when you specify a 20 percent tint in your document, you get a 20 percent tint on your film (unless you're adjusting for dot gain, as described above).

If you are working with halftones or tints (and especially color separations) going to film, make sure your service bureau owns a transmission densitometer (as opposed to a reflective densitometer), knows how to use it, and does so frequently, especially when moving between film and paper.

Tip: Some More Questions for Your Service Bureau. Here is a list of a few more questions, which you may want to ask when shopping for a service bureau.

- What imagesetters do they have available and what resolutions can you imageset at?

- Do they have dedicated equipment just for film, and do they calibrate it?

- Do they have an in-house color proofing system?

- What type of film and processing do they use?

- Do they have a replenishing processor, or do they use the same chemicals continually?

- Do they inspect their film before it is sent out?

- How do they normally run jobs created on PCs? Do they have a PC connected to their imagesetter?

There are no right or wrong answers to any of these. However, asking the questions not only tells you a lot about the service bureau, but it also teaches you a lot about the process they're going through to produce your film or RC (resin coated) paper.

You should make decisions about where to run each print job. For example, if a service bureau doesn't calibrate their equipment, you probably don't want to use them for halftoning or color-separation work. If their top resolution is 1270 dpi, you may need to go elsewhere for gray-scale images. You can weigh these items against the cost of the film or paper output, the distance from your office, the friendliness of the staff, and so on.

▼ ▼

Sending Your Document

You have two basic choices in transporting your QuarkXPress document to a service bureau to be imageset: sending the file itself or sending a PostScript dump of the file. Let's be clear right off the bat that we strongly recommend sending a PostScript dump. Why? Mostly because we want to be in control of our documents' printing, but also because the only option the service bureau has to print your PC document may be to download the PostScript file from a Mac to the imagesetter.

When we send the file off to be printed using someone else's system, we don't know whether their fonts are different, whether the text will reflow, whether they'll forget to set up registration marks, or whether they'll print the file at the wrong screen frequency. By sending them a PostScript dump (see "Sending a PostScript Dump," below) you put yourself in the driver's seat: you can control almost every aspect of the print job.

Sending QuarkXPress Files

Though we prefer to send PostScript dumps, we know of service bureaus that prefer to receive the actual QuarkXPress file. And the truth is that many people don't want to be responsible for checking all the buttons and specifications necessary to create a PostScript dump. If you find yourself in either of these situations, you'll need to know what to do in order to optimize your chances of success. Let's look at the steps you need to take.

Use the right driver. The PostScript printer driver (version 3.5) for Windows 3.1 has had a history of problems, most pertaining to high-resolution imagesetters. Even though Microsoft has addressed the problems by releasing driver updates (versions 3.51, 3.52, and 3.53 at this printing), some of the temporary fixes and workarounds that other vendors have made could start causing problems. It's a very shifty, nebulous situation at the moment. If your service bureau handles many Windows documents, they might even have a sign on the wall telling you which version of the PostScript driver you should be using. It's best to tell them about your document—page size, resolution settings, image setting like "Invert", and so on—and see what they recommend.

To see which version you have installed, double-click on the Printers icon in the Windows Control Panel to open the Printers dialog box. Make sure a PostScript printer is selected, and then click the Setup button. In the Setup dialog box, click the About button to see the version number of the PostScript driver along with some copyright information.

As we go to press, QuarkXPress has only been used by a handful of service bureaus, so we haven't pulled together much information on the best driver environment. However, we *can* give you a list of some problems reported with other applications, just in case you run into them with QuarkXPress.

- Even before Windows 3.1 hit the shelves, it was discovered that the "User Defined" paper-size option in the Windows Printer Setup dialog box for driver version 3.5 had problems. The Unit selection buttons in the User Defined Size dialog box were reversed: "0.1 mm" was really "0.01 inches" and vice versa. Obviously, folks got some amazing page-size distortions.

As we mentioned above, according to Quark, Quark-XPress gets around this problem for some imagesetters (Linotronic 330 and Agfa 9000, to name two) by using internal PDF information and taking the law into its own hands. We still advise going with the latest PostScript driver, unless your service bureau recommends otherwise.

- Some service bureaus have also reported problems with EPS graphics printing out at the wrong size on an otherwise normal-looking page. The problem seemed related to the Printer Resolution: setting in the Printer Setup dialog box. Setting the resolution higher than 1270 produced odd-size EPS images. If you reduce the resolution setting in the driver to 1270 or 635, the image usually turns out OK. However, if you do this, you may lose some data in very high-resolution line-art TIFF images.

- The Invert and Mirror image controls in some Windows software have worked erratically, affecting some parts of a page but not others. As we said earlier, it makes more sense to leave Invert and Mirror (or Flip Horizontal, Flip Vertical) turned off in the software and configure the imagesetter to perform those functions, not Windows.

- Color separators using high-resolution bitmapped image files at imagesetter resolutions of 2540 dpi and above (especially on page sizes over 18 inches) had (and may still have) problems with screen angle accuracy and general image quality. That's because the PostScript driver wasn't programmed to deal with such large numbers. It's up to each application to provide a work-around solution (it's another indication that the folks at Microsoft are still a little fuzzy on the concept behind high-quality graphic art).

You get the idea. Suffice it to say that the color-separation and fine-formatting features of QuarkXPress may well push the Windows PostScript driver up to, and possibly over, the edge in some situations. It's just too soon to tell how well the program deals with the shortcomings. This is one area of desktop publishing where Windows lags behind the Macintosh. I guess we've said it at least twice already, but (in theory) your service bureau should know what the current situation is.

Get a PC service bureau. If your service bureau doesn't own a PC, there's not much chance they'll do a good job with your QuarkXPress for Windows document. Increasingly, there are service bureaus that specialize in PC-based publishing, though they're hard to find. Also, some formerly Mac bureaus are coming up to speed on Windows. If a service bureau claims they handle Windows output, ask which PostScript driver they'd prefer you use and whether they have QuarkXPress installed. If they don't know what you're talking about, you can't assume they're "deep" into Windows. It's possible that the best service bureau for you may be in another city, but really sharp bureaus are set up for remote jobs via modem and overnight courier service, so don't overlook this option.

Check your fonts. We can't tell you how important it is to keep track of which fonts you've used and where they are on your disk. Make sure that your service bureau has the same printer fonts (downloadable fonts) that correspond to each and every font you've used in your document. Although sending the fonts that you used in your document to the service bureau technically violates the license agreement that accompanied the fonts when you bought them, many people do this anyway. We've never heard of anyone having any legal problems with this, as long as the service bureau deletes the fonts from their system after running your job.

Printer Setup. We mentioned that this was possibly just superstition, but we've always found it helpful to make sure we've got the appropriate imagesetter driver selected in the Printer Setup dialog box and that we've at least checked the Printer Setup dialog box once before proceeding to the next step.

Look over your document. Take the extra time to perform a careful perusal of your entire document. If you need to, zoom in to 200 percent and scroll over the page methodically. Many problems with printing occur not with the printing at all, but with that one extra word that slipped onto its own line, or the one image that was "temporarily" set to "Suppress Printout," and then never switched back.

Print a proof. If you can print the document on a desktop laser printer, chances are the file will print at your service bureau. That's not a guarantee, but it's usually a pretty good bet. When you print this proof, go over it, too, with a fine-toothed comb. You might have missed something in the on-screen search.

NEW IN 3.3

See page 602

Trap Information. If your document depends on the default trap information that's specified in the Application Preferences dialog box, you need to jot the information down and send it along to your service bureau. The trap information is not actually saved with the document, only with your program.

Include your illustrations. If you have imported TIFF or EPS pictures into your document by using the Get Picture feature, you need to include the original files on the disk with your document. Remember that QuarkXPress imports only a representation image for the screen and then looks for the original at print time. You can use the Picture Usage dialog box to see which graphic images you imported and whether they are missing or present.

The idea is to send your service bureau a whole kit rather than just a file. Give them everything they could ever think of needing, just in case.

▼ ▼

NEW IN 3.3

See page 615

Tip: Catching All the Fonts and Pictures. This is the age of desktop publishing; who has time to write down all the fonts and pictures that they used, one at a time? We sometimes take screen shots of the Font Usage and Picture Usage dialog boxes using Tiffany, SnapPro, or ImagePals Capture, piece them together, and print them out. To tell you the truth, it's often no quicker than just writing them down, but it's usually more fun.

▼ ▼

Tip: Check Your Compatibility. Fonts change, colors change, everything changes except change itself (if you've seen one cliché, you've seen them all). If you're working with a service bureau regularly, you'll want to make sure that their equipment and Windows system setup is compatible with yours. One way of doing this is for you to use the same files; copy every file off their disk onto yours. This is clearly tedious and never-ending. Another way to go is to perform periodic tests; you can use a test sheet. The fonts you regularly use, a gray percentage bar, some gray-scale images, and perhaps some line art (just for kicks) should be on this sheet. The idea is to see if anything changed much between your system and the service bureau's. If fonts come out different, the tints are off, or the density is too light or dark, you can either help them correct the problem or compensate for it yourself.

▼ ▼

Checklist for sending QuarkXPress files. We find checklists invaluable. Not only do they improve your method by encouraging you to perform the appropriate tasks in the right order, they're satisfaction guaranteed, every time. You can check an item off the list, which is in itself a boon to flagging spirits as a deadline looms. Below are examples of checklists we use before sending files to a service bureau.

Fonts.

- What fonts did you use in your document?
- Does your service bureau have the fonts you use?
- Do they have your printer fonts? (If not, send them; see the discussion about the license agreement earlier in this chapter.)

Printer Setup.

- Is "Printer Setup" set to the appropriate printer?

- Have you checked printer options in the Printer Setup dialog box?

Document Check.

- Check for boxes set to "Suppress Printout."
- Check for text box overflows.
- Check for missing or modified pictures (Picture Usage dialog box).
- Check for widows, orphans, loose lines, bad hyphens, and other typographic problems.

Proof.

- Print a proof on a laser printer.
- Check it carefully. Is it what you want?

Relevant files.

New in 3.3 — See page 615

- Did you include EPS and TIFF files?
- Did you include the document itself? (Don't laugh, sometimes this is the one thing people do forget after a long day.)

Calibration.

- Check calibration for gray levels?

Sending a PostScript Dump

It's probably clear that we not only don't trust many service bureaus to do the right thing, but we also don't trust ourselves to always remember everything we need while standing at the service bureau counter. Because of this, we strongly urge you to use PostScript dumps. A PostScript dump, otherwise known as a print-to-disk, when performed correctly, almost always ensures a better print job, and is generally preferred by your service bureau, especially for non-Macintosh, (i.e., Windows) print jobs.

In fact, many service bureaus now give big discounts to people who bring in PostScript dumps as opposed to the actual files (our neighborhood service bureau cuts five dollars a page off their single-page price). Instead of having to open your file, make sure all of the correct fonts are loaded, check all your settings, and then print it, they can send the PostScript dump directly to their imagesetters.

The biggest difference is that you now have the responsibility for making sure your file is perfect for printing. However, this isn't as difficult as it may seem. Let's go through the steps you need to take to create the perfect PostScript dump. At the end, we include a checklist that you can copy or recreate for your own use.

System Setup

To create a successful PostScript dump, you've got to set up your system properly. This requires two main steps: checking your disk space and setting up the destination printer. The first step should be done each time you print a file to disk; the second step you have to set up only once.

Storage. Make sure you have enough storage on your disk to save the PostScript dump. It is automatically saved in the same folder as your copy of Windows (well, sometimes it is arbitrarily saved someplace else, but usually it goes into the Windows subdirectory unless you specify a different directory path name when you enter a name for the PostScript file). PostScript dumps are often not small. They may require anywhere from 10K to 900K (or larger if you're printing scanned images or color separations).

Printer Control Panel. Printing to disk is just like printing to a printer except that instead of funneling the print data down a wire to your printer, you divert it into a disk file. Diverting the data flow is simple enough; just use the Windows Printer Control Panel to change the printer's connection from an actual printer port, like LPT1:, to an imaginary device named FILE:. Here's what you do.

1. Switch from QuarkXPress to the Windows Program Manager. To do this, we like to hold down the Alt key and press the Tab key until the Program Manager icon appears in the center of the screen, then release both keys.

2. From the Main program group in the Program Manager, double-click on the Control Panel icon. When the Control Panel window opens, double-click on the icon labeled Printers.

3. From the Installed Printers list in the Printers dialog box, select the PostScript printer or imagesetter that your service bureau uses. If the appropriate printer doesn't appear in the list, you may need to get the appropriate driver from the printer manufacturer, the service bureau, or from Microsoft. Once you've selected the printer, click the Add button to install it. Don't worry if you have that printer installed once already; you can have two of the same kind of printer installed, but going to different ports (one to LPT1: and another to FILE:, for example).

4. Your new printer selection should read something like "Linotronic 330 on LPT1." Click the Connect button. In the Connect dialog box that opens, scroll down the Ports list and select FILE: as the new printer port. Click OK.

5. In the Printers Control Panel dialog box, click Close, and then exit the Control Panel and switch back to QuarkXPress.

You now have a printer setting that prints to a file, and this setting shows up in the Printer Setup dialog box. Fortunately, you don't have to go through all this *mishegos* every time you want to make a PostScript dump! The printer settings stay loaded until you remove it using the Control Panel (why would you ever want to do that?).

Starting the Print Job

Once your system is ready for the PostScript dump, you can start your countdown to takeoff. You need to take the same steps involved with printing to your own printer: checking the Printer Setup dialog box, checking your fonts and pictures, and finally making sure the Print dialog box is set up just right. Let's go through each of these steps one more time.

Printer Setup. Because you're ultimately printing to a PostScript device, you need to have a PostScript printer selected in the Printer Setup dialog box, preferably the imagesetter model your service bureau uses. This determines how large the printed page can be. Be sure to set the halftone screen frequency you want; this is an area where many people screw up. Read "Printer Setup," above, for more details. It doesn't matter whether you actually have a PostScript printer hooked up or not.

Fonts. You must have a font loaded for every font you use in your document, including fonts embedded in EPS files. One way to check which fonts are in your document is to use the Font Usage feature in the Utilities menu. However, this method won't always give you fully accurate results, so it's best to keep a running list of the fonts you use.

Pictures. Check your Picture Usage dialog box to see if all the pictures you used in your document are available. This is a suggested step, but is not crucial, because if you don't do this, QuarkXPress checks for you at print time and then gives you the opportunity to find any that are missing.

Print. The most common mistakes in creating PostScript dumps are made in the Print dialog box. Be careful with the buttons and menus here. If you want registration marks, you must turn them on here. If you want multiple copies (not likely, for high-resolution output), choose your value here. But if you want only one copy of each page, make sure that you specify "1" here! We've had friends who've accidentally gotten 10 copies back from their service bureau simply because they didn't check this carefully. Expensive mistake.

Be careful, too, with the Tiling features. You may be printing to a roll-fed imagesetter that can handle a full tabloid-size page, and if you were printing tiled proof copies earlier, "Manual" or "Auto Tiling" might have been left on. Once you've inspected the Print dialog box setting and have everything the way you want, click OK.

If you're making color separations, read the color separation section above.

OK. When you are finally ready to print the file, click OK or press Enter. Windows gives you an option for where you want to save the file and what you want to name it (just type the path name into the dialog box; see Figure 10-18). If you've checked the Include Header with Each Job option in the Options dialog box of "Printer Setup," the file that gets saved contains the entire PostScript header. This is really only about 9K of data, so we typically include it with PostScript dumps.

▼ ▼

Tip: When Your File Is Too Big. It's easy to make PostScript dumps that are too big to fit onto a floppy. Add a TIFF or an EPS here and there, use too many auto-downloading fonts, or even just try to print a large file. Don't fret: there's always a workaround.

First of all, if you're going to work with the PC, you must own a copy of PKZIP. It's shareware, which means that you can get it almost anywhere (user group, dealer, on-line service), but if you use it more than once, you are honor-bound to send PKWare, Inc. their money ($25). PKZIP (and PKUNZIP) has become a standard on the PC for compressing and decompressing files. Some TIFF files can compress as much as 90 percent, although most files only compress around 30 to 60 percent. You can also use

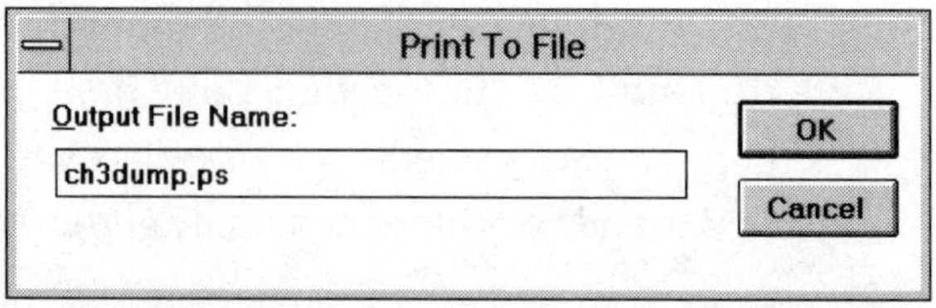

Figure 10-18
Saving a PostScript dump

PKZIP to break up files into several disks, then join them up again to fit back onto a hard disk.

If you're going to be sending lots of large files to your service bureau, we recommend a removable hard disk, such as SyQuest or Bernoulli. Make sure the kind you get is compatible with what your service bureau uses. These removables can hold up to 85MB or 90MB of information. They're also great for backing up your data.

When all else fails, you can use the BACKUP program that ships with Microsoft's DOS system software. In fact, many people prefer this method. We don't. But we did hear of someone who did, once.

▼ ▼

Checklist for sending PostScript dumps

Your service bureau will appreciate you for this one.

System and Font Setup.

- Have you installed a printer in the Windows Printers Control Panel that is set to FILE:?

- Do you have enough memory on your disk to save the PostScript dump?

- Do you have the proper fonts loaded for the fonts that are in your document? EPS files?

- Have you disabled automatic font downloading, so that printer fonts don't get included in the PS dump? In some circumstances, if service bureau doesn't have them, for example, you may want the fonts to automatically download anyway.

Printer Setup.

- Have you selected the appropriate printer?

- Do you have the proper settings in the Printer Setup dialog box? In the Options and Advanced dialog boxes?

Pictures.

- Do you have all of the EPS and TIFF files available? Check the Picture Usage dialog box.

Print Dialog Box.

- Are all of the proper settings made? Registration marks? Page range? Color separations?

Sending the file.

- Do you want to compress or segment the file?
- Rename the file to something appropriate.

Troubleshooting

After all of this, printing should be a breeze, right? Well, we wish it were. Too often, we get phone calls from our service bureaus saying, "Your job wouldn't print." Back in the good old days, a service bureau would offer to fix it for you. Now life has gotten busy for them, and they expect you to do the fixing. Here are some tips that we've found to work over the years.

Graphics Look Awful

One of the most common problems with print jobs from Quark-XPress has never had anything to do with QuarkXPress itself. The problem is with the person sending files. Remember that Quark-XPress does not actually suck in any EPS or TIFF files that you have imported. It only brings in a low-resolution representation for the screen image and maintains a link with the original file. If that file changes or is missing when QuarkXPress tries to print it, the graphic looks different from what you expect.

Two notes to write on your forehead follow.

- If you're going to send your QuarkXPress document, send a whole kit, not just a file. The kit should include the document and all the EPS and TIFF images you used.

- If you can, send PostScript print-to-disk files (PS dumps) instead of the document itself. The PostScript dump does contain the TIFF and EPS files, as well as every other bit of information the imagesetter needs.

Memory Problems

QuarkXPress has gotten a bad rep in the past for causing PostScript errors at print time. Almost all of these errors are the result of printer memory problems (called VMerror), and almost all of them can be avoided with a few tricks.

Reset the printer. Our favorite technique for avoiding memory problems is simply to turn off the printer, wait a few seconds, and turn it back on again. This flushes out any extraneous fonts or PostScript functions that are hogging memory. It's sort of like waking up refreshed after a good night's sleep, but different.

If you're sending a PostScript dump, remember to make sure that the Windows PostScript header file is downloaded first (resetting the printer gets rid of it). A PostScript dump should include the PostScript header information, unless you turned off the Send Header with Each Job option in the Options dialog box of the Printer Setup dialog box (discussed above).

Use minimum settings. Using the minimum settings means turning off all the printer options in the Printer Setup dialog box, including the Image options.

Take care with your fonts. If you play around with a lot of different fonts trying to find one you like, you may inadvertently leave remnants of text formatted with old fonts lying around. For example, a space character may be set to some font that you don't use anyplace else. Nonetheless, QuarkXPress may download that font along with every other font you use. This takes up memory that could be used for something else. Try using the Font Usage dialog box to see which fonts are sitting around in your document. Then purge the ones you don't need.

Clear Memory per Page. Another good way to clear out memory so that your file can print more easily is to select the Clear Memory per Page option in the Advanced dialog box, accessed via the Advanced command button in the Options dialog box of the Printer Setup dialog box (discussed above). (Don't you love these dialog boxes inside of other dialog boxes inside of other dialog boxes? It's like a great Chinese puzzle!) If you must have many fonts on a page, the Clear Memory per Page option tends to keep the minimum number loaded to print each page. Printing may take longer, but at least your page might print without bombing the printer.

Print fewer pages at a time. We have successfully coached long documents out of an imagesetter by printing two to 10 pages at a time rather than trying to get all 500 pages out. This is obviously a hassle, but it's better than not getting the job printed at all. Much of the work can be done early by creating multiple PostScript dumps, then queuing them up on a spooler at the service bureau.

Remove enormous graphics. One of the great promises of desktop publishing was that we could print an entire page with every graphic and text block perfectly placed. Remember that promises are often broken. Case in point: Large graphics (or even small graphics) sometimes choke the printer. These graphics often print all by themselves, but when placed on a page they become the chicken bone that killed the giant. Yes, using every trick possible you might get the page out, but is it worth the time? Perhaps it's more efficient to just let your printer or stripper handle that graphic. Or, god forbid, just hot wax that puppy and paste it down yourself.

PostScript Problems

There are some PostScript problems that aren't memory-related, even though just about everyone at Quark will tell you they don't exist. One is the infamous stackunderflow error. Another is the undefined command error. These are significantly harder to track down and fix. However, here are a few things you can try.

Save as. Logically, resaving your QuarkXPress document under a different name doesn't make any sense, but it does work sometimes.

Selective printing. You can try to pinpoint what page element is causing the error by printing only certain parts of the page. For example, turn on "Rough" in the Print dialog box to avoid printing any pictures or complex frames. If the page prints, chances are one of the graphic images is at fault. You can also use "Suppress Printout" to specify a single image not to print.

If the page still doesn't print after printing a rough copy, try taking out a text box at a time or changing the fonts you used. If you are printing color separations, try printing a single plate at a time.

Shrink the page size. For technical reasons we don't need to get into here, some pages avoid PostScript errors (especially limitcheck errors) when printed at a smaller size. You can use the Reduce or Enlarge setting in the Page Setup dialog box to print the page at 25 or 50 percent of size. Of course, this rarely helps you in the long run. This method is only for really complex graphics or pages.

Re-import. If the problem turns out to be a graphic you've imported, you might try re-importing it. If the image was pasted in, you might have better luck using "Get Picture" instead. If the picture was in some weird format, you might try converting it into a better format, like TIFF (for bitmaps) or EPS (for object-oriented graphics). Then re-import it.

Check printer type. Make sure you have the correct printer type selected in the Page Setup dialog box. Often, this won't have any effect on your output, but it's worth checking.

Big Ugly White Gaps Appear Between Colors

You've output your four-color separations and sent the file off to your lithographer. A few days later you show up for the press check and you see, much to your surprise, big ugly white gaps appearing between each of the colors. What happened? You forgot about traps. It's easy to do, believe us. The remedy? Go read the section on trapping in Chapter 9, *Color*, and redo your negatives.

Wrong Screen Frequency

QuarkXPress can't read your mind nor the mind of your lithographer. If you print out your file with the default halftone screen frequency setting of 60 lines per inch, that's just what you'll get. This is coarse, but fine if you're just going to photocopy your page. However, it looks pretty awful compared to 120 or 133 lines per inch (or higher), which is used in most print jobs. Check with your lithographer for what screen frequency to use, then check your Page Setup dialog box before you print your job. Note that this is not a function that your service bureau can easily change if you provide a PostScript dump.

Not Enough Space Between Pages

If your pages are printing too close together from a roll-fed printer, you may have to adjust the Page Gap value in the Page Setup dialog box. Note that QuarkXPress prints your document only as wide as it needs to. For example, if your page is 4 by 4 inches, QuarkXPress tells the imagesetter to print only four inches of film. This is a great saving for film or RC paper, but sometimes it's a hassle to handle the output.

Fonts Come Out Wrong

Don't forget that you have to have the printer fonts loaded for every font in the document available to QuarkXPress and the printer when you print. That means the fonts you selected, those that were imported, and those that are stuck somewhere in an EPS document. "Available" means that they're installed for ATM and should be referenced in the WIN.INI file..

Also, watch out for EPS files nested inside of EPS files nested inside of EPS files. Depending on which application created each EPS file, QuarkXPress may or may not be able to dig deep enough to find every font used.

Registration Problems

Imagine the Rockettes, kicking their legs to chorus line stardom in perfect synchronization. Then imagine the woman at one end having no sense of rhythm, kicking totally out of sync with the others. This is what happens when one color plate is misregistered with the others. When a sheet of paper is rushed through a printing press and four colors speedily applied to it, there is bound to be some misregistration—sometimes up to a point or two. However, you can help matters considerably by making sure that your film is as consistent as possible.

Whenever we are told that a job printed great "except for one plate that was off register," we immediately ask if that piece of film was output at a different time than the others. The answer is almost always yes. We realize that it's expensive and time-consuming to print four new plates every time you want to make a change to a page, but it is a fact of desktop life that you can almost never get proper registration when you reprint a single plate. Why? The weather, roll stretch, alignment of the stars...all sorts of reasons contribute to this massive hassle.

"Job Finished"

As we said at the beginning of the book, don't give up until you get it to work. If you run into difficulty, there is almost always a workaround solution. Working through to that solution almost always teaches a valuable lesson (as grandma used to say, "It builds character"). However, remember that the solution is sometimes to just print the job in pieces and strip them together traditionally. It feels awful when you have to clean off your drafting table and dust off your hot waxer, but efficiency is often the name of the game.

One last note: when the last page comes out of the imagesetter, don't forget to thank your computer, QuarkXPress, the service bureau, and yourself for a job well done.

APPENDIX A

WINDOWS AND XPRESS

For years, Windows was just plain lame, a rather feeble excuse for a graphic user interface, marred by severe speed and memory limitations and dismal font support. During that dark age, most of the hot desktop publishing and graphics software only ran on the Macintosh computer, and guys like Bob made a living getting Windows to work for publishers.

Perhaps the biggest problem with Windows was that it only let software use the 640K of memory that the underlying MS/DOS operating system apportioned for applications. Sure, there were complicated schemes, such as LIM (Lotus, Intel, Microsoft) that specified "expanded" memory, but software development was unduly difficult. Windows version 3.0 changed all that. Most notably, it gave developers breathing room to create elaborate, graphically oriented programs that could use far more memory.

Memory Lane

But just because you've got the newest version of Windows and a hot machine, don't think that all your memory problems are over. In fact, many of our tips for installing and using Windows with QuarkXPress deal with memory considerations. Although

493

Windows automatically evaluates your system and does a fair job of accommodating what you have, there are often ways to get better speed and reliability.

Use Extended Memory

Windows and Windows applications need to run in *extended* memory, not *expanded* memory. Expanded memory, which we mentioned above, is used to surmount the 1MB (1024K) memory limit of MS/DOS, chiefly for DOS applications. DOS can't use extended memory in most situations, so expanded memory employs a complex scheme to temporarily swap portions of memory from areas that DOS *can't* use into memory areas that DOS *can* use.

Extended memory is more straightforward. It extends in one large block above the 1MB of memory space used by DOS and can be accessed directly by operating systems or programs (like Windows 3.0 and 3.1) that use the extended memory accessing features of the 80286, 386, or 486 microprocessors. Since extended memory entails less rigmarole, it operates faster than expanded memory. If you're using an expanded memory board that's configurable as extended or expanded memory, or both (like an AST RAMPage or Intel AboveBoard), configure it for extended memory, since Windows just won't use expanded memory.

Virtual Memory

If you're using a 386 or 486 computer (and with the demands of QuarkXPress, you ought to be), Windows should be running in 386 Enhanced mode, which takes advantage of several special features of these microprocessors. One feature, virtual memory (or VM), swaps portions of application program code and data from your system's RAM to your hard disk when you run out of extended memory. Windows fools itself into thinking that disk space is also RAM space. More RAM is good (see "RAM's the Thing," below). However, although virtual memory acts in a similar manner to RAM, it's significantly slower. Don't rely on virtual memory for anything you need fast.

If you're curious, double-click the About Program Manager button in the Program Manager's Help menu. Near the bottom of the window, check the Memory: figure under the 386 Enhanced setting. Unless your disk drive is full, you'll probably see a listing of free memory that is much greater than the amount of RAM you've installed.

Permanent Swap File

Here's a further consideration when working with virtual memory. As we said, Windows runs noticeably slower when it has to rely on virtual memory. You can speed up virtual memory a bit by setting a *permanent swap file*, which gives Windows quicker access to the disk space.

Windows uses a swap file as a virtual memory storage space. A *temporary swap file* is created when you start Windows, and erased when you quit. The file (named WIN386.SWP) shrinks or grows as needed. A permanent swap is a specially reserved area of uninterrupted disk space, which Windows can hop onto faster. It's a fixed size, and it's always there, though invisible, even when you're not running Windows. Here's how to set up a permanent swap file in Windows 3.1.

1. In the Main program group in Program Manager, double-click on the Windows 3.1 Control Panel icon.

2. In the Control Panel window, double-click on the 386 Enhanced icon to open the 386 Enhanced dialog box. Then click the Virtual Memory command button to open the Virtual Memory dialog box.

3. In the Virtual Memory dialog box, first check out what your current situation is. The Drive: setting should be your main hard drive, preferably the fastest one installed in your system. (It should *not* be a mounted network drive).

4. If the Type: setting is "None" or "Temporary," change it to "Permanent." To do that, click the Change button to expand the Virtual Memory dialog box to include the Change Settings options.

5. The Space Available: figure refers to the largest clump of available disk sectors, unbroken by random sectors of

stored information. This is often referred to as "contiguous" or "unfragmented" disk space. A permanent swap file must use contiguous disk space. You may find that the maximum swap file size is smaller than the total free space on your disk. This means that your disk is fragmented, to some extent, with free space interspersed between blocks of recorded data. If the maximum "Space Available" is less than what you want, you should use a disk defragmenting utility like those provided with The Norton Utilities, PC Tools 8.0, Disk Optimizer Tools, and others, to tighten things up. You can also defragment your hard drive by backing it up on a file-by-file (archive) basis (not a disk dump), reformatting the drive, and restoring your files.

The "Recommended Maximum Size" that Windows suggests is usually about half of the "Space Available." This may be way too big, depending on how much space you have available. Obviously, the amount of virtual memory you need depends on how much RAM you have and the kind of applications you intend to run. If you have only 4MB of RAM and plan to use lots of scanned images in QuarkXPress, and run your word processor simultaneously, you might try a 10MB permanent swap file to see how it works out. An over-size permanent swap file, on the other hand, is wasted disk space. If you have 16MB of RAM, you might need only a 4MB to 6MB swap file (just for the hell of it), or none at all.

6. Once you've decided what you need, enter the size in the New Size edit box. Then restart Windows for the changes to take effect.

The Use 32-bit Access option (the check box at the bottom of the Virtual Memory dialog box) is new in Windows 3.1. Also known as "Fast Disk," this option increases virtual memory performance when you're running DOS applications under Windows. If you don't see the option, Windows determined during its installation that your hard drive controller isn't compatible with Fast

Disk. 32-bit access is only compatible with Western Digital or compatible drive controllers. If you see the option and run DOS applications in Windows (and you're short on memory), give 32-bit access a try. If it doesn't work, an alert box displays the next time you start Windows, telling you your controller isn't compatible. Go back to the Virtual Memory dialog box and turn off the Use 32-bit Access option.

As an interesting side note, the Fast Disk option is sensitive to changes in your disk software. In Bob's case, it once refused to invoke itself because it detected a software change or possible virus. Bob then discovered he'd gotten the Michelangelo virus during the previous Windows session, possibly from installing some sleazy software. Michelangelo infects disk boot sectors, hence it interfered with 32-bit access.

RAM's the Thing

Nothing speeds up Windows like more memory. If you've been running on a minimal 3 or 4MB RAM configuration, you'll be amazed how QuarkXPress and your other programs sail along when you move up to 6 or 8MB. QuarkXPress uses up about 600K to load itself and a short, simple document. Add a couple of 24-bit TIFF images, and you're easily up to about 2.5MB, by our tests. And that's just QuarkXPress! What about your word processor? If you decide you need to edit some text, do you really want to take the time to save your document, quit QuarkXPress, load your word processor, edit the document, save it, quit the word processor, and reload QuarkXPress? If you're really publishing for a living, you can't afford to do this.

Get some RAM. In fact, get as much as you can afford. At the time we go to press, it runs about $40 per megabyte. Bob's got 20MB in his clone PC. But then at any one time he may be running QuarkXPress, Word for Windows, and CorelDRAW, and possibly a screen capture utility. He checks his e-mail regularly, so he'll load a communications program on top of that, not to mention Super Mario VGA (a habit he can't seem to kick after picking it up from his 5-year-old). If some file alchemy is required, he might even need Aldus PhotoStyler running on top of all that. Each of these programs requires memory, and all together they take up gobs of it.

And that's not all. QuarkXPress and other publishing programs run even faster with a larger disk cache. A disk cache keeps areas of your hard disk, especially those you've recently accessed, in memory. Instead of going to the disk for the next piece of information it needs, Windows is likely to find it in the cache. The end result is better speed. A 2MB disk cache is optimal. Windows SmartDrive disk cache automatically increases the size of your disk cache to 2MB once you've installed 6MB or more of RAM in your system.

ATM also maintains a font cache, where it holds onto the typefaces it's already rendered. This way it can use them again on screen without having to render them from scratch. If all the fonts used in your document are in the cache, screen redraw speeds up radically. If you're using lots of fonts at different sizes and have enough RAM to spare, go for a 1024K (1MB) font cache in ATM. Just use the ATM Control Panel and increase the Font Cache setting. You'll need to quit and restart Windows for the change to take effect. Of course, if you're using only one font in one size, raising this cache value doesn't help at all.

▼ ▼

Tip: Increase Your Picture Memory One of the benefits of having loads of RAM is the ability to improve the quality of the on-screen representation of pictures that appear while you're dragging a picture box. You can do that by allocating more memory to this function. Simply open the QUARK.INI file using Windows Notepad or another text editor that can save text in plain, ASCII format, and add the following on a line by itself. "MaxTempPicKB=*number of kilobytes*" (no quotation marks, of course).

The default value is 8,000K (8MB), and you can specify anywhere from 500K to 64,000K. If you increase the value, it takes QuarkXPress a little bit longer to generate the superior representation (that lag you notice between the moment you click and the moment you can start dragging the picture). But if you need the higher-quality image, you just need to take that performance hit. The truth of the matter is that we typically don't even bother changing this.

Windows Resources

Even with a zillion megabytes of RAM in your PC, Windows can still run out of memory. That's because there are two kinds of memory: the standard kind we've been talking about so far, and a more precious type called *system resource* memory. In Windows 3.1 there's 128K of system resource memory, period. Windows uses system resource memory to keep track of open windows, icons, and much of the desktop stuff you see on your screen. To check how much system resource memory you've already depleted, use the About Program Manager command under the Help menu in Program Manager. At the bottom of the window you'll see "System Resources:" listed as a percentage, like "60% free." Load QuarkXPress and a blank document, and that figure could easily plunge to 44 percent. Every application you open takes another bite, as does every additional window you open within an application. We start getting nervous when system resources get down to 15 percent, because at that point, something could blow. If you're lucky, you'll get a nice polite "Not enough memory to complete operation" alert, but you could also crash your application or Windows itself.

Here are a few things we do to conserve Windows resources.

Keep just a few program groups. Each group you create in Program Manager uses system resources, so avoid using too many. We now keep all of our main applications in one large group, though in our more frivolous days we had a Word Processing, a Page Layout, a Graphics, and a Spreadsheet group, just because we could. Most Windows applications create a group for themselves during installation. Just drag the application icons to your main application group and delete the new groups.

Reduce the number of icons you use. Delete nonessential icons, like the "Release Notes" that an application may install for your convenience, and other cute stuff you won't use. You can also delete the icons for applications that you only use once in a while. Just run them using the Run command under the Program Manager's File menu. The Run command's Browse dialog box makes it pretty easy to find the application.

Strip the Wallpaper. Windows lets you do a fair amount of interior decorating. The Wallpaper feature lets you substitute a bitmapped graphic for the bland, monotone default background used by Windows. You can even line your screen with a picture of your loved one, which they'll really appreciate (not!). Unfortunately, Wallpaper blows a lot of memory and system resources. Unless you never strain the Windows system resources and have more RAM than you know what to do with, don't bother with the wallpaper.

Quit. We saved the obvious for last. Close applications when you're not using them. Even when "Minimized," programs still draw on system resources. In QuarkXPress, close documents that you're not working on.

Clip the Clipboard

When you cut or copy something to the Windows Clipboard, it stays there until you cut or copy something else. Meanwhile, it takes up memory (standard memory, not system resource memory). Cutting several pages of text or a graphic can add up to a big chunk of memory. What to do? First, you can delete the contents of the Clipboard by using the Clipboard accessory in the Accessory group. Double-click the Clipboard icon. Then select Delete from the Clipboard Edit menu and quit the Clipboard accessory.

The second method is significantly easier: Just cut or copy something else that is much smaller. For example, copy one word onto the Clipboard. That clears out most of what was there, and the small item takes only a fraction of the memory.

That said, don't bother doing this unless you've really stretched your memory and feel that you're in danger of running out. Especially, if you're cutting and pasting fairly frequently, it could end up simply wasting time.

Speed-Ups

As you've probably noticed, we're kind of fixated on speed and efficiency. One of the best ways we know of to be efficient and get where we're going fast is to use keyboard shortcuts. Here are a few shortcuts that Windows gives you that can help in any program.

Next, please. Typing Alt-Tab switches to the next loaded application. (That includes the Program Manager, which is also an application.) Contrary to what it says in the Windows User's Guide, the first application it switches to is usually the one you used last. Shift-Alt-Tab does the same thing as Alt-Tab, only in reverse, taking you to the last application in the order. To be honest, we're not sure how Windows maintains this order, but if you get tired of playing Solitaire or Minefield you could try figuring it out (let us know if you do).

Alt-Tab is preferable to an alternate shortcut, Alt-Esc, which does the same thing, but in a different way. Alt-Tab presents the next application as an icon in the middle of your screen, not the live window; hold down the Alt key and repeatedly press the Tab key until you see the icon of the program you want, then release both keys. That application's window then pops open. Alt-Esc simply switches from application to application in whatever state you left them, as open windows or icons. It takes longer to get to the application you want.

What are my options?. You can get to the Task List by typing Control-Esc. From here, you can select any of the currently running applications, using the arrow keys or a click of the mouse. Since it requires more moves than Alt-Tab, it's not as fast (read: not as good). However, Bob has used it on occasions when, after Windows crashed and started taking on water, Alt-Tab was frozen. Strangely enough, Control-Esc successfully got him to another application to save the file he'd been working on.

Quittin' quickly. You can get out of QuarkXPress really quickly by typing Alt-F4 (that's the fastest way we know of short of pulling the plug out of the electric socket). The problem is that we sometimes can't remember this, so we typically just type Alt-F X (which accesses the File menu, then selects Exit).

Help!. If you use QuarkXPress's built-in, on-line help, you should remember the F1 key. Pressing this opens the help dialog box.

Closing windows. Don't forget that you can quickly close an open document window by pressing Control-F4. Then, if QuarkXPress prompts you to save changes, you can simply type Y or N.

Next window, please. Back in Chapter 1, *QuarkXPress Basics*, we mentioned that one of the best ways to move between documents was to type Alt-W, then the number that corresponds to the window. An even faster method is to type Control-F6. We use this particularly when we're switching back and forth between two documents.

Shortcuts

We'll finish up this little appendix with just a few more shortcuts that we've found helpful in the Windows environment. If you have other ideas, let us know! We're always trying to get more efficient.

Loading several applications at once. If you know you're going to use several applications in your session, try this: Go to the relevant application group and double-click on each application icon while holding down the Shift key. (The mouse pointer may switch to an hourglass, but keep going.) Most applications load fine this way.

Auto-loading at startup. If you know you're usually going to use one or more applications in each Windows session, here's an easy way to automatically load them: drag each application icon into the StartUp group. The group has a special property: Any and all applications in that group are automatically loaded when you start Windows. You can quickly and easily change the startup applications to suit whichever project you're doing.

Quick edit of system files. You power users already know this one, but initiates should know that the easiest way to peek into or edit the WIN.INI, SYSTEM.INI, CONFIG.SYS, and AUTOEXEC.BAT system configuration files is the Windows SYSEDIT program. To start SYSEDIT, just use the Run command in the Program Manager File menu and enter "SYSEDIT" as the Command Line entry. Four edit Windows, one for each file, cascade onto your screen, ready for you to fiddle with. You can also add the program to your main application group by dragging it from File Manager. Then a quick double-click opens all those files for editing.

Choosing groups. You can open an application group without clicking on its icon by using the Windows menu in Program Manager. The Windows menu lists your groups, so you can open one from there instead of double-clicking on a group icon. By relying on the Windows menu, you can tuck the icons out of sight, or at least not worry if they're obscured by another open window.

Window Maximus. We can't afford dual-page monitors, so we like to Maximize the windows of the applications we're running. You can use the control box menu accessed by clicking the control box at the top-left corner of the window. If you're a good shot with a mouse pointer, you can click the Maximize button at the upper-right corner. (It looks like a little upward-facing pointer.) For an easier target, simply double-click the title bar that runs across the top of the window. You'll get instant Maximization.

Faster thinking through blinking. If you like strong coffee and edit text with intensity to match, then increase Window's cursor blink rate to its maximum. You'll be amazed how much faster you can locate the quickly flashing insertion point on a full page of solid text. From the Windows Control Panel, double-click the Desktop icon. From the Desktop dialog box, move the Cursor Blink Rate slider bar all the way over to the right, for Fast blink.

Skip startup screen. We get tired of seeing the cool, blue Windows startup screen. If you do also, try starting Windows by typing "WIN :" (that's followed by a space and a colon). We haven't pulled out our stopwatches to see if Windows actually loads faster, but that moment of visual silence while Windows loads itself, *sans* startup screen, helps us prepare for the grueling session ahead.

APPENDIX B

IF YOU USE A MACINTOSH

It can't be denied that there are lots more Windows boxes out there than Macs, and an increasing number of them are running the Windows version of QuarkXPress. Although many hard-core Macintosh users may prefer to wear cloves of garlic (or rubber gloves) when working with Windows machines, they'll have to deal with you sooner or later.

From the outset, QuarkXPress for Windows could open files saved by QuarkXPress for Macintosh version 3.1. But it was a one-way trip until QuarkXPress for Macintosh version 3.2 came out. Now, at last, there's two-way transferability of files between Macs and Windows machines.

Or is there? While bringing files from your Macintosh to a PC and back again is possible, it certainly isn't a no-brainer. In this section, we want to take a quick tour of the obstacles in your way when transferring files.

You May Get There From Here

There are many ways of transferring files between PCs and Macs, and QuarkXPress is happy with the result no matter how you

505

move your files. If your PCs and Macs share a hard drive on a network through any kind of network software, you can just copy the file, or open it directly. If you have a modem link between the machines, you can use your communication program's file-transfer capabilities.

However, the most popular way to transfer files is via floppy disk. This is easy enough to do if the Macintosh can read 1.44Mb floppies. This kind of floppy drive is called either a SuperDrive or a High-Density Floppy Drive; almost every Mac and PC sold in the past five years has one. The high-density drives can read from and write on PC-formatted floppies as well as the standard Macintosh-formatted ones.

However, even though the Macintosh can theoretically read and write PC floppies doesn't mean that the operating system itself can. Every Macintosh comes with a simple program called Apple File Exchange that lets you access PC disks. Unfortunately, you can only read and write on them from within the program (the disks don't show up on your desktop). When you're running Apple File Exchange, you can insert a PC disk, select files to copy or remove, and so on. The built-in "default translation" usually works pretty well. When you quit Apple File Exchange, any PC disks in your drives are automatically ejected.

This is admittedly kludgey, albeit free. If you're doing a lot of transfers between your PC and a Macintosh, you should purchase one of three relatively inexpensive programs for the Mac. PC Exchange, DOS Mounter, and AccessPC let you insert disks and they appear right on the desktop, like Macintosh disks. All three of the programs let you map PC extensions (see "PC Naming Conventions," below) to Macintosh application file types so that you can double-click on PC files to open them (again, just like from Macintosh disks). DOS Mounter and AccessPC let you mount PC SyQuest cartridges, too.

Note that all the programs we just talked about can format PC disks, too. In fact, the Macintosh usually reads PC disks that were formatted on a Macintosh even better than the disks that were formatted on a PC.

There are also programs that let PCs mount Macintosh disks. We use Mac-in-DOS with pretty good results. However, for various technical reasons we don't really need to get into, we typically recommend that people store and transfer their files using PC-formatted disks only.

▼▼▼▼▼▼▼▼▼▼▼▼▼▼▼▼▼▼▼▼▼▼▼▼▼

Tip: Translations vs. Universal File Formats. While you can now move QuarkXPress files between PCs and Macs, there's still no such thing as a "universal" QuarkXPress document format that's identical on both platforms. Each time QuarkXPress opens a document saved on the opposite platform, it must translate the file. The file name doesn't change, but—as one Quark tech-support person puts it—"the dirty bit is on," so you should immediately save the file. And since some information gets lost (as we'll describe) or needs to be fixed when you translate files, we'd recommend you keep your cross-platform transfers to the minimum necessary to finish a job. Remember: fewer translations equals less clean-up.

▼▼▼▼▼▼▼▼▼▼▼▼▼▼▼▼▼▼▼▼▼▼▼▼▼▼▼▼▼▼

File Names, Types, and Creators

The first hassle (though minor) in moving files from one platform to another is that PCs and Macintoshes "see" files differently. On the Macintosh, every file has several attributes attached to it, including file type and creator. These are four-letter keys that tell the Macintosh what sort of file it is and what program generated it. For example, when you double-click on a file, the Mac looks at the file's creator to see what application to start up.

In the PC world, of course, it's simpler: no file types, no file creators—only file names. PC files all have names that are eight-dot-three. That means that the name can be no longer than eight letters, followed by a period, and ending with a three-letter extension; for example, 8LTRBLUS.TXT. This extension provides all the information (and it ain't much) about the file's type and creator.

Moving from Pc to Mac

When you're trying to open a QuarkXPress for Windows document on a Macintosh, you must make certain that the document has either the correct three-letter extension or the correct file type and creator. If you move a file from the Macintosh to Windows without the right extension, and can't see the file in an Open dialog box, you should switch the File Types popup menu option in the dialog box to "All Files *.*".

If you move the file from Windows to the Macintosh, the document icon may look like a blank page. But as long as the file has the proper DOS extension (.QXD) QuarkXPress can still "see" and open the file on the Macintosh.

If you want the file to open when you double-click on it in the Finder, or your PC disk mounter doesn't map the extensions to the proper file type, you have to change the file type and creator. The easy way is to open it with QuarkXPress, if possible, and do a Save As, renaming it if you want (otherwise it overwrites the original). This works as long as the file is a proper QuarkXPress file and has the .QXD file name extension.

You can also use Macintosh utilities such as PrairieSoft's Disk-Top (in the Technical mode), Apple File Exchange, ResEdit, or the shareware program FileTyper to manually change the type and creator. Also, the three utilities for mounting PC disks all have a cool feature that lets you automatically assign a proper file type and creator based on the PC file's three-letter extension (see Figure B-1).

So what are the appropriate file types and creators? Documents created in QuarkXPress 3.1 or later on the Macintosh have a creator code of XPR3; documents created in version 3.0 have a creator code of XPRS. The file type depends on what kind of file it is: documents are XDOC, templates are XTMP, and libraries are XLIB. These are the only kinds of documents on the Mac that will ever show up in QuarkXPress's file-opening dialog box; you'll never see a Microsoft Word or FileMaker Pro file in there, because QuarkXPress filters out all files except those which have these three specific file types.

Figure B-1
Mapping extensions to applications and document types

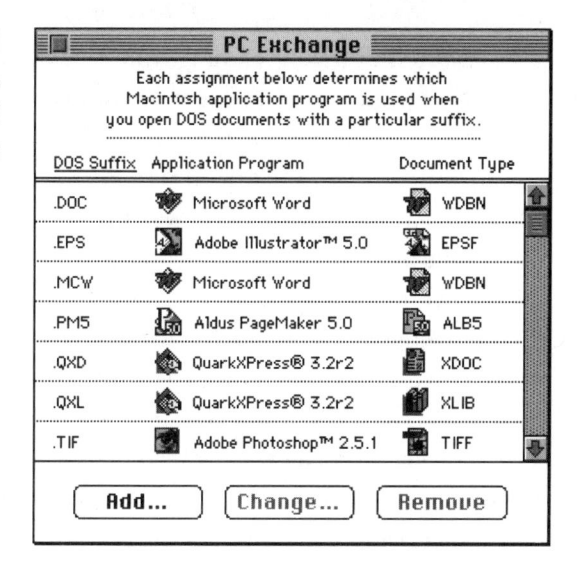

DOS Suffix	Application Program	Document Type
.DOC	Microsoft Word	WDBN
.EPS	Adobe Illustrator™ 5.0	EPSF
.MCW	Microsoft Word	WDBN
.PM5	Aldus PageMaker 5.0	ALB5
.QXD	QuarkXPress® 3.2r2	XDOC
.QXL	QuarkXPress® 3.2r2	XLIB
.TIF	Adobe Photoshop™ 2.5.1	TIFF

Note that when you open a QuarkXPress for Windows file on the Macintosh, the Open dialog box tells you that it's a PC file; when you click Open, it gives you a message saying it's converting the file.

Mac to Pc: Filenames and Extensions

While Macintosh users who are used to 31-character names find the eight-dot-three filename limit for PC files absolutely infuriating, for us PC users, it's just another creative opportunity. You can use almost any combination of characters you want in a PC filename except punctuation (see "Tip: Careful with Your Naming," below).

It's really easy to change the file type and creator for a PC file while on either a Macintosh or a PC: just change the three-letter extension. The eight-character filename can be whatever you want, but the relevant extensions are .QXD for documents, .QXL for libraries, and .QXT for templates. If you assign a legal name to a document using these extensions, it should be easily opened by QuarkXPress for Windows, either by double-clicking in the Windows File Manager, or from QuarkXPress for Windows. You can also select "All Files *.*" in the popup menu in the Open dialog box, and it shows even files with the wrong extensions.

Note that if you (or your colleagues) are using a Mac-based PC-disk mounter or a file server, you can save a little trouble by always adding the dot-three extension name to the Macintosh file. Even though the first part of the name is truncated, the dot-three part is retained. (This won't work when you use communications programs or other means to transfer files.)

If you don't give a proper DOS name and extension to a document while it's still on the Macintosh, its name appears strangely altered and truncated when it's transferred to the PC.

▼▼▼▼▼▼▼▼▼▼▼▼▼▼▼▼▼▼▼▼▼▼▼▼▼▼▼▼

Tip: Careful with Your Naming. The filenaming conventions used by the Macintosh and the PC are so different that, for some people, they become the central issue in cross-platform compatibility. Macintoshes use 31-character names, while PCs use eight characters plus three extension characters after a period (eight-dot-three). The two most dangerous traps in file naming are name size and characters within the name.

▶ **Name size.** When you move a document from the Macintosh to the PC and the name of that document is longer than eight letters or numbers (alphanumerics), the operating system generates a new name in eight-dot-three form. For instance, if you use Apple's PC Exchange software on the Macintosh, and move a document called "David's Document" to a PC floppy disk, the name comes across as !DAVID'S.DOC.

If you open this file in QuarkXPress for Windows and then save it again with the same name, chances are the file will return to the Macintosh with its full name. That's because PC Exchange (and other similar utilities) stores the full name inside a directory called RESOURCE.FRK. However, if you either move the file to a disk without moving RESOURCE.FRK or save the file with a different name, the full name is lost.

▶ **Characters.** The only character you can't use in a Macintosh file name is a colon. That's because the Macintosh operating system uses colons internally to keep track of file paths (what files are within what folders). DOS-based systems, however, use lots of these "internal" characters for all sorts of stuff. That means you can't use spaces, question marks, asterisks, slashes, backslashes, equal signs, plus signs, or angle brackets in DOS filenames.

Because of these limitations, we reluctantly recommend that—if you have to move your files around a lot—you use the lowest common denominator for all your graphics and document names. That means only PC files names (your Mac friends will just have to suffer).

What Does (and Doesn't) Transfer

Physically moving your QuarkXPress files between platforms and successfully opening them is only half the job of transferring files. In general, all page-layout, text, and picture information comes across just fine in either direction, as do any changes you've made to the General, Typographic, and Tool preferences. Also, any colors, style sheets, and H&J settings you've defined in the document generally transfer without a hitch. However, you'd better be aware of what doesn't get transferred. QuarkXPress documents on each platform are almost identical, but that "almost" can trip you up if you're not careful.

Frames. We have very mixed feelings about the Frame Editor program on the Macintosh. It can do some nice things, but mostly we think it fits best in the Trash. But who listens to us? Lots of people are using custom frames and getting reasonable results. However, Frame Editor doesn't exist in QuarkXPress for Windows. In version 3.1 of the Windows version, custom frames didn't even show up correctly on the screen, let alone print properly. Now, in version 3.3, any special frames you've created or assigned on the Mac will travel over to the PC, and usually show up and print fine. Of course, you still can't edit those bitmapped frames, as there's no Frame Editor utility on the PC (thank goodness).

Color-contrast adjustment. In QuarkXPress for Windows, you can't adjust the contrast of color bitmap images, as you can in the Macintosh version (See Figure J on the color pages for an example of why you won't care that you can't do this). However, any brightness/contrast adjustments made to a bitmap in the Mac version aren't lost when you transfer your file to Windows; you just can't change them unless you bring them back to a Mac. But let's get serious for a moment: why would you want to use QuarkXPress's color-contrast functions? Photoshop is a much better tool for this sort of thing.

XPress Preferences. On the Macintosh it's called XPress Preferences; on the PC it's called XPRESS.PRF. Either way, they do the same thing, but are not interchangeable. There is no good way to move a preferences file from one platform to the other, but fortunately, that's not something that many people need to do. All the document-level preferences are saved within the document itself, and almost all of them translate perfectly (Auto Ligatures is one notable exception). When you open a Macintosh file in QuarkXPress for Windows, you're almost always prompted with the "XPress Preferences does not match" dialog box. We typically just click the Use Document Preferences button.

Character set remapping. Probably the biggest hassle in transferring files between platforms is character-set remapping. The problem here is that Macintosh and Windows font character sets don't match completely. All the basic "low-ASCII" characters (letters, numbers, punctuation) map just fine, but special characters can sometimes get messed up.

If a special character shows up in both Macintosh and Windows typefaces, QuarkXPress does its best to map them correctly. But there's only so far it can go. Table B-1 shows a list of characters that are commonly found in Windows and Macintosh fonts that have no equivalent on the opposite platform (unless you switch to a special typeface). You can also use this table to select special characters if you know you'll be printing on the other platform.

Table B-1
Special characters that map differently in Windows and on the Macintosh

Windows	ANSI code	◄ maps to ► Macintosh	ASCII Code
Š	138	˘	255
š	154	π	185
¦	166	ı	245
²	178	≈	197
³	179	Δ	198
¹	185	◊	215
¼	188	⁄	218
½	189	fi	222
¾	190	fl	223
Ð	208	￼	240
×	215	˘	249
Ý	221	˙	250
ý	253	˝	253

Note that the mathematical symbols that seem to appear in every PostScript font on the Macintosh are often just mapped from the Symbol font. So unless the font you're using has the math symbols built in—unfortunately there's no good way to find this out without Fontographer or another font-editing program—several characters won't transfer correctly. See Table B-2 for where the mathematical symbols are found in standard Macintosh encoding, and where you can find them in the Symbol font itself. (Key combinations are listed for the Macintosh; see Appendix C, *ANSI Codes*, for the ANSI code in Windows.).

Ligatures. One of the biggest losses in going from Mac to PC is ligatures. The "fi" and "fl" ligature characters on the Macintosh are not to be found on the PC. That's right: any ligatures used in a Mac document go bye-bye when they're opened by QuarkXPress for Windows. If you've used them in a Macintosh document, or aren't sure whether you did, you should use Find/Change to change them back to normal character pairs before transferring the file.

However, Quark 3.2 and later on the Macintosh introduced the automatic ligatures option, which keeps the characters as "f," "i," and "l" in the text but substitute the ligature character on

Table B-2
Commonly used math symbols

These symbols are found in most Macintosh fonts. Press the listed keystrokes on the Macintosh to create these symbols.

Name	Looks like	In most fonts	Symbol font
Division	÷	Option-/	Option-Shift-P
Plus or minus	±	Option-Shift-=	Option-Shift-=
Greater or equal	≥	Option-period	Option-period
Lesser or equal	≤	Option-comma	Option-3
Approximate equal	≈	Option-X	Option-9
Not equal	≠	Option-=	Option-P
Infinity	∞	Option-5	Option-8
Partial differential	∂	Option-D	Option-D
Integral	∫	Option-B	Option-Shift-;
Florin	ƒ	Option-F	Option-7
Capital omega	Ω	Option-Z	Shift-W
Capital delta	Δ	Option-J	Shift-D
Product	Π	Option-Shift-P	Shift-P
Summation	Σ	Option-W	Shift-S
Pi	π	Option-P	P
Radical	√	Option-V	Option-/

screen and in output. However, this feature isn't supported under Windows since the ligature characters don't exist. If you move a Mac file with automatic ligatures over to Windows, the ligatures go away (and because of that, you may get some text reflow; see Figure B-2). But at least you have fi, fl, or ffi, rather than some strange little character that you have to search for and replace.

Figure B-2
Windows warning about automatic ligatures

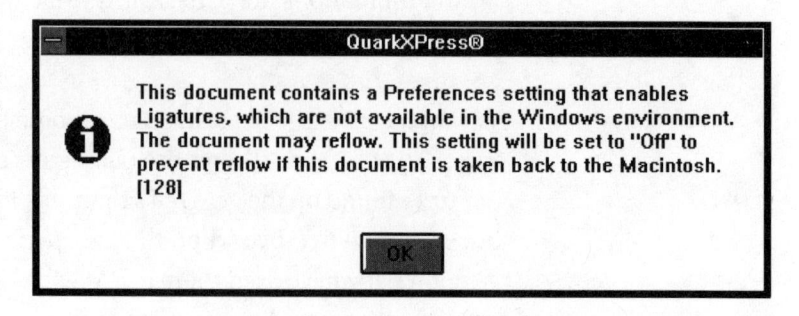

> **QuarkXPress®**
>
> ⓘ This document contains a Preferences setting that enables Ligatures, which are not available in the Windows environment. The document may reflow. This setting will be set to "Off" to prevent reflow if this document is taken back to the Macintosh. [128]
>
> [OK]

The second solution is to use a program like Fontographer or FontMonger to either mess around with the ASCII numbers assigned to ligatures in Windows fonts, or create new fonts on the PC that include the ligatures. We only recommend the latter if you're particularly brave, and aren't working on a deadline. Or you can resort to Expert Set fonts from Adobe and other font vendors, and use the Find/Change dialog box to replace fi's and fl's with Expert Set characters. The Expert Set characters are typically the same in both Macintosh and Windows versions of the fonts.

Font metrics. Font metrics describe the width of each character in a font, and the kerning pairs for those characters. On the Macintosh, PostScript fonts store their character widths and kerning pair values in the screen font files. Macintosh TrueType fonts store metrics entirely in the printer font (the screen fonts contain just bitmaps). On the PC, the font metrics for PostScript fonts are located in .PFM files; metrics (and outlines) for TrueType fonts are found in .TTF files.

However, no matter where the metrics of a font may reside, you need to be aware that the metrics of a PC font may differ from those of a Macintosh font, even if they're from the same company. We don't know why this is, but it's certainly a major problem when moving files back and forth. If the metrics change, then the text in a document reflows. Sometimes this is hardly a problem, and other times it can spell hours of work.

It's a good idea to have a printed proof of a Macintosh document handy after you've imported it into your Windows version of QuarkXPress (or vice versa). That way you can check to see if the layout got altered in the transfer. When proofing the document, look for any widows or orphans that may result from minute differences in font metrics. If you notice a problem, you can sometimes adjust the spacing parameters through kerning or tracking to compensate for the differences in font metrics.

Forbidden fonts. There are certain typefaces that exist only on Macs or only on Windows machines. You should never use them on documents that you intend to shuffle between platforms, unless you enjoy spending a lot of time staring at the Font Usage dialog box. On the Macintosh, avoid using system fonts such as Chicago, Geneva, Monaco, and New York (a good rule, with some exceptions, is never to use a font named after a city). In Windows, avoid fonts such as "Helv", "System", or "Tms Rmn".

If you open a file and its document fonts are missing, Quark-XPress gives you a chance to immediately change them. If you click Continue, it ignores the missing fonts and replaces them with a default font. If you click List Fonts, you get the Missing Fonts dialog box (see Figure B-3). You can then select fonts that you want changed, and replace them with an available font.

Figure B-3
Missing Fonts dialog box

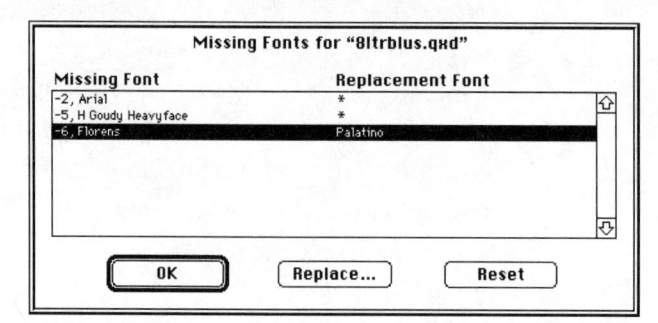

QuarkXPress catches missing fonts if you've used them anywhere in your document, including in style sheets and on master pages. In other words, even if you don't use a particular style sheet or master page anywhere in your document, you get notified.

Kerning information. If you've spent a lot of time making kerning tables within QuarkXPress's Kern/Track Editor, you might want to save the hassle of doing them over on another platform. We're happy to note that you can move the kerning information from the PC to the Macintosh (or vice versa) by exporting the information as a text file (click the Export button in the Edit Kerning dialog box) and importing into the other program (use the Append button in the same dialog box in the Windows version).

The only problem with this technique is that the fonts on each platform are sometimes different, even if they're the same font from the same company—just like with the metrics. Therefore, the kerning used on the Macintosh might not always apply precisely to the PC font.

Transferring Graphics

The last (but certainly not the least) of your problems when transferring files between platforms is graphics. In fact, this is one of the least-understood issues in cross-platform compatibility. The basic problem is that graphics, like fonts, are described in different formats on the two platforms.

The good news is that QuarkXPress is smart enough to do most of the translation work for you. No matter which platform you're working on, QuarkXPress can import files in either IBM or Macintosh format. It simply doesn't care whether you're on a Macintosh importing a PC format file, or on a Windows machine importing a Macintosh TIFF file. This is great, but if you're using pictures in your documents, you still might have some work ahead of you.

Graphic links. The first and most basic problem is that links to EPS and TIFF images can get messed up in the transfer—the Picture Usage dialog box shows the image as either missing or modified. You can remove the chance of this happening by keeping the images in the same folder as the QuarkXPress document you're opening, and by always naming files with the PC eight-dot-three convention.

If you send a document to the Mac to work on it temporarily, the picture links to the files on the PC are retained (as long as they aren't changed on the Mac). Similarly, links within Macintosh documents are retained when you move a file to your PC and back, as long as you don't change them on the PC. The trick is to update a picture only if you're certain you won't be sending the QuarkXPress file back to its original location, or if you absolutely must print with current versions of artwork regardless of the platform.

EPS screen previews. The next thing you need to be careful of is how images are transferred between the Macintosh and PC. Screen previews are handled differently on each platform. When you create an EPS with Macintosh preview, the screen preview is stored in what's called the file's resource fork. The problem is that resource forks don't exist on the PC, so if you move the graphic over and try to import it into QuarkXPress for Windows, you can't see the preview. In fact, without a screen preview, all you see on the screen is a gray box where the picture should be. Note that the picture still prints properly, even if you can't see it on screen.

There are two solutions to this problem: importing into Mac XPress and then transferring the document to the PC, or saving the picture as PC EPS.

▶ **QuarkXPress for Macintosh.** Because QuarkXPress saves a preview image of each picture within your documents, you can bring those documents to the PC and still see the preview image on screen. The images are linked to the EPS files, so even if you move the image and the QuarkXPress document to the PC, you can print properly, as well. Even auto-runarounds are transferred okay.

▶ **PC EPS files.** The second solution for the EPS screen preview problem is to give your EPS files PC previews. Adobe Illustrator, Aldus FreeHand, Adobe Photoshop, the new Apple/Adobe laser printer driver, and a slew of other programs let you save or export a file as a PC EPS—with a preview that's saved in the data fork rather than the resource fork. Therefore, when you move it over to the PC, you can import it, screen preview and all. This is our favorite method because most of the Macintosh and PC applications that we use can read or import this PC format just as easily as the Macintosh format. Again, this is working with the lowest common denominator, but there's hardly a penalty paid except for the anemic file name.

File names and extensions. Just as QuarkXPress documents need to have their names changed, graphics that get transferred to the PC also need appropriate file extensions or else the program won't be able to recognize them as graphics. That means they'll often need to be renamed to have a three-letter .TIF, .EPS, or .PCT extension.

File types to avoid. Some formats to avoid: PICTs contained in Mac documents and transferred to PCs sometimes print poorly or not at all (just like on Macs!), and, WMF pictures in PC documents may (similarly) not print correctly on the Mac. Sometimes EPS images from the Mac look wrong on screen after they're transferred. Often if you simply re-import the picture, it'll clear up any problems. And when it comes to OLE linked files, forget it. If you've used OLE to link to a file on your PC, that link gets lost for all time as soon as the file is opened and saved by QuarkXPress for Macintosh. Similarly, if a Macintosh user has subscribed to an edition using Publish and Subscribe, that information is lost when the document's opened on your PC.

▼▼▼▼▼▼▼▼▼▼▼▼▼▼▼▼▼▼▼▼▼▼▼▼▼▼

Tip: Transferring Libraries. We love it when the folks at Quark say things like, "You can't do that." We take it as a personal challenge. For example, Quark said, clear as a Texas sky in June, that you can't move libraries between a Macintosh and a PC. After some intense thought, sweat, and caffeine, what we found was that Quark really should have said, "You cannot move libraries between a Macintosh and a PC *easily*."

If you have a library that you absolutely must take from one platform to another, you can. However, it's what we call a kludge—pronounced "kloodge." (Our friend Steve Broback recently came up with the best definition of "kludge" we've heard: "It's Yiddish for 'duct tape.'" It's something you use at the last moment to fix a problem, but for which you hope there'll be a better solution soon.) The trick is in understanding what libraries really are.

A QuarkXPress library is simply a QuarkXPress document with some additional preview and labeling information. That means that you can actually open a QuarkXPress library within Quark-XPress as a document. If you move a Macintosh library to the PC, open it by either selecting "All Types *.*" in the Open dialog box or by changing the file name extension to .QXD.

What you see is each library entry on a separate page of a big QuarkXPress document. Each page is the maximum size allowable—48 inches by 48 inches. If you don't see the library entry, look in the upper-left corner of the page. Now you can open a new library in QuarkXPress for Windows and use the Item tool to drag the old page items into the library, one page at a time. Of course, this is not only a pain in the lower back, but you also lose all your labels.

Modern Myths

We have very mixed feelings about cross-platform compatibility. On the one hand, moving document and graphics between Macintoshes and PCs sometimes works like a charm. On the other hand, sometimes the strangest things happen and it can cause horrible nightmare scenarios (of course, right on the eve of a deadline). Although QuarkXPress is very similar on the two platforms, and tries its hardest to make cross-platform issues irrelevant, there are clearly issues that are beyond its control.

Nonetheless, because more and more people are finding themselves in that "third-culture" arena—where they are literate on two or more platforms—transferring files is becoming almost commonplace. With the introduction of Power Macintoshes that can emulate both Windows and Macintosh, we may see an explosion of compatibility problems—or (thinking optimistically) solutions. Whatever the case, with a dose of experience and a patient hand, you may soon find yourself making the process more or less painless.

APPENDIX C

ANSI CODES

ANSI Code	Times	Symbol	Zapf Dingbats
1–45 No characters			
46	.	.	✎
47	/	/	✏
48	0	0	✐
49	1	1	✇
50	2	2	✈
51	3	3	✓
52	4	4	✔
53	5	5	✕
54	6	6	✖
55	7	7	✗
56	8	8	✘
57	9	9	✢
58	:	:	✣
59	;	;	✤
60	<	<	✥
61	=	=	†
62	>	>	✞
63	?	?	✟
64	@	≅	✠
65	A	A	✡
66	B	B	✢
67	C	X	✣

521

ANSI Code	Times	Symbol	Zapf Dingbats
68	D	Δ	♣
69	E	E	❖
70	F	Φ	◆
71	G	Γ	◇
72	H	H	★
73	I	I	☆
74	J	ϑ	✪
75	K	K	☆
76	L	Λ	★
77	M	M	★
78	N	N	★
79	O	O	★
80	P	Π	☆
81	Q	Θ	✱
82	R	P	✲
83	S	Σ	✳
84	T	T	✴
85	U	Υ	✵
86	V	ς	★
87	W	Ω	✷
88	X	Ξ	✸
89	Y	Ψ	✹
90	Z	Z	✺
91	[	[	✻
92	\	∴	✼
93	]	]	✽
94	^	⊥	✾
95	_	_	✿
96	`		❀
97	a	α	❁
98	b	β	❂
99	c	χ	❃
100	d	δ	❄
101	e	ε	❅
102	f	φ	❆
103	g	γ	❇

ANSI CODES

ANSI Code	Times	Symbol	Zapf Dingbats
104	h	η	✳
105	i	ι	✲
106	j	φ	✴
107	k	κ	✶
108	l	λ	●
109	m	μ	○
110	n	ν	■
111	o	ο	❏
112	p	π	❐
113	q	θ	❑
114	r	ρ	❒
115	s	σ	▲
116	t	τ	▼
117	u	υ	◆
118	v	ϖ	❖
119	w	ω	❘
120	x	ξ		
121	y	ψ		
122	z	ζ	∎
123	{	{	'
124	|	|	'
125	}	}	"
126	~	~	"
127–129 No characters			
130	,		
131	*f*		
132	,,		
133	…		
134	†		
135	‡		
136	ˆ		
137	‰		
138	Š		
139	‹		
140	Œ		
141–144 No characters			

ANSI Code	Times	Symbol	Zapf Dingbats
145	'		
146	'		
147	"		
148	"		
149	•		
150	–		
151	—		
152	~		
153	™		
154	š		
155	›		
156	œ		
157–158 No characters			
159	Ÿ		
160 No character			
161	¡	ϒ	✁
162	¢	′	✂
163	£	≤	✃
164	¤	/	♥
165	¥	∞	✄
166	¦	f	✆
167	§	♣	✇
168	¨	♦	♣
169	©	♥	♦
170	ª	♠	♥
171	«	↔	♠
172	¬	←	①
173	-	↑	②
174	®	→	③
175	¯	↓	④
176	°	°	⑤
177	±	±	⑥
178	²	″	⑦
179	³	≥	⑧
180	´	×	⑨
181	µ	∝	⑩
182	¶	∂	❶

ANSI CODES

ANSI Code	Times	Symbol	Zapf Dingbats
183	.	•	❷
184	,	÷	❸
185	ı	≠	❹
186	º	≡	❺
187	»	≈	❻
188	¼	…	❼
189	½	|	❽
190	¾	—	❾
191	¿	↵	❿
192	À	ℵ	①
193	Á	ℑ	②
194	Â	ℜ	③
195	Ã	℘	④
196	Ä	⊗	⑤
197	Å	⊕	⑥
198	Æ	∅	⑦
199	Ç	∩	⑧
200	È	∪	⑨
201	É	⊃	⑩
202	Ê		
203	Ë	⊄	❷
204	Ì	⊂	❸
205	Í	⊆	❹
206	Î	∈	❺
207	Ï	∉	❻
208	Ð	∠	❼
209	Ñ	∇	❽
210	Ò	®	❾
211	Ó	©	❿
212	Ô	™	→
213	Õ	∏	→
214	Ö	√	↔
215	×	·	↕
216	Ø	¬	↘
217	Ù	∧	→
218	Ú	∨	↗
219	Û	⇔	→

Ansi Code	Times	Symbol	Zapf Dingbats
220	Ü	⇐	➔
221	Ý	⇑	→
222	Þ	⇒	→
223	ß	⇓	➡
224	à	◊	➡
225	á	⟨	➡
226	â	®	➢
227	ã	©	➣
228	ä	™	➤
229	å	∑	➥
230	æ	⎛	➡
231	ç	⎜	➧
232	è	⎝	➡
233	é	⎡	⇨
234	ê	⎢	⇨
235	ë	⎣	⇨
236	ì	⎧	⇨
237	í	⎨	⇨
238	î	⎩	⇨
239	ï	⎪	⇨
240	∂		
241	ñ	⟩	⇨
242	ò	∫	⊃
243	ó	⌠	➤
244	ô	⎮	➘
245	õ	⌡	➤
246	ö	⎞	➚
247	÷	⎟	➘
248	ø	⎠	➤
249	ù	⎤	➚
250	ú	⎥	→
251	û	⎦	↔
252	ü	⎫	➤
253	ý	⎬	➤
254	þ	⎭	⇒
255	ÿ		

APPENDIX D

XPRESS TAGS

The following is a complete listing of the XPress Tags coding and tagging language. By inserting these tags in text files, you can specify almost every typographic control in QuarkXPress. Use at your own risk (and to your own advantage).

Every XPress Tags text file should start with a version and platform code. For the XPress Tags filter included with QuarkXPress for Windows version 3.3, the first line of the file should read: "<v1.70><e1>".

Both the "v" and the "e" should be lowercase. If you're moving an XPress Tags file from the Macintosh, the code will read "e0" instead of "e1". If you change the code to "e1", QuarkXPress handles character mapping for you. Don't change the code, and it doesn't.

If you don't include a version code at all, the meaning of baseline shift values is reversed. With no version code, "<b2>" means text is shifted down two points. With the version code, "<b2>" means text is shifted up.

All codes that are in angle brackets can be combined within one set of angle brackets. For example, "<BI*d(1,3)>" changes the formatting to bold, italic, and with an initial cap.

Character Formats

Style	Code[1]
Plain	`<P>`
Bold	`<B>`
Italic	`<I>`
Outline	`<O>`
Shadow	`<S>`
Underline	`<U>`
Word underline	`<W>`
Strikethrough	`</>`
All caps	`<K>`
Small caps	`<H>`
Superscript	`<+>`
Subscript	`<->`
Superior	`<V>`
Type style of current style sheet	`<$>`

Attribute	Code[2]	Value
Typeface	`<f"name">`	Name of font
Size	`<z#>`	Points
Color	`<c"name">`	Name of color (the four process colors and white can be specified by C, M, Y, K, and W, without quotes, as in `<cY>`)
Shade	`<s#>`	Percentage
Horizontal scale	`<h#>`	Percentage
Kern next 2 characters	`<k#>`	1/200 em
Track	`<t#>`	1/200 em
Baseline shift	`<b#>`	Points

[1] *These codes act as toggle switches; the first time they're encountered, the format is activated. The second time, the format is deactivated. Note the similarity to formatting keystrokes.*

[2] *In these codes, "#" should be replaced with a number. This number can be set to the same precision as QuarkXPress's measurements (tenths, hundreths, or thousandths of a unit). The measurement units used are shown. If you replace "#" or any other code value with a dollar sign ($), QuarkXPress uses the formatting of the current style sheet.*

Paragraph Formats

Attribute	Code[3]	Value
Left-align	<*L>	None
Center-align	<*C>	None
Right-align	<*R>	None
Justify	<*J>	None
Paragraph formats	<*p(#,#,#,#,#,#,G or g)>	Left Indent, First Line, Right Indent, Leading, Space Before, Space After, Lock to Baseline Grid (G=lock, g=don't lock)
Drop cap	<*d(chars,lines)>	Character Count and Line Count
Keep With Next ¶	<*kn1> or <*kn0>	1=keep with next, 0=don't keep with next
Keep Lines Together	<*kt(A)> or <*kt(start,end)>	"A"=all; start and end are number of lines
Set Tab Stops	<*t(#,#,"character")>	Position, Alignment (0=left, 1=center, 2=right, 4=decimal, 5=comma), Fill character[4]
H&J	<*h"name">	Name of H&J specification
Rule Above	<*ra(#,#,"name",#,#,#,#)>	See "Rule Below"
Rule Below	<*rb(#,#,"name",#,#,#,#)>	Width, Style (from 1–11), Name of color, Shade (percent), From Left, From Right, Offset (if you specify Offset as a percentage place a percent sign after the number)

Special Characters

Character	Code
Soft return	<\n>
Discretionary return	<\d>

[3] In these codes, "#" should be replaced with a measurement in points. If you replace "#" or any other code value with a dollar sign ($), QuarkXPress uses the formatting of the current style sheet. If the code requires multiple values, every value must be present and delineated by a comma.

[4] Align on is specified by replacing the alignment number by the character contained within quotation marks. QuarkXPress 3.3 allows two-character tab leaders.

Character	Code
Indent Here	<\i>
Previous text box page #	<\2>
Current text box page #	<\3>
Next text box page #	<\4>
New column	<\c>
New box	<\b>
@	<\@>
<	<\<>
\	<\\>
ASCII character	<\#decimal value>[5]
Standard space	<\s>[6]
en space	<\f>[6]
Flex space	<\q>[6]
Punctuation space	<\p>[6]
En dash	<\#208>[7]
Em dash	<\#209>[7]
Return (new paragraph)	<\#13>[7]
Tab	<\#9>[7]
Right-aligned tab	<\t>

Style Sheets

Description	Code	Values
Define style sheet	@name=	Name of style sheet; follow the equal sign with definition
Use "Normal"	@$:	
Use "No Style"	@:	
Apply style sheet	@name:	Name of style sheet

General codes

Code	Means...
<v#>	XPress Tags filter version number. QuarkXPress 3.2 came with version 1.60; QuarkXPress 3.3 comes with 1.70.
<e#>	Platform version number. 0=Mac, 1=Windows.

[5] Note that the number sign must precede the ASCII character value.
[6] Precede these codes with an exclamation point to make them nonbreaking. For example, <\!s>.
[7] You can also type type the character itself on the Macintosh.

APPENDIX E

RESOURCES

We just can't emphasize it enough: QuarkXPress does not exist in a vacuum. There are literally hundreds (thousands?) of utilities and applications to use alongside QuarkXPress, not to mention fonts, clip art, and great doo-dads to make computing more fun. In this appendix we cover almost all the programs that we've discussed throughout the book, along with others that you should at least know about, if not run right out and buy.

XTensions

We first covered XTensions and how they can add functionally to QuarkXPress back in the *Introduction*. We mentioned several commercial vendors, but there's no way we could talk about them all. At press time, there are over 60 different XTensions shipping for the Windows version of QuarkXPress. They range anywhere from $30 to $400, and while many of them are pretty simple utilities (such as NudgeIt, which lets you move objects around your page by preset amounts by clicking in a small palette), many add a significant amount of functionality to QuarkXPress.

To find out more about what XTensions are available, contact The XChange at the address below, and ask for their Quark XTensions catalog. You can also find freeware or shareware XTensions on electronic bulletin boards such as CompuServe.

One of the primary developers of XTensions is Quark itself. They're committed to releasing a similar if not identical XTension on the Windows platform for every XTension they do for the Macintosh edition. And on the Macintosh the list is extensive (no pun intended). These are all free if you get them from a bulletin board system or a users group (they alone may justify the cost of getting a modem).

▼▼▼▼▼▼▼▼▼▼▼▼▼▼▼▼▼▼▼▼▼▼▼▼▼▼

Bob and his many relatives
Quark Inc.
1800 Grant St.
Denver, CO 80203
303/894-8888
Product Information Line: 800/788-7835

Quark has produced some of the most widely-used XTensions, partly because many of them are "free" (if you buy them directly from Quark, they charge you around $25 for disk duplication, shipping and handling) and partly because they're really useful. Several of them are simply XTensions we think you *must* have.

Bob and Son of Bob. The Bob and Son of Bob XTensions—BOB.XXT and SOBOB.XXT—are for version 3.1 only. They add a number of features—such as a keystroke for jumping to the View percentage field and the ability to do multiplication and division in QuarkXPress's palettes and dialog boxes—that Quark has now included in the newest version of the program. A few of them haven't been bundled in, but it doesn't matter; you shouldn't use these with version 3.3 anyway.

Thing-a-ma-Bob. Thing-a-ma-Bob—called TOMBOB.XXT—includes Make Fraction/Make Price, Value Converter, Remove Manual

Kerning, and Word Space Tracking. It's free, so why not add these functions? This is also available on the Quark Goodies Disk (see the card in the back of the book for more information).

Bobzilla. Bobzilla—called BOBZILLA.XXT—includes Go-To-Page (what we call popup page), Line Check, Super Step & Repeat, and Full Resolution TIFF. Many people get by without this, but you shouldn't: it's free, it's cool, it's on our disk.

Cool Blends. Cool Blends—COOLBLEN.XXT—is now included with QuarkXPress, though it's still a separate file in QuarkXPress's XTENSION subdirectory. This XTension adds five blend types to QuarkXPress (in addition to Linear, which is built in): Mid-Linear, Rectangular, Diamond, Circular, and Full Circular. See Appendix F, *What's New in 3.3*, for more information. If you use a Cool Blend and give the file to someone else, they must have the same or a later version of the XTension for the blends to work correctly.

▼ ▼

XTension of the Month Club
XPress XPerts XChange (X3)
The XChange
PO Box 270578
Fort Collins, CO 80527
(800/788-7557 or 303/229-0620; Fax 303/229-9773
CompuServe: 75300,2337 or America OnLine: XChange

If great companies develop out of great needs, then the XChange is destined to fly. One of the biggest problems with getting quality XTensions has been where to go for information, sales, and technical support, since Quark itself doesn't sell third-party XTensions. The XChange is now here on the scene to help. They have agreements with most commercial XTension developers to be XTension Central: they market and sell XTensions (the developers love this because they're usually small shops without the resources to get the word out). And they also handle tech support for many of the XTensions (what they don't know, they know how to find out).

If you need an XTension, but don't know who makes it, or if it even exists, call the XChange. If they don't know of it, they'll pass the idea on to a XTension developer who might create it down the line (or do a custom job for you).

The XChange also has an XTension of the Month Club. As a subscriber ($99 per year), each month you get a free XTension, a demo version of new or existing XTensions, and other software. They'll even send you a newsletter with all sorts of XTension information in it.

The XChange is also the central hub of the XPress XPerts XChange, an international users group for people using QuarkXPress. At the time of this writing, X^3 ("ex-cubed") is in its initial formation stages, but it looks like it will be a great place to acquire QuarkXPress information.

Quark Lab-Paks

If you're teaching or creating a student publication at a college or university, or are a Quark Authorized Training Center or Consultant, you might qualify to buy a 15-user Lab-Pak from Quark that you can use to teach the program. There are a number of restrictions and difficulties with the Lab-Pak, but there are great benefits as well. Most of all, it's a way to get 15 registered, educational-use-only copies of the program for the retail price of a single copy of QuarkXPress (about $800).

Do You Qualify?

The criteria for qualifying to buy the Lab-Pak are pretty simple.

- You plan to use the Lab-Pak copies of QuarkXPress in a course for credit; to produce a student publication; or as part of training offered by an authorized training center or consultant.

- You agree not to use any of the Lab-Pak copies for anything but learning purposes. That is, the Lab-Pak copies can't be used in offices or outside of classrooms (except to produce student publications).

There are a few other particulars which Quark provides as part of the application form. You can call Quark's Education Product Manager at 303/894-8888 to get an application form.

▼▼▼▼▼▼▼▼▼▼▼▼▼▼▼▼▼▼▼▼▼▼▼▼▼▼

Tip: Managing the Lab-Pak. When you get the Lab-Pak, you'll find 15 individually serialized, fully functional copies of QuarkXPress. Because they're individually serialized, you should immediately make backup copies of the 15 installation disks with the serial numbers on them. Quark doesn't devote a lot of time and effort to these educational programs, so if one of your serialized disks goes south, it can take four to six weeks to get a replacement.

▼▼▼▼▼▼▼▼▼▼▼▼▼▼▼▼▼▼▼▼▼▼▼▼▼▼

Tip: Answer Your Mail. Quark's support for the Lab-Pak, as we noted, is pretty minimal. However, they take all correspondence very seriously. They send you a questionnaire every fall, which you must fill out in its entirety, enclose the proper documentation, and return within some stated period of time. If they don't receive the form back by the deadline, they may "unregister" your Lab-Pak. It reverts to a single registered copy of Quark; the other 14 serial numbers are removed as authorized numbers from their database. This is an expensive mistake, so make sure and immediately reply to all mail from Quark.

▼▼▼▼▼▼▼▼▼▼▼▼▼▼▼▼▼▼▼▼▼▼▼▼▼▼

Quark Multi-Paks

While the Lab-Pak is intended and priced for educational use, Quark does offer a "pack" approach for commercial users, too. If you purchase in increments of five copies, you can get a single serial number that works with multiple copies over a network. The pricing in this system is typically not advantageous until you start purchasing 10 or more copies.

On the other hand, the administrative burden is lower: you can install all users from a single set of installation disks. Note that if you sign up for this, Quark registers the program for you and ships it direct from Denver. Of course, sometime their typists are less than perfect; one of David's colleagues at Kodak purchased a 10-pack and for the next year he saw "Eastman Koday" every time he ran QuarkXPress.

Software

QuarkXPress only goes so far, and XTensions—while stretching farther—don't fill all our needs. So we turn to other programs, utilities, and system extensions to make our lives better. In this section, we provide contact information for all of the software we've talked about throughout the book, as well as a few other programs or companies you should probably know about.

Font Downloader
Illustrator
Photoshop
Adobe Dimensions
Adobe Type Manager (ATM)
Adobe Type Reunion (ATR)
Adobe Systems Inc.
1585 Charleston Road
PO Box 7900
Mountain View, CA 94039-7900
415/961-4400

FreeHand
PageMaker
PrePrint
TrapWise
Aldus Corporation
411 First Avenue S., Suite 200
Seattle, WA 98104
206/622-5500

Fontographer
Altsys Corporation
269 W. Renner Road
Richardson, TX 75080
214/680-2060

FontMonger
FontMinder
Ares Software Corp.
561 Pilgrim Drive, Suite D
Foster City, CA 94404

EfiColor profiles
Electronics for Imaging
2855 Campus Drive
San Mateo, CA 94403
415/286-8600

Precision Imagesetter Linearization Software
Kodak Electronic Printing Systems, Inc.
164 Lexington Road
Billerica, MA 01821-3984
508/667-5550

PS Plot
DoubleUP
Legend Communications
54 Rosedale Avenue West
Brampton, ON L6X 1K1, Canada

Microsoft Word
Microsoft Excel
Microsoft
1 Microsoft Way
Redmond, WA 98052-6399
206/882-8080

Mac-in-DOS
Pacific Micro
201 San Antonio Circle, C250
Mountain View, CA 94040

PKZIP
PKWare, Inc.
7545 N. Port Washington Rd.
Glendale, WI 53217

LaserCheck
Advanced PostScript Error Handler
Systems of Merritt, Inc.
2551 Old Dobbin Drive East
Mobile, AL 36695
205/660-1240

Color Calibration Software for Postscript Imagesetters
Technical Publishing Services, Inc.
2205 Sacramento
San Francisco, CA 94115
415/921-8509

Images with Impact
3G Graphics
114 2nd Ave. S, Suite 104
Edwards, WA 98020
800/456-0234

User Groups

X³ (X-cubed)
The XChange
PO Box 270578
Fort Collins, CO 80527
800/788-7557 or 303/229-0620 or fax 303/229-9773
CompuServe: 75300,2337 or America Online: XChange

QuarkXPress Users International
PO Box 170
1 Stiles Road, Suite 106
Salem, NH 03079
603/898-2822 or fax 603/898-3393

Color-Matching Systems

Pantone
55 Knickerbock Rd.
Moonachie, NJ 07074
201/935-5500

TruMatch
25 West 43rd St., Suite 802
New York, NY 10036
212/302-9100

ANPA
Newspaper Association of America
11600 Sunrise Valley Drive
Reston, VA 22091
703/648-1367

Focoltone
Springwater House
Taffs Well, Cardiff
CF4 7QR, United Kingdom
44/222-810-962

Toyo Ink Manufacturing Co. Ltd.
3-13, 2-chome Kyobashi
Chuo-ku, Tokyo 104
81/3-2722-5721

Magazines and Publications

PostScript Language Reference Manual
PostScript Language Program Design
PostScript Language Tutorial and Cookbook
(also known as the Red, Green, and Blue books)
Addison-Wesley Publishing
6 Jacob Way
Reading, MA 01867
617/944-3700

***Digital Color Prepress* volumes 1 and 2**
Agfa Prepress Education Resources
PO Box 7917
Mt. Prospect, IL 60056-7917
800/395-7007

Step-By-Step Electronic Design
Dynamic Graphics
6000 N. Forest Park Drive
Peoria, IL 61614-3592
309/688-8800

The Form of the Book
Hartley & Marks, Inc.
79 Tyee Drive
Point Roberts, WA 98281

U&lc
International Typeface Corporation
2 Hammarskjold Plaza
New York, NY 10017
212/371-0699

Before and After
PageLab
331 J Street, Suite 150
Sacramento, CA 95814-9671

PC World
PC World Communications Inc.
501 Second Street
San Francisco, CA 94107
800/825-7595

How To Boss Your Fonts Around
Learning PostScript
The Little PC Book
The PC is not a typewriter
The Photoshop Wow! Book
QuarkXPress Tips & Tricks
QuarkXPress Visual Quickstart Guide
Real World FreeHand
Real World Scanning & Halftones
The Windows 3.1 Bible
WYSIWYG . . . and many, many more
Peachpit Press
2414 Sixth St.
Berkeley, CA 94710
800/283-9444 or 510/548-4393; Fax: 510/548-5991

Publish!
501 Second Street
San Francisco, CA 94107
800/274-5116

QuarkXPress Unleashed
Random House Electronic Publishing
400 Hahn Road
Westminster, MD 21157

Seybold Report on Desktop Publishing
Seybold Publications
PO Box 644
Media, PA 19063
215/565-2480

PC/Computing
Ziff-Davis Publishing Company
950 Tower Lane, 19th Floor
Foster City, CA 94404

APPENDIX F

WHAT'S NEW IN 3.3

Everything changes. The seasons change, the interest rate changes, even the matzoh-brei at Rose's Deli in Portland has changed (they said it'd never happen). Fortunately, at least one thing has changed for the better: QuarkXPress. Version 3.1 was good, and 3.3 is, well, *g-r-r-r-reat*. We can't be sure, but it sometimes seems like version 3.3 of QuarkXPress has all the great features that Quark's software engineers really wanted to put into version 3.1 but didn't have the time for. We can understand that: we included piles of tips, tricks, and useful production techniques in this appendix that didn't make it into the first edition of this book.

In this appendix we're going to fully cover every feature that's been added to QuarkXPress since version 3.1, plus we're going to throw in a bunch of these great tips. All of the new 3.3 features are detailed in Table F-1, and you'll find "New in 3.3" markers in the margins throughout the book to flag key areas that have changed in this version.

Table F-1
New features in 3.3

Feature	Page
Accents for all caps	581
Alternate Em	581
Appending styles improved	585

ASCII and Binary options	605
Auto Backup	568
Auto Save	566
Collect for Output feature	615
Cool blends additions	597
Copying linked text boxes	562
DIC inks	604
Didot measurement unit change	571
Display Correction	566
Document Layout palette changes	572
Drag-and-drop color swatches	598
Drag-and-drop editing	570
Drag-and-drop picture import	592
Drag-and-drop text import	576
EfiColor	619
EPS colors import	599
Flipping items	556
Font list updating	579
Font substitution	579
Forced justification mode	584
Get Text settings sticky	576
Grabber Hand changes	565
Indent Here improved	579
Installing 3.3	546
Interactive text resizing	558
JPEG import filter	594
Keep with Next ¶ improved	583
Kern to spaceband	592
Low Resolution TIFF	566
Mutliple-Item Undo	563
Next Style	584
Non-PostScript printing changes	606
OLE support	597
Pantone Process and ProSim	603
Photo CD import filter	596
Picture box skew	556
Picture previews	590

Polygonal text boxes	557
PostScript Printer Description files (PPDS)	611
Print dialog box changes	613
Printer Setup changes	611
Q measurement unit	571
Quick item deactivation	550
Revert to last minisave	568
Saving pages as EPS files	609
Smart Quotes	569
Speed Scroll	564
Text box skew	555
Tiling document windows two directions	560
Toyo inks	604
Trapping Preferences	602
Two-character tab leaders	579
Upgrading to 3.3	546
Vertical scaling	581

▼▼▼▼▼▼▼▼▼▼▼▼▼▼▼▼▼▼▼▼▼▼▼▼▼▼▼▼▼▼▼

What Happened to 3.2?

A brief historical note. Many of the improvements we describe here were actually planned for a version that never was: QuarkXPress 3.2 for Windows. Yes, it was slated for delivery—the documentation was even being printed—when Quark quite wisely decided to synchronize the Mac and Windows 3.3 releases of QuarkXPress from now on. So, though the Mac release of the Macintosh version of QuarkXPress 3.2 had been on the streets a while, Quark decided to scrap Windows 3.2 entirely and jump right to 3.3. That's the edition we're exploring here.

Note that this appendix is structured in much the same way as the book's chapters: from *QuarkXPress Basics* (Chapter 1) through *Printing* (Chapter 10). This should make it easy for you to quickly find the information you need.

EfiColor. One improvement in 3.3 that isn't covered in this appendix is the EfiColor color-management system (introduced on the Macintosh in version 3.2). EfiColor is a combination of an XTension and a background processor that improves the relationship between the colors you see on screen and what comes out of a printer or off a printing press. We discuss EfiColor thoroughly in Appendix G.

QuarkXPress Basics

Quark hasn't changed XPress's graphical user interface (GUI) too much since version 3.1. However, they did listen carefully to their users' wish lists and added some really cool features, like improved palettes, a bunch of new preferences, nifty commands for arranging windows, and some subtle differences in magnifying parts of a page. Let's look at each new change.

Installing and Upgrading

Let's start from the very beginning. If you registered your copy of QuarkXPress for Windows before March 31, 1993, you're going to get an "automatic upgrade" (that is, a free one) in the mail. If you haven't, call Quark and make sure they have your latest address and other information. (If you bought your copy from someone and didn't fill out the ownership transfer forms then see "Tip: If You Sell Out," below.) This is Quark's way of rewarding early adopters of the Windows version of the program.

If you registered your copy of 3.1 after March 31, 1993, the upgrade to 3.3 costs $150 if you order within 90 days of 3.3's ship date. If you wait and order after 90 days from the ship date, the upgrade costs you $195.

Once you have your disks, installing or upgrading to QuarkXPress 3.3 is a snap. It's the same procedure we describe on page 10, although there are new XTensions to consider. You can choose what items to install by selecting or deselecting them in the Items list in the Customize dialog box of the Installation window.

▼ ▼

Tip: Full Install with an Upgrader. You can, by the way, use the QuarkXPress 3.3 update disks to do a full install, though there are a few steps involved. Here's how.

1. Launch the updater. When the first screen appears, click Continue.

2. At the second screen, a message appears saying, "Please enter the directory which contains the installed version of QuarkXPress you wish to update." Don't enter anything. Click Stop in the lower-left corner of the window.

3. You'll then see the message, "Application installation is not yet complete. Are you sure you want to exit install?" Hold down the Control and Alt keys and click the Yes button.

4. The first screen of the Updater reactivates. Click Continue.

5. The second screen of the Updater will reappear, this time bearing the message, "Please enter the directory in which you'd like to install QuarkXPress." Accept the default directory C:/XPRESS or enter the name of the directory you want to install to.

6. Click Continue. You'll notice that the Updater now functions like an installer.

Note that this technique won't install the tutorial sample files.
▼ ▼

The QuarkXPress installer installs the EfiColor dynamic link library (.DLL) background processor and the EfiColor XTension, along with all other XTensions, in the XTENSION subdirectory of your QuarkXPress directory. The EfiColor device profiles that come with your copy of QuarkXPress are placed in the EFICOLOR subdirectory of your QuarkXPress directory.

Dynamic Link Libraries are program code that run as though they were part of Windows once they're started up. EFI created the EfiColor DLL (EFICOLOR.DLL), Storm Technologies created the JPEG DLL (JPEGLIB.DLL), and Kodak developed the Photo CD DLL

(PCDLIB.DLL). Quark, in turn, developed an XTension (.XXT) that works in conjunction with each respective DLL. The XTension automatically loads the DLL when activated.

▼▼▼▼▼▼▼▼▼▼▼▼▼▼▼▼▼▼▼▼▼▼▼▼▼▼▼

Tip: Turning XTensions Off. The EfiColor and new JPEG and Photo CD import filters and their related dynamic link libraries (DLLs) use up a fair amount of memory and could cause memory deficiency problems if you're trying to run QuarkXPress on a machine with limited memory (like if you have less than 5Mb of RAM).

If you already installed the DLLs with the installer or upgrader, you can deactivate them by using Windows File Manager to rename the EFI.XXT, JPEG.XXT, and PHOTOCD.XXT XTension files with different file name extensions, such as ".xxx". QuarkXPress won't try to load an XTension named EFI.xxx, for example, but you can rename it to EFI.XXT if or when you need to use EfiColor. Of course, you need to restart QuarkXPress for the change to be made because the program loads the XTension information in at launch time. This technique will deactivate any Quark XTension.

▼▼▼▼▼▼▼▼▼▼▼▼▼▼▼▼▼▼▼▼▼▼▼▼▼▼▼

About that About box. When you hold down the Control key and select About QuarkXPress from the Help menu, the Environment dialog box you get tells you familiar information about your PC system, your Windows setup, and your version of QuarkXPress just as with previous versions (see pages 6–7). There are a few changes here in version 3.3 to make it easier for you and Quark to keep track of your configuration (see Figure F-1).

If you click on a listed XTension name in the Environment dialog box in version 3.3, you'll see the XTension's serial number (if it has one). There's also a button for displaying your own user registration information, and another for creating a registration disk with that information that you can send back to Quark. Quark uses these disks to plug your information directly into its customer-support database.

Why create a registration disk if it's already created as part of the installation process (see page 10)? Sometimes Quark receives registration disks that have been damaged in transit. Until now, there was no way they could ask you to easily recreate such a damaged disk; once you installed and mailed in your disk, it was

Figure F-1
Environment dialog box

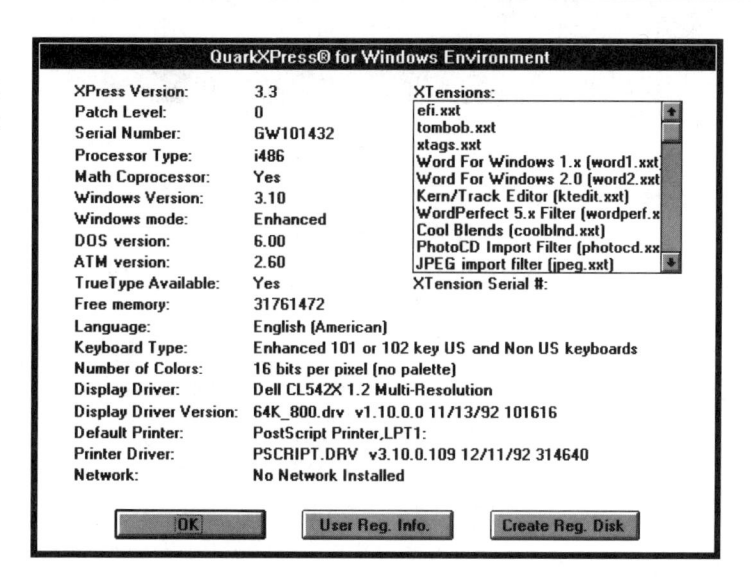

QuarkXPress® for Windows Environment	
XPress Version:	3.3
Patch Level:	0
Serial Number:	GW101432
Processor Type:	i486
Math Coprocessor:	Yes
Windows Version:	3.10
Windows mode:	Enhanced
DOS version:	6.00
ATM version:	2.60
TrueType Available:	Yes
Free memory:	31761472
Language:	English (American)
Keyboard Type:	Enhanced 101 or 102 key US and Non US keyboards
Number of Colors:	16 bits per pixel (no palette)
Display Driver:	Dell CL542X 1.2 Multi-Resolution
Display Driver Version:	64K_800.drv v1.10.0.0 11/13/92 101616
Default Printer:	PostScript Printer,LPT1:
Printer Driver:	PSCRIPT.DRV v3.10.0.109 12/11/92 314640
Network:	No Network Installed

XTensions:
efi.xxt
tombob.xxt
xtags.xxt
Word For Windows 1.x (word1.xxt)
Word For Windows 2.0 (word2.xxt)
Kern/Track Editor (ktedit.xxt)
WordPerfect 5.x Filter (wordperf.x
Cool Blends (coolblnd.xxt)
PhotoCD Import Filter (photocd.xx
JPEG import filter (jpeg.xxt)
XTension Serial #:

[OK] [User Reg. Info.] [Create Reg. Disk]

gone! Now you have the option of creating a new one. Kind of obscure, rarely needed, but a lifesaver when you gotta do it.

▼ ▼

Tip: If You Sell Out. Why you'd ever want to sell your copy of QuarkXPress is beyond us. However, in case you do, you'd better know Quark's rules about such things. First of all, you have to notify Quark that you want to sell their product (the closest thing to this that we've encountered in real life is someone telling their parents that they wanted to buy birth control pills). Quark's customer service sends you a Transfer Request form. After both you and the purchaser sign the forms, and you send them back with a $25 fee, Quark updates their databases and the deed is done. The only reason we even bring this up is that the purchaser may not get "automatic" or paid upgrades unless they do this (Quark checks addresses and other registration information rigorously).

▼ ▼

The New File and Library Commands

There's something new about Quark's New command. It's hierarchical. Look under the File menu, and you'll see a small submenu attached to the New command (see Figure F-2). You can either create a new document or a new library file from this submenu.

There's a logic to this. Since the two kinds of files you can create from within QuarkXPress are either documents or libraries

Figure F-2
The new New submenu

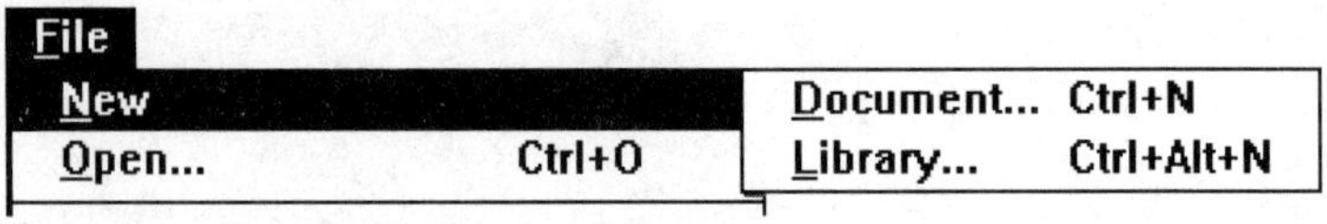

File		
New		Document... Ctrl+N
Open... Ctrl+O		Library... Ctrl+Alt+N

(not counting the many kinds of files you can export from a document), it makes a certain amount of sense to group the commands for creating these files under the New command.

Of course, you can always use the Control-N shortcut to make a new document and avoid the submenu, or Control-Alt-N for a new library.

Also note that the Library command is gone from the Utilities menu. In version 3.3, you open Library files via the Open command, as you would any other QuarkXPress file. How do you know whether a file displayed in the Open dialog box is a document, a library, or a template? Easy: Click on the document's name, and the file's type appears at the bottom of the dialog box.

▼ ▼

Tip: Send your Libraries, Not Your Pictures. If you're preparing templates and picture libraries so that someone else can do the actual page-layout work, remember that you might not need to send them the picture files on disk. QuarkXPress captures a low-resolution preview image for each picture when you imported it into a picture box, and that's saved within the library.

If you send just the library file, the person making pages can place, see, and print the screen representations. When the document file comes back to you, QuarkXPress remembers the locations of all the original graphics files on your disks, and uses those for printing.

▼ ▼

Quick Item Deactivation

This is another nice little feature for those times you want to deselect (deactivate) any or all selected items in your document. Just press the Tab key while the Item tool is selected. We use this to get rid of the handles that appear on selected items, but you may also feel better deselecting everything so that you don't inadvertently alter an item.

Palettes

If you've worked with version 3.1 much, you know how great those floating palettes are. You can have them open or closed, move them around the screen, and get lots of functionality in very little space. There are some additions to the Measurements palette in version 3.3, and Quark also dramatically revamped the Document Layout palette, which we'll describe later in "Document Construction."

Measurements palette changes. The changes to the Measurements palette are minor, but as the palette is so vital to your day-to-day use of QuarkXPress, we'll mention them here briefly.

First, when you have the Content tool active and a text or picture box selected, you'll notice two new small arrow-shaped icons: to the left of the scaling fields for a picture box, and to the left of the leading and tracking/kerning fields for a text box. You can use these icons to flip the contents of these boxes horizontally or vertically (see "Flipping Out," later in this appendix).

When you have the Content tool active and a text box selected, you'll see a fifth justification mode icon, for the new forced-justification mode, which we'll also explain later in "Type and Typography."

▼ ▼

Tip: Keeping Your Tools Around. After you use a tool like the text or picture box tool, the Tool palette automatically reverts back to either the Content or the Item tool (depending on which of the two you last used). This becomes a hassle if you want to use the same tool again. Instead, you can hold down the Alt key as you select a tool. The tool remains selected until you select another.

▼ ▼

By the Numbers

QuarkXPress has always stood out for its ability to use numeric specifications—you can type in numbers for positioning, scaling, and the like. Of course, this feature has often required that you keep the good ol' Windows Calculator accessory open to do mundane arithmetic tasks (so when you needed to make a box exactly two-thirds of its current size, you could figure out just what number to enter in the appropriate field). Or, if you were a low-tech type like some of us, it's meant keeping paper and pencil (or fingers) handy. Well, you can almost kiss your calculator (or pencil or fingers) good-bye.

QuarkXPress 3.1 performed simple arithmetic operations for you—nice, as long as you only understood addition and subtraction. Now you can take it to a second-grade level, since Quark has added multiplication and division. With a full array of basic arithmetic operators (+, -, * and /), you're in business. If, for example, you have a text box that measures 4.323 inches, and you want to make it two-thirds as wide, just enter "*2/3" to the right of the inch mark and press Enter.

Arithmetic works in almost any field in any dialog box.

▼▼▼▼▼▼▼▼▼▼▼▼▼▼▼▼▼▼▼▼▼▼▼▼▼▼▼

Tip: Mix and Match Measurements. Even better, when you're adding or subtracting values, you can mix and match any measurement system that QuarkXPress recognizes, something we touched on briefly in Chapter 1. Even if you've specified in Preferences that inches be the measurement unit used for horizontal dimensions, you're not restricted to using inches in any horizontal measurement box. If you want to make our hypothetical 4.323-inch-wide text box three picas narrower, all you have to do is type "-3p" after the inch mark.

▼▼▼▼▼▼▼▼▼▼▼▼▼▼▼▼▼▼▼▼▼▼▼▼▼▼▼

Tip: Moving an Item's Origin. PageMaker lets you set the origin of a page element from a number of locations, rather than just the upper-left corner. Until QuarkXPress does the same, we can only offer a somewhat weak workaround for specifying alternate origins: use the built-in math functions. If you want the right side of a 12-pica-wide picture box to be set at the 2.75-inch mark, type "2.75"-12p" into the x-origin field of the Measurements palette. That is, simply subtract the width of the box from the right point. Or, if you want the center of a 16-pica-wide text box to be at the 18 cm mark, you can type "18cm-16p/2".

▼ ▼

Tip: Proportional Resizing by the Numbers. Don't forget that Quark-XPress can do a lot of math work for you. This can come in handy in situations where you're trying to resize items on a page. For example, if you know that the one-by-two-inch box (two inches tall) on the page should be five inches wide, you can type "5" in the width field. But what do you put in the height field? If you want to keep the aspect ratio, you can let the program do a little math for you: just type *newwidth/oldwidth* after the height value. In this example, you'd type "*5/2" after the height. This multiplies the value by the percentage change in width (if you divide 5 by 2, you get a 250 percent change, or 2.5 times the value).

▼ ▼

Tip: Spacing with Percentages. You don't have to type an absolute value into the Space field of the Space/Align dialog box. You can type a percentage, too. For instance, if you want the tops of two lines to be twice as far apart as they already are, you can type "200%" and click OK. When you're working in percentages, the Apply button has an additional function: it lets you apply that percentage more than once. If you type "150%" and click Apply, the objects are spaced one-and-a-half times their existing distance. Then, if you click Apply again, they're moved *another* one-and-a-half times, and so on.

▼ ▼

Viewing Changes as You Make Them

Another relatively subtle but extremely helpful change is the ability to view page items while moving, cropping, rotating, or sizing them. You might remember that previously you were only shown the outline of a picture or text box while you altered it. Now, if you hold the mouse button down on a picture box handle for half a second before dragging it, you can see the picture crop (or scale, if you have the Control key held down, too) as you move the handle.

Similarly, if you move or rotate the box, you can see the text or picture rotate while dragging if you simply pause for half a second before starting to drag. No, you don't have to count out half a second; just wait until you see the object flash quickly before you start dragging.

More Better Shortcuts

We've always loved the many keyboard shortcuts built into QuarkXPress. With Version 3.3, there's much more to love. We've even added a tear-out keystroke shortcut card in the back of the book that you can use as a handy reference. If that isn't enough, though, Table F-2 lists the many new shortcuts that Quark has added. Table F-3 lists all of the new function key shortcuts.

Table F-2 New keyboard shortcuts

To get ...	Press ...
Single straight quote with Smart Quotes on	Control-'
Double straight quote with Smart Quotes on	Control-Alt-'
Increase line width by one point	Control-Shift-Alt-period
Decrease line width by one point	Control-Shift-Alt-comma
Document Setup	Control-Alt-Shift-P
Application Preferences	Control-Alt-Shift-Y
Edit H&Js	Control-Alt-H
Force justify	Control-Alt-Shift-J
Check spelling in document	Control-Alt-Shift-W
Increase Horizontal/Vertical Scaling one percent	Control-Alt-]
Decrease Horizontal/Vertical Scaling one percent	Control-Alt-[
Breaking punctuation space	Shift-spacebar
Nonbreaking punctuation space	Control-Shift-spacebar
Em dash	Control-Shift-=
Nonbreaking em dash	Control-Alt-Shift-=

Table F-3 Function key shortcuts

Keystroke	What you get
F1	QuarkXPress Help
F2	Font Usage
Shift-F2	Picture Usage
F3	Expand/shrink document window
Shift-F3	Fit in Pasteboard
F4	Show/hide Document Layout palette
Alt-F4	Exit program

Control-F4	Close window
F5	Bring to Front
Control-F5	Bring Forward
Shift-F5	Send to Back
Control-Shift-F5	Send Backward
F7	Show/hide Guides
Shift-F7	Snap to Guides
Control-F7	Show/hide Baseline Grid
F8	Show/hide Tool palette
Shift-F8	Previous tool
F9	Show/Hide Measurements palette
Shift-F9	Font Field in Measurements palette
Control-F9	Next font in list
Control-Shift-F9	Previous font in list
F11	Show/hide Styles palette
Control-Shift-F11	Edit H&Js
Shift-F11	Edit Style Sheets
F12	Show/hide Colors palette
Control-F12	Show/hide Trap Information
Control-Shift-F12	Trapping Preferences
Shift-F12	Edit Colors

Box Skew

Here's another terrific feature we've been eagerly awaiting. Box Skew lets you skew text and picture boxes and their contents (we talk about skewing on page 315). You can skew a text box, and all the text within the box is skewed to the same angle—and you're still able to edit the text. By combining QuarkXPress's ability to skew and rotate text boxes, you can create some interesting effects, like a 3-D cube with angled text on each side (see Figure F-3).

Text box skew. To skew a text box and its contents, select the box and choose the Modify command from the Item menu, press Control-M, or double click with the Item tool to open the Text Box Specifications dialog box. Go to the Box Skew field, and enter the number of degrees you want the box to be skewed (it only lets you

Figure F-3
Text box skew

Oh my goodness gracious, I'm falling to the right, I'm falling! Help me! I'm caught in a skewed text box and I can't get out. Please call for help before I am skewed too far... Oh my goodness gracious, I'm falling to the right, I'm falling! Help me! I'm caught in a skewed text box and I can't get out. Please call for help before I am skewed too far... Oh my goodness gracious, I'm falling to the right, I'm falling! Help me!

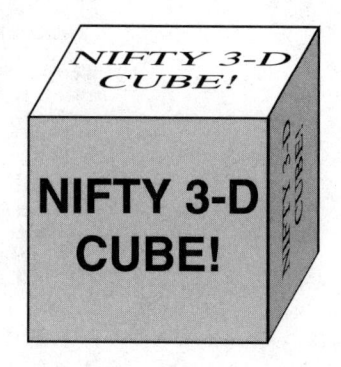

NIFTY 3-D CUBE!

enter values between -75 and 75 degrees). Enter a positive number to skew the box and its contents to the right; a negative number skews them to the left.

Picture box skew. You were able to skew the contents of picture boxes in QuarkXPress version 3.1, but now you can skew the box and its contents, all in one fell swoop. Just go to the Picture Specifications dialog box and enter a Box Skew value exactly as described above for text boxes. The only difference is that you can still skew the contents of a picture box independently of the box itself, using the Picture Skew field in the dialog box or Measurements palette.

Of course, if you're really bored, you can even play dueling skewing by setting values in Box Skew and Picture Skew that cancel each other out.

▼ ▼

Tip: The Polygon Blues. Here's a quick one that can help you out of a jam. If you're drawing a complex polygon and can't find the first point of the polygon, don't fret, and—whatever you do—don't restart your PC! You've got two reasonable choices. First, you can press the Escape key to cancel the polygon operation. However, that kills the polygon entirely. The second choice is better: just double-click somewhere. Double-clicking automatically closes the polygon for you.

▼ ▼

Flipping Out

Here's another dream come true. It used to be that if you wanted to flip a picture or text along the vertical or horizontal axis—so that you could mirror it on facing pages, for instance—you had to dive into a graphics program, flip the image, save it as a picture, then bring it into your QuarkXPress document.

Well, no longer. Just select the object, then go to the Style menu and choose Flip Vertical or Flip Horizontal. Not only does this command let you flip pictures and text, but flipped text remains fully editable (to do this, you have to practice reading the newspaper in the mirror).

You can also use the new icons for flipping contents in the Measurements palette (see Figure F-4). The top icon controls horizontal flipping; the lower one controls vertical flipping. Note that Flip Vertical and Flip Horizontal only flip the contents of boxes, not the boxes themselves (subtle difference).

Figure F-4
Flip Horizontal/Vertical

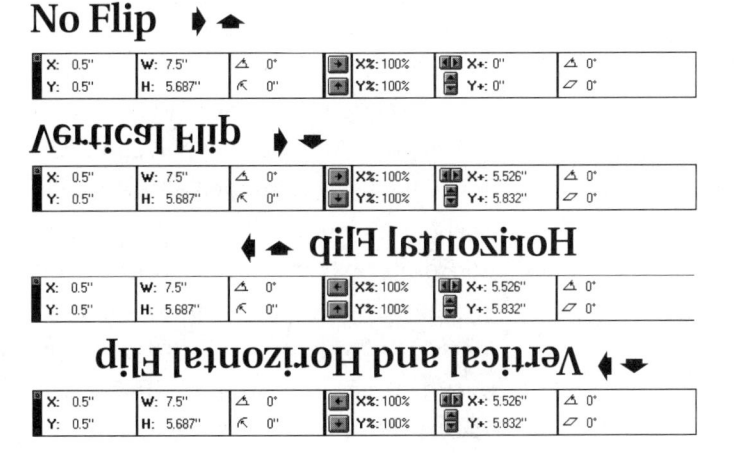

Polygonal Text Boxes

In QuarkXPress 3.1 you could have any shape of text box you wanted, as long as it was rectangular. Now, you can have any shape you want, provided it's not a Möbius strip. The Text Box tool itself still only creates rectangular text boxes. But after you've created a text box, the new Box Shape submenu under the Item menu lets you further alter its shape.

You'll notice, in fact, that the Box Shape submenu stands in for Picture Box Shape submenu when you've selected a text box. It works for text boxes the same way we described for picture boxes back on page 42. First create a rectangular text box as you normally would using the Text Box tool. With the text box selected, choose any of the shape options from the Box Shape submenu (round-corner, mitered-corner, or scallop-corner rectangles, or circular/oval; see Figure F-5).

Figure F-5
Box Shape submenu

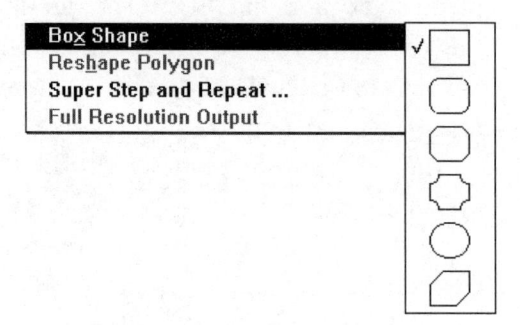

```
Box Shape
Reshape Polygon
Super Step and Repeat ...
Full Resolution Output
```

But you can create many more shapes beyond these basic six. You can, in fact, turn any of these prefab shapes to an editable polygon and modify the heck out of it. To do that, select the text box—rectangle, oval, whatever—and then go to the Box Shape submenu and select the Polygon icon at the bottom of the list. From the Item menu make sure the Reshape Polygon command is checked; if not, select it.

Your text box will now appear with control handles along its perimeter. A rectangle will have only four points, but the curved portions of other shapes will have many (note that when you convert a curve to a polygon, the curves turn to straight line segments). Click on a handle or an entire line segment and drag, just as you would with a polygonal picture box, as we described on page 34.

You can create additional handles by holding down the Control key while clicking on the box perimeter, or delete one by clicking on it while holding down the Control key.

Note that the Vertical Alignment controls of the Text Box Specifications dialog box become inactive for text boxes once you've applied a box shape (XPress is smart, but it isn't that smart).

Interactive Text Resizing

For quite a while you've been able to scale a picture box and its contents by holding down the Control key while dragging on a handle. Ever caught yourself attempting to do the same to a box of display type that just needs a little bit of tweaking? Now you don't have to feel sheepish, because you actually can scale text within a box by Control-dragging on the box's handles. As you resize the box, the text size increases or decreases to fit your changes. Depending on how you reshape the box, the type size changes, as well as the type's horizontal or vertical scaling (see Figure F-6).

Figure F-6
Text resizing by Control-dragging text box handles

Stretch Me!!!!!

All the rules for resizing and scaling picture boxes now apply to text boxes. In addition to Control-key scaling, Shift-Control turns rectangular boxes into squares (scaling contents appropriately), and Shift-Control-Alt scales the box and its contents but maintains existing horizontal and vertical proportions. And if you wait half a second after you click on a handle before you begin to drag, you can see the type change on screen as you drag (see "Viewing Changes as You Make Them," above).

There are two catches to this neat new feature. First, it only stretches type to the limits you could ordinarily. For example, you can't stretch type wider than 400 percent, because horizontal scaling won't go any further than that. Second, this scaling only works on unlinked text boxes, not on text boxes that are part of a longer story, as it's intended for use on headline and display type.

Think about how easily you could mess up the formatting of a long story, if by resizing a text box through which it flowed, you ended up scaling some (but not all) of the text in a paragraph. Although we're sure that someone out there will take issue with us, we agree wholeheartedly with Quark's decision to limit this feature to unlinked boxes!

Doing Windows

We're not talking about household chores here (QuarkXPress won't vacuum under the furniture either); we're talking about opening multiple documents in QuarkXPress. In version 3.3 you can open a whole mess more document windows at once—25 to be exact. Goodbye seven-window limit! However, having so many document windows open at once could mean massive clutter and confusion (especially for Bob, who thinks that the Windows "desktop metaphor" was created to let him make his virtual desktop as messy as his physical one); fortunately, Quark has provided some ways to cut the clutter.

The Windows menu, discussed on page 18, is the prime implement. Just selecting a window from the menu makes it active, which is particularly convenient if the window you want happens to be hidden beneath a slew of other windows. Also, version 3.3 will display—and let you select—the Clipboard in the Windows menu if you've opened the Clipboard via the Show Clipboard command under the Edit menu. No dice if you're displaying the Clipboard via Windows' Clipboard accessory.

If you've ever sprained your mousing wrist moving and resizing windows in order to drag items between documents, you'll really love the new tiling options in the Windows submenu, Tile Horizontally and Tile Vertically. Tiling resizes every document window so that each takes up an equal portion of your screen. So if you have three document windows, tiling sizes and arranges them so that each takes up one-third of your screen. The Tile Horizontally command arranges your three documents as tall, narrow windows, with their title bars adjacent to each other. The Tile Vertically command does the opposite, stacking your three documents short and wide, one on top of the other.

Once you open more than three documents on a standard 640-by-480-pixel VGA monitor the differences between the two options are less straightforward. Four windows, for example, will be arranged in a two rows, two windows per row, regardless of whether you choose Tile Horizontally or Tile Vertically. Nevertheless, we often use these features when dragging objects or pages from one document to another.

▼ ▼

Tip: Fitting More in Your Window. If you select Fit in Window from the View menu (or press Control-zero), QuarkXPress fits the current page to the window. Holding down the Control key while selecting Fit in Window will center the spread, but in a reduced view that encompasses the width of the pasteboard as well. You can minimize that reduction by entering a small percentage value in the Pasteboard Width field of the Application Preferences dialog box—provided you don't need much Pasteboard to work with.

▼ ▼

Tip: Centering on Item when Zooming. Quark has an even cooler feature that centers a selected page item when you change the zoom percentage. To be precise, QuarkXPress centers any selected page item if any part of the page that contains that item is in your document window, or—if the item is on the pasteboard—if any part of that item is shown in the document window.

For example, if you select a short rule on a page while viewing at Fit in Window size, and then select Actual Size, QuarkXPress zooms in and centers that rule on your screen. If the selected item is a text box and you have the Contents tool selected, then Quark centers on where the cursor is or on whatever text is highlighted. This makes zooming in and out on a page much easier: if you're editing some text, you can use Fit in Window to see the "big picture," then select 100 percent to zoom back to where your cursor is in the text.

▼ ▼

Tip: Jump to View Percent. Version 3.3 adds another handy keyboard shortcut: pressing Control-Alt-V selects the View Percent field of your active Quark window. To change your magnification, just type in any value between 10 and 400, and press Enter. You can also type "T", "Th", or even "Thumb" to get Thumbnails view.

▼ ▼

Ultimately, we still like to use the Control-drag shortcut (see Chapter 1, *QuarkXPress Basics*, pages 60–61) to zoom to where we want to go, but these new features are often helpful in bouncing quickly back and forth between percentage views.

Copying Linked Text Boxes

The ability to easily copy objects between documents was one of the greatest new features put into QuarkXPress. The only problem has been when you were trying to copy a linked text box, in which case QuarkXPress would refuse to let you copy or cut it to the Clipboard, or drag it to another page. In version 3.3, this problem has almost been solved.

Copying single linked text boxes. You can copy a single linked text box to a new document, and QuarkXPress copies, along with it, the entire text chain, from the beginning of that box on. None of the text preceding that box in the chain moves to the target; only the text from the ensuing linked boxes (and any overflow text, which wasn't in any boxes).

Also note that if you have Automatic Page Insertion turned on, and your new document's master page has an automatic text box, QuarkXPress creates as many new pages as necessary to contain all of the copied story. So if you move a box that's part of a long story, you may end up with quite a stack of new pages to deal with. It'd be nice if QuarkXPress could automatically break the chains when you copy, bringing to the new document only the text within the box you're moving (if you'd like, that is), but we have to leave Quark some refinements to work on for the next version.

Copying groups of linked text boxes. Believe it or not, you can now also easily copy as a group text boxes that are linked to each other. But if you want to copy multiple text boxes that are linked to each other, as well as to boxes that you haven't selected, QuarkXPress will still refuse to copy or move them, giving you instead the familiar message: "This text box or a text box in the group has linkages that can't be duplicated." You have to copy either one box or all boxes in a text chain. If you're in Thumbnails view, and copy multiple pages from one document to another, links between boxes on different pages are also maintained in your target document.

Multiple-Item Undo

Deleting a group of items in QuarkXPress 3.1, whether grouped via the Group command or simply Shift-clicked, was a one-way street to item oblivion. That's because 3.1 couldn't Undo deletions of grouped items, and even gave you a warning message if you tried.

Now, it's no problem. Or almost no problem, since there are a couple of minor limitations. For one thing, if one of the deleted items is a text box that was part of a linked chain, but you're not deleting all of the text boxes in the chain, the links to and from that deleted text box are not restored when you Undo the deletion. Also, when the deleted items are on different layers in the document, all items you deleted will end up below the layer of the topmost deleted item. So the Undo is not a true reversion to the previous state. Still, that's better than losing all of them.

Visually Accurate Rulers

One other subtle change in the area of rulers that you might like: Rulers are now visually accurate. What does that mean? It means that when a box or a rule looks like it is directly over a tick mark in the ruler, it really is. For example, if you want to visually place a box at the two-inch mark (as opposed to using the Measurements palette), you can follow the gray lines in the rulers as you drag the box. When the gray line is over the two-inch mark, the box is truly at two inches, even when you're at a view other than 100 percent or if you've changed the Points/Inch value.

This might not seem like a big deal, but in earlier versions, you could never really be sure unless you checked the Measurements palette or the Item Specifications dialog box. It might be at 1.998 or 2.01 inches.

▼ ▼

Tip: Getting Rid of Ruler Guides. No matter how easy it is to move guides around, it's always a hassle to add 20 guides to a page and then remove them one at a time. Well, take a shortcut: hold down the Alt key while clicking once in the horizontal ruler, and all the horizontal guides disappear. Alt-clicking in the vertical ruler has the same effect on vertical guides. If the page is touching the ruler when you do this, only the page guides disappear; if the pasteboard is touching the ruler, then only the pasteboard guides (the ones that go all the way across spreads and the pasteboard) disappear. This works in version 3.1, too.

▼▼▼▼▼▼▼▼▼▼▼▼▼▼▼▼▼▼▼▼▼▼▼▼▼▼▼

Tip: Scale-Specific Guides. Apparently some programmer threw this feature in without telling anyone, because we found out that it's not even documented internally at Quark. If you hold down the Shift key while dragging a ruler guide rule out on the page or spread, it becomes magnification-specific. That is, if you pull it out in Actual Size view, you'll only be able to see it at Actual Size view or higher (more zoomed in) magnification. If you zoom out (let's say to Fit in Window view), it disappears. This is great for those times when you want to see a thumbnail of the page without guides, but need the guides to work with.

▼▼▼▼▼▼▼▼▼▼▼▼▼▼▼▼▼▼▼▼▼▼▼▼▼▼▼

Application Preferences

You thought you could set a lot of preferences before, but get ready for more! As you may recall, any selections you make in the Application Preferences dialog box are application-wide; that is, they aren't just for the document you have open. Let's jump in and discuss each new element (see Figure F-7).

Speed Scroll. Here's another wonderful enhancement in 3.3 that makes us want to bow down and give thanks in the general direction of Denver (where Quark lives). If you turn on Speed Scroll (not to be confused with Scroll Speed, covered on page 82 and below), QuarkXPress automatically greeks the display of pictures, graphics and blends as you scroll through a document. Only when you stop scrolling does it take the time to properly display these elements. This may not sound like a big improvement at first, but if you've died of boredom while scrolling through a long document with lots of big four-color TIFFS, you'll appreciate how much time Speed Scroll can save you (that is, unless you liked taking a coffee break while you were scrolling).

Figure F-7
The new Application Preferences dialog box

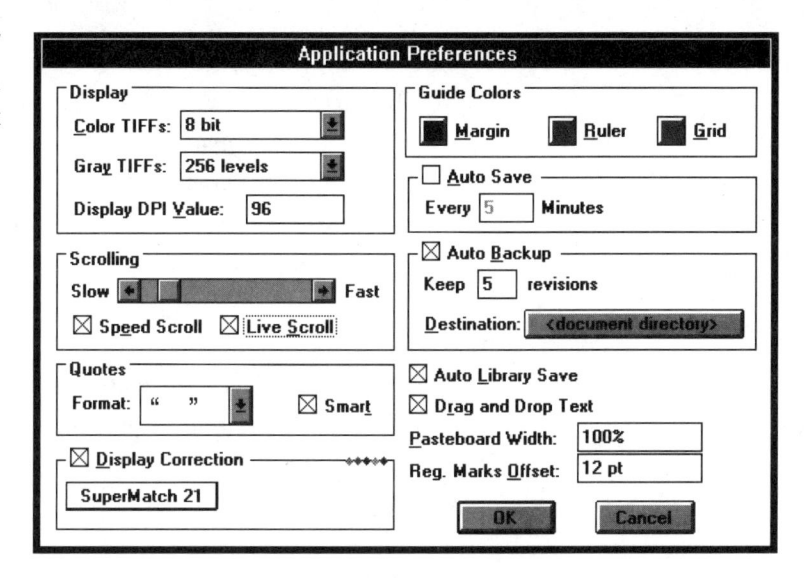

> **Tip: Scroll Speed.** If you do use the scroll bar arrows to get around, you definitely want to examine the Scroll Speed feature in the Application Preferences dialog box. This feature lets you control how far each click in a scroll-bar arrow takes you. For example, if you have the Scroll Speed set to Fast, then clicking an arrow may move you an entire screen or more. If you have it set to Slow, a click may only move the screen one or two pixels.

Grabber Hand. Back in Chapter 1, *QuarkXPress Basics*, we talked about the Grabber Hand (hold down the Alt key and drag; see page 59). The Grabber Hand is still there in 3.3, but it's permanently on; there's no option to turn it off in the Application Preferences dialog box. We can't imagine why you'd want to, anyway.

Color TIFFs/Grayscale TIFFs. These updated controls first saw life as a simple checkbox in version 3.1 that would allow you to choose whether, on eight- or 24-bit monitors, imported grayscale TIFFs would be displayed using 256 or 16 levels of gray. This proved to be so popular that the interface was revised (it's a popup menu now) and similar choices extended to color TIFFs. Specifically, you can select 16 (four-bit) or 256 (eight-bit) levels of gray for grayscale TIFFs, and 256 colors (eight-bit), or millions of colors (24-bit) display for color TIFF images.

Once again, it's a time-versus-quality issue. The lower the bit depth, the faster your screen redraw will be; the higher the bit depth, the better the onscreen display. You can recoup some of the performance hit from higher-quality image displays by selecting Speed Scroll (see above). You should also note that many Windows-accelerated vga-compatible display adapter cards don't offer nearly as much display acceleration when you're working in bit depths beyond 256 colors.

Of course, if you don't have eight- or 24-bit images, you can't display them in those modes, anyway. Note that these features don't affect the images themselves or how they print—just how they're displayed on the screen.

Low Resolution TIFF. This preference item first appeared in version 3.1, but has disappeared in version 3.3. Back in 3.1, when you had Low Resolution TIFF checked, imported TIFF images would be shown on the screen at half the screen resolution (whatever you entered in the Display DPI Value field), unless you held down the Shift key while importing them; see Chapter 8, *Image Modification*, page 358).

In version 3.3, the opposite is now the default. TIFFs come in at screen resolution (screen redraws take longer) unless you hold down the Shift key while importing, in which case you get half the screen resolution.

Display Correction. If you've installed the EfiColor XTension and system, you'll see a checkbox entitled Display Correction in the Application Preferences dialog box. This lets you turn on or off the part of EfiColor that attempts to match your onscreen display of color to what's available from your selected printer. When you turn on Display Correction, you can select your monitor (if you have a profile installed for it) from a popup menu of monitors your EfiColor system knows about. We explain this process in more detail in Appendix G, *EfiColor*.

Auto Save. At first glance, Auto Save looks like a yawner. As it turns out, it's anything but. There are plenty of commercial and shareware utilities that will automatically save a document you're working on, as you're working on it. But all these utilities work by generating the equivalent of QuarkXPress's Save command at predefined intervals. Now suppose you mistakenly delete all of a story; then, before you can undo your deletion, some macro kicks in, saving your document—and your mistake—for all eternity (or until you fix your mistake, or lose your job because of it!). For this reason, we've stayed away from autosaving utilities.

Until now. The folks at Quark really got the design of this feature right. You turn Auto Save on by checking its box, and you can specify any interval you want between saves (the default is every five minutes). But—and here's the great part—autosaves don't automatically overwrite your original file. That only happens when you use the Save command. So if you use the Revert to Saved command or close and then reopen the document without saving changes, you revert to the last saved version of your original file—just as you would expect—not to the last autosaved one.

Auto Save exists to help you recover from a dreaded system crash or network communications failure (when you lose the connection to your file server with a document open, QuarkXPress sometimes refuses to let you do a Save As.) After you have a crash, you can restart QuarkXPress and open the autosaved file in most cases.

Whenever QuarkXPress does an autosave, it creates a temporary backup file (.ASV) in the same folder as your document, and keeps track of every change you've made since the last time you saved the document. Whenever you save your document, QuarkXPress deletes that incremental file, and starts over again.

Once you've restarted QuarkXPress after a system crash, use the Open command to open your document (you can open either the .QXD or the .ASV file). You'll get an alert box stating that the document will be restored to the point at which the last Auto Save occurred. Click the OK button. If you decided you'd rather work with the last Saved version then use the Revert to Saved command from the File menu.

Note that any changes made to your Application Preferences are lost in the event of a system crash, regardless of whether your current document was saved or autosaved. Application Preferences are only saved when you exit QuarkXPress by selecting Quit from the File menu.

The problem with Auto Save is that it creates a file the same size as the one you're working on. If your file is 12Mb, then you'd better have at least 12Mb available on your hard drive when you turn Auto Save on. It's a nice system, but far from perfect.

Even if you don't have Auto Save turned on, QuarkXPress writes a .ASV file when you do an actual Save. It does this to prevent the original file from being damaged during a Save. After the .ASV file is written successfully, the original file is deleted and the .ASV file is renamed. If you crash while the file's actually being written, the .ASV file is usually trashed—so you lose all the changes since your last save—but the original document file is intact.

▼▼▼▼▼▼▼▼▼▼▼▼▼▼▼▼▼▼▼▼▼▼▼▼▼

Tip: Revert to Last Minisave. Auto Save goes by another name, too: PageMaker calls these things minisaves. Sometimes you want to use a minisave as something other than crash insurance. For instance, you may want to go back to the changes you made 10 minutes ago, and ignore the ones you made five minutes ago. Quark has included a command that lets you revert to the last autosave instead of going back all the way to the last full save. Just hold down the Alt key when you select Revert from the File menu.

▼▼▼▼▼▼▼▼▼▼▼▼▼▼▼▼▼▼▼▼▼▼▼▼▼

Auto Backup. Until now, revision control with QuarkXPress has been strictly up to you. If you wanted to keep previous versions of a document, you had to be sure to copy them to another location, or use Save As frequently, slightly changing the name of your file each time (we always name our files with version numbers—"1.1", "2.4", etc.).

With version 3.3, those days are gone. You can use the Auto Backup function to tell QuarkXPress to keep up to 100 previous versions of your document on disk (the default is five). By clicking the Destination button, you can specify exactly where you want revisions to be stored. The default, "<document directory>", is the subdirectory in which your original document resides. If you need to open a previous version of a file, look in the destination subdirectory. The file with the highest number appended to its name is the most recent revision. Every time you save, the lowest numbered backup is deleted, and a backup is created with the next higher number.

▼▼▼▼▼▼▼▼▼▼▼▼▼▼▼▼▼▼▼▼▼▼▼▼▼

Tip: Fill 'Er Up with Backups. After working with Auto Backup for a couple of weeks, you may find your hard drive mysteriously filling up. Remember, those backup files (as many per file as you've specified in Application Preferences) don't go away by themselves. You need to delete them when you're done with them. One suggestion: Set your Auto Backup to save to a special backup subdirectory on a seldom-used drive.

▼▼▼▼▼▼▼▼▼▼▼▼▼▼▼▼▼▼▼▼▼▼▼▼▼

Smart Quotes. If you want QuarkXPress to insert curly quotes instead of straight quotes when you press the quote key (who doesn't?), the Smart Quotes feature in the Application Preferences dialog box is for you. It both turns on the Smart Quotes feature and lets you specify which characters will be used for open and closed quotes. Smart Quotes works by looking to the left of the insertion point to determine if an open or closed quote character should go there. If the character to the left is a white space character, such as a spaceband, tab key, or return, QuarkXPress enters an open single or double quote when you press the ' or " key.

The popup menu lets you choose some alternative quote characters, including all closed quotes, Spanish alternatives, and inside and outside guillemet combinations, all of which can be useful if you're formatting foreign-language documents (see Figure F-8).

▼▼▼▼▼▼▼▼▼▼▼▼▼▼▼▼▼▼▼▼▼▼▼▼▼

Tip: Toggling Quotes. Smart Quotes are really cool if you type a lot in QuarkXPress. However, if you ever want to enter a single or double "neutral" straight quote character, it's a hassle to turn Smart Quotes off first. Instead, hold down the Control key when typing the quote key to get a single straight quote; when it's off, you get a curly quote. To do the same but with double-quotes (normal quotation marks), type Control-Alt-'.

▼▼▼▼▼▼▼▼▼▼▼▼▼▼▼▼▼▼▼▼▼▼▼▼▼

Figure F-8
Smart Quotes alternatives available in Application Preferences

"This is an example of Smart Quotes," he said.
"This is a different kind of Smart Quotes," he added.
„Here's yet another kind of Smart Quotes," he continued.
«These quotes are called guillemets,» he went on.
»So are these, but they're reversed,« he concluded.

Drag-and-Drop Text. We thought drag-and-drop text editing was pretty cool when it was introduced to the PC world in Microsoft Word for Windows 2.0. We think it's even cooler now that it's in our favorite program, introduced in version 3.3. Drag and drop is an easy way of copying or moving text from one location in a story to another.

To use drag-and-drop text editing, select some text, then drag the selection to another location in the text chain. As you move the mouse, you'll get an insertion point and a little rectangle. When the insertion point reaches the place where you want the selected text to go, release the mouse button, and—*presto:* your text is cut from its original location and placed at the insertion point.

If you want to copy a selection (instead of just moving it), hold down the Shift key as you drag. Note that any text you drag-move or drag-copy also gets placed in the Windows Clipboard (replacing whatever was there). Also, at least for now, you can't drag-copy text between unlinked text boxes or between documents—only within a single text chain.

▼ ▼

Tip: Erasing Preferences You've Made. Suppose you create custom information for a document, but don't want that information to be used in the next document you create. When you save and close that first document you can reset kerning or tracking tables, or clear out the hyphenation exceptions dictionary for the next document. If you don't clear and reset these controls, the XPress Preferences file (XPRESS.PRF) remembers them, and they are used for each document that you create.

▼ ▼

Tip: Resetting and Switching Preferences. If you delete the XPRESS.PRF file (or move it out of the QuarkXPress directory), then Quark-

XPress creates a clean, new one for you. This is a great method for starting over from scratch with the default tracking and kerning tables, and with no items in hyphenation exceptions.

If you have two or more XPRESS.PRF files with varying information, you can move them in and out of your QuarkXPress directory. However, you do have to quit and relaunch QuarkXPress for the new items to take effect.

▼▼▼▼▼▼▼▼▼▼▼▼▼▼▼▼▼▼▼▼▼▼▼▼▼▼

The Q and Didot Measurements

No, Q doesn't refer to some character in a James Bond movie or *Star Trek: The Next Generation*. It refers to a little-known-in-the-West measurement used mostly in Japan and Korea, which is exactly .25 millimeters. Although Q doesn't show up in the Vertical and Horizontal measurements popup menus, you can type any measurement as a Q in the palettes and dialog boxes (either upper- or lowercase is okay).

And speaking of measures, the Points/Inch field in the General Preferences dialog box has had a subtle update which will help you conform to the Euro-scene; namely the Didot system, which we mentioned back on page 84. The Didot system uses different-sized points. To make it easier for you to accommodate that system in QuarkXPress, the Points/Inch field is no longer restricted to entries in the 72–73-point range; it now lets you enter anything in the 60–80-point range. Didot points number 67.43 to the inch.

▼▼▼▼▼▼▼▼▼▼▼▼▼▼▼▼▼▼▼▼▼▼▼▼▼▼

Document Construction

Way back at the beginning of this appendix, we noted that everything changes. Well, here we go contradicting ourselves again. One thing that never changes is the need to create good, solid infrastructures for your documents. Out of all the tools available to do this, only a couple of things have changed since version 3.1.

The first is that you can now print master pages by selecting Print while the master page is displayed in the document window. The second change is in the Document Layout palette.

Note that when you print master pages, both the left and right pages print if the document has facing pages (you can't print only the left or the right alone). Unfortunately, you have 12 different master pages and you want them all printed, you have to print them one spread at a time.

Document Layout Palette

The Document Layout palette has undergone significant changes in version 3.3. For one thing, it's just a heck of a lot easier to use. You'll notice that the Document/Masters and Apply menus are gone, as is the toggle icon for changing between master-page and document view (see Figure F-9). Master-page and document-page icons now each have their own section of the palette to romp in, so you can view both at the same time.

At the top of the palette below the title bar are two icons for generic blank pages which you can use to create new master pages—single-sided on the left and double-sided on the right. To their right are two new buttons, Duplicate and Delete, whose functions we'll get into shortly. Below these buttons is the master page area. You can scroll through this area to see additional master pages that aren't displayed, or you can grab the divider bar that separates the master-page area from the document-page area and drag it down to display more master pages.

Making and duplicating pages. Creating a new document page is now much simpler than before: drag a master page icon into the document-page area. This certainly beats using the former Insert command under the Document/Masters menu. You can create new master pages the same way. To create a new master page based on an existing master, first click on the master you want to copy, and then click the Duplicate button.

If you're in the mood to insert multiple pages, hold down the Alt key, then drag a master page icon into the document-page area, positioning the pointer where you want to begin adding

Figure F-9
The revised Document Layout palette

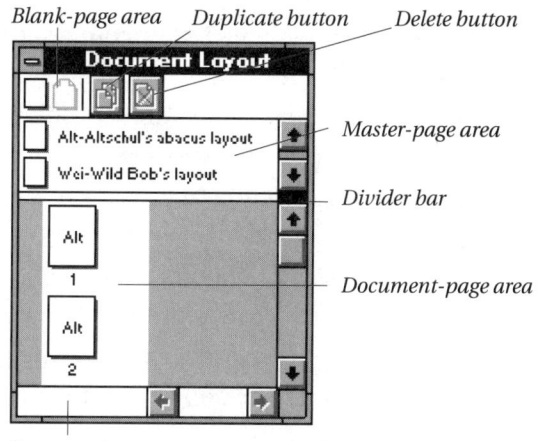

Blank-page area *Duplicate button* *Delete button*
Master-page area
Divider bar
Document-page area
Page number

pages. When you release the mouse button, the Insert Pages dialog box appears, and you can enter the number of pages you want to add.

Applying a master page. As we've said, there's no more Apply menu, and life is the better for it. To apply a master page to an existing document page you have a couple of ways to go, both simple. One way is to select the document page, then hold down the Alt key and click on the master page you want to apply. The other way is to drag the master-page icon on top of the document page.

Which do we prefer? Although there is a certain drag-and-drop elegance to the latter method, a slight slip of the mouse could result in your adding a new page when you really want to apply a different master to an existing page. Furthermore, you can't apply a master page to several document pages at once.

The Alt-click technique, however, makes this simple. Just click with the Shift or Control key to select multiple pages (the latter lets you select discontiguous pages), and then Alt-click on the master page. Similarly, if you want to apply one master page to another existing master page (replacing all its items with those of the source master page), you select the target master page, then Alt-click on the source. An alert box pops up asking if it's "OK to replace" the selected master page with the one you've just Alt-clicked. Think about it for a second—unless you feel lucky—and then click OK or Cancel.

Deleting pages. With the Delete command under the defunct Document/Masters menu replaced by the Delete button, you can be sure that deleting procedures are different in version 3.3. To delete a page or pages, just select what you'd like to delete, then click the Delete button. (Big surprise, eh?)

▼▼▼▼▼▼▼▼▼▼▼▼▼▼▼▼▼▼▼▼▼▼▼▼

Tip: Avoiding Alerts. We don't know about you, but we often spout spontaneous invectives when our computer alerts us to a dangerous procedure. Because we've used the program for so long, we *know* that what we're doing can't be undone or is potentially life-threatening to our document. One example is the "Are you sure you want to delete these pages" prompt when you click the Delete button in the Document Layout palette. QuarkXPress is trying to be helpful, because you can't reverse this action. But it annoys us. However, if you Alt-click the Delete button, the pages are deleted without a prompt. Hooray for progress.

▼▼▼▼▼▼▼▼▼▼▼▼▼▼▼▼▼▼▼▼▼▼▼▼

Sections. Creating a new section is also slightly different in the new palette. To start a new section, you can bring up the Section dialog box by clicking the page number displayed at the bottom left of the palette window; or you can click the absolute page number beneath each page icon.

▼▼▼▼▼▼▼▼▼▼▼▼▼▼▼▼▼▼▼▼▼▼▼▼

Tip: Big Page Numbers. The problem with checking thumbnails on screen is that you can hardly ever figure out what page number is what. One reader, Carole Wade, notes that she sometimes adds big automatic page numbers (Control-3) that hang off the edge of the pages onto the pasteboard for the left and right master pages (see Figure F-10). You can set these text boxes to have no runaround and turn Suppress Printout on, and QuarkXPress acts as if they aren't even there. However, even at tiny sizes, you can see them attached to each page.

▼▼▼▼▼▼▼▼▼▼▼▼▼▼▼▼▼▼▼▼▼▼▼▼

Tip: Copying Master Pages. Have you ever wanted to copy a master page from one document to another? Kinda' difficult, isn't it? Well, no, not really. Put both documents into Thumbnail view and drag a page from the first document into the second. The master page

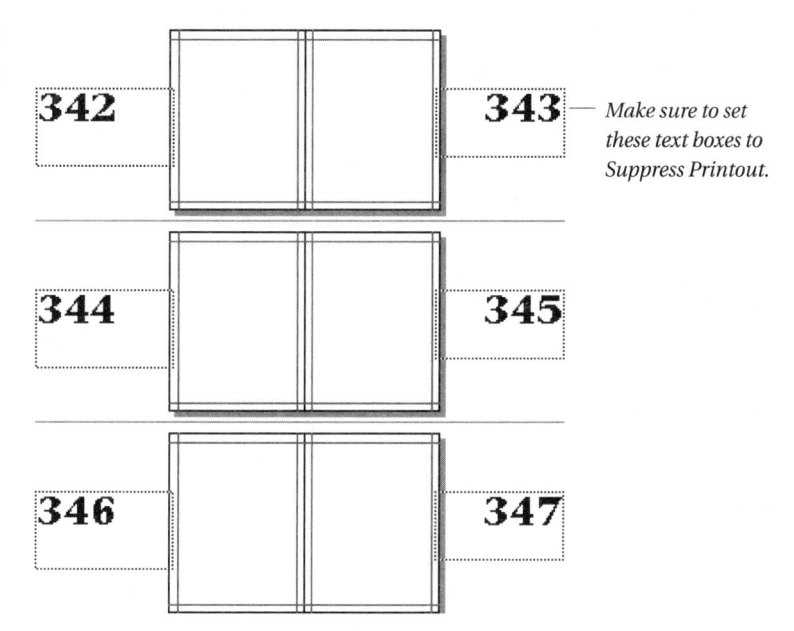

Figure F-10
Big page numbers

Make sure to set these text boxes to Suppress Printout.

that was assigned to that page comes over along with the page itself. Then you can delete the page itself, and the master page stays in the second document.

▼ ▼

Tip: Basing a New Master Page on Another. If you need a new master page but don't want to format it from scratch, you can base it on another that carries at least some formatting that you wish to retain. There are two ways to do this. First, you can create a new master page. Then, select the icon of the particular master page whose formatting you wish to copy, and drag it over the icon of the just-created master page, releasing the mouse button when that icon is highlighted.

However, an even easier way is simply to select the master page you want to duplicate, and click the Duplicate button at the top of the Document Layout palette.

▼ ▼

Tip: Unintentional Multipage Spreads. There are problems in moving pages around in spreads that are just waiting to unfurl. If you insert the pages next to an existing page, you may be unknowingly creating a multipage spread instead of adding pages the way you'd want. The trick is to be careful about what icons you see when you're dropping the page. If you see a page icon, you'll get a spread; if you see a black arrow icon, you'll add pages to the document flow.

Word Processing

There's one major and a few minor changes to version 3.3's word-processing features. The coolest new feature in this area is drag-and-drop text import and editing.

Drag-and-Drop Editing

We mentioned this earlier, in "Application Preferences," so here's a quick recap. When this option is active in the Application Preferences dialog box, you can move selected text by dragging it to another location within its text chain. Holding down the Shift key as you drag copies the selected text.

Drag-and-Drop Text Import

If you want, you can now import a text file by dragging its icon from the Windows File Manager and dropping it into a text box in QuarkXPress. This might be worth the effort if you have to place a lot of short text files for some reason. You'd simply arrange the File Manager and QuarkXPress document windows so that you could see a list of files in File Manager and the relevant page or pages in QuarkXPress. We don't see this situation arising very frequently in relation to text files. (However, see "Drag-and-Drop Picture Importing," later in this chapter.)

Get Text

The Get Text dialog box now lets you know something about a text file before you start to import it. Select a file from the File Name scroll list and QuarkXPress displays the file's format (Word for Windows 2.0, WordPerfect 5.1, RTF, etc.), its size, and its last modification date. Also, the options you set for Convert Quotes and Include Style Sheets are now sticky; they keep whatever you set them to last instead of reverting back to the defaults every time bring up the Get Text dialog box.

▼▼▼▼▼▼▼▼▼▼▼▼▼▼▼▼▼▼▼▼▼▼▼▼▼

Tip: Speed Spell-Checking. If you've ever tried to spell-check an enormous document, you've probably too often found yourself waiting for the screen to redraw. Only after the screen redraws can you decide to move on to the next word. One reader, Bob Martin, points out that the process goes more quickly if you first reduce the window size considerably and then zoom in to 400 percent. QuarkXPress hardly has to redraw anything on the screen each time. Plus, the found text is almost always more visible in the small window.

▼▼▼▼▼▼▼▼▼▼▼▼▼▼▼▼▼▼▼▼▼▼▼▼▼

Tip: Formatting Tabs Quickly. Another reader pointed out to us that you can sometimes format tabs for a number of lines more easily by just working on a single line. If you set the proper tab settings for the first line first, you can quickly apply those settings to the rest of the lines by selecting all the lines (including the first one), opening the Tabs dialog box (Command-Shift-T), and clicking OK (or pressing Enter). The tab setting for the first line automatically gets applied to all the rest of the lines.

▼▼▼▼▼▼▼▼▼▼▼▼▼▼▼▼▼▼▼▼▼▼▼▼▼

Type and Typography

There's no denying that QuarkXPress remains the typographic standard against which all other programs are measured. Quark could have sat around on its laurels, but it didn't. Typographic enhancements added in version 3.3 are subtle, but welcome: control over whether accents appear over text formatted with the All Caps character style, vertical as well as horizontal scaling, and forced justification. There are also improvements to both the Keep with Next ¶ and kerning table features.

▼ ▼

Tip: Selecting Paragraphs. We often look over people's shoulders when they work, and what we see could scare a moose. One such scare is the technique of selecting a paragraph so that you can apply some paragraph formatting to it (leading, space before, or whatever). People think that they have to select the whole paragraph first. Not true! When changing paragraph formatting, you only have to have the cursor in the paragraph you want to change. That means you can have one word selected, or three sentences, or half of one paragraph and half of another, or whatever.

▼ ▼

Tip: Formatting Past the Boundaries. As the old Zen master said, "Frustration dissipates like the morning fog when light is shed on the problem." (Actually, we don't know any Zen masters, so we just made that up.) One frustration we still have is QuarkXPress for Windows tab ruler. QuarkXPress for Macintosh has a wonderful tab ruler that pops up inside a text box, and which lets you drag and zoom the underlying page while keeping it onscreen, The Windows version, however, has a tab ruler that reminds us of the awful one found in PageMaker before version 5 (see Figure F-11). Not only is the ruler part of the dialog box instead of showing up as part of the selected text box, it's also not resizable to show more of the ruler, and you can't drag or zoom the underlying page. Windows users deserve better, and we hope Quark could fix this in a micro-update in the near future.

Figure F-11
Paragraph Tabs dialog box

The dialog box is not resizable, nor can you drag the underlying page around while it's displayed.

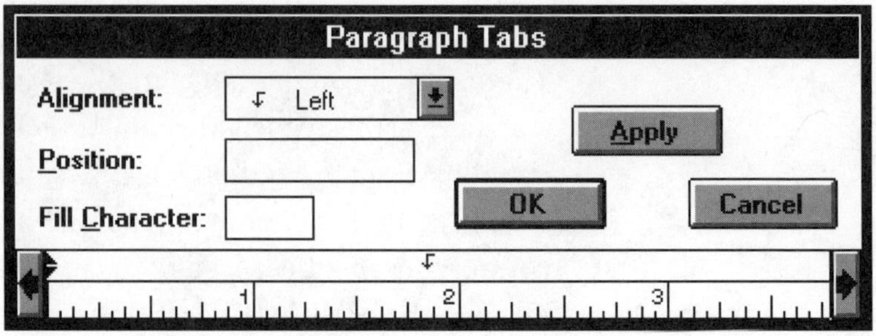

▼ ▼

Fonts

However, before we jump in and discuss all these typographic features, lets look at how QuarkXPress 3.3 now handles fonts.

List updating. You may also notice that version 3.3 loads faster than 3.1. That's partly because, unlike 3.1, version 3.3 doesn't update its internal font list every time you start the program. Font updating only happens now when QuarkXPress detects that fonts have been added or removed from your Windows setup.

The first time you launch QuarkXPress 3.3, it checks for the names of all the fonts you installed in Windows (Type 1 and True-Type) and stores them in a file named PSNAMES.TMP, located in your QuarkXPress directory. QuarkXPress updates PSNAMES.TMP each time you add or delete fonts. Unless you delete the PSNAMES.TMP file, QuarkXPress won't have to verify font names each time you start it up. The only time you should think of deleting PSNAMES.TMP is if things seem to go screwy with your fonts. In that case, delete or rename the PSNAMES.TMP file. QuarkXPress will then generate a new PSNAMES.TMP file. If the original PSNAMES.TMP file has been corrupted, the fresh file should solve your problem.

Font substitution. Also, if you remove fonts from your system, or try to open your document on another system that doesn't have the same fonts used in your document, QuarkXPress lets you select which installed fonts you'd like to substitute for the missing fonts before opening the document.

Indent Here

A paragraph indented with the invisible Indent Here formatting character (Control-\) now stays indented when the paragraph breaks at the bottom of a text box and continues in the next linked text box. QuarkXPress 3.1 simply forgot about the Indent Here character when a paragraph broke to another linked text box, which proved to be an unpopular "feature."

Two-Character Tab Leaders

You can now enter any two printing characters, instead of one, in the Fill Character field of the Paragraph Tabs dialog box (see

"Tabs," starting on page 200). The characters you enter in the Fill Character field will alternate to fill the tab space (see Figure F-12). You could, for example, increase the amount of space between the dots used in a dot leader by entering a period followed by a word space—a handy refinement for that extra touch of class.

Figure F-12
Two-character tab leaders

Ducks and chicks✽☛✽☛✽☛and geese better⋄⋄⋄⋄⋄⋄⋄⋄⋄⋄⋄⋄⋄⋄⋄⋄⋄⋄⋄⋄⋄⋄scurry

In the second line, the < and > symbols were tightened up by selecting the invisible tab character and applying kerning to it.

▼▼▼▼▼▼▼▼▼▼▼▼▼▼▼▼▼▼▼▼▼▼▼▼▼▼▼

Tip: Adjusting Leaders. You don't have to be content with the size and font of a tab's leaders (otherwise called "fill characters"). If you want the characters to be smaller, select the tab character itself and change the point size. If you want the characters to be in another font, change the font of that tab character. People don't often think of the tab character as a character, but that's just what it is. If you turn on Show Invisibles (select it from the View menu), you can see the character as a little gray triangle.

Changing the font and size isn't all you can do: you can even change the amount of space between the leader characters. Select the tab space and adjust its tracking/kerning value. Typically, when you change the kerning value for a single character it only changes the space between it and the next character; however, in this case it changes the space between each of the leader characters (see Figure F-13).

Figure F-13
Sizing tab characters

Period used as leader characters (18 points; same as other type on the line).

Moishe is.................................not strange.
Oh yes. . . . . he is, too.

Tab reduced to 10 points with a tracking value of 94.

▼▼▼▼▼▼▼▼▼▼▼▼▼▼▼▼▼▼▼▼▼▼▼▼▼▼▼

New Typographic Preferences

Quark added two new checkboxes in the Typographic Preferences dialog box in version 3.3 (see Figure F-14). (We talk about the rest of the dialog box back on pages 221–223.) The two new features are Accents For All Caps and Alternate Em.

Figure F-14
Typographic Preferences dialog box

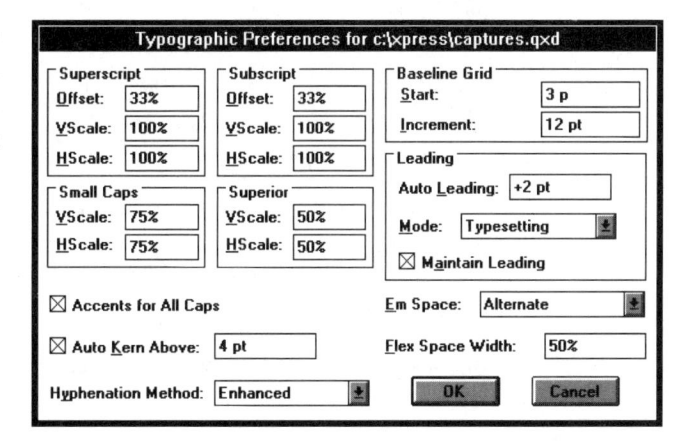

Accents for All Caps. The Accents for All Caps feature is a typographic refinement that lets you specify whether accents appear on accented characters to which you've applied the All Caps type style. Depending on the design of your document or what language you're working in, you may want this feature on or off.

Alternate Em. Quark has always defined an em space as the width of two zeros of the current typeface. However, almost no one else in the world defines an em like that. Quark added the Alternate Em setting to correct this problem in version 3.3.

The Alternate Em sets the em space (and therefore all the settings based on it, such as kerning, tracking, and so on) to the size of the typeface you're using. For example, if you're typing in a 14-point typeface, QuarkXPress's em space (with Alternate Em turned on) is 14 points wide.

Horizontal and Vertical Scaling

You've been able to apply horizontal scaling to type in QuarkXPress from the beginning; now version 3.3 adds vertical type scaling as well. In the Style menu, the Horizontal Scale command is now Horizontal/Vertical Scale.

The dialog box now includes a menu you can use to choose horizontal or vertical scaling. You can enter a value between 25 and 400 percent for either horizontal or vertical scale.

Note that you can't apply both horizontal and vertical scaling to a block of type. You can't, for example, specify "150%" Vertical Scaling and "200%" Horizontal Scaling to the same selection of text. If you apply "150%" Vertical Scaling and then apply "200%" Horizontal Scaling, you end up with "200%" Horizontal—the Vertical Scaling defaults back to "100%". You have to apply either one or the other, and, if necessary, change the type's point size to adjust it in the second direction.

Also, the type scaling keyboard shortcuts remain the same, Control-[and Control-], with one change: these keystrokes scale text either horizontally or vertically, depending on which direction was last selected in the menu in the dialog box.

Kern to Space

Have you ever felt that for certain typefaces a lowercase italic t, f, or l at the end of a word leans too far across the word space, so it's distractingly close to the first letter of the following word? Bob's noticed this problem, especially on justified text, and has dealt with it by occasionally adding a thin space after the offending character. Now there's an easier way. The Kerning Table Editor, discussed back on page 224, now lets you include a word space or en space in a kerning pair and adjust the spacing just as you would any other pair of characters.

To enter an en space in the Pair field of the Kerning Values dialog box, you must first enter the en space character in a QuarkXPress text box (Control-Shift-6), copy it to the Windows Clipboard, and then paste it into the field by pressing Control-V (the Paste command under the Edit menu won't be accessible).

▼ ▼

Tip: Adjusting Space After Caps. We often find that the space between a drop cap and the text that's flowing around it is too small. People have tried all sorts of weird workarounds for moving the two apart, but we prefer the simple method: add kerning between the drop cap and the character after it. The more kerning you add, the farther away the flow-around text is set.

▼▼▼▼▼▼▼▼▼▼▼▼▼▼▼▼▼▼▼▼▼▼▼▼▼▼

Keep With Next ¶

The Keep With Next ¶ and Keep Lines Together controls in the Paragraph Formats dialog box, which we discussed back on page 215, have been improved in version 3.3. In 3.1, subheads that were paragraphs of two or more lines would separate at page or column breaks, even if you'd specified the Keep With Next ¶ and Keep Lines Together options. Now, the Keep With Next ¶ feature keeps such subheads together when a column or page break would have previously separated them.

The H&Js of Paragraph Formatting

This new version of XPress has two minor changes in the way it handles H&Js: deleting/replacing and forced justification.

Deleting/replacing H&Js. When you delete an H&J setting that's currently applied to one or more paragraphs in the document you're working, QuarkXPress 3.3 now prompts you to select a replacement H&J specification. A dialog box will pop up stating "OK to delete this H&J and replace it with another H&J wherever it is used?" You can choose an alternate H&J specification from the Replace With popup menu.

▼▼▼▼▼▼▼▼▼▼▼▼▼▼▼▼▼▼▼▼▼▼▼▼

Tip: Find/Change H&J settings. There's just no way to find and replace H&J settings throughout a document. Or is there? Let's say someone was working on your document and applied an H&J setting called "Really Tight" to paragraphs when you weren't looking. You want to clear them out. This isn't something you need to do every day, but if you do need to do it, you can try the technique we talk about in "Tip: Replacing Style Sheets," later in this chapter. Everywhere we say "style sheets," just mentally replace it with "H&Js."

▼▼▼▼▼▼▼▼▼▼▼▼▼▼▼▼▼▼▼▼▼▼▼▼▼

Forced justification. Speaking of justification, QuarkXPress 3.3 has a new alignment mode: Forced. When you select Forced (from the Style menu, the Measurements palette, or by typing Control-Alt-Shift-J), QuarkXPress forces every line in a paragraph to be justified, including lines that wouldn't ordinarily extend to the margin, such as a single word on the last line, or a single-line paragraph (you still need to have a return at the end of the paragraph; single-line text boxes ignore this command).

Forced justification has basically the same effect as creating a H&J setting with a large Flush Zone (see page 212). It takes a lot of steps to define and apply such an H&J setting, however, so Quark made it easy with the Forced mode.

Copy Flow

Styles are one of the most important features in any text-handling application. And, while QuarkXPress has pretty good styles, they have a ways to go in our opinion. They've certainly taken some solid steps toward getting style right with this release, however. There are four new features that apply to style in version 3.3: a local-formatting indicator, Next Style, improved appending, and improved deleting of styles.

Styles and Local Formatting

In version 3.3, if there is any local formatting in the text containing the insertion point—formatting that overrides the current style's formatting—a plus sign appears to the right of the style's name in the palette. This is a handy way of knowing if you're looking at a paragraph formatted according to its style, or at formatting that's been applied locally (see Figure F-15).

Next Style

Word processors have had this feature for years, and we're delighted to see it now in version 3.3. In the Edit Style Sheet dialog box, there's a popup menu you can use to select the style that

Figure F-15
Local formatting indicator in Style Sheets palette

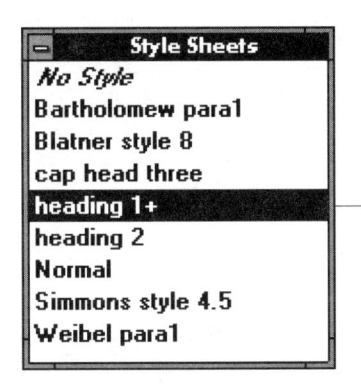

Style Sheets
No Style
Bartholomew para1
Blatner style 8
cap head three
heading 1+
heading 2
Normal
Simmons style 4.5
Weibel para1

The "+" here shows that there's local formatting in the current text selection.

QuarkXPress automatically applies to the next paragraph you create after one with the style you're defining. For example, if you've created a style called "Heading" to be followed by one called "Normal", you can apply the "Heading" style to a paragraph. When you press Enter after you've typed your heading copy, the new paragraph is automatically set to the "Normal" style.

Note that this only works if the insertion point is at the very end of a paragraph when you press Enter. If the insertion point is in the middle of a paragraph when you press Enter, you'll simply break that paragraph in two, and both new paragraphs will have the same style as the original one.

Also, when you're defining a new style, one of the choices in the Next Style popup menu is "Self". If you want to define the Next Style as the style you're currently defining, select "Self". Because you haven't yet named the style and clicked OK, "Self" is just a stand-in for the style name. If you click OK, and then Edit the style you just defined, the style's name now shows up in Next Style instead of "Self".

Appending Styles

Prior to version 3.3, if you wanted to import styles into your document that had the same name as a currently defined style, you were out of luck. QuarkXPress wouldn't do it (and wouldn't even alert you to the problem) until you first deleted the style with the same name in your target document. Since this would replace that style with "No Style" wherever you'd applied it, deleting a style was a pretty drastic step (you had to go through and restyle all the paragraphs; see "Tip: Deleting Styles," below).

It was usually easier to simply redefine the style by hand in your target document rather than to delete it and import the style with the same name. If you brought in text with the same style names as existing styles, QuarkXPress brought the text in with the original formatting intact, but as local hard formatting, overlaying the style-sheet formatting (see page 267, "Appending Styles"). Pretty annoying.

In version 3.3, Quark has taken the first step towards solving this problem. Now, if you bring styles into a document by using the Append command, QuarkXPress checks to see if there are styles in your target document with the same name (but different formatting attributes) as any you're importing. If it finds such a conflict, it displays a dialog box showing the name and characteristics of the conflicting styles and gives you the option of renaming the style that's being imported, or simply ignoring it and using the existing style (see Figure F-16). If you rename the style, QuarkXPress appends an asterisk to its name and imports it.

Note that if you import a style sheet by dragging a page or a text box from one document to another, QuarkXPress won't alert you that there is a style-name conflict; it reverts to the old hard-formatting routine.

Although the ability to rename and import styles is a step in the right direction, we'd still love to see QuarkXPress allow you to actually replace style definitions when there are style-name conflicts (see "Tip: Overwriting Existing Styles," below). Most word processors let you do it, and it's a handy way to quickly change all the formatting in a document.

▼ ▼

Tip: Deleting Styles. When you delete a style sheet in QuarkXPress 3.3, the program asks you if you want to replace it with another one. That is, all the text that is tagged with the deleted style is assigned a new style sheet, rather than going to "No Style". The dialog box is similar to the one you now get when you delete a color or an H&J setting. We think this is one of the coolest features about style sheets in version 3.3.

Figure F-16
Appending styles with different definitions from Microsoft Word

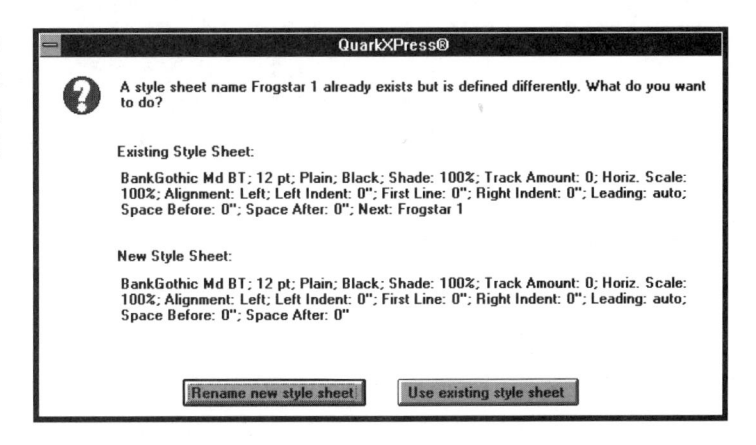

▼▼▼▼▼▼▼▼▼▼▼▼▼▼▼▼▼▼▼▼▼▼▼▼▼

Tip: Overwriting Existing Styles. As we said earlier, we wish that there were a little more control over how QuarkXPress handles importing style sheets. But take heart: there are always workarounds. For example, here's a little number that lets you import style sheets that override the ones within your document.

1. Import the new style sheets from another document by clicking Append in the Style Sheets dialog box. When it asks you whether you want to rename the incoming styles or use the existing styles, click Rename. As we said earlier, QuarkXPress adds an asterisk after the name of each renamed style. For instance, if the style were named "Callout", the program would add a new style called "Callout*".

2. Delete the original style (in this case, "Callout"), and tell QuarkXPress to replace all instances of that style with the new asterisked style ("Callout*").

3. Select "Callout*", click Edit, and remove the asterisk from the Name field.

4. Click Save.

Now the old style is the same as the newly imported style. In effect, the old style sheet name has been overwritten by the new one. This technique works great as long as you don't have to go through it for 125 different styles. We still wish there were an Override Existing option when importing styles.

▼▼▼▼▼▼▼▼▼▼▼▼▼▼▼▼▼▼▼▼▼▼▼▼▼▼▼

Tip: Replacing Style Sheets. We find it rather odd that you can search and replace style sheets in Microsoft Word but not in QuarkXPress. Or can you? Here's a quick search-and-replace procedure to change all instances of one style to another. Let's say you want to replace every instance of "Heading3" with "RunInHead".

1. Open the Style Sheets dialog box and duplicate "Heading3" (select the style and click the Duplicate button).

2. When the Edit Style Sheets dialog box appears, leave the name set to "Copy of Heading3" and click OK.

3. Select the style you want to replace (in this case "Heading3") and click the Delete button. Don't worry; because you created a duplicate of this style, you'll be able to get it back after deleting it.

4. QuarkXPress asks you what style you want to give to the paragraphs tagged "Heading3"; specify the replacement style in the popup menu (in this case "RunInHead"). This is the key to this tip.

5. Click Save.

6. Go back to the Style Sheets dialog box and edit the duplicate style sheet: remove the "Copy of" from the front of the name, and click OK.

You have now replaced all instances of "Heading3" with "RunInHead". Note that this tip also works for replacing colors and H&J settings.

▼▼▼▼▼▼▼▼▼▼▼▼▼▼▼▼▼▼▼▼▼▼▼▼▼▼▼

Tip: Style Sheet Page Breaks. PageMaker has a kind of cool feature that we like: you can specify a paragraph style that breaks to a new page. That is, any paragraph that is tagged with this attribute will always start at the top of a page or column. As it turns out, you can do a similar thing in QuarkXPress. Many readers pointed out that you can simply make the Space Before value in the Paragraph Formats dialog box as large as the text column is tall. For example, if your text box is 45 picas tall, set Space Before to 45 picas. You can set this as a paragraph style or as local formatting.

▼▼▼▼▼▼▼▼▼▼▼▼▼▼▼▼▼▼▼▼▼▼▼▼▼▼

Tip: Based on Differences. Note that styles that are based on other styles are primarily defining differences between the base style and the new style. Let's say you have a style called "Head1" and it's 18-point Futura with the bold style applied, and a style called "Head2" that's based on "Head1", except that it's 12-point Futura and is not bold. The difference between the two is the point size and the style.

If you change the font of "Head1" to Franklin Gothic, then the font of "Head2" changes, too, because they're linked by their differences. There's one exception: if you change the parent style to have attributes that are the same as the child style, the difference link is broken. If you change "Head1" to "not bold," for example, then there's no difference in style between the two and the link is broken. Then, if you go back and change "Head1" to bold again, "Head2" follows suit and becomes bold. This is much the same as what happens when local formatting within a paragraph matches the formatting of the style (see page 265).

▼▼▼▼▼▼▼▼▼▼▼▼▼▼▼▼▼▼▼▼▼▼▼▼▼▼▼▼
Where Text Meets Graphics

There's only one little change in the area of text and graphics interaction in version 3.3. Back in Chapter 7, *Where Text Meets Graphics*, we described ways to use anchored text boxes for things like initial caps, hanging subheads, and the like. The bug in the ointment, however, was an actual software bug, described on page 344. This critter caused funny things to happen if you anchored a text box in front of a left- or right-indented paragraph. Fortunately, the bug swatters at Quark came down hard on version 3.3, and now the bug is gone; anchored text boxes are finally free to hang.

▼ ▼

Tip: Use Polygonal Text Boxes. Instead of using complicated inverted text wraps, we like to use the polygonal text-box feature introduced in QuarkXPress 3.3. Make a regular text box, then select the last item in the Box Shape submenu (under the Item menu). This turns the text box into a polygon. To alter its shape, you have to turn on Reshape Polygon (select it from the Item menu).

▼ ▼

Tip: Adjusting Runarounds for Anchored Boxes. It took us almost forever to figure out that QuarkXPress ignores any runaround specification you give an anchored box except for one: the Top field when Runaround is set to Item. If you want to set a runaround for an anchored box, you have to set it before you paste it into the text block (you can't change it once it's pasted in). Whatever you have set for the Top runaround value is set for all four sides of the runaround box.

▼ ▼

Pictures

Earlier in this appendix, we looked at various Application Preferences such as the bit-depth options for color and grayscale TIFFs. These aren't the only new features in QuarkXPress that have to do with pictures. There are a few others; each of them is minor, but useful nonetheless.

Previews

It's not that these first two features aren't useful, it's just that they don't shake the very foundations of how we've come to know QuarkXPress. The first is an image TIFF/RIFF previewer. This means that when you are importing pictures, you can now see a preview of TIFF, JPEG, PCX, BMP, or GIF pictures as well as EPS graphics—everything QuarkXPress will import, except CGM, HPGL, and DRW (Micrografx Designer) formats. To see the preview portion of the dialog box click the Unfold button (see Figure F-17). The lower part of the Get Picture dialog box will then display the

Figure F-17
Unfolded
Get Picture
dialog box

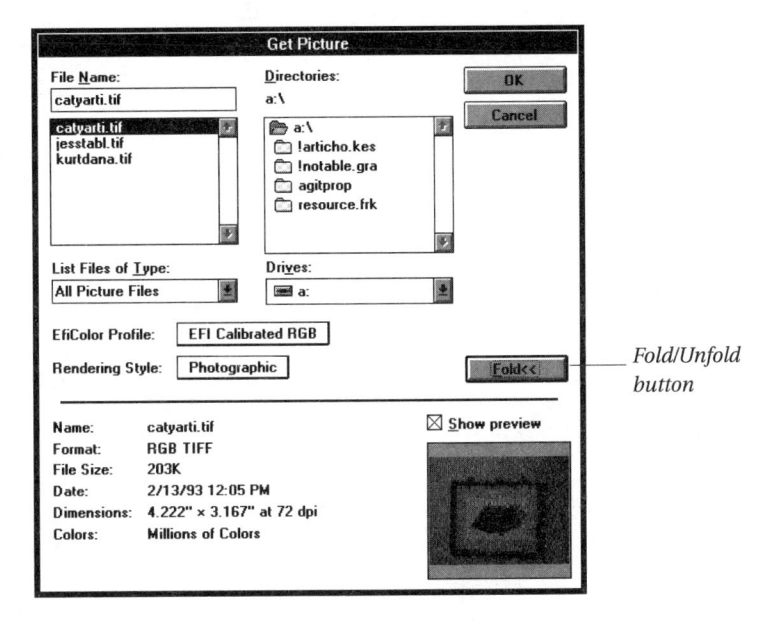

Fold/Unfold button

Show Preview checkbox and data concerning a graphic file's name, format, file size, date, dimensions, and color depth. This latter information will show for any graphic file you select, whether or not you've toggled on the Show Preview option. To hide this lower portion of the dialog box, click the Fold button. Quark has done a pretty good job of optimizing the preview speed, but if you don't need to see the picture to pick it, you're still better off not turning on Show Preview.

The second new picture-oriented feature is the Show Preview window in the Find Missing Picture dialog box, for when you need to find missing pictures—typically from the Picture Usage dialog box (see Figure F-18). This previewer works in the same way as the Picture Preview in the Get Picture dialog box: a Fold/Unfold button extends the Find Missing Picture dialog box, exposing the Show Preview checkbox, which turns it on and off.

Suppressing Printout in Picture Usage

Sometimes a change in QuarkXPress doesn't seem like a big deal until you realize how much time it can save you under the right circumstances. One of these sleeper changes is version 3.3's addition to the Picture Usage dialog box. There's now a column at the far right labeled Print, which you can use to turn on or off the

Figure F-18
Find missing picture dialog box with unfolded picture preview

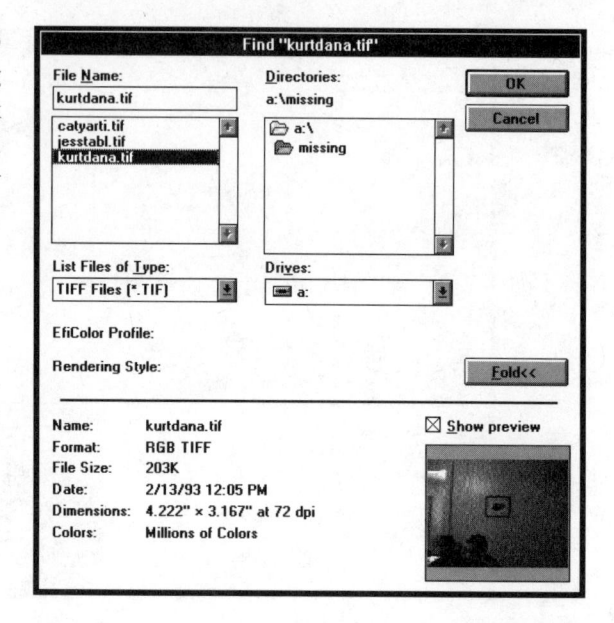

printing of each picture individually (see Figure F-19). When you think of a document that has lots of pictures, some that you want to print sometimes, others that you want to print other times, you can see how valuable this feature really is. Don't forget to turn the pictures back on before making PostScript dumps or sending your files to a service bureau—as we did with the second pass of the color pages for this book!

Drag-and-Drop Picture Importing

You can now import picture files by dragging a file icon from the File Manager and dropping it on an active picture box. Of course, this only works with file formats that QuarkXPress can import via the Get Picture command. Such a feature may seem a little esoteric to some of you, but this little baby could save some big time if your document, say a catalog, calls for several picture imports per page.

For example, suppose you have six picture boxes per page, and 20 pages of them. Instead of performing the Get Picture command 120 times, just do the following: Open your document in QuarkXPress, press Alt-Tab to switch to the Windows Program Manager, and then launch File Manager from the Program Manager. Adjust the sizes of the QuarkXPress and File Manager win-

Figure F-19
Picture Usage dialog box with the new Print column

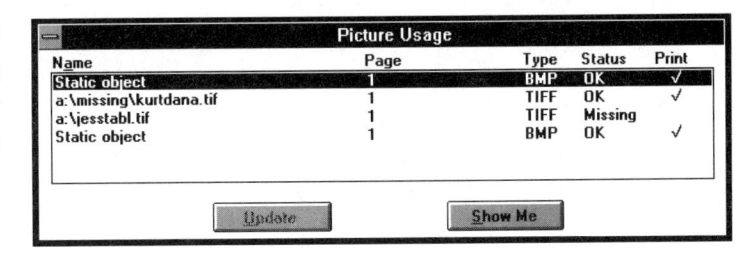

Name	Page	Type	Status	Print
Static object	1	BMP	OK	✓
a:\missing\kurtdana.tif	1	TIFF	OK	✓
a:\jesstabl.tif	1	TIFF	Missing	
Static object	1	BMP	OK	✓

dows so you can see them both on screen at the same time. (The File Manager window can actually be quite narrow, so you can just see the list of picture files.) Now click on a picture file in the File Manager, drag it over to the corresponding picture box in the QuarkXPress window, and let go. The picture pops right into place in one smooth move.

▼▼▼▼▼▼▼▼▼▼▼▼▼▼▼▼▼▼▼▼▼▼

Tip: Finding Picture Paths. The Picture Usage dialog box is helpful in an indirect way, too. If you're trying to find where a picture came from—that is, where it is on disk—you can select the picture on the page and open the Picture Usage dialog box. That picture is highlighted in the list, so if you have a whole mess o' pictures in your document, you don't have to go scrolling through the list to find the one you want (this also works if you have multiple picture boxes selected). The disk path name is displayed on the left side of the dialog box.

▼▼▼▼▼▼▼▼▼▼▼▼▼▼▼▼▼▼▼▼▼▼

Tip: Finding a Bunch of Missing Files. If you move image files or rename the subdirectories they reside in (or even rename the volume they're on), you can wind up with all of your pictures missing. There are two easy ways to relink images.

The first method is coarser, and works if all of your image files are in one subdirectory. Move your QuarkXPress document inside that subdirectory and open it. QuarkXPress looks for missing pictures first inside the subdirectory where the document is located; it automatically relinks them. Save the document, and then move it wherever you like; the images stay linked.

The second method is more subtle, and works if you have clumps of missing files in one or more subdirectories. When you find one missing file inside a subdirectory, QuarkXPress "sees" the other missing files and prompts you whether or not you want to relink them all in one fell swoop (see Figure F-20). You can then repeat this for other subdirectories with missing images in them.

Figure F-20
Additional missing pictures dialog box

▼ ▼

New Graphic File Formats

QuarkXPress has always been fairly omnivorous when it comes to importing graphics files, and it's even more so in the latest version. New formats supported (or supported better) include JPEG, Photo CD, and OLE.

JPEG. QuarkXPress now imports JPEG-compressed image files via its new JPEG DLL and Quark XTension. To import JPEG files, you must have the JPEGLIB.DLL file as well as JPEG.XXT in your Quark-XPress XTENSION subdirectory when you launch QuarkXPress.

JPEG is an industry-standard method for compressing image files at very high compression ratios, even up to 100:1 in some cases. Several popular photo-editing applications, such as Aldus PhotoStyler and Adobe Photoshop, can save images as JPEG files.

Almost anyone working with 16- or 24-bit color images will appreciate JPEG compression. It compresses image files to an incredible degree. A 10:1 compression ratio is considered conservative, and 20:1 and 30:1 are commonly used.

You'd rather save a 60Mb color image file in six megabytes of disk space, wouldn't you? Well, you may or you may not, depending. Since 3:1 compression is considered pretty good for compression utilities like PKWare's PKZIP, how does a JPEG compression routine crunch things even further? It does it by discarding redundant image data, data that you may or may not miss when you view the decompressed file (that's why it's called "lossy" compression). The higher a compression ratio you use, the more likely it is you'll notice some undesirable changes in the image. It all depends on the type of image and what you want to use it for.

Bob's talked to lots of professional photographers who routinely use JPEG compression at about a 10:1 compression ratio and swear that they can't see a difference between the printed results using JPEG compressed and uncompressed files. One photographer once even swore he'd never use a technology that loses image data, like JPEG; but after being forced into using JPEG on a project he immediately went out and bought JPEG software and a hardware accelerator that speeds the compression/decompression process. The message is clear: if you've heard some negative things about JPEG, check it out for yourself. You may be surprised.

With the XTension and DLL installed, QuarkXPress can read in files that are saved in JFIF (JPEG File Interchange Format). That's the one that QuarkXPress and most other PC-based programs work with. When it comes time to print, XPress decompresses the image and sends it to the printer (if it didn't do this, the printer probably couldn't image it correctly).

There are two problems with going this route. First, if you're sending your document and JPEG files for printing on someone else's system, they'd better have the JPEG XTension installed. If not, only the low-resolution screen images will print out. Second, the decompression time can be significant; and because QuarkXPress has to go through it every time you print the page, it can add up quickly unless you have a DSP accelerator board.

Note that JPEG EPS files can be imported by QuarkXPress even if you don't have the XTension and DLL (it looks just like an EPS file on the "outside," but inside it's in a JPEG format). However, you can't print them unless you use a PostScript Level 2 printer (they can decompress JPEG data). Desktop laser printers with this version of PostScript are more common these days, but there are few imagesetters out there that can read these files.

One last thought on the subject: JPEG is really a specification for an image data stream. It's not necessarily considered a file format, since the JPEG data stream itself is incorporated into other image file formats, such as TIFF 6.0. The JPEG XTension reads files that contain JFIF (JPEG File Interchange Format) markers, which provide applications specific information about the file contents. Most PC and Mac JPEG import/export filters interpret JFIF markers.

Photo CD. If you have the Photo CD dynamic link library (PCDLIB.DLL) loaded in your QuarkXPress directory and the Photo CD XTension (PHOTOCD.XXT) loaded in your XTENSION subdirectory, you'll be able to open images saved in Kodak's Photo CD format through the Get Picture dialog box. Specifically, you'll be opening Photo CD Image Pac files, either directly from a Kodak Photo CD or from a regular CD-ROM, your hard drive, a server, or any kind of cartridge.

Image Pac files on the plain Photo CD (Photo CD Master) actually contain image data at five different resolutions from 128 by 192 pixels up to 2,048 by 3,072 pixels. Image compression reduces the size of a single Image Pac to 4.5Mb. (A newer format, Pro Photo CD, can store 4096 by 6144 pixels in a sixth resolution; this isn't accessible using this XTension yet.)

By default, QuarkXPress imports the 256-by-384-pixel image for your screen display, but grabs the higher resolution data, if needed, when it's time to print. Since the Photo CD XTension is required for image output as well as import, your service bureau must have the Photo CD XTension installed.

While the ability to import Photo CD files directly is kind of cool, we find it somewhat useless. First of all, whenever you print, QuarkXPress has to be able to find the Image Pac, which typically means you have to have the Photo CD loaded (or your service bureau does). Second, and even more to the point, while EfiColor can separate the color Photo CD images, they probably won't look very good because almost all scanned images need tonal correction and sharpening (see David's book, *Real World Scanning and Halftones*, for more on this). It makes much more sense to import the image into a program like Adobe Photoshop first (preferably using Kodak's Acquire module), and then save it as a TIFF or EPS image after performing tonal correction and sharpening (as well as any other modifications you want to make).

OLE. Back on page 305, we griped that pictures brought into QuarkXPress via OLE (Object Linking and Embedding) don't appear in the Picture Usage dialog box. Well, by golly, now they do! Instead of seeing a file name in the Name column of the Picture Usage dialog (OLE links aren't named), you'll see its OLE status listed in one of the following ways: either Linked Object, if you used the Paste Link command; Embedded Object, if you used the Paste command in the Paste Special dialog box on an OLE object; or Static Object, if you used the Paste command in the Paste Special dialog box for the generic Picture item. Items that you've simply pasted into QuarkXPress from applications that aren't OLE servers also show up as Static Objects. This update to the Picture Usage dialog box does improve one of the considerations we had against pasting (OLE-based and otherwise) as a form of picture importing, but there are others (see pages 299 and 304).

Color

When we ask people why they use QuarkXPress, the answer (as often as not) is, "It's the program to use for color work, and that's what we do." It's true that QuarkXPress has become the leader in color page layout, but it's still not perfect for working with color. And, frankly, practically no software is, mainly because working with color throws together so many separate sciences and technologies: perceptual studies, computer-display characteristics, and color printing and prepress.

Still, the improvements in 3.3 alleviate several headaches and make it easier to work with different color models: spot colors in EPS files now import seamlessly, the Edit Color dialog box sports five new color models, the Colors palette sports a handful of cool new blends, and a few other goodies. In this section we'll look at each of these new features. We discuss the capabilities added by the EfiColor XTension in Appendix G, *EfiColor*.

▼ ▼

Tip: Duotones from Photoshop. Many people create duotones or tritones in Photoshop, and then save them as EPS files (you have to save them as EPS files) before importing them into QuarkXPress. If the duotone uses spot colors, such as Pantone colors, you have to make sure you've got the same-named color in your QuarkXPress document. People have had difficulty with this in the past because the two programs sometimes named their Pantone colors differently.

Fortunately, QuarkXPress 3.3 now automatically imports the color names into your document so you're sure to get a match. Even though Photoshop's Pantone color names can be slightly different from QuarkXPress's (Photoshop's have an extra letter at the end of some the colors), QuarkXPress is smart enough to import them in the way it names them.

Also note that if your duotones are set to a spot color and a process color (like black), you have to adjust the halftone screen for the spot color so that you don't end up with moiré patterns.

▼ ▼

Tip: Find/Change Colors. If you need to replace every instance of "Red" in your document with "Blue", you'll find yourself frustrated. Fortunately, you can find and replace colors in QuarkXPress 3.3 using the same technique we talked about back in "Tip: Replacing Style Sheets." Where it says "style sheets," think "colors." It works just the same.

▼ ▼

Drag-and-Drop Color Application

The Colors palette, discussed on page 401, gives QuarkXPress much versatility in creating and applying colors and tints, and it's gotten a bit better. Sometimes we think the folks at Quark like to toss in features just because they're cool—for example, drag-and-drop color application. Try it: hold your mouse down on one of the tiny color squares on the Colors palette, and drag it over your page. Notice that as you drag, the image of that color square stays attached to your pointer. As you move the pointer over objects, their color changes to the color you're dragging. Move the pointer past an object and its color reverts to whatever it was before. It really doesn't add a tremendous amount of what we in the software-pontificating business like to call "functionality," but it's a heck of a lot of fun to play with.

To apply a color to an object, just let go of the mouse button. Note that you can apply a color in this way to backgrounds and borders, but not to text, even if you have the text icon selected in the Colors palette. And since the palette is grayed out until you select an object, you can't drag anything until you've selected at least one object. Of course, if you have a black-and-white monitor, those color squares aren't displayed, so you can't use this tip.

Automatically Adding EPS Spot Colors

When you import an EPS (Encapsulated PostScript) picture containing spot colors, QuarkXPress now automatically adds those colors to the Colors palette and to the Colors scroll list in the Colors dialog box. You'll also find the automatically added spot colors in the Plate menu in the Print dialog box (provided you've set Separations to On).

▼▼▼▼▼▼▼▼▼▼▼▼▼▼▼▼▼▼▼▼▼▼▼▼▼▼

Tip: To Import or Not To Import. Unless you're really in control of the graphics you're importing you may not want this palette update to happen. If not, hold down the Control key when you click OK in the Get Picture dialog box under the File menu.

▼▼▼▼▼▼▼▼▼▼▼▼▼▼▼▼▼▼▼▼▼▼▼▼▼▼

One note of caution: since the name of the QuarkXPress color and the name of the color stored in the EPS file must match exactly, don't edit the name of an imported spot color. If you do, QuarkXPress won't be able to separate the renamed color onto the correct plate when you print separations.

Cool Blends

The Colors palette is also the home of the new blends feature. The linear blend came in 3.1; five others arrived with 3.3. Blends are often called vignettes, fountains, or graduated fills, but the concept is always the same: the background of a text or picture box can make a gradual transition from one color to another (see Figure F-21). Unlike some other programs that create graduated fills, in QuarkXPress you can blend any combination of spot colors, process colors, "White", or "Registration".

Figure F-21
Blending from one color to another

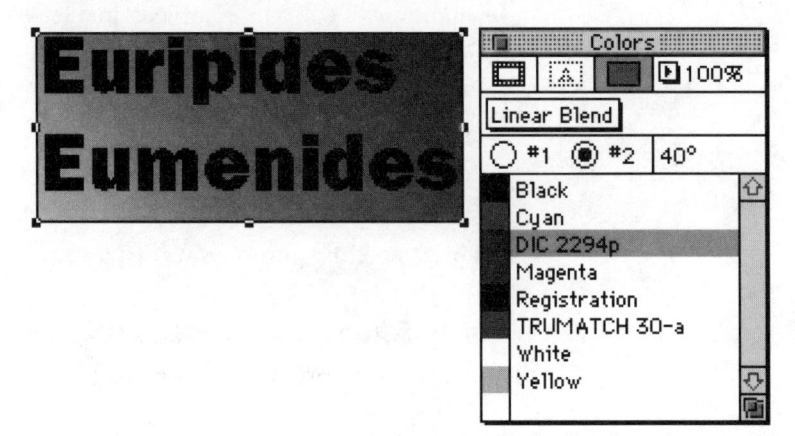

With Version 3.3, Quark's added a dizzying array of blends, not just Linear, but also Mid-Linear (goes from one color to another, then back again), Rectangular, Diamond, Circular, and Full Circular. See Figure F-22 and Figure D in the color plates for examples of these various blends.

Figure F-22
New cool blends

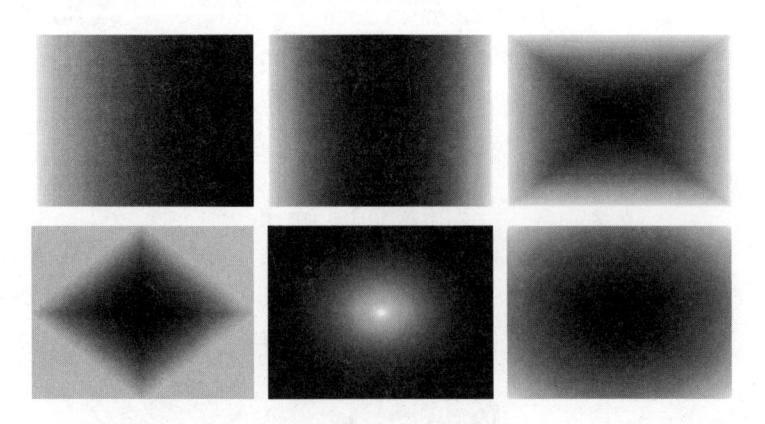

▼ ▼

Tip: A New Dimension. Okay, maybe we're just easily amused, but we think this trick for creating three-dimensional buttons in QuarkXPress is pretty keen.

1. Draw a rectangle or oval (we think it looks best with a square or circle).

2. Give it a straight linear blend. We like to set it at 45 degrees, but it's up to you.

3. Duplicate the object, and make it smaller. The amount you make it smaller is up to you. Remember that if you want to reduce it to 80 percent, you can simply type "*.8" in the width and height boxes.

4. Reverse the blend order of the second object. For instance, if the first object blends from "Cyan" to "White", then the second object should blend from "White" to "Cyan".

5. Space/Align the two objects so that their centers are equal (set Vertical and Horizontal alignment to zero offsets from the objects' centers in the Space/Align dialog box).

You can really see the effect best when the page guides are turned off (see Figure F-23). It's even nicer when you add a .3-point white frame around the inside object (sort of a highlight to the button's ridge).

Figure F-23
Making 3-D buttons

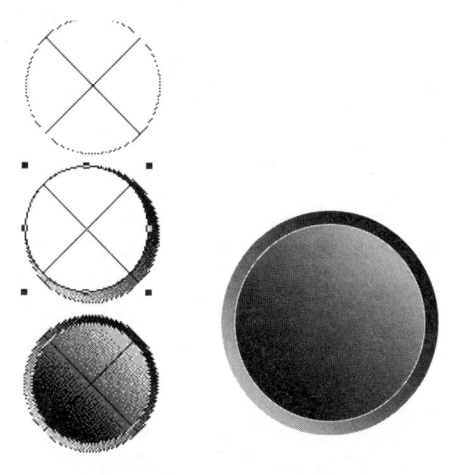

Trapping Preferences

To keep the Application Preferences dialog box from getting too crowded, Quark broke out trapping preferences into its own dialog box in version 3.3. In the earlier version, Quark forgot to save trapping preferences info in your file. That oversight's been fixed in Version 3.3, we're happy to report.

▼▼▼▼▼▼▼▼▼▼▼▼▼▼▼▼▼▼▼▼▼▼▼▼

Tip: Just (Don't) Do It. Trapping is as much art as science—in fact, if you look up "difficult" in the dictionary, it offers the synonym: "trapping." We often don't have time to mess around to make sure our traps are proper throughout a document, and sometimes even if we have time, it'd just be too much of a hassle.

QuarkXPress's trapping is pretty good, all in all, but it's lacking in some important areas, such as blends, choking type, and partially overlapped objects. Ultimately, QuarkXPress isn't designed to be a great trapper. If you want to spare yourself a lot of hassle, you can turn auto trapping off (see "Tip: Turning Auto Trapping Off," below), and use a program like Aldus TrapWise.

You probably won't want to own TrapWise yourself (it costs $5,000), but your service bureau will. Find out how much it costs for them to trap the page for you, and then compare that with how much it's worth to you not to worry about it anymore.

▼▼▼▼▼▼▼▼▼▼▼▼▼▼▼▼▼▼▼▼▼▼▼▼

Tip: Turning Off Auto Trapping. Depending on your page design, trapping can occasionally cause problems or slowdowns at print time. You can turn it off entirely, however, by setting the Auto and Indeterminate trapping values to zero in the Trap Preferences dialog box. If you're having strange slowdowns at print time and are working with colored type on colored backgrounds, you might try this. Note that you won't get any trapping, which causes its own problems.

▼▼▼▼▼▼▼▼▼▼▼▼▼▼▼▼▼▼▼▼▼▼▼▼

Color Models

QuarkXPress now lets you choose colors from among eight different color swatch books: Pantone, FocolTone, and TruMatch—all originally in QuarkXPress 3.1—plus five additional ones, Pantone Process, Pantone ProSim, Pantone Uncoated, and the Japanese systems Toyo and DIC.

Pantone Uncoated is basically the same as the regular Pantone colors; they're just used to spec color for printing onto uncoated or matte paper stocks. Pantone Process and ProSim are process color-matching systems. This means that they're like Pantone spot colors insofar as you use a swatch book to choose colors that can easily be communicated to a lithographer, but they're based on the four process colors rather than on solid "spot" colors. As we've said 300 times before: if you use these, don't rely on the screen representation of the colors. It is almost assuredly wrong. Buy the swatch books (see Appendix E, *Resources*), and use those. Okay, now let's take a look at each of these color models.

Pantone Process and ProSim. When Pantone realized that they were being left behind (by TruMatch; see page 388) in the process-color game, they shifted into first gear and released two process-color libraries. The first, ProSim, is designed to simulate the PMS spot colors with the four process colors. It's based on the Pantone Process Color Simulator swatch book, which shows Pantone spot colors printed side-by-side with their process simulations. The second, Pantone Process, is a process-color matching system much like TruMatch. It has no relationship to the Pantone spot colors; it's just a CMYK swatch book.

There are three problems with spot-color simulation systems like ProSim. The first problem is that it's really hard to simulate spot colors with the four process colors. The second problem is that the team of people Pantone hired to create these simulations seemed to include one person who was (in Steve Job's infamous words) brain-damaged. It's very strange . . . many of the simulations are as good as they could be. Others are so far off the mark that we really had to marvel at the scheme. The third problem is that these systems still use the incredibly strange numbering system that Pantone spot colors use.

Note that ProSim's two primary benefits are that it tries to be more consistent between screen and final output, and that it tries to simulate the PMS colors more closely. The first, as we know, is a lost cause (see "What You See and What You Get," page 380). The second benefit is marginal. We feel that trying to match spot colors is typically difficult and unwieldy at best. You're best off using a swatch system that was designed from the start to be used for process color.

Pantone Process, on the other hand, is process color from the ground up (it doesn't try to match anything but itself). It has a new numbering scheme, but this is hardly worth describing because it doesn't appear to make any sense. Fortunately, this system does have a few things going for it. First, it's generally easier to find colors in it than in the Pantone spot-color swatch books (which are arranged with some semblance of order). Second, there are more colors to choose from than in any previous color-matching system. Third, because Pantone is so well established, it's sometimes easier to find Pantone's swatch books.

We personally feel that the TruMatch system is the best process-color system for designers; it's more intuitive and easier to use than Pantone's. However, both work in more or less equivalent ways. They're just process-color swatch books, though both are produced with rigorous quality-control standards.

Toyo and Dic. Toyo and DIC are both spot-color matching systems from Japan, created by the Toyo Ink Manufacturing Co. and DIC (Dainippon Ink and Chemicals, Inc.), respectively. These spot-color inks have a built-in feature which is helpful: their names reflect how closely you can simulate them in process colors. If the name (number, really) is followed by one asterisk, it means that the color cannot be closely matched in process colors. If the number is followed by two asterisks, it means that the color that you see on screen isn't even close to the spot color. For instance, metallic colors can never be represented on screen, so they're followed by two asterisks.

If you're creating documents that will be printed in Japan, then you may want to specify spot colors in either of these systems rather than with an American system like Pantone (so the proper spot-color name prints on each overlay). Otherwise, you can probably relax and keep reading.

Printing

Let us not forget the ultimate feat of electronic publishing: printing out our documents. Version 3.3 of QuarkXPress adds a few new features to our printing possibilities, none of which by itself is particularly earth shaking. In sum, though, they add up to a much more reliable and efficient printing experience.

There are several new printing features, including more PostScript output options, improvements in non-PostScript printing, and improved access to Printer Description Files (PDFs), among many others. Read on.

New PostScript Options

PostScript has always been plain, simple, and easy to understand, right? Well, QuarkXPress's PostScript options just got more complicated and powerful in version 3.3. So here's a rundown on the changes from version 3.1 and how they affect you.

ASCII or Binary. Version 3.3 gives you control over the data format QuarkXPress uses when it creates PostScript: ASCII or Binary. When you select one of these, QuarkXPress writes all bitmap image information in one form or the other.

What's the difference? Bitmapped images saved in Binary format are half the size of ASCII. So why use ASCII? You need to if the image will ever be printed over a serial connection (from a DOS or UNIX box, for instance). Binary images won't print over a serial connection.

There are two places where QuarkXPress offers you this choice. In the Save Page as EPS dialog box, there's a popup menu labeled Data from which you can choose ASCII or Binary. Similarly, the Printer Setup dialog box has a Data Format menu from which you can select ASCII, Binary, and a third called PC Binary.

The PC Binary data format tries to deliver both the compact data of binary and the communications compatibility of ASCII. That's because the standard binary format inadvertently sends codes that interfere with direct parallel and serial port connections. PC Binary overcomes this problem by avoiding these codes. If you're connected to a printer via a network, you can still use the Binary or ASCII options.

Non-PostScript Printing

Earlier in the book, we said darn little about non-PostScript printing in relation to QuarkXPress 3.1 because, frankly, there wasn't much to say. QuarkXPress was and still is geared to working with PostScript. However, Quark has discovered that a lot people without PostScript printers have bought QuarkXPress for Windows and definitely intend to print with it. Similarly, some folks (even those who do own PostScript printers) want to print to their non-PostScript fax boards. So Quark got it together and beefed up XPress's non-PostScript printing a bit.

Let's assume you've got a Hewlett-Packard LaserJet printer, one without additional PostScript circuitry. These printers understand their own set of codes, known as PCL (Printer Control Language), which works with bitmapped PCL fonts.

When most other programs print to PCL printers, they send streams of PCL codes and PCL fonts. QuarkXPress doesn't. Instead, it generates a giant 300-dpi bitmapped image of each page and sends that premade image down the wire to the printer. In version 3.1, QuarkXPress used your Windows video driver to generate this bitmap. Given the number of video drivers on the Windows market, incompatibilities and anomalies were myriad. Fortunately, in 3.3, it now builds the high-resolution bitmap in memory by using Microsoft's DIB (Device Independent Bitmap) driver, which is automatically installed when you install QuarkXPress. You'll find it as filename DIB.DRV in the SYSTEM subdirectory of your Windows directory.

There are several important ramifications related to Quark's approach to non-PostScript printing.

- ▶ For LaserJets, QuarkXPress doesn't use PCL bitmapped fonts or Infinifonts; it doesn't even know whether you have them installed. This relates to what we discussed back on pages 159 and 160: For all practical purposes, QuarkXPress only works with fonts installed for ATM (Adobe Type Manager) or TrueType. Ahhh, no wonder QuarkXPress doesn't employ PCL codes and fonts when printing to LaserJets!

- ▶ Even if you're using one of the new 600-dpi printers, you're still limited to printing at 300 dpi.

- ▶ QuarkXPress version 3.1 printed graphics on non-PostScript printers only at screen resolution; i.e., very badly. With the change in version 3.3 to use the DIB driver mentioned above, the non-PostScript rendering process now uses the full-resolution data of image files. QuarkXPress itself does the halftone rendering of grayscale images and, frankly, they come out looking pretty good for 300 dpi. You can alter the halftone line-screen frequency in the Printer setup box, though raising it much above 53 lpi will limit the gray-level response to the point where you'd notice strong banding in contours.

For the LaserJet drivers supplied with Windows, the dithering and intensity controls in the Printer Setup Options dialog box do zilch—no effect on printing. That's no problem; we'd rather handle such adjustments from within QuarkXPress anyway. We also found that the Setup dialog box in the Windows Printers control panel allows you to change printing resolution from 300 dpi to either 150 dpi or 75 dpi. Though, for aesthetic reasons, we don't recommend lowering the resolution, we also discovered another problem. Instead of printing the full page at a lower resolution, at

75 dpi we ended up with about a quarter page at 75 dpi, useless unless you're interested in closeup views of halftone patterns—halftone cells appeared proportionately larger.

Fax boards and dot-matrix printers. The first release of QuarkXPress 3.1 processed ("rasterized") non-PostScript pages in bands, sometimes referred to as "strips," instead of single full-page bitmaps. When Quark released their 3.12 update, they switched to the full-page method. However, this caused problems with fax boards and dot-matrix/inkjet printers, which need to get their print data in strips. They just can't chew through a full-page bitmap.

Version 3.3 solves this problem by automatically switching between strip and full-page bitmap methods as needed, though you may need to coax it along. Here's the story.

When you print, QuarkXPress looks at the QUARK.INI file under a section headed "[AlternatePrintMethod]". In that section is a list of printer or fax card drivers that need to get print data in strips. If the driver with which QuarkXPress is trying to print is listed there, QuarkXPress automatically switches to strip mode.

Why do we bother you with all this arcana? Because if you have trouble printing to your fax card or inkjet printer (or LaserJet with only 512K of memory) there's something you can do about it. Open the QUARK.INI file in a text editor (the Windows Notepad does nicely), and scroll down until you see an entry like this:

[AlternatePrintMethod]
WINFAX=1
FAXAbility=1
HP DeskJet=1

The number "1" after the equal sign enables the old "strip" method, which is what you want. A zero disables it.

If you don't see your device among the list of printer and fax drivers, then you can enter it on a line by itself. You'll need to enter the full, exact name of the printer driver in question (see "Tip: Finding Your Device Name," below). Then, follow it with an equal sign and the number "1" (no spaces). Save the file again, and when you restart QuarkXPress you should be in business.

▼ ▼

Tip: Finding Your Device Name. There are a couple of way to find the exact name of the device you're outputting to. One way is to check the Printers control panel. Open the Control Panel in the Windows Main group, and then open the Printers control panel. You'll see a list of printers in the Installed Printers scroll box. Entries read something like "Canon Bubble-Jet BJ-10e on LPT1:". Ignore the " on LPT1:" part and just use the driver name listed.

A second method is to examine the drivers listed under the "[devices]" heading in your WIN.INI file. They'll look something like this:

[devices]
Canon Bubble-Jet BJ-10e=CANON10e,LPT1:
HP DeskJet=HPDSKJET,LPT1:
Linotronic 330=pscript,LPT1:
LM WinPrint 800 PS=pscript,WinSpool:
PDFWriter=PDFWRITR,FILE:

The driver name you want is the one *before* the equal sign.

▼ ▼

Saving a Page as EPS

In Version 3.3, when you save a page as EPS, the dialog box gives you some new options, such as the ability to save the file in four different formats: color, black and white, DCS, and DCS 2.0. Let's look at these (see Figure F-24).

Color/B&W. If you choose either Color or B&W, you get a normal PC-compatible encapsulated PostScript file, just like we described back on page 292. One addition, though: we said that the choice between Color and B&W (black and white) is only for the screen image. As it turns out, the choice also affects the way that QuarkXPress writes the PostScript code. If you choose B&W, color items are actually changed into black-and-white (or gray) items.

DCS. We talked a little about Desktop Color Separation (DCS) back in Chapter 9, *Color* (on page 418), but let's go over it here one

Figure F-24
Save Page as EPS dialog box

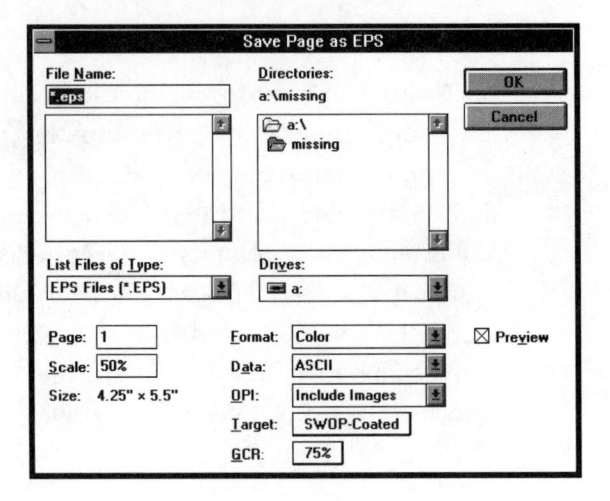

more time. The DCS method is based on preseparating color images into five separate EPS files (which is why DCS is sometimes called EPS-5). Four of the files contain high-resolution information for the process colors (cyan, magenta, yellow, and black). The fifth file contains a low-resolution composite image (for proofing), a screen representation of the picture, and pointers to the four higher-resolution files. This fifth file is what gets imported into QuarkXPress.

When you print your file, QuarkXPress replaces this representation file (sometimes called the "main file") with the four high-resolution files. This means you can print the separations directly from QuarkXPress to an imagesetter. This is great for situations where the color images are not huge, and can be transmitted in a reasonable amount of time over a small bandwidth network.

Choosing DCS results in QuarkXPress saving all five files to your disk. If you set the Target Profile in the Save as EPS dialog box to SWOP-Coated (or to some other process-color profile), the EfiColor processor converts RGB bitmaps into CMYK (see Appendix G, *EfiColor*). That means you can save an EPS file that will separate properly in other programs.

Note that because the DCS file format only handles the four process colors, any RGB spot colors end up getting separated via EfiColor and placed on the CMYK plates.

Dcs 2.0. Dcs 2.0 handles cyan, magenta, yellow, black, plus as many spot colors—or varnish plates, or whatever—as you want. All your spot colors get put on their own plates. Dcs 2.0 saves the entire image in one file rather than in five. (Not all DCS 2.0 images have to be one file, but that's the only kind that XPress makes.) That means that the file is big. Sometimes very big.

The only other program we know of that exports DCS 2.0 files is Adobe Photoshop 2.5 on the Mac with the PlateMaker plug-in export filter. You can build CMYK images in Photoshop and make additional channels that represent each spot color or varnish plate. Then PlateMaker exports the image in DCS 2.0 and Quark-XPress can separate it.

Printer Setup Changes

There are a few new options in the Printer Setup dialog box (see Figure F-25). If you aren't producing color work, then these may not be of much use to you; but if you are, they could be crucial.

EfiColor. First—and perhaps foremost—if you have EfiColor installed you can select the EfiColor profile you want to use for your printer (see Appendix G, *EfiColor*). For high-resolution imagesetters, such as the Linotronic 330, EfiColor lets you select a GCR, or gray component replacement percentage.

Printer Description Files (PDFs). Other changes have to do with information available in the Printer Description File (PDFs, discussed on page 440) for the printer you've selected. Version 3.3 has a new menu for selecting PDFs. You can actually select a PDF for a printer or imagesetter other than the one you're connected to. That way, if Quark hasn't provided a PDF for your precise model of printer, you can choose one that's similar to it. The Select PDF For menu is active whenever you've selected a PostScript device as the Default or Specific printer.

PostScript Printer Description files (PPDs). Adobe Systems released a new PostScript printer driver for the Macintosh in summer 1993, and followed that with the Windows version in early1994. This

Figure F-25
Printer Setup
dialog box

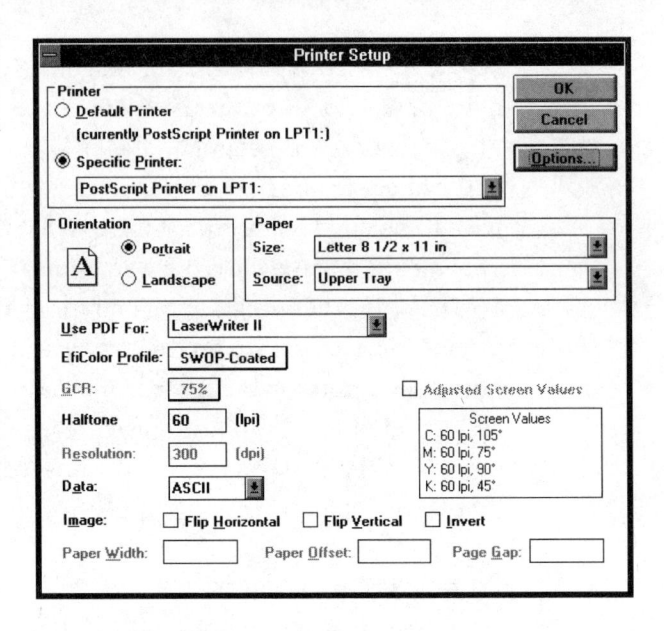

```
┌─ Printer Setup ─────────────────────────────────┐
│ ┌─Printer──────────────────────────┐   [  OK  ] │
│ │ ○ Default Printer                │             │
│ │   (currently PostScript Printer  │  [ Cancel ] │
│ │    on LPT1:)                     │             │
│ │ ● Specific Printer:              │  [Options...] │
│ │   [PostScript Printer on LPT1: ▼]│             │
│ └──────────────────────────────────┘             │
│ ┌─Orientation──┐ ┌─Paper──────────────────────┐  │
│ │  ● Portrait  │ │ Size:  [Letter 8 1/2 x 11 in ▼]│
│ │ A            │ │ Source:[Upper Tray         ▼]│
│ │  ○ Landscape │ │                            │  │
│ └──────────────┘ └────────────────────────────┘  │
│                                                  │
│ Use PDF For:   [LaserWriter II    ▼]             │
│ EfiColor Profile: [SWOP-Coated]                  │
│ GCR:           [75%]      □ Adjusted Screen Values│
│ Halftone       [60]  (lpi)   ┌Screen Values────┐ │
│ Resolution:    [300] (dpi)   │ C: 60 lpi, 105° │ │
│ Data:          [ASCII ▼]     │ M: 60 lpi, 75°  │ │
│                              │ Y: 60 lpi, 90°  │ │
│                              │ K: 60 lpi, 45°  │ │
│ Image:  □ Flip Horizontal □ Flip Vertical □ Invert│
│ Paper Width:[    ] Paper Offset:[    ] Page Gap:[ ]│
└──────────────────────────────────────────────────┘
```

driver uses Adobe's standard PostScript Printer Description files (PPDS) which they've used with Illustrator and other programs for years. QuarkXPress 3.3 now supports these files by automatically converting them to PDFs at program startup, and placing them in the PDF subdirectory. The program uses a PDF in preference to a PPD for the same printer. Call Adobe at 800/833-6687 to order the driver; it's about$24.95 plus shipping, handling, and tax.

Adjusted Screen Values. Also, the dialog box now has a field that displays screen angles for each process color. The default degrees are cyan at 105, magenta at 75, yellow at 90, and black at 45. If the PDF for the printer you've chosen contains alternate screening information, and you've checked the Adjusted Screen Values box, the new screen angles for your Halftone Frequency setting appear in this field. Sometimes this means that QuarkXPress will override the halftone screen frequency value you've entered in the Halftone Screen field. For example, the LaserWriter IIf-g PDF uses a halftone screen of 106 lpi (to take advantage of Apple's Photo-Grade technology in those printers). Also, see "EfiColor or PDF Screen Values" in Appendix G, *EfiColor*.

Print Dialog Box Changes

The Print dialog box in QuarkXPress 3.3 contains four new print-related features: Low Resolution output options, Blank Pages, Calibrated Output, and Print Status. One of these saves money, the other three save frustration. First, we should mention that in Version 3.3, Quark cleaned up the dialog box considerably (see Figure F-26). Gone are the many buttons, replaced by a cleaner array of popup menus for many familiar options (of course, if you don't like popup menus, you're out of luck).

Figure F-26
Print dialog box

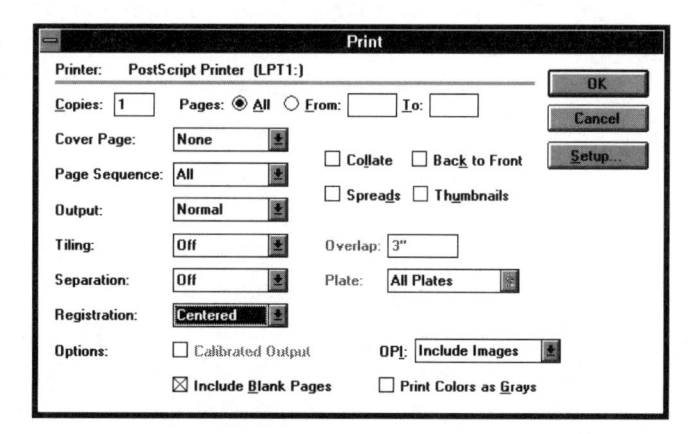

Low Resolution, Rough, or Normal Output. Like many other additions, the new Low Resolution and Rough options in the Output menu may not seem like much at first glance, but they can be tremendous time-savers. If you check Low Resolution in the Print dialog box, QuarkXPress prints a document using the picture preview image built into the document, rather than the source picture file. If you select Rough when you print, QuarkXPress replaces pictures with boxed X's, and replaces complex box frames—from Mac versions of XPress—with simple ones.

These are godsends if you have to make many proofs to a low-resolution desktop printer. We can't tell you how much time we've wasted either sending documents with high-resolution pictures to low-resolution devices (it can take forever for them to print), or hiding the pictures somewhere on our hard disks so QuarkXPress can't find them, then telling it to print anyway (that was the old trick for making QuarkXPress use the internal low-res image).

Calibrated Output. If you've ever printed a 50-percent gray box on your desktop laser printer, you've probably noticed that the box often comes out looking much lighter when printed on an imagesetter. That's because laser printers (being toner-based) use larger, sloppier dots than imagesetters. The Calibrated Output option is designed to compensate for this, making your laser printer kick out gray tints that more closely match the imagesetter output.

When you select the Calibrated Output option, gray tints and grayscale images should print more lightly than normal on your laser printer. To tell you the truth, we avoid the Calibrated Output option, mainly because we don't have any control over what it does. True, laser tints do normally seem to come out on the dark side, but Calibrated Output, in our experience, tends to overcompensate. When we're serious about printing scanned photographs, for example, we'd rather make our adjustments in the Picture Contrast Specifications dialog box or in a image-editing program, so that we know exactly what's going on.

Still, it might work in your situation. You'll notice, however, that the Calibrated Output is only an option if you've chosen a PDF that contains the calibration data. Since Calibrated Output only applies to laser printers, it's not an option if you've chosen a PDF for an imagesetter or a color printer. And not all laser printer PDFs have the calibration data. Of the laser printer PDFs shipping with QuarkXPress, the LaserWriter II f-g, LaserWriter Pro 600 & 630, and Generic B&W PDFs lack calibration data, so Calibrated Output isn't an option if you've chosen one of those, either.

Print Status. In version 3.1, you needed to hold down the Shift key as you clicked on the Print button in order to view the Print Status windows during printing. Now in version 3.3 it's just the opposite: you get Print Status automatically every time you print, unless you hold down the Shift key, in which case Print Status only shows the document file name and selected printer. The full Print Status dialog box not only tells you what page it's printing, but also what color plate, tile, and EPS/TIFF images it's working on (see Figure F-27).

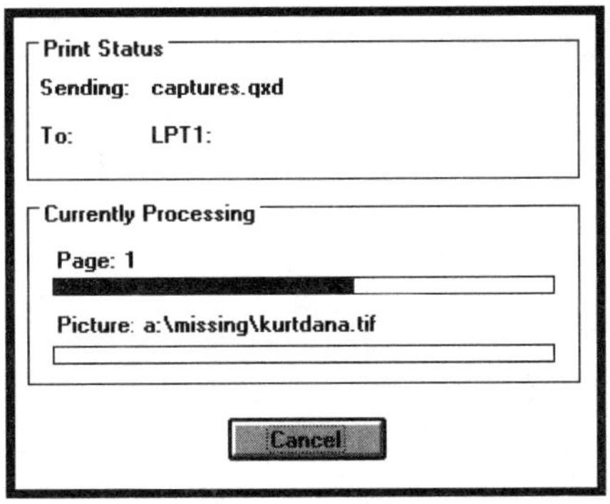

Figure F-27
Print Status dialog box

▼ ▼

Tip: Jump to Absolute Page Numbers. If you play around with sections and page numbers, you may find yourself in a quagmire when you try to print a page range. For example, let's say your document begins on page 56 and you want to print the 16th through the 20th pages. You could sit around and try to figure out what numbers to plug in to the Print dialog box's page range fields or you could just type "+16" and "+20". The plus sign before the number means that the numbers are absolute; the first page is "+1", the second page is "+2", and so on.

This is also helpful when moving to a page using Go To page. You can quickly jump to the 20th page by typing "+20".

▼ ▼

Collect for Output

If you send files to a service bureau a lot, you're going to love this feature. The Collect for Output command under the File menu copies your document and all the picture files necessary for its output to a subdirectory of your choice. It also creates a report containing detailed information about your document, from what fonts and pictures you used to what trapping preferences are set to. Then all you have to do is send that subdirectory to your service bureau or color prepress house by disk, modem, or carrier pigeon.

Using this command is simplicity itself. When you select it, it prompts you to select a subdirectory. You can also click the New Directory button to create a new subdirectory. You also specify a name for the report. We typically just use QuarkXPress's default name; it's simply the name of your document with .XTG (XPress Tags format) stuck on the end. Then click the Collect button or press the Enter key, and QuarkXPress copies your document and all picture files, wherever they might reside, to that target folder. Note that you must first save your document file or Quark will prompt you to do so (as the good *QuarkXPress Book* tells us, you've got to be saved before collection).

Note that to avoid potential copyright problems, QuarkXPress doesn't copy any fonts to the folder. That's up to you to do yourself, if necessary. The legal ramifications are between you, your service bureau, and your font vendor. We don't blame Quark for wanting to stay out of this one!

Collecting files for output takes longer than manually copying each file, as QuarkXPress does a very thorough search for each file it needs. This may take a bit more time, but the process does give you the satisfaction of knowing you haven't forgotten to copy that little bitty logo illustration hidden at the bottom of page 32.

Note that the document report saved in the subdirectory is saved in the XPress Tags format (see Chapter 5, *Copy Flow*). That means you can read it in a word processor, but there'll be a bunch of weird codes in there. Instead, try importing it into a QuarkXPress text box with the Include Style Sheets checkbox turned on in the Get Text dialog box. That way you can format the various parts of the document using style sheets.

The Big 3.3 Picture

What we don't understand is why Quark persists in numbering its new versions only in .1 increments. With all the new features introduced since 3.1, we feel we should be up to 3.6 or 3.7 by now! It's impressive how the increased functionality has speeded up our production work. And with features such as separation of CMYK and RGB TIFFS and the new palettes, it gets easier and easier to create high-quality artwork.

But this isn't the end of the line! The future of QuarkXPress is bright. Products like QuarkPrint and the Quark Publishing System are making printing and networking more efficient. And then there are the many XTension developers who are making our lives even easier (see Appendix E, *Resources*). But don't worry: as quickly as the world of electronic publishing changes, we'll be right there, acting as your all-night consultants.

APPENDIX G

EFICOLOR

For years, "What You See Is What You Get," or WYSIWYG (pronounced "wizzywig") has been one of the key buzzwords of desktop publishing. It meant that the page layout you saw on your computer screen was, more or less, what you'd get out of your printer. WYSIWYG works fine for a page with any color of ink—so long as it's black (to paraphrase Henry Ford). But it's significant that nobody's felt the need to come up with a similarly cute acronym for describing color fidelity between computer and printer. We did consider "Color You See Is Color You Get," but we wouldn't want to be responsible for unleashing "kissykig" upon the world. Our editor, Steve Roth, says he prefers WYGIWYG: "What You Get Is What You Get."

Silliness aside, the main reason nobody's come up with such an acronym is that until fairly recently, it would have described a condition that didn't exist. If you've ever tried creating color pages, you've learned—probably with no little pain—that the colors you see on your computer have little more than a passing resemblance to what comes out of your printer or off a printing press. In fact, a major part of working with color on personal computers has been learning through trial and error that when you see color A on your PC screen, you'll actually get color B out of your color proofing printer, and color C off of a four-color press run. Your only guides were process color swatch books, test prints, and bitter experience.

▼▼▼▼▼▼▼▼▼▼▼▼▼▼▼▼▼▼▼▼▼▼▼▼▼▼▼▼▼▼▼▼▼▼▼
Managing Color

Well, the times they are a-changing, and the hottest things on the PC market today are color-management systems (CMSes) that promise to provide fidelity between the colors on your computer screen and those of your printed output. Apple, Kodak, Pantone, and Electronics for Imaging, among others, have management systems that sometimes actually cooperate with each other. Frankly, we're more than a little skeptical of some of the claims made by marketers of these products ("No more MatchPrints; proof colors right on your computer screen!"), but color-management systems are clearly a step in the right direction.

And if you've upgraded to or purchased QuarkXPress 3.3, you already own one such system, or at least major components of it: EfiColor from Electronics for Imaging (EFI), supported in QuarkXPress by the EfiColor XTension.

You should note, however, that EfiColor, and color-management systems in general, are far more advanced on the Macintosh than they are on Windows. QuarkXPress is one of the very first EfiColor-capable applications for Windows, whereas entire suites of such applications exist on the Macintosh—including programs like EfiColor Cachet, a color-correction program. You may find that your strongest motivation for using the EfiColor XTension is when you're working with images created with EfiColor-capable applications on the Macintosh.

What EfiColor Attempts

As a color-management system, EfiColor is designed to make the colors on your document's page consistent—from your computer screen to a color proof to your final output device. If you're creating a document to be output on a four-color press, EfiColor makes the colors on your screen look more like those that will emerge from your press run. If you use a color printer such as a QMS ColorScript or Canon CLC 500 with an EFI Fiery RIP for comps, EfiColor ensures that your color printout also bears more than a passing resemblance to your final four-color output.

Note that we're saying "look like" and "passing resemblance." EfiColor can remove a lot of the guesswork from working with color. So instead of few of the colors on your screen looking like your final output, many of the colors you see may be significantly closer to what you'll be getting than they would otherwise. In photographic images—images that use a lot of subtle tonal changes, not flat tints—you'll have a better idea of what the overall look and color cast of the final image will be.

EfiColor's other great claim to fame is its ability to separate RGB bitmaps to CMYK for process-color output. Prior to the arrival of the EfiColor XTension, you had to preseparate your files into CMYK using Photoshop, PhotoStyler, or the like (in fact, you may still want to use that method; see "Before You Use EfiColor," later in this chapter).

Why Color Management "Can't" Work

If there's one thing we want you to get out of reading this appendix, it's that it's just plain not possible for computer monitors, thermal-wax color printers, color copier/printers, and four-color printers to exactly match each other, color for color. Each device uses different technology to create color, and each uses differing methods of specifying its colors.

Monitors display colors as values of red, green and blue (RGB). Printers usually use cyan, magenta, yellow, and black (CMYK). The colors emitted from a monitor use light and are additive: the more color you add, the closer to white the screen gets. On the other hand, printers that apply ink, wax, or toner to paper generally create colors by combining values of cyan, magenta, yellow, and black. This color model is subtractive: the more of each component you add, the darker your final color becomes. When you create a color with two different methods, there's really no way that the two can look exactly the same.

Plus, the same RGB values on two different monitors might not look like each other at all, because the screen phosphors and technology might be slightly different. Similarly, the same CMYK values printed on a thermal wax transfer printer such as a QMS ColorScript look very different from "identical" values printed on a four-color press on coated stock, and those colors also look different than colors printed on newsprint.

We call each of these color systems *device dependent* because the color is specific to only one device—a brand of monitor, color printer, or whatever. EfiColor tries its best to create consistency among various devices, but you need to understand that it's not entirely possible.

"I Only Paint What I See"

Matching colors might be a hopeless comparison of apples, oranges, and grapefruits, except that there's one constant shared by every method of creating colors: the human eye. The fact is that your eyes don't care what technology a monitor or printer uses to create a color; they just see colors. Just as monitors and printers are device *dependent*, your eyes are device *independent*. They're the one constant in this whole *mishegoss*, and not surprisingly, they're the key to many color-management systems, including EfiColor.

No, EfiColor doesn't try to calibrate your eyes with some sort of cybernetic gizmo. Rather, it uses a color-space model based on statistical analysis of how most people perceive differences between colors. This model was developed by the Commission Internationale de l'Eclairage (International Commission on Color, or CIE to you and me) in the 1930s. The CIE color space describes every color the human eye can see, using a mathematical model that isn't dependent on fickle things like the density of phosphor coatings or the amount of ink spread on certain paper stocks.

Unlike RGB or CMYK values, which don't really describe a color (the same values might look quite different on different devices), CIE values actually describe a color's appearance, not just the values that make it up.

Color-Management Concepts

Before we go too much further into this discussion, we have to take a break and define a couple of important words: *gamuts* and *profiles*. We'll use these words a lot throughout this chapter.

Gamuts. A device's color *gamut* describes the range of colors that device can create or sense, and how the colors are distributed within that range.

Since the CIE color space describes every color you can see, by default it has the largest gamut. No device—monitor, scanner, or printer—can come close to reproducing this range of colors, and so the gamut of any specific device is smaller than the CIE gamut. Plus, different devices are able to image different sets of colors (the available colors are spread out differently). So one device may be able to reproduce many hues of red, while another may be weak in reds, but especially competent in producing a wide range of blues.

Profiles. EfiColor uses files called *device profiles* to keep track of not only the color gamut of particular devices, but also other information about their capabilities and limitations.

Most of the profiles you use with EfiColor are actually device characterizations, rather than calibrations. In other words, they're a generic description of a 13-inch monitor, or a printing press that uses SWOP (Standard Web Offset Press) coated inks, not a specific description of your personal device or your lithographer's press. With the pending release (at this writing) of EfiColor Works on the Macintosh, however, tools will be available to build custom scanner and monitor EfiColor profiles for your devices. (Unfortunately, we don't yet know of any plans to release this on Windows).

Another development promises to provide even more flexibility in choosing, using, and customizing profiles. As of March 1994, the four primary color-management software companies (EFI, Eastman Kodak, Apple, and Pantone) have agreed in principle to standardize on Apple's ColorSync profile system. The profiles to be provided in EfiColor Works are actually ColorSync profiles. Many scanner- and monitor-calibration systems can already create ColorSync profiles. And because other color-management vendors are starting to sell their hand-built output profiles in ColorSync format, in the not-so-distant future (perhaps by the time you read this) you'll be able to mix and match profiles from every company, or even make your own.

Like your Uncle Jack used to say, you can buy your razors from one company, and your blades from someone else. Again, how this relates to the Windows market is still unclear; we hope the format crosses over quickly.

From Device to Device

EfiColor actually adjusts colors depending on what it knows about certain printers and monitors. It does this by converting color information to and from its native CIE color-space format (see Figure G-1). If you've installed the appropriate device profiles on your Mac, EfiColor can transform the color you see on your screen into CIE color, then turn around and convert it to a similar color on your color printer.

Note that a color monitor can display a different set of colors than a desktop color printer, which, in turn, has a much greater gamut than a four-color press. EfiColor's color transformations, for instance, work best when they reduce one device's gamut to match another; it's just not possible to *increase* a device's gamut to match another's, although there are ways of faking it. A color monitor is good at displaying the limited gamut of a four-color press, but a four-color press is hard-pressed (no pun intended) to simulate a display.

Perhaps the most important aspect of this technology is the conversion between RGB and CMYK color models. Once EfiColor transforms a color into its internal CIE color space, it can transform it to any other color model and device space it knows about. And while the RGB-to-CMY conversion is relatively simple (see Chapter 8, *Color*, page 407), converting from RGB to CMY *plus* K has traditionally been quite difficult. EfiColor does this for you behind the scenes.

Figure G-1
EfiColor's transformations

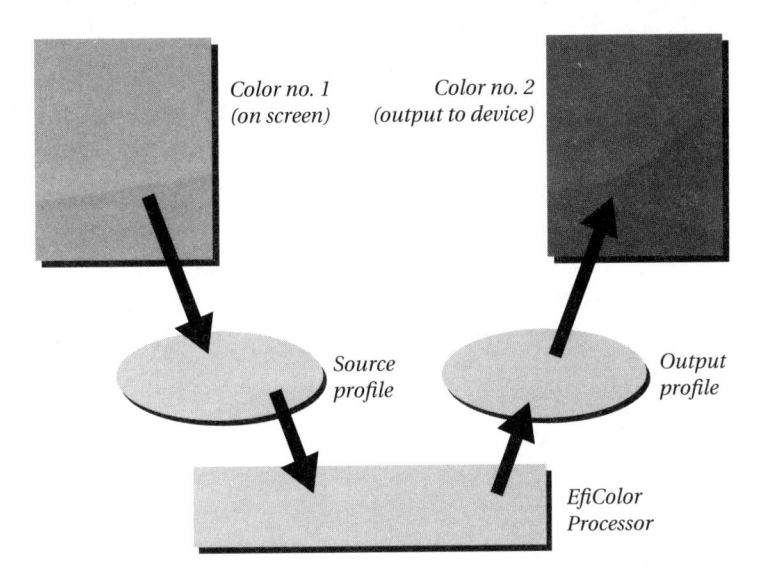

Color no. 1 (on screen)   *Color no. 2 (output to device)*

Source profile   *Output profile*

EfiColor Processor

Whether or not you want EfiColor to do this conversion is a legitimate question; people have argued for years over which program does the best conversion. Some say Adobe Photoshop, some say EfiColor, and some say forget all desktop solutions and hire a traditional color separator to do it for you. You'll forgive us if we just stay out of this argument. But do note that EfiColor gives you the choice by letting you turn its transformations on or off.

Metric Color Tags (MCTs)

If all the colors you ever use are created on your own PC using QuarkXPress, then the color transformations we just described would be all you'd ever need. But life (and desktop publishing) is more complicated than that. Most of the time you'll be importing artwork created or scanned elsewhere. How will your EfiColor XTension know on what sort of display this artwork was created, and for what kind of printer it was designed?

The answer is supplied through the Metric Color Tag (MCT) format: applications that support EfiColor can tag a graphics file with profile information. Then, when you import a picture into QuarkXPress, the EfiColor XTension automatically reads the MCT information from the picture and uses the appropriate device profile to transform the picture's colors when it's displayed and printed to simulate the colors of the output device you've specified. At least that's the way it's supposed to work.

The important thing to understand here is that specifying a color with RGB or CMYK values alone doesn't really mean anything. For example, it's meaningless to say "This color has such-and-such RGB values," because there's no basis for comparison. The RGB values as displayed on one device are totally different from those values displayed or printed on other devices. However, if you say "This color is defined by these RGB values *as displayed on this particular device,*" then you've got something to work with. Knowing both the values and the device profile sets the groundwork for knowing what the color really looks like.

Using EfiColor

OK, so now that you have an idea of what EfiColor's supposed to do, let's talk about how it works with QuarkXPress 3.3, and how you tell it what you want.

Installing EfiColor

Note that EfiColor is not built into the QuarkXPress application itself. Rather, it's a combination of an XTension and a dynamic link library (DLL). Therefore, in order to use EfiColor, you must first make sure it's installed properly. As we discussed in Appendix F, QuarkXPress automatically installs the EfiColor XTension files unless you click the Customize button in the installation dialog box to deselect EfiColor. Since you've already told the Installer that you want the system installed, you'd better tell it that you want the XTension and help file as well.

What You Get

The two components of the EfiColor system are the EfiColor dynamic link library (EFICOLOR.DLL) and the EfiColor XTension (EFI.XXT). The EfiColor DLL sits in the same directory as your QuarkXPress program, and the XTension goes into the XTENSION subdirectory.

EfiColor Processor. The EfiColor XTension (from Quark) calls the EfiColor DLL (created by EFI), and both are needed. There's also an EFICOLOR subdirectory under your QuarkXPress directory which contains all the EfiColor profiles currently installed on your PC as well as ancillary files used by EfiColor.

Profiles. QuarkXPress ships with a number of profiles, including profiles for two scanners, five printing devices, and a bunch of different monitors. If your monitor's or printer's profile is not included with QuarkXPress, then you should contact Quark to see if they have one available. Though EFI sells profiles for the Macintosh, they don't plan to make them available for Windows.

For example, QuarkXPress comes with the SWOP-Coated profile, but there's no profile for uncoated stock. You can purchase that profile separately, or you can get it by buying EFI's Cachet program when it becomes available for Windows. Monitor profiles may be available free from online services and user groups.

The monitor-profile situation in Windows-land is pretty insane, we should warn you. That's because a good profile should really take into account your combination of display monitor *and* display adapter card. Put another way, your monitor may display colors somewhat differently depending on whether you plug into a SpeedStar HiColor adapter or a Hercules Graphite Card.

Now, picture the huge variety of color display adapters and display monitors currently for sale, and then consider all the possible combinations. EFI representatives we spoke to admit that neither they nor anyone else is likely to produce monitor profiles covering every possible combination. The solution to this problem will be do-it-yourself EfiColor profile kits. Monitor calibrators, such as the SuperMatch Display Calibrator, will let you create custom profiles for your monitor. But again, this stuff has only just arrived on the Mac, and it will be a while before it's common on the PC.

Remember that in order to transform colors correctly, the EfiColor XTension must have profiles available for whatever monitors, color printers, and whatnot that you're using.

The EfiColor XTension

The EfiColor XTension adds many dialog boxes and commands to QuarkXPress. Rather than tackle them on an item-by-item basis, we'll take you on a tour of how we think you'll most likely use the XTension's features.

Although the range of choices you can specify with EfiColor seems daunting, you can break EfiColor's choices into three broad categories: telling it about your monitor, telling it about your printer(s), and telling it about your images and how it should modify colors within XPress. When the EfiColor XTension knows all these variables, then it can correctly transform color between color spaces and gamuts, resulting in closer color matching between all the devices.

Telling EfiColor About Your Monitor

The first step in getting consistent color is to tell EfiColor about your monitor. When EfiColor is turned on, the Display Correction checkbox is active in the Application Preferences dialog box under the Edit menu (or type Control-Alt-Shift-Y). You can then turn Display Correction on or off, and select the profile for your monitor from the popup menu (see Figure G-2).

Figure G-2
Monitor selection in Application Preferences

☒ Display Correction
Apple 13" RGB

Because EFI's monitor profiles are designed to work with properly calibrated monitors, your screen color looks best when you have calibrated your monitor to match the values specified in the reference card for your monitor's profile (these reference cards come with the profiles and with the EfiColor XTension's documentation). On most monitors, in fact, if you haven't calibrated properly, chances are that turning Display Correction on won't make any difference.

Telling EfiColor About Your Printers

The next step in the consistent color dodge is to tell EfiColor what printer you're printing to. Of course you don't need to do this until you're actually ready to print a proof or your final piece. You give EfiColor this information in the Page Setup dialog box (see Figure G-3). The EfiColor XTension adds two items to the Printer Setup dialog box: one popup menu for selecting the desired EfiColor profile, and another for specifying the percentage of gray component replacement (GCR) you want to use. In some circumstances, when you've selected a color printer, for example, it also changes the Use PDF Values checkbox to Use EfiColor Screen Values.

Figure G-3
EfiColor controls in the Printer Setup dialog box

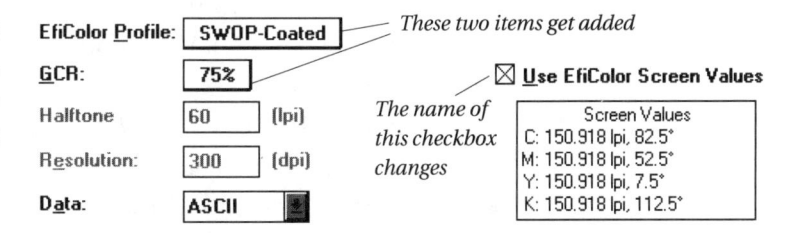

EfiColor Profile: SWOP-Coated — *These two items get added*
GCR: 75% ☒ Use EfiColor Screen Values
Halftone: 60 (lpi) *The name of this checkbox changes*
Resolution: 300 (dpi)

Screen Values
C: 150.918 lpi, 82.5°
M: 150.918 lpi, 52.5°
Y: 150.918 lpi, 7.5°
K: 150.918 lpi, 112.5°

Data: ASCII

EfiColor Profile. After you use the Printer Type popup menu to select your printer, you can use the EfiColor Profile popup menu immediately below to select that device's profile. However, note that you should always choose the profile associated with the printer you've selected. If you select the QMS ColorScript from the Printer Type popup menu, then you should always pick a ColorScript profile, too (EfiColor helps you out by making an educated guess as to which profile you want). If you select a profile that isn't set up for the printer—for example, if you select SWOP-Coated—you'll probably end up with garbage.

Note that the EfiColor Profile popup menu changes, depending on what printer type you have selected. If you're printing to a black-and-white imagesetter (which, by definition, prints only black and white), you can't select a profile for a color printer.

Gray Component Replacement (GCR). If you select SWOP-Coated or another four-color process profile, QuarkXPress lets you specify a value for Gray Component Replacement (GCR). You can choose zero, 25, 50, 75, or 100 percent. This process replaces areas of neutral gray that are made up of cyan, magenta, and yellow inks with equivalent tints of black. The two greatest benefits of GCR are saving ink on long press runs and creating rich, crisp dark areas.

Some people argue that EfiColor's GCR isn't precise enough for high-quality work. If you feel that way, you probably want to use a different program for your color separations, such as Color Access or Photoshop. For most color work, one of the five preset GCR values is reasonable. We typically leave this set to 75 percent. When you set GCR to 100 percent, you often lose some of the soft, natural-looking shadow areas because black is replacing almost all the cyan, magenta, and yellow tones. (The color pages of this book were made with 75-percent GCR.)

The key to GCR—curiously enough, they don't talk about this in the documentation—is that it only works for RGB-to-CMYK conversions. Colors and images that are already specified in the CMYK color model don't get adjusted at all. If you specify a GCR value, QuarkXPress either applies those GCR values to your process-color separations or simulates the effect when printing to a color printer.

EfiColor or PDF Screen Values. Whenever you select a color printer in the Printer Type popup menu, QuarkXPress changes the checkbox labeled Use PDF Screen Values in the Printer Setup dialog box to Use EfiColor Screen Values. When this checkbox is turned on and you're making color separations, QuarkXPress prints your document using the halftone screen frequency and angle values built into the EfiColor profile, rather than using either QuarkXPress's built-in values or those in the PDF or PPD. We prefer to use the EfiColor values (they're probably overridden by the imagesetter's screening method, anyway—Agfa's Balanced Screening or Linotype-Hell's HQS), but it's really up to you.

No matter what you pick in this checkbox, the angles and screen frequencies are displayed in the Halftoning field at the lower-right corner of the dialog box.

▼ ▼

Tip: Non-PostScript Printers. If you're using a non-PostScript printer, you can still specify an EfiColor profile. Once you've selected the printer in the Printers Control Panel, you can select the EfiColor Profile you want from the popup menu in the Printer Setup dialog box. You'll get more accurate color if you use the inks and papers specified on the printer's profile reference card.

▼▼▼▼▼▼▼▼▼▼▼▼▼▼▼▼▼▼▼▼▼▼▼▼▼▼
Tip: Turn Calibrated Output Off. If you're using the EfiColor XTension, we recommend that you turn off Calibrated Output in the Print dialog box. Some people use the calibrated output feature to adjust for dot gain, but the way that QuarkXPress handles it just isn't as powerful as other calibration software such as the Precision Imagesetter Linearization Software from Kodak. Whatever the case, if you leave Calibrated Output on, then it may further adjust your color correction, messing up what the EfiColor XTension is trying to do.

▼▼▼▼▼▼▼▼▼▼▼▼▼▼▼▼▼▼▼▼▼▼▼▼▼▼▼▼▼▼
Telling EfiColor About Pictures

Once you've told EfiColor about your monitor and printer, you need to tell it a little about the pictures you're importing. You can do this in several ways, but when you import a picture, typically you'll assign it a profile and rendering method in the Get Picture dialog box.

Selecting a Profile
The EfiColor XTension adds two popup menus to the Get Picture dialog box (see Figure G-4). These popup menus let you assign both an EfiColor profile and a *rendering style* to pictures as you import them (we'll explain what rendering style is in just a moment).

If a picture didn't have a profile or rendering style assigned to it, then EfiColor can't transform its colors because it doesn't know what to transform *from* (it doesn't know what the colors are supposed to look like). Therefore, no color matching is possible. Again, the point is that when you tell EfiColor where the image came from, here in the Get Picture dialog box or elsewhere, you're telling it how the colors should really look.

Figure G-4
EfiColor popup menus in the Get Picture dialog box

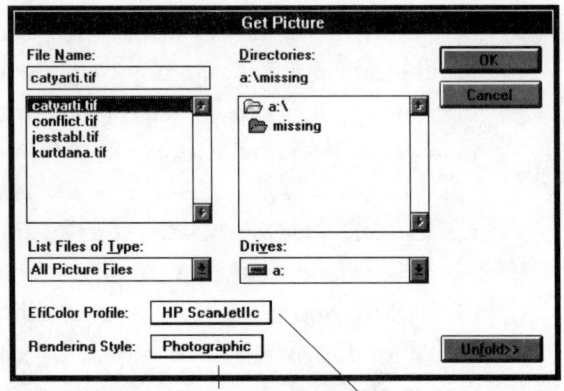

These two popup menus appear for appropriate images.

For instance, when we scan an image on our Hewlett-Packard ScanJet IIc, we can assign the ScanJet IIc profile when we import it into a picture box. EfiColor then knows not only the RGB values in the image but also what device created those values—hence, what the colors really look like.

In general, you should select a profile that corresponds to how the picture was saved. EfiColor is smart enough to examine the format of a file and only display acceptable profiles. That is, it lets you choose process-color profiles such as SWOP-Coated only when you're importing a CMYK image, and RGB color profiles when the image is stored in an RGB mode.

You can change the default settings (the ones that come up automatically) by going to the EfiColor Preferences dialog box (see "EfiColor Preferences," later in this appendix).

Note that if the picture you're importing has a Metric Color Tag (MCT) attached to it, the Profiles popup menu automatically changes to that profile. Also, its name is displayed with an underline, just to show you that it's a special case. You can change it to a different profile if you want to, but we wouldn't advise it.

Rendering Style

What are rendering styles, anyway, and how do you know what kind to assign to a picture? The rendering style of a picture tells EfiColor how to convert colors in a picture when the gamut of your printer isn't big enough to print those colors. For example, it's easy to pick an RGB color that cannot be printed in CMYK on a press. So the EfiColor XTension can transform that color into a color that a press can print. EfiColor has two methods for converting colors like this: Photographic and Solid Color.

Photographic. If the image you're importing is a scanned photograph, you probably want to use the Photographic rendering method. That seems obvious enough. But why?

When EfiColor needs to transform a color into a smaller gamut, it has to deal with colors that fall outside that gamut—and their relationships to other colors. Photographic rendering compresses the entire color range of your picture to fit into your printer's gamut (see Figure G-5), maintaining the balance of color throughout the picture. All the colors in the picture change, but they maintain their relationships to each other, resulting in a more true-to-life rendition of color photographs.

Balance, it turns out, is often more important to maintain in photographic images than the colors themselves. For example, the colors in a picture of a face can be pretty far off, but as long as the colors maintain a relative balance—among the skin, the eyes, and the hair, for instance—our eyes adjust to it fine.

Solid Color. If your picture contains only a few colors that must be matched as closely as possible between your proofs and your final output, select Solid Color for the rendering style. When Solid Color is selected, colors in your image that are within the output device's gamut stay just the same; no color adjustment is made. Any color that is outside the printer's gamut gets mapped to the nearest possible color.

You end up with fewer colors using the Solid Color rendering method, because some colors are mapped to the same values as existing colors. Most colors don't change at all, and every color is mapped to its closest equivalent. The relationship between colors changes, but that's less important with a nonphotographic image.

Images from FreeHand or Illustrator that have been turned into TIFFs are often perfect for Solid Color rendering (especially if they don't include graduated fills), because you want the colors to be as close as possible to your original specifications. On the

Figure G-5
Solid versus Photographic rendering

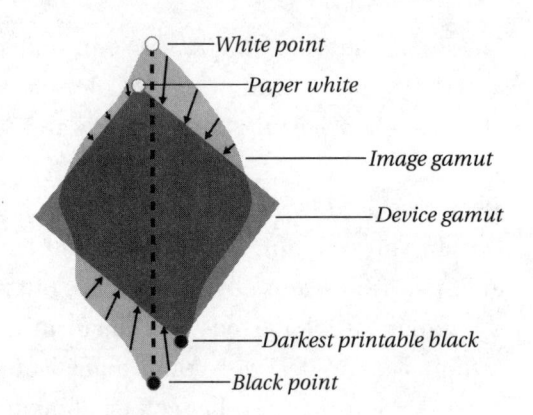

- White point
- Paper white
- Image gamut
- Device gamut
- Darkest printable black
- Black point

Solid rendering

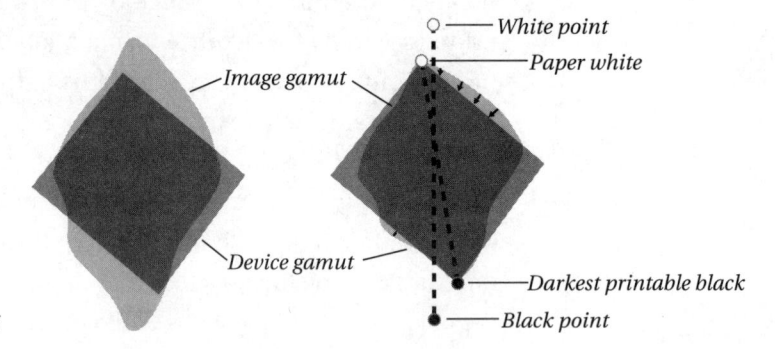

- Image gamut
- Device gamut

- White point
- Paper white
- Darkest printable black
- Black point

Photographic rendering

other hand, if you specify that a photograph should be transformed with Solid Color rendering, the colors in the picture that are inside the printer's gamut will be maintained perfectly, whereas any color outside the printer's gamut will be mapped, throwing the balance way off.

Changing the Profiles for a Picture

What happens if you've imported a picture, and then realize you've chosen the wrong profile or rendering style for it? You could reimport the picture and spend a lot of time (importing pictures takes somewhat longer with EfiColor; see "Before You Use EfiColor," later in this appendix), or you could select the picture and choose the Profile command from the Style menu. The Picture Profile dialog box (see Figure G-6), has the same two popup menus—Profiles and Rendering Styles—as the Get Picture dialog box.

Figure G-6
Picture Profile dialog box in the Style menu

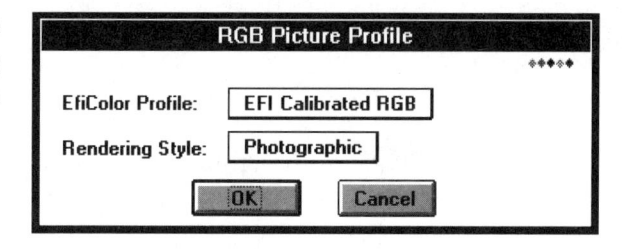

If you want to change a lot of pictures at the same time, you can use the Profile Usage dialog box (see Figure G-7), found under the Utilities menu. You look for and replace profiles in much the same way that you identify and update missing pictures or fonts.

Figure G-7
Profile Usage dialog box from the Utilities menu

The Profile Usage dialog box contains information about your document's pictures and profiles, and lets you replace profiles quickly.

Profile. The first column in the Profile Usage dialog box lists all the profiles used in the current document. Even if you don't have any items in a document, the default profiles for RGB and CMYK images are always listed in the dialog box. Note that a profile can be listed more than once, depending on the kinds of objects to which it's applied. For example, all the QuarkXPress items that have a profile assigned to them are listed, as are all the pictures that have a certain profile, and so on. That makes it easy to change all of one kind of object from one profile into another.

Objects. These are the kinds of color models to which a profile's been applied in a document. The possibilities are pictures (imported graphics), RGB/HSB colors, and CMYK colors. Note that you can't apply the same profile to both RGB/HSB and CMYK colors.

Status. Status in the Profile Usage dialog box means almost the same thing as in the Picture Usage dialog box. However, instead of pictures, QuarkXPress is looking for the availability of profiles. "OK" means that the necessary device profile has been installed in your EFICOLOR subdirectory; "Missing" means it's not there (see "Missing Profiles," later in this chapter).

Show First. The Show First button is active only when you've selected a profile that's applied to pictures. Clicking on it takes you to the first picture in a document that uses the profile you've selected. After you've displayed the first picture, the button changes to Show Next, so you can use it to cycle through all the pictures that use a specific profile. Of course, if there's only one picture in a document that uses that profile, the button remains Show First. And, just as in the Find/Replace dialog box, you can change the button back to Show First at any time by holding down the Option key.

Replace All. This button lets you automatically replace a profile you've selected for the entire object class on that line. When you click the Replace All button, the Replace Profile dialog box appears. For instance, if you want to change all the CMYK pictures in your document from a SWOP profile to a Canon CLC500 profile (we don't know why you'd want to do this), you can select SWOP-coated-profile pictures and click Replace All.

This dialog box has the familiar popup menus for selecting profiles and rendering styles. If you've selected a profile that's missing, it appears grayed-out in the menu. If you've chosen Replace All for several pictures that use different rendering styles, then the word Mixed appears in the Rendering Style popup menu.

Note that it's possible to change the profiles for RGB/HSB Colors and CMYK Colors. If you change these, QuarkXPress goes through your document and changes both the colored elements (the ones you colored in QuarkXPress) and the default profiles in the EfiColor Preferences dialog box.

Replace. This button is only active when you've selected a profile that is applied to pictures. Use the Show First or Show Next button to select the picture you want to change, then click the Replace button. This brings up the Replace Profile dialog box (see Figure G-8).

Figure G-8
Replace Profile dialog box

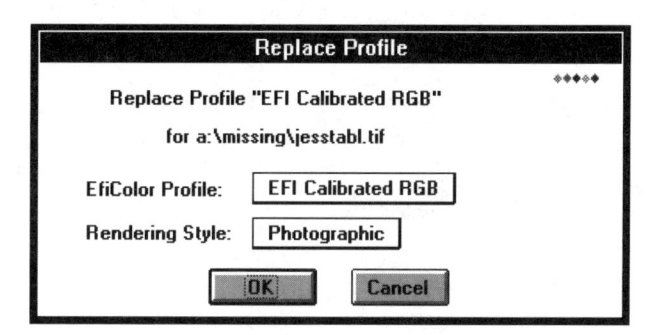

Picture Info. Underneath the profiles section of the Profile Usage dialog box are two pieces of information titled Picture Info. These fields display the path leading to a selected picture and the rendering style applied to it. Note that you can only see Picture Info after you've selected a picture with Show First or Show Next.

Pictures That EfiColor Understands

The EfiColor XTension performs both color transformation and color separation (if you're printing separations) for almost every graphic file format that you can import into QuarkXPress, both bitmapped *and* object-oriented. The two exceptions are pictures stored as EPS or those containing OPI comments. All the rest work fine, including RGB PICT, RGB TIFF, DRW, JPEG, HPGL, CGM, GIFF, Scitex, BMP, PCX, and WMF. CMYK TIFF and DCS files are already separated, so EfiColor passes them through unchanged.

Although the EfiColor XTension can recognize EPS and DCS images that have had MCTs assigned to them, you can't change the profile for these pictures, nor can you assign a profile to an EPS or DCS file that doesn't already have one. Also note that the profile name for an MCT file will appear grayed out if it's a profile not available on your system.

By the way, the EfiColor documentation says that when you print your document using the preview image of an EPS or DCS picture—that is, if either the high-res picture is missing or if you turn Low Resolution on in the Print dialog box—then EfiColor transforms the colors of the preview image. They're wrong. Apparently, that's an error in the documentation; it only works sometimes. Oh well. Perhaps someday.

▼▼▼▼▼▼▼▼▼▼▼▼▼▼▼▼▼▼▼▼▼▼▼▼▼▼▼▼▼▼▼
Editing Colors in QuarkXPress

Objects that are built or colored directly in QuarkXPress can always be transformed by the EfiColor XTension. The key to making this work is correctly setting up the Edit Color dialog box for each color (see Figure I on the color pages). The EfiColor XTension adds a few new features to this dialog box: Target, Gamut Alarm, and Rendering Style.

Note that every color you create in the Edit Color dialog box is automatically assigned a profile based on the defaults you have selected in the EfiColor Preferences dialog box. If the color is set using CMYK, TruMatch, Focoltone, or Pantone ProSim, Quark-XPress assigns the default CMYK profile. If the color is set using RGB, HSB, or one of the spot color matching systems (Pantone, DIC, or Toyo), the RGB/HSB default is assigned.

Target
Before you even begin to pick a color, you should select a profile from the Target popup menu; the profile that you select should be for your final output device. If your final artwork is on a Canon CLC500 with a Fiery RIP, then select Fiery. If your final destination is a four-color press, then select SWOP-Coated or another four-color profile.

You want to set the target profile because that's how EfiColor figures out which colors are within the device's gamut (see "Gamut Alarm," below). If the Gamut Alarm box is unchecked, then you don't need to set the target profile—in fact, the menu is grayed out.

Gamut Alarm

The Gamut Alarm checkbox lets you turn on and off one of the neatest features of the EfiColor XTension. The gamut alarm actually shows you whether the color you specify can be printed on the target printer. There are two ways to see if your color is within gamut: the gamut alarm and the gamut map.

Alarm. The gamut alarm is a triangle with an exclamation point in it, sitting to the left of the New and/or Old color field. When either the old color (if you're editing a color) or the new color is out of gamut (outside of the possible color spectrum of the target device), the gamut alarm appears, warning you that the color cannot be printed on the target printer.

The gamut alarm takes two profiles into consideration: the default color profile and the target profile. The EfiColor XTension essentially compares the two profiles to see if a color created with the default profile falls inside the gamut of the target profile. If the color is outside that gamut, then the gamut alarm shows up. (The default profile set up in the EfiColor Preferences dialog box is the source profile automatically assigned to all colors created within the program.)

Gamut outline. The second part of the gamut alarm system is the gamut outline, which is basically a graphic representation of the available color gamut. If you're specifying an HSB, RGB, or CMYK color, the EfiColor XTension displays a red border on the color wheel that shows you where the edges of the gamut are (see Figure I in the color pages). Note that if you select a color near the border of the gamut outline, the border and the triangular gamut alarm might disagree. The gamut alarm is always the final judge in these disputes. If you're using color swatches—such as TruMatch, Pantone, or Focoltone—diagonal lines cross out swatches that don't fit in the gamut of the target device.

Once again, this gamut outline takes into account both the default color profile (the one assigned to the color) and the target printer. If you change one or the other, the gamut outline changes, too.

Rendering Style for Colors

Sometimes you want to use a color even if the gamut alarm says it won't print correctly. Perhaps you don't have the correct profile to select in the Target popup menu, or perhaps you trust yourself more than you trust the gamut alarm. (Who are we to stop you if you know what you're doing?) If the color you pick *is* inside the gamut, you can just leave the rendering style set to Solid (see "Rendering Style," earlier in this chapter). However, if it isn't, you need to think for a moment about which rendering style you want.

You can determine which rendering style to choose based on the source of the color and how you'd like it to finally appear.

Solid Color. If you're specifying a color using a matching system such as TruMatch or Pantone, you probably want your final output to appear to be as close to those colors as possible. In that case, you should probably select Solid Color in the Rendering Style popup menu. Likewise, if you're trying to match a color to a color in an imported graphic to which the Solid Color rendering style is assigned, you should also apply the Solid Color rendering style to your color. Otherwise, the picture's color and the color you're creating may not match properly.

Photographic. On the other hand, if you're creating a color that you want to match to another color in a continuous-tone image (a scanned photograph or piece of artwork), you should select the Photographic rendering style (see "Matching Colors in Pictures" below). EFI also advises that if your color doesn't fit in your device's gamut, you should select the Photographic rendering style. However, while this does maintain the overall color balance of your document's colors, it may not provide the best match to that one particular color.

Note that the Rendering Style popup menu is only available when your color is set to Process Separation. That's because EFI figures that if you're creating a Pantone solid spot color, you're always going to want Solid Color rendering. So that's what it gives you. We can't think of a reason why you wouldn't want this, but if you like, you can call them and complain.

▼ ▼

Tip: Matching Colors in Pictures. Suppose you've imported a picture into your QuarkXPress document, and you want to create a color in QuarkXPress that exactly matches a color in the picture. If you've used named colors such as TruMatch or Pantone to define a color in a graphics program, all you need to do in QuarkXPress is specify the same color with exactly the same name, and assign to it the same rendering style and device profile as you've used for the picture.

However, if you're matching colors in a scanned photograph, you have a little more work cut out for you. The problem is that your graphics program probably defines color differently than QuarkXPress does. Therefore, you have to convert the color from the way it's described in your graphics program to the way it's described in QuarkXPress.

1. Open the image in a program like Photoshop or Photo-Styler.

2. Use the Eyedropper tool to find the exact RGB or CMYK values of the color you want to match. Write those values down (yes, you may have to actually use a pen—so much for the paperless office).

3. In QuarkXPress, create a color based on those RGB or CMYK values and set it to the Photographic rendering style. Some photo-manipulation programs define RGB colors as numbers on a scale from zero to 255, while QuarkXPress defines them as percentages from zero to 100. To convert the former to the latter, divide the color's value by 255 and multiply by 100; for example, the color value 129 divided by 255 and multiplied by 100 gives you 50.6 percent.

4. Make sure that Process Separation is turned on.

EfiColor Preferences

The EfiColor Preferences dialog box (found under the Edit menu) is the Command Central of the EfiColor XTension (see Figure G-9). Here's where you set both the default EfiColor settings and also tell EfiColor how and when to do its thing. Note that this preferences dialog box works just like QuarkXPress's: if a document is open, then any changes you make in the EfiColor Preferences dialog box affects only that document. If no documents are open when you change something, then that change is good for all subsequent documents you open (older documents retain their settings). Let's examine what the various options in this dialog box do.

Figure G-9
EfiColor Preferences

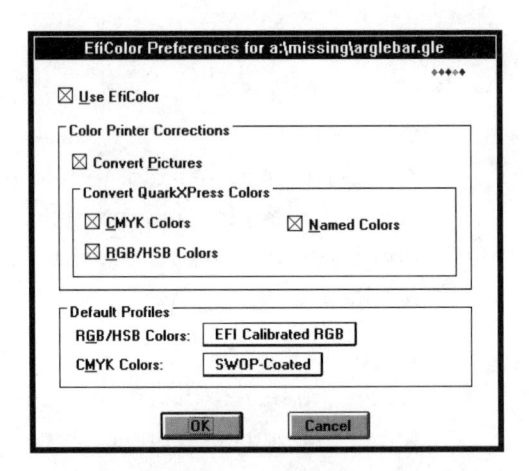

Use EfiColor. The first item in the EfiColor Preferences dialog box is Use EfiColor. This is almost entirely self-explanatory: check this box to turn EfiColor on; uncheck it to turn EfiColor off. When EfiColor is off, the XTension doesn't transform any colors at import, on screen, or during printing. Note that any pictures you've already imported into your document look the same on screen even after you turn EfiColor off. You can't reset them to a pre-EfiColor screen rendition without re-importing them. However, if EfiColor is turned off, the picture won't be transformed when you print the document.

Convert Pictures. The upper half of the EfiColor Preferences dialog box is labeled Color Printer Corrections, which is really a misnomer because it's not just color printers that this affects. The changes you make in this area of the EfiColor Preferences dialog box alter the way that EfiColor transforms colors anytime you use a profile.

The first checkbox in the Color Printer Corrections section is Convert Pictures. Check this box to have EfiColor convert colors in imported TIFF, PCX, or other bitmap-format pictures.

Convert QuarkXPress Colors. The three checkboxes in the Convert QuarkXPress Colors section let you tell EfiColor which kinds of colors created within QuarkXPress to convert. Turning these on or off won't change anything except tint builds or colors that you actually specify in QuarkXPress. The three checkboxes are labeled CMYK Color, RGB/HSB Colors, and Named Colors.

The trick here is that while Pantone is a named color, TruMatch and Focoltone are not. Why? Because the Pantone system actually defines a set of distinct, named ink colors, whereas TruMatch and Focoltone colors are built from CMYK inks, as are Pantone Process and ProSim colors, for that matter.

Default Profiles. The Default Profiles section of the EfiColor Preferences dialog box lets you set which profiles the EfiColor XTension will use whenever you create new colors or import artwork. You can always override these profiles for individual pictures later, but you can't override them for colors created within QuarkXPress (those are always assigned with whatever you have Default Profiles set to). Also, pictures that already have profiles assigned to them via a MCT ignore the default profiles on import.

If you don't want CMYK colors that you specify within QuarkXPress to be modified at all on your final output device, be sure to select that device's profile as your CMYK default. For instance, we send our final film to an imagesetter and then take that film to a printer, so we set the default CMYK profile to SWOP so that EfiColor doesn't alter the CMYK values when we print; it assumes that they're already set up for that output. However, when we print to a color printer, the colors *do* get altered (because we're not printing seps).

Missing Profiles

Progress is never without a price. When you use a new typeface, you have the burden of making sure your service bureau and other people who receive your documents have that typeface as well. It turns out that EfiColor profiles are the same way. When you send a file to another QuarkXPress user, you must make certain that your recipient has legal copies of all the EfiColor profiles you've used in your document (see "Tip: Moving Profiles," below). Just as with fonts, the Collect for Output feature (see "Collect for Output" in Appendix F, *What's New in 3.3*) doesn't automatically assemble all the profiles used in a document. You're on your own there, although profiles are listed on the output report.

What To Do

So let's say you've received a document without all the needed profiles. How will you know? What can you do about it? If you're familiar with the ways QuarkXPress handles missing fonts and pictures, you should have no trouble coping with missing profiles.

When you open a document that uses one or more profiles that are not in your EFICOLOR subdirectory, an error message appears indicating the missing profile or profiles (see Figure G-10). If you can obtain the proper profile from someone—perhaps the person who sent you the QuarkXPress document, or from EFI, or maybe even the manufacturers of the device—then do it (see "Tip: Moving Profiles," below). You just have to put that profile in your EfiColor subdirectory, and relaunch QuarkXPress.

However, if you can't obtain the profile, you can either go ahead and do nothing about it, or replace it with a profile that is active in your system. If you're only interested in a fast and dirty

Figure G-10
Missing profile when opening alert

*[Dialog box: Missing Profiles — c:\quarkcap\arglebar.gle uses profiles not installed in your EfiColor Database: * HP ScanJetIIc — OK]*

proof—let's say you're proofing page geometry or type—then there's no need to replace profiles. But if you need EfiColor's color matching, you must replace the missing profiles (see "Changing the Profiles for a Picture," earlier in this chapter).

▼ ▼

Tip: Moving Profiles. EfiColor profiles are little pieces of software. And, like most pieces of software, they're copyrighted. Like fonts, you're not really supposed to copy them from one machine to another; you're supposed to buy a profile for each machine you use. However, EFI is being somewhat generous: they're encouraging people to freely pass around monitor and scanner profiles. But restraint is the name of the game when it comes to output device profiles.

▼ ▼

Printing with Missing Profiles

If you attempt to print a file that uses profiles which are missing from your system, you'll get an alert very similar to the one displayed when you try to print a document with missing or modified pictures (see Figure G-11).

You've got three options in this dialog box: click Cancel to cancel the print job, click OK to proceed with printing despite the missing profiles, or click List Profiles to display the missing profiles. If you choose the third option, you get the Missing Profiles dialog box, which is almost identical in appearance and function to the Profile Usage dialog box, with a few changes.

First of all, it only displays missing profiles and the items associated with them. There's also an OK button, to let you proceed with printing the file regardless of the number of profiles you've replaced. And there's a Cancel button, to stop replacing profiles; however, this also stops your print job.

Figure G-11
Missing profile when printing alert

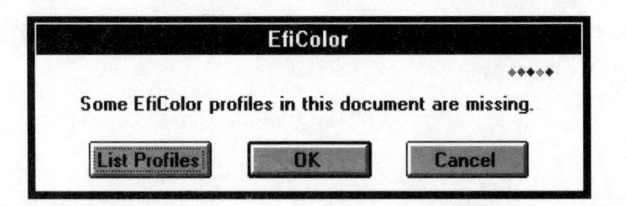

▼▼▼▼▼▼▼▼▼▼▼▼▼▼▼▼▼▼▼▼▼▼▼▼▼▼▼▼
Tip: Pre-EfiColor Documents. It's pretty simple to take advantage of EfiColor's capabilities in a document created by previous versions of QuarkXPress. When you open an old document, the EfiColor XTension may be turned off. Go to the EfiColor Preferences dialog box and turn it on. Once EfiColor's on and you've chosen appropriate profiles for the colors in your document, EfiColor converts the document's colors when you print. If you're not happy with the results and would rather have the colors print as they did in previous versions of QuarkXPress, simply turn EfiColor off in the Preferences dialog box.

▼▼▼▼▼▼▼▼▼▼▼▼▼▼▼▼▼▼▼▼▼▼▼▼▼▼▼▼▼▼▼▼▼
Before You Use EfiColor . . .

If EfiColor is so great and wonderful, why would you ever *not* want to use it? There are lots of reasons, from speed to consistency. In this last section of this appendix, we want to look at a few things that you should think about before you jump in and start using EfiColor.

Performance

Every time EfiColor transforms a color to look right on your screen or your proofing printer or your final output device, the color gets *processed*. That takes time. And time is something we often don't have enough of.

Imagine converting a 30Mb image from RGB mode to CMYK mode in Adobe Photoshop. It takes a long time, doesn't it? EfiColor can't do it any faster than Photoshop can, and that's just what it's doing when you print an RGB TIFF from QuarkXPress with EfiColor turned on. And it has to make that conversion every time you print.

Similarly, when you import any sort of TIFF or PCX image, Efi-Color has to convert the screen preview to look correct on the screen. That can easily make importing pictures take four or five times as long as without EfiColor. You can speed the process a little by holding down the Shift key while clicking Open in the Get Picture dialog box; that imports the picture at half the screen resolution. However, you then get a low-resolution image to look at onscreen, which sort of defeats the purpose.

Dollars and Sense

Time, we all know, is money. And if EfiColor is a hit to our performance at output time, then money may be at stake. Many service bureaus were bewildered soon after EfiColor first appeared on the scene when they started receiving documents that took five or 10 times longer to output than they expected. The culprit? The EfiColor XTension. Although EfiColor Cachet had been released months before, and Quark had announced the incorporation of EfiColor support with the XTension, service bureau operators weren't prepared for the amount of time it could take to convert even moderately sized RGB images to CMYK separations. Their clients weren't prepared for the kinds of charges they could incur.

Service bureaus usually charge a per-page amount, which is based on how much an average page takes to imageset. If your job goes over their time limit—say 10 minutes—the service bureau might charge you an additional per-minute charge that can range as high as two or three dollars a minute. If you're relying on the EfiColor XTension to separate your RGB images, and that adds an additional ten minutes to the print time . . . well, you can see the dollars adding up.

So for those of you who operate a service bureau: warn your clients in advance about using the EfiColor XTension (or against it, if you aren't willing to support it). You might suggest they make PostScript dumps, so it's *their* machine time that's being eaten. For those of you using a service bureau, investigate the excess-time charges to see if it's worth the extra money. Plus, you should consider doing PostScript dumps rather than paying per-minute charges on the service bureau's computer.

Incompatible File Formats

What happens when you import a color EPS image from Aldus FreeHand, CorelDraw, or Adobe Illustrator onto your page and surround it with colors that you've matched exactly within QuarkXPress? You can throw the words "matched exactly" out of your vocabulary. The colors you assign in QuarkXPress are transformed according to the profiles you choose. The colors in the EPS image are not transformed at all. Why? Because the EfiColor XTension never transforms EPS or DCS images. Never ever. Well, maybe their screen-preview renditions, but probably not even those.

You have to understand the philosophy of EPS images. The whole idea of Encapsulated PostScript originally was that a program should never need to look "inside" them and should certainly never change anything inside them. Therefore, according to this school of thought, EfiColor should never adjust the colors inside an EPS or DCS image.

The problem is that people use these images all the time and go nuts when the colors don't match what comes out of QuarkXPress. Unfortunately, we don't really have a good answer for how to handle this situation right now. If you're using images built with Photoshop or Cachet, you can assign either an MCT or an EfiColor profile to the image (EFI is selling color-separation sets for Photoshop that help you do this). This allows EfiColor to adjust the screen preview image to more closely match what will come out of the printer. It has no effect on the printed output, however.

Until Aldus, Corel, and Adobe decide that color management is really worth their time (read: their customers want it), we'll all just have to hold our breath and wait for a whole, integrated color-management system.

▼▼▼▼▼▼▼▼▼▼▼▼▼▼▼▼▼▼▼▼▼▼▼▼▼

Tip: Don't Convert Pantone Colors. A funny thing happens if you convert a Pantone color to RGB and then try to print it using EfiColor: you get a different color. Now theoretically, this shouldn't happen. However, because of the way that EfiColor "sees" Pantone colors, you get a more accurate Pantone color by leaving it in Pantone mode (you can change the name if you want) rather than converting it to RGB or CMYK.

▼▼▼▼▼▼▼▼▼▼▼▼▼▼▼▼▼▼▼▼▼▼▼▼▼

The Problem with OPI

Trying to manage color with OPI images (see "Using OPI" on page 323) is even more difficult than with EPS, because QuarkXPress never even touches the final image. Remember that with OPI, you export PostScript from QuarkXPress without image data; only little tags are inserted in the PostScript saying what the name of the image is and how it should be adjusted (rotation, cropping, and so on). That's why QuarkXPress is only called an *OPI writer*.

The PostScript that comes from QuarkXPress gets passed on to another program—an *OPI reader*—that interprets the PostScript and strips in high-resolution images where appropriate. Until OPI readers include the EfiColor color-management system, those images will never get adjusted properly. The solution, again, is to adjust for the target printer when the image is scanned or saved from an image-manipulation program.

Quality of Character

Blends, vignettes, fountains . . . whatever you want to call them, they're a hassle when it comes to color management. The problem, put simply, is that you can get a nice clean blend, but the colors may be slightly different from what you want. Or you can get a weird looking printed blend, but the colors all along the blend will be as close as they can be to the original screen colors. EfiColor takes the first path, making the blend look smooth. We agree that this is probably what people want, but you need to at least be aware of it so that you don't get snagged down the road.

Pros and Cons

When it comes right down to it, we think that the EfiColor XTension is not only really cool but incredibly useful. However, it obviously has limits and isn't for everyone all the time. One of the most important things to note is that color management works best when you're comparing apples to oranges rather than to salmons or coffee beans. You'll get a better idea of a final color by looking at a printed color proof than at the screen. You can calibrate all you want, and you'll still always get a more reliable image from a printer than from the screen. It still won't be a perfect match to your final output, of course, but it's that much closer. Clearly, as with just about every other aspect of desktop publishing, WYSIWYG color is a relative thing.

Index

3G Graphics 538
256 Levels of Gray 81

A

Accents for All Caps 581
Access PC 506
Actual Size. *See* Zooming
Adjusted Screen Values 612
Adobe Document Structuring Conventions 450
Adobe Illustrator 291, 421–422, 518, 536, 633, 648
Adobe Photoshop 417, 419–420, 518, 536, 598, 611, 621, 630, 641
Adobe Type Manager (ATM) 5, 154–157, 159–161, 428, 498, 536
Adobe TypeAlign 245, 536
Agfa Balanced Screening 630
Aldus FreeHand 47, 291, 300, 421–422, 518, 537, 633, 648
Aldus PhotoStyler 287, 291, 293, 365, 417, 497, 507, 537, 621, 641
Aldus PrePrint 324, 420, 537
Aldus TrapWise 537, 602
Aligning items. *See* Space/Align
Alternate em 581
Amazon jungles viii, 1, 7
Ami Pro 274
Anchored boxes 338–346
　alignment 341–343
　deleting 345
　moving 345, 346
　resizing 340
　runaround 590
　what you can't do 339
Anchored rules 346–353
　Rule Above/Below 346–351
　vertical rules 350–353
ANSI codes 238–240, 513, 521–526

Apple File Exchange 506, 508
Apple 56–157
Application Preferences 58–59, 78, 564–565
Apply 27–28, 364
Arithmetic. *See* Math
Arrow keys 39, 132
Arst, Mike xv
ASCII 243, 274, 513, 605–606
ATM. *See* Adobe Type Manager (ATM)
Auto Backup 568–569
Auto constraint. *See* Constrain; between items
Auto Kern Above 50, 218, 228
Auto Library Save 78, 80
Auto Page Insertion 82, 121–122, 562
Auto Picture Import 319
Auto Save 566–568
Auto Trap Preferences 412–416
AUTOEXEC.BAT 444, 503
Automatic text box 97–98, 102–106
Auxiliary dictionaries 43–146

B

Background color 31–32, 51, 328
Balanced Screens 630
Ballot boxes 242
Baseline grid 218–219
Baseline shift 80–181
Bernoulli 485
Binary versus ASCII 605–606
Bitmapped images 286–289, 356–357
Bitstream Makeup 245
Blends 402–403, 533, 599–601, 649
BMP. *See* Windows Bitmap
Bob XTension 532
Bobzilla XTension 533

651

Box shape submenu 557–558
Box skew 555–556
Bring to Front 49
Broback, Steve 519
Brown, Russell 381
Burnt sienna 382
Buttons 600–601

C

Calibrated output 463, 470–471, 614, 631
Cancel 27–28
Carriage return. *See* Return
Cascade 8–19
Centering
    pictures 308–309
    text 182–185, 187
CGM. *See* Computer graphics metafile (CGM)
Chaining. *See* Linking
Character formatting 64–181
    baseline shift 80–181
    color and shade 71
    dumb/smart ways 260
    horizontal scale 72–173, 218, 559
    indeterminate 70
    kerning 73–178, 516, 582
    reversed type 71, 350
    tracking 78–180, 218
    typeface 65–166
    shadowed 255
    size 66–167
    styles 67–171
Character sets 243–245, 510, 512–515
Character spacing 211
Character styles 38–139, 271
Check boxes 27
Check spelling. *See* Spelling checker
Cheshire Group 472
Choking. *See* Trapping
Chopped liver ix
Ciceros/cm 84. *See also* Measurement systems
Clear Memory per Page 449, 488
CIE color 622. *See also* EfiColor
Clipboard. *See* Cut, Copy, and Paste
Clone 47
Closing documents 4
CMYK TIFF. *See* TIFF
Collect for Output 615–616

Color
    additive 384
    appending 397–398, 599
    blends 402–403, 533, 599–601, 649
    CMYK 385–386, 393
    composite 384
    creating 390–395
    default 390, 398–399
    deleting 397
    drag-and-drop 598–599
    editing 395, 638
    EfiColor 619–650
    EPS files 599
    find/change 598
    Focoltone 388, 540, 639, 643
    halftones 383
    HSB 386–387
    indeterminate 400–401, 413–414
    libraries 398, 519
    models 384–389
    naming 391
    palette 401–402
    Pantone 380, 387–388, 393–394, 421, 539, 598, 603–604, 639, 643, 648
    registration 400, 462
    RGB 384–385
    rich black 409–410
    separation 383, 417–422, 466–470
    spot versus process 382–384, 421–422, 640
    subtractive 385
    trapping 398, 403–416, 490, 602
    TruMatch 381, 388–389, 393–394, 539, 603–604, 639, 643
Color Access 630
Color-management systems (CMSes) 620–626. *See also* EfiColor
Color proofing 620
Color of text 96–197
Color separation 398, 403–422, 466–470
Column guides 95–97, 102, 120
Columns 32
CompuServe 4, 296
Computer graphics metafile (CGM) 294–295
Constrain
    movement 42, 44–45
    between items 48, 52–54
Content tool 30, 164, 551
"Continued" lines 25–126
Continuous Apply 27–28, 364
Contrast control 361–370, 512
Conventions used xiii

Converting files 505–520
Cool Blends XTension 533, 599–600
CorelDraw 248, 291, 301–302, 311, 421, 648
Corner radius 34–36
Crayola crayons 382
Crop marks 27–128
Cropping 310. *See also* Pictures
Current Box page number 107, 236, 574–575
Custom trapping. *See* Trapping
Customizing. *See* Preferences
Cut, Copy, and Paste 46–47, 75, 148, 299–305, 500, 562

D

Dainippon Ink and Chemicals (DIC) 604–605
David's dog 379
Decimal tab. *See* Tabs
Default pages. *See* Master Pages
Defaults. *See* Preferences
Delete changes 10. *See also* Master pages
Deleting pages 63–66, 574
Densitometer 473
Deselecting page items 550
Desktop Color Separation (DCS) 418–419, 609–611, 648
Dialog boxes 27–29
Diddley, Bo 81
Didot system 84, 571. *See also* Measurement systems
Dingbats 242–243
Discretionary hyphen 234–235
Disks 9
DiskTop 508
Display Correction 628. *See also* EfiColor
Display DPI Value 81, 566
Display Halftoning 378. *See also* Halftones
Distributing items. *See* Space/Align
Document Layout palette 26, 62, 64–65, 111–115, 117–118, 122, 572–576
Document Setup 118–119
Documents
   and master pages 109–110, 115, 573
   automatic text box 97–98
   closing 14
   creating 92–98, 116–118
   deleting pages 63–66, 574
   locking 17–18
   margin guides 93–95, 119–120
   moving pages 63–66
   opening 13–14, 18–20

   page size 92–93, 118–119
   Revert to Saved 18, 133, 399, 568
   saving 15–16
   selecting 19
DosMounter 506
Dot gain 470
Dot-matrix printers 608
Downloading fonts 427–429
DPI. *See* Display DPI Value and Resolution
Drag-and-Drop
   color application 598–599
   text 570, 576
   importing pictures with 592–593, 631–632
   importing text with 576
Drivers 475–476
Drop caps. *See* Initial caps
Dummy documents 150–152
Duotones 598
Duplicating items 45–47, 105
Dynamic Link Libraries 547–548, 626

E

Early days of DTP viii
Ebrahimi, Fred xiv
Edit Auxiliary 143–146
Edit Trap. *See* Trapping
EfiColor 619–650
   default profiles 643–644
   definition 620–621
   device-independent color 622
   Display Correction 566
   dynamic link library 626
   file formats 637–638
   gamuts 623, 639
   Get Picture dialog box 631–632
   gray-component replacement (GCR) 629–630
   halftone screen values 629–630
   installing 547, 626–627
   Electronics for Imaging 537
   matching colors in pictures 641
   missing profiles 644–646
   monitors 627–628
   Metric Color Tags (MCTs) 625–626, 632, 637
   performance 646–647
   picture info 637
   preferences 642–644
   printer setup 611
   profiles 623–625, 627, 631–632
   Profile Usage 635–637
   processor 627

EfiColor *(continued)*
  rendering style 631–634, 640–641
  replacing profiles 636–637
  RGB to CMYK translation 621, 630, 646
  Solid versus Photographic rendering 634
  target device 638
  turning it off 642
Eight-plus-three file names. *See* File types
em and en dash 237
Em and en units 174, 176, 581
Embedding 302–305
En space 235
Encapsulated PostScript 74, 292–293, 307, 318, 420–423, 442, 486, 517–518, 599
End of Story. *See* Auto Page Insertion
Endcaps. *See* Lines and arrows
End 63, 452
Enter. *See* Return
Environment dialog box 6–7, 548–549
EPS. *See* Encapsulated PostScript
Exporting text 278–283. *See also* Text
Extensions. *See* File types, XTensions

F

Facing pages 94–95, 97, 117–119
Faith 13
Families 170, 226
Fax boards 606–609
File management 13–20
File Manager 12, 14, 18, 509, 548, 592–593
File types 14–17, 291–292, 507–510, 518. *See also* Graphic file formats.
Fill character. *See* Tabs
Find/Change 133–140
  colors 598
  find next/find first 139
  hyphenation and justification 583
  profiles 635–637
  run-in heads 272–273
  special characters 134–135
  style sheets 588
  typefaces 166
  wild card 135
First Baseline 200–201
First line indent 189–190
Fit in Window. *See* Zooming
Flex space 222–223, 236
Flip Vertical/Horizontal 556–557

Focoltone 388, 540, 639, 643
Fold/Unfold button 591
Folio. *See* Page numbers
Font Usage 166
FontMinder 163, 537
FontMonger 157, 248, 514, 537
Fontographer 248, 513, 537
Fonts 154–163
  definition 154
  downloading 427–429
  families 170, 226
  forbidden 515–516
  managing 158–163, 429
  missing 516
  printer fonts 155–156, 427–429
  rendering 156
  screen fonts 155, 257
  selecting 165–166
  TrueType 154–159, 427, 445–448, 515
  Type 1 156–157, 427–429
  updating 579
  Vector Above 256–257
Footers. *See* Headers and footers
Force Vector Fonts 294–295
Forced justification 584
Foreign accents and punctuation 240–241, 581
Fractions 245–248
Frames 31–32, 51, 72–73, 511
Function keys 554–555

G

Gamma curves 365–366
Gamuts 623, 639. *See also* EfiColor
GCR 629–630
General preferences 82–84
Geschke, Chuck 426
Get Picture 300, 592, 631–632, 647. *See also* Pictures
Get text 273–278, 576–577. *See also* Text
GIF. *See* Graphics Interchange Format
Gill, Tim vi, xiv
Go to 62
Grabber hand 59, 565
Grabbing through items 49
Graduated fills 402–403
Graphic file formats 286–298. *See also* File types.
  altering 360
  bitmapped images 286–289
  computer graphics metafile (CGM) 294–295

Graphic file formats *(continued)*
    desktop color separation (DCS) 418–419, 609–611, 648
    and EfiColor 637–638
    encapsulated PostScript 292–293, 300, 307, 318, 420–423, 442, 486
    Graphics Interchange Format (GIF) 296, 356
    Hewlett-Packard Graphic Language (HPGL) 296–297
    Macintosh 517–518
    Micrografx Designer (DRW) 295–296
    PCX 294, 356
    PICT 298, 356, 518
    TIFF 293, 300, 318, 331, 356, 358, 385, 417, 419–420, 486, 565–566
    object-oriented graphics 289–291
    Scitex CT 298
    Universal versus Translation 507
    Windows Bitmap (BMP) 297, 300, 356
    Windows Metafile (WMF) 297–298, 300
Graphics Interchange Format (GIF) 296, 356
Gray-component replacement (GCR) 629–630
Greeking
    pictures 322
    text 256
Grouping items 49–52
Guides 69–72, 80. *See also* Margin guides and Columns
Guillemets 240
Gutter 96

H

H&Js. *See* Hyphenation and Justification
Halftones 370–378
    display halftone 378
    dots 370
    gray levels 372
    preset combinations 374–375
    screen angle 372–373, 376, 612, 629
    screen frequency 371, 376, 438, 490, 612, 629
    spots 370–371, 377–378
Hanging drop caps. *See* Initial caps
Hanging indents 190–191
Hanging tabs 203
Hard disks 5–6, 481, 569
Harvard Graphics 295
Headers and footers 98
Help 22, 502
Hewlett-Packard Graphic Language (HPGL) 296
High Quality Screening (HQS) 630
HiJaak ColorSet 420

Horizontal alignment 182–184, 584
Horizontal scale 172–173, 218, 559, 581–582
HPGL. *See* Hewlett-Packard Graphic Language
Hyphenation and Justification
    applying 213–214
    automatic hyphenation 209–211, 218
    basics 207–208
    deleting/replacing 583
    exceptions 229–230
    find/change 583
    flush zone 212
    forced justify 584
    hyphenation zone 210
    justification 211–212, 584
    setting your own 212–214
    single word justify 212
    speeding typing 149
    suggested hyphenation 229

I

Ignore Attributes. *See* Find/Change
Ignore Background 295
Ignore White 414–415. *See also* Trapping
ImageIn 293, 365
Importing pictures 299–308, 358, 592–593, 631–632
Importing text 273–278, 576–577. *See also* Text
Imposition 459. *See also* Printing
Indent here 232–233, 579
Indents 187–191
Indeterminate type style 170
Indeterminate color. *See* Trapping
Indexed color 296
Initial caps 248–254, 344–345, 582–583
Inline graphics. *See* Anchored boxes
Inline rules. *See* Anchored rules
Insert pages 116–118
Inset Systems 420
Installation 9–11, 546–547, 626–627
Integral scaling 313–314
Inter ¶ Max. *See* Vertical alignment
Inverting pictures 361, 436. *See also* Pictures
Item tool 30, 551

JK

JPEG 547–548, 594–595
Joining lines 44
Jump lines 125–126

INDEX • JUSTIFY

Justify. *See* Horizontal alignment
Keep changes 110. *See also* Master pages
Keep lines together 215–217, 583
Keep with next ¶ 215–216, 583
Kerning tables 87, 223–226, 516, 582
Kerning. *See also* Tracking
  automatic 174–175, 178
  manual 175–178
  spacebar 582
  speeding typing 149
Keystrokes 25–26, 28, 266, 501–502, 554
Kodak Precision Imagesetter Linearization Software 471, 537, 631

L

Lab-Paks 534–535
LaserCheck 471, 538
LaserMaster 445
Launching 12, 14
Layering 48–49
Leaders. *See* Tabs
Leading 192–198
  absolute 193
  automatic 194
  modes 195–196
  relative 195
  solid 195
Left indent 189
Legend Communications 429, 537
Letter spacing 211
Libraries 26, 73–78, 519, 549–550
  adding entries 74
  converting 519
  grouping items 77
  labeling items 76–77
  moving entries 74–75
  opening 74
  removing entries 75–76
  saving 78
Ligatures 237–238, 513–515
Line screen. *See* Halftones
Lines and arrows 36–39, 43–44
Linking 66–69, 102–105, 117, 302–305, 562
Linotype-Hell's High Quality Screening (HQS) 630
List Files of Type. *See* File Types
Live scrolling 59, 80
Local formatting. *See* Character formatting, Paragraph formatting, Style sheets; versus local formatting

Locking documents 17–18
Locking items 45
Low Resolution output 613
Low Resolution TIFF 80, 358, 566. *See also* TIFF

M

Mac-In-DOS 507, 538
Macintosh 145, 223, 244, 281, 298, 361, 417–418, 440, 473, 505–520
  Access PC 506
  Apple File Exchange 506, 508
  character set 512–516
  color contrast 512
  file naming 509–511
  font metrics 515–516
  Frame Editor 511
  graphics 516–519
  kerning tables 516
  libraries 519
  ligatures 513–515
  Publish and Subscribe 519
  resource forks 510, 517
  transferring files 505–520
Magnification
  onscreen. *See* Zooming
  when printing 454, 465
Maintain leading 219–220
Managing copy 259–261
Margin guides 93–95, 102, 119–120
Master guides 102, 119
Master page preferences 110
Master pages 98–115
  applying to pages 109–110, 115, 573
  automatic text linking 102–106, 117, 121–122
  basing on another 114–115, 572, 574–575
  compared to PageMaker 99–100
  copying to another document 574
  changing 108–110
  definition 98
  deleting 112, 574
  displaying 100–101, 112
  document layout palette 111–115, 122, 572–575
  graphics on 108
  headers and footers 106–107
  items on 103, 106–107
  master guides 102, 119
  multiple 112–114
  preferences 110
  naming 113–114
  viewing 100–101
MathType 241

Math 29, 514, 552–553

Matrox 81

Measurement systems 28–29, 40, 70, 83–84, 552, 571

Measurements palette 24–25, 31, 551–553

Memory 5–6, 19–20, 448–449, 487

Menus 20–22

Metric Color Tags (MCTS) 625–626, 632, 637. *See also* EfiColor

Micrografx Designer (DRW) 295–296, 311

Micrografx Picture Publisher 287, 293

Microsoft Word 146–147, 264, 274–275, 277–280, 538, 570, 587

Microsoft 157, 538

Missing fonts 516

Missing pictures. *See* Picture Usage

Möbius strip 557

Moby Dick 285

Modes. *See* Lines and arrows

Moiré pattern 469–470

Monitors 81, 382

Monitor profiles. *See* Profiles *and* EfiColor

Moving pages 63–66

Moving. *See* Navigating

Multiple documents 18–20, 65–66, 560

Multiple-page spreads 122, 456

Multiple-up copies 127–128

Munsil, Don xv

N

Navigating
  files 16
  through document 57–62
  text 130–132

NEC 81

New column/box character 235

New documents 92–98

New in version 3.3 543–617

Next Text Box page number 126, 236. *See also* Page numbers

No style. *See* Style sheets

Noncontinuous pages 64

Non-PostScript printing 606–609, 630–631

Norton Utilities 496

Nudge 310

O

Object linking and embedding (OLE) 301–305, 519, 597. *See also* Pictures

Omit TIFF. *See* OPI

Opening documents 13–14, 18–20

OPI 323–326, 420, 649

Orthogonal line tool. *See* Lines and arrows

Ovals. *See* Picture boxes

Overflow. *See* Linking

Overprint. *See* Trapping

Overview
  of book x–xiii
  of QuarkXPress 2–7

P

Page grid 96

Page guides 69–72, 80

Page items
  cloning 47
  creating 30–38
  deleting 47–48, 563
  deselecting 550
  duplicating 45–47, 105
  grouping 49–52
  layering 48–49
  locking 45
  moving 39–40, 45
  resizing and reshaping 41–44, 553, 558–559
  rotating 40–41
  selecting 49, 52
  Space/Align 44, 54–57, 553
  Step and Repeat 46–47, 105

Page numbers 98, 107–108, 122–124, 236, 574–575, 615

Page size 92–93, 118–119

Palettes 23–26

Pantone 380, 387–388, 393–394, 539, 598, 603–604, 639, 643, 648

Paperless office 425

Paragraph formatting 181–220
  baseline grid 218–219
  copying 270
  dumb/smart ways 260–261
  horizontal alignment 182–184
  hyphenation & justification 207–214, 584
  indents 187–191
  keep lines together 215–217, 583
  keep with next ¶ 215–216, 583
  leading 192–198
  maintain leading 219–220

Paragraph formatting *(continued)*
   selecting a paragraph 578
   space before/after 199
   tabs 200–206, 232, 577, 579–580
   vertical alignment 184–187, 558
Paragraph styles. *See* Style sheets
Parent/child relationship. *See* Constrain
Paste Special. *See* Object linking and embedding
Paste. *See* Cut, Copy and Paste
Pasteboard guides 71, 80
Pasteboard 47, 57, 59, 61, 119, 561
PCL fonts 606–607
Pc Tools 496
PCSEND 429
Peachpit Press 541
Photo CD 547–548, 596
Photographic rendering. *See* EfiColor; rendering style
PhotoStyler. *See* Aldus PhotoStyler
PICT files 298, 356, 518
Picture boxes 33–36, 74, 555–556. *See also* Page items
Picture Usage 305, 319–322, 517, 591, 593, 597
Pictures 285–326
   centering 308
   coloring 359
   contrast control 361–370, 512
   cropping 310–311
   displaying 498
   flipping/mirroring 555–556
   importing 299–308, 358, 592–593, 631–632
   inverting 361
   linking 318–322, 517–519
   management 318–322
   memory 498
   moving 309–310
   multiple changes 316
   object linking and embedding (OLE) 301–305, 519, 597
   OPI 323–326, 420, 649
   perspective 316–317
   Picture Usage 319–322, 517, 591, 593, 597
   previewing 591–593
   resizing 311–313, 553
   rotating 314–315
   save as EPS 323–326, 609–611
   skewing 314–317, 555–556
   transparent 360
   suppress printout 323, 326, 478, 591–593
   upgrading screen quality 358–359
Picture Info 637
PinPointXT 472

Pixels 287, 331
PKZIP 484, 538, 594
PMS. *See* Pantone
Points/Inch 83–84, 571. *See also* Measurement systems
Polygonal text boxes 557–558, 590
Polygons 34–35, 42–43, 332–336, 339, 360, 556–558, 590
Popup menus 27
Posterizing pictures 362–363, 367
PostScript dumps 480–486, 647
PostScript errors 428, 450, 472, 489–491
PostScript fonts. *See* Fonts; Type 1
PostScript-5. *See* Desktop Color Separation (DCS)
PostScript 158–160, 291–293, 426, 595, 606
PostScript Printer Descriptions (PPDS) 611–612, 630
Precise Bounding 295
Preferences
   application 58–59, 78, 80–82, 86, 564–565
   document vs. application 86
   general 82–84
   tools 84–86
   XPress Preferences 87–89, 512, 570–571
Prefixes. *See* Page numbers
Previous Text Box page number 126, 236. *See also* Page numbers
Print Colors as Grays 467
Print Status 465–466, 614–615
Printer description files (PDFS) 440–441, 611, 630
Printer name 609
Printer Font Metrics (PFM) 162, 427, 515
Printing
   advanced options 445–450
   back to front 455
   basics 451–452
   choosing a printer 430–432
   calibrated output 463, 470–471, 614, 631
   collating 456
   Collect for Output 615–616
   colors 467
   cover page 452
   dot gain 470
   double-sided documents 455
   drivers 475–476
   EfiColor. *See* EfiColor
   encapsulated PostScript 442
   halftone frequency 438, 490, 612, 629
   header 443–445
   imposition 459
   inverting/flipping 436–437, 476
   job information 462
   Low Resolution output 613

Printing *(continued)*
　memory 448–449, 487–488
　non-PostScript 606–609, 630–631
　offset 440
　options 441–445
　orientation 432–433
　page gap 440, 490
　paper size 434, 439
　PostScript dumps 480–486, 647
　PostScript errors 428, 450, 472, 489–491
　PostScript Printer Descriptions (PPDs) 611–612, 630
　printer description files (PDFs) 440–441, 611, 630
　printer resolution 439
　printer setup 430–450, 611–612
　printing status 465–466, 614–615
　registration marks 459–462
　roll-fed printers 437–441
　rough 453, 613
　saddle-stitched binding 458
　saving film and paper 432–433
　scaling 454, 465
　service bureaus. *See* Service bureaus
　spreads 456–458
　source 435
　status 465–466
　TESTPS.TXT 449
　thumbnails 453–454
　tiling 463–465, 484
　troubleshooting 486–491
　TrueType fonts 445–448
Process color. *See* Color
Process Trap 414–416. *See also* Trapping
Profiles 623–625, 627, 631–632. *See also* EfiColor
Profile Usage 635–637
Program Manager 19–20
PSDOWN 429
PSNAMES.TMP 579
PSPlot 429, 537
Publisher's Prism 420
Publisher's Type Foundry 248
Publisher's Paintbrush 287, 294

Q

Q measurement 571
Quark, Inc. 532
QUARK.INI 498, 608
QuarkXPress
　Bill Clinton and 694
　customizing 79–86
　installation 9–11, 546–547
　launching 12, 14
　New in version 3.3 543–617
　overview 2–7
　registration 10, 548–549
　requirements 4–6
　selling your copy 549
　upgrading 546–547
　users group 539
　and Windows 493–504
Quit 502
Quotation marks 238, 569–570

R

RAM. *See* Memory
Range kerning. *See* Tracking
Real World PostScript 376, 470
Real World Scanning & Halftones 596
Registration color 400, 462
Registration disk 10
Registration Marks 82, 128, 459–462
Registration, copyright, and trademark symbols 238–239
Relinking with pictures 322, 517
Rendering fonts 156
Rendering style 631–634, 640–641. *See also* EfiColor
Requirements 4–6
Resizing
　anchored boxes 340
　items 41–44
　pictures 311–313, 553
　text 558–559
Resolution
　display value 81, 566
　printer 430, 439
　of bitmapped images 287–288
　screen 358
RGB to CMYK translation 621, 630, 646. *See also* EfiColor
Return 145, 231–232
Reversed type 171, 350
Revert to Saved 18, 113, 399, 568
Rich black 409–410
Rich Text Format (RTF) 274–275, 279–280
Right indent tab 205
Right indent 189
Rivers 208
Roman numerals. *See* Page numbers
Rough printing 453, 613
Rosette 469

Rotation 40–41
RTF. *See* Rich Text Format
Rule Above/Below 346–351
Ruler guides 69–72, 80, 563–564. *See also* Margin guides and Columns
Rulers 69–72, 563
Run-in heads 272–273

S

Save Page as EPS 323–326, 442, 609–611
Saving documents 15–16, 18
Scale-specific guides 564
Scitex CT 298
Screen captures 478
Screening. *See* Halftones
Scroll Speed 58–59, 82, 565
Scrolling 57–59
Sections 122–124, 574
Seeing items change 39
Selecting items 49, 52, 550
Selecting text 130–132, 578
Selling QuarkXPress 548
Send Header 443–445. *See also* Printing
Send to Back 49
Serial printer connection 605
Service bureaus 87–88, 304, 472–486, 647
Shadowed type 255
Show/Hide Invisibles 231
Single-sided pages 95, 117–118
Skewing boxes 555–556
Small caps 222
Smart Quotes 569–570
Snap to Guides 71–72, 96, 120
Soft fonts 162
Soft return 232
Solid rendering. *See* EfiColor; rendering style
Son of Bob XTension 532
Space before/after 199
Space/Align 44, 54–57, 553
Special characters
   ASCII 243, 513
   ANSI codes 238–240, 513, 521–526
   ballot boxes 242
   character sets 243–245, 510, 512–515
   dingbats 242–243
   discretionary hyphen 234–235

discretionary new line 233
em and en dash 237
en space 235, 581
enter (return) 231
finding 134–135
flex space 236
foreign accents and punctuation 240–241, 581
guillemets 240
indent here 232–233, 579
ligatures 237–238, 513–515
Macintosh 512–516
new column/box 235
page numbers 236, 574–575, 615
punctuation and symbols 236–241
quotation marks 238, 569–570
registration, copyright, and trademark 238–239
show/hide invisibles 231
soft return 232
tab 232
UNICODE 245
Specifications dialog box 32–33
Speed Scroll 565
Spelling checker 140–146
   auxiliary dictionaries 143–146
   document 143
   fast 577
   story 141–143
   word 140–141
Spot color. *See* Color
Spreading. *See* Trapping
Spreads
   multiple page 122
   printing 456–457
Step and Repeat 46–47, 105
Sticky tools 551
Storm Technology 547
Style sheets 259, 261–273
   appending 267–268, 585–586
   basing on 269–270, 589
   by example 268–269
   defining 264–266, 271
   definition of 261–262
   deleting 586
   find/change 588
   keystrokes 266
   local formatting 584–585
   menu 263
   and multiple documents 152
   Next Style 584–585
   normal and no style 267, 271
   overwriting existing styles 587
   palette 263, 270–271

Style sheets *(continued)*
  tags 262–263
  versus local formatting 263–264, 270, 584–585
  word processors 276–278
Subdirectories 11–12
Suggested hyphenation 229
Super Mario 497
Superscript and subscript 221
Suppress Printout 323, 326, 478, 591–593
Suspect word. *See* Spelling checker
Symbols 236–241, 513, 521–526
SyQuest 485
SYSEDIT 161, 503
System resources 19–20, 499–500
Systems of Merritt 471–472

T

Tabs 200–206, 232, 577, 579–580
Tagging. *See* Style sheets
Tailfeathers. *See* Lines and arrows
Target device 638. *See also* EfiColor
Taub, Eric xv
Technical Publishing Service's Color Calibration Software 471, 538
Templates 16–17
TESTPS.TXT 449
Text
  deleting 133
  finding and changing 133–140
  entering 130, 147–148
  exporting 278–283
  flipping/mirroring 556–557
  importing 273–278, 576–577
  navigating through 130–132
  resizing 558–559
  selecting 130–132, 578
  skewing 555–556
  XPress tags 280–283, 527–530
Text boxes 30–33, 150, 200, 555–559, 562. *See also* Page items
Text box polygons 557–558, 590
Text inset 32, 188
Text link arrow. *See* Linking
Text outset 330. *See also* Text runaround
Text overflow. *See* Linking
Text runaround 328–338
  anchored boxes 590
  auto image 330–331

  both sides of a graphic 336–337
  introduction 328–329
  inverted 334–336
  item 330
  manual image 331–334
  none 329
  polygons 332–336, 339
  with no picture 334
Thing-a-ma-Bob XTension 532–533
Thumbnails
  on screen 60, 63–64, 562
  when printing 453–454
TIFF 293, 318, 331, 356, 358, 385, 417, 419–420, 486, 565–566
Tiling 18, 66, 70, 442, 463–465, 484, 560–561
Tool palette 23, 29–30, 551
Tool preferences 84–86
Toyo inks 540, 604–605
Tracking tables 87, 223, 226–228
Tracking 178–180, 218
Transferring files 505–520
Transparency 31, 328, 360
Trapping 398, 403–416, 490
  Aldus TrapWise 537
  automatic 406–408
  choking 404
  definition 403–404
  ignore white 414–415
  indeterminate color 413–414
  manual 410–412
  palette 411–412
  process trap 414–416
  overprinting 404, 408–409, 414
  preferences 412–416, 478, 602
  small objects and type 408, 416
  spreading 404
  turning it off 602
Trip marks. *See* Crop marks
TrueImage 157, 445
TrueType 154–159, 445–448, 515
TruMatch 381, 388–389, 393–394, 539, 603–604, 639, 643
Type 1 fonts 156–157, 427–429, 515
Type styles 167–171
Typefaces. *See* Fonts
Typographic preferences 219, 221–223, 581
Typography. *See* Character formatting, Hyphenation and Justification, Paragraph formatting

U

Undo 28, 563
UNICODE 245
Unlinking 67–69, 105
Unlocking items 45
Upgrading QuarkXPress 546–547
Use PDF/EfiColor Screen Values 629–630. *See also* EfiColor *and* Printer Setup

V

Vector Above 256–257
Ventura Publisher 282–283
Vertical alignment 184–188, 558
Vertical scaling 581–582
View percent field 561. *See also* Zooming
Vignettes 402–403
Viruses 497

W

Warnock, John 426
Wilde, Oscar 428
WIN.INI 159–163, 491, 503
Window management 18–20, 58, 502
Windows and QuarkXPress 493–504
   disk cache 498
   extended memory 494
   keyboard shortcuts 501–502, 554
   permanent swap file 495
   RAM 497–498
   system resources 19–20, 499–500
   virtual memory 494–495

Windows Bitmap (BMP) 297, 300, 356
Windows Calculator 551
Windows Character Map 239, 241
Windows Control Panel 158, 163, 431–432, 481–482, 503
Windows File Manager 12, 14, 18, 509, 548, 592–593
Windows menu 18, 560–561
Windows Metafile (WMF) 297–298, 300
Windows Notebook 148–149
Windows Paint 287
Windows TrueType. *See* TrueType
WINPSX 429
WMF. *See* Windows Metafile (WMF)
Word count 143
Word for Windows. *See* Microsoft Word
Word spacing 211
WordPerfect 274, 277–278
WYSIWYG 380–381, 619

X

XChange 532–533, 539
XPress Preferences 87–89, 223, 512, 570–571
XPress Tags 274, 280–283, 527–530
XPress XPerts XChange (X^3) 533–534, 539
XTensions 4, 78–79, 274, 531–534, 548
XyWrite 274

Z

Zapf Dingbats 241, 521–526
Zooming 60–61, 561

The QuarkXPress Book Doesn't Stop Here Anymore

▼▼▼▼▼▼▼▼▼▼▼▼▼▼▼▼▼▼▼▼▼▼▼▼▼▼▼▼▼▼▼▼▼

We couldn't do it. We just couldn't steer though the twists and turns of all those wild jungle roads just to stroll off at the end of the line. So we ain't stoppin' here! We've hijacked the bus, we're painting it pink and green and we won't stop drivin' until we reach the top. Stay on board! Give us a shout and let us know how you've liked the ride so far. Tell us if you've picked up any new XPress Demon machete techniques. We're always looking out for a new trick or two from a young tyro or a seasoned pro. You can find David and Bob at these addresses.

David Blatner
1619 Eighth Avenue N
Seattle, WA 98109-3007
CompuServe: 72647,3302
AOL: Parallax1

Bob Weibel
775 East Main Street
Ashland, OR 97520
CompuServe: 71730,2600

Colophon

▼▼▼▼▼▼▼▼▼▼▼▼▼▼▼▼▼▼▼▼▼▼▼▼▼▼▼▼▼▼▼▼▼

This book was created using every technique and many of the tips that we divulge throughout the chapters. Text was written using Microsoft Word for Windows and Macintosh, and Microsoft Works (on a little Heath-Zenith DOS laptop). Artwork was created using Aldus FreeHand, Adobe Illustrator, Adobe Photoshop, and Aldus PhotoStyler. Screen shots were made using Tiffany and HiJaak. Fonts were handled expertly through the use of Ares Software's FontMinder.

David uses either a Matrox 24-bit color board or a SuperMac Thunder/24 graphics accelerator (depending on how he's feeling that day), with an NEC 4FG color monitor. Bob uses Diamond SpeedStar HiColor 16-bit color board on his "nothing-fancy" Gateway 2000 CrystalScan monitor.

Body copy is set in Adobe Utopia and heads in Bitstream's Futura Condensed Bold. Chapter heads are set in Adobe's Bodoni Poster Compressed.

Pages for the first edition were sent as PostScript files to Seattle ImageSetting and Datatype and Graphics in Seattle, where they were imageset on Linotronic 300s and 330s at 1270 dpi.

New pages for the second edition were output on an Agfa ProSet 9800 and imposed using ImpoStrip at Consolidated Printers in Berkeley, California. The "New in 3.3" graphics were manually strippe. The book was printed by Consolidated on Husky Vellum.

More from Peachpit Press...

CorelDRAW 4: Visual QuickStart Guide
Webster & Associates

Our CorelDRAW 3 QuickStart was so popular that we've put together a new edition covering CorelDRAW 4, the latest version of this versatile drawing program. The guidebook covers the latest features of CorelDRAW, along with CorelTRACE and CorelMOSAIC. $15 *(350 pages)*

Desktop Publishing Secrets
Robert Eckhardt, Bob Weibel, and Ted Nace

Here's a compilation of hundreds of the best desktop publishing tips from five years of *Publish* magazine. It covers the major graphics and layout programs on both the PC and Macintosh platforms and offers valuable tips on desktop publishing as a business. $27.95 *(550 pages)*

Dr. Daniel's Windows Diet
Daniel Will-Harris

Put Windows on a high-performance diet! This little book offers simple solutions to a universal problem—Windows can be slow. These easy-to-follow prescriptions cover the essentials of making Windows work faster—from autoexec.bat to virtual memory. It helps you work faster, with keyboard shortcuts, file tips and more. $8.95 *(96 pages)*

Everyone's Guide to Successful Publications
Elizabeth Adler

This comprehensive reference pulls together the essential information needed to develop and produce printed materials that get your message across. Packed with ideas, advice, examples, and graphic illustrations, it covers planning, design, writing, desktop publishing, printing, and distribution in a clear, friendly manner. $28 *(412 pages)*

Four Colors/One Image
Mattias Nyman

Step-by-step procedures for reproducing and manipulating color images using Photoshop, QuarkXPress and Cachet. *Four Colors* (printed in color throughout) is filled with before-and-after examples, making it an invaluable resource for those who need great color output. $18 *(84 pages)*

FrameMaker 4 for Windows: Visual QuickStart Guide
Jann Tolman

This guidebook to FrameMaker 4 is a wise choice for beginners and intermediate users. Relying heavily on graphics and simple, step-by-step directions, this book is chockfull of tips and techniques that are sure to make learning FrameMaker easier. $18.95 *(360 pages)*

And here's even more selections,

Jargon: An Informal Dictionary of Computer Terms
Robin Williams

Finally! A book that explains over 1200 of the most useful computer terms in a way that readers can understand. This straightforward guide not only defines computer-related terms but also explains how and why they are used. *Jargon* covers both the Mac and PC. $22. *(688 pages)*

The Little PC Book
Larry Magid

Magid offers friendly advice on the basic concepts of operating a computer in non-technical, bite-sized pieces. *The Little PC Book* won rave reviews for providing a painless way to become PC literate without being buried in details. Rather than covering a wide range of non-essential information, this book helps make a novice more comfortable with his or her PC. $17.95 *(376 pages)*

The Little WordPerfect for Windows Book
Kay Yarborough Nelson

This book gives you the basic skills you need in order to create simple and effective documents using WordPerfect for Windows. You'll also learn about WordPerfect's new Windows interface. $12.95 *(200 pages)*

Mastering CorelDRAW 4
Chris Dickman

Like its earlier versions, this terrific tutorial book is studded with tips and undocumented features: it also covers topics such as imagesetting using service bureaus and default customizing. Includes two disks with utilities and 26 commercial-grade TrueType fonts. $34.95 *(750 pages)*

The PC is not a typewriter
Robin Williams

PC users can now learn trade secrets from author Robin Williams, whose best-selling *The Mac is not a typewriter* introduced tens of thousands of Mac users to the secrets of creating beautiful type. Covers punctuation, leading, special characters, kerning, fonts, alignment, and more. $9.95 *(96 pages)*

Photoshop in Black and White
Jim Rich and Sandy Bozek

An illustrated guide to reproducing black and white images using Adobe Photoshop 2.5. Provides detailed information on how to adjust the tonal range of grayscale images for optimum reproduction and tips on how to best use Photoshop with scanned images. $18 *(489 pages)*

For a full listing of Peachpit titles, call 1-800-283-9444 and request our full-color catalog.

all available from Peachpit Press.

**Photoshop for Windows:
Visual QuickStart Guide**

Elaine Weinmann and Peter Lourekas

The author of our award-winning *QuarkXPress for Windows: Visual QuickStart Guide* does it again: an accessible way to learn how to use masks, filters, colors, tools, and more. $18.95 *(264 pages)*

**QuarkXPress for Windows:
Visual QuickStart Guide**

Elaine Weinmann

Take an easy, visual approach to learning the basics of QuarkXPress. This handy *QuickStart Guide* covers everyday features of one of the most popular and powerful desktop publishing programs around. $15 *(224 pages)*

**The QuarkXPress Book,
2nd Edition for Windows**

David Blatner and Bob Weibel

The Mac version of this book has been a bestseller for two years—so useful that Quark's own support staff uses it. It tells you everything you need to know about QuarkXPress—importing and modifying graphics, creating large documents, printing, and more. $29.95 *(542 pages)*

Real World Scanning and Halftones

David Blatner and Steve Roth

Master the digital halftone process—from scanning and tweaking images on your computer to imagesetting them. You'll learn about optical character recognition, gamma control, sharpening, PostScript halftones, Photo CD, Photoshop and PhotoStyler. $24.95 *(296 pages)*

Windows 3.1 Font Book

David Angell and Brent Heslop

This hands-on font guide for Windows users explains managing, choosing, and using fonts, with instructions for working with TrueType and PostScript fonts. And it also contains suggestions for building a font library, and over 100 font samples. $12.95 *(184 pages)*

Word 6 for Windows Essentials

Geoffrey Mandel

This book is a handy reference to Word for Windows: loaded with useful tips and tricks. It explains both basic and advanced features. You'll also learn how to customize your program and use math and graphics features. $29.95 *(375 pages with disk)*

**WordPerfect:
Desktop Publishing in Style, 2nd Edition**

Daniel Will-Harris

This popular guide (over 90,000 in print) to producing documents with WordPerfect opens with a tutorial and proceeds through 20 sample documents. Humorous and fun to read, this book is invaluable to people who use WordPerfect. $23.95 *(672 pages)*

⊙ Order Form

to order, call:
(800) 283-9444 or (510) 548-4393 or (510) 548-5991 (fax)

Qty.	Title	Price	Total

SHIPPING:	First Item	Each Additional			
UPS Ground	$ 4	$ 1	Subtotal		
UPS Blue	$ 8	$ 2	8.25% Tax (CA only)		
Canada	$ 6	$ 4	Shipping		
Overseas	$14	$14	**TOTAL**		

Name		
Company		
Address		
City	State	Zip
Phone	Fax	
❏ Check enclosed	❏ Visa	❏ MasterCard
Company purchase order #		
Credit card	Expiration Date	

Peachpit Press, Inc. • 2414 Sixth Street • Berkeley, CA • 94710